fast guide to
Cubase SX

Simon Millward

Third edition

D1471376

PC Publishing

PC Publishing
Keeper's House
Merton
Thetford
Norfolk IP25 6QH
UK

Tel 01953 889900
Fax 01953 889901
email info@pc-publishing.com
web site http://www.pc-publishing.com

First published 2003
Second edition 2004
Third edition 2005
Reprinted 2005, 2006

© Simon Millward

ISBN 1 870775 98 8

British Library Cataloguing in Publication Data
A catalogue record for this book is available from the British Library

Cover design Hilary Norman Design

Printed and bound in Great Britain by Biddles, Kings Lynn, Norfolk, UK

Introduction

Welcome to the *Fast Guide to Cubase SX*.

Musicians, sound engineers and producers have for some time dreamt of the idea of the affordable, personal desktop recording studio. With Cubase SX/SL, this concept is now a reality. Cubase SX/SL is a radical new Cubase which takes software-based music creation and production into the 21st century.

This book aims to give users the skills and knowledge to be able to operate the main elements of Cubase SX/SL and also helps take your music and sound production to a higher level. It is designed to be the ideal companion to the user documentation and suits all levels of users, including musicians, producers, sound recordists and audio professionals.

The *Fast Guide to Cubase SX* is not a retread of the manual. It supplies the essential information to get you up and running in the shortest possible time but, more importantly, covers a wide range of practical techniques and theoretical knowledge which help you get the most from the software. The book is packed full of hints, tips and tutorials and includes an extensive website list and glossary. Audio and MIDI recording, editing, mixing, sound processing and mastering are all covered in detail, and a unique tips and power tools chapter takes your programming skills to the next level. All this ensures that you get the very best out of Cubase SX/SL.

Contents

Description and overview

This chapter provides an overall description of Cubase SX and gives a brief preview of the Project window, Transport panel and Mixer. This helps you become familiar with the main points of contact before moving on to a more detailed exploration of the program.

What is Cubase SX?

Cubase SX is a professional music creation and production system for the recording, editing and processing of MIDI data and digital audio. It belongs to a type of software sometimes referred to as a 'MIDI+audio' sequencer and, when installed on your computer, is also known as a 'digital audio workstation' (DAW). A sequencer, in its simplest form, is a device which allows you to chain together 'sequences' of musical notes or events. However, Cubase SX is infinitely more capable than this. It allows you to perform a multitude of music production tasks within a single, streamlined software environment. Cubase SX is at once a MIDI sequencer, a powerful multitrack digital audio recorder, a fully featured mixing console, a music for video production workstation, a post production workstation, an audio analysis tool, an audio loop creation tool and a multimedia tool.

Cubase SX can be interfaced with the usual range of MIDI devices, such as synthesizers, samplers and drum machines, and is also a digital audio recorder for recording vocals, acoustic musical instruments, line level signals from electronic musical instruments like electric guitar and bass, and anything else you can imagine. In addition, it allows the mixing of both audio and MIDI recordings in a virtual mixing console offering comprehensive effects, EQ and automation. The program features the use of 'native audio processing' which means that most of the audio processing is performed by the CPU (central processing unit) of the computer. Audio recording and processing can therefore be performed with less hardware. The program runs on PC and Macintosh computers.

Cubase SX provides simultaneous playback of hundreds of audio and MIDI tracks (depending on the overall speed and efficiency of the host computer). It incorporates a streamlined Project window which allows the management of most routine recording, editing and processing within a single-page environment. The virtual mixing console provides adaptable screen views within which all audio or MIDI tracks can be viewed and mixed in the same order in which they appear in the Project window. Each audio track features 4-band parametric EQ, eight real-time send effects and eight real-time insert effects. Other features include VST and Direct X plug-in architecture for audio effects and VST Instruments, and MIDI plug-in architecture with four send and four insert effects per MIDI track. A comprehensive range of audio effects, MIDI processors and VST Instruments are supplied with the program. For mixing purposes, there is sample accurate automation for all mixer, VST Instrument and effects parameters and an audio mixdown facility. Offline audio processes include time-stretch, pitch shift, envelope, fade, noise gate, normalise, reverse and other processes. Special audio manipulation tools include groove extraction, audio looping, audio warping and audio quantize. For MIDI, there are Key, In-place, Drum, List, Logical, Score and Sysex editors. Unlimited undo/redo, off-line process history, user-configurable key commands and workspaces help complete the picture.

Cubase SX supports all standard digital audio recording resolutions up to 32-bit float/96kHz. Support for ASIO allows the use of low-latency audio cards and hardware.

When was Cubase SX developed?

The Cubase family of sequencers already has a long history. Steinberg developed their first sequencer, the Pro 16, in 1984 on the Commodore 64 computer. This was followed by the Pro 24 for the Atari computer in 1986. The very first version of Cubase began life in 1989 as a radical new update to the Pro 24. It featured the (at the time) revolutionary Arrange window which allowed musicians to visualise and 'arrange' their musical compositions in a dynamic graphical display of time (on the horizontal axis) against tracks (on the vertical axis). All these early applications were concerned with the recording of MIDI data only. However, as the processing power of computers increased during the 1990's Steinberg was able to add audio recording capability to the program. During the same period, the code was ported to PC and Apple Macintosh computers.

In 1996, Steinberg introduced the concept of VST (Virtual Studio Technology) and Cubase became known as Cubase VST. VST aims to bring all those elements normally found within a real-world recording studio into a single virtual environment inside your computer. This design principle remains one of the cornerstones of Steinberg's software development strategy and now, more than ever, the virtual studio concept has become a reality.

With Cubase SX (introduced in 2002), Steinberg further refined and streamlined the Cubase concept into a package which is more powerful, more flexible and more logical than its predecessors. It brings the idea of the virtual desktop recording studio into the 21st century.

Who can use Cubase SX?

Newcomers to the software and also experienced sequencer users may have to learn new skills in order to have meaningful contact with the many aspects of Cubase SX. The MIDI sequencer element of the package requires knowledge of the normal techniques associated with MIDI recording but the audio aspects require knowledge from a wider range of music technology disciplines.

Of course, anyone can use Cubase SX but, since the package involves the concept of a self-contained virtual recording studio, it follows that having knowledge of the skills required to operate a real-world recording studio is useful. This encompasses such things as sound engineering and music production. However, even users with limited sound recording skills are able to quickly benefit from the advantages of SX.

Why use Cubase SX?

There are many reasons why Cubase SX is an excellent music software choice. The seamless integration of MIDI and audio recording and real-time processing together with the possibility of recording large numbers of tracks, the inclusion of 4-band parametric EQ on every audio channel and the supply of a wide range of effects and processors are just some of the advantages encompassed by the program. The package is also very cost-effective since most of the audio processing takes place in the computer's main processor, so there is no need for additional DSP (digital signal processor) hardware. Cubase SX can produce excellent results using a fast PC or Mac computer and an ASIO low-latency audio card. The convenience of this compact arrangement is an obvious advantage.

How do I use Cubase SX?

This is the key question! Before you can use Cubase SX you must have some idea of how to record and manipulate MIDI data, how to record and manipulate audio signals, how you are going to get an audio signal into the computer and how you are going to feed it back out into the real world. These matters, and many other details related to Cubase SX, form the subject matter of this book.

The big picture

A simple graphical representation of the system helps us understand what is included in the Cubase SX package (see Figure 1.1). On the one hand, there is the MIDI sequencer functionality of the program. This does *not* involve the recording of the actual audio signal itself. MIDI (Musical Instrument Digital Interface) is mainly a note-based interface, originally devised so that elec-

Figure 1.1
Simple visualisation of Cubase SX

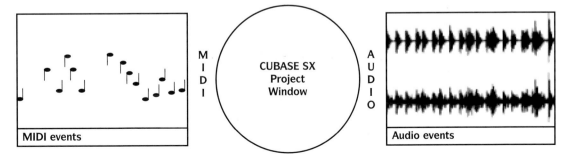

tronic keyboards and synthesizers could 'talk' to each other. MIDI data includes information about the pitch and velocity of the notes being played and travels through a cable from one keyboard to another. This data can also be recorded into a computer-based sequencer like Cubase SX. Music recorded in this way is represented as individual note events. What we see in Cubase SX is a representation of these events in the form of notes on a score, or graphical blocks in a piano-roll style editor.

On the other hand, there is the audio recording capability of the program. This involves the recording of the actual audio signal itself. The audio is represented as waveforms of the sound signal, referred to in Cubase SX as audio events. The audio side of the program also includes the virtual studio features of mixing, routing, processing and adding effects to the material.

The MIDI and audio functions of Cubase SX are seamlessly integrated. For example, the recording of both kinds of data can take place in the Project window, the main window of Cubase SX, and both kinds of data can be mixed

Figure 1.2
Cubase SX: graphical overview

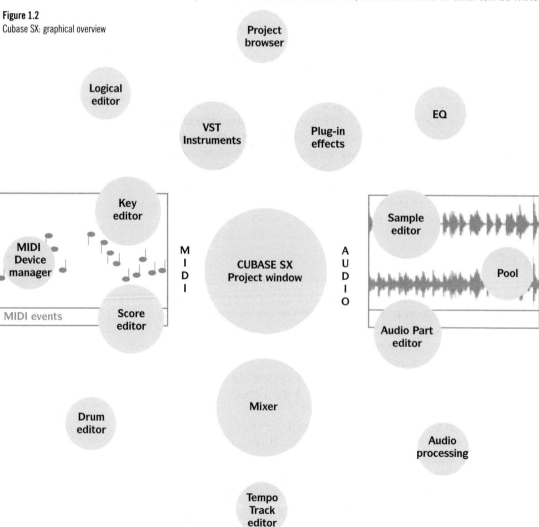

in the same virtual mixing console, known as the Mixer. The Project window and associated Mixer form the central hub of activity for most Cubase SX projects. In the Project window, MIDI recordings are displayed as graphical blocks, usually containing symbols representing the notes, and audio recordings are displayed in similar graphical blocks, usually as waveforms representing the recorded signal. You can fulfill most routine recording, editing, mixing and processing tasks within the Project window and Mixer, but for editing in fine detail the system contains a wide range of specialist editors and functions (see Figure 1.2 for a basic overview).

On the MIDI side of matters, Figure 1.2 shows the main MIDI-based editors; the Key, Score and Drum editors. These are used to edit note and controller data in fine detail and the Score editor can also produce professional-quality printed scores. More distant from the central area of activities we find features like the Logical editor and the MIDI Device manager. There is also a comprehensive range of other features for the editing and processing of MIDI data including the List editor, SysEx editor, MIDI plug-in effects and processors and sophisticated quantize functions (not shown in the diagram).

In the audio domain, the Sample editor forms the main editing environment for audio material. There are also many audio processing features such as EQ, plug-in effects and off-line audio processing. The management of audio files and events takes place in the Pool.

Somewhere in between the MIDI and audio sides of Cubase SX we find VST Instruments (Virtual Studio Instruments) which are played using conventional MIDI data but produce their sounds using the system's audio engine. Some plug-in effects also respond to MIDI data but process audio. You can use the Mixer to mix audio, MIDI, VST Instrument, Group and other tracks. The mixer channels are displayed in the same order as the corresponding tracks in the Project window. For overall project management there is the Project browser. This allows you to take a look at all events and files contained within a project.

Brief preview

Figure 1.2, above, provides a graphical overview of the main parts of Cubase SX which is useful for an appreciation of what the system includes. But what does Cubase SX actually look like on screen, where are the main areas of activity and how do you interact with the program?

You can change the appearance of Cubase SX to suit your own requirements but when you first launch a project you might see the Project window displayed in a similar manner to Figure 1.3, (the Project window is the uppermost window). By default, computer keys F2 and F3 open the Transport panel and Mixer. These are also shown in Figure 1.3.

The Project window is where you see a graphical representation of your audio and MIDI material in the form of rectangular blocks known as 'parts' or 'events'. Parts are containers which can hold either audio or MIDI events. MIDI data is always contained within a part but audio data can appear directly in the Project window as events. Parts and events are found on tracks which can be designated as audio, MIDI or other data types. Other data types include automation, marker and video tracks. Track names are dis-

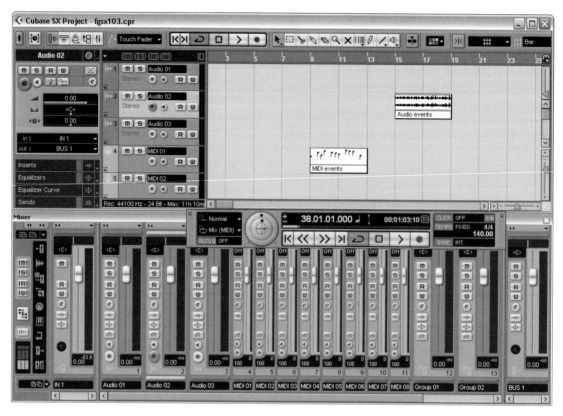

Figure 1.3
Cubase SX Project window, Mixer and Transport panel

played vertically in the track list and time is represented horizontally on a ruler which, by default, displays bars and beats. There is a toolbar at the top of the display and an optional control area to the left of the track list, known as the Inspector. The Inspector shows additional details for the currently selected track. The Project window is the centre of activity for most Cubase SX operations.

The Mixer displays the tracks in the same order as they appear in the Project window but laid out as channels with volume faders, pan controls, EQ controls, effects sends and so on, similar to a conventional mixing console. Both audio and MIDI tracks are mixed in the Mixer and the mixing environment can be configured and scaled to suit your requirements and the available screen space.

The Transport panel features the normal rewind, fast-forward, stop, play, cycle and record controls and manages most playback and recording functions. The stop, play, record and cycle buttons are duplicated in the Project window toolbar. The current song position is shown by a vertical line which moves across the Project window. This is known as the Project cursor.

Cubase SX's user interface is intuitive and direct. It features a comprehensive set of menus and icon buttons, and a large number of mouse functions, user-configurable keyboard shortcuts, and drag-and-drop editing techniques with which to control operations in the Project and other windows. These functions and a whole lot more are described in detail throughout the course of this book.

Patience, practice and understanding

This chapter gives you a foretaste of the power and elegance of Cubase SX, but before proceeding further it is worth being aware of the following: the streamlined design of Cubase SX is the result of many years of research and development and the program represents the leading edge in native audio music software. It provides a logical and adaptable framework within which you can operate intuitively and creatively. However, despite being one of the more user-friendly music software applications, there is still a learning curve and there are still techniques with which to become familiar and concepts to understand. This requires some initial effort from the user. Achieving the best results requires patience, practice and understanding.

Setting up the system

This chapter describes the hardware you need to run Cubase SX, how to install the software and what kinds of overall system setups are suitable for the program.

General computer requirements

Info

For those who need more details about computer requirements see Appendix 1 at the back of this book and also consult your user manuals and the latest computer and music technology magazines.

Cubase SX runs on PC or Apple Macintosh computers. In order to use the program comfortably you are advised to choose a computer with a very fast processor, a particularly large and fast hard drive and a large amount of RAM. The more audio tracks, effects and VST Instruments you wish to use, the more powerful your computer must be. The system should also include suitable audio hardware (often in the form of an audio card), preferably featuring its own dedicated ASIO driver, and a suitable MIDI interface if you intend to record MIDI data in Cubase SX. Your computer should also feature a USB port since Cubase SX is protected by a special key which plugs into a USB socket.

The program has been optimised for the latest operating systems on both platforms. Windows 2000 or XP is required for the PC and OS X (10.2 or higher) is required for the Mac. The recording of multi-track digital audio makes special demands of a computer system so it is worth considering the details (see Appendix 1). PC users are advised to obtain a PC which has been built specifically for audio purposes. Your choice of platform (PC or Mac) is purely a matter of personal preference.

Installation

Before proceeding

Before proceeding with the installation of any audio hardware and software, ensure that you already have one of the recommended operating systems running on the computer and that it is functioning correctly. Before installing Cubase SX itself, the intended audio hardware (audio card) and associated driver should already have been installed on the computer.

Audio hardware and drivers

There are various ways in which Cubase SX can communicate with your audio hardware. This depends as much on the hardware's drivers as on the design of the hardware itself. A driver is a short software program which provides the communication link between the hardware device and the operating system (or a specific application like Cubase SX). The hardware is set up and initialised via the driver software. In the case of Cubase SX, the program communicates with the audio hardware according to what kind of driver has been installed. The main options include:

1   A dedicated ASIO (Audio Stream Input Output) driver supplied with, and written exclusively for, the audio hardware. This provides direct communication between Cubase SX and the hardware. This is the preferred choice since it reduces the delay between user input and the time it takes for the computer to respond and process the data through the software and hardware. This delay is commonly known as latency. Lower latency means smoother and more accurate real-time operation of Cubase SX. A well-written dedicated ASIO driver should provide a latency of less than 10ms.
2   A Direct X driver supplied with the audio hardware allowing communication with Microsoft Windows Direct X. Direct X handles multimedia operations under Windows. When Cubase SX is installed on a PC computer system, its own ASIO Direct X driver is automatically installed. There are, therefore, two drivers involved with this option, one for the audio hardware and one for Cubase SX. To communicate with the audio hardware via Direct X you must choose the ASIO Direct X Full Duplex driver option for your audio device within Cubase SX. This option provides adequate performance but with inferior latency figures to dedicated ASIO drivers.
3   A standard Windows multimedia driver allowing communication between Windows compatible audio cards and the Windows multimedia system. This is supplied with the audio card. When Cubase SX is installed on a PC computer system, its own ASIO Multimedia driver is automatically installed. There are, therefore, two drivers involved with this option, one for the audio hardware and one for Cubase SX. To communicate with the Windows multimedia compatible hardware you must choose the ASIO Multimedia driver option for your audio device within Cubase SX. This option provides inferior latency performance and is not recommended for professional applications.

Option 1 is strongly recommended for all Cubase SX systems. The best audio cards and professional audio hardware are supplied with dedicated ASIO drivers.

MIDI interface and drivers

If MIDI functionality is not included in your audio hardware, you may need to install a separate MIDI interface (assuming that you intend to record MIDI-based music as well as audio). Installation of MIDI devices is usually a simple procedure involving the connection of the hardware interface to the computer, switching it on (if it has a power switch) and installing the driver (usually supplied on a CD-ROM). All standard MIDI interfaces function with Cubase SX. See the documentation supplied with the MIDI interface for full details.

Before installing Cubase SX

Before installing Cubase SX you should:

- Preferably defragment the hard disk.
- If you have not already done so, install your audio hardware and driver(s) according to the supplied documentation (see 'Audio hardware and drivers', above).
- Test the functionality of the audio hardware outside of Cubase SX if you have other suitable software already installed (as part of the operating system, for example). This assumes that you already have your hardware's audio outputs connected to an amplifier and loudspeakers (or headphones).
- If needed, install your MIDI interface and driver according to the supplied documentation (see 'MIDI interface and drivers', above).

Installing Cubase SX

Cubase SX is supplied on a DVD-ROM and is easily installed onto a suitably prepared computer. The following steps outline what you need to do:

- Ensure that the supplied Steinberg copy protection key is *not* plugged into the computer's USB port. This should be plugged in *after* the installation of Cubase SX and re-starting the computer.
- Insert the Cubase SX DVD-ROM and explore its contents. Double-click on autorun.exe to open the install dialogue. Select 'install' or 'setup' to start the installation procedure.
- Follow the on-screen instructions to proceed through the installation procedure.
- The installation only takes a few minutes and once complete you are invited to re-start your computer.
- After re-starting the computer, insert the supplied Steinberg copy protection key into the computer's USB port. A driver needs to be installed for the key. This usually takes place automatically.
- You can now launch Cubase SX by double-clicking on the Cubase SX logo on the desktop.

That's the nasty bit over! From here on things become more musical and slightly less technical. Inevitably, some users run into difficulties during the setup process, but do not despair since even the most experienced user can have installation problems.

System verification

Upon first launching Cubase SX you may immediately ask one important question. 'Where, within Cubase SX, do I find the audio hardware and MIDI interface I have just installed?' The first part of the answer is to have a clear idea of the design features of the hardware, with particular attention to the type of ASIO driver you have installed, the number of audio inputs and outputs provided, and the number of MIDI input and output ports provided. You can then set about finding the locations within the software where the ASIO driver and the various inputs and outputs are activated.

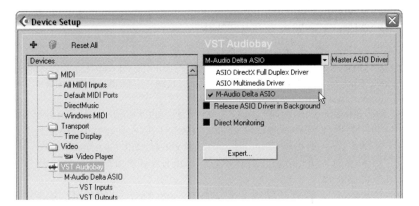

Figure 2.1
Finding the ASIO driver in the Device setup window

Verifying the ASIO driver

Cubase SX chooses its ASIO driver according to what hardware and driver(s) are already installed in the computer. To verify or change the ASIO driver select 'Device Setup' from the Devices menu. Choose 'VST Audiobay' in the device list and verify which ASIO driver has been installed in the ASIO driver field (Figure 2.1). If supplied with your audio hardware, make sure that its dedicated ASIO driver is selected here. A special ASIO driver written exclusively for the hardware gives better latency performance than the other options.

Finding the audio inputs

The inputs of your audio hardware are connected within the software at two locations (see Figure 2.2). Firstly, the input ports are enabled or disabled in Device setup / VST inputs (Devices menu). By default, all available ports are enabled ('Yes' selected in the 'visible' column). Input ports that you do not need may be disabled here (by selecting 'No' in the 'visible' column). The number of input ports depends upon the number of physical inputs on your audio card/hardware. Secondly, the activated inputs are connected in the input section of the VST Connections window (Devices menu). This is where you assign the inputs to one or more input busses (added using the 'Add bus' button). An input buss added here appears in the Mixer as an input channel strip (to the left of all other channel strips).

Info

In Cubase SX, audio input and output routing is based upon busses. Input signals must enter the program via an input buss and output signals must exit via an output buss.

Figure 2.2
The inputs from your audio hardware are routed via the VST inputs section of the Device Setup window followed by the inputs section of the VST Connections window

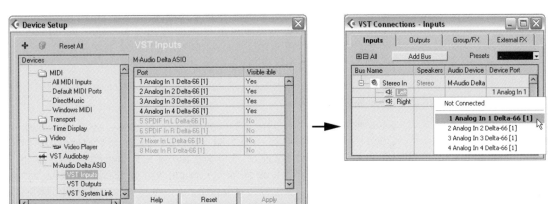

Finding the audio outputs

Similar to the inputs, the outputs of your audio hardware are also connected within the software at two locations (see Figure 2.3). Firstly, one or more output busses is assigned to the currently active output ports in the output section of the VST Connections window. An output buss may be added using the 'Add bus' button and this appears in the Mixer as an output channel strip (to the right of all other channel strips). Secondly, the output ports are enabled or disabled in Device setup / VST outputs (Devices menu). By default, all available ports are enabled ('Yes' selected in the 'visible' column). Output ports that you do not need may be disabled here (by selecting 'No' in the 'visible' column). The number of output ports depends upon the number of physical outputs on your audio card/hardware.

Figure 2.3
The outputs to your audio hardware are routed via the outputs section of the VST Connections window followed by the VST outputs section of the Device Setup window

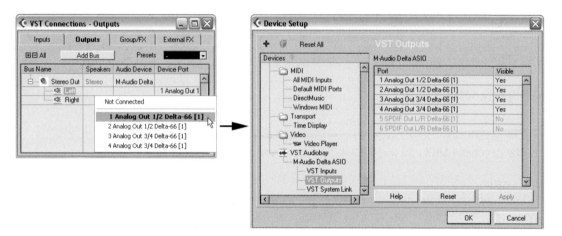

Finding the MIDI inputs and outputs

Under Windows, the available MIDI input and output ports are found in Device Setup/DirectMusic and under Mac OSX they are found in Device Setup/MIDI system page (Devices menu). Here you can show/hide the available ports by clicking in the Show column. Verify that the required MIDI ports are active and visible, i.e. marked 'Yes' in the active and show columns (see Figure 2.4).

Figure 2.4
The Device setup window showing the available MIDI ports

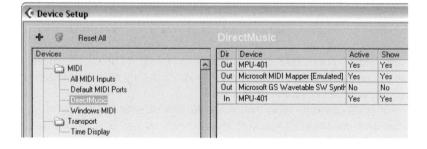

The active MIDI ports are available in the pop-up 'in' and 'out' menus of each MIDI track (opened by clicking in the 'in' or 'out' fields). In systems with multiple inputs it is possible to assign a number of MIDI inputs in Device Setup/All MIDI inputs. In such a system, selecting 'All MIDI inputs' in the MIDI track's 'in' pop-up menu helps get MIDI input into the program by ensuring reception of MIDI data simultaneously for all assigned inputs.

Default input and output ports are given to newly created MIDI tracks according to what is assigned in Device Setup/Default MIDI Ports. To assign your own default MIDI ports for new MIDI tracks, make a selection from the MIDI input and output menus (Figure 2.5).

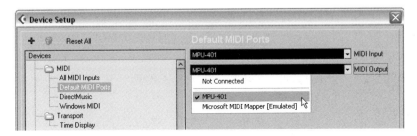

Figure 2.5
Assign default MIDI input and output ports in Device Setup/Default MIDI Ports

Overall system setup

The overall system used for Cubase SX may vary enormously and depends on the precise requirements of each user. By overall system we mean Cubase SX and all the peripheral MIDI and audio equipment which may surround it.

A simple system

Unless you intend to monitor on headphones alone, you normally need some kind of amplifier and speaker system. In the simplest of cases, the stereo outputs from an audio card pass directly to the amplifier and all playback from Cubase SX is heard through the speakers.

In order to make MIDI-based recordings, you need some kind of MIDI input device such as a MIDI keyboard/synthesizer or a MIDI guitar. For audio recording, the bare minimum is a single microphone connected to a microphone input of the audio hardware. This describes the minimum setup needed to record and playback both MIDI and audio material and is shown in Figure 2.6.

Microphone matters

The microphone is the very first stage in the recording path when you are recording live vocals, musical instruments and other real-world sources so, if you are serious about your recording, it is worth investing in a well-specified model. A bad quality input signal cannot be corrected in Cubase SX and cannot be improved later, no matter how good the quality of the analogue to digital conversion of your audio hardware.

For good all-round performance and for the recording of vocals, large-diaphragm condenser (capacitor) microphones usually produce the best results. These invariably require phantom power to drive the microphone. However, microphone choice depends very much on the source which is being recorded and only knowledge and experience can help make the appropriate decision.

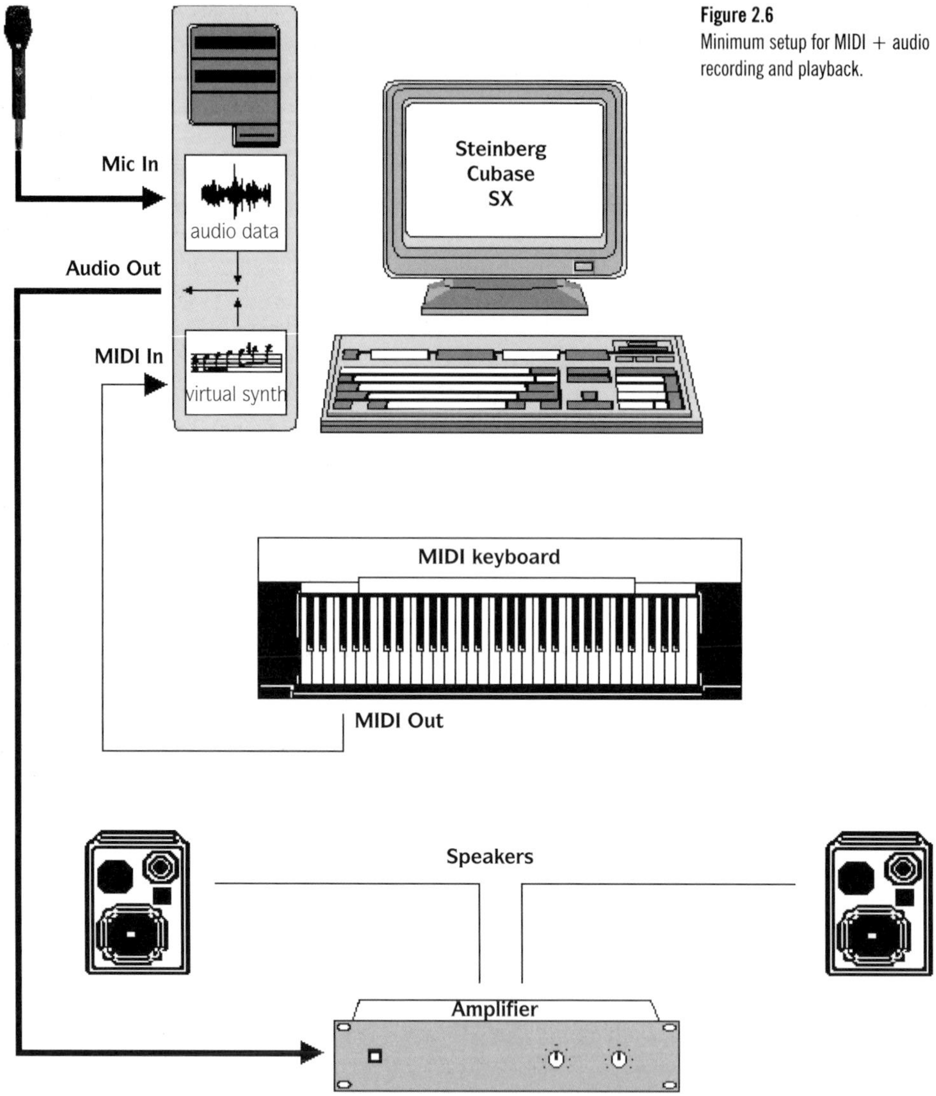

Figure 2.6
Minimum setup for MIDI + audio recording and playback.

The basic techniques for connecting a microphone to a Cubase SX system include the following:

1   *Connection of the microphone directly to the microphone input of the audio hardware device or audio card.* Many high-end audio devices feature mic inputs (or mixed mic/line inputs) with phantom power which are suitable for the direct connection of professional microphones.

2   *Connection of the microphone to the audio hardware device via a separate mic pre-amp.* A mic pre-amp is a unit specialised in optimising the signal from a microphone. The inputs of the mic pre-amp are suitable for the connection of professional microphones and line level or digital outputs provide the connection to the audio hardware device.

3 *Connection of the microphone to an external mixing console.* Professional mixing consoles provide microphone and line inputs for the connection of a variety of sources. A line level output signal from the console (e.g. a group out) is then routed to the line inputs of the audio hardware device.

For small-scale systems which do not feature a mixing console, option 2 is the preferred choice. A mic pre-amp can significantly improve the quality of the source signal and professional units often include compression, EQ, gating and valve simulation effects. However, for non-mixing console systems, option 1 also provides good results but with less flexibility. The quality of the results of option 3 depend very much upon the quality of the mixing console.

There is an additional practical problem when using a microphone connected to a small-scale computer recording system: fan noise. Most computers make enough noise to interfere with a microphone recording taking place in the same room. The immediate solution is to place the microphone as great a distance away from the computer as is practical and acoustically desirable, or to use screening between the computer and the microphone. Never attempt to dampen the noise of the fan by blocking the ventilation of the computer case as this could cause your computer to overheat. Of course, the ideal solution is to make all the recordings in a separate (preferably acoustically treated) room, as takes place in a professional recording studio.

Other input sources

If you are an electric guitarist or bassist, it is possible to record directly into the line inputs of your audio hardware via a guitar or bass pre-amp. Many of the mic pre-amps mentioned above are dual mic/line devices which can be used for both kinds of sources. This is particularly useful for the small home recording setup and for guitarists who wish to take advantage of computer-based recording technology, which has, until recently, been MIDI and keyboard centred.

MIDI keyboard choice

To make real-time MIDI recordings you need some kind of MIDI triggering device. In most cases this means a MIDI keyboard but it could also be a MIDI guitar, MIDI drum pads or a MIDI wind-blown instrument. The device should preferably be velocity sensitive and, in the case of a keyboard, have at least a five octave key span, although two octave mini-keyboards are excellent for small desktop systems where space is limited. Those keyboards which have their own sound-making circuitry should be equipped with MIDI in, out and thru sockets (now standard on regular MIDI keyboards). Some budget keyboards with no sound-making circuitry may only feature a single MIDI output, which may be all you need to trigger the other MIDI devices within a simple system.

Other things to look out for in MIDI keyboards are high quality on-board sounds and effects, ease of programmability and keys which are comfortable to play.

Info

A high-quality professional microphone can radically improve the fidelity of the input signal. Large-diaphragm condenser models supplied by Neumann, AKG, Shure, Beyer, Sennheiser, Sony, Calrec, Rode and Audio Technica are highly recommended.

Info

In a computer-based recording setup, the input signal from a microphone is often further improved by using a high-quality mic pre-amp. The best mic pre-amps feature a superior signal path to many mixing consoles and often provide compression and EQ parameters. They are, therefore, desirable even if you already own a mixing console. The mic pre-amps supplied by Focusrite, Joe Meek, SPL and DBX are highly recommended.

Info

It is difficult to recommend specific keyboard models since there are so many to choose from and many different levels of functionality. However, you are likely to find what you need among those instruments manufactured by Roland, Yamaha, Korg, Alesis, Emu and Evolution.

A complex system

Larger-scale overall setups for Cubase SX involve a wide range of variables. A large-scale setup is likely to include a mixing console and/or external control hardware, external sound processing equipment and effects, one or more mic pre-amps, professional studio monitors and a network of MIDI devices. These items significantly improve the functionality of Cubase SX. An example setup is shown in Figure 2.7.

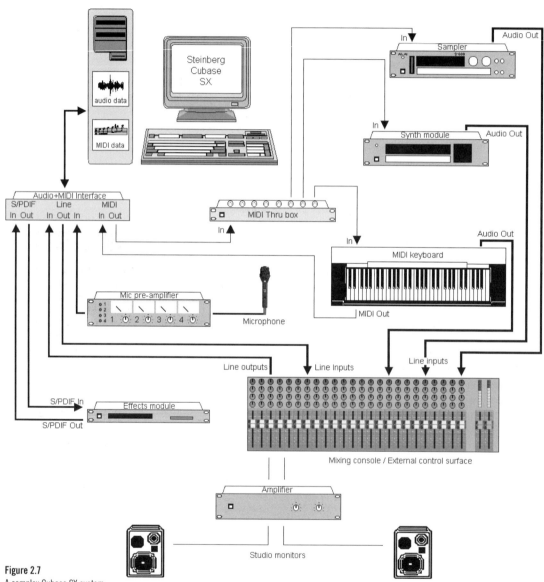

Figure 2.7
A complex Cubase SX system

Do I need a mixer?

One of the first questions which might be asked when setting up the overall system surrounding Cubase SX is 'why do I need an external mixer when there is a virtual mixer in Cubase SX?' The answer is that it all depends on how you want to link Cubase SX to the external world. Cubase SX's interconnectivity with the external world is limited by the installed audio hardware and the equipment in the overall system. Simple systems featuring a microphone and mic pre-amp, for example, do not really need an external mixer. In this case, Cubase SX's mixer might be viewed as being primarily concerned with playback and mixing.

However, an external mixing console is often more flexible for all kinds of recording, playback and routing tasks. For example, the majority of users need a way of interfacing and routing the wide range of equipment which is commonly used in the recording process. This might include one or more microphones, a lead or bass guitar, a keyboard, a multi-track recorder, a CD player or any number of other musical instruments or sound sources. Any combination of these sources might then be routed into Cubase SX via the line-outs of the external mixer. The use of an external mixer also provides direct, hands-on control of multiple faders and control knobs, which is especially convenient for recording multiple sources.

The choice of mixer is dependent upon the application and, of course, if you do not have a vast amount of external recording equipment or complex routing requirements you may still decide that you do not really need an external mixer. In any case, a project studio may require only a small mixer, providing enough inputs for several microphone and line signals (such as those from MIDI keyboards and modules) and enough I/O sockets to be able to interface external units and Cubase SX (as shown in Figure 2.7). For Cubase SX, a small, high quality external mixer with flexible routing functions is often preferable to a large console with many channels. A small mixer is fine for most recording purposes although it may not be able to handle a large-scale automated mix. In this context, the mixing facilities of Cubase SX become extremely useful since its virtually unlimited number of mixer channels and advanced automation facilities mean that the mix can be performed entirely within SX. The use of Cubase SX with a small mixer therefore cuts down on the cost and extra space requirements of a large console.

External control surfaces

One of the limitations of computer-based multi-track audio systems is that manipulation of the controls is achieved mainly via the mouse and keyboard. This is not practical or convenient for the manipulation of some of the common audio control parameters. This is immediately apparent if you try to simultaneously move two faders in Cubase SX's Mixer. A mouse only allows you to move one fader at a time and a conventional computer keyboard does not feature hardware sliders. The installation of an additional hardware control surface can overcome these problems.

Hardware control surfaces include a number of hardware buttons, faders and control knobs designed for various levels of functional integration with the software. For example, the more sophisticated dedicated control surfaces include transport controls, faders, pan pots and control knobs which can be assigned to the majority of Cubase SX's functions. They may also provide microphone and line inputs, MIDI I/O and routing capability and may therefore replace the necessity for more traditional external mixing console solutions. Alternatively, some regular mixing consoles can double as control surfaces for Cubase SX (e.g. Yamaha's 01v).

Cubase SX includes support for CM Motormix, JL Cooper MCS-3000 series, Mackie Control, Radikal SAC 2.x series, Roland MCR8, Steinberg Houston, Tascam US-428, Yamaha 01v and DM2000 (among others), many of which feature motorised faders which reflect the current settings within Cubase SX and a high level of functional integration with the program. A generic remote setup option allows communication with a wide range of other control surfaces. Open the Device Setup window (Devices menu) and click on the Add device button to see the available options.

Monitoring

The use of professional audio monitoring equipment is essential for the best results and is a pre-requisite for all professional Cubase SX installations. This normally includes a power amplifier and studio monitors (or active monitors), placed in an acoustically balanced room. A professional monitoring system is designed to give a clear, neutral sound so that you can make truly accurate judgments during each stage of the recording process.

Large, highly accurate monitors with a wide, flat frequency response which does not significantly colour the sound are normally chosen for professional recording studios. A pair of small nearfield monitors are often sufficient for home studio setups. These also serve as a second reference in larger setups where the monitoring can be switched between the main speakers and the nearfield speakers. The final choice of monitor is based upon its technical specifications and your own judgments about its fidelity.

The positioning of the monitors is extremely important. A good starting point is that of an equilateral triangle formed by the listening position and the two speakers. Traditionally, the sound path from the two monitors produces a 60 degree angle at the listening position. The distance between the two monitors should not exceed the distance from the monitors to the listener as this can seriously affect the perception of the stereo image. It is also desirable to have the monitors placed on a non-resonant, rigid surface which does not produce any vibrations in the actual structure of the room.

Also of primary importance is the use of a high quality amplifier which comfortably produces a clear, undistorted signal. The amplifier should not have to be driven to its maximum volume in order to achieve the desired listening level, so a model with sufficient headroom above the average listening level should be chosen.

CD and DVD recording

Of all the peripheral equipment surrounding Cubase SX, CD and DVD recorders are among the most useful. Using a CD recorder you can create your own Red Book audio CDs for demo or mastering purposes. CD and DVD are also invaluable for routine data backup where the audio is stored as computer data files. DVDs are particularly appropriate for backup and archiving due to their large storage capacity (around seven times the capacity of regular compact disc).

For the creation of audio CDs, audio material is mixed down directly as an audio file onto hard disk using SX's Export/Audio mixdown function. The audio files are later burnt onto CD using a separate mastering/burning application, such as Steinberg Wavelab. For mastering purposes the chosen application must be capable of burning Red Book audio CDs. For reliable results a good quality CD burner is required.

MIDI networks

Many Cubase SX systems include some kind of MIDI network. Larger networks may feature a MIDI thru box (also called a MIDI splitter box) which enables the channeling of MIDI data to specific locations in the system. The MIDI network in Figure 2.7 features a master keyboard from which the MIDI Out is sent to the MIDI In of the computer. The MIDI input data passes through Cubase SX and is passed back out, along with any other data which has already been recorded, to the MIDI input of the MIDI thru box. The data is connected to the respective outputs of the thru box to be passed back to the master keyboard and to the other modules in the system.

Cubase SX is supplied with a number of VST Instruments and others can be installed from the vast range of VSTi products available from Steinberg and other developers. These are triggered via MIDI in much the same way as their external counterparts and considerably expand the available sound palette.

Summary

The above has explained some of the variables involved in setting up a Cubase SX system but readers should be aware that the art of sound recording and the science of studio design embrace a wide range of subjects, which are beyond the scope of this book. It should also be apparent that any combination of the above elements might be included in a Cubase SX system, depending on the application. Some users might require a very comprehensive MIDI network with just one extremely high quality microphone for the recording of vocals. Others may opt for a very basic MIDI system of one master keyboard for triggering VST Instruments, coupled with a large external mixing console and a comprehensive range of microphones and devices for recording audio into the program. Many professional applications would include all of the above and a whole lot more besides.

Info

Red Book refers to the technical specifications which govern the correct creation and manufacture of an audio CD, as defined by Sony and Philips. An actual copy of the Red Book is usually only available to CD manufacturing plants. Other CD types have similar colour-coded books which govern their creation, such as Yellow Book for CD-ROM, Green Book for CD-i, Orange Book for write-once CD-R, White Book for video CD and Blue Book for CD-Extra.

3

First steps

This chapter shows you how to set up a new project, how to record MIDI and audio tracks, and explores some of the general features of the system. Most users are keen to make their first recording as soon as possible and many attempt to do this without ever having read the manual. This is certainly possible since Cubase SX has been designed to make the recording process as trouble-free as possible. However, it is not always certain that things will go according to plan since the recording process is controlled by many parameters.

The following step-by-step guides help avoid some of the common problems which may arise during the recording process.

Recording in Cubase SX

Creating a new project

The Cubase SX environment is based upon the idea of organising all your recording, editing and processing endeavours into a 'project'. All the data for a project is normally stored in a single directory on your system's hard disk, the location of which is chosen before you start recording. The directory for the project contains the project file itself (recognised by its .cpr file extension) and all the associated audio, edit, fade and image files.

To ensure a trouble-free journey through the recording processes outlined below it is best to set up a new empty project. Proceed as follows:

1 Select 'New Project' from the File menu and choose 'Empty' from the dialogue which appears on screen (Figure 3.1).

Figure 3.1
Create an empty new project

2 In the Select directory dialogue which appears, choose your audio drive or an appropriate existing directory (usually the location where you intend to store all your Cubase SX projects) and click on the Create button to create a new directory for this particular project (Figure 3.2). Choose an appropriate name, (like 'First recordings', for example). The directory is created on the hard disk.

Figure 3.2
Create a directory for the new project

3 Click on OK to leave the Select directory dialogue. An empty Cubase SX project with various default settings is opened on the screen (Figure 3.3).

Figure 3.3
The resulting empty project in Cubase SX

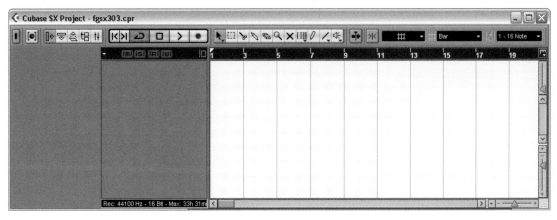

Project setup

When you create a new project, Cubase SX gives you a working environment with various default general settings. Many of these are found in the Project setup window (Figure 3.4). This is opened by selecting Project setup from the Project menu. Whenever you start a serious project you should verify that the Project setup values are suitable. The Project setup determines the settings for a number of fundamental global parameters. Most of the settings could be changed half-way through a project but the sample rate should be set once only before commencing. For the purposes of making your first recordings, as outlined below, configure your Project window to match the values shown in Figure 3.4.

Figure 3.4
Project setup window

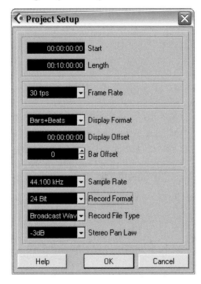

The values in the Project setup window are saved as part of each Cubase SX project file. The parameters include the following:

- Start – determines the start time of the project (hours:minutes:seconds:frames). This allows you to set the start time to values other than zero and to regulate the start time when Cubase SX is synchronised to an external device.
- Length – determines the overall length of the project (hours:minutes:seconds:frames). Ten minutes is a good default length but this depends entirely upon the kind of project you are creating.
- Frame rate – sets the frame rate for Cubase SX when it is slaved to external time code.
- Display format – sets the global time line format for all ruler and position displays in Cubase SX.
- Display offset – allows you to set an offset for the ruler display when working with Cubase SX slaved to external time code (hours:minutes:seconds:frames).
- Bar offset – allows you to set a bar offset value relative to the start time chosen above. Only relevant when bars and beats are displayed in the ruler.
- Sample rate – determines the sample rate for the project. All audio playback and recording occurs at this sample rate. Here you would

normally use 44.1kHz for audio-only projects and 48kHz for sound-to-picture projects. 88.2 and 96kHz help optimise audio quality and suit projects destined for high-end mastering and high-resolution formats such as DVD-Audio and SACD (see the section entitled 'What bit resolution and sample rate should I use?' on page 117 in Chapter 7 for more details).

- Record format – determines the sampling resolution (bit depth) for the project. All choices available here give excellent recording quality but 24-bit and 32-bit float are recommended for serious projects.
- Record file type – sets the file format for all audio files recorded within the project.
- Stereo pan law - determines how the level is attenuated when audio signals are panned centre. The default setting is -3dB..

Your first MIDI recording

1 Connect your MIDI keyboard

Ensure that the MIDI Out of your MIDI keyboard (or other MIDI controller device) is connected to the MIDI In of your MIDI interface/sound card. This is verified by checking the MIDI activity indicator on the Transport panel while playing the MIDI keyboard. Reasons for no activity indication include a badly installed interface or a faulty/incorrectly connected MIDI cable. Also ensure that the MIDI Out of your MIDI interface is connected to the MIDI In of the keyboard.

2 Add a MIDI track

Add a new MIDI track by selecting Add track/MIDI in the Project menu. A new MIDI track is added to the track list and automatically selected. MIDI tracks are displayed with a five-pin DIN socket symbol to the left of the track's mute and solo buttons.

3 Set MIDI input/output ports and MIDI channel

If it is not already visible, open the Inspector for the selected MIDI track by clicking on the 'Show Inspector' button in the top left corner of the Project window. Set the MIDI input port to your chosen MIDI input device in the MIDI 'in' field. Set the MIDI output port to the desired MIDI output device in the MIDI 'out' field (i.e. the MIDI output port to which your external MIDI device is connected or VST instrument port if you are triggering a VST instrument).

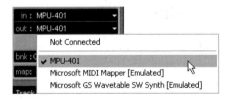

Remember that there could be several input and output ports available, depending on the hardware and software you have installed or activated in your computer. Select an appropriate MIDI channel in the channel field.

4 Activate record enable and verify MIDI thru

Activate the record enable button of the selected MIDI track by clicking on it once. When activated the record enable button is illuminated in red. Recording takes place on all record enabled tracks in the Project window when you press the record button on the Transport panel. The record enable button is activated by default when each track is selected (unless you have unticked 'Enable record on selected track' in File/Preferences/Editing). When

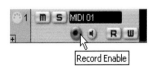

a track is record enabled MIDI Thru is automatically selected for the track allowing you to monitor the MIDI device you are triggering.

For routine MIDI recording applications the global MIDI Thru of Cubase SX should be made active. The global MIDI Thru function is found in File/Preferences/ MIDI.

5 Set metronome

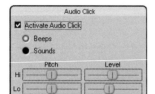

Before recording anything, set up an appropriate precount and guide click by activating Precount and adjusting the settings of the Metronome setup dialogue (Transport menu/Metronome setup). Try ticking 'Precount' in the Transport menu and 'Activate Audio click' in the Metronome setup dialogue. Select 'Beeps' if you prefer a standard audio 'beep' or, alternatively, select 'Sounds' to assign your own custom click using any audio file on your hard disk. Set a precount of 2 bars. If you would prefer to use a MIDI device for the click sound, tick 'Activate MIDI click'. Set the MIDI click channel and output port to an appropriate drum or percussion MIDI device (the supplied LM7 VST instrument is a good choice). Set the MIDI notes as required (C#1 usually triggers a rimshot sound and F#1 triggers a closed hi-hat).

6 Adjust the tempo and activate click

Ensure that the tempo is adjusted to 'Fixed' mode in the Transport panel. Enter the desired value in the tempo field. Activate the click button on the Transport panel. This provides a guide click from the selected MIDI device or from the audio output, as set above. Ensure that the punch in and punch out buttons on the Transport panel (Locators section) are de-activated. Leave all other Transport panel settings in their default positions.

7 Start recording

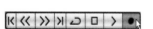

To record, select the record button on the Transport panel. Cubase SX outputs a two bar count, as set in the metronome, before recording commences from bar 1. The selected track turns red to indicate that recording has been implemented. Anything played on your MIDI keyboard is recorded by Cubase SX.

8 Stop recording

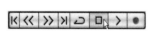

Stop recording by selecting the stop button on the Transport panel. A graphical strip known as a 'part' remains on the track and this contains the MIDI events you have just recorded.

9 Rewind

Rewind the song position in the conventional manner using the Transport panel rewind button or, alternatively, select '.' on the computer's numeric keypad which takes you back to the beginning of the project.

10 Now play it back

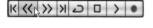

To play back the performance select the Transport panel's play button.

Save your work by selecting save from the file menu or use Ctrl + S (PC) / Command + S (Mac) on the computer keyboard. The above ten steps should get you into MIDI recording with the minimum of fuss. Cubase SX has been

supplied with most of the parameters already
sensibly set so, in most cases, only steps 6,
7, and 8 are necessary to actually make the
recording. The other steps outlined here help
you become aware of some of the other
parameters involved. Once the parameters
have been set up to suit your own recording
needs, many of the above steps can be ignored and the routine recording
process becomes much easier.

Figure 3.15
Resulting MIDI part in the Project window

If you experience problems with this process you should ensure that:

- the MIDI cables are not faulty and have been connected correctly
- the MIDI interface has been correctly installed and is selected in the MIDI
  in and out fields of the selected MIDI track
- the MIDI channel is appropriate in the channel field
- any external equipment connected to the system is switched on and
  configured to receive MIDI information on the appropriate channel(s)

Your first audio recording

Audio recording is managed in a similar manner to MIDI recording and normally takes place in the Project window. The following steps outline the basic
procedure. It is assumed that a stereo audio signal is being routed to the first
pair of line inputs of your chosen audio hardware and that you are already
familiar with MIDI recording, as outlined above.

1 Check your audio hardware

Before proceeding with the recording, make sure that your audio hardware is
installed correctly. Open the control panel for the audio hardware (if supplied) and verify the settings. Ensure that the audio outputs of the audio
hardware are connected to your amplifier and speaker system or external
mixer so that you can hear any audio output. Decide what you are going to
record and connect the source signal cable to the first pair of line inputs of
your audio hardware. It is assumed here that you are recording a stereo line
level source (such as the stereo audio output from an electronic keyboard
instrument, or a CD player).

2 Verify the VST input connections

Select VST Connections from the Devices menu and click on the inputs tab.
Click on an entry in the ASIO Device port column to show a list of the available input ports. The number of available input ports depends upon the number of physical inputs on your audio hardware. Ensure that the input pair into
which you have routed your external signal is assigned to an input buss. The
input buss appears in the Mixer to the left of all other channels.

3 Add an Audio track and activate the monitor and record enable buttons

Add a new Audio track by selecting Add track/Audio in the Project menu.
Select stereo in the configuration menu of the pop-up Add dialogue. A new
stereo Audio track is added to the track list. Audio tracks are displayed with
a wave symbol to the left of the track's mute and solo buttons. For monitor-

ing purposes, select 'Tapemachine Style' in File/Preferences/VST/Auto Monitoring. Make sure that the monitor button for the newly created audio track is active (illuminated). This allows you to hear the input signal and visually monitor the level on the channel's level meters. Also make sure that the record enable button is active (illuminated in red). This makes the channel record ready. In Tape Machine Style mode, activating the record enable button also automatically activates the monitor button when you are in Stop or Record modes. Recording takes place on all record enabled tracks in the Project window/Mixer when you press the record button on the Transport panel. By default, the record enable button is activated when a track is selected (unless you have de-selected 'Enable record on selected track' in File/Preferences/Editing).

4 Open the Mixer and select 'Meter input' in Global meter settings

Open the Mixer from the Devices menu or select F3 on the computer keyboard. Here you find the input buss which is connected to your audio hardware inputs (on the left) and the channel strip for the Audio track you created in step 3 (to the right). Right-click (PC) / Control + click (Mac) in blank space in the Mixer and select 'Meter input' in the Global meter settings section of the pop-up menu. In the input buss you now see the level of the incoming signal at the input of your audio hardware (before any level changes or other processing takes place within Cubase SX).

5 Adjust the input level while monitoring the signal in the input buss

The signal level at the input of your audio hardware is visually monitored in the meters of the input buss when the Global meter settings have been set to 'Meter input'. At this stage, the level is adjusted using the output fader of your external mixer or directly on the output faders of the device or instrument you are recording. Some audio hardware allows adjustment of the input signal via its own control panel. *The source level at the input is NOT adjusted using the input buss fader.*

Carefully adjust the input level so that no clipping occurs on the level meter of the input buss channel strip. Clipping has occurred if the clipping indicator to the lower left of the fader is illuminated in red. The level should not exceed 0dB. Signals which exceed this level produce an unpleasant audible distortion. The precise amount of headroom is shown just below the channel meters. For most applications set the signal level for a safety margin of around -1 to -6dB. The final decision for the precise input level is a matter of judgement and experience and is highly dependent upon the characteristics of the input signal. For example, a signal such as slow synthesiser strings might be easier to predict and control than live vocals, since string sounds are normally quite smooth whereas vocals are likely to feature sudden transient peaks. While it is desirable to avoid distortion you need to also avoid recording signals too low.

To aurally monitor the signal make sure that the monitor enabled audio channel you created in step 3 is set to receive the signal from the appropriate input buss in the Input/Output settings shown above the channel strip (see step 7 below for details). There may be a delay between the moment the signal enters the audio hardware and the moment you hear it via Cubase

Info

In Cubase SX, audio input and output routing is based upon busses. Input signals must enter the program via an input buss and output signals must exit via an output buss.

SX. This delay is known as latency and varies according to the audio hardware and driver which is installed on your system. Audio hardware devices with special dedicated ASIO drivers give the best performance and are the preferred option. Some ASIO drivers allow the use of the Direct Monitoring option in the VST Multitrack section of the Device setup dialogue. This virtually cuts out the latency altogether but does not allow the monitoring of the whole signal path which passes through Cubase SX.

Overall, this step ensures that the incoming signal is not producing distortion at the input of your audio hardware. This is often a once-only calibration.

6 Switch to Meter post-fader setting

Now that you know that there is no distortion at the input of your audio hardware, it is appropriate to switch the meter setting back to the default 'Meter post-fader' position. You are now monitoring the signal after it has passed through the input gain, fader and any other processing on the input buss and it is this signal which is recorded to hard disk. If you have not changed any of the controls on the input buss then the post-fader output signal is identical to the input signal. If you are suffering from a particularly weak source signal, you may at this stage wish to adjust the input gain on the input buss. Hold Shift or Alt and adjust the input gain control as required. You may also apply insert effects or EQ on the input buss. This allows you to 'print' effects and processing to hard disk (such as a signal with compression and EQ, for example).

7 Select an input on the record channel

Make sure that the record enabled audio channel you created in step 3 is set to receive the signal from the appropriate input buss (i.e. that to which you have connected your stereo audio source). The input buss for audio channels is chosen by clicking in the Input/Output fields above the channel strip (found in the Mixer or in the Inspector). You may need to click on the 'Show input and output settings' icon in the lower left corner of the Mixer if the Input/Output routing fields are not visible. The default names for the first pair of inputs for your audio hardware usually read 'IN 1' or 'BUS 1'. Here they have been renamed as 'Stereo In 1'.

It is also on the target record channel where you set the output routing for the signal. By default, a stereo audio channel is routed to the first stereo output buss found in your system which, in turn, is connected to the first pair of outputs on the audio hardware.

Note that the fader and all other controls of the target record channel are used purely for monitoring and mixing purposes. The level and quality of the audio signal which is to be recorded to hard disk is not affected by any settings you make here.

8 Adjust the metronome and tempo

As with the MIDI recording process outlined above, adjust the Metronome to give the desired pre-count before recording commences. It is possible to record audio with no concern for the current tempo but here it is assumed you are using the tempo of the click to keep in time. Ensure that the click is activated and the tempo adjusted to the desired setting in the Transport panel (use fixed mode). This provides a guide click from the selected MIDI device or

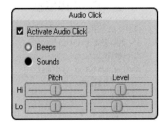

from the audio output, as set in the Metronome. Ensure that the punch in and punch out buttons on the Transport panel are de-activated. Leave all other Transport panel settings in their default positions.

9 Start recording

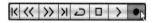

To record, select the record button on the Transport panel. After the pre-count, commence the musical performance (or send the audio signal). In this exercise, recording commences at bar 1. The selected track turns red to indicate that recording has been implemented.

10 Stop and play back the recording

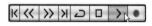

Stop recording by selecting the stop button on the Transport panel. A graphical strip remains on the track containing a waveform which represents the audio you have just recorded. This is known as an audio event. To play back the audio, rewind and press the play button (note that in 'Tapemachine Style' mode, as chosen in step 3 above, playback automatically de-activates the monitor button so that you can hear the recorded audio).

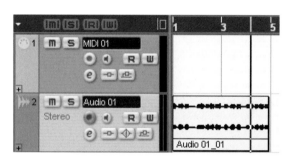

The resulting audio event appears in a similar manner to that shown in Figure 3.26. Save your work by selecting save from the file menu or use Ctrl + S (PC) / Command + S (Mac) on the computer keyboard.

Figure 3.26
Resulting Audio event in the Project window

First impressions

Creating a new project and recording with Cubase SX reveals some of the primary features of the program. The MIDI and audio recording processes operate in a similar fashion and, once you have been initiated, recording can actually be accomplished with far fewer steps than those outlined above. You may have already noticed that you can achieve a great deal without ever leaving the Project window. The Project window is at once a powerful multi-track recorder and a sophisticated multi-track editor in a single ergonomic environment. Its streamlined approach speeds up your production time and enhances your creativity. However, before exploring the Project window in more detail, let's first look at the system in a more generalised way.

Testing the controls

Some users miss many of Cubase SX's peripheral features in their quest for a quick result. Relying on the mouse alone is not always the best way of using the program. Remember that there are also a substantial number of key commands which make navigating around the system faster and easier (Table 3.1). The key commands can be explored and edited in the Key Commands dialogue (File/Key commands).

Table 3.1 Default key commands

Typewriter keyboard		Function
PC	Mac	
F2	F2	open/close Transport panel
F3	F3	open/close Mixer
F4	F4	open/close VST Connections
F8	F8	open/close video
F9	F9	select previous tool
F10	F10	select next tool
F11	F11	open/close VST instruments rack
F12	F12	open/close VST performance meter
ctrl + O	command + O	open project
ctrl + S	command + S	save project
ctrl + W	command + W	close current window
ctrl + Q	command + Q	quit program
ctrl + E	command + E	open default editor associated with the event type
ctrl + R	command + R	Score edit
ctrl + X	command + X	cut
ctrl + C	command + C	copy
ctrl + V	command + V	paste
ctrl + Z	command + Z	undo
ctrl + P	command + P	open Pool
ctrl + T	command + T	open Tempo track
alt + I	option + I	show/hide Inspector
backspace	backspace	delete selected track, part or event
return	return	open/close editor
C	C	metronome click on/off
F	F	autoscroll on/off
I	I	punch in on/off
O	O	punch out on/off
J	J	snap on/off
M	M	mute on/off
P	P	move locators to start and end points of selected part/event
R	R	record enable track
S	S	solo on/off

When you create a new project within Cubase SX, the Project window appears on the computer screen governed by various default settings. From here we can use some of the default key commands to move around the system. We are not following any particular logic here, but just becoming familiar with the controls. It's rather like learning to drive a car – it's a good idea to get the feel of the controls before actually going out on the road. Try using the new project you created in the recording exercises outlined above.

Without attempting to achieve anything musically constructive, let's try various combinations of the key commands on the computer keyboard. Pressing the up/down arrows allows you to select different tracks in the Project window track list. Pressing F2 opens/closes the Transport panel. Leave the Transport panel open on screen. Now press F3 to open the Mixer. The Mixer displays all tracks as channel strips in the same order in which they appear in the Project window track list. With the Mixer still open on screen press the M key on the computer keyboard to mute the currently selected track. Press M again to un-mute the track. Now do the same with the S key to solo and un-solo the track. You can select different channel strips in the Mixer using the left/right arrows. Pressing F3 a second time closes the Mixer. Note that many of the key commands behave like on/off or open/close switches for their respective functions. You can therefore handle Cubase SX in a very logical fashion. Other immediately useful key commands include the C key for turning the guide click on and off, the forward slash key for turning cycle on and off, and the G and H keys for horizontal zoom out and zoom in. The escape key normally closes the currently active window and exits from a dialogue.

The numeric keypad

Table 3.2 Numeric keypad shortcuts

Numeric keypad		Function
PC	Mac	
*	*	record
Enter	Enter	play
0	0	stop
–	–	rewind
+	+	fast forward
1	1	go to left locator
2	2	go to right locator
•	•	go to bar 1.1.1.0
/	/	cycle on/off

The numeric keypad may be viewed as a kind of tape recorder remote control. Although all the controls are already available within the Transport panel (and the most important are also available in the toolbar above the Project window display), their repetition on the keypad provides a handy alternative (see Table 3.2). This is invaluable for managing the transport functions when the Transport panel is hidden from view.

Using the mouse

The mouse is, above all, useful for the drag-and-drop functions, changing values, using tools, and fine editing in the editors. It provides a convenient method of setting the project cursor position by clicking in the ruler above the track display. Double clicking in the ruler initiates playback from the point at which you clicked. Double clicking a second time in the ruler stops playback. The mouse is also used to open Cubase SX's menus.

The menus

The menus are found under various headings at the top of the computer screen and Figure 3.27 shows most of the menu contents at once.

File	Edit	Project	Audio	MIDI	Scores	Pool	Transport	Devices
New Project	Undo	Add Track	Process	Open Key Editor	Open Selection	Open Pool Windo	✔ Transport Panel	MIDI Device Manage
New Library...	Redo	Remove Selecte	Plug-ins	Open Score Editor	Edit/Page Mode			Mixer
Open...	History...	Remove Empty	Spectrum Analyzer	Open Drum Editor	Symbol Palettes	Import Medium..	Locators to Selection	Mixer 2
Open Library...		Show Used Auto	Statistics	Open List Editor		Import Audio CD	Locate Selection	Mixer 3
Close	Cut	Hide All Automat	Advanced		Global Settings	Import Pool...	Locate Next Marker	Plug-in Information
	Copy		Event or Range as	Over Quantize	Layouts	Export Pool...	Locate Previous Marker	Time Display
Save	Paste	Pool	Events from Regio	Iterative Quantize	Staff Settings		Locate Next Event	VST Connections
Save As...	Paste at Origin	Markers	Create Region(s)	Quantize Setup...		Find Missing Files	Locate Previous Event	VST Instruments
Save Project to	Delete	Tempo Track	Events to Part	Advanced Quantize	Global Functions	Remove Missing		VST Performance
Save as Templat	Split at Cursor	Browser	Dissolve Part		Layout Functions	Reconstruct	Play from Selection Star	Video
Save Library...	Split Loop	Beat Calculator.	Snap Point to Curs	Transpose...	Staff Functions	Convert Files...	Play from Selection End	
Revert	Range	Set Timecode at	Bounce Selection	Merge MIDI in Loop		Conform Files...	Play until Selection Star	Show Panel
		Notepad	Detect Silence	Dissolve Part	Auto Layout	Extract Audio fro	Play until Selection End	
Page Setup...	Select	Project Setup...	Find Selected in Po	O-Note Conversion	Align Elements		Play until Next Marker	Device Setup...
Print...	Duplicate	Auto Fades Sett		Repeat Loop	Text	Create Folder	Play Selection Range	
	Duplicate		Functions	Repeat Loop		Empty Trash	Loop Selection	
Import	Repeat...		Crossfade	Functions	Move to Voice	Remove Unused		
Export	Fill Loop		Remove Fades		Move to Staff	Prepare Archive.	Use PreRoll	
Replace Audio in	Move to		Open Fade Editor(:	Logical Editor ...	Move to String	Set Pool Record	✔ Use PostRoll	
Cleanup...	Convert to Real Copy		Adjust Fades to Ra	Logical Presets			✔ Start Record at Left Locator	
	Group		Fade In to Cursor	Drum Map Setup...		Minimize File		
Preferences...	Ungroup		Fade Out to Curso	Insert Velocities...		Update Origin	Metronome Setup...	
Key Commands.				Reset		New Version	Metronome On	C
	✔ Automation follows Events		Offline Process History...			Insert into Proje	✔ Precount On	
Recent Projects	Auto Select Events under Cursor		Freeze Edits...			Select in Project		
						Find in Pool...	Sync Setup...	
Quit	Zoom ▶						Sync Online	T
	Macros ▶						Retrospective Record	Shift+Pad *

It is apparent from the range of menu items that Cubase SX is extremely comprehensive. Some of the most important elements include the file save and open functions; the import options; the undo and select options; the pool, tempo track and project setup; audio processing; MIDI editors; the quantize functions; and the score, transport and VST functions. Most of the important menu items are explored throughout the course of this book but before we go any further let's consider the options for managing how Cubase SX behaves each time you launch the program.

Figure 3.27
Cubase SX menus

Cubase SX startup options

You can set Cubase SX to behave in various different ways when the program is launched by changing the selection in the 'On Startup' option in File/Preferences/ General (Figure 3.28).

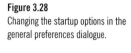

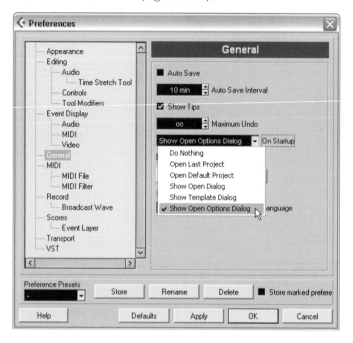

The available options are as follows:

- Do nothing – Cubase SX is launched as an empty environment with no open Project window.
- Open last project – opens the last project which was worked upon in Cubase SX.
- Open default project – opens the Cubase SX default project file (named as 'default.cpr').
- Show open dialogue – automatically opens a Project file selection dialogue when Cubase SX is launched, (as though you have already selected Open in the File menu).
- Show template dialogue – opens a project template dialogue.
- Show open options dialogue – opens an options dialogue, allowing you to choose from a list of your most recent projects.

These options help manage how you start your Cubase SX sessions. If you are working on a single long-term project then 'Open last project' is the best option. If you are using Cubase SX as a musical notepad then you may prefer to start with the same default project at the beginning of each session, in which case you should select 'Open default project'. If you continually change between a number of simultaneous projects on the same system then try using 'Show open options dialogue'.

The Project window

This chapter provides information on the Project window, the Project window tools, the Transport panel, the Inspector, event and part editing, and file handling. The Project window is the centre of activity for many of Cubase SX's functions and, as such, this chapter is essential reading for those not yet familiar.

The Project window

Project window basics

The Project window (Figure 4.1) features time on the horizontal axis and tracks on the vertical axis. Tracks are added to the project using the Add command in the Project menu. A number of different track types are available including audio, FX, folder, group, MIDI, marker, play order, ruler, automation and video types. Each track has a name and this can be changed by double clicking in its name field and typing in a new name. Various buttons surround the track name including (for audio and MIDI tracks) the mute and solo buttons ('M' and 'S'), the record and monitor buttons (red circle and speaker icons), and the read and write buttons for track automation ('R' and 'W'). Tracks contain data which is shown in the central area of the Project window (arranged as graphical blocks, lines, waveforms and symbols). This central area is known as the event display.

The current time position is shown by a vertical line known as the project cursor. When in play mode, the project cursor moves along the horizontal time line which is marked by a ruler located just above the event display. By default, the ruler displays time in bars and beats but by clicking on the arrow to the right of the ruler you can also find options for displaying time in seconds, samples or a number of common time code formats. There can be only one active Project window at any one time. An active Project window is designated by an illuminated blue indicator in the top left corner on the toolbar. (However, a Project folder can contain several project files, each of which might be a variation of the same song or musical arrangement). A new project may be created at any time by selecting New Project in the File menu (or by pressing Ctrl (PC) / Command (Mac) + N on the computer keyboard).

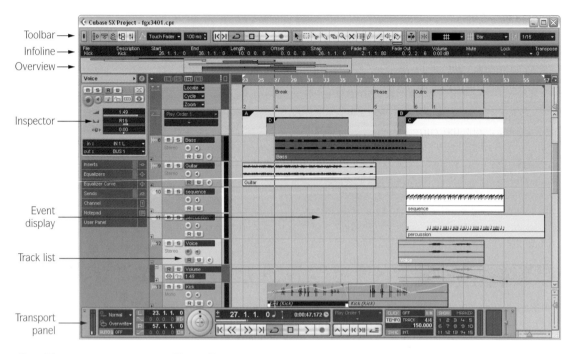

Toolbar →
Infoline →
Overview →

Inspector →

Event
display →

Track list →

Transport
panel →

Figure 4.1
The Project window

The toolbar

The Project window features a toolbar above the event display which contains a number of function buttons and tools (Figure 4.2). These provide among the easiest methods of getting into the details of the Project window.

Figure 4.2
The Project window toolbar

Let's firstly concentrate on the operation of the most commonly used buttons and the editing tools. From left to right the first five buttons include:

The show Inspector button

This shows/hides the information and editing area to the left of the event display known as the Inspector (see 'The Inspector' (page 49) for more details).

The show Info line button

This shows/hides an information line above the display which shows the details of the currently selected event.

The show Overview button

This shows/hides an overview strip above the display used for sizing and navigating within the event display.

The Open Pool button

This opens the Pool, a file display and organisation window which shows all the audio and video clips used in the active Project (see Chapter 10 for more details).

The Open Mixer button

This opens the Mixer, a virtual mixing console for the mixing of all audio, MIDI, VST Instrument and Group tracks and the setting up of EQ, effects and automation (see Chapter 11 for more details).

The Infoline

The Infoline (shown by clicking on the Infoline button in the toolbar) displays information about the currently selected event or part. The contents vary according to what kind of event or part is chosen. For a MIDI part the Infoline includes (from left to right) the name, start time, end time, length, offset, mute status, lock status, transpose and velocity values. Most of these are self explanatory. Offset is an amount by which the contents can be moved back and forth in time relative to the start and end of the part. Lock allows various attributes of the part, such as position and size, to be locked to avoid accidental changes to important material.

Name	Start	End	Length	Offset	Mute	Lock	Transpose	Velocity
MIDI 01	43.01.01.000	53.01.01.000	10.0.0.0	0.0.0.0	-	-	▼ 0	0

Figure 4.3
Infoline for a MIDI part

The infoline is particularly useful for detailed editing since all fields can be directly edited using the mouse and computer keyboard. When more than one event is selected the infoline text is shown in yellow and contains the information relevant to the first of the selected events. Editing any of the yellow text values applies the changes relatively to all selected events (i.e. changing the start position from, for example, bar 17 to bar 18 moves all selected events one bar later than their current position). To apply the edits in an absolute sense hold down Ctrl while making the changes (this time, changing the start position from bar 17 to bar 18 moves all selected events to the same absolute position at bar 18).

The Infoline for an audio event is very similar but contains a greater number of data fields including the file name which is referenced by the audio event; a description field; the start, end and length; offset, snap and volume fields; and fade, mute and lock fields. See Chapter 8 for more information about the audio event Infoline.

The Overview strip

The Overview strip (shown by clicking on the show overview button in the toolbar) shows a 'thumbnail' view of the event display. The blue selection box outlines the horizontal bar range shown in the event display and by grabbing either end of the selection box (a double arrow appears) you can change the range. You can also grab the whole box (a hand symbol appears) and drag it to a new position within your arrangement.

Figure 4.4
Overview

Other toolbar functions

The buttons and functions visible on the toolbar may be shown/hidden using the options shown in the pop-up menu which appears when you right click

Tip

When playing a VST instrument or recording live audio and monitoring via Cubase SX from a channel using insert plug-ins, the automatic delay compensation of the program may sometimes result in added latency. To cure the problem, try activating the Constrain Delay Compensation button on the toolbar while recording. When activated, insert VST plug-ins in the live signal path (with a higher delay than the setting in 'Preferences/VST/Delay compensation threshold') are turned off. De-activate the button after use.

Tip

To show the 'classic' Cubase toolbox rather than the Quick menu tick 'Popup toolbox on right click' in File/Preferences/Editing.

(PC) / Ctrl + click (Mac) anywhere on the toolbar. Other functions include Constrain delay compensation, Performance meter, Locators, Time display, Markers, Nudge palette and the Color menu. Constrain delay compensation helps minimise additional latency which may be caused by the automatic delay compensation of the program while monitoring live audio or a VSTi on channels with insert effects. The Performance meter allows you to see the current load on the CPU and hard drive. The Locators option shows the left and right locator positions. The Markers option provides a numerical display of the first ten markers. The Nudge palette allows you to trim the start and end points of the current event selection or move the event back and forth in time. The colour menu provides a colour palette for changing the colour of the currently selected track or event. The order in which the buttons and functions appear on the toolbar is edited in the Setup dialogue.

The Project window tools

To choose a tool in the Project window make a selection from the tool buttons in the toolbar or click with the right mouse button (PC)/ Ctrl + click (Mac) in the event display to open a pop-up tool selection menu (a context sensitive menu known as the Quick menu). The tools are for the manipulation and editing of events and parts and they include the following:

Object selection tool (pointer tool)

The object selection tool (or pointer tool) is the default, general purpose tool for the selection, moving and copying of events and parts, and for the manipulation of data anywhere in the Project window. Its button has a small downward pointing arrow in the lower right corner. This indicates a multi-function tool. Click on the tool button a second time to reveal the other functions. There are two additional options for the object selection tool; 'sizing moves contents' and 'sizing applies time stretch'. 'Sizing moves contents' moves the contents of an event or part forward or backward in time according to whether you size the object by sliding the start or end handles, (this effectively locks the start or end of the contents to the start or end of the object). 'Sizing applies time stretch' stretches (or compresses) the contents of an object when you re-size it. For MIDI parts the notes are re-positioned accordingly and for audio events the audio is time-stretched (or compressed).

Range selection tool

The range selection tool is for making event-independent selections of any material in the Project window. Once selected, the material can be cut, copied and pasted as required and all events are automatically split where applicable. This is in contrast to the object selection tool (outlined above) which always selects whole events and parts.

Split tool

The split tool is for splicing events/parts into smaller portions. Events/parts are split at the mouse position and according to the current snap settings. Holding Alt while clicking with the split tool automatically divides the event/part into a number of smaller events at the resolution of the snap settings.

Glue tool

The glue tool is used to join together two or more events/parts. In the case of MIDI material, parts are joined to make one longer MIDI part. In the case of audio material, events/parts are grouped into one longer audio part.

Erase tool

The erase tool is for deleting events by clicking on any single object or select-ed group of objects in the event display. Holding Alt while clicking on an event (or while clicking in blank space) deletes all the following events on that track.

Zoom tool

The zoom tool is for zooming in and out of the event display. To zoom in, select the zoom tool and click in the event display. This zooms in to the dis-play horizontally around the position at which you clicked. Holding Alt while clicking with the zoom tool zooms back out again. By clicking and dragging a selection box with the zoom tool you can zoom in to specific areas of the event display. To zoom back out again hold Ctrl (PC) / Command (Mac) while clicking in the event display with the zoom tool. This steps you back through the previous zoom views you have used. Holding Shift while clicking in the event display with the zoom tool gives you a full zoom on the whole of the currently used area of the event display. By default, the zoom tool acts upon the display horizontally. For simultaneous horizontal and vertical zooming de-activate 'zoom tool standard mode' in File/Preferences/Editing.

Mute tool

The mute tool is for muting events and parts. Click on objects individually or drag a selection box over several to implement muting. When an object is muted it is displayed in grey. Muting actions are not stored in the undo list and so cannot be undone using Ctrl/Command + Z. To undo a mute, click on the muted object a second time.

Time warp tool

The time warp tool is for dragging a bar position to a time position. This might be used to line up the start or end of a musical passage to a visual cue in a video or it might equally be used to make a musical sequence fit a specific time dura-tion. The time warp tool operates between the left and right locators in two modes; 'default' mode and 'musical events follow' mode. In the default mode, all tracks are automatically switched to linear time base and do not move when you drag the warp tool in the display. In 'musical events follow' mode, the events on all tracks which are set to musical time base mode are moved as you drag the warp tool in the display. The time warp tool is used most effectively when you set the snap mode to Events, at which time it becomes easier, for example, to drag a bar position to the start or end of an event. Inserting markers in the Marker track also helps navigate the Warp tool to the desired time position.

Holding Shift while clicking in the Project window display with the Time warp tool inserts a tempo event. Holding Shift with the time warp tool in the ruler allows the deleting of tempo events. To use the time warp tool, 'tempo track' mode must be selected in the Transport bar (time warp does not function in fixed tempo mode). For more details on the use of the time warp tool see Chapter 18.

Draw tool

The draw tool is used for drawing new empty parts by dragging the tool in the event display, adding markers in the Marker track (see below for details) and freely drawing such things as volume and pan curves on automation tracks.

Line tool

The line tool features straight line, parabola, sine, triangle and square forms which may be used to draw their respective shapes on automation tracks according to the current snap resolution.

Play/scrub tool

The play/scrub tool is a dual function tool. In its default play mode, clicking on an audio or MIDI event plays back the material from the position at which you click and continues for as long as you hold the mouse button. In scrub mode clicking and dragging over an audio or MIDI event plays back the material at the speed with which you drag, much like rocking the tape back and forth over the playback heads of a tape machine. You can change the characteristics of the scrub behaviour in File / Preferences / VST / Scrub response.

Colour tool

The colour tool allows you to apply different colours to events in the display. The colour is chosen from a pop-up colour palette which appears when you click on the colour strip just below the tool button. Double-clicking on the colour strip opens the event colour dialogue where you can create your own custom colours. To change an event back to the default colour chosen for the track, click on the event with the colour tool with 'default colour' chosen from the colour palette.

Autoscroll and snap functions

Autoscroll button

The autoscroll button is found to the right of the Project window tools and is activated/de-activated using the mouse or by pressing 'F' on the computer keyboard. When activated, the event display follows the project cursor. When de-activated, the event display remains at the position you choose regardless of the position of the project cursor.

The snap button

The snap button is found to the right of the autoscroll button and is activated/de-activated using the mouse or by pressing 'J' on the computer keyboard. When activated, all tool manipulations and editing moves are sensitive to the snap settings. Snap describes the manner in which event manipulations and editing with the tools is pulled onto the nearest bar or beat (or other subdivision) of the grid. This occurs according to a chosen snap resolution.

The snap mode, grid and quantize selectors

There are a number of menus and parameters which govern snap behaviour. Most of these are found to the right of the snap button in three menus known as the 'Snap mode menu', the 'Grid type menu' and the 'Quantize type menu' (Figure 4.5).

Snap mode menu

The Snap mode menu contains the following options:

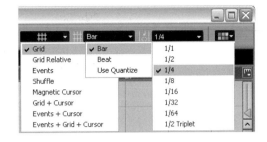

- Grid – the snap resolution is governed by the setting of the Grid type menu to the right.
- Grid relative – the snap resolution is governed by the setting of the Grid type menu but dragged objects maintain their relative position to the nearest snap point. For example, dragging an event whose initial position is bar 1 beat 2, with Grid relative enabled and Bar selected in the Grid type menu, snaps the event to bar 2 beat 2, bar 3 beat 2, bar 4 beat 2 and so on, as you drag the event across the display. This mode is excellent for moving and copying events whose positions do not begin on precise divisions of the bar.
- Events – the start and end positions of objects become magnetic. Any events dragged near to these points are snapped onto the start or end of the nearest object.
- Shuffle – objects moved on a track are snapped tightly one against the other with no space in between. This mode may be used for changing the order of tightly grouped events by dragging and inserting objects in between eachother.
- Magnetic cursor – the project cursor becomes magnetic and any objects dragged nearby are snapped to its position.
- Grid + cursor – grid and magnetic cursor modes combined.
- Events + cursor – event and magnetic cursor modes combined.
- Events + grid + cursor – event, grid and magnetic cursor modes combined.

Figure 4.5
The Snap mode selector, Grid selector and Quantize selector menus

Tip

To make adjacent events follow when you resize any event in the Project window, select shuffle in the snap mode menu before resizing. This results in gapless resizing of adjacent events since they remain tightly 'glued' together. This is particularly useful when editing speech or the gaps between the musical phrases of a solo instrument.

Grid type menu

The Grid type menu changes according to which timeline format has been chosen in the ruler. Click on the downward pointing arrow to the right of the ruler to change the time format. This is most commonly set to bars and beats, in which case the menu contains the following:

- Bar – tool editing and event placement snaps to the nearest 1 bar division on the ruler.
- Beat – tool editing and event placement snaps to the nearest 1 beat division on the ruler.
- Use quantize – tool editing and event placement snaps to the nearest division as chosen in the Quantize type menu (see below).

The Grid type menu choice affects the snap behaviour only when 'grid' is selected in the Snap mode menu (above).

Quantize type menu

The Quantize type menu contains a list of note values which may be used to define the snap resolution. However, the quantize value is only relevant to snap behaviour when all three of the following selections are made:

- 'grid' is selected in the Snap mode type menu (see above)
- 'use quantize' is selected in the Grid type menu (see above)
- bars and beats is chosen as the time format on the ruler.

If any of these is not the case then the Quantize type becomes irrelevant to the snap behaviour.

This is an alternative function for the Quantize type menu, which is usually used in association with Cubase SX's main quantize functions (found in the MIDI menu). When used to govern the snap resolution in the Project window, quantize allows the editing and moving of events to be locked to musically meaningful positions along the time scale. This helps you complete your musical arrangement with maximum speed and accuracy.

The main quantize functions (MIDI menu) automatically move recorded musical events onto the divisions of the bar chosen in the Quantize type menu. Quantize was first devised as a purely corrective function for MIDI recordings but, in Cubase SX, it may also be used to affect the timing of audio material and, as you can see, govern the snap resolution. Cubase SX provides two main types of quantize functions known as Over quantize and Iterative quantize (see the MIDI menu). Over quantize moves recorded events onto the exact divisions of the bar as chosen in the Quantize type menu, whereas Iterative quantize moves recorded events *towards* the chosen value according to a strength percentage (see Chapters 5 and 6 for more details about quantizing).

Split, divide, size and track colour functions

Vertical split point

The Project window features a vertical split point at the left edge of the event display. Pulling the split point to the left maximises the size of the event display, giving you more space to work. Pulling the split point to the right reveals more of the buttons and functions associated with the tracks.

Divide track list

Clicking on the Divide track list button divides the track list into two separate displays. This is useful when working with video tracks where the video track can be placed in the upper display while all the audio and MIDI tracks are placed in the lower display. This allows you to freely scroll within the musical arrangement while always keeping the video track visible in the upper part of the display. Similarly, the Marker track might be better placed in the upper display so that it is always visible. The divided track list is also good for using Ruler tracks set to different time displays (e.g. one set to SMPTE time in the upper display and another set to bars and beats in the lower display).

Track size

The vertical size of the tracks is scaleable. By default, Cubase SX sizes the tracks in terms of rows. Clicking and dragging on the lower edge of a track allows you to change its vertical size. Holding Ctrl (PC) / Command (Mac) while dragging on the lower edge sets all tracks to the same row size. Greater track size reveals more of the track's buttons and expands the waveform/MIDI events view in the event display.

Track colours

Clicking on the small colour palette above the track list toggles between standard and colour-coded track displays. When colour is activated, the tracks show their default colours both in the Project window and in the Mixer. This helps clarify the screen display and allows you to change the default track colour from the pop-up colour palette which appears when you click in each track's colour box in the track list. Colour may be applied to regular MIDI and audio-based tracks and is also helpful for automation tracks.

The ruler and the left and right locators

The Project window features a ruler above the event display to help you navigate within your project and to specify the timing divisions which Cubase SX takes into account for transport and editing operations. Click on the downward pointing arrow to the right of the ruler to change the time format (Figure 4.6). This is most commonly set to bars and beats but the time line may also be displayed in seconds, samples and various time code formats.

The ruler also displays the left and right locators. These are shown as pointers at each end of a shaded area in the ruler and event display. The locators are used for defining the positions you want to start and stop recording and for setting up cycle playback and cycle recording operations (Figure 4.7). The positions of the left and right locators are set in the Transport panel (see below) or by clicking and dragging in the upper half of the ruler (a pencil tool appears). Moving the right locator to before the left locator implements 'skip' mode where playback jumps between the start and end points of the shaded area. This is good for quickly testing alternative musical arrangements.

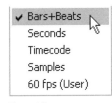

Figure 4.6
Choosing the time format in the Project window ruler

Figure 4.7
The left and right locators in the ruler

Info

An alternative method of setting the positions of the locators is to click in the ruler while pressing Ctrl (PC) / Command (Mac) to set the position of the left locator and click in the ruler while pressing Alt to set the position of the right locator.

The Transport panel

The Transport panel is a user-configurable strip for the control of standard transport operations such as record, play, stop, rewind, and various record, playback and cycle modes. It is opened by selecting 'Transport panel' in the Transport menu or by pressing F2 on the computer keyboard (Figure 4.8). It can be dragged to any screen position and each section of the panel can be shown/hidden by right clicking (PC) / Command clicking (Mac) anywhere on the panel and making the desired selection from the pop-up menu. All of its parameters may be updated or manipulated in some way using either the mouse or various computer keyboard commands.

Tip

Ctrl/Command click on the Click, Tempo and Sync buttons to open the Metronome, Tempo and Sync Setup windows respectively.

Figure 4.8
The Transport panel

Apart from the obvious tape recorder style controls the Transport panel also features the following:

Linear record mode selector

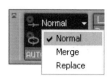

This determines how Cubase SX behaves when recording audio or MIDI events which overlap existing events in the project. There are three modes as follows:

- Normal – any audio or MIDI recording which takes place over a passage where there is existing material does NOT overwrite the previously recorded events. It produces a new event which overlaps the existing material. In the case of MIDI events, both the new and previously recorded material is heard simultaneously. In the case of audio events, only the audio event which takes playback priority is heard (normally the event which is 'on top' in the event display).
- Merge – for audio recording, merge produces identical behaviour to normal mode (as described above). For recording MIDI over an existing MIDI part, any new events are merged with the existing events in the part and no new MIDI part is created.
- Replace – any audio or MIDI recording which overlaps a passage where there is existing material replaces the previously recorded events in the overlapped section.

> **Tip**
>
> Right click/Command click on the Transport panel to open a pop-up menu where you can show/hide the various elements of the panel.

Cycle record mode selector

The cycle record mode selector determines the manner in which recordings are made when in Cycle mode. Mix and Overwrite modes are relevant mainly to MIDI recording. Keep Last and Stacked modes are relevant to both audio and MIDI recording. The modes function as follows:

- Mix (MIDI) – in mix mode, the current MIDI input is added to any existing recording in the same part. This is the default mode for quickly building up a rhythm part, for example, when different elements of a drum kit can be added on each lap of the cycle.
- Overwrite (MIDI) – in overwrite mode, any MIDI input replaces any existing recordings in the same part and deletes any data which occurs after the drop-in point for the current lap of the cycle.
- Keep Last (audio and MIDI) – for MIDI recordings, each completed lap of the cycle in which there is MIDI input replaces the previously recorded lap. If you do not play anything, the existing events recorded on a previous lap are kept. For audio recordings, the last lap in the cycle which is recorded up to the end of the cycle range is kept as an audio event. All previously recorded laps are kept within the audio file and may be accessed via the regions settings or other manipulations of the audio event (see Chapter 8 for more details).
- Stacked (audio and MIDI) – for MIDI recordings, a MIDI part for each lap of the cycle appears on its own lane within the vertical space of the MIDI track. The stacked MIDI parts can be directly spliced, muted or otherwise edited in the Project window, or edited in the Key editor. Edited parts may be later merged into a single composite part using Merge MIDI in Loop (MIDI menu). For audio recordings, an audio event for each lap of the cycle appears on its own lane within the vertical space of the audio track. The stacked events can be edited directly in the event display, making it easy to quickly build up a composite take while remaining in the Project window.
- Stacked 2 (no mute) – similar to the regular stacked mode outlined above except that previous takes are not automatically muted on each lap of the cycle. This is relevant mainly to MIDI recording and means that all recorded events are heard simultaneously (similar to overwrite mode except that the recordings are stored in separate events).

The left and right locator positions

These show the current positions of the left and right locators. Clicking on either of the 'L' and 'R' boxes moves the project cursor to the respective positions in the event display. Clicking on any part of the locator positions or double-clicking either of the locator positions allows you to enter a numerical value from the computer keyboard. The left and right locators can also be set by dragging the locator pointers in the ruler (see 'The ruler and the left and right locators' above).

The automatic quantize button (AQ)

Used to automatically quantize a performance as it is recorded according to the quantize value set in the Quantize type menu.

The punch in and out buttons

For automatically dropping in and out of record mode at the left and right locator positions. Cubase SX always starts recording from the left locator position and when record mode is implemented the punch in button is automatically selected. However, if Cubase SX is rewound to a point some bars before the left locator and put into play with the punch in button manually selected, Cubase SX drops in to record when it reaches the left locator position. If the punch out button has also been selected, Cubase SX drops out of record at the right locator position. Otherwise it remains in record mode until you stop the sequencer.

Pre and post-roll parameters

The pre-roll field determines the number of bars of pre-roll which occurs when you implement playback or record. The post-roll field determines the number of bars of post-roll which occurs after dropping out of record. The latter is only relevant when you use the punch out button. To enable pre and post-roll, activate 'pre/post roll' in the Transport menu or click on the pre/post roll buttons on the Transport panel.

Shuttle speed and jog wheels

The Transport panel features a useful dual dial control which helps you find specific audio material and locations within your project based upon what you hear. This is useful for lining up the project cursor to audio cues prior to using the 'split at cursor' or 'add marker' functions, for example. The outer dial is the shuttle speed dial which allows you to monitor the audio as you move the project cursor forwards or backwards within the material. This is a bit like standard fast forward and rewind except you can still hear the audio. The further round you drag the dial from its centre position the faster the playback speed (normal or reverse playback depending on which side of the centre position you drag the dial). The inner dial is the jog wheel. This also allows you to move the project cursor while still hearing the audio but, this time, is designed for jogging back and forth over a smaller section of material, much like a traditional jog wheel designed for lining up the playback heads of a tape machine to a specific location on tape. The jog wheel is an infinite wheel with no minimum or maximum positions so you can continuously rotate it in either direction to find the desired audio point. The centre of the dial features '+'

and '–' nudge buttons. These allow you to nudge the project cursor position backwards or forwards one frame at a time (according to the current time code frame rate). These buttons are useful for fine tuning the position of the project cursor to very precise locations within the arrangement.

The position display and position slider

The position display shows the current project cursor position in two displays; the primary and secondary time displays. The primary time display is selected for the project in Project menu/Project setup or by making a selection from the pop-up menu to the right of the primary time display or to the right of the ruler. The secondary time display is selected from the pop-up menu to the right of the secondary time display. Clicking on any part of the position display or double-clicking on it allows you to enter a numerical value from the computer keyboard. The '+' and '-' buttons allow you to move the cursor position forwards or backwards one bar, one frame, one second or one sample at a time depending on which time format has been chosen. The position slider is found just below the position display and can be used to quickly slide back and forth within the project.

The Click on/off button

This enables/disables the guide click for Cubase SX (as set up in the Metronome dialogue).

The Tempo track mode and tempo/time signature displays

The tempo track mode allows the changing of the tempo behaviour between 'fixed' and 'track' modes. In fixed mode, the tempo follows the single tempo and time signature settings as shown in the Transport panel. In tempo track mode, the tempo follows any tempo and time signature changes as found in the Tempo track. The tempo is shown in beats per minute (BPM).

The sync button

For activating or de-activating synchronisation to an external time code generating device. When de-activated (set to 'INT'), Cubase SX uses the internal timing clock of the computer for all tempo and time-based functions. When activated, Cubase SX may be slaved to an external clock for synchronisation with other sequencers, tape machines and drum machines.

Track types

Cubase SX features a number of different track types, each specialised in the handling of its own kind of data, and each displayed with a unique graphical symbol in the track list of the Project window (Figure 4.8a).

Audio and MIDI tracks are explored in the recording exercises in Chapter 3. The Marker track, Folder tracks and the Play Order track are described in the following sections.

The Marker track and Marker window

The Marker track and Marker window are for managing guide markers inserted along the time line of your project. Markers allow you to quickly move to

Info

When the time format is set to bars and beats the position display shows the project cursor position in bars, beats, sixteenth notes and ticks (by default, there are 120 ticks in each sixteenth note).

Figure 4.8a
The different track types in the track list

any position within your project and to set up cycle loops (for recording and playback purposes). The Marker track is opened in the event display using the 'Add track' option in the Project menu. However, the difference between the Marker and other types of tracks is that only one Marker track can be present for each project. The Marker window provides a list-based overview of all markers and allows you to edit and name them as desired.

There are three different types of markers: the left and right locators, cycle markers and standard markers. The Marker track and Marker window essentially deal with the same data but the Marker track allows a graphical approach whereas the Marker window provides a text-based list.

Opening the Marker track

Select 'Add track' from the Project menu and choose 'Marker' to open the Marker track in the event display (Figure 4.9).

Figure 4.9
The Marker track in the event display

Adding markers

There are a number of ways to add markers as follows:

1. To add standard markers, click on the add marker button found in the track list section of the Marker track or press the insert key on the computer keyboard. Standard markers are placed at the current location of the project cursor and are automatically numbered in ascending order as they are added. Standard markers appear as vertical blue lines. They can be added on the fly (while in playback mode) or while Cubase SX is static. Standard markers are named in the Infoline.

2. To add cycle markers, click on the add cycle marker button found in the track list section of the Marker track. Cycle markers are placed between the current positions of the left and right locators and are automatically numbered in ascending order as they are added. They appear as vertical grey lines at the left and right locator positions joined by a single horizontal grey line. Cycle markers are named in the Infoline.

3. You can also use the draw tool to add standard markers by clicking at the desired position within the Marker track (this also functions by clicking with the pointer in the Marker track while holding Alt). Holding Ctrl (PC) / Command (Mac) and dragging with the pencil tool allows you to insert a cycle marker over the selected range. If the snap button is active, markers are magnetic to the current snap resolution.

Editing markers

Markers are edited in a similar manner to other events in the event display. Marker events are selected by clicking on them with the object selection tool, they are deleted using the erase tool, and cycle marker events are split into two by clicking with the split tool on the horizontal line between the two cycle points.

The Marker window

The Marker window displays the Marker track data in list format. Any changes made in either the Marker window or the Marker track are reflected in both. Select 'Markers' from the Project menu or Ctrl + M (PC) / Command + M (Mac) to open the Marker window (Figure 4.10).

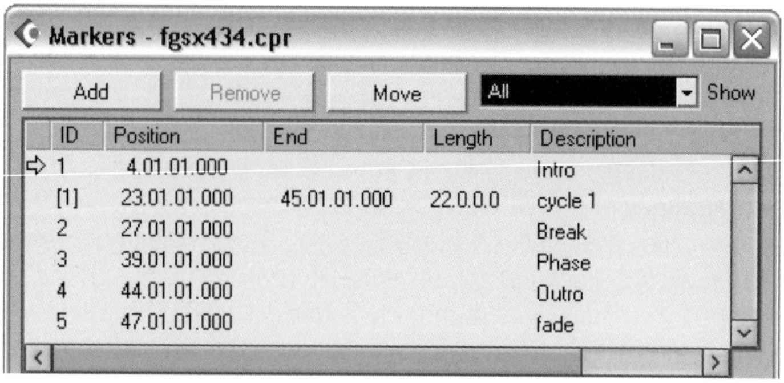

Figure 4.10
The Marker window

The Marker window features a number of columns for the display of marker information. These include the following:

- ID – shows the ID number for the marker.
- Position – shows the ruler position for the marker (or the start position in the case of cycle markers).
- End – shows the end position of cycle markers.
- Length – shows the length of cycle markers.
- Description – allows you to enter a description or name for the marker or cycle marker. The left and right marker names cannot be changed.

The Marker window is useful for getting an overview of all the markers in the project and provides a way of filtering the different marker types in the show menu.

Using the markers

There are a wide range of uses for markers including marking points of interest within your music, labelling sections of your arrangement so that you can see its structure more clearly and setting up cycle loops for playback and recording purposes. For example, one classic use of markers is to mark the intro, verse, chorus, bridge, break (and so on) of a song structure. In addition, there are a number of techniques associated with markers which make navigating within your project a whole lot easier. Try the following:

- Double click between any two markers with the pointer tool to select all events in the bars between them.
- Double click between any two markers with the range selection tool to select the precise range in the bars between them.
- Double click on any standard marker to move the project cursor to the marker's location.
- Double click inside any cycle marker to move the left and right locators to the start and end of the cycle range.
- Select numeric keypad numbers 3 to 9 to move the project cursor to marker numbers 3 to 9.

Info

Markers are also viewed and edited in the Inspector and the Project Browser. Note that removing the Marker track from the event display does not remove the marker data. All data remains intact and the markers are still available in other parts of the program.

Tip

By default, the numeric keypad numbers 3 to 9 are the key commands for standard marker numbers 3 to 9 and are used for quickly moving the project cursor to the respective locations. Also try using the markers box in the toolbar.

- In the Marker track header in the track list, open the locate pop-up menu to navigate to any one of the available markers. Open the cycle marker pop-up menu to move the left and right locators to the start and end of a chosen cycle marker range. Open the zoom pop-up menu to zoom in to a chosen cycle marker range.

Folder tracks

A folder track is a special kind of track which acts as a container for any number of other tracks, much like the folders you use to store files on your hard disk. In the same way that organising a filing system on your hard disk helps keep track of your data, creating folder tracks in Cubase SX helps clarify complex musical arrangements and keeps the event display uncluttered.

To create a folder track, use 'Add track' in the Project menu and select 'Folder'. A new folder track appears in the event display. Once the folder track is available you can drag and drop other tracks into the folder track. A green arrow appears over the folder track each time you drag another track into the appropriate position to be dropped. All track types may be dragged into a folder track, including other folder tracks. A closed folder track looks similar to that shown in Figure 4.11. Note that the folder track can be sized and named like any other track and most tool editing techniques are still valid, such as splitting, erasing, muting and so on.

You can open or close a folder track by clicking on the folder icon or on the +/- box in the lower left corner of the track header. Figure 4.12 shows the event display when the folder track in Figure 4.11 is opened.

Info

Cubase SX also supports group channel, input/output channel automation and video tracks. Group channels are sub-groups to which the signals from any number of regular audio tracks can be routed. The input/output channel automation tracks are for the management of any mix automation data from the input/output buses. Video tracks are for the display of video files when you are working on sound to picture projects. These elements are covered in other chapters.

Figure 4.11
A closed folder track

Folder Tracks might be used for grouping together different elements in order to clarify the musical structure of your music (such as drums, percussion, strings, brass and vocals). If you are working on a vocal part, you might like to put the backing tracks into their own folder so that you can focus on the vocal track in the event display. In addition, using folder tracks frees up more space in the Project window and is excellent for soloing and muting purposes where you might like to solo or mute whole sections of the arrangement rather than individual tracks.

Figure 4.12
The same folder track opened in the event display

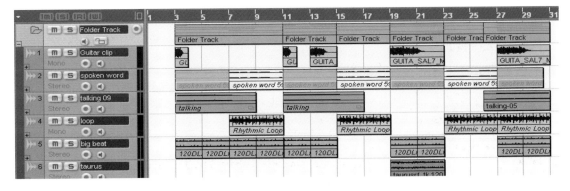

Play Order track

The Play Order track is a special non-linear playback track which allows you to play different sections of your musical arrangements in any order and with any number of repeats. This could be likened to a pattern-based sequencer where various preset patterns can be chained together to form a musical composition.

There can be only one Play Order track in each Cubase project. It is managed in the Project window and in the Inspector or Play Order editor. The main steps you need to take to start using the Play Order track are as follows:

- Add the Play Order track to the project by selecting Add Track/Play Order in the Project menu. The Play Order track appears in the Project window.
- Create some parts in the new Play Order track which correspond to the desired sections of your existing musical arrangement by dragging across the display with the draw tool (Figure 4.13). By default, new play order parts are named with the letters of the alphabet but, if you need to, the name may be changed on the infoline.

Figure 4.13
Play order parts in the event display

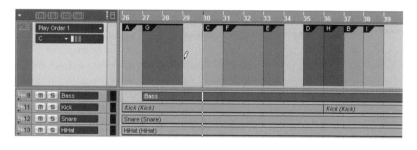

- Open the Inspector for the track by clicking on the Show Inspector button in the Project window toolbar. (Alternatively, open the Play Order editor by clicking on the edit button in the Play Order track header).
- Drag and drop Play Order parts from the 'Play Order parts' section of the Inspector (or Play Order editor) into the 'Current Play Order List' (Figure 4.14). You can arrange the parts in any order you wish and adjust the number of repeats for each part in the right-hand column.
- Activate Play Order mode by clicking on the Play Order mode button in the track header of the Play Order track. Playback is now governed by the order of events in the current Play Order list.

Figure 4.14
Drag and drop play order parts into the current Play Order list in the Inspector

Using the Play Order track

The Play Order track is a great tool for remixing and loop-based dance styles. In this context, it would normally be used to re-order the sequence of events in an existing musical arrangement. For example, rather than start at the beginning of the song, you could start on the ad-lib chorus section at the end, and if the second and third bar of the solo section contains a great hook line, you could loop it twice before the start of the first verse. And if you are working with repetitive loops, it is easy to chain your patterns together with the desired number of repeats in the Play Order list. There are a wide range of possibilities for creatively re-arranging any existing musical structure. However,

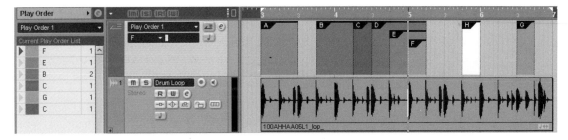

the Play Order track may also be used in a more experimental way to generate new ideas. For example, take any drum loop and manipulate the play order
using relatively short Play Order parts of one, two and four beats in length.
This is a good loop mangling technique and can help create new drum rhythms
(Figure 4.15). The same technique can be used for the creative manipulation
of abstract and time-stretched sound effects. Remember that Play Order parts
can be nested inside each other allowing you to use parts of varying lengths
over the same passage (see parts E and F in Figure 4.15).

Figure 4.15
Experimenting with Play Order parts on a
drum loop to create a new rhythm

Playback and manipulation of the Play Order track can also be achieved in
the Transport panel by activating the Play Order section (right click/Ctrl click
on the Transport panel to open the pop-up menu). Note also that several Play
Order lists may be held in memory at the same time allowing you to build up
a number of different musical arrangements within the same project.

When you are happy with a new play order you may wish to convert it into
a conventional linear arrangement. This is achieved by selecting 'Flatten Play
Order' in the pop-up Play order menu in the Inspector (or by clicking on the
'Flatten Play Order' button in the Play Order editor). Upon selection, all relevant events are re-arranged, split and repeated as necessary across the event
display in a linear manner corresponding to the order of events in the current
play order list, and the Play Order track itself is closed. All material which is
not used in the Play Order list is deleted from the event display. If you are
likely to need the original linear version of the project at a later date, you are
strongly advised to save the project under another name before using the
'Flatten Play Order' command.

The Inspector

The Inspector is found in the Project window to the left of the track list. It is
opened and closed by clicking on the Show Inspector button in the toolbar. The
Inspector contains a number of parameters and sub-sections associated with
the currently selected track. The contents of the Inspector vary according to
what type of track is selected. The two most important Inspector configurations
are those for MIDI and audio track types and these are outlined below.

The Inspector for MIDI tracks
For MIDI tracks, the Inspector features five sections which are opened by
clicking on the corresponding tab. The sections include the following:

Basic track settings
The basic track settings section features the MIDI track name as shown in the

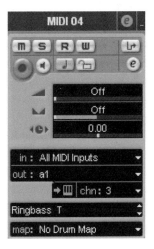

Figure 4.16
Basic track settings (Inspector for MIDI
tracks)

track list, various function buttons and a number of other parameters. The buttons include the mute and solo buttons ('M' and 'S') for muting or soloing the track, the read and write buttons for track automation ('R' and 'W'), the Input Transformer button for opening a real-time MIDI data transformation tool, the record and monitor buttons for record-enabling and monitor-enabling the track, the linear/musical timebase button for switching between time (non-tempo dependent) or beat based (tempo dependent) positioning of events, the lock button for locking the name, position, length etc. of events on the selected track and the edit MIDI channel button for opening an overall parameters window featuring channel fader, insert and send effects.

Below the buttons there are mini-faders for controlling the MIDI volume, pan and delay time (in milliseconds). There are also fields for setting the input, output, MIDI channel, program name (or number) and MIDI drum map setup.

Volume and pan are useful for quickly setting up the basic level and pan position for the chosen track while still remaining in the basic settings section. Delay might be used for changing the feel of the chosen track in relation to the others, by shifting the data backwards or forwards in time. This might include adjusting a snare or hi-hat track to be late or early to give the drum arrangement a special feel, or shifting a slow strings sound earlier to anticipate the beat. The program field changes the program number / patch in the target MIDI unit / VST instrument. This is useful for quickly searching for the desired patch on a synth while still remaining within the convenient environment of the Project window.

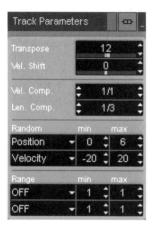

Figure 4.17
Track parameters (Inspector for MIDI tracks)

Track parameters

The Track parameters section features controls for the real-time manipulation of MIDI data. These include the following:

*   Transpose – for the transposing of MIDI notes up or down (range: –127 to +127)
*   Velocity shift – for the adding or subtracting of an amount to the velocity of MIDI notes (range: –127 to +127)
*   Velocity compression – for the compression or expansion of the velocity of MIDI notes according to a compression/expansion ratio.
*   Length compression – for the compression or expansion of the length of MIDI notes according to a compression/expansion ratio.
*   Random – for the adding or subtraction of random numbers between a chosen minimum and maximum value. Random acts upon a choice of the position, pitch, velocity or length of MIDI events and features two independent random fields.
*   Range – for the limiting or filtering of MIDI notes or notes of a chosen velocity between a minimum and maximum value. Range features a choice of velocity limit, velocity filter, note limit or note filter and features two independent range fields.

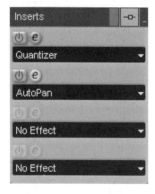

Figure 4.18
Inserts section (Inspector for MIDI tracks)

Transpose can be used for trying out simple harmonies or shifting the octave for any given sound, as well as corrective transposing. Velocity shift affects the overall velocity of the MIDI data and is used when you need to increase / decrease the perceived force with which the notes in a performance are played. Velocity shift and velocity compression might be used together to flatten out the dynamics of an over-excited track (try settings of +60 for velocity shift with 2/3 for velocity compression). Length might be used to increase the staccato feel of a track by using a setting of 1/3 or 1/4. To increase a track's legato try a value of 3/1 or more. The random section is good for 'humanising' a MIDI performance by introducing random inaccuracies into the data. Try setting the first random field to 'position' with minimum at 0 and maximum at 6, and the second random field to 'velocity' with minimum at –20 and maximum at +20. This avoids robotic MIDI parts.

Inserts

The Inserts section features four slots for inserting MIDI effects plug-ins into the MIDI data path. This is a 'mirror' of the MIDI Inserts section for the track as found in the extended part of the Mixer. The supplied MIDI effects include Arpache, Autopan, Chorder, Compress, Control, Density, Micro Tuner, MIDIEcho, Note to CC, Quantizer, Step Designer, Track Control, Track FX and Transformer. You can get a good idea of the functions of these effects from their names. To find out more, choose a MIDI track and experiment with one or more MIDI effects in the Inserts section. To load a MIDI effect, click on an empty effects slot to open the effects menu. Choose the desired effect from the list. When an effect is chosen from the menu it is immediately activated and its GUI is automatically opened. Adjust the parameters as required or choose an existing preset from the presets menu of the chosen effect. Activate playback to hear the results. MIDI insert effects transform the data in real-time. The original MIDI data remains intact unless you use 'Merge MIDI in loop' in the MIDI menu. Note that with Insert effects the MIDI data is routed 'through' each activated effect in turn. (See Chapter 13 for more details about MIDI effects).

Sends

The Sends section (Figure 4.19) features four slots for assigning MIDI send effects to the chosen MIDI track. This is a 'mirror' of the MIDI Sends section for the track as found in the extended part of the Mixer. Each MIDI track can have its own unique set of send effects and settings. The supplied effects are the same as those for the MIDI Insert effects (see 'Inserts' above). To find out more, choose a MIDI track and experiment with one or more MIDI send effects. MIDI send effects transform the data in real-time. The original MIDI data remains intact unless you use 'Merge MIDI in loop' in the MIDI menu. Note that with send effects both the original MIDI data and the effect data appear at the output of the MIDI track. (See Chapter 13 for more details about MIDI effects).

Channel

The Channel section (Figure 4.20) features a 'mirror' of the channel strip as found in the Mixer. This can be used to change the level and pan position for the track and to apply mute, solo, read, write, bypass inserts, disable sends, record and monitoring functions. You can also edit the name for the track.

The Inspector for audio tracks

For audio tracks, the Inspector features five sections which are opened by clicking on the corresponding tab. The sections include the following:

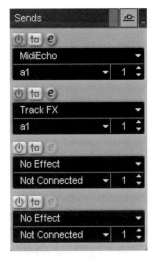

Figure 4.19
Sends section (Inspector for MIDI tracks)

Figure 4.20
Channel section (Inspector for MIDI tracks)

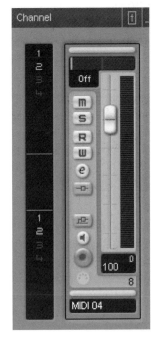

Figure 4.21
Basic track settings (Inspector for audio tracks)

Figure 4.22
Inserts section (Inspector for audio tracks)

Info

Auto fade produces glitch-free transitions between adjacent audio events by applying a short automatic crossfade (see Chapter 8 for more details). This is set globally for the project in 'Auto fades settings' in the Project menu or it can be adjusted individually for the track in the Inspector by clicking on the auto fades settings button.

Basic track settings

The basic track settings section features the audio track name as shown in the track list, various function buttons and a number of other parameters. The buttons include the mute and solo buttons ('M' and 'S') for muting or soloing the track, the read and write buttons for track automation ('R' and 'W'), the auto fades settings button for adjusting the auto fade characteristics for the track, the record and monitor buttons for record-enabling and monitor-enabling the track, the linear/ musical timebase button for switching between time (non-tempo dependent) or beat based (tempo dependent) positioning of events, the lock button for locking the name, position, length etc. of events on the selected track and the edit audio channel button for opening a channel edit window for the adjustment of channel fader, pan, insert, send and EQ parameters.

Below the buttons there are mini-faders for controlling the audio volume, pan and delay time (in milliseconds). There are also fields for setting the audio input and output ports.

Volume and pan are useful for quickly setting up a basic level and pan position for the chosen track while still remaining in the basic settings section. Delay might be used for changing the feel of the chosen track in relation to the others, by shifting the data backwards or forwards in time.

Inserts

The Inserts section (Figure 4.22) features eight slots for inserting audio effects plug-ins into the audio signal path. This is a 'mirror' of the audio Inserts section for the track as found in the extended part of the Mixer. To find out more, choose an audio track and experiment with one or more audio effects in the Inserts section. To load an audio effect, click on an empty effects slot to open the effects menu. The menu features a wide range of audio effects organised into various categories including delay, distortion, dynamics, filter, modulation, reverb and others. When an effect is chosen from the menu it is immediately activated and its GUI is automatically opened. Adjust the parameters as required or choose an existing preset from the presets menu of the chosen effect. Activate playback to hear the results. The effects processing takes place in real-time. Note that with Insert effects the audio signal is routed 'through' each activated effect in turn. (See Chapter 13 for more details about audio effects).

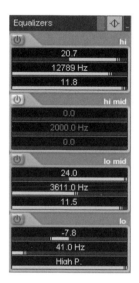

Figure 4.23
Equalizers and Equalizer curve sections (Inspector for audio tracks)

Equalizers

The Equalizers section (Figure 4.23) features a four band parametric EQ for adjusting the equalisation of the chosen track. This is a 'mirror' of the audio track EQ section as found in the extended part of the Mixer. The controls include low, low mid, high mid and high sections with Q, frequency and gain controls for each. Adjustments are made by dragging the mini-faders or double clicking on the parameters field to enter a precise value directly. There is also an Equalizer curve section which displays the equaliser settings visually as a simple curve (Figure 4.23). Click directly in the display to change the shape of the curve using the equaliser handles which appear. To delete a handle drag it out of the display. (For more information about EQ see Chapter 11).

Sends

The Sends section (Figure 4.24) features eight slots for audio send effects each with a mini-fader for regulating the amount of audio track signal which is sent to the effect. The choice of send effects is determined by the number of FX channel tracks which have been created for the project. Edit buttons for each effect allow you to open its GUI directly from the Inspector. The sends section is a mirror of the audio Sends section for the track as found in the extended part of the Mixer. The supplied effects are the same as those for the audio Insert effects (see 'Inserts' above). To find out more, choose an audio track and experiment with one or more audio send effects. Audio send effects transform the signal in real-time. With send effects the original audio signal ('dry' signal) is mixed with the FX channel signal ('wet' signal) at the master output faders. (See Chapter 13 for more details about audio effects).

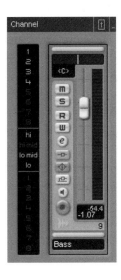

Figure 4.24 (left)
Sends section (Inspector for audio tracks)

Figure 4.25 (right)
Channel section (Inspector for audio tracks)

Channel

The Channel section (Figure 4.25) features a 'mirror' of the channel strip as found in the Mixer. This can be used to change the level and pan position for the track and to apply mute, solo, read, write, edit, bypass inserts, bypass EQ, disable sends, record and monitoring functions. You can also edit the name for the track.

Using the tools

Arranging and editing the events in the event display is among the principal functions of the Project window and once you have recorded a number of audio events or MIDI parts you will almost certainly wish to edit them in some way. This requires a good knowledge of how to use the tools in the toolbar. Using the tools is among the most important skills in the confident handling of Cubase SX. See Table 4.1 for a summary of the main tool functions.

Table 4.1 Tool function table

Tool	Keys held		Mouse action	Result
	PC	Mac		
object selection	-	-	double click between locators	creates a new empty part
	-	-	click on event	selects event
	-	-	click in empty space and drag	opens rectangular selection box
	-	-	click on event(s) and drag	moves event(s)
	alt	alt	click on event(s) and drag	copies event(s)
	alt + shift	alt + shift	click on event and drag	copies event as a shared copy
range selection	-	-	click and drag	selects an 'event-independent' range
erase	-	-	click on event(s)	erases event(s)
	alt	alt	click on event	erases event and all those following
split	-	-	click on event	splits event at mouse position
	alt	alt	click on event	splits event into several smaller events
scrub	-	-	drag over event	plays event's contents at drag speed
speaker	-	-	click on event	plays event contents at normal speed
pencil	-	-	click in empty space and drag	creates a new empty part
mute	-	-	click on event	mutes the event
glue	-	-	click on event	joins selected event to the next event

Among the most common event editing operations include selecting, moving, duplicating, splitting, joining, resizing, fading, muting and erasing. If you have not yet recorded a number of events in the Project window use the events created in the recording exercises outlined in Chapter 3 as test material.

Tip

Click with the right mouse button (PC)/ Ctrl + click (Mac) in empty space in the event display to open a context sensitive pop-up menu (known as the Quick menu) containing the tools and a wide range of editing functions.

Selecting

Selecting, in itself, does not involve the direct editing of events but it is often an important step before other editing operations take place. The object selection tool is the tool most often used for the routine selection of events. Any object in the event display may be selected by clicking on it with the object selection tool. Dragging a selection box around a number of events allows you to select a number of objects in one move. Holding the Shift key on the computer keyboard allows you to add to (or subtract from) an existing selection by clicking on single objects one at a time. All selections made with the object selection tool involve whole events. Alternatively, you may implement event-independent selections using the range selection tool. Select the range selection tool and drag the capture zone across the required bar range.

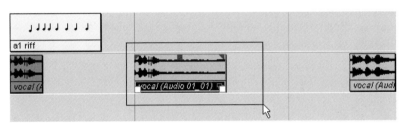

Figure 4.26
Selecting an event in the event display

Moving

To move an event to a new position in the display, select the object selection tool, click on the event and drag it to a new position. More than one event can be moved simultaneously by clicking in empty space and dragging a selection box around several events. Clicking and dragging on any one of the selected events allows you to move all the events to a new location. Alternatively, try using the range selection tool to select an event-independent range within the display. The selection can then be moved to a new position in the same way, (events are automatically split at the appropriate positions). If the snap button is active, dragged events are magnetic to the snap resolution.

Figure 4.27
Moving an event

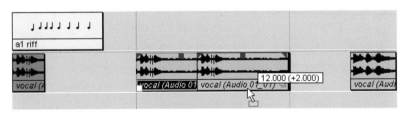

Duplicating

To duplicate an event, select the object selection tool, click on the event and drag while holding Alt on the computer keyboard. A duplicate event is created

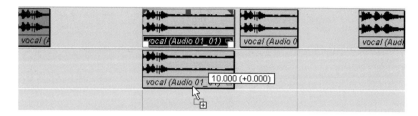

Figure 4.28
Duplicating an event

To duplicate a number of consecutive events (i.e. to repeat the events) select Repeat in the Edit menu (Ctrl/Command + K) and enter the number of repeats required in the pop-up dialogue. Alternatively, select Duplicate in the Edit menu (Ctrl/Command + D).

which can be placed at a new location in the event display. Holding Shift + Alt while dragging the event creates a shared copy. Any subsequent audio or MIDI processing which takes place on one of the shared copies affects all the others simultaneously. Duplicating audio events always results in shared copies since the events are always referenced to the same audio clip. Shared copies can be converted to independent events by selecting 'convert to real copy' in the edit menu (see Chapter 8 for more information).

Splitting

To split an event, select the split tool (scissors) and click on the event at the point you wish to implement the split. If the snap button is active, the split point is magnetic to the snap resolution. The event is divided into two separate events. Holding Alt while clicking on an event, splits the event into a number of smaller parts at the resolution of the snap setting.

Selecting a number of events and clicking on any one with the split tool, splits all events at the same point.

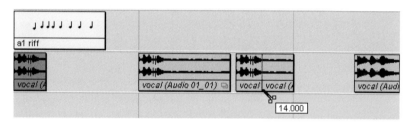

Figure 4.29
Splitting an event

Joining

To join one event to a following event, select the glue tool and click on the first of the events. In the case of MIDI material, the first part is joined to the second to make one longer MIDI part. In the case of audio material, the audio events are grouped together within a single audio part.

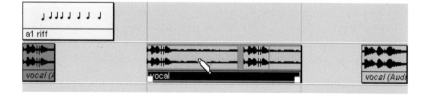

Figure 4.30
Joining events

Resizing

To resize events drag one of the small square handles which appear in the lower corners of the start and end point of the event. The handles become visible when the event is selected and a double arrow appears when you have placed the mouse in the correct position to begin resizing. For this purpose,

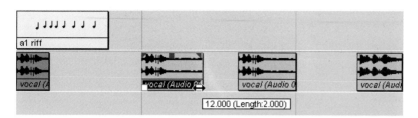

Figure 4.31
Resizing an event

the object selection tool is available in three modes; 'normal sizing', 'sizing moves contents' and 'sizing applies time stretch'. Normal sizing resizes the object without making any changes to the data; it simply hides existing data when you reduce the size and adds blank space when you increase it. 'Sizing moves contents' moves the contents of an event forward or backward in time by locking the start or end of the contents to the start or end of the object. 'Sizing applies time stretch' stretches (or compresses) the contents of an object when you re-size it.

Normal resizing is helpful when you need to quickly top and tail an event to hear only the desired part of the audio. This often applies to audio recordings where extraneous noise may have been recorded before the musical performance begins. 'Sizing moves contents' allows you to slide the contents of an event backwards or forwards in time. This might apply to situations where you are happy with the attack (first part) of an event but wish to shorten it overall. In this case you would move the first part of the event to the right. Resizing using the 'sizing applies time stretch' tool is one of the most convenient ways of changing the length and tempo of drum loops to fit the current tempo of Cubase SX. This technique works best on drum loops which are already fairly close to the current tempo since time stretching by more than around 15% may produce undesirable audio side effects.

Fading and volume control

To fade an audio event in or out, select the event with the object selection tool and drag the blue handle in the upper left corner to create a fade in, or drag the blue handle in the upper right corner to create a fade out. The fade curve can be modified by double clicking above the curve in the display and changing the settings in the fade dialogue which appears. Note that the middle blue handle is for modifying the volume of the event. The fade and volume handles are available for audio events only.

If you need to create more elaborate volume curves for audio events, Cubase SX features volume events. These provide a basic alternative/addition to regular automation and have the advantage of being attached permanently to the event.

To create a volume curve for an audio event proceed as follows: select the draw tool and place it within the event (a small volume curve symbol appears

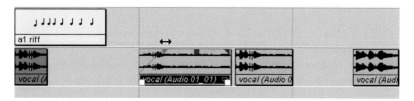

Figure 4.32
Creating a fade in for an event

Figure 4.33
Creating volume events within an audio
event

Figure 4.33
Creating volume events within an audio
event

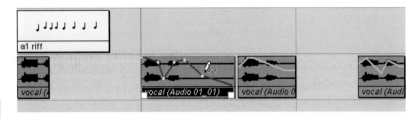

beside the tool). Select the event and click with the tool to insert volume handles. Drag the handles within the event to form the desired curve (see Figure 4.33). Volume events are deleted by holding the Shift key while clicking upon a volume handle.

Muting

To mute an event, select the mute tool and click on the event. You can also drag a selection box over several events to mute a number of objects simultaneously. A muted event is displayed in grey.

Figure 4.34
Muting an event

Erasing

To erase an event, select the erase tool and click once on the event. Multiple events can be deleted by selecting a group of objects and clicking once on any one of them. Holding Alt while clicking on an event deletes the event and all those which follow it on the same track.

Figure 4.35
Erasing an event

Visual clarification

The above outlines the main uses of the tools in the event display. Figure 4.36 provides visual clarification of basic event editing.

Figure 4.36
Basic event editing

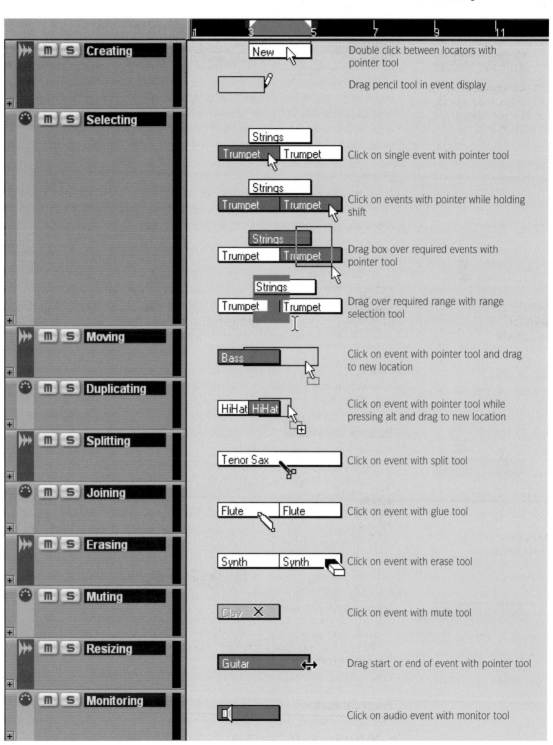

Figure 4.37 (above)
The Quick menu in the event display

Figure 4.38 (right)
The Quick menu in the track list

The Quick menu

The Quick menu is a context sensitive pop-up menu opened by clicking with the right mouse button (PC)/ Ctrl + clicking (Mac) on the area of interest. The contents of the menu vary according to where you click and only include options which are relevant to the chosen area. For example, clicking in the event display opens a menu containing the Project window tools and a wide range of general editing options (Figure 4.37). This menu also varies according to whether there is an event selected and what kind of event this is. When a MIDI part is selected the Quick menu includes more MIDI related items such as the MIDI functions and advanced quantize. When an audio event is selected it contains more audio related items such as the audio processing and audio plug-in options.

Clicking with the right mouse button (PC)/ Ctrl + clicking (Mac) in the Track list opens a menu with functions relevant to tracks such as the Add functions and Show/Hide automation options. Additional functions are added to the menu if you click directly on a track (Figure 4.38).

Zoom functions in the Project window

There are a wide range of functions available for zooming in and out of the event display. This section outlines a number of techniques designed to help you manage the zoom status and general look of the display more easily.

Using the zoom tool

Among the simplest ways to zoom in is to select the zoom tool and click in the event display. This zooms in to the display around the position at which you clicked. Holding Alt while clicking with the zoom tool zooms back out again. Standard horizontal or combined vertical/horizontal zooming takes place according to the zoom tool mode chosen in File/Preferences/ Editing.

Clicking and dragging a selection box with the zoom tool allows you to zoom in to specific areas of the event display. To zoom back out again hold Ctrl (PC) / Command (Mac) while clicking in the event display with the zoom tool. This steps you back to the previous zoom view you have used.

Using zoom in the ruler

Clicking in the ruler and moving the mouse position up or down while keeping the mouse button pressed allows you to zoom in and out horizontally in the event display. Drag down to zoom in and drag up to zoom out. Note that the project cursor is automatically moved to the position of the mouse, and for the function to work correctly, 'Zoom while locating in time scale' must be activated File/Preferences/ Transport.

Using the zoom default key commands

There are a number of default key commands which provide quick and convenient zoom control. Press H to zoom in horizontally and G to zoom out horizontally. Press Alt + H to zoom in vertically and Alt + G to zoom out vertically. Shift + F gives you a full horizontal zoom of all the events present in the event display.

Using the overview strip

The overview strip provides a graphical way of zooming and navigating within your project. The strip is shown by clicking on the Show overview button in the toolbar. The overview features a blue selection box which can be dragged to new positions and re-sized. The selection box outlines the horizontal bar range shown in the event display and by grabbing either end of the selection box (a double arrow appears) you can change the horizontal zoom. (See also 'The Overview Strip' on page 35).

Using the horizontal View presets menu

The View presets menu (Figure 4.39) is revealed when you click on the small downward pointing arrow to the right of the horizontal scroll bar. The menu features a number of presets for full horizontal zoom, zooming to the section inside the left and right locators and, if they are present, you can zoom in to cycle marker positions (see 'The Marker track' below for more details about cycle markers). You can also store your own horizontal zoom presets. To achieve this, set up your desired horizontal zoom (try around 16 bars for example), open View presets, select 'Add' from the menu and name the preset with a name which describes its function in the 'Type in Preset name' dialogue.

Using the Track scale menu

The Track scale menu (Figure 4.40) is revealed when you click on the small downward pointing arrow below the vertical scroll bar. The menu features a number of presets for scaling the vertical zoom in terms of rows. Various preset row values are available and you can also choose a number of tracks with which to vertically scale the event display.

> **Info**
>
> Most of the zoom techniques described in this section can equally be applied to the other editing windows of Cubase SX (where zooming is applicable).

> **Info**
>
> If you prefer the traditional, no-nonsense way of zooming in and out, try using the horizontal and vertical zoom sliders found in the lower right corner of the Project window.

Figure 4.39 (left)
The View presets menu

Figure 4.40 (right)
The Track scale menu

Saving and opening details

Cubase SX provides many ways of opening and saving files, and these should be fully understood before embarking on any serious projects. Most files are handled using the options in the File menu which include regular open and save options for native Cubase SX files and import and export options for file types which are not exclusive to Cubase SX. The type of file to be opened or saved is often recognised by its file extension and the following are the main possibilities:

Tip

Select Ctrl/Command + S to save the project. Select Ctrl/Command + Alt + S to save the project with an incremental number automatically added to the file name. The latter function is valuable for saving different versions of your work as the project progresses. If things go wrong you can always revert to an earlier version.

Cubase project files (file extension: cpr)

Cubase project files are used to save and load all the relevant data of a Cubase SX project, except for the audio files themselves and various Cubase SX global preference settings. Cubase project files are also used to create templates. Templates are preset environments which you can prepare in advance for specific types of projects (such as 24 track audio recording, 16 track surround mixing or stereo mastering). To save a template select 'Save as Template' in the File menu. To open a template select 'New project' in the File menu.

Import audio files (file extensions: wav, aif, aifc, aiff, rex, rx2, sd2, mp3, mp2, mpeg, ogg, wma)

Cubase SX can import and export a wide range of audio file formats. 'Wav' is the standard audio file format used on PC computers, 'aif' is a the standard audio file format used on Mac computers and 'mp3' (mpeg layer 3) is a compressed audio file format designed for use with the internet. Audio files can be imported directly into the event display without opening the Pool (for example, by selecting 'Import Audio file' in the File menu or by dragging and dropping an audio file from the desktop). When using Import Audio File, the audio material is pasted into the event display at the position of the project cursor. When dragging and dropping files the audio is dropped at the position where the mouse was released taking the current snap setting into consideration. 'Mp3' files are first converted into 'wav' files before being used within Cubase SX.

Rex and rx2 are the file extensions for files created in Propellerhead's Recycle program. Recycle is a separate program which is specialised in the processing and manipulation of audio loops. A rex file is an audio file which has been sliced up into its constituent parts thereby making it easier to manipulate in Cubase SX. Once imported into the program, Cubase SX's tempo can be freely changed and the rex file automatically adjusts itself to the new tempo without affecting the pitch of the sound. You can make your own rex files if you have Recycle or alternatively they are supplied on sample CDs. Rex files cannot be created within Cubase SX and it is therefore an import-only format.

Export audio mixdown (file extensions: wav, aif, mp3, ogg, rm, wma, wav [broadcast wave])

Cubase SX's Export option in the File menu allows the exporting of audio in the Project window between the left and right locators in most of the main audio file formats. The Export audio mixdown dialogue allows the exporting of audio files in mono, split stereo and stereo interleaved, and in multi-channel file formats. Bit resolutions between 8-bit and 32-bit float with sample rates between 8 and 96kHz ensure compatibility with just about any possible digital audio standard.

Import and export of standard MIDI files (file extension: mid)

A MIDI file is a special file format designed to allow the transfer of music between different makes of MIDI sequencer and between different platforms.

MIDI files come in two formats: type 0 and type 1. Type 0 files always contain only one track which plays back on many MIDI channels. Type 1 files contain the original track structure of the material and include two or more tracks on separate MIDI channels.

Select File/Export/MIDI file to export a MIDI file. After choosing a name for the file, an Export options dialogue appears. To save as a type 0 file select the type 0 box. De-select the type 0 box to save as type 1. Select the other options in the dialogue as appropriate. All settings in the Tempo track are saved in the MIDI file and all un-muted parts are included.

Select File/Import/MIDI file to import a MIDI file. Cubase SX recognises both MIDI file formats when importing and files may be imported into the current Project at the left locator position or into a new Project.

Key command files (file extension: xml)

Key command files are managed using the presets menu and the store/import options within the Key Commands dialogue (File/Key Commands). Presets allow you to store the current key commands and macros (as assigned within the Key Commands dialogue) in separate files. This is advantageous if several people are using the same Cubase SX system since each can use their own personalised set of key commands. A number of key command files are supplied with the program, as found in the presets menu. Presets are stored on hard disk in System/Documents and settings/User name/Application data/Steinberg/Cubase SX 3/Presets/Key Com- mands. The default Cubase SX key commands may be recalled at any time by clicking on the 'Reset all' button.

Drum map setup files (file extension: drm)

Drum map setup files are used to load and save drum maps. A drum map defines which notes correspond with which drum sounds and the maps are designed and managed within the Drum Map setup window (MIDI menu/Drum Map Setup). Once set up, drum maps are used in the Drum editor.

Cubase song, arrangement and part files (file extensions: all, arr, prt)

Cubase SX can import Cubase song, arrangement and part files from Cubase VST version 5.0 or later. The essential audio and MIDI data is converted but some elements of the older files are either removed or ignored. Those elements which are removed in a Cubase VST5 song import include group, style and chord tracks, MIDI effect devices such as the IPS, MIDI mixermaps, Master track hitpoints, and VST group channels. In addition, all dynamic events, M-points, grooves, sync, mute and solo settings are ignored. VST channel automation is limited to volume, pan and EQ data.

Progress report

This chapter has helped you become familiar with the most important aspects of the Project window, which is of central importance to the successful handling of the program. You may have noticed that you can accomplish most routine recording, playback and editing tasks while still remaining in the Project window and that you can configure the controls to suit your own particular way of working. All this forms part of the design principle of the Project window; 'the ability to comfortably travel a long way without leaving home'. Many of the skills and tools used within the Project window are transferable to other parts of the program. We have only just scratched the surface of the possibilities that are available with Cubase SX but we are now armed with some of the essential tools with which to go on to more musically meaningful pursuits.

MIDI recording

This chapter outlines basic MIDI theory, explains how to set up a MIDI network and features some practical MIDI recording techniques for Cubase SX. Understanding the theory behind MIDI helps you get the most out of MIDI recording and setting up an efficient MIDI network avoids some of the problems which may be encountered with the MIDI aspects of Cubase SX.

What is MIDI?

MIDI (Musical Instrument Digital Interface) is a data communication standard, first established in 1983, for the exchange of musical information between electronic musical instruments and, subsequently, computers. It involves the serial transfer of digital information via cables terminated with 5-pin DIN connectors.

MIDI is governed by a pre-defined set of rules and syntax known as the MIDI Specification. Just as the grammatical rules found in a regular language tell us how to form a sentence, the MIDI specification tells us how MIDI data should be sent and received in packets known as 'MIDI messages'. A MIDI message could describe something as simple as the action of pressing a note on a musical keyboard. In MIDI 'talk', this would be known as a 'Note on' message. A similar message would need to be sent to describe the action of releasing the key, and this is known as a 'Note off' message. Note on and note off messages contain information about the pitch of the key being pressed and the force with which it was pressed (known as the velocity). The duration of each note is governed by the length of time between the note on and note off messages. If a note off message is not sent at some stage after the note on message then the note continues to play indefinitely.

MIDI, therefore, is like a language. MIDI devices, such as synthesizers, samplers and drum machines can effectively 'talk' to each other using MIDI messages. The transmitting of these messages invariably involves two or more MIDI devices, one which is transmitting the data and the other(s) receiving it. It is very important to understand that the transmitted data consists of a series of instructions only, there is NO audio signal within the data. Note on and off messages, for example, instruct the receiving unit(s) about which note should be played, its velocity and duration. The actual sound produced is chosen on the receiving unit by selecting a preset sound program and the resulting sound is output via standard line level audio outputs. MIDI devices normally include MIDI In, MIDI Out and MIDI Thru ports. To transmit messages from one device to another, a MIDI Out is connected to a MIDI In of a second device (using a correctly wired MIDI cable). The MIDI Thru port passes on a copy of the messages received at the MIDI In port. This is often used to daisy-chain several units together in a simple MIDI network. So, in its simplest form, hooking up a MIDI cable from the MIDI Out of your keyboard to the MIDI In of a synth module allows you to play the two devices simultaneously. The MIDI keyboard is being triggered in the normal way from its own keyboard and the synth module is being triggered by the MIDI messages it receives via the MIDI cable.

Great! But how does this help us use the MIDI side of Cubase SX? Well, instead of hooking up the MIDI cable from your MIDI keyboard to a synth module, plug it into the MIDI interface of your computer setup. You can now send MIDI messages into Cubase SX and thereby record a musical performance. If you followed the first MIDI recording project in Chapter 3 then you will have already achieved this. Music recorded in this way is generally represented within Cubase SX as individual note events. These note events are grouped together within MIDI parts in the event display or can be viewed as notes on a score, or graphical blocks on a piano-roll (or drum style) grid within the various MIDI editors. Once the MIDI data has been recorded, it can be transmitted to any of the MIDI devices present in your system, allowing you to mix and match the sounds available, long after the original recording has been made. The available sounds in your MIDI devices are usually stored as programs (presets or patches) which can be changed by selecting a preset manually or by sending a MIDI Program change message.

MIDI message types

You may, at this stage, ask what happens to the outgoing MIDI data if you turn the pitch wheel of your keyboard while playing a note. You might be tempted to think that the MIDI note data itself is modified in some way. In fact, the note data remains the same and the pitch data is sent separately as another kind of MIDI message known, not surprisingly, as a Pitch bend message. Pitch bend messages instruct the receiving unit how to bend the note(s) in question. A similar thing happens if you use the modulation wheel. This sends out another kind of message known as a Control change message (Continuous Controller). Other kinds of messages include Aftertouch (Channel Key pressure) and Program change.

MIDI message types fall into two main categories: Channel and System messages. Channel messages have two sub categories known as Channel Voice messages and Channel Mode messages.

Channel Voice messages

All the message types described so far come under the same category within the MIDI specification and are known as Channel Voice messages. Channel Voice messages are characterised by the fact that MIDI channel information (see below) is embedded within the message. 'Voice' means that this type of message is directed to and controls the receiving instrument's voices (or sounds). Channel Voice messages are arguably the most important part of the MIDI specification and this type of message is likely to be the one with which you most often come into contact in the routine use of Cubase SX. To summarise, Channel Voice messages include the following message types:

- Note off – the releasing of a key to terminate the playing of a note.
- Note on – the pressing of a key to begin the playing of a note.
- Polyphonic Key pressure (Aftertouch) – key pressure taking into consideration the pressure applied to each individual key.
- Control Change (Continuous Controller) – for the control of various non-note parameters like modulation (vibrato), breath control, volume and pan.
- Program change – changes the sound preset in the receiving unit.
- Channel key pressure (Aftertouch) – key pressure taken as an overall pressure reading for the MIDI channel.
- Pitch Bend – instructs the receiving unit to change (bend) the pitch of any currently sounding notes (normally sent using the pitch bend wheel of the master keyboard).

Info

See the glossary and Appendices 2 and 3 for definitions of MIDI terminology and technical data about MIDI messages.

Channel Mode messages

Channel mode messages are a group of reserved control change messages (between controllers 120 and 127). These reset and change the mode of operation of the receiving device. They include the following:

- All sound off (controller 120) – switches off sounds on all channels.
- Reset all controllers (controller 121) – resets all controllers to their default parameters.
- Local on/off (controller 122) – Local off disconnects the keyboard from the sound-making circuitry in the receiving device. Local on re-connects the keyboard to the sound-making circuitry
- All notes off (controller 123) – switches off all currently sounding notes. This is MIDI's panic button and is used to switch off hanging notes.
- Omni mode off, all notes off (controller 124) – the receiving device responds to messages on a single MIDI channel. This message also switches off all currently sounding notes. (Normally corresponds with a MIDI mode 3 status in the receiver, see below).
- Omni mode on, all notes off (controller 125) – the receiving device responds to messages on all MIDI channels. This message also switches off all currently sounding notes. (Normally corresponds with a MIDI mode 1 status in the receiver, see below).
- Mono mode on/poly mode off, all notes off (controller 126) – the receiving device responds to messages monophonically. This message also determines the number of monophonic MIDI channels used to process incoming MIDI notes. It switches off all currently sounding notes. (Normally corresponds with a MIDI mode 4 status in the receiver, see below).
- Poly mode on/mono mode off, all notes off (controller 127) – the receiving device responds to messages polyphonically. This message also switches off all currently sounding notes. (Normally corresponds with a MIDI mode 3 status in the receiver, see below).

Controller messages 124 to 127 can be combined to produce four modes known as MIDI modes. These are operational modes governing how a MIDI device manages data on different channels and whether it responds polyphonically or monophonically. The MIDI modes are as follows:

- Mode 1 (Omni On/Poly) – the receiver responds to messages on all MIDI channels polyphonically. Commonly known as Omni mode.
- Mode 2 (Omni On/Mono) – the receiver responds to messages on all MIDI channels monophonically. Rarely used mode.
- Mode 3 (Omni Off/Poly) – the receiver responds to messages on the chosen MIDI channel polyphonically. Commonly known as Poly mode.
- Mode 4 (Omni Off/Mono) – the receiver responds to messages on the chosen MIDI channel(s) monophonically. In this mode, response to incoming MIDI notes is shared between a number of monophonic channels. Commonly known as Mono mode.

The MIDI modes are slightly outdated but are still implemented in some form on most devices. Mode 1 might be used for troubleshooting and testing. Mode 2 is rarely used. Mode 4 is useful for guitar synthesizers (and similar instruments) since it allows you to assign each string to a different monophonic MIDI channel, thereby more closely approximating the performance behaviour of the real-world instrument. Most MIDI devices power up in MIDI Mode 3.

Multi-timbral functionality (now common in many devices) is not covered by the standard MIDI modes. Multi-timbral mode is therefore assigned on the instrument itself and is normally known as 'Multi Mode'. Multi Mode operation might be viewed as a number of separate polyphonic instruments within a single device (each set to MIDI Mode 3).

System messages

System messages form the other main type of message in the MIDI specification. These include System Common, System Real Time and System Exclusive messages. System Common messages include such things as MIDI Time Code, song position pointer, song select and tune request messages. System Real Time includes timing clock (24 ppqn) and start, stop and continue messages for sequencer synchronisation purposes. System Exclusive involves manufacturer-specific messages and Universal System Exclusive messages like MIDI file dump, sample dump, GM system on/off, MIDI Show Control and MIDI Machine Code.

System Common and System Real Time messages are transmitted globally to all units in the MIDI network and do not use a MIDI channel for transmission or reception purposes. System Exclusive is used for transferring manufacturer and model-specific data to/from individual units and is generally only recognised by a single targeted device. This is typically used for dumping sounds and setup configurations from the MIDI device into a sequencer (like Cubase SX).

MIDI channels

To facilitate the transmitting of MIDI messages to different targets within the same network, MIDI adopts a system of sixteen different channels. Channel Voice messages can be transmitted on any one of these channels. MIDI devices are usually set to receive polyphonically on one channel (Mode 3) or polyphonically on several channels simultaneously (multi-timbral). Messages on all sixteen MIDI channels can be transmitted simultaneously via a single MIDI cable.

To understand MIDI channels, it is helpful to think of your network of MIDI devices as a number of televisions. The signals from the TV broadcasting stations are being transmitted on a continuous basis, but you decide which one you are going to watch on screen by changing the channel on your TV. If you have several televisions you can set each one to a different channel. You can do exactly the same with your network of MIDI devices. Each unit is like a television which can be tuned to the appropriate channel. In such a system, Cubase SX is like a group of TV broadcasting stations. It transmits multiple channel MIDI data to the whole network. However, only those units which are tuned to the appropriate channels produce the appropriate sound. Certain MIDI devices can be set to receive on several channels simultaneously. This is known as multi-timbral or multi mode (as mentioned above) and allows a single unit to perform polyphonically on several channels at once. This means that you can trigger a number of different sounds simultaneously to hear a whole musical arrangement from a single unit (such as drums, bass, piano, strings and brass).

What MIDI is not

MIDI is NOT audio. MIDI data is a set of digital instructions related to a musical performance whereas digital audio is a recording of the actual sound itself.

MIDI network details

Most readers probably have Cubase SX connected to some kind of MIDI synthesizer or piano keyboard and a network of MIDI devices such as rackmount synth modules, samplers, drum machines or effects units (see Figures 5.1 and 5.2). Note that your main keyboard is usually referred to as the master keyboard.

Figure 5.1
A simple MIDI network

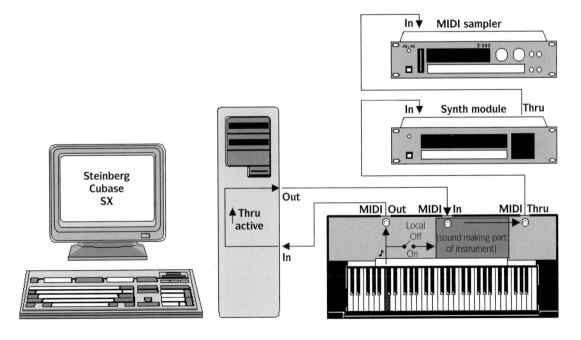

Figure 5.1 shows a very simple MIDI network. The MIDI output from the master keyboard is routed directly into the MIDI In of the computer's MIDI interface. The diagram assumes that a MIDI interface is installed inside the computer (e.g. a PCI sound card featuring MIDI input and output ports). The MIDI input data passes through Cubase SX (via the activated global MIDI Thru in the program, see below) and is routed back out, along with any other data which has already been recorded, to the MIDI input of the master keyboard. A copy of the data arriving at the MIDI In is sent out from the MIDI Thru port of the master keyboard and routed to a synth module. The data arriving at the MIDI In of the synth module is passed on to a MIDI sampler in the same manner (via the MIDI Thru of the synth module). This type of configuration is known as a 'daisy-chain' network.

Although the system shown in Figure 5.1 is easier to set up, it is not as adaptable as that shown in Figure 5.2, and due to the fact that the data passes through several units in the daisy-chain there is more risk of MIDI delays and data corruption.

More complex MIDI networks typically feature a MIDI thru box (also called a MIDI splitter box) which enables the channeling of MIDI data to specific locations in the system. The MIDI network in Figure 5.2 features a master keyboard from which the MIDI Out is sent to the MIDI In of the computer via the MIDI thru box. The diagram assumes that a MIDI interface is installed inside the computer (e.g. a PCI sound card featuring MIDI input and output ports). The MIDI input data passes through Cubase SX (via the activated global MIDI Thru in the program, see below) and is passed back out, along with any other data which has already been recorded, to the MIDI input of the MIDI thru box. The data is split among the outputs of the MIDI thru box and routed to the various devices in the system (including back to the master keyboard itself). This type of configuration is known as a MIDI 'star' network. In such a system,

Figure 5.2
A complex MIDI network

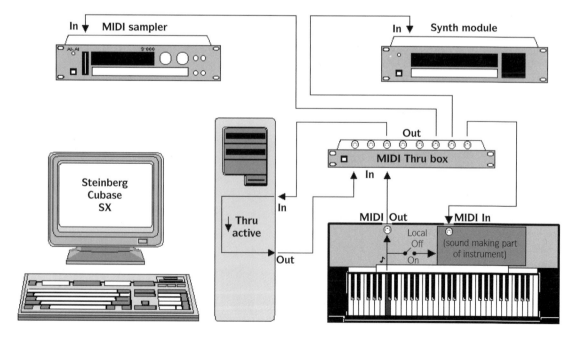

the MIDI thru box allows the connecting of any input to any number of outputs and often includes MIDI data merge functionality so that the MIDI messages from two or more inputs can be merged into one MIDI data stream. Note that the master instrument's keyboard has been disconnected from its sound making circuitry (commonly known as Local off mode, see page 72). In this mode, the sound making circuitry is triggered by incoming MIDI messages only. The master keyboard, therefore, triggers its sound making circuitry via Cubase SX. Note also that MIDI outputs are always connected to MIDI inputs and involve single cables between each output/input pair of sockets.

A MIDI star network is recommended for ensuring better MIDI timing, particularly for systems featuring more than two modules in addition to the master keyboard. It is also more flexible since, with a sufficiently well-specified MIDI Thru box (e.g. 8 in, 8 out with MIDI merge), any MIDI output can be routed to any MIDI input, allowing sophisticated handshaking operations for dumping MIDI data between any unit to the computer and vice versa.

If you have not already done so, it is a good idea to make a clear, logical diagram of your own MIDI network with all the MIDI inputs and outputs clearly labelled. This helps clarify your own setup and can prove invaluable for troubleshooting your system if you run into problems. It is also helpful to include all the peripheral audio equipment and audio connections, once again clearly labelling all the inputs and outputs. (See Figure 2.7 for an example). If you have the time and patience use colour in your diagram to colour code the MIDI and audio connections.

Record modes for MIDI recording

The precise manner in which MIDI recording takes place in Cubase SX is governed by the record mode menus found in the Record Mode section of the Transport panel. You are advised to become familiar with the record modes before commencing any serious recording projects. These affect both the linear and cycle recording behaviour of the program. The linear record modes determine what happens when a new MIDI recording 'overlaps' an existing part on the same track. The cycle record modes determine what happens when you record multiple takes over the same range in a continuous cycle (when the Transport panel cycle button is activated). Note that the linear record modes influence MIDI cycle record behaviour only when you implement a new cycle recording over existing material. Note also that, with MIDI data, you hear the recordings of all parts even if the parts overlap. The function of each record mode is outlined in the following table:

Info

Making a clear, logical diagram of your own Cubase SX MIDI and audio connections and peripheral equipment helps clarify the structure of your system and is invaluable for troubleshooting. In such a diagram, be sure to label all inputs and outputs clearly and, if possible, use colour-coding to differentiate between the MIDI and audio connection cables.

Info

The record modes have a slightly different effect on record behaviour depending on whether you are recording MIDI or audio data.

Record modes for MIDI recording

Linear record modes		Cycle record modes	
Mode	Overlap behaviour	Mode	Cycle behaviour
Normal	pastes new part on top	Mix	mixes with previous lap data
Merge	merges data into existing part	Overwrite	overwrites to end of lap
Replace	replaces data in existing part	Keep Last	keeps last lap only
		Stacked	records laps in lanes

MIDI recording in detail

The following details help clarify the MIDI recording process beyond the level achieved in earlier chapters. Before proceeding any further let's create a new Project, in much the same way as we did at the beginning of Chapter 3.

Create a new project

To create a new project, select 'New Project' from the File menu and choose 'Empty' from the dialogue which appears on screen. In the Select directory dialogue which appears, choose your audio drive or an appropriate existing directory (usually the location where you intend to store all your Cubase SX projects) and click on the Create button to create a new directory for this particular project. Choose an appropriate name. The directory is created on the hard disk. Click on OK to leave the Select directory dialogue. An empty Cubase SX project with various default settings is opened on the screen. We are now ready to start work. It is assumed here that you have read the first three chapters of this book and that you have already made some basic MIDI recordings.

Verify MIDI Thru and set MIDI filter

In Cubase SX, it is standard practice to 'throughput' the MIDI data received at the MIDI IN to the MIDI OUT of the computer. Ensure that the MIDI Thru Active box is ticked in File/Preferences/MIDI. By default, the program is supplied with MIDI Thru activated. Ensure also that SysEx and aftertouch are filtered in the record and thru sections of the MIDI filter (File/Preferences/MIDI/Filter). This avoids recording any unnecessary data in the exercise outlined below.

Set Local Off

At this point, it is also desirable to set your master keyboard to Local Off. Local Off means that the musical keyboard is disconnected from the sound making part of the instrument (your master keyboard should include a parameter for Local on/off control). All sound is now triggered via MIDI only. This avoids double notes and stops the master keyboard being triggered inappropriately when other instruments in the network are being played live via MIDI.

Add some MIDI tracks

Select 'Add Track/Multiple' in the Project menu and choose MIDI and a track count of '3' to add three new MIDI tracks to the project (Figure 5.3).

Select the first track and choose an appropriate MIDI input and output in the 'in' and 'out' fields of the Inspector (Figure 5.4) in order to test your sys-

Figure 5.3 (left)
Adding multiple MIDI tracks in the Project window

Figure 5.4 (right)
Set the MIDI in, out and channel fields to test the devices in your MIDI network

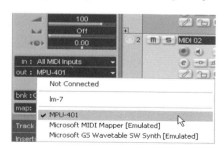

tem. These would normally correspond to the MIDI input and output ports of the MIDI interface you have installed in your computer (see 'Finding the MIDI inputs and outputs' on page 12 for more details). It should now be possible to play any of the devices in the MIDI network by changing the MIDI channel in the channel field. It is also possible to play any of Cubase SX's internal VST Instruments (Virtual Studio Instruments) by selecting the instrument in the 'out' field. For a VST Instrument to be available in the 'out' menu it must have already been activated in the VST Instruments panel opened from the Device menu (see Chapter 16 for more details about VST Instruments).

Troubleshooting

If you experience difficulties with triggering your real-world or virtual instruments verify that:

- the record enable or monitor enable button for the chosen MIDI track is active. This allows MIDI data to pass from the MIDI input to the MIDI output.
- the MIDI activity indicator in the Transport panel registers MIDI input and output activity when you play your keyboard.
- the target devices are switched on and are functioning correctly.
- the MIDI cables are of the approved type and are not faulty.
- the MIDI cables are correctly connected between Cubase SX and the devices in the network (i.e. MIDI outputs connected to MIDI inputs).
- the target devices are set to the correct MIDI channels.
- the correct output device and channel is selected in the 'out' and channel fields of the MIDI track.

Preparing the system

To adjust the system to suit your MIDI network and prepare for recording, proceed as follows:

1 Adjust the settings of the Metronome dialogue (Transport menu). Set a precount of two bars, activate the MIDI click and de-activate the audio click. Set the MIDI click channel and output port to an appropriate drum or percussion sound source. If you do not have an appropriate external sound source try using the LM7 VST Instrument supplied with Cubase SX. To use the LM7, activate the instrument in the VST Instruments rack (Devices menu/VST Instruments or F11 on the computer keyboard) by clicking on the VST instrument field in an empty slot in the rack and selecting LM7 from the 'Drums' folder (Figure 5.5). Select the '909' drum kit.

   In the Metronome dialogue, set the output port to 'LM7', and select either C#1 (MIDI note no.37) or F#1 (MIDI note no.42) in the high note and low note fields. These correspond to either the rimshot sound or the hi-hat sound of the LM7.

Figure 5.5
Activate the LM7 drum module in the VST Instruments rack

Figure 5.6 (below)
Set the output device and output notes in the Metronome

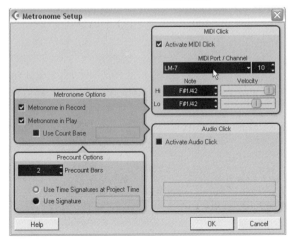

To ensure that you achieve predictable results, activate 'Precount on' and 'Start Record at Left Locator' in the Transport menu.

2 Activate 'Click' on the Transport panel by pressing 'C' on the computer keyboard (or by clicking on the Click button with the mouse).

3 Test the click and verify the tempo of Cubase SX by pressing enter on the numeric keypad (or by clicking on the Transport panel play button with the mouse). In Fixed tempo mode you can adjust the tempo on the fly by double-clicking on the Transport panel tempo field and pressing the up or down arrows on the computer keyboard to increase/decrease the tempo. When you are satisfied with the tempo, press enter on the computer keyboard.

Figure 5.7
Name and choose MIDI inputs and outputs for each of the three MIDI tracks

4 Double-click on the name of the first of the three MIDI tracks you created in the Project window and enter 'drums' in the name field (for example). Name the second track as 'bass' and the third track as 'piano' (for example). Choose appropriate MIDI inputs and outputs in the 'in' and 'out' fields of the Inspector and appropriate MIDI channels to route your playing to the appropriate MIDI devices in your MIDI network for each track. This is important for the recording operation outlined below. You can, of course, choose different names and instruments as you see fit. Your project now resembles Figure 5.7.

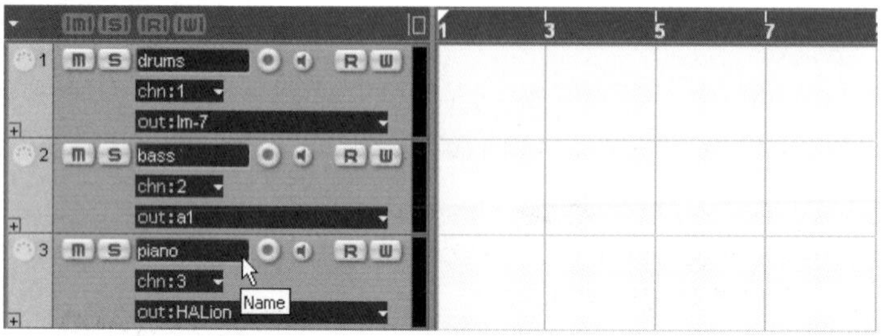

5 Select an appropriate sound for each MIDI device either on the unit itself or remotely using the program field ('Prg') in the Inspector (Figure 5.8). The program field sends out MIDI program change messages when you change its value.

Figure 5.8
Selecting a program remotely by name, using the program field of an installed MIDI Device

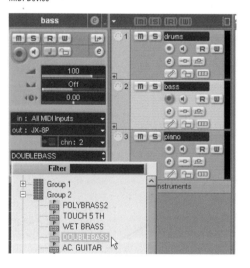

Using the program field for remote selection of sounds by name depends on whether the chosen device is supported in the MIDI Device Manager (Device menu/MIDI Device manager). Click on 'Install Device' in the MIDI Device Manager for a list of supported MIDI devices. To install a device, simply click on the desired device in the list (Figure 5.9). The device is now available in the 'out' field of the MIDI track and, when selected, a pop-up presets list is available from the program field from which you can choose the desired sound. The presets for VST instruments are automatically shown in the pop-up programs menu.

6 Set the left and right locators in the ruler above the event display by clicking and dragging in the upper half of the ruler (a pencil tool appears). Set the left locator to bar 3.1.1.0 and the right locator to bar 7.1.1.0 (4 bars). It is assumed here that you have set you default ruler display to bars and beats. In this mode, the bar display figures refer to the time position in bars, beats, sixteenth notes and ticks.

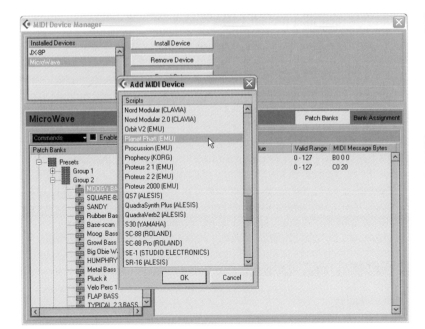

Figure 5.9
Installing a MIDI device in the MIDI
Device manager

Info

The pop-up presets list is good for auditioning sounds on the fly. You can step through the sounds in the list using the up/down arrow keys on the computer keyboard while Cubase SX is in play mode. Also try entering the name of the type of sound you are looking for into the filter at the top. All sounds containing the text you enter are then shown in the list.

7 Activate Cycle on the Transport panel by pressing the divide key (/) on the numeric keypad (or by clicking on the Cycle button with the mouse). Cubase SX is now set to cycle between the left and right locators positions (in record or playback modes).

8 Ensure that the cycle record mode on the Transport panel is set to mix. In mix mode, the current MIDI input is added to any existing recording(s) in the same part when recording in cycle mode. This is the default mode for quickly building up a rhythm part, for example, when different elements of a drum kit can be added on each lap of the cycle.

9 If you are feeling lazy, activate the automatic quantize button (AQ) on the Transport panel and select 1/16 note in the Quantize selector above the event display. This auto-corrects your playing to the nearest sixteenth note. (This is OK for this project but is not suitable as a default setting since it can result in rather lifeless, robotic music).

Tip

An alternative, sometimes quicker, method of setting the left and right locators is to click once in the ruler while holding Ctrl (PC)/Command (Mac) on the computer keyboard to set the left locator, and click once in the ruler while holding Alt to set the right locator.

The advantages of recording in cycle mode

In cycle mode the punch in and out buttons can be largely ignored since the punch in button is auto-selected when Cubase SX is put into record mode and the punch out point (the position of the right locator) is never actually reached since Cubase SX cycles back to the left locator position. Recording is de-activated only when Cubase SX is stopped manually.

When recording in cycle mode, Cubase SX automatically remains within the segment which is being recorded upon without any further effort, and any recorded material can be instantly monitored on the next lap of the cycle. Cycle recording in mix mode is particularly useful for continually adding to the material without dropping out of record and is convenient for building up a rhythm pattern.

Tip

If you are happy with the way the system is configured so far and often work with MIDI-only recordings you might like to save what we have achieved so far as a template. This could serve as a startup blank project whenever you start a new MIDI project. Select 'Save as template' in the File menu and choose a suitable name like 'MIDI startup', for example.

MIDI cycle recording project 1 (Mix mode)

Let's start by recording a drum part using the first MIDI track we created, above. For this first project we are recording in cycle recording mix mode as chosen in steps 7 and 8, above. The idea in this project is to gradually add to the recording on each lap of the cycle without dropping out of record mode.

Start recording

Select the drums track. Click on the record button of the Transport panel or select the multiplication key (*) on the numeric keypad. A pre-count is heard according to what has been set in the metronome. When recording commences, the track header turns red and the project cursor starts to move. Anything played on your keyboard (or other master instrument) is now recorded into Cubase SX. Try recording something simple using, for example, a bass drum and snare. Cubase SX cycles between the left and right locators (as set above), and you may add to the recording on each lap of the cycle.

Track switching

Once you are satisfied with what you recorded on the drums track, switch to the next track (the bass track) by pressing the down arrow key on the computer keyboard. Do this without dropping out of record. Record your bass part and then switch to the piano track, once again, without dropping out of record. Record your piano part and stop Cubase SX when all recording is complete. If necessary, you can go back and add further data to any of the tracks by switching between them using the up/down arrows of the computer keyboard (see Figure 5.10). When you are happy with your recording, don't forget to save it by selecting the save function in the File menu (Ctrl/Command + S).

Info

If you prefer, you can set up Cubase SX to record without cycle. In this mode recording begins from the left locator position and ends when Cubase SX is stopped or, if the punch out button has been activated, when the project cursor reaches the right locator position.

Figure 5.10
Cycle recording multiple MIDI parts in mix mode allows you to quickly build up a MIDI arrangement

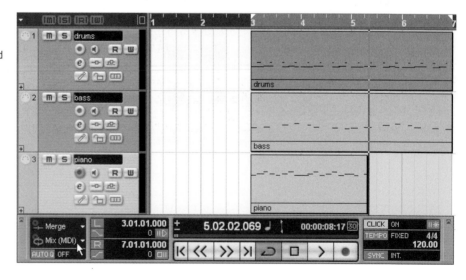

MIDI cycle recording project 2 (Overwrite mode)

Delete the events recorded in project 1, above, and switch off automatic quantize (AQ) in the Transport panel. This time, select 'Overwrite' in the cycle record mode selector. In overwrite mode, the current MIDI input replaces any existing recordings in the same part and deletes any data which occurs after the drop-in point for each subsequent lap of the cycle.

Start recording

This time we are recording a single piano part. Select the piano track. Click on the record button of the Transport panel or select the multiplication key (*) on the numeric keypad. A pre-count is heard according to what has been set in the metronome. When recording commences, the track header turns red and the project cursor starts to move. Anything played on your keyboard (or other master instrument) is now recorded into Cubase SX. Try recording a fairly complex piano part.

Practice makes perfect

Your piano performance may be lacking the first time around the cycle. DO NOT drop out of record just start playing again on the next lap of the cycle. Your previous recording is replaced since you are in cycle record overwrite mode. All notes which come after your drop in point are replaced by the new performance. This allows you to keep practising the part until you play it 'perfectly'. When you get it right, your performance is already captured since you are still in record mode (see Figure 5.11). When you are happy with your recording, don't forget to save it by selecting the 'save as' function in the File menu.

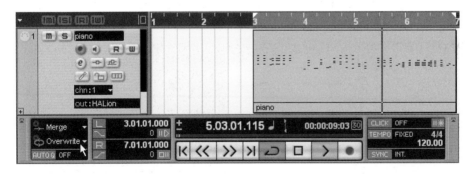

Figure 5.11
Cycle recording in overwrite mode allows you to capture a great musical performance

MIDI cycle recording project 3 (Stacked mode)

Delete the events recorded in the previous projects, above. This time, select 'Stacked' in the cycle record mode selector. In stacked mode, a new MIDI part is created for each lap of the cycle. The parts are automatically 'stacked' on separate lanes within the vertical space of the MIDI track. Each of the previous takes is also automatically muted as each new take commences.

Start recording

We are now recording a single piano part again. Select the piano track. Click on the record button of the Transport panel or select the multiplication key (*) on the numeric keypad. A pre-count is heard according to what has been set in the metronome. When recording commences, the track header turns red and the project cursor starts to move. Anything played on your keyboard (or other master instrument) is now recorded into Cubase SX. Try recording a fairly complex piano part.

Relax while you play

This time you can feel really free to experiment since all your playing is automatically and conveniently captured in separate stacked parts, one for each lap of the cycle. These are also automatically numbered and arranged within the vertical space of the MIDI track (Figure 5.12). When recording is complete, editing the parts with the splice, mute and other tools allows you to assemble a 'perfect' take while still remaining in the Project window. If desired, you can merge all the wanted material into a single composite part using Merge MIDI in Loop (MIDI menu). When you are happy with your recording (and editing), don't forget to save your work under a new name by selecting the 'save as' function in the File menu.

Figure 5.12
Cycle recording in stacked mode gives you maximum flexibility at the editing stage

Combining techniques

The techniques from the above three projects can be combined. How to record largely depends on what kind of recording you are making. For example, using cycle recording in mix mode is probably best suited to drum and percussion parts where you may wish to build up the rhythm on each lap of the cycle. Unless you are an excellent musician this same technique may not be so useful for recording your bass and piano parts. These might benefit more from cycle record in overwrite mode. This gives you the opportunity to keep on repeating your part until you get a good take. Stacked mode probably gives you the most flexibility since it effortlessly organises your recording into neat, separate segments and leaves all your options open until you decide which takes to keep at the editing stage. Remember that you can freely switch between mix, overwrite and stacked modes on the fly without dropping out of record.

Other MIDI recording techniques

Linear recording

Cycle recording is best suited to relatively short passages. Linear recording (meaning when you are NOT recording in cycle mode) is often better for longer performances and for detailed punching in over specific segments. Linear recording behaviour depends upon the setting made in the Linear recording mode menu on the Transport bar (mix, merge or replace) and the pre-roll, post-roll and punch button settings (mix, merge and replace modes are explained in Chapter 4). Recording is also affected by 'Start Record at Left Locator' in the Transport menu which, when activated, ensures that all recording starts at the left locator position. Various combinations of these settings can be applied to tackle your chosen MIDI recording task. For example, when punching in over an existing recording, it is preferable to actually hear the music in the bars before the punch in point (rather than just a metronome precount). This allows you to play along with the music before you reach the punch in point, often resulting in a better take. To set this up in Cubase SX, proceed as follows:

- drag the left and right locators in the ruler to select the segment in which you wish to record.
- activate the pre and post-roll buttons in the Transport bar and enter '1' (one bar) in each.
- activate the punch in and punch out buttons on the Transport bar (click on the buttons or use the 'I' and 'O' key commands on the computer keyboard).
- choose the appropriate mode in the linear record mode menu on the Transport panel. If you are punching in over a badly played section which you definitely wish to replace it might be appropriate to choose 'Replace' mode.
- choose the track upon which you wish to record and activate its record enable button.

Selecting record automatically rolls the Project cursor back one bar before the punch in point and starts playback. When the punch in point is reached

Cubase SX automatically drops into record mode. Recording continues up to the punch out point. After the punch out point playback continues for a further one bar. Using a post-roll as well as a pre-roll helps you hear your take in context. In 'Replace' mode, all existing MIDI data in the recorded segment is replaced by your new performance.

Retrospective record

When Cubase SX is in stop or play mode, any MIDI input is still recorded by the program, as long as one MIDI track is record enabled. This helps capture the magical performance you might produce when you are practising before starting to record or when you are playing along with an existing arrangement without recording. Retrospective record helps you avoid the 'if only I had recorded that!' syndrome which afflicts some recording sessions. Selecting Retrospective record from the Transport menu instantly creates a MIDI part beginning at the project cursor on the current record enabled track and this contains your recently played MIDI performance. If the MIDI input took place alongside an existing arrangement the data is synchronised with the other MIDI parts as if you had recorded it in the normal way. The amount of data which can be recorded by the Retrospective record function is chosen in File/Preferences/Record.

Quantize

If your piano part (above), or any other MIDI recording, was played extremely accurately it may not need any further attention, but many recordings benefit from quantize.

Quantize is a kind of timing correction which is applied at the moment of recording (automatic quantize) or, more commonly, after the part has been recorded. It involves the moving of recorded musical events onto pre-defined beats according to a position-based grid. In Cubase SX, the resolution of these pre-defined beats is chosen in the quantize selector above the event display. This is like imposing a grid of vertical lines across the event display which become 'magnetic' for the surrounding recorded notes whenever you select a quantize function. It was first devised as a purely corrective function for MIDI recordings but has now assumed the role of a creative tool.

Using quantize

Simple corrective uses of quantize might include moving all the hi-hats in a MIDI drum recording onto the exact nearest $1/16^{th}$ note divisions of the bar (known as 'over-quantize' or 'hard quantize') or it might concern moving the hi-hats *towards* the nearest $1/16^{th}$ note divisions according to a strength percentage (known as 'iterative quantize'). Over quantize and iterative quantize functions are found in the MIDI menu of Cubase SX.

To quantize a MIDI part, select it and choose a quantize value in the quantize selector above the event display. Try 1/16 and select iterative quantize in the MIDI menu (Figure 5.13). Iterative Quantize tightens up parts that were loosely played but retains the feel of the original performance.

Quantize your part until it sounds musically correct. You can undo any quantizing action using the main undo command in the Edit menu (Ctrl/Command+Z). This takes you back to the previous quantized state if you have implemented more than one quantizing action. You can go back to your original unquantized performance using 'Undo quantize' (found in the Advanced quantize sub-menu of the MIDI menu). If you wish to make adjustments to the quantize effect select 'Setup' from the Quantize type menu or select 'Quantize Setup' from the MIDI menu. These open the Quantize Setup dialogue. In Quantize Setup you can fine tune the quantize function with a range of control parameters. For example, this allows the application of a swing factor for imposing a swing feel upon your performance, or the adjustment of the magnetic area within which the quantize function is sensitive (Figure 5.13). Clicking on the store button stores your settings in the Quantize selector menu under a new name.

Info

Swing occurs when every second note position on the quantize grid is pushed to the right. The more the notes are pushed, the more the music swings.

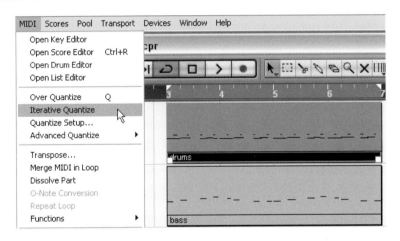

Figure 5.13
Quantizing a MIDI part using iterative quantize

To experiment with the quantize functions, select a MIDI part and commence playback in cycle mode. Open the Quantize Setup window and make some adjustments to the controls. Leave the window open and apply your settings to the selected part by clicking on the Apply button. Try adjusting the swing factor to 100% with a grid setting of 1/8, for an obviously audible effect. Working directly out of the Quantize Setup window is a good way of becoming familiar with the quantize functions. Quantize Setup is also explored in Chapter 6.

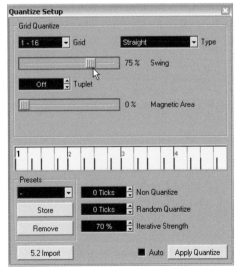

Figure 5.14
Adding swing in Quantize Setup (Grid mode)

Info

In recent times, the popular music charts have been full of songs where the rhythm has a distinctive swing or shuffle feel. This is as a direct result of the quantize features of modern sequencers. The shuffle feel became fashionable some years ago and is a pre-requisite for certain styles of music. A shuffle feel is easy to implement in Cubase SX using the swing slider in the Quantize Setup window.

Quantize health risks

Heavy use of the quantize functions is not always good for your musical health. It is not always desirable to have all the notes in all parts occurring on exact divisions of the beat, so quantize should be used with some care. Iterative quantize is often a better option than Over quantize. Too much quantize can result in music which is robotic and lifeless.

How do I include my MIDI recordings when I use Export/Audio Mixdown?

This is probably the most frequently asked Cubase-related question of all time! Cubase SX includes a sophisticated virtual mixing console where both audio and MIDI tracks can be mixed and automated. When you have finished your latest musical masterpiece and set up a killer mix you can mix down your efforts to an audio file on hard disk using the Export/Audio mixdown function found in the File menu. There's just one catch. The MIDI tracks which trigger your external MIDI devices are NOT included in the mixdown!

The Audio mixdown function includes all audio tracks and automation between the left and right locators. It also converts all MIDI tracks which trigger VST Instruments. However, it does NOT convert regular MIDI tracks which trigger MIDI devices external to Cubase SX. The program has no way of knowing what audio signals these external devices are producing.

The solution to the problem

The audio signals of all external MIDI devices must be recorded onto regular audio tracks before using Export/Audio mixdown. The details of achieving this need not be over-complicated. The essential thing to bear in mind is the manner in which the audio outputs of your MIDI devices are routed into your overall system. Most of us use an external mixing console of some kind in order to manage the audio signals from the MIDI network. If you followed the advice (above) of making a clear, logical diagram of your MIDI network and audio system (with all the inputs and outputs clearly labelled), you can make good use of it here.

Assuming that the line outputs of your MIDI devices are routed into the line inputs of your external mixing console, the following is what you need to do:

1 Set up the sound of each MIDI instrument on the external mixing console. If you intend to bounce the audio from the instruments to a stereo pair in Cubase SX then you should take some time setting up the mix. However, for the best results you are advised to record each instrument on a separate track of Cubase SX as explained in the following points.

2 Connect one (or two if you are recording in stereo) of the group outs of the external mixing console to the desired physical input(s) of the audio hardware you have connected to your computer. Route the first instrument you wish to record to the chosen group output(s).

3 Put Cubase SX into play mode so that you can hear the MIDI sequence of the chosen MIDI device and set up an audio track for recording in the

Info

See Chapter 11 for more details about Export/Audio mixdown.

normal way. On the chosen audio track, choose the input buss into which you have routed your MIDI device. Record the audio output of the first MIDI device (via the chosen group output(s) of your external mixing console).

4   Proceed in a similar manner to record all the MIDI parts of your external units onto separate audio tracks of Cubase SX. If you have multiple input audio hardware then you may prefer to record all your MIDI devices in a single pass.

5   When all the MIDI parts have been recorded onto regular audio tracks, mute all the original MIDI tracks in the Project window.

6   Set up your mix in the normal way, including the new audio tracks, and adjust the left and right locators to the start and end points of the music. Use Export/Audio mixdown to create an audio file on hard disk. The mix is now complete and includes all the audio signals from your MIDI devices.

Summary

Armed with the recording and editing techniques outlined in this and previous chapters, you are now ready to tackle more elaborate MIDI recording projects. With a little practice, you quickly find your own preferred method of recording and, using the techniques outlined above, you can go on to build up a number of tracks. Remember that the recording projects outlined here are only exercises and can, of course, be adapted to suit your own needs. To help clarify the basic recording process Figure 5.15 presents the essential steps in the form of a flowchart.

Tip

Use the tools and other techniques, as outlined in Chapter 4, to arrange and edit your newly recorded parts in the event display. Do not forget to save your work at regular intervals.

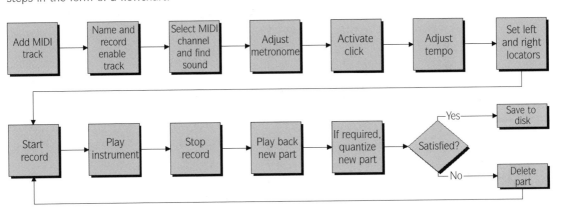

You can achieve an awful lot while still remaining in the Project window both in the recording and editing sense, and you may be surprised how quickly you can build up an entire musical arrangement. However, there are times when you need to process and edit MIDI data in fine detail and this forms the subject matter of the next chapter.

Figure 5.15
MIDI recording flowchart

MIDI editing

In Chapters 3 and 5 we explored some of the main techniques associated with the recording of MIDI-based music. This helps you to record and manipulate MIDI data at the event level. A wide variety of editing functions can be carried out on MIDI parts while still remaining at the event level in the Project window, but to look at a part's contents in fine detail we must open it in one of the MIDI editors. This chapter covers the Key editor, Edit In-Place editor, List editor and Drum editor.

General features of the MIDI editors

To open a MIDI editor, select a MIDI part and choose one of the editors from the MIDI menu. Each editor includes a toolbar, an infoline, a grid (where the MIDI notes and events are displayed) and a MIDI Controller display. The notes (or events) are shown as graphical strips in the Key and List editors and as diamond-shaped symbols in the Drum editor. The Edit In-Place editor is similar to the Key editor but opens up in the Project window within the expanded vertical space of the chosen MIDI track. This has the advantage of allowing you to edit and line up MIDI events relative to the events on the other tracks in the Project window (see the 'Edit In-Place' section below for more details).

The grid is a series of horizontal and vertical 'guide lines' which help you place notes at the correct pitch and at meaningful positions along the time line. This is particularly relevant when the snap button is activated, at which time the vertical lines of the grid become 'magnetic' for all newly input or edited notes. To get a better idea of how the grid behaves try selecting different values in the quantize menu (when bars and beats is chosen as the display format in the ruler). The distance between the vertical grid lines is modified for each new value chosen. De-activating the snap button might be viewed as switching off the 'magnetic' behaviour of the grid lines, at which time notes may be freely inserted or dragged to any position along the time line.

The MIDI editor toolbar

All the MIDI editors feature a toolbar which varies slightly for each editor (Figure 6.1). The common features of the toolbars include the following (left to right):

- solo button – for soloing the currently selected part.
- acoustic feedback button – for automatic playback of selected and inserted notes via MIDI.

Figure 6.1
MIDI editor toolbar (Key edit)

- info button – for showing or hiding the infoline.
- tool buttons – for selecting various editing tools (see below).
- autoscroll button – to automatically scroll the display to follow the project cursor position.
- show part borders button – for activating flags which show the start and end position of the part currently being edited.
- edit active part only button – restricts all editing operation to the active part only
- part list menu – you can select more than one part (or a whole track) for editing when you open a MIDI editor. This menu provides a list of all selected parts (or all parts in the track) allowing you to quickly choose which part you wish to edit next. The display automatically scrolls to the start of each part you choose.
- insert velocity field – for selecting the default velocity for inserted notes.
- snap button – for switching on the 'magnetic' action of the grid.
- quantize menu – for choosing the resolution of the grid and the division of the bar to which notes are attracted when you select a quantize function in the MIDI menu.
- length quantize menu – for changing the length of existing notes when using length quantize from the MIDI menu and for choosing a default length for inserted notes.
- velocity colours menu – for selecting the manner in which colour is used for velocity in the Controller display.
- step input and MIDI input buttons – to allow the input of notes one at a time according to the current quantize resolution and to allow the input of MIDI note and velocity data to change the values of existing events via MIDI.

Infoline

When the infoline button is activated a horizontal information line appears between the grid and the toolbar (Figure 6.2). It displays the details of the currently selected note, including the start position, end position, length, pitch, velocity, channel and note-off velocity. Position and length information is displayed according to the time line format you have chosen in the ruler. The infoline is particularly useful for detailed editing since all fields can be directly edited using the mouse and computer keyboard. When more than one event is selected the infoline text is shown in yellow and contains the information relevant to the first of the selected events. Editing any of the yellow text values applies the changes proportionally to all selected events, (i.e. changing the velocity value from, for example, '75' to '80' adds five to the velocity of all selected events). To apply the edits in an absolute sense hold down Ctrl while making the changes (this time, changing the velocity from '75' to '80' sets the velocity of all selected events to the absolute value of '80').

Figure 6.2
MIDI editor infoline

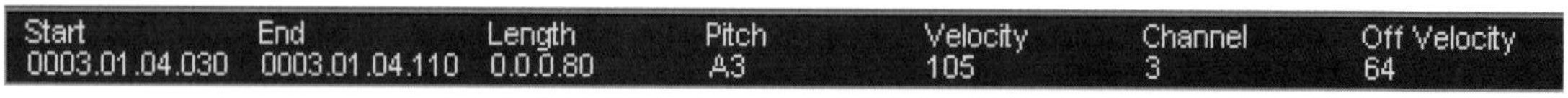

Start	End	Length	Pitch	Velocity	Channel	Off Velocity
0003.01.04.030	0003.01.04.110	0.0.0.80	A3	105	3	64

The MIDI editor tools

Info

To select a tool in any of the editors, click on one of the tool buttons in the toolbar or click with the right mouse button (PC) / Ctrl + click (Mac) in the grid to open the pop-up Quick menu. The tools are for the manipulation and editing of MIDI notes and Controller events and most of the tools listed here are relevant for all the MIDI editors. They include the following:

When the snap button is activated and bars and beats is set as the time format in the ruler, all tool editing in the Key, List and Drum editors is 'magnetic' to the current quantize settings (as set in the quantize and length quantize menus). With snap active and bars and beats in the ruler, the quantize setting is mirrored by the position of the vertical lines on the grid.

Object selection tool (pointer)

Similar to the Project window, the object selection tool (or pointer tool) is a general purpose tool for the selection, moving and copying of MIDI notes and events and for the manipulation of parameters anywhere in the MIDI editors. It is particularly useful for re-sizing in the Key editor where either the start or end of a note can be dragged to a new position (a double arrow appears when you position the pointer over the start or end points of the note). Unlike the Project window, the object selection tool for the MIDI editors is not a multi-function tool.

Draw tool

The draw tool is for inserting new events onto the note grid or into the Controller display. The lengths of existing notes may be changed by dragging the end point and velocity and Controller data can be individually modified in the Controller display.

Paint tool

The paint tool is a multi-function tool. Click on the button a second time to reveal the other options. The paint brush allows the free drawing of events on the note grid or in the Controller display. The line, parabola, sine, triangle and square tools impose their respective shapes on inserted or edited events. Note that the size of the shapes imposed by the sine, triangle and square tools is regulated by the current quantize value (when the snap button is activated).

Erase tool

The erase tool is for deleting events by clicking on one event or a selected group of events. Pressing Alt while clicking with the erase tool deletes all following events in the Part.

Zoom tool

The zoom tool is for zooming in and out of the grid display. To zoom in, select the zoom tool and click in the event display. This zooms in to the display horizontally around the position at which you clicked. You can zoom in to specific areas of the display by dragging a box around the area of interest with the zoom tool. To zoom back out hold Ctrl (PC) / Command (Mac) while clicking in the event display with the zoom tool. This steps you back through the previous zoom views you have used.

Mute tool

The mute tool is for muting events. Click on events individually or drag a selection box over several to implement muting. Click on or drag over the muted events to un-mute them. When an event is muted it is displayed in white.

Split tool

The split tool is for splicing notes into two shorter notes. Notes are split at the mouse position and according to the current snap/quantize settings.

Glue tool

The glue tool is used to join together notes of the same pitch to create one longer note.

Time warp tool

The time warp tool in the MIDI editors functions in a similar manner to the time warp tool in the Project window. In order to function correctly, the MIDI editor's ruler must be set to bars and beats. The time warp tool operates within the active part in two modes; 'default' mode and 'musical events follow' mode. In the default mode, the events in the MIDI editor do not move when you drag the warp tool in the display. This might be used to match the tempo to MIDI material which was not played to a strict click. When the snap button is activated on the toolbar the time warp position snaps to the start and ends of note events. This is useful for lining up beat positions to note events. In 'musical events follow' mode, all MIDI events are moved as you drag the warp tool in the display. This could be used for tempo manipulations which must take place within a given time frame.

Holding Shift while clicking in the grid with the time warp tool inserts a tempo event. Holding Shift with the time warp tool in the ruler allows the deleting of tempo events. When you first drag in the grid with the warp tool, a tempo event is automatically inserted at the start of the active part. This ensures that the tempo of material which occurs before the active part is not changed. Note that to use the time warp tool 'tempo track' mode must be selected in the Transport bar.

Drumstick tool

The drumstick tool is only relevant to the Drum editor. The Drum editor does not include a pencil tool in its toolbar. Instead, the drumstick tool is used for inputting events and re-sizing controller events. The drumstick tool behaves slightly differently to the pencil tool in that clicking on an event a second time removes it from the grid and dragging horizontally inputs repeated notes at the current quantize setting (if the snap button is activated).

Step input and MIDI input buttons

The six step/MIDI input buttons are concerned with the input of notes one step at a time (step input) and the entering of note and velocity data via MIDI. The buttons function in two modes according to which of the step and MIDI input buttons has been activated.

With the step button activated, when you play a note on your MIDI keyboard it is recorded onto the grid one step at a time at the resolution of the quantize menu setting and with the note length at the length quantize menu setting. The input data is also modified according to which of the note, velocity on and velocity off buttons (the rightmost three buttons) you have selected in the toolbar. With the note button activated the pitch of the input notes follows the keys you play on your keyboard. With the note button de-activated the pitch of the input notes remains at C3/60. With the velocity on button activated the velocity of the input notes follows the velocity with which you play the notes on your keyboard. With the velocity button de-activated the velocity of the input notes matches that set in the insert velocity field. The velocity off button functions in a similar manner. A 'move insert mode' button allows you to insert notes into an existing sequence by pushing existing notes to the right.

With the MIDI input button activated, when you select an existing note on the grid and play a note on your MIDI keyboard, this imposes the received MIDI information onto the selected note according to which of the note, velocity on and velocity off buttons (the rightmost three buttons) you have selected in the toolbar. When the incoming MIDI information has been registered the editor moves on to the next note automatically. This allows you to re-record note and/or velocity data for an existing sequence in step-time.

General tips on using the MIDI editors

The following tips are designed to help you get started in the MIDI editors.

- Once you have selected one note event in a MIDI editor, try using the left and right arrow keys on the computer keyboard to scroll through consecutive notes. This is often easier than using the mouse. In order to be able to hear each event as it is selected, activate the acoustic feedback button (loudspeaker symbol) in the toolbar. Use the up and down arrow keys to change the pitch of a selected note.
- Adopting a two hand approach speeds up tool selection and editing. Use the left hand to select the tools with the computer typewriter keys 1 to 9 (or F9 and F10 to step through the tools) and use the right hand for all mouse manipulations.
- To gain an initial understanding of the function of the grid, open a MIDI editor (the Key editor, for example), make sure bars and beats is chosen as the display format in the ruler, activate the snap button and change the quantize menu to different values. For each new value selected in the quantize menu the distance between the vertical grid lines is modified. When the snap button is activated the grid becomes 'magnetic' and any inserted notes are pulled onto the nearest vertical grid line. This also helps you get to grips with the quantize functions. Selecting Over quantize from the MIDI menu pulls all recorded notes in the part onto their nearest vertical grid lines. You can see the effect of the quantizing action on the grid. Observing the effect of quantizing in a MIDI editor provides excellent visual feedback of what actually happens when you use the quantize functions, and is a helpful learning aid for getting to know what quantize is all about.
- Clicking once in the ruler moves the project cursor to the position at which you clicked. Double clicking in the ruler starts playback from the point at which you clicked. Double clicking a second time stops playback and re-positions the project cursor to the point at which you clicked. This helps you navigate within your chosen MIDI editor.
- Use the G and H keys for horizontal zoom control in the grid display. Use Alt + G and Alt + H for vertical zoom control (may need to be assigned in File/Key Commands/Zoom). At higher vertical zoom settings the MIDI note name/number appears inside the note strip.

- Click with the right mouse button (PC)/Ctrl + click (Mac) in the grid to open the Quick menu. This allows quick tool selection and provides rapid access to the menu items relevant to MIDI editing.
- Cubase SX benefits from unlimited undo/redo. Use Ctrl + Z (PC)/ Command + Z (Mac) to undo an edit. Use Ctrl + Shift + Z (PC)/Command + Shift + Z (Mac) to redo an edit. To see the current edit history open the 'History' dialogue (Edit menu). Move the blue line to step back and forth within the edit history. Note that the edit history is cleared when you close the project.

Tip

Increasing the Key editor vertical zoom resolution reveals the note names inside each event on the grid.

Figure 6.3
The Key editor

Key editor

The Key editor (Figure 6.3) is a piano roll style editor featuring time on the horizontal axis and pitch on the vertical axis. The main display area is the grid where notes are represented as graphical strips. There is a mini piano keyboard to the left of the display, which corresponds to the pitch, and a

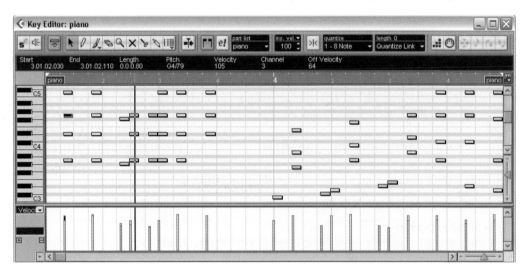

Controller display below where velocity and various non-note events, such as Pitch Bend and Modulation, are shown. Similar to the Project window and the other MIDI editors, there is a ruler which marks the time line in the currently chosen format (bars and beats, for example) and a toolbar and infoline (as outlined above).

To open the Key editor from the Project window either double click on a MIDI part, select a MIDI track or part and select 'Key editor' from the MIDI menu, or press Ctrl (PC)/Command (Mac) + E on the computer keyboard (the default key command). Pressing the Return key on the computer keyboard also opens/closes the Key editor for a selected MIDI part. Note that you can select more than one part from the same or different tracks and all notes in all parts are visible in the Key editor. However, the notes from only one part at a time are active and all other non-active notes are displayed in grey. Use the part list to select the active part and the 'show part borders' button to highlight the active part.

Tip

When using the Key editor, try pressing 'P' on the computer keyboard to set the left and right locators to the start and end points of the selected part. Also select Cycle on the Transport panel, (use the divide key on the numeric keypad). Cubase SX now cycles within the selected part (between the left and right locators) ensuring that the project cursor does not disappear from view while you are in the Key editor.

Controller display

The Key editor features a Controller display for velocity and non-note MIDI data such as Pitch Bend, Aftertouch, Program Change, Modulation, Main Volume and Pan. Right click (PC)/Ctrl + click (Mac) in the Key editor grid to 'create a new controller lane' from the pop-up Quick menu. By default, velocity is displayed when you create a new lane. To change the type of event shown, click on the menu to the left of the Controller lane to open the pop-up menu. If the type of data you wish to see is not present in the menu, click on 'Setup' to open the Controller menu setup dialogue, and add the required data type to the menu using the left pointing arrow button.

Events are shown as vertical strips which, by default, are colour-coded according to their value, (where low values are shown in blue and high values are shown in red). This is particularly useful for velocity since it gives an immediate idea of the intensity of the musical performance. The velocity colour is also applied to the note itself on the grid, which conveys the velocity status even if the Controller display is hidden from view. More controller lanes may be added by, once again, selecting 'Create New Controller Lane' from the Quick menu. This allows the simultaneous display of a number of controller lanes which is invaluable for high precision multiple controller editing.

Figure 6.4
The Controller display allows multiple controller lanes to be shown

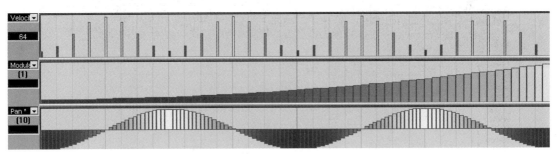

Key editor basic techniques

Most routine editing in the Key editor revolves around inserting, selecting, moving, re-sizing and deleting notes and controller events using the tools.

The draw tool is the standard tool for drawing new note events onto the grid. Notes are pulled onto the nearest vertical grid line when the snap button is activated. Their velocity is determined by the insert velocity value on the toolbar and, with single click inserts, their length is determined by the length quantize value. Clicking and dragging to the right with the pencil tool allows you to insert a note of a longer length. Clicking and dragging in the Controller display with the pencil tool inserts new controller events. If there are events already in the Controller display these are updated according to the new shape drawn by the pencil tool (Figure 6.5).

The pointer tool would normally be used for the selection of notes on the grid and events in the controller display. The standard selection procedures as outlined in Chapter 4 also apply to the

Figure 6.5
Inserting new notes and new controller events using the draw tool

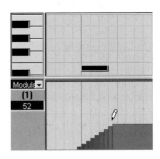

selection of events in the Key editor. The principal methods include dragging a box around a number of events or clicking on individual events. Selected notes may be moved by clicking on one of them and dragging to a new position. Holding Alt on the computer keyboard copies the notes instead (Figure 6.6).

Figure 6.6
Selecting and moving notes

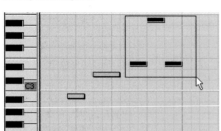
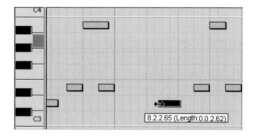

The pointer tool may be used for re-sizing notes by clicking and dragging on their start or end points. A double arrow appears when the tool is placed above the appropriate position (Figure 6.7).

Figure 6.7
Re-sizing notes using the pointer tool

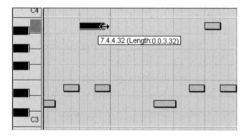
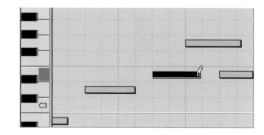

Deleting notes is achieved either by dragging over the notes with the erase tool or selecting the notes and pressing backspace on the computer keyboard. If your deletions are of an experimental kind, you may prefer to temporarily mute the notes using the mute tool.

Key editor close-ups

Editing a bass line

You have recorded a perfect bass line with a great feel but some notes are too long, some are too short and some overlap. The Key editor provides a solution as follows:

- Select the draw tool.
- Click and hold the draw near the end point of each offending note and drag the length to the desired duration.
- If the snap button is activated, the new length is snapped to

Figure 6.8
Editing the lengths of overlapping bass notes

the nearest vertical grid line. De-activating the snap button allows you to freely adjust the length of the note and may be a better option for this exercise.
- 'Delete overlaps' in the MIDI functions menu may also provide a partial solution to the problem.

Editing note start positions within a chord
The start positions of the notes in the chords you recorded are inaccurate and misplaced. To cure the problem in the Key editor proceed as follows:

- Click and hold on the misplaced note using the pointer tool. Drag the note to a new position.
- Alternatively, change the start position of the note by clicking and dragging the start point with the pointer tool (a double arrow appears).
- For a more natural result, the Snap button could be de-activated to allow the placing of notes or start positions with greater subtlety on the grid.
- If very subtle changes in position are required try entering new values into the start position field in the infoline. Double click on the existing value and enter a new value using the typewriter keyboard. Alternatively, click and hold on the value and drag the mouse up or down to increase/decrease the setting. This works only if you select 'Increment/Decrement on Left-click and Drag' in File/Preferences/Control/ Value Box.

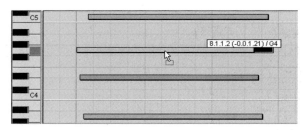

Tip

To nudge MIDI notes back and forth, select the note and press Ctrl/Command + the left or right arrows on the computer keyboard. Alternatively, use the nudge buttons on the toolbar. The nudge resolution is determined by the current quantize value in the quantize menu and/or the ruler format. (To move a note one tick at a time, place the pointer over the start tick value on the info line and turn the wheel of your mouse).

Figure 6.9
Editing the start positions of notes within a chord

Editing note velocities
The synthesizer sound you are using produces an unwanted percussive attack on certain notes within a sequence due to their having been recorded with a higher velocity. To correct the situation proceed as follows:

- Select velocity in the Key editor Controller display by clicking on the downward pointing arrow to the left of the Controller lane to open the pop-up controller selection menu. Normally, velocity is displayed by default when you first open the Key editor.
- The velocities of the recorded notes are now visible in the display as vertical strips.
- Select the draw tool and click and drag on the offending velocities to set them to appropriate new values.

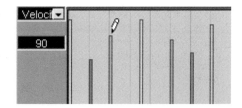

Figure 6.10
Changing velocity values using the draw tool

Producing crescendos
If crescendos (or decrescendos) are required after the notes have been recorded then the Controller display of the Key editor is one of the best places to create them. This technique is particularly useful for drum rolls and snare fills. Proceed as follows:

- Select velocity in the Controller display.
- Select the line tool and click and drag a line at the appropriate angle

Tip

To hear a MIDI note as you change its velocity in the Controller display or on the infoline, activate the acoustic feedback button on the Key editor's toolbar. This also allows you to hear the note if you change its pitch.

across the note velocities to which you wish to apply the crescendo.

- When the mouse is released a velocity ramp matching the straight line appears.

- For a more exponential crescendo try using the parabola shape tool.

- This technique can be used on other types of data, such as Main Volume events for the creation of MIDI volume fade ins and fade outs.

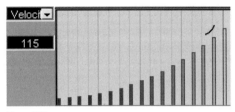

Figure 6.11
Producing a crescendo using the parabola shape of the draw tool

Producing special effects with modulation

The Modulation Controller is often used with synth patches to produce real-time modulation of some aspect of the sound, such as increasing the brightness, modifying the cut-off frequency of the filter or adding more vibrato. Using the draw tool shapes, like sine and triangle, you can create special effects by drawing automated shapes in the Controller display. Proceed as follows:

- Select modulation in the Controller display. De-activate the snap button on the toolbar.
- Select the triangle shape draw tool and click and drag to the right from the upper left corner of the controller lane (when the value field should read 127) to the lower right corner (when the value field should read 0).
- When the mouse is released a triangular-shaped sequence of modulation events appears in the display.
- Try re-activating the snap button and choosing different quantize values and different tool shapes (e.g. sine and square) to create other kinds of special effects.

Figure 6.12
Drawing modulation shapes in the Controller display for special effects

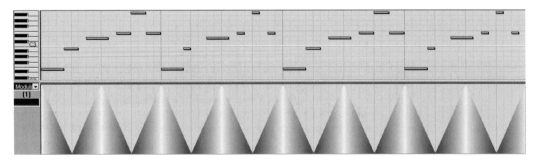

Multiple controller lanes for high-precision editing and special effects

If your target synthesizer responds to Controllers 70-74, several controller lanes can be used simultaneously to set up tightly co-ordinated special effects. Proceed as follows:

- Open the number of controller lanes required using 'Create New Controller Lane' in the Quick menu.
- Select the controllers you intend to use in the pop-up controller selector

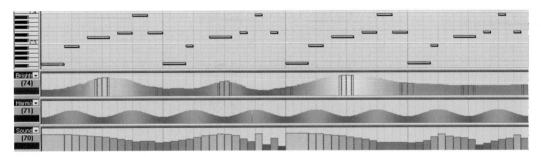

menus to the left of the lanes. Try starting with three controller lanes showing Controllers 70, 71 and 74.

• Select a draw tool and draw the required data in the display. Try using combinations of the paintbrush, parabola, sine, triangle and square tools.

Figure 6.13
Tightly co-ordinated editing in multiple controller lanes

Edit In-Place

The Edit In-Place editor (Figure 6.14) is similar to the Key editor except that it is opened "in-place" in the Project window. This means that you can look inside a MIDI part while still remaining in the Project window and, more importantly, you can line up individual MIDI events to events on other tracks in the event display (or vice versa). To open the Edit In-Place editor select a MIDI part (or MIDI track) in the event display and select 'Edit In-Place' from the MIDI menu or press Ctrl/Command + Shift + I on the computer keyboard. Usefully, the keyboard shortcut toggles between opening and closing the Edit In-Place editor. Alternatively, try using the Edit In-Place button in the track list (this can be made visible by activating it in the Track Control Settings dialogue, opened by clicking on the small downward pointing arrow at the top left of the track list).

The Edit-In Place editor opens within the vertical space of the selected MIDI track which expands to accommodate the grid. The vertical grid lines in the editor line up perfectly with the grid in the main part of the Project window. It is therefore a relatively easy task to line up MIDI events to other

Figure 6.14
Edit In-Place editor

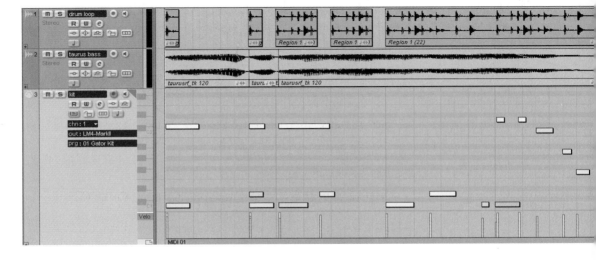

Tip

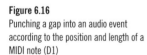

When using the Edit In-Place editor, setting the snap type menu to 'Events' allows you to snap MIDI notes to marker positions. This is excellent for lining up MIDI notes to markers which were created using 'Create markers from hitpoints' (Audio menu), thus allowing you to fine tune the positions of MIDI notes to the hitpoints of an audio recording.

events along the time line. The other features of the editor include a Controller display below the grid, a virtual keyboard to the left, and a toolbar above which is opened by clicking on the grey triangle found at the upper left side of the virtual keyboard.

Edit In-Place basic techniques

To zoom in vertically in the Edit In-Place editor, place the pointer in the left part of the virtual keyboard to the left of the grid so that a hand appears. Drag the hand to the left or right to zoom in and out. Drag the hand up or down to scroll the key range shown in the editor. To zoom in and out horizontally, use the standard Cubase zoom controls (by default, key commands G and H).

Clicking on the grey triangle in the upper left corner of the Edit In-Place editor opens a toolbar. The toolbar is a reduced version of the toolbar found in the other MIDI editors. Here you have access to the acoustic feedback button, part list, insert velocity, length quantize, velocity colours, transpose and chord recognition parameters.

The snap and quantize behaviour is governed from the main Project window toolbar using the snap type and quantize type menus. (The grid type menu has no function in the Edit In-Place editor). Setting the snap type menu to 'Events' is particularly helpful for lining up MIDI events to other events on other tracks in the display (or vice versa).

Edit In-Place close-ups
Snapping to events

As mentioned above, activating the snap button and selecting 'Events' in the snap menu is particularly useful in the Edit In-Place editor. For example, this makes it easy to move a MIDI note which triggers a crash cymbal to coincide with the start of an audio event, as shown in Figure 6.15.

Figure 6.15
Lining up a MIDI crash cymbal (C#2) with the start of an audio event in the Edit In-Place editor

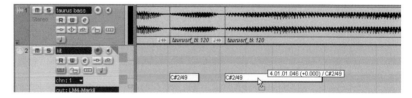

Moving audio events in relation to individual MIDI events is equally useful. For example, Figure 6.16 shows how you can 'punch a hole' in an audio event for the precise duration of a MIDI event. In this case, a gap is punched into an audio event (a drum loop) according to the position and length of a MIDI snare drum (D1). To achieve this the drum loop is split and the end of the resulting first event is dragged to the start of the MIDI note, while the start of the second event is dragged to the end of the MIDI note.

Figure 6.16
Punching a gap into an audio event according to the position and length of a MIDI note (D1)

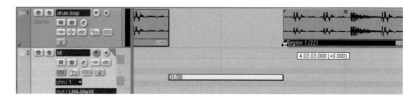

Selective moving and copying

Another advantage of the Edit In-Place editor is the ability to selectively move or copy specific MIDI events within a part along with other selected events in the general event display. For example, this would allow you to copy audio events along with just the MIDI notes which trigger a cymbal in a MIDI part, as shown in Figure 6.17. All non-selected MIDI notes are not copied/moved with the selection.

Figure 6.17
Selectively copying the cymbal crashes in a MIDI part along with some audio events

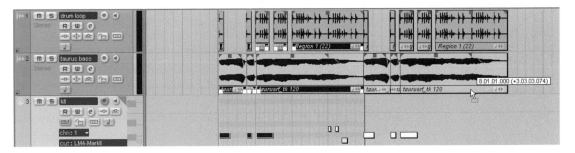

The List editor

The List editor (Figure 6.18) is a list-based editor where all data is presented in a list of time-consecutive events. It differs from the other editors in that all kinds of MIDI data, score and standard MIDI file events may be viewed and edited.

The List editor is opened from the MIDI menu or you may like to assign a Key command in File/Key Commands (try Ctrl/Command + Alt + L). Similar to the Key editor, the List editor features a grid and a toolbar containing a similar set of tools. However, the most important feature of the List editor is the list itself. There are a number of columns hidden behind the grid which can be revealed by moving the split point to the right of the screen. This reveals more details about the events in the list.

The columns contain information about each event including its type, start position, end position, length, data values 1, 2 and 3, MIDI channel and associated System Exclusive or text data in the comment column. For example, regular note events feature their pitch in the data 1 column followed by their veloc-

Info

The List editor displays a simple time ordered list of the MIDI events. Unlike the Key editor, the vertical axis of the grid does NOT represent pitch. Changing the pitch in the List editor data 1 column therefore produces no visible change to the events in the grid. Time is shown on the horizontal axis of the grid.

Figure 6.18
The List editor

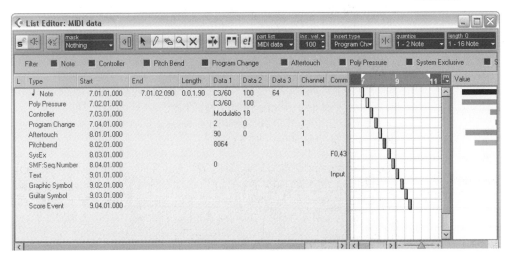

ity on in the data 2 column and velocity off in data 3. Controller events feature the controller name (or number) in the data 1 column followed by the value of the controller in the data 2 column. Most events have no entry in the comment column. However, the comment column for a System Exclusive event contains the System Exclusive message itself.

Features which are unique to the List editor include the Insert menu, the Mask menu, and the Filters. These are found in the toolbar.

The Insert menu

The Insert pop-up menu on the toolbar contains a list of event types. Any chosen event type may be inserted into the List by clicking with the draw tool on the grid. The event types include Note, Controller, Program Change, Aftertouch, Pitch Bend, SysEx, SMF and text.

The Mask menu and display filters

The Mask menu is used to force a display of:

1 all data of the same event type as the currently selected event
2 all data with the same event type and the same data 1 value as the currently selected event.
3 all data with the same MIDI channel as the currently selected event.

All other events are hidden from view. Alternatively, the events in the list may be filtered according to Logical editor presets.

The display filters are comprised of nine tick boxes, one for each of the main event types and for SMF and score events. These are hidden or shown using the toolbar's 'Show filter view' button. When a box is ticked the corresponding event type is filtered out of the event list.

The Mask menu and display filters are among the most useful features of List edit. They can be used to clarify the list and to expose certain types of data for deletion or other editing.

List editor basic techniques

In the List editor, events may be edited by clicking on the column values and entering a new value with the computer keyboard (depends upon the value box setting in File/Preferences/Controls). Type a new value directly or use the up/down arrow keys to increment/decrement the value.

When the mouse pointer is moved into the grid area to the right of the list, it is automatically changed to a pencil tool. The horizontal bars in the display represent the data 2 values of events. These values may be changed graphically in the display in much the same way as in the Controller display of the Key editor.

Clicking in the comment column for a System Exclusive event opens the MIDI Sysex editor. This is for editing System Exclusive data in fine detail and requires a good knowledge of SysEx theory in order to be successful. The user manual of your MIDI device normally lists the details of its SysEx messages.

The essential difference between the List and the Key editors is that the Key editor is directed towards the graphical editing of note data on the grid and controller data in the Controller display, whereas the List editor is directed towards the more detailed editing of any type of event and its various values in the display list. As a general rule, the List editor is more useful for the

Tip

If you select 'Increment/decrement on left-click and drag' in File/ Preferences/Controls, you can change any of the values in the List editor columns simply by clicking at the appropriate location and dragging the mouse up or down.

editing of non-note events and helps when a more scientific approach is required. List edit is excellent for sorting events for analytical and troubleshooting purposes and might help you find undesirable events which are causing problems with your MIDI devices.

List editor close-ups

Editing System Exclusive messages

For the editing of System Exclusive messages proceed as follows:

- Click once in the comment column of the System Exclusive event in the list. The first part of the SysEx message is always visible in the comment column.
- The whole message is displayed in the MIDI Sysex editor which opens automatically. The data is shown in hexadecimal notation (Figure 6.19).
- Edit the data as desired and click on the OK button to keep the changes. A good knowledge of System Exclusive is required to make any meaningful changes.

Figure 6.19
Editing System Exclusive data

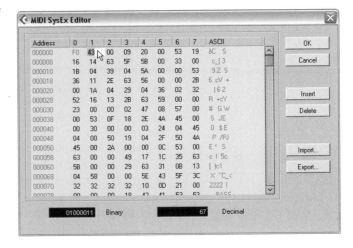

Finding unwanted Program Change messages

At some time in their use of the program, most Cubase SX users suffer from the problem of an unwanted or incorrect program change (or some other data type) embedded somewhere among the rest of the data. This is not always easy to find for deletion or editing. With the List editor filters the task is made easier. Proceed as follows:

- Activate the filter button on the toolbar. Tick the filter boxes of all those data types you do not wish to see.
- The unwanted event(s) can now be found more easily among the remaining unfiltered data displayed in the list.

Figure 6.20
Exposing Program Change events using the List editor's filters

Filter	☑ Note	☑ Controller	☑ Pitch Bend	■ Program Change	☑ Aftertouch			
L	Type	Start	End	Length	Data 1	Data 2	Channel	Comment
	Program Change	0007.04.01.000			3	0	1	
	Program Change	0010.01.01.000			54	0	1	

Inserting a Local Off Controller event

Most users set their master keyboard to Local Off for use with Cubase SX. This disconnects the keyboard from the sound-making circuitry of the instrument. Finding the Local Off control in the instrument itself is not always obvious and some instruments power up in Local On mode. To overcome these problems it is helpful to embed a Local Off message into a MIDI part which can be used within a default startup project to make sure that the master keyboard is always set to Local Off. To insert a Local Off event in List edit, proceed as follows:

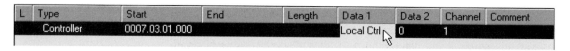

L	Type	Start	End	Length	Data 1	Data 2	Channel	Comment
	Controller	0007.03.01.000			Local Ctrl	0	1	

Figure 6.21
Creating a Local Off Controller message
in List edit

- Create an empty MIDI part in the Project window, select it and open List edit.
- Select Controller in the Insert menu of the List edit toolbar.
- Select the draw tool and click once in the grid with the mouse at the beginning of the part. A new controller event with various default values is inserted into the list.
- Click once in the data 1 column of the new event and enter the number '122' using the computer's numeric keypad (Controller 122 is the Local On/Off Controller).
- Make sure that '0' is entered into the data 2 column ('0' is the off setting and '127' is the on setting for Local Control).
- Make sure that the MIDI track containing the part is transmitting to your master keyboard. When the newly created MIDI part is played, the Local Off message is sent to the keyboard and it is set to Local Off mode accordingly.

The Drum editor

The Drum editor is a 'drum machine' style editor featuring time on the horizontal axis and pitch in the form of drum names on the vertical axis (Figure 6.22). Like the Key editor there is a grid but, this time, notes are represented by diamond-shaped symbols. The drum names are shown as a list to the left of the display and there is a toolbar above the grid and a Controller display below, similar to those found in the Key editor. To open the Drum editor, select a MIDI part and then select 'Drum editor' from the MIDI menu.

As the name implies, the Drum editor is designed for the editing of drum and percussion data. It operates in two modes depending on whether or not you have activated a drum map. Without a drum map, the editor functions

Figure 6.22
The Drum editor

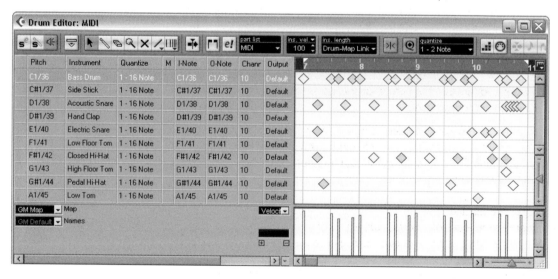

in a similar way to the Key editor. When a drum map is activated, more columns appear in the display and the editor features the names and note positions of specific drum setups, such as those found in external drum machines and modules or in a standard GM drum map.

Drum maps are assigned on a track-by-track basis and each track can be assigned a different drum map. Maps are chosen from the map menu in the Drum editor or in the Inspector for the track. When a map is assigned for a track in the Project window, the data display format switches to diamond-shaped symbols for all parts on the track. New maps are added to the menu using the Drum Map Setup dialogue.

Drum editor columns

When a drum map has been assigned, pulling the split point to the right reveals a number of columns which are unique to the Drum editor. These include the following:

- Selection – a blank column for triggering/selecting each instrument with the mouse.
- Pitch – defines the base note for each instrument. This is the actual note which gets recorded and the settings in this column cannot be modified. There are 128 pitches available matching the 128 possible MIDI notes. The note in the pitch column often matches that found in the I-Note column but this may not always be the case.
- Instrument – for naming each instrument (drum) in the map.
- Quantize – for assigning an individual quantize value for each instrument which governs the resolution of any inserts or editing for the instrument on the grid.
- Mute – for muting individual instruments. Muting also occurs when you activate the 'solo instrument' button on the toolbar.
- I-Note (input note) – defines the pitch of the note you use to trigger each instrument. This is the source note you play on your master keyboard (or other controller instrument).
- O-Note (output note) – defines the pitch of the note which is transmitted from the MIDI output of Cubase SX when its corresponding input note is received. This is the note which is transmitted to the target MIDI device.
- Channel – for the selection of a MIDI channel for each instrument.
- Output – for the selection of a MIDI output port for each instrument. When set to 'default' the output for the instrument is transmitted via the MIDI port set for the track.

When a drum map has not been assigned, only the pitch, instrument and quantize columns are available. In this mode, you can still select the list of names and quantize values for the available maps using the Names menu (below the Map menu).

Setting up a Drum map

A Drum map is a set of 128 instrument slots each assigned to one of the 128 possible MIDI notes, and each with their corresponding name and values in the columns. Drum maps are assigned to MIDI tracks using the map menu which is found in the Drum editor or in the Inspector for the track. To

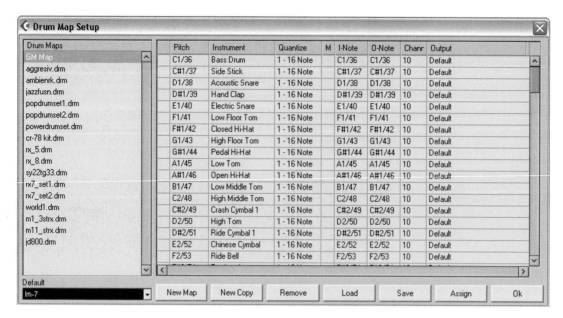

Pitch	Instrument	Quantize	M	I-Note	O-Note	Chanr	Output
C1/36	Bass Drum	1 - 16 Note		C1/36	C1/36	10	Default
C#1/37	Side Stick	1 - 16 Note		C#1/37	C#1/37	10	Default
D1/38	Acoustic Snare	1 - 16 Note		D1/38	D1/38	10	Default
D#1/39	Hand Clap	1 - 16 Note		D#1/39	D#1/39	10	Default
E1/40	Electric Snare	1 - 16 Note		E1/40	E1/40	10	Default
F1/41	Low Floor Tom	1 - 16 Note		F1/41	F1/41	10	Default
F#1/42	Closed Hi-Hat	1 - 16 Note		F#1/42	F#1/42	10	Default
G1/43	High Floor Tom	1 - 16 Note		G1/43	G1/43	10	Default
G#1/44	Pedal Hi-Hat	1 - 16 Note		G#1/44	G#1/44	10	Default
A1/45	Low Tom	1 - 16 Note		A1/45	A1/45	10	Default
A#1/46	Open Hi-Hat	1 - 16 Note		A#1/46	A#1/46	10	Default
B1/47	Low Middle Tom	1 - 16 Note		B1/47	B1/47	10	Default
C2/48	High Middle Tom	1 - 16 Note		C2/48	C2/48	10	Default
C#2/49	Crash Cymbal 1	1 - 16 Note		C#2/49	C#2/49	10	Default
D2/50	High Tom	1 - 16 Note		D2/50	D2/50	10	Default
D#2/51	Ride Cymbal 1	1 - 16 Note		D#2/51	D#2/51	10	Default
E2/52	Chinese Cymbal	1 - 16 Note		E2/52	E2/52	10	Default
F2/53	Ride Bell	1 - 16 Note		F2/53	F2/53	10	Default

Drum Maps: GM Map, aggresiv.drm, ambienrk.drm, jazzfusn.drm, popdrumset1.drm, popdrumset2.drm, powerdrumset.drm, cr-78 kit.drm, rx_5.drm, rx_8.drm, sy22tg33.drm, rx7_set1.drm, rx7_set2.drm, world1.drm, m1_3strx.drm, m11_strx.drm, jd800.drm

Default: lm-7

Buttons: New Map, New Copy, Remove, Load, Save, Assign, Ok

Figure 6.23
The Drum Map Setup dialogue

set up a new map or save and load maps to/from disk, open the Drum Map Setup dialogue from the map menu (Figure 6.23).

Even though changes can be made to the drum map while remaining in the Drum editor, the Drum Map Setup dialogue has everything you need for drum map editing purposes. You can create an empty new map using the New Map button. You can copy an existing map using the New Copy button. The Save and Load buttons allow you to save and load maps to/from disk and the Remove button allows you to delete the currently selected map from the list. The Assign button assigns the chosen map to the Drum editor.

Any value in the columns is edited by clicking on it once with the mouse and entering a new value using the computer keyboard. The quantize, channel and output columns feature pop-up menus. The pitch column values are fixed and cannot be changed. Holding Ctrl (PC)/Command (Mac) while entering a value in the quantize, channel or output columns changes all instruments to the same value for that column. The columns themselves can be moved within the display by dragging the column header to a new position with the mouse.

The general use of the Drum Map Setup dialogue is not particularly difficult but understanding the details of the I-Note, O-Note and pitch columns requires considerable effort. It makes things clearer to view the I-Note column as a representation of where the sounds are being played on the keyboard and the O-Note column as a representation of where the sounds are found in the target MIDI device. The pitch column is a series of fixed MIDI note values tagged on to each row (the value in the pitch column is what actually gets recorded in Cubase SX). Imagine that you wish to set up a drum map which corresponds with the bass drum, snare and hi-hat of an external drum module. This might mean that you need to adjust the note positions in the O-Note column to match the positions of the drums in the module, so that you can continue to play the drums in the standard GM key positions, as found in the I-note column (for example) (Figure 6.24.)

Imagine that you now wish to change the sound of the snare to the snare found in the 909 kit of the LM7 virtual drum module supplied with Cubase SX. Firstly,

Instrument	Quantize	M	Pitch	I-Note	O-Note	Chanr	Output
bass drum	1/16 Note		C1	C1	B0	12	Microsoft MPU-401 (WDM)
snare	1/16 Note		D1	D1	F#1	12	Microsoft MPU-401 (WDM)
closed hi-hat	1/16 Note		F#1	F#1	G1	12	Microsoft MPU-401 (WDM)
pedal hi-hat	1/16 Note		G#1	G#1	A1	12	Microsoft MPU-401 (WDM)
open hi-hat	1/16 Note		A#1	A#1	B1	12	Microsoft MPU-401 (WDM)

Figure 6.24
Adjusting the O-Note values to match the drum note positions of a target drum module

make sure that the LM7 is activated in the VST Instruments panel (opened from the devices menu or press F11 on the computer keyboard). Change the preset drum kit to '909'. To assign the snare to the LM7, select LM7 in the output column for the snare and adjust the note value in the O-Note column to match the location of a snare sound (Figure 6.25). Triggering multiple MIDI devices via the drum map might also mean that you need to change the MIDI channels in the Channel col-

Instrument	Quantize	M	Pitch	I-Note	O-Note	Chanr	Output
bass drum	1/16 Note		C1	C1	B0	12	Microsoft MPU-401 (WDM)
snare	1/16 Note		D1	D1	E1	12	lm-7
closed hi-hat	1/16 Note		F#1	F#1	G1	12	Microsoft MPU-401 (WDM)
pedal hi-hat	1/16 Note		G#1	G#1	A1	12	Microsoft MPU-401 (WDM)
open hi-hat	1/16 Note		A#1	A#1	B1	12	Microsoft MPU-401 (WDM)

Figure 6.25
Assigning the snare to the LM7 VST Instrument

umn as well as the output ports for each of the sounds concerned.

Now let's think about the details of what actually happens when you trigger your drum sounds via a drum map. Firstly, the incoming MIDI note finds its corresponding pitch in the I-Note column. It is then instantaneously transposed to the value found in the pitch column on the same row, (when recording, it is always the pitch column value which gets recorded). From there, it is instantaneously transposed a second time to the value found in the O-Note column on the same row (the O-Note value is the final output note sent to the target MIDI device). If the bass drum in your target MIDI device is found on B0 but you wish to play it using C1, set the O-Note value to B0 on the row which corresponds to I-Note value C1 (usually the row named as a bass drum and corresponding with a pitch column value of C1). You can now play the bass drum using the standard C1 key on the keyboard even though it is found on B0 in the target unit. Alternatively, if the first three drum sounds of a kit are found on MIDI notes F0, F#0 and B0 but you wish to play them in the middle of your keyboard, change their I-Note values to C3, D3 and E3 (for example).

Drum editor basic techniques

The Drum editor features a drumstick tool which replaces the functions of the draw tool found in the other editors. The drumstick tool is used for inserting notes onto the grid. It differs from the draw tool in that it cannot be held and dragged on the grid to adjust the length of a note as it is being inserted. Instead the length is governed by the Insert Length setting on the toolbar. However, if you click and drag the drumstick horizontally along the grid, for one sound, a series of events are inserted at the resolution set by the quantize column for that sound (if global quantize is de-activated on the toolbar), or at the resolution set by the quantize value on the toolbar (if global quantize is activated on the toolbar). If the drumstick tool is clicked over an existing event, the event is deleted.

The toolbar also features a 'solo instrument' button. This solos the currently selected instrument in the drum map. When the drum solo button is

---

Tip

It is always the pitch column note which gets recorded in Cubase SX. Therefore, with a map containing O-Note data which does not match the pitch column data, the recorded notes only trigger the correct sounds when the correct drum map is active. There may be times when you no longer wish to use the drum map but wish to retain the recorded data suitably transposed to trigger the correct sounds (such as when you export your MIDI sequence as a Standard MIDI File). To achieve this, use O-Note Conversion in the MIDI menu.

activated all instruments other than the one which is currently selected are muted in the mute column. This is excellent for soloing individual drum sounds for fine tuning in a mix.

Like the Key editor, the Drum editor features an Infoline, where existing events can be updated in terms of their position, length, pitch, velocity and channel. The Drum editor also has a Controller display but it differs from the Key editor in that it shows the controller data for the currently selected instrument only. This is useful for creating velocity ramps for snare rolls, for example (see below).

Drum editor close ups

Inserting 1/16th note hi-hats

A common requirement for drum parts is the insertion of a hi-hat at regular 1/16th note intervals. To achieve this in the Drum editor, proceed as follows:

- Select an Insert Velocity and an Insert Length in the toolbar.
- Activate global quantize on the toolbar and set the quantize value to '1/16 note'. This governs the resolution of any inserted events. Alternatively, de-activate global quantize and set the quantize column value for the hi-hat instrument to '1/16 note'. When global quantize is de-activated the resolution for inserted events is governed by the values found in the quantize column.
- Select the drumstick tool and click and drag horizontally across the grid in the row corresponding to the closed hi-hat instrument. Drag for the desired number of bars. A series of events are inserted at the chosen resolution.

Figure 6.26
Inserting hi-hat events using the drumstick tool

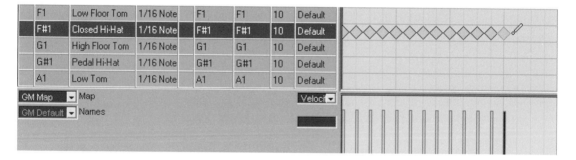

Creating crescendos for drum rolls and fills

The advantage of creating drum related crescendos in the Drum editor is that you can see the velocity data separately for each instrument in the Controller display. Proceed as follows:

- Select the instrument for which you wish to create a crescendo in the instrument list.
- Select velocity in the Controller display.
- Select the line tool and click and drag a line at the appropriate angle across the appropriate note velocities.
- When the mouse is released a velocity ramp matching the line appears.
- For a more exponential crescendo try using the parabola shape of the draw tool.

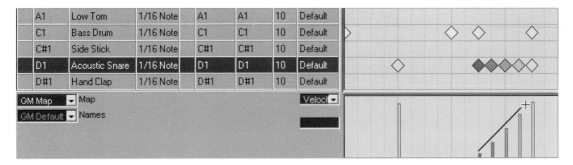

A1	Low Tom	1/16 Note	A1	A1	10	Default
C1	Bass Drum	1/16 Note	C1	C1	10	Default
C#1	Side Stick	1/16 Note	C#1	C#1	10	Default
D1	Acoustic Snare	1/16 Note	D1	D1	10	Default
D#1	Hand Clap	1/16 Note	D#1	D#1	10	Default

GM Map ▼ Map
GM Default ▼ Names
Veloci ▼

Combining loop and solo

It is often helpful to replay a single drum sound repeatedly while you are adjusting its EQ and effects settings. This is particularly true of bass drum and snare sounds and could also apply to tom rolls when you are setting up pan positions. With the Drum editor this is a two stage process. Proceed as follows:

Figure 6.27
Using the line tool to create a crescendo in the Drum editor's Controller display

- In the Drum editor, select the events you want to hear soloed. This could be one event or the events from several bars. Click with the right mouse button (PC)/Ctrl + click (Mac) in the grid to open the Quick menu and select 'Loop selection' from the Transport section. Loop playback commences.

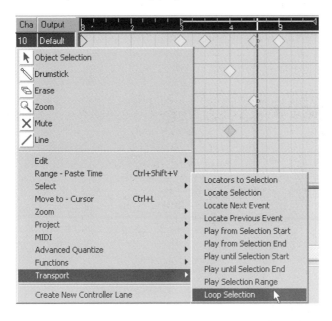

Figure 6.28
Select the events and activate 'Loop selection' from the Quick menu

- Activate the solo editor and solo instrument buttons on the toolbar. Select the instrument you wish to hear. If you wish to hear several instruments, un-mute them in the mute column.

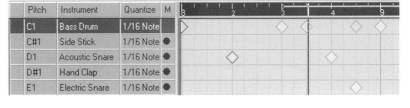

Pitch	Instrument	Quantize	M
C1	Bass Drum	1/16 Note	
C#1	Side Stick	1/16 Note	●
D1	Acoustic Snare	1/16 Note	●
D#1	Hand Clap	1/16 Note	●
E1	Electric Snare	1/16 Note	●

Figure 6.29
Solo the instrument you wish to hear

Smart moves

To help you remember the basic moves for using the MIDI editor tools, Table 6.1 summarises the main tool editing techniques. These are applicable to all the editors outlined in this chapter. As well as opening a single MIDI editor from the Project window, you can also open multiple editors on the screen and switch between them at will. Changes made in one editor are immediately reflected in the others. This is extremely useful for detailed work.

Table 6.1 Smart moves for the MIDI editors

Tool	Keys held		Mouse action	Result
	PC	Mac		
Pointer	-	-	click on event	selects event
	-	-	click on event and drag	moves event
	alt	alt	click on event and drag	copies event
	alt	alt	click and drag in grid	inputs note of length dragged
	-	-	click on start/end point of note and drag	re-sizes note
	-	-	click and drag in grid	opens rectangular selection box
	shift	shift	double click on note	selects all notes on same pitch
Erase tool	-	-	click on event	deletes event
Line/parabola tool	-	-	click and drag in Controller display	changes values in straight/curved lines
Draw	-	-	click/hold on note end and drag	changes length of note
	-	-	click and drag in grid	inputs note of length dragged
	-	-	click and drag in Controller display	inputs/changes values of events
Drumstick	-	-	click and drag horizontally in grid	inputs multiple notes at quantize resolution
Paintbrush	-	-	click and drag in grid	paints events freely on grid
Zoom tool	-	-	click in grid	zooms in horizontally
	ctrl	cmnd	click in grid	zooms out horizontally

More about the MIDI menu

The MIDI menu contains a number of other important commands and a functions sub-menu for the editing of MIDI data. These complement the use of the main MIDI editors and help handle some of the common MIDI editing tasks with maximum speed and convenience.

Transpose

The transpose function opens a simple dialogue where you can specify the amount by which you wish to transpose the currently selected part or notes. You can also specify an upper and lower barrier for the transposition which keeps the transposed notes within a chosen range of octaves. Transpose is good for making global transpositions of whole parts or a number of selected parts.

Merge MIDI in Loop

Merge MIDI in Loop merges all MIDI data between the left and right locators into a single new MIDI part on the currently selected track. If there is already a part on the destination track you can choose to merge this with the other data or erase it. Options are provided for including MIDI send and insert effects. Merge MIDI in Loop is the function to use when you wish to make your MIDI effects a permanent part of the data.

Dissolve Part

Dissolve Part allows you to split the data in the chosen MIDI part(s) onto separate tracks according to either the channel or pitch of events. Channel is useful for splitting the multiple MIDI channel elements of a musical arrangement which have already been merged into a single part, such as a Type 0 Standard MIDI file. Pitch is excellent for splitting a drum or percussion part into its constituent instruments.

The MIDI Functions

The MIDI functions are found in the Functions sub-menu of the MIDI menu. The MIDI functions are a convenient set of editing commands which can be used in combination with the MIDI editors or directly on MIDI parts in the Project window. The functions include the following:

- Legato – increases the lengths of all selected notes to the start positions of the next note. Useful for pads and strings when you need smooth chord changes and a continuous sound.
- Fixed lengths – fixes the lengths of all selected notes to the same value as chosen in the Length quantize selector of the toolbars of the Key and List editor. This function is available in the Key and List editors only. It is not available in the Project window.
- Delete doubles – deletes all doubled notes which occur on the same pitch and at exactly the same position. Always operates on whole MIDI parts. Delete doubles is useful for 'cleaning up' after you have been recording in cycle mode.
- Delete controllers – deletes all controller, aftertouch and pitch bend data from the currently selected part. Always operates on whole MIDI parts. Delete controllers is useful when you need to strip a MIDI part back down to its notes-only state.
- Delete notes – the Delete notes function is designed to find and delete low velocity and short ghost notes which were not intended as part of the performance. The Delete notes dialogue allows you to set thresholds for length and velocity, below which offending notes are deleted.
- Restrict polyphony – allows you to match the polyphony of your MIDI parts to the polyphony available in the target MIDI device. It functions by reducing the lengths of certain overlapping notes. This function may cause undesirable side effects and so should be used with care.

- Pedals to note length – finds all sustain pedal controller events (Controller 66) and changes the length of the notes concerned to match the on and off points of the pedal. After modifying the notes the sustain pedal events are deleted.
- Delete overlaps (mono) – adjusts the lengths of all overlapping notes which occur on the same pitch.
- Delete overlaps (poly) – adjusts the lengths of all overlapping notes in the part (regardless of pitch).
- Velocity – processes the velocity of the notes in a part according to a number of settings in a pop-up dialogue. You can add or subtract a fixed velocity, compress or expand the velocity according to a percentage, or restrict the velocity range between an upper and lower limit.
- Fixed velocity – sets all selected notes to the same velocity (as chosen in the Insert velocity field of the Key and Drum editors).
- Thin out data – reduces the density of recorded MIDI controller data. Helpful when large amounts of data are causing MIDI timing problems.
- Reverse – reverses the playback order of the notes in the part.
- Merge tempo from tapping – uses the distance between the notes found in the selected MIDI part to calculate a tempo map. In the MIDI merge options dialogue which appears when you use this function, you decide what timing resolution the notes in the part represent. This is most often used when you wish to create a tempo map which matches the tempo changes of an audio or MIDI performance which was created without a strictly regulated click track. To record the part which is to be used for the 'Merge tempo from tapping' function you simply 'tap' the MIDI note of your choice in time with the music (see chapter 18 for more details).

More about quantize

As outlined in Chapter 5, using the quantize functions involves moving recorded musical events onto pre-defined divisions of the bar (or beats) according to a position-based grid. In the MIDI editors, the resolution of these pre-defined divisions is chosen in the quantize selector on the toolbar. This imposes a series of vertical lines across the display which you can actually see in the MIDI editors and, as already outlined, this is known as the grid. Try changing the quantize value in the toolbar and you will see the grid modified accordingly. Whenever you use a quantize function, the grid becomes 'magnetic' for the recorded notes in the part and they are pulled onto or towards the nearest vertical line. The MIDI editors provide excellent visual feedback of what is actually happening when you use the quantize functions.

In Cubase SX, the quantize functions are available in two overall modes; grid quantize and groove quantize. Grid quantize mode is concerned with quantizing templates based upon regular grid spacings between 1/128 and whole notes (with variations in between). Groove quantize mode is concerned with more complex quantizing templates which have been 'extracted' from audio and MIDI events. 'Grooves', as the name suggests, are generally based upon the 'feel' of the music from which they are derived. But before we get into the details, let's start with the basics.

Basic quantize

Quantize was first devised as a purely corrective function for MIDI recordings but has now assumed the role of a creative tool. However, before becoming creative it is a good idea to become familiar with the basics. It helps to understand the basics if we look at Over quantize and Iterative quantize graphically in the Key editor. Figure 6.30 shows the before-and-after case for the quantizing of an inaccurately played hi-hat to 1/16th note divisions of the bar, using Over quantize (selected in the MIDI menu) and quantize set to '1/16 note' on the toolbar. The first two beats of the bar are shown where each vertical line represents the 1/16th note divisions. The original part contains notes which occur at different points either side of the 1/16th note pulse. After quantization, all notes line up exactly to the grid.

Figure 6.30
Using Over quantize to 'hard quantize' an inaccurately played hi-hat (upper grid) to exact 1/16th note divisions of the bar (lower grid)

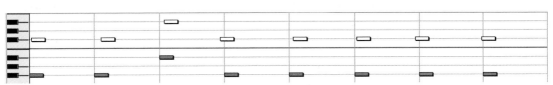

Figure 6.31 shows what happens if we were to use Iterative quantize on the same hi-hat part. In this case, the corrected notes do not fall directly onto the $1/16^{th}$ note divisions of the bar. Instead, they are moved slightly closer to the divisions, thus tightening things up while still retaining the original feel of the playing. This particular Iterative quantize function has a strength percentage of 50% which means that notes are moved towards the pulse by reducing the current distance from the $1/16^{th}$ note grid lines by 50%. Note that, unlike Over quantize, Iterative quantize can be used several times in succession, on each occasion moving the notes slightly closer to the chosen quantize resolution. Iterative quantize gives us a clue as to the nature of the more creative uses of the quantize functions.

Figure 6.31
Using Iterative quantize to quantize an inaccurately played hi-hat (upper grid) moves the notes *towards* the $1/16^{th}$ note divisions of the bar (lower grid)

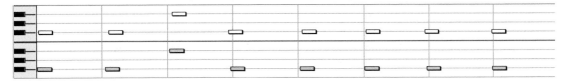

Quantize Setup in detail

The Quantize Setup dialogue allows you to adjust the quantize parameters and create/edit presets. It functions in 'grid quantize' or 'groove quantize' modes, depending upon how the quantize data is created.

Quantize Setup (Grid mode)

To become more familiar with the quantize functions of Cubase SX it is best to start with the Quantize Setup dialogue in standard grid quantize mode (Figure 6.28). Choose the '1–16 Note' preset from the Quantize Type menu on the toolbar.

The Quantize Setup dialogue in grid quantize mode includes the following parameters:

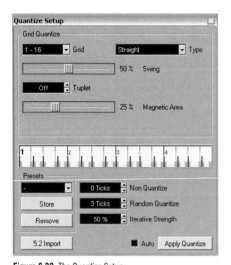

Figure 6.32 The Quantize Setup dialogue in grid quantize mode

- Grid selector – a quantize selector menu containing a list of the possible note divisions of the bar between 1/128 and whole note values.
- Type selector – a quantize type menu with straight, triplet or dotted options.
- Swing slider – for adding a swing (shuffle) factor to the quantize function.
- Tuplet – for setting up complex quantizing functions based upon tuplet, triplet, quadruplet and more complex divisions of the bar.
- Magnetic area – determines a magnetic capture area within which notes are pulled onto or towards the grid. Notes outside the magnetic area are not affected by the quantizing action.
- Non-quantize – determines an area around each grid line within which notes will not be affected by the quantize function.
- Random quantize – adds a random number of ticks to the position of notes affected by the quantize function in order to humanise the correction effect (particularly when using Over quantize).
- Iterative strength – regulates the strength of the Iterative quantize function in terms of a percentage. For example, a strength setting of 50% means that notes are moved towards the grid by reducing the note's current distance from the grid lines by 50%, each time the Iterative quantize function is used.
- Auto – when auto is activated all changes made to the parameters are applied in real-time.
- Apply button – applies the edited quantize parameters using the Over quantize function.
- Presets section – allows the saving and loading of quantize presets and the removal of presets from the current list. These appear in the quantize type menu on the toolbar.

Adjusting any of the main parameters updates the Quantize Setup window's grid display. This provides graphical feedback of the overall quantizing function you have created and helps understand the function of each parameter as it is adjusted. The grid display shows one bar with blue lines indicating the positions of the quantize grid.

Experimenting with grid quantize

Experimentation while listening to the results is one of the best ways of getting to know the quantize functions. In order to experiment with the quantize functions, it is recommended that you set up some key commands and work with the Quantize Setup dialogue open and visible on the screen. Proceed as follows:

1 Open the Key commands dialogue (File menu) and select MIDI in the categories list. Select the Iterative quantize command and assign the key combination 'Shift + Q'. Select the Undo quantize command and assign 'U'. Verify that Over quantize is assigned the 'Q' key. This is the default setting as supplied with the program.

2 Select a MIDI part which contains notes which have not been recorded accurately (if necessary, create a special test part of badly played material)! Drum or rhythmic parts make good test material for the quantize functions.

3 While still in the Project window, open the Quick menu and select 'Loop selection'. You are now in cycle playback on the chosen MIDI part.

4 Open the Key or Drum editor and adjust the grid so that you can see the notes clearly on the screen.

5 Open the Quantize Setup dialogue (from the MIDI menu or from the quantize menu on the toolbar). You are now ready to start experimenting. Remember, it is important to be able to hear and see the results of your experiments.

The idea with this setup is to use the right hand with the mouse to manipulate the parameters in the Quantize Setup dialogue and the left hand on the computer keyboard to initiate the quantize functions with the key commands. This two-handed approach is a valuable technique which can serve you well in all your quantizing operations.

Experiment 1

Check out the differences between Over quantize and Iterative quantize and learn how to use the key commands you created in step 1 above. Proceed as follows:

• In the Quantize Setup dialogue, select 1/16 in the grid menu and 'straight' in the type menu.

• Press Q on the computer keyboard to apply Over quantize to the part. Press U to undo the quantizing. Listen carefully to the difference. Note that the undo command restores the part to its original state before any quantizing was applied.

• Press Shift + Q (as set up in step 1, above) to apply Iterative quantizing to the part. Try applying this several times and note how the notes gradually move closer to the grid lines. Adjust the iterative strength parameter in the Quantize Setup dialogue to change the intensity of the iterative quantizing action. Listen carefully to the results. Press U to undo the quantizing.

• Try experimenting with the grid and type menu settings in the Quantize Setup dialogue and check out the effect of adding swing using the Swing slider. Swing works well with rhythmic parts and you might like to try it on 1/16th note hi-hats (as outlined in the quantize section in Chapter 5).

Experiment 2

Check out the effect of the quantize settings in the Quantize Setup dialogue in real-time as you adjust the parameters. Proceed as follows:

• Activate auto in the Quantize Setup dialogue.

• Adjust the Random quantize parameter to 10 ticks.

• Move the magnetic area slider while listening to the part. Notice how the notes bob back and forth as you increase the magnetic area and also how they gradually move closer to their nearest grid lines. The small movements are due to the random quantize setting. Each time you move the magnetic area slider the part is quantized again (from its original

---

Info

Swing is when every second note position on the quantize grid is pushed to the right. The more the notes are pushed, the more the music swings.

Info

You can undo/redo all MIDI editing using the undo/redo functions in the Edit menu or by pressing Ctrl+Z (undo) or Ctrl+Shift+Z (redo). You can also step back through your edits using the Edit history window (select 'history' in the Edit menu). The edit history is cleared when you close the project.

unquantized state) using the new slider value and other values and, each time, applying a small random value to the quantized position. This technique applies the Over quantize function. Iterative quantize cannot be applied in this way.

- Experiment with the other parameters while listening to the results in real-time.

These experiments are designed to help you explore the quantize functions in grid mode and encourage an understanding of the more creative aspects of quantizing. If, while experimenting, you stumble upon a combination of settings which gives particularly pleasing results, be sure to save it using the Store button. You can always use it at a later stage in a more serious project.

Quantize setup (Groove mode)

What is groove quantize?

In Cubase SX, groove quantize involves adjusting the timing and accent characteristics of musical material according to the natural 'groove' or 'feel' of a recorded musical performance (extracted from audio or MIDI recordings). While grid quantize (outlined above) processes material based upon 'regular' note values between 1/128 to whole notes, groove quantize processes material in a more 'irregular' way. This irregularity usually involves a succession of events whose timings fall at slightly different points around the beat. This is comparable to the kind of timing nuances we might find in any real-world musical performance. Cubase SX allows us to 'extract' such timing nuances from existing audio recordings or from MIDI parts and store the information as a groove template. Quantization using groove quantize thus allows the feel of one passage of music to be imposed upon another.

A groove can be quite simple, as in the case of a one bar 1/16th note shuffle groove or it can be a highly complex succession of timing events which vary over a number of bars. Groove quantize can be applied to whole arrangements or to selected elements, and different elements can be treated with different grooves.

Extracting a groove

There are two methods of creating your own groove quantize template, as follows:

1 To extract a groove from a MIDI recording proceed as follows:
   • Select a MIDI part in the event display (one, two or four bar patterns work well).
   • Select 'Part to groove' in MIDI / Advanced Quantize.
   • Open the Quantize type menu to reveal the newly added groove which appears last in the list with the same name as the part from which it was extracted.
2 To extract a groove from an audio event proceed as follows:
   • Select an audio event in the event display.
   • Double click on the event to open the Sample editor. In the Sample editor set up a loop of the desired length using the Range selection tool while in loop playback mode.

• Select the Audio tempo definition tool. Select Transport / 'Locators to selection' (or press P) to set the blue tempo definition ruler bar to the range selection. Define the number of bars / beats of the audio in your chosen range selection.
• Select Audio / Hitpoints / Calculate hitpoints.
• Adjust the sensitivity slider so that one hitpoint appears for each hit in the rhythm.
• Select Audio/Advanced/'Set audio event from loop'. Select Audio/Advanced/'Set tempo from event'.
• Select Audio/Hitpoints/'Create groove quantize from hitpoints' to create the groove template.
• Open the Quantize type menu to reveal the newly added groove which appears last in the list with the same name as the audio event from which it was extracted.

Get into the groove

To explore the groove quantize functions of Cubase SX, open the Quantize setup dialogue (MIDI/Quantize setup) and switch to 'groove' mode by choosing an existing groove quantize preset (Figure 6.33). If you cannot find an existing groove, create your own using one of the methods described above.

The Quantize Setup dialogue in groove quantize mode includes the following parameters:

• Position, velocity and length sliders – these determine how much the position, velocity or length of the events in the groove template affect the target material (where 0% is no effect and 100% is maximum effect).
• Pre-quantize – allows the 'regular' quantizing of material before it is groove quantized. This is helpful if Groove quantize produces undesirable results due to irregularities in the target Part.
• Max. move in ticks – determines the maximum amount by which notes in the target are moved. Helpful for restricting the quantizing action within defined limits.
• Name and details field – gives the name of the original event/part from which the groove was extracted and details of the original tempo, time signature and part/event length. Knowing the original details can help judge whether the groove is likely to suit the target material.
• Presets menu – allows the storage and recall of quantize presets. These appear in the quantize type menu on the toolbar.
• Store, remove and Import 5.2 buttons – allows the storage of the current settings as a new preset or the deletion of the currently chosen preset. Removal involves a permanent deletion of the information and as such should be used with great care. The Import 5.2 button allows the importing of groove templates which were saved in Cubase VST 5.2 format.
• Non-quantize – determines an area around each event in the groove within which notes in the target part are not affected by the quantizing action.

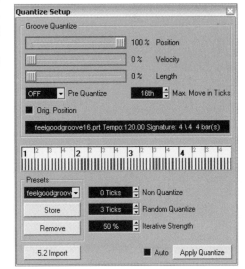

Figure 6.33
The Quantize setup dialogue in groove quantize mode

- Random quantize – adds a random number of ticks to the position of notes affected by the quantize function in order to humanise the correction effect (particularly helpful for humanising the over-quantize settings).
- Iterative strength – regulates the strength of the Iterative quantize function in terms of a percentage. For example, a strength setting of 50% means that notes in the target part are moved towards the groove template events by reducing the note's current distance from the groove template events by 50%, each time the Iterative quantize function is used.
- Auto – when auto is activated all changes made to the parameters are applied in real-time.
- Apply quantize button – applies the edited quantize parameters using the Over quantize function.

Adjusting any of the main parameters updates the Quantize Setup window's central display. This provides graphical feedback of the overall quantizing function you have created and helps understand the function of each parameter as it is adjusted. The display shows the number of bars in the groove and contains blue lines indicating the positions of the events in the groove template.

Advanced quantizing techniques

The quantizing tools of Cubase SX may be used purely for corrective purposes but, when used in a more creative manner, provide a powerful tool for injecting new life into your MIDI and audio recordings. The following outlines a number of advanced techniques and ideas for enhancing and experimenting with the feel of your tracks (relevant to both grid and groove modes).

Groove quantize can be used to match the timing characteristics of a MIDI part to an audio event by extracting the groove from the audio and applying the resulting groove template to the MIDI material. This is useful for making MIDI parts fit precisely alongside an existing audio arrangement. Much of the time, however, you might create a groove from an existing MIDI or audio event simply because you like the feel of the music. It is also possible to manufacture your own grooves by editing and manipulating the data in a MIDI part in the Key editor. You can then quickly create a groove template from this 'manufactured' MIDI part using 'Part to groove' (MIDI menu / Advanced). The latter technique is particularly relevant in the light of the various tips supplied below. These help understand what is going on 'inside' the groove. Quantize may be applied to both MIDI and audio material, as long as the target audio has been divided up into separate rhythmic components using Cubase SX's audio slicing techniques.

Pushing a bass drum ahead of the beat produces a sense of urgency and delaying a snare to fall after the beat produces a lazy, 'laid back' feel. Conversely, a late bass drum produces a relaxed effect and an early snare makes things sound 'tight' and anticipated. Groove templates are best applied individually to separate bass drum and snare tracks to achieve the latter late/early effects. Experiment with your collection of grooves to hear which combinations work well together. Manipulation of the position of the snare in relation to the second and fourth beats can have a major effect on the groove of the whole song and making sure that the hi-hat part is not playing repetitions of exactly the same part throughout helps maintain the interest of the

Tip

Not all material is suitable for groove quantizing and only certain groove templates may suit a given musical passage. You may be able to improve upon the results by experimenting with the position, velocity and length sliders and the random field in the Quantize Setup dialogue.

Tip

Generally, there is no one element which is responsible for the groove. Each instrument might emphasise different beats in the bar and the groove of each element might vary. You could have late bass drums on the first and third beats of the bar combined with early snares on the second and fourth. This makes things sound tight and tense.

Info

See Chapter 8 for more details about audio slices

listener. To avoid exact repetitions of the same hi-hat part in Cubase SX, use the Random quantize field in the Quantize setup dialogue to introduce a slight variation in the quantizing action (try between 3 and 5 ticks). The hi-hat itself plays a major role in the character of the groove, especially when manipulating shuffle and swing feels. Shuffles are concerned with delaying every other note in a succession of regularly spaced note events. In Cubase SX the amount of swing can be controlled in fine detail using the swing slider in the Quantize setup dialogue (Grid mode). In a similar manner to the kick and snare, moving the hi-hat ahead of the beat produces a sense of urgency and moving it late produces a looser feel. You might also be concerned with rhythmic punctuations in the arrangement such as cymbal crashes and drum rolls. Moving crashes to occur ahead of the beat can produce excitement and moving them to be late produces a sense of expectation. Some styles of music rely on specific grooves with specific relationships between the bass drum, snare and hi-hat. For example, many shuffle grooves rely on a bass drum and snare which are quantized tightly to the beat while the hi-hat alone is quantized to the shuffle groove. Quantize is often best applied to specific parts of the arrangement rather than to the whole kit or rhythm section. For this reason, detailed quantizing works better when the constituent parts of the rhythm section are on separate tracks (particularly the kick, snare and hi-hat).

In real-world performances, the relative timing positions of the constituent parts of a drum rhythm are often in a constant state of change but the overall characteristics of the changes remain fairly constant. In other words, the kick might always be played ahead of the beat, the snare might fluctuate on and around the beat and the hi-hat might always be behind the beat. It is also often the case that the bass drum and snare are rarely played at precisely the same moment in each bar and all the instruments are in a constant state of subtle change in terms of accent. Approximating similar behaviour with both grid and groove quantize helps humanise and enliven the material. Try experimenting with the position, velocity and length sliders (groove mode) or the swing and magnetic sliders (grid mode) along with the random field in the Quantize setup dialogue to simulate similar behaviour in your MIDI parts. When applied to sliced audio events, similar slider manipulations can help you to mangle drum loops beyond recognition or to find a new, original feel for the rhythm. Once processing like this has been applied successfully, an A-B comparison usually reveals just how dull the original parts were sounding.

The use of quantize does not exist in isolation from other techniques such as tempo, accent and overall musical arrangement manipulations. All these latter elements can be used to create the right feel. For example, classic tempo manipulation might involve slowing the tempo on the verses and speeding it up for the choruses. You can create still more excitement by combining an early snare with a tempo increase. The musical arrangement often benefits if the events are not too dense. Many sequencer-based musicians fall into the trap of programming extremely busy drum parts which leave no space for the rhythm to breathe. Also, don't forget that the relative timing positions of different elements can be changed by simply moving whole tracks backwards or forwards in time using the track delay parameter in the Inspector. And, of course, quantize itself is not confined to the drum kit alone, it can be applied to any instrument in the arrangement.

Audio recording

Chapter 3 outlined the basic audio recording process. This chapter provides more detailed information about audio recording, routing and the general handling of audio data within Cubase SX.

Although this chapter is mainly concerned with the audio recording process within Cubase SX, it was also considered useful to include information about digital audio and the larger recording process. Cubase SX does not exist in isolation from the rest of the sound recording world and it is essential to keep this in mind when using the software to record audio. The following section is for the benefit of those with little experience in sound recording. More experienced users may prefer to move on to the section entitled 'Audio routing'.

Digital audio and audio recording techniques

What is digital audio?

Audio recording in Cubase SX is of the digital variety. This means that the sounds you record are converted into a numerical representation of the signal using an analogue-to-digital converter (ADC). These numbers are stored in a data retrieval system (e.g. your hard disk), and you can hear the sounds again by converting the numbers back into the analogue domain using a digital-to-analogue converter (DAC). With a Cubase SX system these converters are found on your audio card or some other part of the audio hardware.

The quality of the audio is dependent on the general performance of the converters, the sample rate and the bit resolution. The sample rate is the number of times the analogue signal is measured, or 'sampled', per second. The bit resolution, (also referred to as the bit depth), is a measure of the accuracy of the system. The greater the number of bits the more levels of resolution are available to measure the analogue signal. Popular bit resolutions include 8, 16, 20, 24 and 32-bit float. Regular audio CDs are 16-bit with a sample rate of 44.1 kHz.

Cubase SX normally operates in 16, 24 or 32-bit float resolutions with a sample rate choice of 11.25 to 96kHz. Theoretically, you can therefore achieve very high quality recordings with the system. However, there are many other factors which affect the sound quality and paramount among these is how you actually make your recordings.

Some differences between analogue and digital recording

If you were recording onto an analogue multi-track tape recorder your approach to sound recording might be different to when using a digital system like Cubase SX.

For example, analogue systems are more forgiving of extreme peaks in the signal than digital systems. When recording onto analogue many sound engineers might record certain sounds with the level meters pushing up into the red on certain peaks in the signal. Although, strictly speaking, the sound is distorting, the kind of mild distortion produced is not displeasing to the ear. The extreme peaks alone are distorting and in the analogue system these are rounded off to closer to the level of the rest of the signal, bringing about a natural compression effect and, some would say, adding a certain warmth to the sound.

This is not the case with digital audio. Digital audio systems generally use full-scale (FS) meters, as opposed to the VU (Volume Unit) meters often found in analogue systems. The maximum level for a digital audio system is 0dB FS. There is no additional headroom above this maximum point. Once the level goes into the red, (above 0dB FS), the distortion produced is extremely unpleasant to the ear. There is also no graduated distortion response with digital systems; it sounds bad whether you are 10dB or 0.1dB above 0dB FS. For this reason, when you record with Cubase SX you must ensure that no clipping occurs on the input buss.

Recording digitally sometimes results in recordings with a lower average level than may have been the case if you were recording the same sources onto analogue tape. The digital version needs more headroom to avoid distortion on the peaks in the signal whereas the analogue recording may benefit from pushed levels and natural tape compression. Recording digitally at lower levels can be problematic with 16-bit systems where there is limited dynamic range to capture the low level detail (the theoretical dynamic range of 16-bit is 96dB). However, capturing low-level detail is not an issue at higher bit depths like 24-bit and 32-bit float since these feature greatly improved dynamic range (due to less quantising errors), adding 48dB or more dynamic range at the lower end of the scale when compared to 16-bit (the theoretical dynamic range of 24-bit is 144dB).

Overall, the advantages of digital audio far outweigh the disadvantages. It suffers less from background noise and hiss, it has a better dynamic range than analogue, it can be conveniently stored on hard disk, it can be easily processed in the digital domain using digital signal processing techniques (as in Cubase SX's plug-ins), and exact copies of the original can be made with no loss of quality.

What bit resolution and sample rate should I use?

The short answer

The short answer is to use the highest bit resolution and sample rate that your system can manage. For standard audio applications, 24-bit/44.1kHz is a good choice for most users. For greater fidelity assurance use 32-bit float/44.1kHz or 24-bit/96kHz.

The long answer

Although the short answer given above is adequate for the needs of many Cubase SX users, in reality, the issues are slightly more complicated. Bit res-

Info

As a general rule, Steinberg recommend that there is no point recording at a higher bit depth than that of your audio hardware's A/D converters.

Info

One negative aspect of digital audio is that it can seem 'harsh' or 'brittle' when compared to analogue tape recordings (although subjective opinions on this subject vary greatly). PSP Audioware's Vintage Warmer (or Cubase SX's Magneto) help counteract this phenomenon by emulating tape saturation. This adds warmth and character to the signal. However, a truly authentic emulation of tape saturation has proved particularly difficult to reproduce digitally.

Tip

Recording at 32-bit float/44.1 can help preserve the quality of recordings which you expect to subject to plug-in processing or off-line audio processes at a later stage.

olution (also known as bit depth) describes the range of values (quantising steps) available to measure the signal (16,777,216 values for 24-bit and 65,536 values for 16-bit). Sample rate describes how many measurements of the signal are made per second (for example, 44.1kHz measures the signal 44,100 times per second). The first thing to consider is the bit resolution and sample rate of the final media for which the recording is intended and then work at preferably a greater resolution within Cubase SX. Greater audible improvements are to be made by increasing the bit resolution rather than the sample rate, so the primary consideration is to maximise the bit resolution. The maximum possible resolution also depends upon the resources of your host computer since not all systems are capable of recording at high bit resolutions and sample rates. If you are aiming to produce a standard audio CD then the final resolution is going to be 16-bit/44.1kHz, but the whole recording process benefits if you do all the initial work at a higher resolution, such as 24bit/44.1kHz (or even 32-bit float/44.1kHz). You only apply dithering and truncate to 16-bit at the very last stage. This results in a significant improvement in the fidelity of the final audio signal, (a 16-bit audio signal produced in this way might have an apparent bit resolution of 18 or 19 bits which equates to 12 to 18dB increased dynamic range). The whole idea with digital recording is to start with high resolution sources and maintain this high resolution for as long as possible until the mastering stage (until the point just before dithering and truncation to 16-bit, for example).

The above advice suggests that if the sample rate of the destination media, like a CD for example, is at 44.1kHz then we should start out recording at 44.1kHz in Cubase SX. This works as a rule of thumb. The objective here is to avoid the possibly detrimental effect of sample rate conversion. Working at a higher sample rate, such as 96kHz, and then converting to 44.1kHz at a later stage may result in more damage to the audio signal than if you had started out with 44.1kHz in the first place. This is especially true if you use sub-standard sample rate conversion. To ensure optimum quality, if you must use sample rate conversion, you are advised to use a high quality conversion plug-in such as Steinberg Wavelab's Crystal Resampler or similar. Otherwise, play safe and set your Cubase SX project to the same sample rate as the final destination media (as suggested above).

It is also worth considering that you may in the future wish to release your music on one of the higher resolution audio formats such as DVD-A (Digital Versatile Disc - Audio) or SACD (Super Audio Compact Disc). DVD-A boasts a maximum resolution of 24-bit/96kHz and SACD uses an alternative high quality digital audio format known as DSD (Direct Stream Digital) which gives an equivalent performance. Working at 96kHz uses more computer resources but is likely to produce recordings with subtly improved transparency and detail. However, there is much debate on whether we can actually perceive the difference between 44.1 and 96kHz sample rates. 44.1 digital audio successfully produces signals up to 20kHz (the upper limit of human hearing) so, theoretically, we cannot improve matters any further by using a 96kHz sample rate, which raises the upper limit to 48kHz (we cannot hear in this region). However, researchers suggest that the upper threshold is not the factor which directly compromises the signal. It is rather the steep filters in the 44.1 D/A conversion process which can be detrimental. The use of a higher sampling frequency like 96kHz allows the use of gentler filters which are less detrimental. In any case, many professional mastering engineers argue that they can hear the difference between 96 and 44.1kHz but most also admit that any improvement is subtle. Regardless of the debate, if your material is destined to be mastered in a professional mastering house they may well request the source files in 24-bit/96kHz format.

Recording vocals and live instruments – microphone recording techniques

The first stage in making a recording of a vocalist or live instrumentalist is deciding where they are going to perform. The acoustic environment for the performance plays a major part in giving the recorded sound its particular characteristics. In a professional recording studio this environment is often an acoustically treated performance area which is isolated from the control room and the outside world. If you are lucky enough to have a similar facility as part of your Cubase SX system then so much the better.

The second stage is deciding which microphone to use and where to place it in relation to the vocalist or instrumentalist. The microphone is the very first stage in the recording path when you are recording live vocals, musical instruments and other real-world sources so, if you are serious about your recording, it is worth investing in a well-specified model. For good all-round performance and for the recording of vocals, large-diaphragm condenser (capacitor) microphones usually produce the best results. Inexperienced sound recordists may have the impression that you can place any kind of microphone anywhere in front of the source and then start recording. Unfortunately, it is not quite as simple as this, since there are a multitude of different microphone models designed for different purposes and, even if you have chosen an appropriate model, a change of even a few centimetres in microphone position can affect the sound quality. It is wise, therefore, to experiment with the microphone position and, if you have several models, the microphone type. Don't be afraid to take a little time to get the right sound at the time of the actual recording. This might also involve the application of EQ or compression using your external equipment. If you are recording vocals, a pop shield reduces the 'explosives', (the 'p' and 'b' sounds which cause pops and low frequency rumbles), and can simultaneously help set the distance that the vocalist should be from the microphone.

A third consideration is the possibility of using a microphone pre-amp before the signal reaches your mixing console or Cubase SX, and this is certainly highly recommended. In general, you should try to limit the number of devices through which the signal has to pass before it arrives within Cubase SX so it is recommended that, when using a mic pre-amp, you pass the signal directly from there into Cubase SX. The best mic pre-amps feature a superior signal path to many consoles and often provide high-quality compression and EQ controls.

Recording live sounds via microphones is generally more difficult than recording line level signals like synthesizers and samplers. This is because the sound signal is in a constant state of change and is likely to feature unpredictable peaks and lows in the amplitude of the signal. The level of difficulty is increased when you are using more than one microphone simultaneously, as in the case of recording a drum kit.

A high-quality professional microphone can radically improve the fidelity of the input signal. Large-diaphragm condenser models supplied by

Info

See the section entitled 'Microphone matters' in Chapter 2 for more information about connecting a microphone to a Cubase SX system.

Tip

You can normally safely roll off the low frequencies in a vocal recording (below 60Hz) to avoid low frequency rumbles.

Info

Using microphones very close to the source (close-miking) results in a phenomenon known as the proximity effect, where lower frequencies are disproportionately boosted. The proximity effect can be actively used to create a more intimate feel but, where it is not desired, EQ might be used to adjust the spectrum for a more 'open' sound.

Info

A mic pre-amp is highly recommended for recording vocals and live instruments. Check out the mic pre-amps supplied by Focusrite, Joe Meek, SPL, M-Audio and DBX.

Tip

You can normally safely roll off the upper frequencies in bass guitar recordings (above 8 – 10kHz) to cut out hiss and high frequency interference. A similar technique can be employed with electric guitar depending on the precise nature of the material.

Neumann, AKG, Shure, Beyer, Sennheiser, Sony, Calrec, Rode and Audio Technica are highly recommended.

Recording electric guitars, electric basses, synthesizers and samplers

The recording of electric guitars and basses presents a whole new set of potential problems to the sound recordist. Both instruments can be recorded using DI (Direct Injection) or microphone techniques or both simultaneously. You can also use a guitar or bass pre-amp which produces a convenient line level signal as output. This can be routed to the line inputs of your external mixer or directly into your audio hardware.

When placing microphones around a guitar speaker cabinet it is common practice to use two microphones, one placed close to the speaker and the other further back to pick up more of the room sound. A bass guitar cabinet is more likely to be recorded using a single microphone designed for lower frequencies and this signal is often mixed with a DI line signal from the bass amplifier or a DI box.

One of the problems when recording electric guitar and bass is that of noise interference. This manifests itself as a background buzz or hum which varies according to the relative positions of the guitar, amplifier and speakers. This is due to electromagnetic interference between the pickups of the guitar and the amplifier and speakers (or any other electronic equipment near to the guitar). Single-coil pickups are more prone to interference than humbucking pickups. Popular solutions include minimising the interference by experimenting with the relative positions of the guitar, amplifier and speakers and using gate and noise filtering processors after the recording has been made. CRT type computer monitors also cause significant hum when used near electric guitar instruments. The preferred solution for minimising this effect in a Cubase SX system, is to use an LCD/TFT flat-screen monitor. Otherwise, play your guitar at some distance from the computer equipment or, if you have the facilities, use a separate room for the guitar performance.

Info

For information on how to reduce the background noise in an electric guitar recording in Cubase SX, see the section entitled 'Detect Silence' in Chapter 8.

Once again, the sound signal from these instruments is often unpredictable as there can be significant changes in level from one note (or chord) to the next due to the instrument's resonant behaviour and changes in the player's technique and playing intensity.

Synthesizers and samplers are easier to record since they are generally more predictable and, if they are controlled via the MIDI sequencer of Cubase SX, you can re-play the parts many times over until you are satisfied that you have set the optimum record level. They also have the convenience of line outputs which are easy to handle when routed into your external mixer or directly into your audio hardware. However, synthesizer and sampler sounds can often seem lifeless and lacking in character when compared to 'real' acoustic instruments so care needs to be taken in how you record them. The use of effects and processing is a popular method of livening things up and some sound recordists will go as far as adding noise and distortion to the signal in order to give it more character. Effects added in this way are often intended to be an integral part of the recorded sound. If you are not sure of what the final sound should be, it is better to add the effect at the mixing stage (for example, subtle use of Cubase SX's supplied Quadra Fuzz effect produces good results for this kind of processing).

Info

See the 'Ten golden rules for recording and mixing' in Chapter 11 for more audio recording tips.

The magic formula for making great sounding recordings?

Sorry! There is no magic formula for making great sounding recordings, there are only guide lines. Despite enormous technological advances in all areas of the audio and recording industries and the availability of digital audio recording tools like Cubase SX, it remains impossible to devise a fixed set of rules which ensure a high-quality recording. One of the problems is that each individual has a different idea of what actually 'sounds good'. Another is that recording equipment (such as microphones and loudspeakers) and sound itself behave differently according to the acoustic environment and temperature. And, of course, when recording a live musician, no two musical performances are ever exactly the same.

So, what are the guide lines? We've already touched upon some of them in this chapter and in Chapter 2 but one of the major requirements is to learn how to use your ears. These are actually the only tools you have to judge whether or not you are making what is, in your opinion, a great sounding recording. Once you've got your ears up and running, your task is to get the best possible sounding signal recorded into Cubase SX. This starts at source and may encompass a wider range of elements than just the sound itself.

For example, is the vocalist singing in tune? Is the guitar in tune with the synthesizer you recorded on a previous session? Is everybody playing in time? Have you minimised any noise interference at source? Have you selected the best acoustic environment in which to make your microphone recording? Is the microphone placed in the optimum position relative to the source and the acoustic space? Once you have answered these and other questions relevant to preparing your session, you can then start to judge if you are achieving the sound quality you require in Cubase SX. It is important to capture a good performance and to get the right sound at the time of recording; it is not advisable to expect to be able to 'fix it in the mix'. Try to get the optimum signal level recorded whilst also avoiding distortion. Unpredictable sound sources, like vocals, might benefit from compression before the signal arrives in Cubase SX. Take your time getting things right in the early stages of the recording process and never hesitate to experiment with microphone placement before resorting to EQ.

EQ might be used for creative effects but, at the recording stage, is best used in a corrective sense to filter out any low frequency rumbles, high frequency hiss or other interference which does not form part of the required signal or to flatten out the frequency response of instruments recorded using close-miking techniques. For low frequency rumbles, many microphones incorporate low frequency roll off filter switches and these might provide a better option than using EQ. When using a high or low pass filter to roll off the high or low frequencies above or below the required sound, great care must be taken to ensure that you do not shave off parts of the actual signal.

You can sometimes safely reduce the top end (above around 10kHz) of such instruments as bass drums, bass guitars, bass synths, electric pianos and electric guitars. Similarly, you can normally safely roll off the low end (below 60Hz) of such instruments as vocals, violins, hi-hats and cymbals. When using close-miking techniques, particularly on live drums, the lower frequencies are disproportionately boosted due to a phenomenon with cardioid or figure-of-eight pattern microphones known as the 'proximity effect'. The proximity

Tip

You cannot make judgements about sound without an accurate monitoring system in an acoustically balanced environment. One of the keys to making good recordings is accurate monitoring.

Tip

Using Cubase SX in cycle record mode might help you capture that once-only magical performance (see 'Audio recording in cycle mode' below).

effect can be actively used to create a more intimate feel but, where it is not desired, a high-pass filter and/or low frequency shelving EQ (in the region below around 200Hz) might be used to adjust the spectrum for a more 'open' sound. Another corrective technique includes using a narrow band parametric EQ to reduce certain over-emphasised harmonics which occasionally become apparent in bass guitar, electric guitar, organ, drum and percussion performances due to resonances in the instrument itself or in the performance space. The use of EQ in these contexts would normally be that found on your external console or pre-amp. Bear in mind that the EQ sections of budget equipment often create more problems in the sound than they solve.

Many experienced sound engineers prefer to use a minimum of EQ at the time of recording and there are some very good reasons for this. As soon as you switch in an EQ section you are routing the signal through another set of control circuits which can potentially degrade the signal. Degradation might be particularly apparent if you are using the EQ section of a budget mixing console. EQ also affects the phase of the frequency components within the signal and this can result in undesirable side effects and harshness. The guideline here is to get the sound as right as possible before it even enters your external console or mic pre-amp and, certainly, before it enters Cubase SX. EQ at the recording stage might be viewed as a last resort, when there is no other solution, but there are no hard and fast rules.

Last but not least, in all of the above recording techniques, monitor your sounds through high quality loudspeakers in an acoustically balanced room and avoid excessive monitoring levels.

This provides you with a very brief taste of what is involved in the larger recording process outside of the direct domain of Cubase SX. As you have probably realised, specific sound engineering skills are required if you intend to do a lot of audio recording using microphones. Microphone choice and placement is a big subject and it is beyond the scope of this book to cover it in detail.

Audio routing

Part of understanding the manner in which a traditional recording studio functions involves knowledge of all the inputs and outputs of the mixing console, where the audio signals are going to, and where they are coming from (otherwise known as routing). Things are similar with Cubase SX. Knowledge of how the signal travels from the source into your audio card/device, through Cubase SX, and finally back out again can help you understand the audio recording process in more detail. This seems like common sense but it is surprisingly easy to get confused when there are a large number of inputs and outputs in an audio system.

The input path

Figure 7.1 shows an example of the input path using a system with multiple input audio hardware.

The signal is traced from its arrival at two of the physical inputs through to its destination as a stereo recording on one of Cubase SX's audio tracks. Although this is simple enough when presented in this graphical form it is

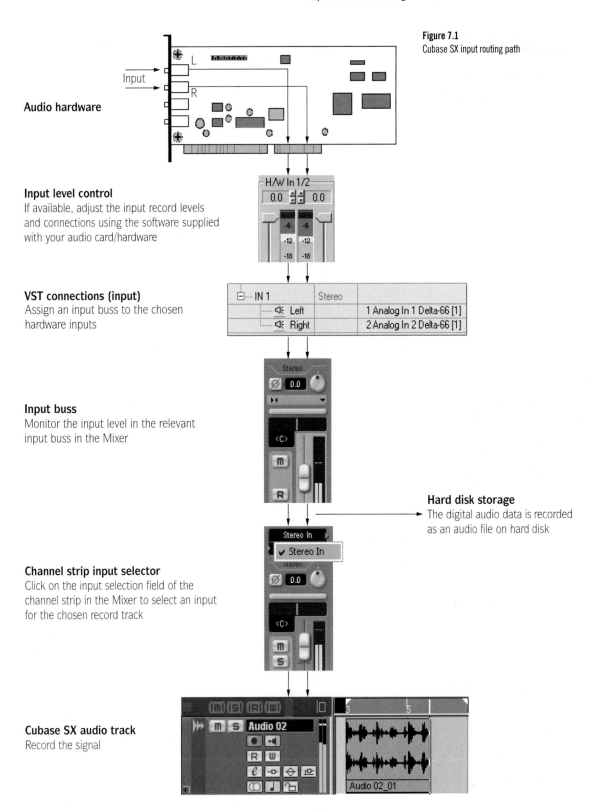

Figure 7.1
Cubase SX input routing path

Audio hardware

Input

Input level control
If available, adjust the input record levels
and connections using the software supplied
with your audio card/hardware

VST connections (input)
Assign an input buss to the chosen
hardware inputs

Input buss
Monitor the input level in the relevant
input buss in the Mixer

Hard disk storage
The digital audio data is recorded
as an audio file on hard disk

Channel strip input selector
Click on the input selection field of the
channel strip in the Mixer to select an input
for the chosen record track

Cubase SX audio track
Record the signal

perhaps not quite as easy when you are using the program. Looking at the signal path graphically allows you to stand back and think about what is actually taking place.

In this example, a stereo signal is connected to the line inputs of the audio card/hardware. It is first converted into digital form via the analogue-to-digital converters of the audio hardware. It then passes through the software audio mixer associated with the audio hardware. This is where settings which govern the operation of your audio hardware are made and, depending on the hardware in use, where the source level at the input of your audio hardware is adjusted.

Next, the signal passes via the input section of the VST Connections window where the input ports of the audio hardware are connected to a chosen input buss. By default, at least one input buss is already present in the VST Connections window and this is normally connected to the first two audio inputs found in your audio hardware device. An input buss can be renamed in the Bus Name column and, although this is not essential, it often helps clarify the source of the audio signal in other parts of the program (intelligent labelling can help when your hardware features multiple inputs). Further input busses may be added by clicking on the Add bus button.

Now that the input buss is connected to a physical input, the input signal can be seen in the chosen input buss channel strip in the Mixer. Input busses appear to the left of all other channels in the Mixer. At this point you can visually monitor the level at source or the level being recorded to hard disk according to the Global meter settings (Meter Input or Meter Post-fader). This is seen as activity in the level meter of the input buss. The input buss post-fader signal is what gets recorded to hard disk and the same signal is also simultaneously routed to one or more audio channels for monitoring and recording purposes.

To actually hear the input buss post-fader signal, at least one audio track/channel must be monitor enabled and its input set to the appropriate input buss (when monitoring via VST). For this we move on to the next stage in the input routing path where the input selector of the chosen audio channel is selected. This opens a pop-up menu containing the available inputs, as activated in the VST Connections window. Normally, the chosen channel is also record enabled so that you can actually make your recording. Finally, when you make your recording it is represented by a waveform inside an audio event in the event display.

The output path

Once recorded to hard disk, pressing the playback button sends the signal back through the system to the outside world. Figure 7.2 shows the output routing path for three stereo and three mono audio tracks which are routed to four outputs of a multiple I/O audio card/device.

In Cubase SX, tracks are assigned as either mono or stereo when they are first added to the project using the Add track command (Project menu). A stereo track contains two audio signals, (the left and right channels of the stereo signal), and a mono track contains a single signal. The signals arrive at their corresponding channels in the Mixer in the same order in which they appear in the track list.

After the Mixer channel stage the various audio signals are routed, in this case, to a Master buss (synths and drum loop) and to a Group channel

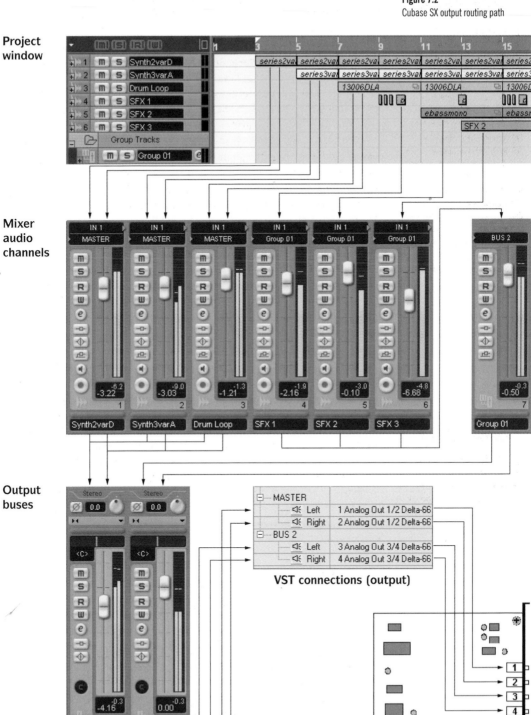

Figure 7.2
Cubase SX output routing path

Project window

Mixer audio channels

Output buses

(SFX 1,2 and 3). The Group channel output is, in turn, routed to a second output buss. The various signals are heard on the left or right of the stereo image according to each channel's pan control setting. Overall level changes and master insert effects may be applied in the output buss channel strips which appear to the right of all other channels in the Mixer. Finally, the master buss is routed to physical outputs 1 and 2 and Bus 2 is routed to physical outputs 3 and 4 of a multiple I/O audio hardware device in the output section of the VST Connections window. By default, at least one output buss is already assigned in the VST Connections window and this is normally routed to the first two audio outputs found in your audio hardware device. Further output busses are added by clicking on the Add bus button. After being converted back into the analogue domain via the D/A converters of the audio hardware, the composite audio signal arrives back in the real world where it can be amplified and monitored as required.

Viewing the audio system of Cubase SX in terms of the signal path as it passes through the program helps clarify the processes of routing and recording audio. The rest of this chapter is dedicated to solving some of the problems you may be having with routing and handling audio, and to outlining some of the key audio concepts of Cubase SX.

Key steps for routing an input signal onto an audio track

This chapter assumes that you are already familiar with basic recording techniques and that you have already attempted to make an audio recording in Cubase SX using the tutorial in Chapter 3. This should have helped you understand the essentials but the audio recording process sometimes remains difficult to grasp. Among the most important elements and also among the most problematic is the input part of the process. For those readers who may still be having problems with audio recording, the following points outline the key steps to route an input signal onto an audio track:

- Connect the audio signal to the appropriate physical input of the audio card or audio hardware device.
- Verify that the relevant VST input and output ports are visible in Devices / Device Setup / VST Audiobay.
- Connect the input of the audio hardware to an appropriate input buss in the VST Connections window.
- Verify that there is level activity in the meters of the chosen input buss in the Mixer.
- Adjust the input level using one or more of the following: the output gain of the audio source, the output gain of the send fader on your external mixing console through which the source is routed, the input level fader in the audio hardware's audio mixer (if available), or the input buss gain dial or fader controls.
- Add an audio track in the Project window and select the appropriate input buss by clicking on the input selector field above the channel fader in the Mixer.
- Activate the monitor button for the track (if not already automatically activated). This allows you to hear and see the level of any input signal on the channel meters (assuming that you are monitoring the signal via Cubase SX). Activate the record enable button to make the channel

ready for recording.

• Record the audio in the normal manner using the record button on the Transport panel.

Troubleshooting the recording process

If you have not yet managed to get an input signal showing in the meters or cannot hear your input signal, the following troubleshooting list may help solve the problem:

• Check that the source instrument or device which is supplying the sound signal is not faulty. Ensure that it is switched on/activated and check the audio cables for faulty connections.
• Check that there is not an impedance mismatch between the source signal and the input you have chosen on your audio card/device.
• Check that the audio card/device has been correctly installed and is operating outside of Cubase SX. Test the hardware for audio recording and playback functionality using a software application supplied with your operating system.
• Check that the audio card/device is connected in the VST Connections window (Device menu).
• It is easy to become confused about the left and right inputs of a stereo input device when recording mono sources and the multiple inputs of multiple I/O hardware. Make sure that the audio inputs are clearly labeled in the VST Connections window and that the correct input has been selected on the chosen audio track.
• To hear and see the signal on the channel level meter of the chosen audio track make sure that the monitor button is activated (illuminated).

Monitoring in Cubase SX

The above troubleshooting steps solve the majority of problems with the setting up of the input routing of Cubase SX. However, you may also be encountering difficulties due to confusion about how best to monitor the signal (in both the visual and audio sense) and the manner in which Cubase SX behaves when you select an audio track. There are three basic audio monitoring techniques, as follows:

Via an external mixer
If you have an external mixing console as part of your Cubase SX system then you may wish to monitor the signal directly from there before it arrives in the program. Most consoles allow you to do this. For this technique, choose 'Manual' in Preferences/VST/Auto Monitoring (File menu) and do not activate the monitoring button for the chosen audio channel. However, you need to manually activate the record enable button on the channel to make your audio recording.

Via Cubase SX
In this mode, you monitor the audio after it has passed through the input and output stages of your audio hardware and Cubase SX. For this technique,

Tip

By default, the record enable button is automatically activated whenever you select a track. If you wish to record several sources simultaneously, select a number of tracks by clicking on them while holding the Shift key. In this way, a number of selected tracks are automatically record enabled. Of course, the number of simultaneous sources you are actually able to record depends entirely on how many physical inputs are present in your audio hardware.

choose either 'While record enabled', 'While record running' or 'Tapemachine style' in Preferences/VST/Auto Monitoring (File menu). (See below for a full explanation of these options). All three cases automatically activate the monitor button (in the chosen circumstances) so that you can automatically hear the input signal.

Via the audio card/device using Direct Monitoring

Some ASIO 2.0 audio hardware drivers allow the use of Direct Monitoring. This allows the routing of the audio signal in the audio hardware to be controlled from within a music software application like Cubase SX. Direct Monitoring is activated in the VST Audiobay section of the Device setup dialogue by ticking the Direct Monitoring option (if the option is greyed out this means that it is not available with your audio hardware). Direct Monitoring re-directs the input signal from its usual path within the audio hardware so that you can hear it with minimum latency (see below for an explanation of latency).

With Direct Monitoring, you can still choose a monitoring mode in Preferences/VST/Auto Monitoring ('While record enabled', 'While record running' or 'Tapemachine style') and you can still use the record enable and monitor buttons (as described in step 2, above) but you cannot monitor the whole signal path which passes through Cubase SX (for example, you cannot hear the EQ and effects settings for the channel).

Record enable and monitor buttons in detail

In order that there should remain no doubt as to the precise function of the record enable and monitor buttons, the following outlines the details:

- record enable button activated – activates record-ready status for the track (*you can record on this track*).
- record enable button de-activated – de-activates record-ready status for the track (*you cannot record on this track*).
- monitor button activated – activates monitoring of any incoming signal (*you can hear the input signal and see its level on the meters*).
- monitor button de-activated – activates monitoring of any signal already recorded on the track (*you can hear and see the level of what has already been recorded*).

Monitoring modes in detail

The monitoring modes for Cubase SX are chosen in Preferences/VST/Auto Monitoring in the File menu (Figure 7.3). These affect the behaviour of the monitor button relative to the record, playback and record enable status of Cubase SX (thus affecting how you monitor an incoming audio signal when recording). The monitoring modes include the following:

- Manual – the status of the monitor button for the channel is chosen entirely manually. This means that the monitor button is never automatically activated. This mode is suitable when you are monitoring via an external mixing console (when you do not wish to hear the signal via Cubase SX).

- While record enabled – the monitor button is automatically activated whenever the track is record enabled. This means that you are always listening to the incoming audio signal until you manually de-activate the record enable or the monitor button. This is suitable for regular track laying not involving drop-ins and for when you need to rehearse a part before pressing the record button. In this mode, you are monitoring via Cubase SX.

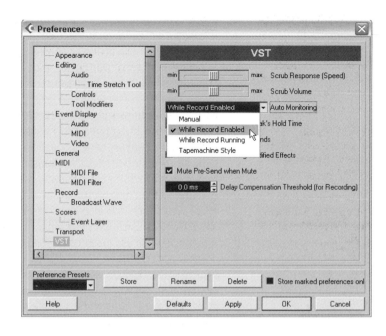

- While record running – the monitor button is only activated when Cubase SX is running in record mode. This means that you are always monitoring what is already recorded on the track unless you start recording. This is useful for dropping in on the fly over a previously recorded track. In this mode, you are monitoring via Cubase SX.

Figure 7.3
Choose your audio monitoring mode in Preferences/VST/Auto Monitoring (File menu)

- Tapemachine style – the monitor button is activated all the time unless Cubase SX is running in playback mode, at which time the monitor button is automatically de-activated. In other words, you monitor the incoming signal whenever Cubase SX is in stop mode or running in record mode. This is a good general purpose mode and useful for dropping in on the fly over a previously recorded track.

Monitoring methods summary

The choice of monitoring method largely revolves around whether you are using an external console for monitoring or wish to monitor via Cubase SX. The advantage of using an external console is that there is no delay in the monitoring of the input signal as you are recording, so you can work with maximum accuracy when overdubbing. This requires a mixing console capable of routing a signal to the input of your audio card/hardware while simultaneously monitoring the signal. Direct monitoring via the audio card/hardware (as outlined above) has a similar advantage of minimal delay when monitoring the input signal while recording and is also excellent for timing-critical overdubs. However, the disadvantage of these methods is that they do not allow the monitoring of the input signal via Cubase SX as it is being recorded. Monitoring via Cubase SX is helpful if you wish to, for example, record a dry signal while monitoring it with added reverb (a popular technique when recording vocals). The disadvantage of monitoring via Cubase SX is that the signal suffers from a slight delay. This delay is known as latency.

Latency

Latency is the delay between the input and output of a digital audio system (expressed in samples or milliseconds). All digital audio systems take a small amount of time to respond to a user input and process the data through their hardware and software. This affects real-time performance. It not only imposes a slight delay between the audio input and output signals, it also affects the delay between the moment you move a channel fader on the screen and the moment you hear the audible result, and it imposes a slight delay between the moment you press a note on your MIDI keyboard and the moment you hear the sound from a VST Instrument. If the delay is too long then it becomes difficult to play accurately in real-time performance.

So where does the latency come from? Latency is actually imposed by a combination of factors in the signal chain. Paramount among these are the audio buffers of the audio card. The audio buffer size can usually be adjusted and is often quoted in a control panel utility supplied with your audio card. Typical figures include 64, 128, 256 and 512 samples. These sample values can be converted to actual delay times (in milliseconds) by dividing the quoted figure by the sample rate you are using.

For example, at a sample rate of 44.1kHz:

$$64/44.1 = 1.45ms$$
$$128/44.1 = 2.9ms$$
$$256/44.1 = 5.8ms$$

and so on. Typically, you may also expect to add another 0.5ms to this figure for each of the A-to-D and D-to-A converters, and other elements in the signal chain may also add a small amount of delay. Thus, for a quoted buffer size of 128 samples you could expect a real-world latency of around 3.5 – 4ms each, for both the recording and playback parts of the signal chain. This equates to a total latency of around 7 – 8ms when monitoring in real-time via Cubase SX. It is important to understand here that this latency only affects the monitoring of a real-time performance. Any tracks which are already recorded are not subject to the same latency issues.

It is a fact that real-world machines and electronic musical instruments also suffer from similar delays, and a delay of a few milliseconds is imposed each time you move further away from your monitoring loudspeakers (around 3ms per metre). Musicians naturally compensate for the delays they hear while playing in real-time, as long as the delay remains minimal and fairly constant. However, virtuoso performers, drummers and percussionists can pick up on even the slightest irregularities when monitoring during a live performance so the effect of latency must be minimised. To provide optimum real-time performance, professional audio hardware with a dedicated ASIO driver which can achieve overall latency times of less than 10ms are highly recommended.

Record modes for audio recording

The precise manner in which audio recording takes place in Cubase SX is governed by the record mode menus found in the Record Mode section of the Transport panel. You are advised to become familiar with the record modes before commencing any serious recording projects. These affect both the linear and cycle recording behaviour of the program. The linear record modes determine what happens when a new audio recording 'overlaps' an existing event on the same track. The cycle record modes determine what happens when you record multiple takes over the same range in a continuous cycle (when the Transport panel cycle button is activated). Note that, in certain circumstances, 'Replace' linear record mode can influence audio cycle record behaviour but, on almost all occasions, it is preferable to perform audio cycle recording with 'Normal' activated in the Linear record menu. Note also that, with audio data, when events overlap you only hear the event which takes playback priority. The function of each record mode is outlined in the following table:

Record modes for audio recording

Linear record modes		Cycle record modes	
Mode	Overlap behaviour	Mode	Cycle behaviour
Normal	pastes new event on top	Mix	creates one region/event per lap
Merge	pastes new event on top	Overwrite	creates one region/event per lap
Replace	replaces existing event	Keep Last	keeps last complete lap in display
		Stacked	records laps in lanes
		Stacked 2	records laps in lanes (no muting)

Audio recording strategies

Basic recording

By this stage, you are familiar with the essential steps of recording an audio signal in Cubase SX. Most of the settings you make to route a signal through to the chosen channel do not have to be reset every time you record a new track. However, at the start of a new project you may have to specify various default settings in the Project Setup window (such as the sample rate and record format).

How is my recording processed and where is it stored?

Once the preliminaries are over, it is usually sufficient simply to select an audio track and press the record button. This gets your track recorded, but it is also helpful to bear in mind how your input signal is being processed and where it is stored. Many readers are already familiar with these processes but it is worth revising them.

Firstly, the analogue sound signal is converted into digital information using the audio hardware's analogue-to-digital converter. Once converted, the information is stored in a buffer (a temporary storage area). When the buffer is full, the system collects the data and stores it on your hard disk. This process happens repeatedly and very quickly. The actual speed depends upon the size of the buffer, the CPU power of the computer and the efficiency of the hard drive. As you may have realised, this process contributes to the latency of the system (as outlined above). To increase the speed of the process, and therefore reduce the real-time monitoring latency of your system, you might like to try setting a smaller buffer size in your audio hardware driver software when you are recording. Smaller buffer size means less latency, and less latency means that you can monitor in real-time via Cubase SX with greater accuracy. However, a smaller buffer size also means that the drain on your CPU power is much greater and, in extreme cases, may cause other operational elements in the computer to slow down or fail. In reality, the juggling of buffer size against CPU power is a compromise but at least it is a compromise which is under your own control.

As for storage, most high performance hard drives can adequately handle the recording of digital audio. The audio files themselves are stored in the folder for the project as chosen when you first created it (by default, within a sub-directory named Audio). If you wish to verify the location of the project folder on the hard disk, open the Pool (Ctrl/Command + P) where the project folder is shown in the information line at the top of the window. For keeping track of how much space you have available, Cubase SX features a handy info line directly below the track list which shows the chosen sample rate and record format, and the remaining recording time in hours and minutes (Figure 7.4).

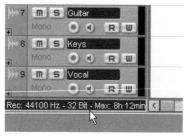

Figure 7.4
Keep track of the available recording time on your hard disk using the info line below the track list

Visual feedback

When recording audio, it is also extremely useful to have clear visual feedback of the whole operation. To achieve this in the Project window, work with the Inspector for the audio track open and the Channel section selected. You can now clearly see the level of the incoming audio signal in the channel strip's meter (Figure 7.5). Alternatively, work with a reduced Mixer opened below the Project window (similar to Figure 7.6). Monitor your signal according to your chosen monitoring method as outlined in 'Monitoring in Cubase SX', above.

Multitrack recording

For multitrack recording, it may be appropriate to open the Mixer on screen to see a number of channels simultaneously. This might suit the simultaneous recording of several inputs on separate tracks or an overdubbing session where you may wish to change the mix of the backing tracks to suit the needs of a live performer. In these cases, open the Mixer in Normal mode below the Project window by selecting it from the Devices menu or pressing F3 on the computer keyboard (Figure 7.6).

Normal mode, (as opposed to Extended mode), displays only the channel faders in the mixer and takes up less vertical space on the screen. It may also be useful to see the input and output busses. These are shown/hidden by clicking on the relevant icons in the panel to the left of the mixer channels. When recording multiple tracks, you need to record enable the appropriate number of tracks and make sure that each is set to the appropriate input.

The number of separate sources which can be recorded simultaneously depends on the number of active hardware inputs available on your system. The Mixer gives easy access to the inputs in the Input/Output section above the channels, allowing you to make quick adjustments when setting up the session. Figure 7.6 shows an eight track recording taking place in Cubase SX.

While in the Project window, you can select tracks using the up/down arrow keys. While in the Mixer, you can select tracks using the left/right arrow keys. Several tracks/channels can be selected simultaneously by hold-

Figure 7.5
When recording audio tracks, work with the Channel section open in the

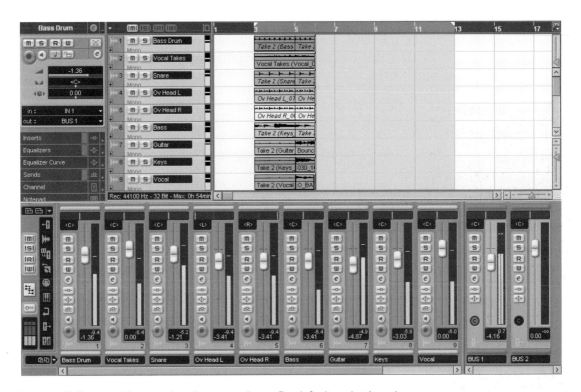

Figure 7.6
For overdubbing and multi-track recording, try opening the Mixer in Normal mode below the Project window. This screenshot shows an eight track recording taking place in Cubase SX.

ing the Shift key while pressing the arrow keys. By default, selecting also record enables the tracks and the Shift and arrow combinations therefore provide a quick method of record enabling multiple tracks.

Mono or stereo

The mono or stereo configuration for audio tracks is chosen when you add a new track by selecting the Add Audio track command from the Project menu. In the Add Audio Track dialogue which appears, you can also choose a multi-track or surround configuration (Figure 7.7). The chosen format is fixed at the time of creation and you cannot change the status later. However, it is possible to drag a stereo event onto a mono track (for example), at which time the stereo recording is played back in mono (you hear the left and right channels merged together). This is useful for quickly checking out the mono compatibility of a stereo recording. Equally, you can drag a mono event onto a stereo track, at which time you hear the same mono signal in both channels. (Further mono/stereo manipulations are possible using 'Flip Stereo' in the Audio Process menu).

Figure 7.7
Choose the configuration for the new audio track in the Add Audio Track dialogue

Tracks, channels and playback priority

In Cubase SX, tracks are listed vertically in the Project window. Audio tracks might contain any number of digital audio recordings represented as graphical events along the time line of the event display. When it is created, each audio track is automatically assigned its own audio channel and you can see these in the Mixer where they appear in the same order as they are found in the Project window. The tracks and channels in Cubase SX are not unlike those found in traditional multi-track recording setups where the tracks on the tape of a multitrack tape machine are routed to the channel faders and controls of a mixing console. The difference with Cubase SX is that there can be literally hundreds of audio tracks and an almost infinitely wide mixing console! (depending on the available processing power). The assignment of tracks to channels takes place invisibly, so in the routine recording process, you do not need to be concerned with it. Cubase SX manages the available resources behind the scenes, leaving you to concentrate on the music and the recording, as you proceed with your session.

You can record several times on the same track over the same section but, with audio recording, the previously recorded material is never overwritten. The audio file which has been recorded on hard disk still exists, regardless of how you chop and change, cut and paste or otherwise manipulate events in the event display. The audio file is only ever deleted if you instruct Cubase SX expressly to do so. However, playback on the same audio track occurs according to a strict rule: an audio track can only play back one audio event at any one time. If events overlap, only one of them is heard. When working with multiple takes on the same track, use the 'To Front' and 'Move to' options in the Quick menu (or Edit menu) to choose which take you want to hear (Figure 7.8). Takes can later be merged into a single audio part and edited in fine detail in the Audio Part editor (see Chapter 8 for more details).

Figure 7.8
Use the 'To Front' option in the Quick menu to choose the take you wish to hear

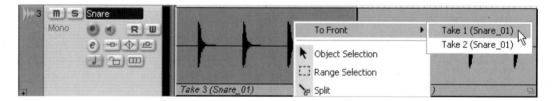

Of course, nothing prevents you from moving to a new track for each take to avoid recording events on top of eachother. However, there are far easier ways of dealing with multiple takes. Multiple take audio recording in cycle stacked mode is outlined further below, but first let's take a look at a more basic technique which pre-supposes that you wish to stop between each take. Stacked cycle record mode, as we shall see below, automatically divides the vertical height of the track into 'lanes', one for each take. If you click on the 'Lane display type' button and select 'Lanes fixed' mode, you can use a similar display style in normal linear record mode (Figure 7.9). When a track is set to 'Lanes fixed' mode, takes are recorded onto separate lanes within the vertical space of the record track, allowing you to see the subsequent events

Figure 7.9
Selecting 'Lanes Fixed' mode allows you to record takes onto separate lanes within the same track

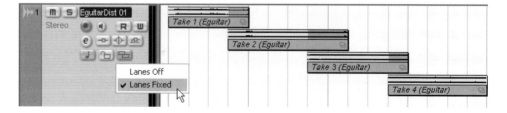

in the event display with greater clarity. Moreover, those sections of the audio that take playback priority are highlighted in green. The most recent take appears in the lowest lane and priority is ordered from the lowest lane upwards. This arrangement makes it extremely easy to edit the events directly in the event display and means that you can quickly assemble a composite take without ever leaving the Project window.

Using punch in and punch out

Automatically punching in and punching out of recording is a common requirement with multitrack recording systems. The technique can be ideal for replacing specific sections of a recording and, if you are using Cubase SX on your own, gives you a hands-free technique for dropping into record, leaving you to concentrate on the musical performance.

The punch in and punch out buttons are found on the Transport panel. They are activated/de-activated by clicking on the buttons themselves or pressing the 'I' and 'O' keys on the computer keyboard. Punch in and out work in conjunction with the left and right locators of the ruler. The left locator marks the punch in point and the right locator marks the punch out point. To use automatic punch in and punch out, proceed as follows:

- select and record enable the track upon which you wish to record.
- set up the left and right locators to encompass the section you wish to record.
- activate the punch in button (press 'I' on the computer keyboard).
- activate the punch out button (press 'O' on the computer keyboard).
- rewind to some point before the left locator.
- start playback. When the project cursor reaches the left locator position Cubase SX automatically starts recording.
- record the new segment. Cubase SX automatically stops recording when the project cursor reaches the right locator position.

The punch in and punch out buttons might also be used in conjunction with pre-roll and post-roll on the Transport panel (the two symbols below the left/right locator positions). Try setting each of these to one bar (enter '1' into the pre and post roll fields). Activate the pre and post roll buttons in the Transport panel. Activate 'Start record at left locator' in the Transport menu. Activate the punch out button. Now when you click on the record button the project cursor immediately jumps back one bar giving you a neat pre-roll each time you perform your automatic punch in. This allows you to play along with the music before the punch in point.

Figure 7.10
Using automatic punch in and out to record a guitar performance in bar 6

Dropping in 'on the fly'

While automatic punch in and out is useful when you know exactly where and when you want to start recording, it is also useful to be able to punch into record mode at any moment on the currently selected (and record enabled) track. Such a situation might occur when your vocalist or other performer decides to produce a superb performance when you are monitoring a rehearsal but not actually recording. To drop in 'on the fly' without interrupting the flow of the music, simply click on the record button on the Transport panel or press the '*' key on the numeric keypad. To drop back out of record, click on the record button a second time (Cubase SX drops out of record and continues in play mode), or simply click on the stop button to stop the sequencer. If you propose to do a large number of takes over a specific segment, it is often more appropriate to record in cycle mode (see below).

Audio recording in cycle mode

Recording multiple takes over the same segment of music was touched upon in 'Tracks, channels and playback priority', (above) but recording audio in cycle mode elevates this technique way beyond what you can achieve manually (in 'linear' recording mode). Cycle recording is implemented by activating the cycle button on the Transport panel and clicking on the record button. Recording takes place in a continuous cycle between the left and right locators until you click on the stop button. Audio recording in cycle mode is an excellent method of capturing a magical performance since you can leave Cubase SX in record mode while you perform the same segment of music over and over again. This is particularly useful for vocalists, who might be having difficulty with one particular section of the song or with the ad-libs at the end. Or it might suit the recording of a guitar or saxophone solo where the musician would like to try a number of solos one after the other. You can later choose the best take or compile the best parts of a number of takes into a final composite version. You can even set up a cycle over the whole length of your musical creation and perform the whole thing several times (assuming that you have the necessary hard disk space). Cubase SX makes all this very easy and benefits from an intuitive set of tools to select and edit the takes after recording has been completed.

Audio cycle recording takes place between the left and right locators and its behaviour varies according to two main factors: the 'Audio cycle record mode' chosen in Preferences/Record/Audio Cycle Record Mode (File menu) and the 'Cycle record mode' chosen in the Transport panel. All the options record one long audio file which is automatically divided up to match the length of each take.

Audio cycle record mode (Preferences)

The Audio cycle record mode in Preferences governs the audio aspects of the cycle recording process (as opposed to the MIDI aspects, which are managed elsewhere). There are three options, which operate as follows:

• Create regions – regions are sections within audio clips. These are areas within your audio material which are marked as sections of interest, much like you might highlight or underline sections of interest within the text of a book (see Chapter 8 for more details about regions). When 'Create regions' is selected, one region is automatically created for each lap of the cycle and each region is automatically named with a sequential take number. When recording has been completed a single event appears between the left and right locators containing the last take. Other takes can be selected from the 'Set to Region' option in the Quick menu. This is the default setting for Cycle record mode.

- Create events – a separate audio event is created for each lap of the cycle. When you have finished recording, the events appear on top of eachother between the left and right locators. You can select takes by using the 'To Front' option in the Quick menu. Create events has the advantage that all the events are immediately available in the event display and if the material is not too complicated you can quickly edit the events to assemble a composite take while still remaining in the Project window.
- Create events and regions – creates both events and regions simultaneously which gives you the choice of using either regions or events for the manipulation of your multiple takes.

Cycle record mode (Transport panel)

Clicking on the cycle record mode selector in the Transport panel opens a menu with four options which determine the manner in which recordings are made when in Cycle mode (i.e. when the cycle button is activated on the Transport panel). 'Mix' and 'Overwrite' modes are relevant mainly to MIDI recording but also affect audio recording (at the time of writing). The modes function as follows:

- Mix and Overwrite modes – in these modes the Audio cycle record mode (Preferences) is taken into consideration. If 'Create regions' has been chosen only a single event which contains the currently chosen region remains in the display after recording is completed. If 'Create events' has been chosen separate events for each lap of the cycle are created and appear in the same 'event space' on the audio track (pasted on top of eachother). See Audio cycle record mode, above, for details.
- Keep Last – in this mode the Audio cycle record mode (Preferences) is NOT taken into consideration. Regions are created for each lap of the cycle but only the last complete lap in the cycle (i.e. that which is recorded up to the end of the cycle range) is kept as an audio event. Other takes can still be selected from the 'Set to Region' option in the Quick menu.
- Stacked – an audio event for each lap of the cycle appears on its own lane within the vertical space of the audio track. In this mode, the Audio cycle recording mode (Preferences) is NOT taken into consideration since separate new events are created automatically. When recording is complete, the stacked events may be edited directly in the event display, making it easy to quickly build up a composite take while still remaining in the Project window. Here, it is easy to see which parts of which events take playback priority since they are highlighted in green.
- Stacked 2 (No mute) – the same as stacked mode except that no muting of events takes place.

Practical audio recording projects in cycle mode

Audio cycle recording project 1 ('Keep Last' mode)

The following outlines the procedure for cycle recording in 'Keep Last' mode. To record your multiple takes, proceed as follows:

- Click on the cycle record mode selector in the Transport panel and select 'Keep Last' from the pop-up menu.
- Set the left and right locators to the appropriate segment of your musical arrangement. Depending on the precise nature of the material, you may wish to leave some pre and post roll space at the start and end of the target segment so that you can prepare yourself before each take commences.
- Activate the cycle button on the Transport panel (press '/' on the numeric keypad).
- Select the target record track and make sure it is record enabled.
- To commence recording, click on the record button on the Transport panel (press '*' on the numeric keypad).
- Record the performance as many times as you wish. On each lap of the cycle a new region is automatically created, suitably named with a new sequential take number. Only the last complete take is kept as an audio event in the event display (Figure 7.11).

Figure 7.11
Recording a vocal line in 'Keep Last' cycle record mode. Here, the fourth lap of the cycle is shown.

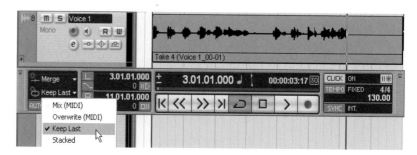

Keep Last mode was designed with the idea of recording the musical performance over and over again until you get a good take. When you think you have your good take you stop recording and it is only the good take which remains in the event display. However, should you need to, you can still select any one of your takes by right clicking (PC)/Ctrl clicking (Mac) on the event to open the Quick menu. Here you find a 'Set to Region' option in the top part of the menu where you can choose from any of the previous takes.

Figure 7.12
Use the 'Set to Region' field in the Quick menu to select a previous take

Audio cycle recording project 2 ('Stacked' mode)

The following outlines the procedure for cycle recording in 'Stacked' mode. To record your multiple takes, proceed as follows:

- Click on the cycle record mode selector in the Transport panel and select 'Stacked' from the pop-up menu.
- Set the left and right locators to the appropriate segment of your musical arrangement. Depending on the precise nature of the material, you may wish to leave some pre and post roll space at the start and end of the target segment so that you can prepare yourself before each take commences.

- Activate the cycle button on the Transport panel (press '/' on the numeric keypad).
- Select the target record track and make sure it is record enabled. In order to be able to see the stacked lanes in the vertical space of the audio track try expanding its vertical size by clicking and dragging on the lower limit of the track in the track list.
- To commence recording, click on the record button on the Transport panel (press '*' on the numeric keypad).
- Record the performance as many times as you wish. On each lap of the cycle a new event is automatically created, suitably named with a new sequential take number and automatically arranged on lanes within the vertical space of the track (Figure 7.13).

Figure 7.13
Recording a vocal line in 'Stacked' cycle record mode. Events are stacked onto separate lanes.

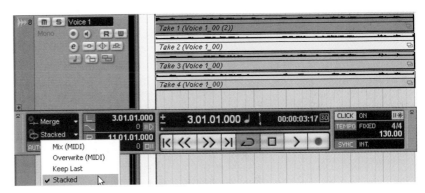

Stacked mode was designed with the idea of recording a musical performance over and over again and retaining all events so that you can later choose the best sections for a 'perfect' composite take. When you have completed your 'Stacked' cycle recording it is easy to edit the events directly in the event display using the standard tools. Playback priority works from the lowest lane upwards and those parts of the events which take priority are highlighted in green. In other words, you only hear the highlighted sections. This makes editing directly in the event display very intuitive. Therefore, on most occasions, when using stacked cycle record mode, a 'perfect' composite version of your takes can be assembled while remaining in the Project window.

Editing audio recordings made in cycle mode

As outlined above, you can edit your cycle record mode recordings directly in the event display and this is especially true of stacked mode. Alternatively, you may wish to edit in the Audio Part editor. This has the advantage that you can set up the editor's environment with the specific tools necessary to do the job (for example, you can set up the tools, nudge buttons and independent track loop settings to be visible on the toolbar). Should you wish to do this, you must first place the events in an audio part. For this purpose, select 'Audio/Events to Part' from the Quick menu (choose 'Regions' if the 'Create Part using Regions?' dialogue appears). This transforms the currently selected audio events into a single audio part. Double click on the part to open the Audio Part editor where the takes appear on separate lanes (Figure 7.14). The bottom lane in the Audio Part editor takes playback priority. You can assemble the best composite version of your takes by splitting, muting, deleting or moving the material, working from the lowest lane upwards. It is true to say that the Audio Part editor is more useful for audio cycle recordings made in Keep Last mode than for those made in Stacked mode. The Audio Part editor is explained in more detail in Chapter 8.

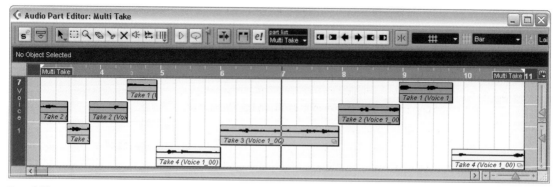

Figure 7.14
Your multiple take recording in the Audio
Part editor

Audio events, audio clips and audio files

The concepts of audio events, audio clips and audio files need to be fully
understood in order to appreciate exactly how Cubase SX handles audio data.
Luckily, you do not need to be aware of these details for routine audio
recording and editing but knowledge of what is going on behind the scenes
can help when you are troubleshooting or when you are involved at a deeper editing level.

Whenever you make an audio recording, there are three things which
occur in Cubase SX as follows:

1   an audio file containing the actual audio recording is created on the hard disk.
2   an audio clip which points to this audio data is created in the Pool (see
    Chapter 10 for more details about the Pool).
3   an audio event which points to the clip is created in the event display of the
    Project window.

Figure 7.15
An audio event points to its
corresponding audio clip which, in turn,
points to its corresponding audio file on
hard disk

These three elements are shown in Figure 7.15. This shows the state of
affairs just after you have made an audio recording in Cubase SX.

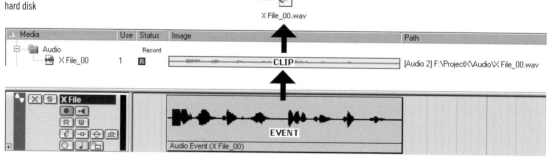

The details of this figure can be explained in three steps as follows:

1   an audio file called 'X File_00' is created on the hard disk in the 'Audio'
    folder of a project called 'ProjectX'. The audio file takes its name from
    the name of the audio track at the time of recording.
2   an audio clip, also called 'X File_00', is created in the Pool and, at this
    stage, this audio clip provides a reference to, or points to, the whole
    audio file stored on hard disk. Like the audio file, the audio clip also

takes its name from the name of the audio track at the time of recording. The audio clip and the audio file always begin with the same basic name (but the overall name may change after certain kinds of editing operations). If you change the name of the audio clip, the basic name of the audio file on disk is changed accordingly.

3   an audio event is created in the event display which provides a reference to, or points to, the audio clip (at this stage it points to the whole audio clip).

Let's imagine that we are only interested in the second half of the recorded audio event. We decide to split it in two and normalise the second half (using the split tool and the normalise function of the processing section of the Audio menu). When you process a recording, Cubase SX asks you exactly how you would like to proceed in a pop-up dialogue (Figure 7.16).

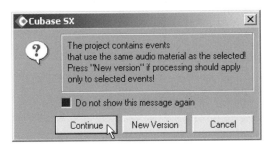

Figure 7.16
'New version' dialogue for processing audio

In this dialogue, the two options function as follows:

• 'Continue' means that all events referring to the same audio clip are updated to reflect the applied processing.
• 'New version' means that a new, exclusive event and a corresponding new audio clip are created. In this case only the one event features the processing you apply.

Let's choose 'Continue' since we are only interested in creating one version of this audio material. The result of the editing is shown in Figure 7.17.

You could happily go on splitting and processing your events without too much concern about the number of audio files and clips you are creating behind the scenes. You can undo your processing in the normal way, using Ctrl/Command + Z. You can even undo it at a later date using Cubase SX's Offline Process History (Audio menu). But let's take a look at what has actually happened in Figure 7.17.

Figure 7.17
The relationship between the events, clip audio files after splitting and processing event

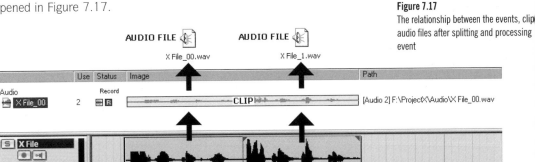

When you split the event, you produced two events which point to the same audio clip. The first event points to the first half of the clip and the second event points to the second half of the clip. Before you applied the processing, the clip was still pointing to the whole of the audio file. However, when you applied the processing, something unexpected happened. Rather than change the original audio file, a completely new audio file was created (X File_1). Finally, you have two events which point to the same clip and a clip which points to two different audio files. The audio clip knows at which moment it should start pointing to the second audio file.

You may ask why Steinberg designed this part of the software like this. The main reason is that you always preserve your original recording on the hard disk in an unchanged state. This is re-assuring and means that, if things go wrong, you can always go back to it. Another reason is that when you process an audio file several times, each process is stored in a separate edit file. This allows the use of the Offline Process History to go back to a clean version of a guitar recording, one month after you applied compression, distortion and reverb to it (for example).

The following provides a summary of the above information:

Info

All audio files created by audio and plug-in processing are stored in the 'Edits' sub-directory of the main project folder.

- audio events are what you see in the event display and provide the means by which you visualise your audio recordings. Audio events appear at various points in time within your project and feature a start time and an end time. The placement and size of events can be edited at any time after recording has been completed. Audio events point to the whole of, or part of, an element in the Pool known as a clip. Each audio event points to a single clip – it *cannot* be associated with more than one.

- an audio clip is an element which points to an audio file on the hard disk. An audio clip provides an interface between the audio events in the event display and the audio files on the hard disk. It decides which section of which audio file gets accessed by which audio event.

- an audio file is the raw audio material stored on hard disk. There are two categories of audio files; those containing the original data as captured at the time of the original recording (stored in the Audio sub-directory), and those containing edited audio data as created when audio processing is applied (stored in the Edits sub-directory).

Audio editing

This chapter describes how to edit audio material in general and in particular using Cubase SX's two main audio editors, the Audio Part editor and the Sample editor.

A number of general event-based audio editing operations using the tools and other techniques have already been described in Chapter 4 but here we progress to a deeper level. As well as exploring the editors, this chapter outlines specific techniques for direct editing in the Infoline, creating fades and crossfades between events, time stretching, handling audio loops and using the options in the Audio menu.

The Audio Part editor and Sample editor offer ways of viewing and editing audio data which are not possible in the Project window. The Audio Part editor is for the editing of audio events grouped inside an audio part. It is often more convenient to edit audio events in groups rather than as separate events. Manipulations of data in the Audio Part editor most often involves splicing, trimming and moving events in much the same way as takes place in the Project window. This editor also features special functions for manipulating events which have been recorded in Cycle Record mode, and for editing audio slices which were created in Hitpoint mode (see below for a full explanation). Editing in the Audio Part editor is non-destructive. This means that the actual audio file on hard disk is not altered by any editing actions.

The Sample editor allows you to edit at the audio clip level. Here, you are working with the actual waveform of the audio data in terms of defining regions, calculating hitpoints, cutting, copying and pasting, and performing other detailed audio processing tasks. In the Sample editor, you edit and view your audio data in fine detail at the sample level. Editing is non-destructive in the sense that you can revert to a previous version of the file at a later date using the Offline Process History (Audio menu) and, for as long as you are working in the same continuous session, you can use the Undo command (Edit menu).

General audio editing techniques

Using the Audio event Infoline

An Infoline appears above the display when you activate the info button on the toolbar in either the Project window or the Audio Part editor. This displays the details of the currently selected audio event or for the first of a multiple event selection (Figure 8.1). The Infoline is useful for directly editing various parameters associated with the audio event in both the Project window and

File	Description	Start	End	Length	Offset	Snap	Fade In	Fade Out	Volume	Mute	Lock	Transpose	Finetune
Trumpet	Take 2	3. 1. 1. 0	5. 2. 3.105	2. 1. 2.105	0. 0. 0. 0	3. 1. 1. 0	0. 0. 0. 0	0. 0. 0. 0	0.00 dB	-	-	-1	-5

Figure 8.1
The Infoline for an audio event

the Audio Part editor. You can edit the values directly in the fields by double clicking on the value and entering a new value using the computer keyboard. Alternatively, activate 'Increment/Decrement on Left click and drag' in File/Preferences/Editing–Controls/ Value Box and simply click and drag up or down in the field to change the value. In this case, the changes are sensitive to the current Snap resolution when the Snap button is activated.

When more than one event is selected the infoline text is shown in yellow and contains the information relevant to the first of the selected events. Editing any of the yellow text values applies the changes relatively to all selected events. For example, changing the start position moves the start position of all the currently selected events but maintains their relative positions. However, if you wish to apply the same absolute start position to all the selected events hold down Ctrl while making the change. In this case, the start times of all selected events snap instantly to the same position. Note that applying the same file name in the File field to a number of audio files is NOT possible since all audio files must retain a separate and unique name. However, it is possible to enter an absolute name for all descriptions in the Description field.

Useful direct editing actions on the Infoline include the following:

- Edit the name of the audio file and clip associated with the audio event by entering a new name into the File field. Similarly, a description for the event may be entered in the Description field. The description appears first in the audio event followed by the name of the audio file in brackets.

Important

Changing the name in the File field of the Infoline changes the name of the clip in the Pool *and the name of the actual audio file on hard disk*. This is significant if you are working with a file from an audio library since you may change the name of the file on hard disk without really wanting to. Other applications in your system which accessed the same file may then have difficulty finding it. For this reason, you are advised to always make a copy of the file for use in the Project when you first import it.

- Edit the start, end and length fields to precise numerical values in (you guessed it!) the start, end and length fields. This is applicable to situations where you know the precise point at which you want the event to start or end, or the precise length. When bars and beats are shown in the ruler, these values are displayed in bars, beats, sixteenth notes and ticks (each sixteenth note contains 120 ticks).
- The offset for the audio event provides a way of sliding the contents back and forth within the audio event. There are two reasons why you might want to do this. Firstly, Cubase SX slightly anticipates the record drop-in point to make sure that you don't miss any of the start of your intended take. You can see this in the Sample editor as a small segment of audio before the audio event starts. Normally you don't hear this but if, after recording, you needed to change the feel of the timing by bringing some of the pre-recorded attack into the audible part of the event, adjusting the offset in the Infoline provides one way of doing it. Secondly, if you

have re-sized the audio event so that there are substantial parts of the associated audio clip which are not visible within the event, the offset value allows you to slide the contents around without moving the position of the audio event. If the audio event already plays the whole clip, the offset value cannot be adjusted. The contents may also be moved by pressing Ctrl + Alt and dragging within the event.

- The Snap point value provides another way of moving an audio event to a new position in the display. This is an absolute value corresponding to a point on the ruler and does not move the position of the Snap point within the event.

- The volume field provides an alternative numerical method of changing the volume of the event, providing +24dB of boost or infinite attenuation. The volume is normally adjusted by moving the blue volume handle in the centre of the event.

- The fade in and fade out fields provide quick numerical methods of adjusting the fade in and out characteristics of the event. The fade characteristics are normally adjusted using the blue fade handles at each end of the event (as described in 'Using the tools' in Chapter 4).

- The Mute field offers a quick method of muting the currently selected event or group of selected events.

- The Lock field allows you to lock the position, size and any other kind of editing of the audio event such as volume changes, fades and audio processing. When you are happy with the audio events in a Project, possibly when it is near to completion, Lock is invaluable for protecting those audio events which you no longer wish to move or change.

- Transpose allows you to apply real-time pitch shifting to the selected audio event(s) in semitone steps in the range -24 to +24 semitones. This could be used if you change the key at a later date after having completed the recording and remains reasonably transparent if the pitch change is between -5 to +5 semitones, depending upon the material. Alternatively, Transpose provides an easy method of experimenting with more extreme pitch changes for the creation of sound effects.

- Finetune is similar to Transpose but allows pitch change in one cent steps (100th of a semitone) between -100 and +100 cents. Useful for re-tuning instruments within an arrangement. Also excellent for the instant creation of phasing and ADT effects by creating a copy of an event on a spare track and detuning the second event by a small amount (try between -3 to -40 cents).

Useful Audio menu options

There are a number of very good audio editing tools in the Audio menu of Cubase SX. These are accessed via the main Audio menu itself or using the Audio section of the Quick menu. Editing is generally directed to one or more selected audio events or parts.

Events to Part

It is often appropriate to group a number of audio events into a single audio part so that they can be moved around and edited as a single block within the event display. First, ensure that all the events are on the same track and then select the events by dragging a selection box around them, (or use

'Select all events' from the Quick menu opened on the Track list). Once selected, choose 'Events to Part' in the Audio menu (or in the Quick menu).

Events to Part is also applicable when you have a number of overlapping events on a single track or on different tracks and you wish to edit them in the Audio Part editor. First, drag all the events onto a single track and then select them. Select 'Events to Part' to convert the events into an audio part. Double click on the audio part to open the Audio Part editor (see 'Editing miscellaneous takes in the Audio Part editor', below, for more details).

Dissolve Part

Dissolve Part provides the opposite function of Events to Part, above. This is applicable when you wish to have access to the individual audio events inside a part while still remaining in the Project window. Such a case may occur if you decide to change the structure of a musical arrangement.

Bounce selection

Figure 8.2
Bounce Selection Replace Events
dialogue

Bounce selection creates a single new audio file and clip from the currently selected audio events or parts and, if chosen, a single new audio event which replaces the original events/parts. All auto-fades, fades and other audio processing are included in the bounce and, for multiple selections over several tracks, the function operates on a track by track basis. Audio events, and the associated audio file and clip, created with Bounce are named according to the source track name. Bounce Selection may also be used to bounce the current range selection in the Sample editor to a new file and clip. In this case, a second instance of the Sample editor is automatically opened containing the bounced audio.

When using Bounce Selection in the Project window or Audio Part editor, a dialogue appears asking if you wish to replace the currently selected material (Figure 8.2). If you click on Replace the original selected audio events or parts are replaced with a single audio event. If you click on No, the events are not replaced. In both cases, a new audio file is created on the hard disk and a new audio clip is created in the Pool. The original audio files and clips associated with the selected events/clips from which the bounce was made are not deleted or modified in any way.

Detect silence

Detect silence (Audio/Advanced sub-menu) allows you to process your audio material in various ways based upon a definition of what should be judged as silence within the chosen audio event. This takes place in a graphical dialogue window which opens when you select the function. As well as detecting the silence itself, the Detect Silence function is equally applicable to finding the useful non-silent segments within your audio material. Let's imagine two typical audio editing scenarios:

Scenario 1

You have made a recording of a lead guitar and between the wanted lines of the performance there is noise and interference. How can you quickly and automatically eradicate the unwanted noise, without resorting to noise gates or manual editing in the Sample editor? Detect Silence provides an answer. Select

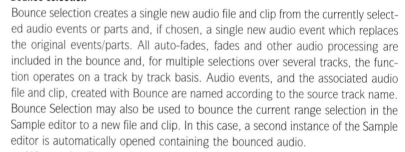

Tip

Detect Silence is excellent for dividing up audio tracks of drum loops after having imported the audio from CD (using File/Import/Audio CD).

the audio event containing the lead guitar and then select the Detect Silence function in the Audio menu. As a starting point, adjust the parameters as shown in Figure 8.3.

The Open Threshold parameter governs the level at which the audio should not be treated as silence (i.e. it governs the threshold for opening the gate to allow the wanted part of the signal through). The Close Threshold parameter governs the level at which the audio material should be treated as silence (i.e. it governs the threshold for closing the gate to

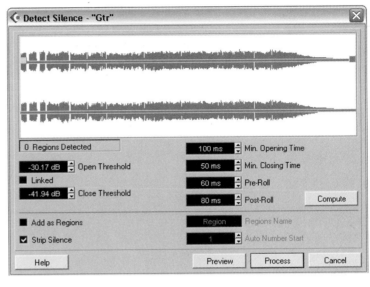

Figure 8.3
Finding the unwanted noise between the wanted notes of an electric guitar performance in the Detect Silence dialogue

block the unwanted part of the signal). In this case, these two parameters have been set to around −30dB and −40dB, respectively. The Minimum Opening time holds the gate open for a prescribed length of time after the Open threshold level has been reached to avoid the gate opening and closing too many times during passages featuring staccato notes or other 'quick-fire' material. The Minimum Closing time holds the gate firmly shut for a prescribed length of time after the Close threshold level has been reached and is usually set to a relatively small value to avoid cutting out any wanted material. The pre and post-roll parameters set a value in milliseconds which is added to the wanted part of the signal before and after the opening and closing of the gate to make sure that you do not lose any of the attack or decay. Here, values of 100ms, 50ms, 60ms and 80ms have been chosen.

Make sure you have activated Strip Silence and de-activated Add as Regions. Click on the Compute button followed by the Process button. Close the dialogue to go back to the Project window where your original audio event has now been automatically split into a number of separate events, with all those sections containing the noise eradicated from the performance (Figure 8.4). You might like to group all such events together within a single audio part using 'Events to Part' in the Audio menu. If you choose the values in the Detect Silence dialogue carefully, this technique is very effective for cleaning up noisy electric guitar recordings.

Figure 8.4
A cleaner electric guitar performance in the Project window after treatment using Detect Silence

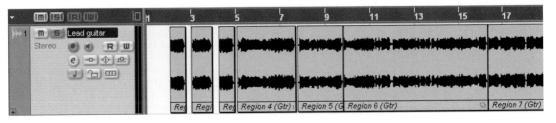

Scenario 2

You have imported an audio file into Cubase SX which contains a series of consecutive drum and percussion loops with silence in between each loop. How can you automatically mark the wanted audio sections as regions? (See below for more details about regions). Detect Silence provides a very quick and effective answer. Select the audio event containing the drum loops and then select the Detect Silence function in the Audio menu. Adjust the main parameters to the same values as in the electric guitar example outlined above but activate Add as Regions and de-activate Strip Silence. If you want your regions to start tightly cut to the first beat of each loop, try a value of Øms for the pre-roll setting. Enter a generic name into the Regions Name field (Figure 8.5).

Figure 8.5
Finding the relevant audio for the creation of automatic regions in the Detect Silence dialogue

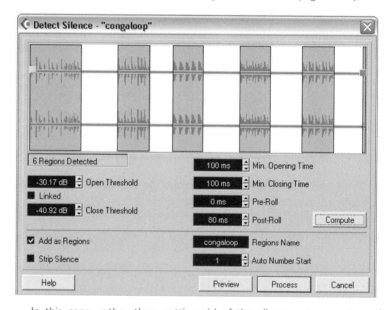

In this case, rather than getting rid of the silence we are automatically marking the areas of interest within the audio material. Click on the Compute button followed by the Process button. Close the dialogue to go back to the Project window. Double click on the audio event to open the Sample editor. Activate the Show Regions button in the Sample editor. The regions you cre-

Figure 8.6
The resulting regions in the Sample editor

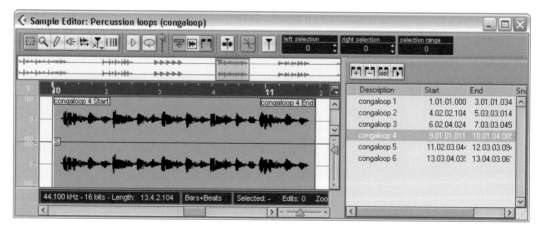

ated in the Detect Silence dialogue are now visible in the list and can be selected, played and manipulated as desired (Figure 8.6). This technique is excellent for automatically marking areas of interest within your audio material and can save a lot of time when working with loops.

Loop manipulation with Loop Selection and the Beat Calculator

When working with audio loops and any other material that you wish to play in a repeated cycle, one of the most convenient commands is 'Loop selection' in the Transport menu. This is best activated using the default key command: Shift + G. When used in the Project window or the Audio Part editor, Loop selection automatically sets the left and right locators to the currently selected audio event(s) or range selection and commences playback in cycle mode, starting at the left locator position. When used in the Sample editor, Loop selection initiates cycle playback in the current range selection.

Figure 8.7
The Beat Calculator

The Beat Calculator (Figure 8.7) is also useful when working with loops. This is opened from the Project menu and can be used for matching the tempo of Cubase SX to that of an audio loop.

To match the tempo of Cubase SX to an audio loop, proceed as follows:

- If you have not already done so, make sure that your audio loop has been edited to fit a precise number of beats or bars. You can set up a loop using the range selection tool in the sample editor.
- Alternatively import a ready-made audio loop into the Project window of Cubase SX and select the event.
- Open the Beat Calculator from the Project menu. To make the tempo fit the length of your chosen event you need to know its duration in beats. Enter the beat length into the Beat Calculator and click on 'At Tempo Track Start' to change the tempo of Cubase SX to that of the loop.
- The tempo of Cubase SX now matches the tempo of the loop.

Time stretching

Time stretching allows the changing of the length of the chosen audio material without changing the pitch. The use of the term 'time stretch' is slightly misleading since you can both stretch and compress the length of the target audio.

Time stretching is applied in two ways in Cubase SX; using the Object selection tool or using the Time Stretch option in the Process sub-menu of the Audio menu. The latter case is fully explained in Chapter 9. Time stretching using the Object selection tool was outlined briefly in Chapter 4. The following outlines tool-based time stretching in more detail.

Time stretch is available as the third function of the Object selection tool. It is implemented when you resize the audio event by dragging the start or end points. However, the actual time stretch algorithm used for the operation is chosen in File/Preferences/Editing/ Audio (Figure 8.8).

There are four algorithms available; MPEX2, Standard, Drum mode and Realtime. There are various advantages and disadvantages to each algorithm and, if you are time stretching or compressing important material, it is worth experimenting with the possibilities.

Figure 8.8
Select the time stretch algorithm in the Preferences dialogue

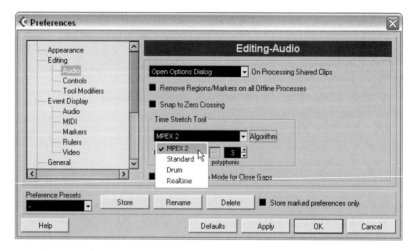

- MPEX2 – MPEX2 is a proprietary time stretch algorithm designed by Prosoniq for optimum audio quality. MPEX stands for "Minimum Perceived Loss Time Compression/Expansion". This gives among the best overall results, particularly if you want your sound to stay true to the character of the original. It is particularly recommended for vocal material and drum loops and does not suffer from too many side-effects, even at high stretch factors. Adjust the mono/poly slider to 1 for monophonic material and to 2, 3 or 4 for progressively better quality time stretching of polyphonic material. Option 4 offers the best quality for polyphonic material but the processing time is slower.
- Standard – this is a good all-round algorithm which processes the target data relatively quickly. It gives a slightly lesser audio quality but is excellent for producing sound effects when stretching audio by large amounts.
- Drum – this is a special algorithm tuned to give the best results for drum and percussion material. It provides a good alternative to the MPEX2 and real-time algorithms and should always be tried when working with drum loops.
- Realtime – uses the same time stretch algorithm as that which is used in Cubase SX's audio warp functions, as managed in the Sample editor (see the section entitled 'The Sample editor', below, for more details). This is a good all-round alternative to the other algorithms.

Time stretching a drum loop

It is recommended that you do not stretch your drum loops by more than around 15% in order to minimise the undesirable side-effects of the processing. It is assumed here that you are inserting a drum loop into a Project which already has a fixed tempo which you do not wish to modify. To make the chosen loop fit the tempo using the time stretch tool, proceed as follows:

- Import your chosen drum loop and place it in the Project window event display. Make sure that it loops for a precise number of bars (in its own original tempo). Popular lengths are one, two and four bars (Figure 8.9).
- Make sure that the Snap button is activated and the Grid selector is set to 'Bar'. Move the drum loop audio event to its intended start position in the musical arrangement.

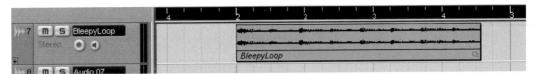

- Choose the MPEX2 or Drum algorithm in File/Preferences/Editing/Audio (as outlined above).
- Select the Object selection tool in time stretch mode and drag the end point of the event to the nearest bar division on the event display. The audio is automatically time stretched according to the chosen algorithm when you release the mouse (Figure 8.10).

Figure 8.9
A one bar drum loop in the event display

Figure 8.10
The one bar drum loop after time stretching

Creating sound effects using time stretch

You can create interesting sound effects using more extreme time expansion and compression. Good source material for this includes vocals, speech, percussion and real-world sounds such as birdsong, animal calls, running water, seawaves and atmospherics. Proceed as follows:

- Choose your source audio material and place it in the event display of the Project window. Edit the event so that there is no silence before and after the signal. This avoids unnecessary processing of silence and speeds up the time stretching operation. Adjust the zoom factor so that you have around 8 bars visible on screen (Figure 8.11).

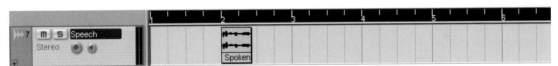

Figure 8.11
Spoken voice as the source for the creation of a special effect

- Choose the Standard or Realtime algorithm in File/Preferences/Editing/Audio.
- Select the Object selection tool in time stretch mode and drag the end point of the event over a large number of bars. (The length all depends on the effect you are trying to achieve. Try between 4 and 16). The audio is automatically time stretched when you release the mouse, according to the chosen algorithm (Figure 8.12). If you are feeling adventurous, you could find a part of the resulting audio event that you like, split it and place it on another track, and then repeat the time stretch process a second time. Alternatively, try creating other effects by taking fairly lengthy audio events and time compressing them.

Figure 8.12
The resulting 'stretched' spoken voice after processing

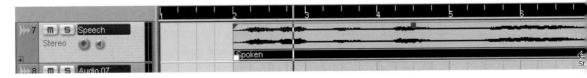

Info

The difference between spline and damped spline curve modes in the fade dialogues - regular spline mode radically affects the shape of the neighbouring parts of the curve as you drag the curve handle within the display and sets up a naturally balanced curve, whereas damped spline mode only has a minimal effect on the neighbouring area and sets up a curve which is more linear. Damped spline mode is therefore easier to control when dragging handles in the display. The curve modes are readily interchangeable so feel free to experiment to get the desired result.

Fades and crossfades

There are many different ways in which fades and crossfades can help you achieve better results in Cubase SX. Simple graphical fade techniques using the fade handles of an audio event have already been described in 'Using the tools' in Chapter 4. The following sections outline some of the other techniques and the use of the various fade dialogues.

Auto fade

There are occasions when splitting events in the Project window or Audio Part editor results in digital clicks. This most often occurs when the edits are not at zero crossing points in the waveform and may be troublesome at the start or end of an event or when one event is placed immediately after another. The cure for this is found in the Auto-fade settings of Cubase SX. The idea with Auto-fade is to impose a short automatic fade-in, fade-out or crossfade for the events in the Project window, to disguise clicks and provide glitch-free transitions between adjacent audio events. This can be set up globally or on a track-by-track basis. Since the fades are applied in real-time, a global setting might result in unnecessary drain on your computer's CPU power. Not all tracks need Auto fades. You are therefore advised to implement auto fades only on single tracks and only when they are needed, unless you have a very powerful CPU with plenty of headroom.

The global Auto fade dialogue is opened by selecting 'Auto Fades Settings' in the Project menu. Since you are being advised here not to use a global setting, leave the parameters in the global dialogue inactive (i.e. do not tick any of the Auto fade in, Auto fade out or Auto crossfade boxes).

The Auto fade dialogues for each track are opened from the Track list Quick menu or by clicking on the Auto fade button in the Inspector (Figure 8.13). The track version of the dialogue is identical to the global version except that it features a 'Use Project settings' tick box. When working on a track-by-track basis, de-activate this tick box since you are setting up the parameters for this track alone.

Figure 8.13
The track Auto fade dialogue

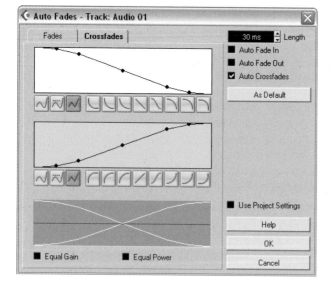

The Auto fade dialogue allows you to set the characteristics of the fade curves by clicking on any of the preset buttons or you can set up custom shapes by dragging directly in the curve displays. The default 30ms length suits most regular auto fade and crossfade requirements. To activate the auto fade functions tick the desired Auto fade in, Auto fade out or Auto crossfade box and click on OK.

Fade in and Fade out dialogues

When you have set up a fade in or a fade out using the blue fade handles at the start and end of an audio event the characteristics of the fade can be modified by double clicking above the fade line. This opens a fade in or fade out dialogue (Figure 8.14). The Fade out dialogue is simply the inverse of the Fade in dialogue shown here.

The fade in and fade out dialogues allow you to modify the characteristics of the fade curve by clicking on any of the eight preset curve buttons or you can set up custom shapes by dragging handles directly in the curve display. Spline, damped spline and linear curve characteristics are available together with a helpful Apply length option which allows you to adjust the length of the fade from within the dialogue. A restore button allows you to reset the dialogue to the default settings. Fades set up using the blue handles are not applied to the audio clip itself. This means that a number of events which refer to the same audio clip can each have an independent fade curve. This differs from the fades which are applied using the Fade in and Fade out functions of the Process menu, which apply the fade to the audio clip itself (described in Chapter 9).

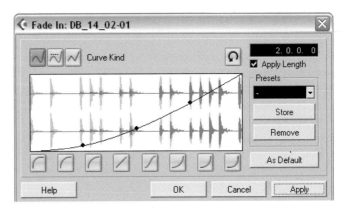

Figure 8.14
The Fade in dialogue

Adjust fades to range

As an alternative to dragging the handles in the event to create fades, Cubase SX provides another more elegant means of achieving the same result. This involves the use of the Range selection tool. To use this technique proceed as follows:

- Select the Range selection tool in either the Project window or the Audio Part editor.
- Select a range over the start of your chosen audio event corresponding to the length of fade in you want to apply. Press 'A' on the computer keyboard (or select 'Adjust fades to Range' in the Audio menu) and a fade in is instantly applied (Figure 8.15).

Figure 8.15
Using the Range selection tool to apply a fade in to an audio event

- Select a range over the end of your chosen audio event corresponding to the length of fade out you want to apply. Press 'A' on the computer keyboard (or select 'Adjust fades to Range' in the Audio menu) and a fade out is instantly applied (Figure 8.16).

Figure 8.16
Using the Range selection tool to apply a fade out to an audio event

- Alternatively, select a range over the central area of your chosen audio event. Press 'A' on the computer keyboard (or select 'Adjust fades to Range' in the Audio menu). A fade in and a fade out are simultaneously applied on either side of the selected area (Figure 8.17).

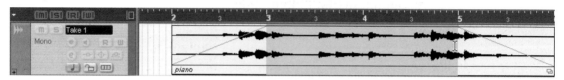

Figure 8.17
Using the Range selection tool to simultaneously apply a fade in and a fade out to an audio event

In addition, if you press the 'A' key command a second time in any of the above techniques, the fade in or fade out (or both) dialogues are automatically opened so that you can edit the curve(s).

Crossfading

Crossfades can be applied between audio events in the Project window if they are on the same track and they overlap. When they do not overlap a crossfade might still be applied if the audio clips they are referenced to overlap. In this case, the events are resized so that the crossfade can be created. If the audio events do not overlap and the whole of the audio clip is referenced by the audio event, no crossfade can be created. Things are similar in the Audio Part editor except that the events are viewed on separate lanes, which makes it slightly easier to set up the crossfades, (see Audio Part editor basics, below).

Let's consider setting up a crossfade between two takes of an 8 bar saxophone melody. Take One is good until an error in bar 5. Take Two plays successfully from bar 4 to the end of the melody in bar 8. We need to create a crossfade somewhere in bar 4. To achieve this in the Project window, proceed as follows:

Figure 8.18
Zoom in to the area of interest

- Select the zoom tool and draw a selection box around the two takes, in this case over the length of the eight bars of the melody (Figure 8.18).

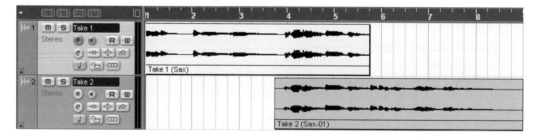

- Activate the Snap button, select Grid in the Snap mode selector, select Use Quantize in the Grid selector menu, and select 1/8 Note in the Quantize selector menu. This helps you when you arrange your overlap (you may often need a smaller resolution). Find a point in bar 4 where the two takes are playing the same note in the same manner. Resize Take One so that it ends (in this case) 1/8 note after this point. Resize Take Two so that it starts 1/8 note before this point (Figure 8.19). You now have a 1/8 note overlap.

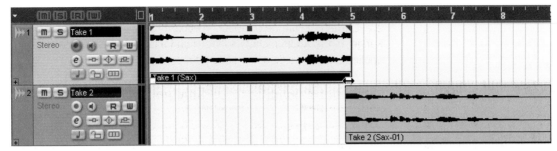

Figure 8.19
Resize each event so that they overlap

- Hold down the Ctrl key on the computer keyboard to limit horizontal movement and drag Take Two on top of Take One (Figure 8.20).

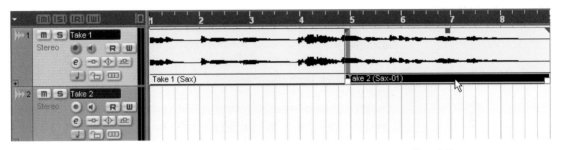

Figure 8.20
Drag one event on top of the other

- Press X on the computer keyboard. The crossfade is automatically created using the current default crossfade settings (Figure 8.21). To adjust the characteristics of the crossfade, press X a second time or double click on the crossfade area to open the crossfade dialogue.

Figure 8.21
Press X to create a crossfade

The Crossfade dialogue

The Crossfade dialogue (Figure 8.22) is opened by double clicking on the cross-fade area. Alternatively, select the events containing the crossfade and press X on the computer keyboard. Several crossfades may be modified in the Crossfade dialogue simultaneously by selecting all the events containing the crossfades.

Figure 8.22
The Crossfade dialogue

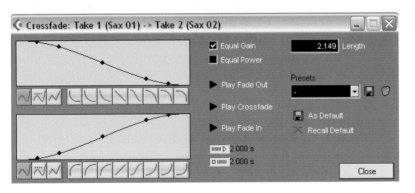

Tip

To remove fades and crossfades, select the events containing the fades using the Object selection tool, or select the range containing the fades using the range selection tool, and then select 'Remove Fades' in the Audio menu.

The Crossfade dialogue features fade out curve and fade in curve displays. You can audition the signal using the Play Fade out and Play Fade in buttons. The resulting crossfade is auditioned using the Play Crossfade button. Eight preset curves are available for each of the fade in and fade out curves with a choice of spline, damped spline or linear characteristics. The fade curves can also be edited manually by clicking and dragging directly in the curve displays.

Activating the Equal Power option ensures that the crossfade contains equal acoustical energy throughout the course of the crossfade. In other words, the perceived loudness remains constant throughout the crossfade. In Equal Power mode, the curve displays have only a single editable point. This is moved horizontally in the display. Equal Power mode might have been applicable to the crossfading exercise outlined above, where you require a crossfade with no change in the perceived loudness of the signal. However, this relies on both the outgoing and the incoming signal having very similar characteristics in order to be successful. Many crossfading tasks might benefit more from Equal Gain (outlined below) or some other configuration.

Activating the Equal Gain option ensures that the summed amplitude of the two curves remains constant throughout the crossfade. This is suitable for a wide range of crossfading tasks where you want the fade in curve to automatically mirror the fade out curve for effortless, 'constant gain' crossfades.

The right panel of the dialogue features a length field where you can adjust the length of the crossfade zone, 'As Default' and 'Recall Default' buttons which allow you to specify the current settings as the default crossfade for future crossfade operations or recall the existing default, and a Preset menu where you can specify and recall your own presets.

The Audio Part editor

The Audio Part editor is opened by double clicking on an audio part or pressing Ctrl + E (PC) / Command + E (Mac) on the computer keyboard while an audio part is selected (Figure 8.23). The editor features time on the horizontal axis and what are known as 'lanes' on the vertical axis. When events within the part overlap, each is shown on a different lane. Events can be dragged between lanes at any time. Playback priority is enforced from the bottom lane

Figure 8.23
The Audio Part editor

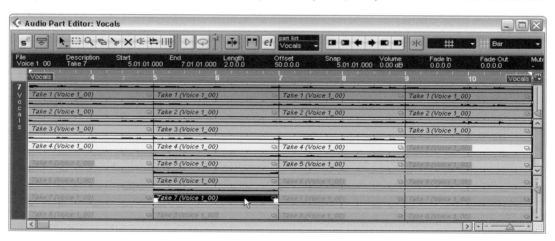

up. Lanes are particularly useful for manipulating multiple takes on the same track, as occurs during cycle recording, or for tidying up after you have been dropping in manually. Multiple parts can be displayed in the Audio part editor.

The editor features a toolbar at the top of the window which contains a similar tool set to the Project window. However, the glue tool is not present and the scrub and play tools are on separate buttons. The operation of all other tools is similar to those found in the Project window (see the section entitled 'The Project window tools' in Chapter 4 for more details).

There is the usual info line button which shows/hides the Infoline (see 'General Audio editing techniques', above, for how to directly edit the values in the Infoline). There is also a solo button and the familiar scroll bars and zoom controls at the lower and right hand edges of the window. Audio events are shown as waveforms inside boxes in the same manner as they are shown in the Project window event display.

Snap points

When the vertical zoom is set to a sufficient factor, the Audio Part editor reveals a 'Snap point' which, by default, is found at the very beginning of each audio event (Figure 8.24).

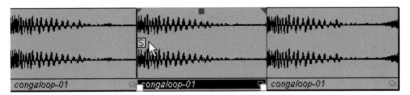

Figure 8.24
The Snap point of an audio event in the Audio Part editor

The Snap point is marked by an 'S' handle attached to a vertical line and this may be dragged to any point within the event. Once set at the desired position, the Snap point is used by Cubase SX to lock the position of the event to the current Snap resolution, whenever it is moved or quantized (assuming that the Snap button is activated). The Snap point allows you to find a musically significant moment within the event, such as the first downbeat in the bar or the precise hit point of a bass drum. This helps line up the audio material to other events and allows you to quantize audio material, especially that which has been divided into smaller sections using the audio slicing techniques of Hitpoint mode (see below).

Audio Part editor play, scrub, audition and loop buttons

The Audio Part editor features separate play and scrub tools which are convenient for quickly auditioning the audio in any part of the display. These operate in a similar fashion to the play and scrub tools in the Project window (as described in Chapter 4).

There are also local audition and loop buttons. These provide local playback of the audio material in the Audio Part editor. When you have selected one or more events, playback takes place over the range of the selected events. Similar playback behaviour occurs when you have made a range selection using the Range selection tool. When no selection has been made, the whole audio part is played back. Pressing the loop button activates the audition button simultaneously, and cycle playback continues until you press the audition button again.

All these functions provide convenient methods of auditioning material in the Audio Part editor. In addition, their use switches the routing of the audio signal to the audition bus. This means that the audio no longer passes through the audio channel and any effects or EQ and you can set a different level on the audition bus fader. The audition bus level is also set using the audition volume mini-fader on the toolbar. This helps with detailed audio editing where effects and EQ might otherwise mask the result. If you wish to hear the audio through the channel in the normal way, use the standard play button of the Transport panel ('Enter' on the computer keyboard).

Editing audio events in the Audio Part editor

Editing audio events in the Audio Part editor is very similar to editing events in the Project window. Please refer to the section entitled 'Using the tools' in Chapter 4 for more details. More specific editing procedures for the Audio Part editor are outlined in 'Audio Part editor basics', below, and in the section entitled 'Creative techniques using the Audio Part editor and Sample editor' later in this chapter.

Audio Part editor basics

In a similar manner to Cubase SX's other editors, it is a good idea to set the left and right locators around the part you are editing in the Audio Part editor. To achieve this, press 'P' on the computer keyboard. This helps keep the Project cursor visible on screen when playing back in cycle mode. Once inside the Audio Part editor, you may prefer to use the local play, cycle and audition tools rather than the main Transport functions, (as described above). When you have selected multiple parts for editing, use the part list menu on the toolbar to switch between parts. Also try activating the 'Show Part Borders' button to help navigate.

To get started with the Audio Part editor let's try creating a sound effect using a cymbal crash. This helps understand the basics and gives a preliminary idea of the creative uses of the editor. This example uses a cymbal crash of four bars in length. The objective is to split the crash into a number of segments and then re-order them in overlapped succession on different lanes within the Audio Part editor. Proceed as follows:

- Record a cymbal crash in the Project window or drag and drop an existing cymbal file onto an audio track. If necessary, split the event and delete the decay so that the cymbal crash has a duration of four bars. With the cymbal event selected, right-click (PC) / Ctrl-click (Mac) to open the Quick menu and select 'Events to Part' in the Audio section (Figure 8.25). This converts the audio event into an audio part.

Figure 8.25
Convert the audio event for the cymbal into an audio part

- Double click on the new audio part to open the Audio Part editor. Select the Split tool in the toolbar and divide the cymbal crash into four 1 bar events (Figure 8.26).

Figure 8.26
Split the cymbal into four 1 bar events in the Audio Part editor

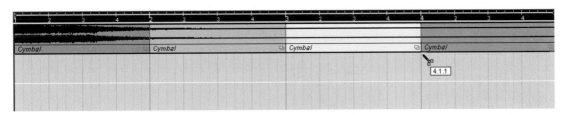

- Select the Object selection tool (pointer) and drag the third bar of the cymbal onto the second lane at position 1.4.1, as indicated by the tool when the event is dragged (Figure 8.27). Activate the Snap button and choose 'Beat' in the Grid selector menu, to make it easier to place the events.

Figure 8.27
Drag the third bar of the cymbal onto the second lane at position 1.4.1

- Drag the second bar of the cymbal onto the third lane at position 2.3.1 (Figure 8.28)

Figure 8.28
Drag the second bar of the cymbal onto the third lane at position 2.3.1

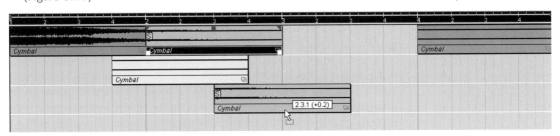

- Finally, drag the first bar of the cymbal onto the fourth lane at position 3.2.1 and drag the fourth bar of the cymbal to position 1.1.1 on the first lane (Figure 8.29). If you found this procedure confusing just remember that all you have done is split your original cymbal into four parts and then re-assembled them in reverse order with one beat overlaps.

Figure 8.29
Drag the first bar of the cymbal to position 3.2.1 and the fourth bar of the cymbal to position 1.1.1

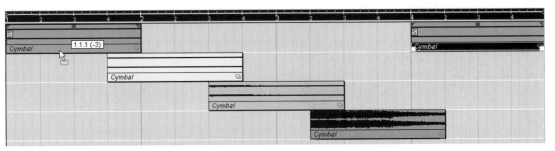

- Resize the event on the fourth lane so that your events span four bars. Put Cubase SX into play to hear the new order of events. The result is a hybrid reverse cymbal effect. To complete the effect, try selecting all events (Ctrl + A / Command + A) and then press 'X' on the computer keyboard. This automatically inserts crossfades between the events giving smooth transitions between each part of the cymbal (Figure 8.30).

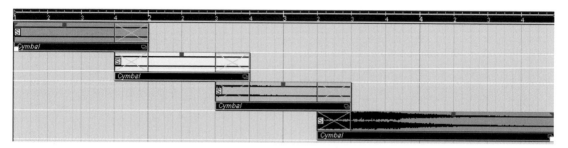

Figure 8.30
Select all the events and press 'X' on the computer keyboard to complete the effect

If you chose the right kind of cymbal for this exercise you should have got a pleasing result. However, some readers may be having difficulty grasping the practical use of this technique. Well, splitting and moving events around is something that occurs frequently in the Audio Part editor (such as when creating composite versions of multiple take material) and overlapping and crossfading is a popular technique for creating smooth transitions between events. The overall technique explained here could be applied to other sounds to create similar special effects and any sustained note could form the target material. The technique could also be applied to two or more different sounds or drum loops to create unique sonic transformations.

The Sample editor

The Sample editor is opened by double clicking on an audio event or pressing Ctrl + E (PC) / Command + E (Mac) on the computer keyboard while an audio event is selected in the Project window or a clip is selected in the Pool (Figure 8.31). The editor window features a specialised toolbar at the top, with tools and buttons which are unique to the Sample editor. The contents of the toolbar are chosen by right-clicking/control clicking in the toolbar and

Figure 8.31
The Sample editor

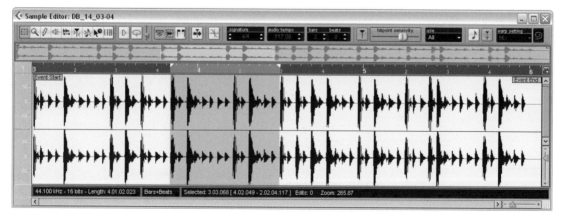

making a selection from the pop-up menu. The main display varies according to the which tool/mode of operation has been chosen. Below the toolbar, there is a thumbnail view which represents the whole of the clip associated with the selected audio data. The main display area shows the waveform of the currently selected material with time on the horizontal axis and amplitude on the vertical axis. When the info button is activated on the toolbar an Infoline appears below the main display area.

Editing in the Sample editor, not surprisingly, is geared towards working at the sample level. Samples are the 'atoms' of digital audio; they are the smallest particles of audio that you can manipulate in Cubase SX. In the Sample editor, you can see these atoms strung together if you view your audio data at maximum resolution, (Figure 8.32), and whenever you make a selection in the waveform display using the Range selection tool, the start, end and length of the selection are shown as samples in the information fields on the toolbar. All this allows you to edit material with surgical precision. However, this does not mean that you need to be permanently concerned with the microcosmic level of your audio material while working in the Sample editor; much of the time you work in an intuitive fashion, using what you hear as the main basis for your editing decisions.

Figure 8.32
A waveform at maximum resolution in the Sample editor

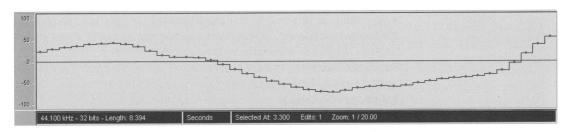

The Sample editor tools

The Sample editor features nine tools, many of which are similar in operation to those found in the Project window (see the section entitled 'The Project window tools' in Chapter 4 for more details). These include from left to right:

Range selection tool

For manually selecting specific areas of the waveform by clicking and dragging in the main display area. Range selections are magnetic to the zero crossing points in the waveform when the 'Snap to zero crossing' button is activated. When this button is de-activated range selections are made freestyle with single sample resolution.

Zoom tool

For zooming in and out of the main display area in standard Cubase SX fashion. The Zoom tool is particularly useful in the Sample editor for zooming in to specific details in the waveform.

Draw tool

For detailed manual re-drawing of the waveform at high resolution (in normal mode). This is designed for detailed repair work such as when manually eradicating a digital click and is only available when the zoom resolution is lower than 1.

Play tool

For auditioning the audio material by clicking on the waveform in the display. Playback commences from the position at which you clicked and continues for as long as you hold the mouse. The playback zone is shown in blue.

Scrub tool

For auditioning the audio material by dragging over any area of the waveform. This plays back the audio at the speed with which you drag, much like rocking the tape back and forth over the playback heads of a tape machine.

Hitpoint edit tool

For the detailed editing of hitpoints. This is a multi-function tool featuring play, insert, move, disable and lock functions. When moved between two hitpoints the pointer changes to a speaker symbol allowing you to audition the audio between the two points. Locating the pointer on a hitpoint's handle in the upper part of the display (at which time the hitpoint is highlighted in green) allows you to drag the hitpoint to a new location. Moving the pointer to the central area of the display while holding Alt (at which time a pencil symbol is shown) allows you to manually insert a hitpoint. Locating the pointer on a hitpoint's handle in the upper part of the display while holding Alt allows you to disable the hitpoint (the hitpoint is highlighted in green and a deletion cross appears). Clicking once on the hitpoint handle locks the hitpoint (at which time it is shown in dark blue). For full details of hitpoint editing, see the section entitled 'Editing hitpoints' near the end of this Chapter.

Audio tempo definition tool

As its name implies, this tool allows you to define the musical length, time signature and tempo of the current audio event or selection in the Sample editor. Once defined, this information is used for audio splicing and the real-time 'warping' of the audio to fit the current tempo. (To implement real-time audio warping, Musical mode must be activated for the audio event). This means that, once the tempo of an audio event has been defined, it follows any tempo changes in the project in real-time, in much the same way as MIDI events. (See the section entitled 'Defining the tempo of the audio and activating Musical mode' below, for more details).

Warp samples tool

The Warp samples tool allows you to attach 'anchor points' known as 'warp tabs' at rhythmically meaningful moments within an audio event. This allows you to stretch or compress specific sections of an audio event to make them fit tightly to the bars and beats. When you stretch or compress the audio in this way, fixed warp tabs are inserted at the start and end of the audio event. (Your audio becomes rather like a curtain attached simultaneously at both ends of the curtain rail. You can stretch or compress the curtain in between for lesser or greater folds in the fabric!). The Warp samples tool is usually used after having already defined the overall tempo of the audio using the Audio tempo definition tool and also after having selected musical mode.

Time warp tool

Similar to its function in the Project window and other editors, the time warp tool is for dragging a bar position to a time position. However, it takes on particular significance in the Sample editor for precisely lining up the tempo to audio material. This can be achieved manually by visually dragging tempo events to specific peaks in the waveform. Alternatively, tempo events can be dragged to hitpoints. This might be used to line up the beats in the bar to each beat as indicated by the hitpoints calculated for a drum loop. To use the time warp tool, hitpoint mode must be switched off. However, when you select the time warp tool any hitpoints that have already been calculated become visible. If the Snap to Zero Crossing button is activated the time warp tool snaps to the hitpoints.

Holding Shift while clicking in the Sample editor display inserts a tempo event. Holding Shift with the time warp tool in the ruler allows the deleting of tempo events. Note that to use the time warp tool, 'tempo track' mode must be selected in the Transport bar (time warp does not function in fixed tempo mode). For more details on the use of the time warp tool see Chapter 18.

Sample editor play and loop buttons

The Sample editor features its own play and loop buttons. These provide local playback of the audio material in the Sample editor. Local playback starts from the current Project cursor position and continues to the end of the clip or the end of the event, depending upon the status of the Show audio event button. When the Show audio event button is de-activated you can play back the current range selection. Pressing the loop button allows looped playback of the selected range or of the whole clip, depending upon the status of the Show audio event button. (Alternatively, try Shift + G to start loop playback of the current range selection and Alt + spacebar to play the current range selection once).

Together with the play and scrub tools, these functions provide a convenient method of auditioning material in the Sample editor. Using any of these functions switches the routing of the audio signal directly to the Audition bus. This means that the audio no longer passes through the audio channel and any effects and EQ. This helps with detailed audio editing where effects and EQ might otherwise mask the result. If you wish to hear the audio through the channel in the normal way, use the standard play button on the Transport panel ('Enter' on the computer keyboard).

Sample editor Autoscroll and Snap to zero crossing buttons

The autoscroll button has the same function as in the other windows of Cubase SX. When it is activated the display automatically follows the position of the Project cursor. Use the 'F' key to enable/disable autoscroll.

When the Snap to zero crossing button is activated all range selection, cutting, copying and pasting, and hitpoint editing snaps to the nearest zero crossing point in the audio waveform. Zero crossing points are where there are the least amounts of energy in the audio signal and editing here reduces the occurrence of audible clicks and makes for a good join when one section of audio is joined to another.

The global Snap to zero function in File/Preferences/Editing–Audio has *no effect* in the Sample editor which is controlled uniquely by its own independent Snap to zero button.

Important

The global Snap to zero behaviour of all windows of Cubase SX other than the Sample editor is controlled using the global Snap to zero function in File/Preferences/Editing–Audio. This function must be used with great caution since, when both the regular Snap button and the global Snap to zero function are activated, splits and other edits in the Project window occur at the nearest zero crossing point to the Snap point and *not* directly on the beat specified by the snap resolution, as usually happens. This may cause unforeseen side-effects when editing events in the Project window, (for example). As a general rule, the global Snap to zero function is best left in its default *disabled* state, unless you have a specific reason for activating it.

Sample editor function buttons

Six more buttons complete the functional layout of the Sample editor's tool-bar. These include from left to right:

- the Info button – when the Info button is activated an Infoline appears below the main display area. This shows the sample resolution, bit depth and length of the associated audio file on disk, the chosen time format in the ruler, and the selection, edit and zoom factor details.

- the Show audio event button – this enables/disables the view and flags of the audio event associated with the waveform. This button is not present if you have opened the Sample editor via an audio clip in the Pool.

- the Show regions button – this shows/hides the Regions list which appears to the right of the main display. Regions are areas within your audio material marked as sections of interest or relevance, much like you might highlight or underline sections of interest within the text of a book. They can be created automatically when recording audio in cycle mode or they can be created manually in the Sample editor (see Chapter 7 'Audio recording in Cycle mode' and the section entitled 'Creating Regions in the Sample editor', below).

- the Hitpoint mode button – this activates/de-activates Hitpoint mode. When first activated, hitpoints are automatically calculated for the whole clip or the current range selection according to the current setting of the hitpoint sensitivity slider. Thereafter, these hitpoints remain attached to the clip and may be viewed or hidden in the Sample editor using the Hitpoint mode button. Hitpoints are those points within the waveform where there are significant peaks in the amplitude of the signal. These peaks usually coincide with the rhythmic pulse of the material and so are useful for establishing the main percussive 'hits' in drum and percussion loops.

- the Musical mode button – this activates or de-activates musical mode. When musical mode is active, the corresponding audio event in the Project window is shown with a small double arrow symbol at the lower right and is automatically stretched or compressed according to the Project tempo. Real-time stretching or compression is calculated using the original tempo and length of the event as defined with the Audio tempo definition tool. (Please note that the small double arrow may be shown in the audio event if warp tabs are present, regardless of the state of the musical mode button).

- the Show warp tabs button – shows or hides any warp tabs within the audio event. When the Warp samples tool is chosen warp tabs are automatically shown in the display but the tabs can also be shown when in hitpoint mode which is helpful if you need to drag a hitpoint to a warp tab.

Modes of operation and display behaviour

The toolbar and main display of the Sample editor are modified according to which tool or mode button is currently active. Most of the behaviour is intuitive. For example, activating the Hitpoint mode button shows all hitpoints, if they have already been calculated, and enables the hitpoint sensitivity slider and 'Use' menu (Figure 8.33). In hitpoint mode, the hitpoints are shown in the display regardless of which tool is currently selected.

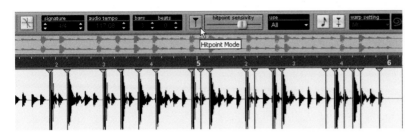

Figure 8.33
Activate the Hitpoint mode button to display all calculated hitpoints

Selecting the Audio tempo definition tool enables the signature, audio tempo and bars and beats fields (Figure 8.34). These parameters remain inactive for all other tool selections since they are irrelevant for all other operations in the Sample editor. However, if musical mode has already been activated the signature, audio tempo and bars and beats fields remain locked unless musical mode is once again de-activated.

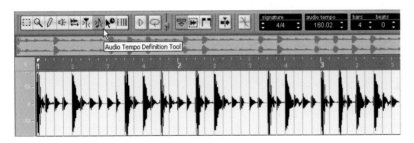

Figure 8.34
Select the Audio tempo definition tool to enable the signature, audio tempo and bars and beats fields

The contents of the Sample editor toolbar are modified by right-click-ing/Control clicking on the toolbar and activating/de-activating the options in the pop-up menu. Activating 'Selection controls' enables left, right and range selection displays at single sample resolution. These are useful for editing in fine detail. Selecting 'Setup' opens a dialogue featuring a helpful presets sub-menu where you can store your own toolbar setups.

Regions

Regions are areas within your audio material marked as sections of interest or relevance, much like you might highlight or underline sections of interest within the text of a book. They can be created automatically when recording audio in cycle mode or they can be created manually in the Sample editor. Click on the Show Regions button to reveal the Regions list to the right of the main display (Figure 8.35). You can create a new region at any time by selecting a range within the waveform and clicking on the Add button above the Regions list. Regions are extremely useful for marking a number of areas of interest within the audio material. Any of the regions may then be played, selected or

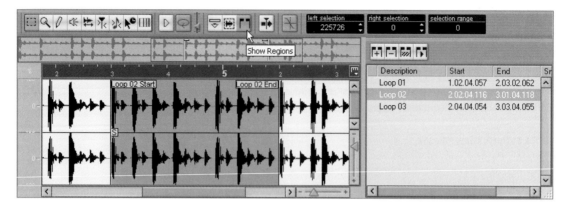

Figure 8.35
Activate the Show regions button to reveal the Regions list in the Sample editor

removed by selecting it in the list and using the corresponding buttons at the top. The start and end points of each region can be directly edited in the list. New audio events can be created from any region by Ctrl/Command dragging directly from the selected area in the waveform display or by selecting and dragging from the region in the Regions list onto a track in the Project window.

Snap points

When the event is visible in the waveform display, the Snap point is shown (marked by a vertical line with an 'S' handle). The Snap point in the Sample editor is particularly useful for finding the precise point of a down beat or other significant moment within the audio material. It can be dragged entirely manually to a significant point within the waveform or it may be dragged to the start point of a region or to the position of the Project cursor, both of which become magnetic to the Snap point when it is dragged nearby. (For more Snap point information see 'Snap points' in the Audio Part editor section above).

Sample editor basics

In a similar manner to Cubase SX's other editors, it is a good idea to set the left and right locator around the event you select for editing. As usual, the quickest way to achieve this is to press 'P' on the computer keyboard. Double-click on the event to open the Sample editor. Once inside the editor, you may prefer to use the local play, loop and audition controls for playback, rather than the main Transport controls.

Helpful key commands

At first sight, navigating within the Sample editor may seem rather confusing. The following key commands help clarify and speed up some of the basic operations:

- Zooming - use Shift + F to zoom to the whole clip associated with the event, Shift + E to zoom to the event itself, and Alt + S to zoom to the current selection (if you have made a selection using the Range selection tool).
- Playback - use Shift + G to loop the current range selection and Alt + Spacebar to play a range selection once. Try also assigning a key command to 'StartStop Preview' in the Key commands dialogue (File/Key commands). This gives you remote control of the local play button.

Tip

For instant range selections of whole events or regions in the Sample editor, double-click on the corresponding event handle or region handle.

The thumbnail view

The thumbnail view above the main display is particularly helpful for navigating to anywhere within the clip. This is similar to the Overview display in the Project window. The current horizontal section of the waveform you can see in the main display is marked by a corresponding blue box in the thumbnail view. You can drag the blue box to different positions within the clip and it can be resized by dragging the start or end points.

First steps in the Sample editor

Probably the best way to get to know the Sample editor is to experiment on a test audio recording. To ease the learning curve it is best to start with something very simple, so here it is suggested that you make a recording of the spoken letters 'VST'. This avoids confusion and you can clearly see the three letters as three significant peaks in the waveform (Figure 8.36). It is suggested that you pronounce the letters in a slow, deliberate fashion in order to get a clear, usable recording.

The idea here is to test various techniques for selection and playback and to re-order the letters using cut, copy and paste techniques so that you hear 'TV' instead of 'VST'. Proceed as follows:

- Take a microphone and record the spoken letters 'VST' onto an audio track in the Project window. Double click on the resulting audio event to open the Sample editor. The waveform should resemble that shown in Figure 8.36.

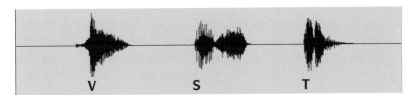

Figure 8.36
Test recording of the spoken letters 'VST'

- Try revealing the event by activating the 'Show Audio event' button. The audio event is highlighted and contains start, end and snap point handles. Try de-activating 'Musical controls' and activating 'Selection controls' using the pop-up toolbar menu (right-click/Control click on the toolbar). The selection controls give you a sample accurate reading of the range selections you make. Activate the 'Snap to zero crossing' button. This helps ensure click-free editing when you copy and paste in the Sample editor.

Figure 8.37
The audio event is revealed by clicking on the Show Audio event button

- Audition the audio by clicking on the play button in the toolbar. The local play button bypasses the channel strip, routes the audio to the Audition buss and provides exclusive playback of what you see in the waveform display. Adjust the playback level using the audition mini-fader on the toolbar (this is a replication of the main Audition buss fader in the Mixer).
- Click on the local play button. Playback commences from the Event start and continues up to the end of the event.
- Select the Range selection tool and drag across the display area. For example, try selecting the letter 'S.' in your audio recording. The selection area is shaded in pale green (see Figure 8.38). Press Alt + Spacebar on the computer keyboard. This is the key command for 'Play selection range' (Transport menu). The 'S' sound is played back once.

Figure 8.38

Select and play the 'S' of your 'VST' test recording

- Still with the 'S' sound selected, press Shift + G on the computer keyboard. This is the key command for 'Loop selection' (Transport menu). The 'S' sound is played back continuously in a loop.
- While still in loop playback, try adjusting the start and end positions of the range selection by dragging on the start or end points with the Range selection tool (a double arrow appears). Each time you release the mouse button, playback re-commences from the start of the range selection. For this to operate correctly in some versions of Cubase SX you must de-activate the Show audio event button. This technique is particularly useful for finding and fine tuning a drum loop (Figure 8.39).
- Now, select 'V', (the first peak in the waveform), by dragging the mouse in the display (Figure 8.40). Copy the selection by pressing ctrl + C (PC) / Mac: command + C.
- Click once on the point just after the 'T.' (the third peak in the waveform) and make sure that there is a zero range selection indicated in the range

Tip

Multiple Sample editors may be opened simultaneously when you are working on several clips at the same time. This is useful for copying, pasting and merging audio between different clips.

Figure 8.39

Try adjusting the start and end position of the range selection while in loop playback

field on the toolbar. Press ctrl + V (PC) / command + V (Mac) on the computer keyboard to paste the 'V' just after the 'T' (Figure 8.41). When the range field on the toolbar reads zero, the contents of the clipboard are *inserted* into the existing waveform at the range selector position (shown by a single pale green vertical line). When the range field on the toolbar reads any value other than zero, the contents of the clipboard *overwrite* the existing waveform beginning from the start position of the range selection.

Figure 8.40
Select and copy 'V'

Figure 8.41
Paste 'V' just after the 'T' at the end of the waveform

- Select the last two peaks in the waveform and audition the selection. The result should be the required spoken letters: 'TV' (Figure 8.42).

- If you are happy with the edit, you could delete the first two peaks in the waveform, the original 'V' and 'S', by selecting them and pressing backspace on the computer keyboard. Alternatively, select the new 'TV' section and activate the Show Regions button. Click on the add button above the regions list and name the new region as 'TV'. If desired, drag the region onto the Project window to create a new audio event.

Figure 8.42
Audition 'TV'

Tip

To merge the current contents of the clipboard with the existing audio in the Sample editor use the Merge Clipboard function in the Process menu (see 'Merge Clipboard' in Chapter 9).

Tip

Sample editor operations such as cut, copy, paste and Draw tool editing can be modified at a later date using the Offline Process History dialogue (Audio menu).

Figure 8.43
A multiple take recording in the Audio Part editor featuring four takes

Creative techniques using the Audio Part editor and Sample editor

Assembling a composite version of a multiple-take recording in the Audio Part editor

The recording of a live performer sometimes requires several takes before a satisfactory result is achieved. Rather than stop Cubase SX after each take, it can often be more convenient to record continuously in cycle mode. In cycle mode, the audio is recorded as one long audio file automatically divided into separate takes, one for each lap of the cycle. When you open the Audio Part editor you find the recording conveniently divided into separate regions and stacked onto separate lanes. Each lane represents the recording from one lap of the cycle and is named with sequential take numbers. A perfect composite take can be assembled by splitting, resizing and muting the material.

The recording part of this process has already been outlined in 'Audio recording in cycle mode' in Chapter 7. Here we concentrate on the editing details. It is assumed here that you have NOT used stacked cycle recording mode. When you have completed your cycle recording and wish to assemble a composite take, proceed as follows:

- Select the cycle recording event(s) in the Project window and then select 'Audio/Events to Part' from the Quick menu. Choose 'Regions' in the 'Create Part using Regions?' dialogue which appears. This creates a multi-lane audio part which is suitable for editing in the Audio Part editor. Press 'P' on the computer keyboard to set the left and right locators to the start and end of the part. Double-click on the part to open the Audio Part editor (Figure 8.43).

- You may firstly wish to audition the takes to establish which versions you prefer. Only one take can be played at any one time and the lowest lane gets playback priority. The most convenient method of auditioning the different takes is to use the Mute tool, working from the lowest lane upwards (Figure 8.44). Activate the Audio Part editor solo button and use the main Transport play and cycle functions for playback.
- To make the task easier, it may be appropriate to colour code the different lanes and to divide all the takes into one or two bar events using the Split tool (Figure 8.45). Alternatively, try splitting the material according to the positions of the musical phrases or vocal lines. To start with, try working with the Snap button activated and the resolution set to bars or beats. To avoid clicks at the split points, try activating 'Snap to Zero crossing' in Preferences/ Editing–Audio (File menu). Do not forget

to de-activate this tick box after editing is complete since this may cause unwanted side-effects in other Cubase SX editing tasks.

- Assemble a basic composite version of the performance by muting those events you do not wish to hear. For clarity, try renaming the 'best' takes and the 'bad' takes in the Description field of the Infoline for each event (Figure 8.46). Try using Shift + G to loop around the currently selected event range.

Figure 8.44
Use the Mute tool when auditioning the material, working from the lowest lane upwards.

Figure 8.45
Use the Split tool to divide the takes into their constituent musical phrases or bars

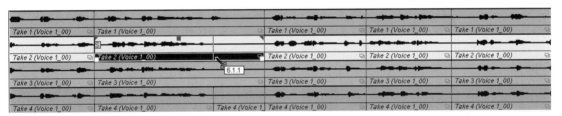

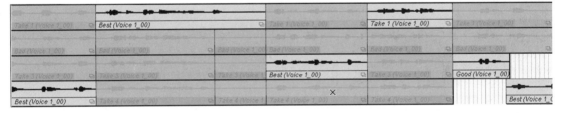

- For detailed composite versions (especially vocal performances), you may need to alternate between very short sections of different takes (such as when using single words in vocal lines). In these cases, it might be appropriate to work at higher zoom factors with the Snap button de-activated (Figure 8.47).

Figure 8.46
Mute those events you do not wish to hear and, if desired, name the best performances

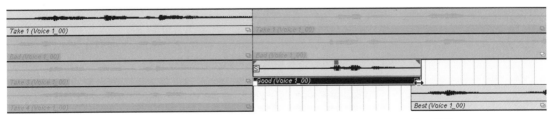

- So far, you have been attempting to chain together all the very best parts of the material, ensuring that there are no dramatic signal level

Figure 8.47
Work at higher zoom factor with the Snap button de-activated for detailed editing

changes and no obvious extraneous noises and interference as you pass from one event to another. When all the edited events produce close to the desired composite version, you may be able to improve matters further by setting up crossfades between all adjacent events. To achieve this, delete all muted events, select the remaining events by pressing Ctrl + A on the computer keyboard, and create automatic crossfades by pressing 'X' (Figure 8.48).

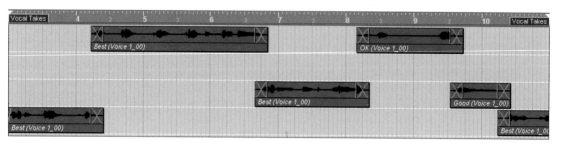

Figure 8.48
Delete all muted events and apply crossfades for smoothing the joins between the remaining events, (the length of the crossfades in this screenshot have been artificially lengthened – in reality they may be much shorter)

- If there are overlaps between the events, the crossfades have the duration of the respective overlaps. If there is *no* overlap between adjacent events, the events are automatically lengthened according to the default length setting in the Crossfade dialogue. If events are not adjacent, no automatic crossfade is created. The crossfade curves may be individually or globally adjusted in the Crossfade dialogue (see 'Fades and Crossfades', above). The crossfade length depends very much on the effect you are trying to produce. For example, if you are aiming for seamless joins on vocal lines try a length of 30ms with a spline-shaped curve (or the default straight line) with or without Equal Gain, as shown in Figure 8.49. Special effects usually benefit from longer crossfade times.

Figure 8.49
Try these settings in the Crossfade dialogue for seamless joins between vocal lines

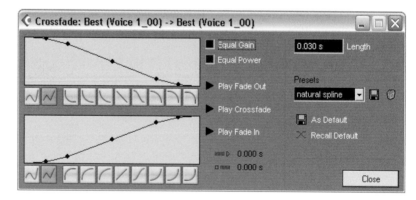

Editing miscellaneous takes in the Audio Part editor

When you have recorded different versions of the same material on several different tracks or when you have recorded a number of takes on the same track as a result of dropping in or punch recording, you may wish to edit the material in the Audio Part editor. Proceed as follows:

- Drag a selection box around the events you wish to edit. These may be on the same track or on different tracks.
- Select 'Events to Part' in the Audio menu (or use the Quick menu).
- Double click on one of the parts to open the Audio Part editor or press Ctrl/Command + E.
- In the Audio Part editor, parts which were on different tracks in the Project window each appear in their own horizontal track in the editor. For multiple recordings which took place on the same track, each take appears in its own lane within the vertical space of its respective track (stacked).
- Use the part list menu to switch between tracks. Alternatively, use the Play tool with the 'Edit active part only' button de-activated, to switch between and audition the contents of each track/lane.
- The events may be edited using similar techniques to those outlined in 'Assembling a composite version of a multiple-take recording in the Audio Part editor', above.

Creating and manipulating regions in the Sample editor

As mentioned elsewhere in this text, regions are areas within an audio clip which are marked as sections of interest or relevance. They are often created, viewed and edited within the Sample editor but are also created automatically when recording audio in cycle mode or when using Detect Silence. Once created, regions provide useful 'signposts' to specific segments of your audio recordings which can be used in different parts of the Cubase SX environment.

Here, we take a look at how regions are handled in the Sample editor. Imagine that you have a recording of some speech or dialogue from the media, some part of which you intend to use as a quotation, or as an effect in a dance track. Regions can help you make your choice more easily. Proceed as follows:

- Double click on the audio event which contains the speech to open the Sample editor. Activate the Show Regions button to open the Regions display (Figure 8.50).

Figure 8.50
Open the Sample editor and activate the Show Regions button

- De-activate the 'Show audio event' button and activate the local loop and audition buttons on the Sample editor toolbar. Playback commences from the current cursor position (Figure 8.51).

Figure 8.51
De-activate the 'Show audio event' button and activate the local loop and audition buttons.

- Listen to the audio and select an area of interest with the Range selection tool. Since you are in local playback and loop mode the cursor jumps to the range you have selected and continues to loop around the selected area. Here, you might be selecting a word, a phrase or a whole sentence. If desired, fine tune the selection by dragging the start and end points of the range. When you are satisfied, click on the Add Region button above the Regions list and enter a name for the region. In this example, you might use the first word of each speech snippet as the region name (Figure 8.52).

Figure 8.52
Select, add and name a region

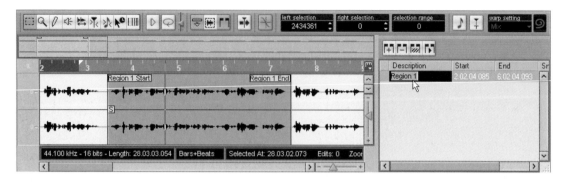

- Select the next area of interest in the audio material and add and name another region for it. You are still in local playback and loop mode so, each time you make a new selection, the cursor automatically loops within it.Continue in the same manner until you have marked all areas of interest. You now have a list of regions (Figure 8.53).

Figure 8.53
Select, add and name other regions to form a list of regions

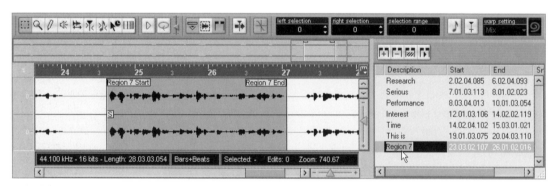

- Stop playback by de-activating the Audition button (toolbar). Do not de-activate the loop button. You can now audition a region in the audio clip by selecting any Region in the Regions list and clicking on the Region list Play button (Figure 8.54). Playback loops around the selected region.

Figure 8.54
Audition each region by selecting it in the list and activating the Region list Play button

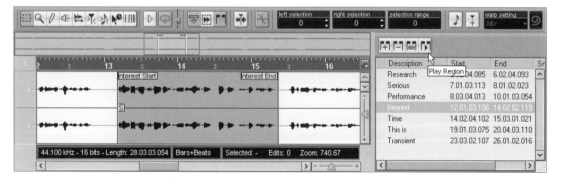

Audition any other region in the list simply by selecting it without dropping out of playback.

- The regions are shown in a time-ordered list but, of course, you can audition them in any order you like. Effectively, you can now jump to any point of interest with greater ease and, by naming each region descriptively, you have created convenient signposts which help you navigate within the audio material. When you have made a decision about which region you intend to use, fine tune its start and end points as desired and drag and drop it from the Regions list into the Project window (Figure 8.55).

Figure 8.55
Drag and drop the chosen region from the Regions list into the Project window

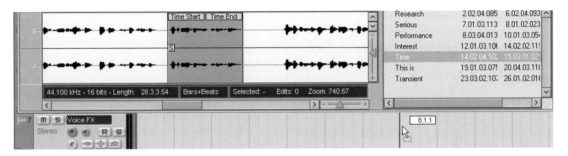

Finding and marking a loop in the Sample editor

This section outlines how to find and mark a drum or percussion loop in the Sample editor. Proceed as follows:

- Double-click on the audio event which contains the drum or percussion loop to open the Sample editor. Use the Range selection tool to mark the approximate region of the loop. You can often 'see' the loop in the waveform display.
- De-activate the 'Show audio event' button and activate the local loop and play buttons on the Sample editor toolbar (or press Shift + G). Playback loops around the selected area.
- Select the Region button and add the selection to the region list. This serves as a backup of your rough loop if you should lose your selection at a later point in this process. De-activate the Region button, if desired.
- Tune the loop by dragging the start or end points of the selected region, (the Range selection tool changes into a double arrow whenever you place it over the start or end points of the selection). Each time you set a new position for either the start or end, playback recommences from the start of the loop. This helps you set the start to the exact downbeat and makes it easier to tune the loop to a precise number of bars or beats.
- If necessary, fine tune the start and end points one sample at a time using the sample start and end fields of the selection controls in the toolbar.
- Once you are happy with the loop, mark it as a new region using the Add Region button and name it appropriately.
- If you wish to create a new event for your loop, select the new region in the Region list and drag it onto the Project window event display. Alternatively, press Ctrl/Command and drag from the range selection in the Sample editor into the Project window.

| **Tip** |

If you are working at high magnification and have lost the start point of your loop proceed as follows: stop playback, ensure that the autoscroll button is activated, and then press L on the computer keyboard. The Project cursor moves to the start point of the current selection. At this point in time, de-activate the autoscroll button and press Shift + G to re-commence loop playback. You can now continue to fine tune the start point of your loop at high magnification.

Digital click removal in the Sample editor

Audio files occasionally suffer from digital clicks and other interference. The Sample editor provides an environment where you can attempt to manually repair the damage. This requires the viewing of the waveform at high magnification. The following provides some guidelines for tackling the problem:

• Double-click on the audio event with the unwanted click to open the Sample editor. Hopefully, the offending click is already visible in the display as a brief spike in the waveform, similar to Figure 8.56. Many kinds of interference are not so obvious and could be far more difficult to locate.

Figure 8.56
Open the sample editor and find the click in the waveform

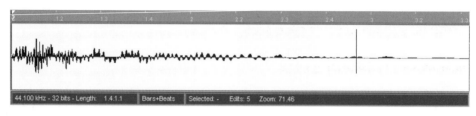

• Locate the mouse in the ruler at the location of the click and drag down to zoom in (activate 'Zoom while Locating in Time Scale' in File/Preferences/Transport). Zoom into a factor of lower than 1 as indicated on the infoline (Figure 8.57).

Figure 8.57
Zoom in to the click

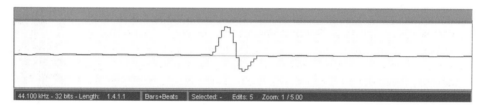

• The offending click is visible in great detail in the display. If you are having difficulty finding your click look out for a small segment of the waveform which has different characteristics to the rest of the audio. One way of eradicating the click is to select the Pencil tool and manually redraw the waveform in the area of the click (Figure 8.58). Draw the new waveform very carefully, attempting to match the characteristics of the new section to the existing waveform which surrounds it.

Figure 8.58
Select the Pencil tool and manually redraw the waveform

An alternative to the above procedure is to select a small portion of the surrounding waveform and to paste this over the click. To achieve this successfully, without changing the length of the audio clip, proceed as follows:

- Activate the Zero crossing point button on the toolbar.
- Working at high magnification, select the range of the click using the Range selection tool. Add the selection as a region in the Regions list. Make a mental note of the length of the selection in samples, as indicated in the range display on the toolbar.
- Search for a suitable adjacent area of the waveform using the Range selection tool. Select an area whose range is the same as, or greater than, the number of samples in the chosen click region.
- When you have found a suitable area, copy it using Ctrl + C.
- Select the range of the click a second time using the region as marked above, and use Merge Clipboard (Audio/Process sub-menu) with the slider set to 100% copy. This overwrites the click.

Audio Warping in the Sample editor

Defining the tempo of the audio and activating Musical mode

Most audio material of a musical nature has some kind of inherent rhythm and the speed of this rhythm can be defined as a tempo (usually expressed in beats-per-minute). You can record your audio to match the current tempo of the project but what happens if you later decide to change this tempo? Or what happens if you decide to use a tempo ramp which gradually increases or decreases? In these cases, the rhythmic pulse of the audio would no longer be synchronised with the tempo of Cubase SX. The solution to the problem is a combination of the Audio Tempo Definition tool and Musical mode, found in the Sample editor. Once you have defined the tempo of the audio and activated Musical mode, real-time time-stretching is applied to the audio events so that they follow tempo changes. This means that changing the tempo of the Project after having recorded all the audio is still a possibility. Moreover, it means that you can import audio from anywhere and by defining its tempo and activating Musical mode you can quickly integrate the material at the current tempo of the project. In essence, the Audio Tempo Definition tool and Musical mode offer you a fuss-free way of locking audio to tempo. This liberates your creativity since you can now easily try out different tempo changes, and use lots of different audio loops from different sources and at different tempi in the same project, without worrying about how you are going to make them fit together. To make all this happen, proceed as follows:

1 Define the tempo of your audio

- Double-click on the audio event which contains the target audio to open the Sample editor. Select the Audio Tempo Definition tool (Figure 8.59).

- If the audio event contains, for example, a drum loop of a known tempo from a sample library which is already precisely edited to fit the length of

Info

Audio tempo definition, musical mode, warp tabs, the warp samples tool, audio quantize and real-time pitch shifting form the main 'audio warp' features of Cubase SX. Most of the details are outlined in this section ('Audio warping in the Sample editor'). Real-time pitch shifting is set up in the Infoline for an audio event (for more details, see the section entitled 'Using the Audio event Infoline' at the beginning of this chapter).

Info

Cubase SX recognises the tempo definition and time signature information contained within Acid-format WAV files. These files are therefore immediately ready for audio warping operations when they are imported into the program.

Figure 8.59
Select the Audio Tempo Definition tool

Figure 8.60

If you already know the tempo, enter it directly in the audio tempo field

the audio event, you could enter the value directly into the tempo field on the toolbar (Figure 8.60).

Info

While it is not always essential for some operations it helps to define the audio tempo before calculating hitpoints or using warp tabs.

- If the loop is precisely edited to fit the length of the audio event but you do not know the tempo, the tempo field may already be showing the correct tempo, which the program attempts to find as soon as you select the Audio Tempo Definition tool. However, to be sure of the tempo, select the audio event using Edit/Select/Select Event, press P on the computer keyboard to set the blue left/right selection zone in the ruler to the length of the event, and enter the bars/beats represented by the audio event in the bars and beats fields. The tempo is calculated from this.

Figure 8.61

Make a range selection and audition and loop it to find the required number of bars/beats by ear

- If the audio event contains non-edited material, use the range selection tool to select a passage which represents an exact number of bars/beats at the audio's own tempo. De-activate the Show audio event button and select Shift + G to audition and loop the selection (Figure 8.61).

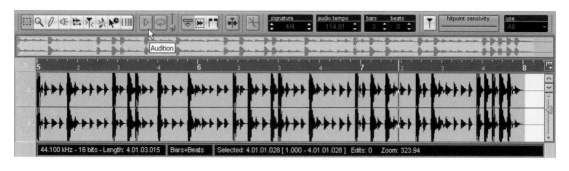

- When you are happy with the accuracy of the loop, press P on the computer keyboard to set the blue left/right selection zone in the ruler to the same passage as the range selection. Enter the number of bars/beats which correspond to the selection you have made, in the bars and beats fields. At this point, the tempo is calculated automatically and appears in the tempo field. (Figure 8.62 shows a range selection which represents four bars at the audio's own tempo).

Figure 8.62

This range selection lasts for 4 bars at the audio's own tempo, which results in a calculated value of 159.22 bpm in the audio tempo field

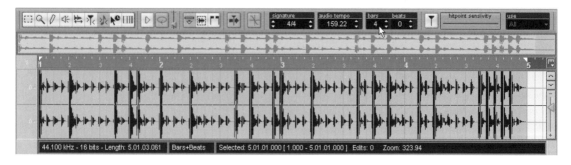

2 Activate Musical mode

- When the tempo of the audio has been successfully defined using the above steps, activate the Musical Mode button on the toolbar (Figure 8.63).

Figure 8.63 (left)
Activate Musical mode

Figure 8.64 (below)
Select a time-stretch algorithm

- In the warp setting menu, select the time-stretch algorithm which most closely corresponds to the type of audio you have processed (Figure 8.64).
- In the Project window, the audio event you set to Musical mode is now shown with a small double-arrow in the lower right corner. If you now change the tempo by imposing, for example, an upward moving tempo ramp between the start and end of the event, the audio follows the tempo precisely using a real-time time-stretch algorithm (Figure 8.65.

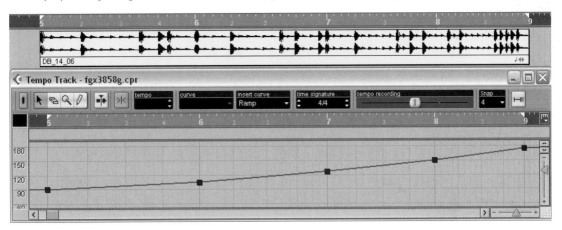

Using Warp tabs and the Warp Samples tool

Audio warping involves the stretching or compressing of the audio between chosen 'anchor points' in the waveform. These anchor points are known as 'warp tabs' and they appear as markers in the ruler and waveform display. Using the warp samples tool, warp tabs may be attached manually at rhythmically meaningful moments within the audio, or they may be generated automatically using the hitpoint positions. Once attached, you can apply audio quantizing or you can stretch or compress specific sections of the audio, normally with the aim of making it fit more tightly to the bar and beat divisions. When you stretch or compress the audio in this way, fixed warp tabs are inserted at the start and end of the audio event. Your audio becomes rather like a curtain attached simultaneously at both ends of the curtain rail. You can stretch or compress the curtain in between for lesser or greater folds in the fabric! By definition, audio warping is a complex and difficult procedure, often requiring detailed knowledge of a number of other editing techniques. To grasp the basics, try the following procedure:

Figure 8.65
An audio event in Musical mode in the Project window follows the tempo curve in the Tempo editor. Note the small double-arrow Musical mode symbol at the lower right of the audio event.

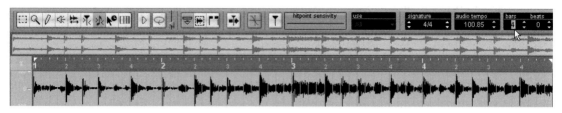

Figure 8.66
Define the audio tempo. Here a four bar
selection gives a tempo of 100.85bpm

- Double-click on the audio event which contains the target audio to open
  the Sample editor. Define the tempo of the audio (Figure 8.66). For
  more details of this step, see the section entitled 'Define the tempo of
  your audio', above.

Figure 8.67
Activate Musical mode

- Activate Musical mode (Figure 8.67) (for more details, see the section
  entitled 'Activate Musical mode', above).
- Calculate hitpoints (for more details, see the section entitled 'Creating
  and editing hitpoints in the Sample editor' below) (Figure 8.68).

Figure 8.68
Calculate hitpoints

Figure 8.69
The resulting hitpoints placed on the
transient peaks of the kick drum and
snare (the first bar is shown)

- Adjust the hitpoint sensitivity slider and the Use menu to produce one
  hitpoint on each quarter note (for example). Here a low sensitivity value
  with Metric bias in the Use menu produces the desired result (Figure 8.69).

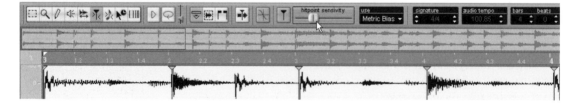

- Select Audio/Realtime processing/Create warp tabs from hitpoints. Warp
  tabs are generated automatically at the positions of the hitpoints. Select
  the Warp samples tool to reveal the Warp tabs (Figure 8.70). Notice
  how the warp tabs/hitpoints are slightly later than the meter time in the
  ruler. The number next to each tab indicates the time-stretch status of
  each segment where less than 1.0 means time compression, more than
  1.0 means time stretch and exactly 1.0 means no audio warping is
  implemented.
- One of the main features of audio warping is the ability to straighten up
  the audio using time-stretching so that the audio fits the meter time
  more tightly. At this stage there are two options. You can use 'Quantize

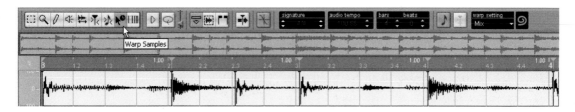

audio' to automatically stretch or compress the audio so that each warp tab lines up exactly to the beat, or you can drag warp tabs manually to the desired positions. Figure 8.71 shows the same audio as above after using Quantize audio (Audio/Realtime processing/Quantize audio). The main 'hits' in the audio now line up with the meter time.

Figure 8.70
Warp tabs created from hitpoints. Here, the warp tabs are shown in the ruler above each hitpoint.

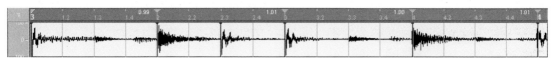

- Figure 8.72 shows the same audio as above, but this time the warp tabs have been dragged manually so that the main 'hits' in the audio fall slightly ahead of the beat. Warp tabs are dragged using the Warp sample tool which snaps to the tab when moved nearby if the 'Snap to zero crossing'

Figure 8.71
'Quantize audio' lines up the warp tabs to the beat. This 'tightens up' the feel of the audio using time stretch or compression.

Figure 8.72
Dragging warp tabs manually to make the 'hits' in the music fall ahead of the beat

button is active. The Warp sample tool may also be used to insert new warp tabs by clicking in the display and dragging to the desired position, at which time the audio on each side of the tab is stretched or compressed as appropriate. When the 'Snap to zero crossing' button is active, the dragged tab snaps to the nearest beat position. To delete a Warp tab, press Shift and click on the tab handle in the ruler (an eraser is shown). To show/hide Warp tabs click on the 'Show Warp tabs' button on the toolbar.

Creating and editing hitpoints in the Sample editor

Hitpoints are special markers which can be assigned to an audio clip based upon the signal peaks in the material. For the uninitiated, a signal peak is a point in the waveform where there is rapid amplitude gain, otherwise known as an attack transient. These points normally correspond to the main performance 'hits' in the signal and can be seen as mountain-like peaks in the waveform display. They might correspond to each note played by a musical instrument, each word sung by a vocalist, or the main percussive 'hits' in a drum or percussion performance. By creating markers at these points we can capture the rhythmic pulse or divide the performance into its constituent parts.

In Cubase SX, a segment of audio found between a pair of hitpoints is known as an audio slice. A common objective, especially when slicing drum and percussion loops, is to finish up with a single sound or drum 'hit' between each consecutive pair of hitpoints.

Info

Warp undo – to undo the audio warping, open the audio event in the Sample editor and select Audio/Realtime processing/ Unstretch audio.
Warp freeze – to make audio warping a permanent part of the audio, select Audio/Realtime processing/Freeze timestretch and transpose. In the dialogue which appears you have the opportunity to use the realtime algorithm or the MPEX2 algorithm. Right click/Command click on the Transport panel to open a pop-up menu where you can show/hide the various elements of the panel.

Calculating Hitpoints

Although not essential, it may help if you define the length of the chosen audio using the Audio Tempo Definition tool before creating any hitpoints, but this depends on what you want to do with them afterwards (for more details, see 'Defining the tempo of the audio and activating Musical mode', above).

Hitpoints are created in the Sample editor when you first click on the Hitpoint mode button or the Hitpoint edit tool in the toolbar. They may also be calculated by selecting 'Calculate hitpoints' in the Audio/Hitpoints menu. For pre-3.1 versions of Cubase, this opens the Hitpoints Detection dialogue (Figure 8.73). 3.1 and later versions feature a new and simplified hitpoint detection algorithm which does not use a dialogue.

Figure 8.73
The Hitpoints Detection dialogue (pre ver 3.1 only)

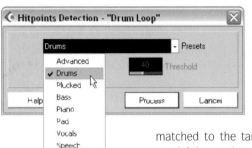

The Hitpoints Detection dialogue operates in a number of preset modes designed for calculating hitpoints according to the type of target audio material (Drums, Plucked, Bass, Piano, Pad, Vocals, Speech and Mix), or operates in Advanced mode where you can experiment with your own settings for the 'Sense' and 'Threshold' parameters (these parameters become active only in Advanced mode). The presets normally work perfectly well when correctly matched to the target material, but if you are not getting the results you need Advanced mode may help. The Sense and Threshold parameters function as follows:

- Sense – governs the sensitivity of the detection to the attack transients in the signal (high setting = more sensitivity).
- Threshold – determines the number of lower level attack transients which are taken into account (low setting = more hitpoints in the low level parts of the waveform).

After you have made your settings click on the process button to commence hitpoint calculation. Hitpoints are calculated for the current range selection, or the whole clip if no range selection has been made. Thereafter, these hitpoints remain attached to the clip and may be shown or hidden in the Sample editor using the Hitpoint mode button. Hitpoints may be re-calculated at any time using Audio/Hitpoints/Calculate Hitpoints. You might need to do this when you have made a new range selection or are not satisfied with the result You can remove existing hitpoints at any time using Audio/Hitpoints/Remove Hitpoints.

The number of displayed hitpoints depends upon the hitpoint sensitivity slider and the setting in the Use menu. The hitpoint sensitivity slider displays more hitpoints the more you move it to the right. When the Use menu is set to 'All', all the calculated hitpoints are visible. When the Use menu is set to one of the note values (1/4, 1/8, 1/16, 1/32 or metric bias) only those hitpoints which are near to the chosen note resolution are shown.

Hitpoints may also be manually entered by selecting the Hitpoint edit tool and clicking in the display while holding Alt. However, wherever possible you are advised to use the calculated hitpoints since normally these more accurately represent the true attack transients of your audio material.

Important

Version 3.1 of Cubase introduced a new hitpoint calculation algorithm which does not use the Hitpoints Detection dialogue shown in Figure 8.73, above. Hitpoints are now detected directly when you select Calculate hitpoints (Audio menu) or the Hitpoints mode button. The new algorithm is more accurate and easier to use than its predecessor.

Info

Calculated hitpoints are *always* placed at zero crossing points in the waveform. This is *not* the case for manually entered or manually moved hitpoints. To ensure that manual manipulations of hitpoints are placed at zero crossing points, activate the Zero crossing point button on the Sample editor toolbar.

Editing hitpoints

Hitpoint editing is managed using the Hitpoint edit tool. This is often used in combination with the Hitpoint Sensitivity slider in order to finish up with the desired number of hitpoints at the appropriate positions in the waveform display. The Hitpoint edit tool is a multi-function tool featuring the following modes:

- Play – when moved between two hitpoints the pointer changes to a speaker symbol allowing you to audition the audio between the two points. This is used to verify the accuracy and suitability of the calculated hitpoints.
- Insert - moving the pointer to the central area of the display while holding Alt (at which time a pencil symbol is shown) allows you to manually insert a hitpoint. Recommended only if regular calculated hitpoints cannot fulfill your requirements.
- Move – locating the pointer on a hitpoint's handle in the upper part of the display (at which time the hitpoint is highlighted in green) allows you to drag the hitpoint to a new location.
- Disable – locating the pointer on a hitpoint's handle in the upper part of the display while holding Alt allows you to disable the hitpoint (the hitpoint is highlighted in green and a disable cross appears). Disabling is useful when your chosen sensitivity setting has given you correctly positioned hitpoints throughout most of the waveform except for a small number of 'rogue' hitpoints. Disabling the offending hitpoints provides a quick and convenient solution (see Figure 8.74). If required, disabled hitpoints can be re-enabled by clicking on the hitpoint's handle a second time. (Note: disabling a manually inserted hitpoint actually deletes it).

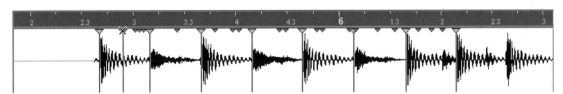

- Lock – clicking once on the hitpoint handle locks the hitpoint (at which time it is shown in dark blue). Locking a hitpoint ensures that it is not affected by further manipulations of the hitpoint sensitivity slider. This is useful when you wish to choose a specific selection of hitpoints which are at the correct positions in the waveform and then remove the rest by lowering the hitpoint sensitivity slider. Any locked hitpoints remain in the display regardless of how low you take the sensitivity slider (see Figure 8.75).

Figure 8.74
Disable 'rogue' hitpoints using the Hitpoint edit tool

Figure 8.75
Lock the best hitpoints and then remove all other hitpoints by lowering the Hitpoint sensitivity slider

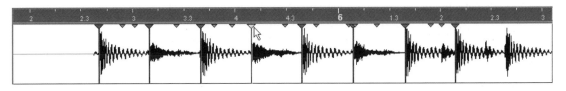

Audio slicing a loop in the Sample editor

As outlined in 'Creating and editing Hitpoints in the Sample editor', above, hit-points allow you to divide your audio material into its main rhythmic components. In Cubase SX, each section marked by a pair of hitpoints is known as an audio slice. In the case of drum loops, this often means that each audio slice contains a single constituent sound or 'hit' for each beat or fraction of a beat in the loop.

Hitpoints and audio slices, therefore, provide a way of breaking up drum loops into their constituent beats. Once audio slices have been created in Cubase SX, the sliced drum loop automatically follows any changes in tempo without changing the pitch of the sound and without the side-effects of time stretching (see 'Gaps in the audio', below, for an exception). This results in more natural sounding loops when you adjust them away from their original tempi and allows you to freely use tempo changes throughout the project. (The other technique which allows you to freely use tempo changes is to define the tempo of the audio using the Audio tempo definition tool and then to activate Musical mode. For more details, see the section entitled 'Defining the tempo of the audio and activating Musical mode', above).

To create audio slices for a drum loop in Cubase SX, proceed as follows:

* Select the audio event which contains the target loop and double click on it to open the Sample editor. Find and select the loop using the Range selection tool. Activate the local loop and play buttons in the toolbar or use Shift + G to commence loop playback automatically (for successful loop playback some versions of the program may require de-activating of the Show audio event button). Fine tune the loop by adjusting the start and end points. Make sure that the start point corresponds with the downbeat of the first beat of the loop and adjust the end point so that the loop plays back over the required number of beats (Figure 8.76). Ignore this first step if you are using a library drum loop which is already tightly edited.

Figure 8.76

Adjust the loop so that it plays for the required number of beats

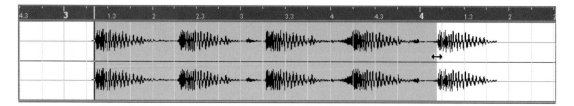

* When you are happy with the loop, click on the Hitpoint mode button to calculate the hitpoints. Adjust the sensitivity slider and other settings so that one hitpoint appears for each beat or sub-division of the beat throughout the loop (Figure 8.77). Attempt to use only those hitpoints

Figure 8.77

Click on the Hitpoint mode button and adjust the Hitpoint Sensitivity slider to calculate the hitpoints

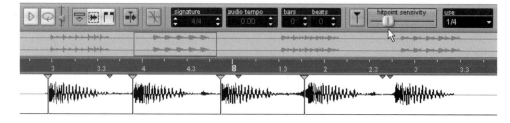

which are created automatically following the techniques outlined in 'Calculating hitpoints' and 'Editing hitpoints', above. The more accurate the audio slices you create, the more accurate will be the handling of the result when played back at different tempos.

- Test each audio slice by clicking between any two hitpoints with the Hitpoint edit tool, at which time the pointer changes to a loudspeaker symbol (Figure 8.78). The slice turns blue as it is played. Attempt to produce slices where one sound is present in each slice. If the results are not satisfactory you may need to re-adjust the hitpoints.

Figure 8.78
Audition each audio slice by clicking between each pair of hitpoints with the Hitpoint edit tool

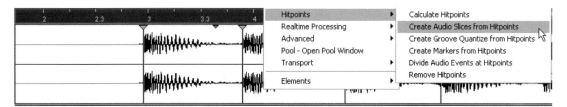

- When you are happy with all the slices, select Audio / Hitpoints / Create Audio Slices from Hitpoints (Figure 8.79). If you have not already done so, a dialogue appears requesting you to enter a tempo for the audio (for details of how to do this, see the section entitled 'Defining the tempo of the audio and activating Musical mode', above).

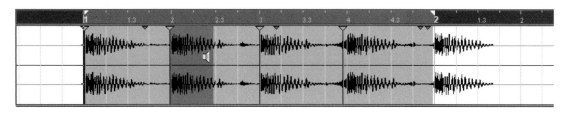

- As soon as you click on Create Audio Slices, the Sample editor is automatically closed and the original audio event in the Project window disappears, to be replaced by an audio part which contains the new audio slices (Figure 8.80). The sliced part is automatically adjusted to the current tempo of the project. Change the tempo of the project and the sliced part follows.

Figure 8.79
Select 'Create Audio Slices from Hitpoints' in the Hitpoints sub-menu

Hitpoints and audio slices might also be used for other purposes, such as extracting, replacing or interchanging individual sounds within a drum loop, extracting a groove template which follows the timing (or feel) of the loop, and also allow you to change the timing of the loop manually.

Figure 8.80
A new audio part containing the audio slices is created in the Project window

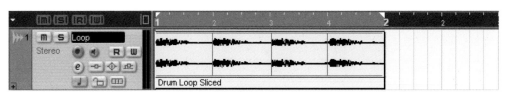

Processing audio slices in the Audio Part editor

Creating audio slices in the Sample editor (outlined above) results in a new audio part in the Project window which contains the sliced data. If you proceed to change the tempo of Cubase SX by a relatively small amount, the results remain fairly transparent. However, more radical tempo changes result in gaps in the audio as the sliced events are moved further apart. This problem is solved in the Audio Part editor. The Audio Part editor is also good for creative manipulations of audio slices, such as quantizing.

Closing the gap

Reducing the tempo by more than a few beats-per-minute results in gaps between each of the audio slices. Figure 8.81 shows the audio slices for a drum loop where the project has been set to the original tempo of the loop, at 120bpm.

Figure 8.81
Audio slices for a drum loop set to its original tempo of 120bpm

When the tempo is reduced to 110bpm gaps appear between the audio slices which interfere with the successful playback of the loop (Figure 8.82).

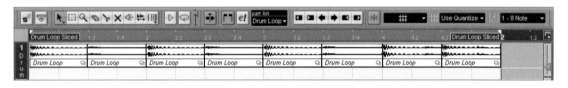

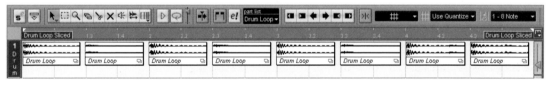

Figure 8.82
Gaps between the slices when the tempo is reduced

To cure the problem, select the part in the Project window (or press Ctrl + A to select all the events in the Audio Part editor) and select 'Close Gaps' in the Audio menu. This applies time stretch to each individual slice and closes all the gaps (Figure 8.83).

Figure 8.83
Close the gaps using the 'Close Gaps' function

The Close Gaps function should be used only when you are sure that there will be no more tempo changes. If at a later date you decide that you wish to change the tempo again, you must revert to the original unstretched audio material.

Increasing the tempo by more than a few beats-per-minute compresses the sliced events more tightly together resulting in overlaps and sometimes occasional clicks. To cure the clicks try setting up auto fades in the Auto fades dialogue for the track. Tick 'auto crossfades' and deselect 'use project settings'. Try between 15ms and 30ms for the crossfade. Alternatively, try activating the fade in and fade out options with a 5ms to 10ms fade time.

Changing the feel of the audio slices using quantize

It is sometimes appropriate to change the timing of the audio slices using the quantize functions. This can result in a loop with a tighter feel or a completely new groove. The results depend very much on how you have sliced the audio. For audio slices which have been divided into 1/8 note segments try the following:

- Double-click on the audio part containing the audio slices to open the Audio Part editor. Select all the slices by pressing Ctrl + A on the computer keyboard.
- Open the Quantize setup dialogue from the Quantize selector menu. Set 1/8 notes in Grid and Straight in Type with a swing factor of between 1 and 100%.
- Click on the Quantize selector menu Apply button. Watch as the events in the Audio Part editor are moved in time and listen to the results.

If you create something you like, try using the 'Close Gaps' function to produce a smoother effect. This technique is highly dependent on the nature of the target material. The results can be subtle or radical and is particularly effective if you need to mangle and transform your loops. Other techniques include the use of fades and crossfades and manipulating the slices manually.

Creating a groove template from hitpoints

As outlined above, hitpoints mark those points in the audio waveform where there is rapid amplitude gain (attack transients). In the case of drum and percussion loops, these points correspond to the rhythmic pulse of the material. Since, by calculating the hitpoints, we have effectively created a rhythmic template of the performance, why not extract this data for use in other parts of Cubase SX? This is indeed what you can do using 'Create Groove Quantize from Hitpoints' in the Audio/Hitpoints menu. To create your own groove quantize template proceed as follows:

- Double-click on the audio event which contains the target loop to open the Sample editor. (To avoid damage to existing material it is best to work on a separate copy of the audio file). Make a range selection in the waveform display using the Range selection tool.
- Commence loop playback by selecting Shift + G. Fine tune the loop so that it matches a precise number of bars and beats (for certain versions of Cubase, de-activate the Show Audio event button on the toolbar to remain within the loop during playback).
- Select the Audio tempo definition tool. Select Transport / 'Locators to selection' (or press P) to set the blue tempo definition ruler bar to the range selection. Define the number of bars/beats of the audio in your chosen range selection. If you already know the tempo of the audio you can enter this directly into the tempo field.

Tip

By default, the 'Close gaps' function in the Audio / Advanced menu uses the current time stretch algorithm selected in File / Preferences / Editing / Audio. If you most often work with drum and percussion audio slices, try activating 'Always use drum mode for close gaps'.

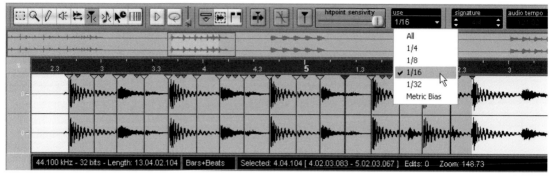

Figure 8.84

Selecting 1/16 notes in the Use menu finds the hitpoints nearest to the 1/16th note divisions of the bar

- Select Audio / Hitpoints / Calculate hitpoints to calculate hitpoints over the chosen passage.
- Adjust the sensitivity slider so that one hitpoint appears for each hit in the rhythm or, if preferred, so that one hitpoint appears at each 1/16 note interval. If the latter is your choice, select 16 in the Use menu and adjust the sensitivity slider as appropriate (as shown in Figure 8.84).

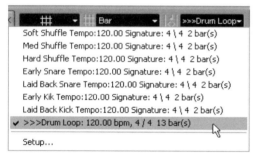

Figure 8.85

Use Create Groove Quantize to create a new groove quantize preset in the Quantize type menu

- Select Audio / Advanced / 'Set audio event from loop'. Select Audio / Advanced / 'Set tempo from event'.
- Select Audio / Hitpoints / 'Create groove quantize from hitpoints' to create the groove template.
- Open the Quantize type menu to reveal the newly added groove which appears last in the list with the same name as the audio event from which it was extracted (Figure 8.85).

Matching the feel of an audio bass line to a MIDI kick drum

Once you have sliced an audio event into its rhythmic components (as outlined in 'Audio slicing a loop in the Sample editor', above) it becomes possible to quantize it using the quantize functions found in the MIDI menu or via the Quantize setup dialogue. This means that you could, for example, impose the timing characteristics of a MIDI drum part onto an audio bass recording (to get the timing of the bass drum and bass line tightly synchronised). To achieve this proceed as follows:

- Select the MIDI kick drum part and select 'Part to Groove' in the MIDI/Advanced Quantize sub-menu. The extracted groove template appears in the Quantize type menu.
- Double click on the audio bass event and calculate hitpoints as described in the section entitled 'Calculating hitpoints' (above). Aim for one hitpoint on each bass note.
- Select 'Create audio slices' in the Audio/advanced sub-menu. The event is split and contained within a new audio part in the Project window.
- Select the resulting audio part and select the groove template as extracted in the first step, above, in the Quantize type menu.
- Select 'Over quantize' in the MIDI menu. The events within the selected sliced audio part are moved according to the feel of the MIDI bass drum groove. (See Chapter 6 for more quantize details).

Info

You can undo/redo all audio editing using the undo/redo functions in the Edit menu or by pressing Ctrl + Z (undo) or Ctrl + Shift + Z (redo). You can also step back through your edits using the Edit history window (select 'History' in the Edit menu). The edit history is cleared when you close the project.

Audio processing

This chapter describes the audio processing functions found in the Process sub-menu of the Audio menu. As well as providing a description of each function, there are explanations of how you might use them for creative and corrective purposes. The audio processing functions are for 'off-line' processing only. Off-line processing is that which does not occur in real-time and usually implies some kind of 'permanent' change to the stored audio files.

The audio processing functions act upon audio data on the hard disk but due to the manner in which Cubase SX has been designed, two types of undo functions are available. Firstly, the normal undo/redo commands in the Edit menu are available while your project is running. Secondly, after you close the project, almost all audio editing can be modified or removed at a later date using the Offline Process History dialogue (Audio menu). This means that you can use offline audio processing techniques with an unprecedented amount of freedom since you can always go back to the original sound of your audio files. However, you may not be able to individually modify, replace or remove each part of the processing. These instances include multiple audio processing operations where the length of the audio clip has been changed at some stage, such as processing which employs time stretch or cut and paste operations at some point in the multiple process. These latter functions can only be individually modified or removed if they were the last editing operations which took place (see Offline Process History, below).

The processing options

Figure 9.1 shows the audio processing options in Cubase SX's Process menu. You can also process your audio in the same manner using the audio plug-in effects in the Plug-ins menu (these are more often used for real-time processing and are described in Chapter 12). The basic operation of the majority of the audio processing functions is fairly easy but it is not quite so obvious how and why you might use them. The 'how and why' forms the subject matter of this chapter.

What gets affected

The processing functions may be applied to audio events, audio clips or range selections. With audio clips, the processing is applied to the whole clip. With audio events, only that part of the associated audio clip which is referenced

| Envelope |
| Fade In |
| Fade Out |
| Gain |
| Merge Clipboard |
| Noise Gate |
| Normalize |
| Phase Reverse |
| Pitch Shift |
| Remove DC Offset |
| Resample |
| Reverse |
| Silence |
| Stereo Flip |
| Time Stretch |

Figure 9.1
The functions in the Process menu

Info

While using audio processing at the event level in the Project window is highly useful, detailed work often benefits from working at the sample level in the Sample editor. For this purpose, you would normally be working with specific range selections made with the range selection tool.

by the event gets processed. With range selections, only that part of the associated audio clip which is referenced by the range gets processed. With multiple event selections, all audio events have the same process applied in equal amounts. For example, if you select two consecutive events and apply fade out processing, the fade does not occur over the whole length of the two events but within each single event.

Common buttons in the audio processing dialogues

Most of the audio processing functions feature a dialogue window which opens when they are selected. Each window has a number of common buttons and menus available. These include, in all windows, the Preview, Process and Cancel buttons and, in the envelope and fade dialogues, the presets menu and Store and Remove buttons. The Preview button allows you to hear the result of the processing before it is actually applied. When in Preview mode, the audio is played back in a continuous loop and you can hear the effect of any changes you make to the parameters in the dialogue on the next lap of the cycle. Some parameter changes re-start the audio instantaneously. All this is very useful for experimenting. The Process button processes the target audio when you are satisfied with the settings you have made. The Cancel button allows you to leave the dialogue without applying any processing. The presets menu and buttons allow you to store (or remove) your own presets. Some dialogues have More and Less buttons for showing or hiding a number of additional parameters.

The Process functions

Envelope

Info

The difference between spline and damped spline curve modes – regular spline mode radically affects the shape of the neighbouring parts of the curve as you drag the curve handle within the display and sets up a naturally balanced curve, whereas damped spline mode only has a minimal effect on the neighbouring area and sets up a curve which is more linear. Damped spline mode is therefore easier to control when dragging handles in the display. The curve modes are readily interchangeable, so feel free to experiment to get the desired result.

The Envelope function (Figure 9.2) applies an amplitude envelope to the selected audio. Spline, damped spline or linear curves are available and you create your own curve by clicking and dragging anywhere within the display, whereupon a new breakpoint is added to the curve. Breakpoints can be dragged to any position within the display and are deleted by dragging them outside of the display window. There are always at least three breakpoints in the display; one at the start, one at the end and one somewhere in between. The uppermost limit of the display represents unity gain so that a straight line drawn at the top of the display results in no change in amplitude in the target audio.

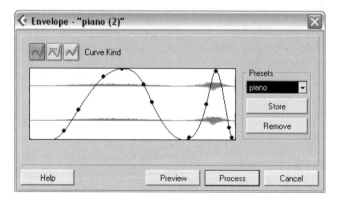

Figure 9.2
Envelope dialogue

The Envelope function is good for applying multiple breakpoint envelopes to audio files in a number of creative and corrective applications. For example, unwanted breaths or syllables which are too loud within a vocal performance can be tamed by carefully reducing the level at the offending points in the waveform. For such correction, select each offending part of the waveform in the Sample editor and apply your chosen envelope to each in turn. If you are deleting unwanted breaths between vocal lines or within speech, a 'bowl' shaped envelope produces more natural results than applying silence. Alternatively, for creating effects and new instrument tones you might try cutting the attack portion of each note of any chosen instrumental recording. Figure 9.2 shows a multiple breakpoint envelope which was used to cut out the attack portion of the notes of two piano chords, producing smooth, volume swells containing only the decay elements of the sound.

Fade in and Fade out

The Fade in and Fade out dialogues provide an alternative method of applying fades when you do not wish to use the usual blue fade handles within the audio events. The advantage of using the blue handles is that a number of audio events which refer to the same audio clip can each have an independent fade curve. Conversely, fades set up from the Process menu are applied directly to the audio clip. This is advantageous when you require global fade settings which are applied to all events which refer to the same section of an audio clip.

The Fade in and Fade out functions open similar dialogue windows, except that one has the inverse fade characteristics of the other (Figure 9.3). The fade dialogues allow you to set the characteristics of the fade curves by clicking on any of the eight preset curve buttons or you can set up custom shapes by dragging handles directly in the curve display. The curve of the Fade in dialogue always starts in the lower left corner of the display and finishes in the upper right corner (the inverse is true for the Fade out dialogue). Spline, damped spline and linear curve characteristics are available and you can save and recall your own presets.

The Fade functions are sometimes useful for applying custom fades to the starts and ends of stereo pre-mastered material, (although if the material has been produced in Cubase SX, fading is sometimes achieved as part of the mix using the master faders, especially if you are using dither after the master faders). Fade in and fade out can also be used over a very short section at

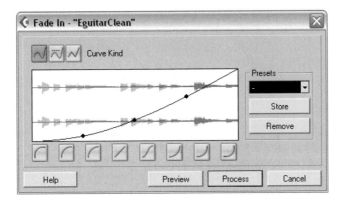

Figure 9.3
Fade in dialogue

the beginning or end of an audio file to mask any sharp transients or digital clicks. This would normally be achieved at a high zoom factor in the Sample editor and results in an audio file which starts and ends more smoothly.

Gain

The Gain function (Figure 9.4) allows you to add gain to (increase) or attenuate (decrease) the amplitude level of the target audio between -50dB and +20dB. The parameters include a main gain slider and pre and post crossfade sliders. As you move the slider, the percentage increase in level is shown as well as the amount of increase/decrease in dBs.

Figure 9.4
Gain dialogue

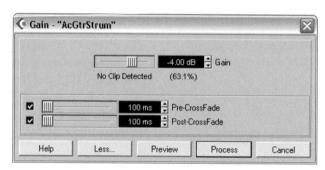

When in preview mode, any audio clipping is indicated in the text line below the main gain slider. This is excellent for warning you of marginal clipping which may otherwise go unnoticed. The pre and post crossfade sliders allow you to apply the gain change gradually either at the start or end of the target audio. A Pre-Crossfade setting indicates that the gain change should start gradually from the onset of the target audio selection and should only reach its full effect at the time specified in the Pre-Crossfade field. A Post-Crossfade setting indicates that the gain change should gradually be removed, starting at the time specified in the Post-Crossfade field before the end of the audio selection.

The Gain function is a powerful level management tool which might be applied to recordings with problematic level changes, such as a vocalist who is occasionally singing either too close or too far away from the microphone or for cutting down sudden extreme peaks or resonances in the audio material. It is also a useful alternative for manually reducing background noise and interference in vocal and lead guitar parts. For detailed editing, it is a good idea to work with the Gain function in the Sample editor (with the Snap to Zero button activated).

Merge Clipboard

Merge Clipboard (Figure 9.5) allows you to merge the contents of the clipboard with the currently selected range when working in the Sample editor. Merge Clipboard is only available if you have used Cut or Copy in the Sample editor (i.e. when the clipboard contains audio data) and no merge operation is possible unless you have made a range selection. The merge operation begins at the start point of the range selection and continues to the end of the selection or until the end of the clipboard contents (whichever comes first).

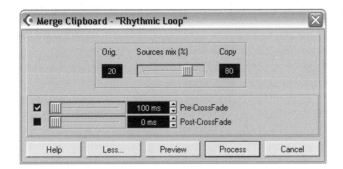

Figure 9.5
Merge Clipboard dialogue

The Merge Clipboard dialogue features a percentage slider where you can select the percentage level of the original audio (the current selection) and the copied audio (the audio data in the clipboard), and pre and post fade options for the merging operation. The pre and post options allow you to merge the clipboard gradually either at the start or end of the target audio. A Pre-Crossfade setting indicates that the clipboard should be merged gradually from the onset of the target audio selection and should only reach its full effect at the time specified in the Pre-Crossfade field. A Post-Crossfade setting indicates that merged audio should gradually be removed, starting at the time specified in the Post-Crossfade field before the end of the audio selection.

Merging audio is good for creating special effects and hybrid instrument, drum and percussion sounds. For example, by merging the audio from a number of different snare drums you can create your own hybrid snare sound. In this context, it is worth experimenting with the pre and post crossfade options of the Merge Clipboard dialogue in combination with the percentage slider, where you might effectively retain the attack of the original instrument and merge the decay of the clipboard. The same technique could be applied to create your own hybrid bass drum sound. This is particularly applicable to working with audio slices in hitpoint mode where it is easier to copy and merge between different slices. When copying and merging between different audio clips try working with two or more Sample editor windows open simultaneously.

Noise Gate

A noise gate is an automatic amplitude level control device which radically attenuates the level of the target signal whenever it falls below a certain threshold. This is commonly used to filter out unwanted background noise and interference in the inactive parts of speech or musical performance. Noise gates are very often implemented as real-time devices but the Noise Gate function in the Process menu allows you to process your audio in a more permanent and detailed fashion.

The Noise Gate dialogue (Figure 9.6) features the common parameters associated with noise gating.

The Threshold parameter sets the level at which the gate begins to close. When the input signal falls below the threshold, the target signal is attenuated (cut). The Attack parameter determines the speed with which the noise gate opens (to allow the signal through) when the signal rises above the threshold. The Minimum Opening Time parameter sets a fixed time for which

Tip

To merge the attack of one drum sound with the decay of another, try setting the Merge Clipboard percentage slider to '100% copy' and adjust the pre-crossfade to between 50 and 100 ms. Activate the pre-crossfade tick box. This mixes the attack of the original with the decay of the copied sound currently in the clipboard.

Figure 9.6
Noise Gate dialogue

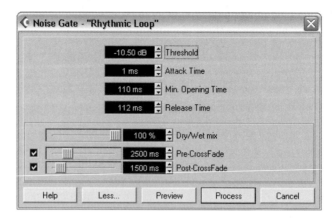

the gate is held open once the threshold has been exceeded. This allows you to impose a time for which the gate is sure to stay open in material featuring radical level changes which might otherwise cause erratic behaviour in the gating action. The Release Time parameter determines how fast the signal is attenuated when it falls below the threshold. The Dry/Wet mix slider allows you to determine the mix between the original signal and the gated signal. The Pre and Post Crossfade options allow you to impose the gating action gradually either at the start or end of the target audio. A Pre-Crossfade setting indicates that the gating action should occur gradually from the onset of the target audio selection and should only reach its full effect at the time specified in the Pre-Crossfade field. A Post-Crossfade setting indicates that the gating effect should gradually be removed, starting at the time specified in the Post-Crossfade field before the end of the audio selection.

Cubase SX's Noise Gate function is a useful alternative to the Dynamics and VST Dynamics plug-ins found in the Plug-ins menu. For the gating of background noise, try setting the Attack, Opening and Release times to 1ms, 100ms and 100ms respectively and then find the best threshold level for your target material. Fine tune the parameters to suit the sound and the gating effect you require. More elaborate use of Noise Gate might involve setting up a tight gate on the target signal which produces an extreme gating effect and then fading this effect in and out using the Pre and Post Crossfade parameters. This works particularly well with drum loops and rhythm material. Figure 9.6 shows the settings used for an eight second drum loop where a tight gating effect is gradually imposed over the first 2.5 secs, remains at its maximum for around 4 secs and is then gradually reduced over the remaining 1.5 secs.

Normalize

Normalisation allows you to increase (or sometimes decrease) the overall amplitude of an audio file according to a specified maximum level. The function is available on most digital audio editors and traditionally involves the boosting of the overall signal up to a chosen maximum. The process functions by finding the current maximum peak in the chosen audio and establishing how many dBs it is below the new maximum level you have chosen. The whole signal is then boosted by this number of dBs.

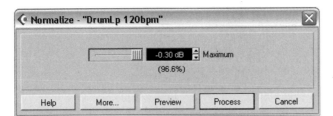

Figure 9.7
Normalize dialogue

The Normalize dialogue (Figure 9.7) in Cubase SX features just one main slider: the maximum level parameter. This is where you choose the new required maximum level for the selected audio material. The processing can also be applied gradually at the start or end of the selection using the Pre and Post Crossfade options. A Pre-Crossfade setting indicates that normalisation occurs gradually from the onset of the target audio selection and only reaches its full effect at the time specified in the Pre-Crossfade field. A Post-Crossfade setting indicates that normalisation should gradually be removed, starting at the time specified in the Post-Crossfade field before the end of the audio selection.

The maximum level possible is 0dB but it is advisable to normalise to slightly below the theoretical maximum, especially for mastering or pre-mastering applications (try -0.3dB). Normalisation is generally used to boost the level of audio files which were recorded at too low a level. While this can help make up for a poorly recorded signal you should be aware that the noise floor is also boosted by the same number of dBs as the rest of the recording. Normalisation should not be used as a routine 'quick fix' for poor recording techniques. The best remedy for sounds recorded at too low a level is to record them again at a higher level.

Normalisation might also be used to boost the signal to its absolute maximum before transferring material to CD. This is common for rock, pop and dance material. However, if you are intending to boost the loudness of the target audio, normalisation is not the best option. Normalisation does not boost signals according to their perceived loudness but according to the highest amplitude peak in the selected material. This means that normalising finished tracks to the same maximum level does not necessarily result in tracks which have the same perceived loudness. Loudness is governed, among other things, by the average signal level of the material and not the extreme peaks. Loudness maximisers, multi-band compressors and other kinds of processing are often a better choice for finished tracks.

Normalize should preferably not be used several times on the same audio file since this can result in degradation of the signal. Also bear in mind that normalisation should not be necessary at all if your audio has already been recorded or mixed at an optimum level.

Tip

Using normalisation to adjust the level of individual songs intended to be included together on a CD release is never a good idea. If you must use normalisation, it is best applied as a single process for all songs at once. This avoids unnatural dynamics changes where the relative perceived loudness between songs may become detrimentally exaggerated.

Tip

If you wish to know the current maximum peak amplitude and the average loudness of an audio clip, select the clip in the Pool and then select Statistics from the Audio menu. The resulting Statistics window shows the maximum peak amplitude (Peak Amplitude), which equates to the single highest peak found in the selection, and the average RMS power (Average), which equates to the average loudness of the signal.

Phase Reverse

The Phase Reverse function inverts the phase of the selection. In effect, this turns the waveform upside down since all positive elements in the signal (those above the zero amplitude line) become negative, and all negative elements in the signal (those below the zero amplitude line) become positive. This is clearly demonstrated if you use Phase Reverse on a small test selection in the Sample editor at high magnification.

Many mixing consoles, including Cubase SX's own mixer, feature a phase reversal button on each channel which produces a similar result. One reason for reversing the phase of a signal is when it forms the left or right channel of a stereo image which has been recorded out of phase. With one of the signals out of phase the stereo image lacks clarity and there may also be a loss of bass frequencies. The situation becomes even worse if you try to mix the two out of phase channels into a mono signal. This can result in some of the frequencies disappearing altogether.

If you suspect that a stereo file is out of phase try applying Phase Reverse to one of the channels and then compare the result to the original. When applied to a mono selection, Phase Reverse has no configurable parameters and so does not feature a dialogue window. When applied to a stereo selection Phase Reverse features a dialogue window and phase reversal can be applied to both channels, or to the left or right channel using the 'Phase Reverse on' menu (Figure 9.8).

Figure 9.8
Phase Reverse dialogue

Pitch shift

The Pitch Shift function allows the changing of the pitch of the selected audio with or without changing its length. It features two pages: a regular Transpose page and an Envelope-based page. These are accessed by clicking on the Transpose and Envelope tabs at the top of the dialogue. The Pitch Shift function is used for corrective pitch manipulation, the creation of basic harmonies and the creation of special effects.

Transpose page

The Transpose page (Figure 9.9) features a virtual keyboard and three parameter sections; Pitch Shift Settings, Pitch Shift Base and Pitch Shift Mode.

The virtual keyboard display

The virtual keyboard offers a visual overview of the pitch shift settings. A red marker shows the position of the base pitch which provides a reference point from which to implement pitch shift operations. A blue marker indicates the amount of pitch shift relative to the base pitch (the red marker). When the Multi Shift box is ticked there may be a number of blue markers in the display forming a chord for creating harmonies. The position of the blue marker(s) may be modified by clicking directly on the virtual keyboard, at which time the pitches at the positions of the red and blue markers are played back so that you can hear the musical interval. If, at any time, you wish to hear the musical interval again, click on the Listen Key button. The position of the red marker (the base pitch) may be modified by clicking directly on the virtual keyboard while pressing Alt.

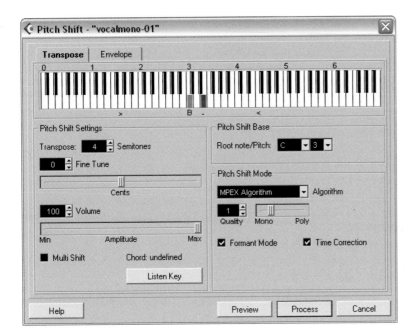

Figure 9.9
The Transpose Page of the Pitch Shift dialogue

Pitch Shift Settings

This section allows you to set a pitch shift amount using a course value of between −16 and +16 semitones and a fine tuning value between −200 and +200 cents. There is also an amplitude slider for regulating the amplitude of the resulting pitch shifted audio. Activating Multi Shift mode allows you to specify a number of simultaneous pitch shifted notes by clicking on the virtual keyboard. A different amplitude may be set for each note in the chord. To include the base note in the result, click on the red marker in the virtual keyboard so that it turns blue. Clicking on the Listen Chord button allows you to hear the resulting harmony in the form of a chord.

Pitch Shift Base

This offers a way of changing the position of the base pitch (the red marker) using note and octave values.

Pitch Shift Mode

This section provides a choice of two pitch shift algorithms, Timebandit Standard and MPEX algorithm, with Formant Mode and Time Correction tick boxes.

- Timebandit Standard – this is a good all-round algorithm which processes the target data relatively quickly. It gives slightly lesser audio quality when compared to MPEX but is excellent for producing sound effects when stretching audio by large amounts.
- MPEX Algorithm – MPEX is a proprietary time stretch algorithm designed by Prosoniq for optimum audio quality. MPEX stands for 'Minimum Perceived Loss Time Compression/Expansion'. This maximises the quality of the results but requires more processing time. Adjust the mono/poly

slider to 1 for monophonic material and to 2, 3 or 4 for progressively better quality pitch shifting of polyphonic material. Option 4 offers the best quality for polyphonic material but the processing time is slower.

- Formant Mode – when activated (ticked), formant mode optimises the processing for vocal material and helps avoid some of the worst side-effects of pitch shifting. For processing most other kinds of audio material, formant mode should be de-activated. Formant mode is available with MPEX only.
- Time Correction – when time correction is activated, pitch shifting does not affect the length of the resulting audio. When time correction is de-activated, pitch shifting changes the length of the audio, resulting in an effect similar to changing the playback speed of a tape recorder.

Envelope page

The Envelope page (Figure 9.10) features a waveform display with a user con-figurable tuning curve and two parameter sections: Pitch Shift Settings and Pitch Shift Mode.

Figure 9.10
The Envelope page of the Pitch Shift dialogue

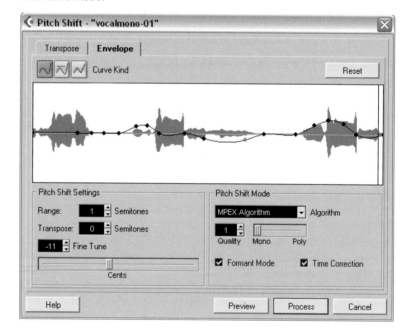

Waveform display

The waveform display features the waveform of the target audio and a user configurable tuning envelope. The horizontal centre line in the display represents zero pitch shift. The shape of the curve is changed by clicking directly in the waveform display, at which time a handle appears at the corresponding point along the curve. The handle is dragged to a new position to change the shape of the curve. When the curve rises above the centre line the pitch rises and when the curve falls below the centre line the pitch descends. To delete a handle drag it outside of the display. The currently selected handle is shown in red. Spline, damped spline and linear curve shapes are available.

Pitch Shift Settings

The Pitch Shift Settings feature Range, Transpose and Fine Tune parameters. Range determines the pitch range, represented vertically in the display, between −16 and +16 semitones. Transpose allows you to transpose the currently selected handle numerically as opposed to graphically in one semitone steps. Fine Tune provides numerical transposition of the currently selected handle in one cent steps.

Pitch Shift Mode

This section is identical to that found in the regular Transpose page (see 'Pitch Shift Mode' in the Transpose section, above, for a full explanation).

Pitch Shift summary

Using Pitch Shift in Envelope mode is excellent for manually re-tuning a melody which a vocalist has sung out of tune, and other kinds of corrective pitch manipulation. It is also excellent for the creation of sound effects when the Time Correction function is de-activated. In this context, try increasing the range of the display and using spline-shaped curves for smooth pitch and speed changes.

Pitch shifting can produce undesirable side-effects, the most common of which is a 'chipmunk' effect when vocals or speech are pitch shifted upwards. When shifted downwards the human voice can take on an equally 'alien' character and may become unintelligible. This is minimised by activating Formant mode but it is impossible to eradicate these side-effects completely. As a rough guide, vocal sounds which are pitch shifted up or down by more than 3-4 semitones begin to suffer undesirable side-effects.

The values you finally choose for any pitch shifting depends upon the audio characteristics of the material being processed and the desired effect you require. For example, if you are producing sound effects, you may be searching for the very audio artifacts which somebody who is transposing a vocal line is attempting to avoid.

Tip

To create an effect of the audio slowing down like reducing the speed on a tape recorder, use the Pitch shift function in Envelope mode. Try a damped spline type curve and a range of 16 semitones. Click in the centre point of the display to enter a new handle and then drag the existing right-most handle to the lower right corner. Select the timebandit standard algorithm, de-activate 'Time correction', and preview the effect.

Remove DC Offset

A DC Offset occurs when there is too much direct current (DC) in the signal. In extreme cases, a DC Offset manifests itself as a waveform which is not visually centred around the zero axis in the waveform display. This is usually due to mismatches between audio equipment at the time of recording. A DC Offset is problematic since it affects where the zero crossing points in the waveform appear and interferes which certain kinds of processing.

The Remove DC Offset function eliminates the DC Offset. It should normally be applied to whole clips or whole audio files since a DC Offset is invariably present throughout an entire recording. If you wish to check a clip for DC offset, select it in the Pool and then select Statistics in the Audio menu.

Remove DC Offset has no dialogue window.

Resample

The Resample function changes the sample rate of the selected audio material. Changing the sample rate has the effect of changing the pitch and the length of the target audio. The interface features two fields where you can allocate a new sample rate directly or change the sample rate in terms of a percentage. The original sample rate of the selected audio is shown at the top of the dialogue. You can change the sample rate directly by double clicking in the 'New rate' field and entering a new rate using the computer keyboard. Alternatively, you can change the percentage value in the 'Difference' field.

Resample allows the changing of the pitch and length over an extremely wide range providing a percentage range of between -99% and +1000%. Negative percentages speed up the sound, making the length shorter and the pitch higher. Positive percentages slow down the sound, making the length longer and the pitch lower. A value of 0% means that the audio is at its original sample rate (i.e. no change), a value of 100% is twice the sample rate, and a value of 1000% is eleven times the sample rate. -50% is half the original sample rate. Using the more extreme settings results in audio played back at ultra slow or ultra fast speeds. Resample is always worth a try for the creation of special effects and is an alternative to the Pitch Shift or Time Stretch functions.

Figure 9.11
Resample dialogue

Reverse

The Reverse function simply reverses the selection. In other words, after processing, you can play the audio backwards. Great! But what could we use this for? Reversing certain kinds of audio material can produce a kind of crescendo, similar to a drum roll, and favourite material for this kind of effect includes snare drum hits, (preferably with a reverb tail), and cymbals. Reversals on any kind of audio material can sometimes produce startling results which are good for special effects, and shorter reversed segments can often find a place in a rhythmic pattern. See 'Combination Processing' below for an example of how to use the Reverse function in combination with other processing.

The Reverse function has no dialogue window.

Silence

The Silence function overwrites the current selection with complete silence. This is most often useful in the Sample editor when working in fine detail. Much of the time you might clean up audio events in the Project window by dragging the start and end points to mask the unwanted material but, if there are a large number of very small and precise sections which need to be silenced, it may be easier to select them in the Sample editor and use the Silence function. When working with the Silence function in fine detail in the Sample editor, activate the Snap to Zero button.

Inserting absolute silence between the lyrics of a vocal track or speech is not always an effective solution for eradicating the background noise in between the wanted parts of the performance since it produces an unnatural effect where the silence actually accentuates the background noise in the wanted material. The technique may be adequate if you have recorded a vocal with minimal background noise. Real-time noise gating or the use of the Noise Gate function (outlined above) often produce better results.

The Silence function has no dialogue window.

Stereo Flip

The Stereo Flip function is for various kinds of stereo processing and therefore works with stereo files only. The Stereo Flip dialogue (Figure 9.12) features a mode selection menu and Pre and Post Crossfade parameters.

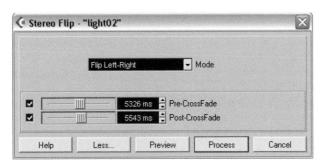

Figure 9.12
Stereo flip dialogue

Stereo Flip includes a number of modes for processing stereo material. These include the following:

- Flip Left-Right – reverses the stereo image by copying the left channel to the right channel and the right channel to the left channel.
- Left to Stereo – copies the left channel to the right channel.
- Right to Stereo – copies the right channel to the left channel.
- Merge – merges the left and right channels into both channels, producing a mono result.
- Subtract – subtracts the left channel information from the right, and the right channel information from the left, thereby attenuating all audio in the centre of the stereo image.

The processing can also be applied gradually at the start or end of the selection using the Pre and Post Crossfade options. A Pre-Crossfade setting indicates that the change in the stereo image occurs gradually from the onset of the target audio selection and only reaches its full effect at the time specified in the Pre-Crossfade field. A Post-Crossfade setting indicates that the stereo processing should gradually be removed, starting at the time specified in the Post-Crossfade field before the end of the audio selection.

Stereo Flip has a number of uses for the processing of stereo material. The most obvious is for the correction of a recording or a mix in which you inadvertently reversed the left and right sides of the stereo image. The second, third and fourth options in the mode menu all provide ways of creating a monophonic result where both channels contain the same signal. This strengthens the centre of the stereo image. In contrast, Subtract effectively eliminates the centre of the stereo image and is therefore useful for taking out the voice from a stereo recording, for karaoke style effects. Using the Pre and Post Crossfade options allows you to gradually fade in or fade out the stereo manipulation and when used with Flip Left Right mode can produce interesting stereo sweeping effects between the left and right channels.

Time Stretch

Time stretching allows the changing of the length of the chosen audio material without changing the pitch. The use of the term 'time stretch' is slightly misleading since you can both stretch and compress the length of the target audio.

Although time stretching may be applied quickly by resizing events using the time stretch function of the Object selection tool in the Project window, using the Time Stretch function in the Process menu (Figure 9.13) allows optimum use of the time stretch algorithms, the adjustment of the length in terms of tempo and gives a wider range of options. The Time Stretch function is the preferred choice when you are processing important material and want to be sure of producing the best possible result.

The Time Stretch dialogue (Figure 9.13) features input and output sections, a Compress/Expand slider and a time stretch algorithm section.

Figure 9.13
Time Stretch dialogue

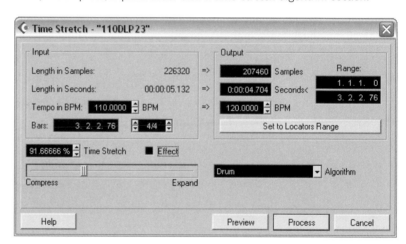

Input section

The input section is where you see the details of the target audio in terms of its current length in samples and seconds. If you know the tempo, or the length of the target selection in bars, you can enter this information into the BPM and Bars fields. The BPM and Bars fields are inter-dependent and changing one always changes the other. A time signature is entered in the time signature field. If you are working with the selection in terms of tempo, this information is essential since it is used as the basis for calculating a new tempo in the output section.

Output section

The output section is where you set a new length or tempo for the selection. The accuracy of the information you see here relies upon the accuracy of the tempo or length entered in the input section. You can change the length in samples, seconds or according to a new tempo in the Samples, Seconds and BPM fields. The Range fields allow you to select a specific range of bars and beats as the new length for the selection and clicking on the 'Set to Locators Range' button allows you to set this range to the current range encompassed by the left and right locators.

Compress/Expand slider

The Compress/Expand slider shows the amount of compression or expansion in percentage terms. It can be adjusted directly by moving the slider handle. The slider functions in two modes. When the Effect box is unticked, compress/expand values between 75 and 125% are available. This is the standard mode when you do not want the time compression or expansion to produce noticeable side-effects. When the Effect box is ticked, compress/expand values between 10 and 1000% are available. This mode is excellent for the creation of sound effects.

The Compress/Expand slider is also adjusted automatically when you update the values in the output section (for example, when you are adjusting the tempo of a drum loop). The Effect box is ticked automatically if the tempo you select in the output section pushes the percentage beyond the 75 or 125% limits. When working with tempo adjustment in the output section this allows you to judge the likelihood of there being noticeable side-effects in the time compressed (or expanded) result.

There are four algorithms available in the algorithm menu as follows:

- MPEX2 – MPEX2 is a proprietary time stretch algorithm designed by Prosoniq for optimum audio quality. MPEX stands for "Minimum Perceived Loss Time Compression/Expansion". This gives among the best overall results, particularly if you want your sound to stay true to the character of the original. It is particularly recommended for vocal material and drum loops and does not suffer from too many side-effects, even at high stretch factors. Adjust the mono/poly slider to 1 for monophonic material and to 2, 3 or 4 for progressively better quality time stretching of polyphonic material. Option 4 offers the best quality for polyphonic material but the processing time is slower.
- Standard – this is a good all-round algorithm which processes the target data relatively quickly. It gives a slightly lesser audio quality but is excellent for producing sound effects when stretching audio by large amounts.
- Drum – this is a special algorithm tuned to give the best results for drum and percussion material. It provides a good alternative to the MPEX2 and real-time algorithms and should always be tried when working with drum loops.
- Realtime - uses the same time stretch algorithm as that which is used in Cubase SX's audio warp functions, as managed in the Sample editor (see the section entitled 'The Sample editor', in Chapter 8, for more details). This is a good all-round alternative to the other algorithms.

Using time stretch

Time stretch can be used to great effect for establishing new tempos for drum loops. Like pitch shifting, time stretching is also excellent for creating sound effects. When audio material is time stretched, Cubase SX must build the audio data required to make the file longer. Depending on the type of material being processed, this may not always sound entirely natural. A similar problem occurs when the audio material is time compressed. In general, stretching or shrinking a file by more than about 15% begins to produce undesirable audio artifacts.

When working with drum loops, the loop should have already been edited so that its duration fits a specific number of bars. The number of bars, or the tempo (if known), is entered in the BPM or Bars fields of the input section. You can then enter a new tempo for the loop in the BPM field of the output section. Alternatively, you can set up a specific range into which you want the time stretched loop to fit by dragging a left/right locator range in the ruler and clicking the 'Set to Locators Range' button in the output section.

For sound effects, try using more extreme time expansion and compression percentages. This is best achieved in the Time Stretch dialogue using the Compress/Expand slider with the Effect box ticked. Good source material for this includes vocals, speech, percussion and real-world sounds such as birdsong, animal calls, running water, seawaves and atmospherics.

Combination processing

One single processing function is not always enough to bring about the desired result, especially when working in a creative context. The following describes a technique for creating a backward reverb effect.

Backward reverb and echo effects were popular in the sixties and seventies for the production of 'psychedelic' effects, particularly with guitar and vocals. It was achieved by playing the multitrack tape backwards and adding reverb or echo effects to the target sound. The reverb or echo was recorded onto another track and the tape was then played in its normal direction. The result was a backward reverb or echo occurring *before* each part of the original audio. This produced the characteristic 'psychedelic' effect. The same technique can be applied to audio material in Cubase SX using the Reverse function and the supplied plug-in effects. Proceed as follows:

Figure 9.14
Select an audio event containing a drum loop or other rhythmic material

• Select the audio material you wish to process. For this exercise, it is best to work with an audio event in the Project window (Figure 9.14). Try using a drum loop or other rhythmic material.

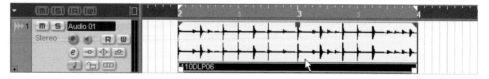

• Select the Reverse function in the Process menu. The selected audio event now plays backwards (Figure 9.15).

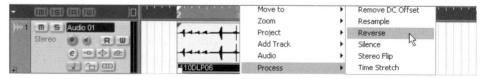

Figure 9.15
Reverse the audio using the Reverse function

• Select Reverb A from the Plug-ins sub-menu (Audio menu). Here you are applying the reverb as an offline process rather than as a real-time effect (Figure 9.16).

• In the Reverb A interface, select the 'Medium' preset in the menu at the top of the display and adjust the mix slider to Wet:100 and Dry:100. Click on the 'More' button and adjust the wet/dry mix to 20% and 80% respectively. Activate the Tail parameter and enter a reverb tail of 1sec (1000ms). These settings ensure a reasonable mix between the wet and dry signals and add a reverb tail to the end of the event (Figure 9.17). Click on the Preview button to audition the result and when you are satisfied click on the Process button to process the audio.

Figure 9.16
Select Reverb A from the Plug-ins sub-menu

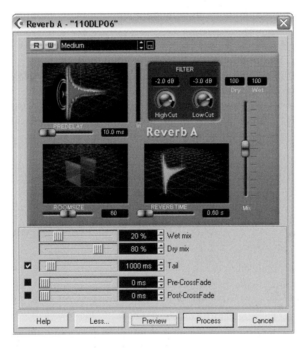

Figure 9.17
Adjust the parameters in the Reverb A interface to add reverb to the selection

• Resize the audio event in the Project window so that it now includes the reverb tail (Figure 9.18).

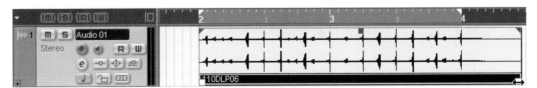

Figure 9.18
Resize the audio event to include the reverb tail

• Apply the Reverse function to the audio event a second time. The original audio now plays back in its normal direction but the reverb effect is reversed and placed in front of the peaks in the waveform. This produces the 'psychedelic' effect described above (Figure 9.19).

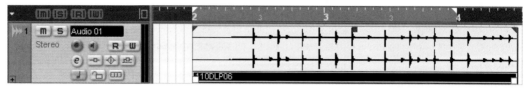

Figure 9.19
Reverse the audio event a second time

- At this point the start point of the drum loop is not on the first downbeat of the bar since the reversed reverb tail is now found in front of the first beat. To make it easier to place the audio event accurately in the event display, drag the Snap point to the first beat of the bar in the Sample editor (Figure 9.20).

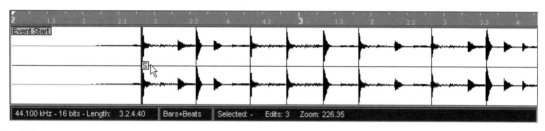

Figure 9.20
Adjust the Snap point of the audio event in the Sample editor

- Moving the audio event in the Project window with the Snap resolution set to 'bar', places the audio event accurately in the event display with the reversed reverb tail occurring before the first beat of the bar (Figure 9.21).

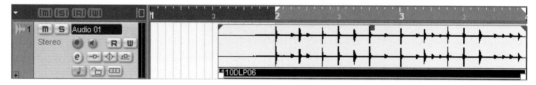

Figure 9.21
Move the audio event to the desired position with the Snap resolution set to 'bar'.

This kind of processing is valuable to those searching for new sound effects and, used in a subtle fashion, it can become a valuable addition to the range of effects you can produce with Cubase SX. The plug-in effect need not be the supplied reverb or echo, you could try any of the additional plug-in effects you may have as part of your Cubase SX system.

Offline Process History

The Offline Process History dialogue (Figure 9.22) provides a way of undoing audio processing at a later date after the session is closed. This means that you can go back and remove the compression, noise gating, reverb and any other offline processing applied to an audio clip many weeks, months (or even years!) after you first applied it. This is assuming that your audio data remains intact at the same locations on the hard disk.

Almost all offline audio processing can be modified or removed at a later date which means that you can use the audio processing functions available in the Process and Plug-in menus with an unprecedented amount of freedom. You can always go back to the original sound of your audio files. However, you may not be able to individually modify, replace or remove each part of the processing. These instances include multiple audio processing operations where the length of the audio clip has been changed at some stage, such as processing which employs time stretch or cut and paste operations at some point in the multiple process. These latter functions can only be individually modified or removed if they were the last editing operations which took place. Functions which cannot be modified or removed are indicated by an icon with a cross in the Status column of the Offline Process History dialogue. For example, the Time Stretch operation in the list shown in Figure 9.21 cannot be individually removed unless the Pitch Shift operation which comes after it is removed first.

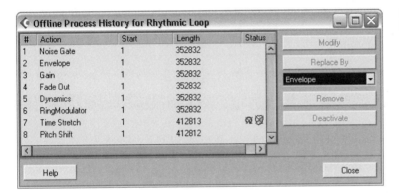

Figure 9.22
The Offline Process History dialogue

The Offline Process History dialogue features a list of all the offline processes which were applied to the current audio selection. You can select any of the processes in the list by clicking on it and the process may then be removed, replaced or modified using the Remove, Replace and Modify buttons (except for the cases outlined above). The Modify button is particularly useful since it opens the dialogue window for the corresponding audio process and recalls the exact settings. Modification is then a matter of tweaking the existing settings. In this context, the Offline Process History dialogue can be used as an interface for fine tuning the overall result of a complex offline multiple audio processing procedure.

The Pool

The Pool is designed for the management of audio and video clips and their associated files on hard disk, known in Cubase SX as the 'media'. It is rather like the folder and file management software which is featured as part of the operating system of your host computer (such as Windows Explorer), except that it handles Cubase SX-related files only.

Each project has its own single instance of the Pool. Here, you see all the audio and video clips associated with the currently active project and you can carry out editing and organisational tasks which affect the clips in the project and the associated files on hard disk. The Pool helps keep track of which clips are currently in use and which file on hard disk is referenced by each clip. It provides a means of importing, auditioning, renaming, copying and deleting clips and files, and finding out which events in the Project window are referenced to the currently selected clip. Conversely, you can find the clip which is referenced by the currently selected event in the Project window. The Pool is also the centre of activities when you are archiving or making safety back-up copies of whole projects.

In order to have meaningful contact with the Pool you should already have a basic understanding of what is meant by events, clips and audio files in Cubase SX. If you are unfamiliar with these concepts, please refer to the section entitled 'Audio events, audio clips and audio files' in Chapter 7. Video clips and their associated files on hard disk are handled in a similar fashion.

The essential thing to bear in mind when you open the Pool is that you are moving one step closer to the raw data on hard disk. You could view this as bypassing the events level of the Project window.

The Pool window

The Pool (Figure 10.1) is opened by selecting Open Pool Window from the Pool menu, by pressing Ctrl + P (PC) / Command + P (Mac) on the computer keyboard or by pressing the Open Pool button on the Project window toolbar.

The Pool displays a list of all the audio and video clips contained within the current Project. The clips are stored within the Audio and Video folders. There is also a Trash folder which serves as a temporary storage area for clips before permanent removal from the project and from the hard disk. The Audio, Video and Trash folders are permanent fixtures and cannot be deleted from the Pool. Any number of sub folders can be arranged within the Audio, Video and Trash folders.

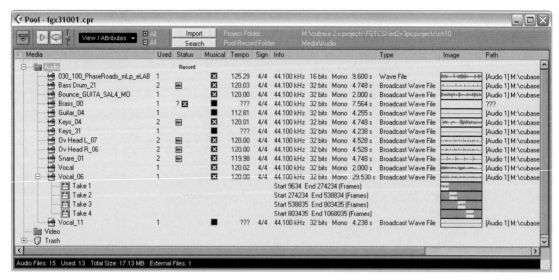

Figure 10.1
The Pool

Figure 10.2
The Pool View
menu

The Pool columns

The Pool's list of clips is arranged across a number of columns. Each column can be hidden or shown using the View menu (Figure 10.2). The columns display a wide range of information about the media used in the project, as follows:

- Media – shows the names of the clips in the Pool arranged in alphabetical order. The clips are stored within Audio and Video folders which may be opened and closed as required. A plus (+) sign next to a clip means that it contains regions. Click on the plus sign to reveal the regions.
- Used – shows the number of times that the clip is referenced within the project. A blank space in this column means that the clip is not currently used.
- Status – indicates the record and file status of clips and the position of the current record folder using various symbols as follows:

Record

The Record symbol shows the position of the current record folder (by default the Audio folder). The Pool allows you to create folders inside the Audio folder, using Create Folder (Pool menu), and should you so wish designate the new folder as the record folder, using Set Pool Record Folder (Pool menu). All new recordings thereafter are stored within the designated folder. The folder chosen as the record folder is indicated by the Record symbol in the Status column and the folder itself is marked with a red record symbol.

The audio wave symbol indicates that the clip has been processed in some way.

The question mark indicates that the clip is referenced by the project but the file associated with it could not be found on the hard disk, (in Cubase SX this is known as a missing file). This occurs if you have deleted, moved or renamed a file outside of Cubase SX or have, at some stage, changed a file common to more than one project.

The X symbol indicates that the clip is referenced to an audio file which is stored outside of the project Audio folder.

The R symbol indicates that the clip has been recorded at some time during the current session. This provides a quick means of finding recently recorded clips.

- Musical mode – shows the musical mode status of each clip. Musical mode is usually activated after having defined the number of bars and tempo for the clip in the Sample editor using the Audio tempo definition tool, but Musical mode may also be activated in the Pool by clicking on the black check box in the column. This activates musical mode only if a tempo has already been defined for the clip. Otherwise, a dialogue appears where you must enter a tempo before proceeding.
- Tempo – shows the tempo of the audio clip as defined using the Audio tempo definition tool. If no tempo has been defined, '???' is displayed in the column. (Note that a preliminary tempo is displayed for the clip as soon as you select the Audio tempo definition tool in the Sample editor. This preliminary tempo may not be the actual tempo for the audio clip and invariably needs further editing to be accurate).
- Signature – shows the time signature of the audio clip. By default, this is set to 4/4 but it may be edited here or in the Sample editor.
- Info – displays the sample rate, bit depth, stereo/mono status and duration (in seconds) of audio clips, and the frame rate, number of frames and duration (in seconds) of video clips. For regions, the start and end time is displayed (in samples).
- Type – indicates the type of audio or video file referenced by the clip.
- Date – shows the date and time when the clip was recorded.
- Origin Time – indicates the original time position at which the clip was recorded. This is useful when you use Insert into Project (Pool menu) since it inserts the clip at the same time position as when it was originally recorded. Imported audio files which were originally saved in Broadcast Wave format have a time position embedded in the file header data and this appears in the Origin Time column. This provides a method by which Broadcast Wave files recorded in other applications can be assembled in Cubase SX at their original time positions.
- Image – displays a waveform of the clip. Click anywhere in the waveform box to audition the clip. Playback begins from the position at which you click. This provides an alternative to using the play button on the toolbar. Note that the waveform display boxes are the same size for all clips and do not reflect their relative durations.
- Path – shows the location on hard disk of the audio or video file referenced by the clip.
- Reel name – a parameter which may be included when you import an OMF file (Open Media Framework Interchange), intended to provide a reference to the original tape or media from which the audio file was taken.

Tip

Click on the title strip of the columns to sort the Pool data by name, duration, type, date, file location and so on. For example, try sorting the clips by date to find the most recently recorded files. Try also using the Optimize Width option in the View menu to clarify the column display.

The Pool toolbar

The Pool's toolbar features Info, Play and Loop buttons. These allow you to show/hide the Infoline below the clip list (see below), audition the currently selected clip or region, or audition the currently selected clip or region in loop mode. The View menu allows you to choose which columns are displayed in

Figure 10.3
The Pool toolbar

the list and the All plus (+) and minus (–) boxes allow you to open or close all folders. There is an Import button for importing audio and video clips directly into the Pool and a Search button for searching for audio files on your system (see below). The toolbar also displays the path of the current project folder and the currently chosen Pool record folder.

The Pool Infoline

The Pool Infoline is shown or hidden using the Info button on the toolbar. The Infoline displays how many audio files are present, how many are actually used

Audio Files: 14   Used: 13   Total Size: 16.80 MB   External Files: 1

Figure 10.4
The Pool Infoline

in the Project, the size of these files in Megabytes and the number of files which are located outside of the Project folder. This is excellent for getting a quick global overview of the file status and hard disk space used in the current project. For example, many experimental projects involve the auditioning of a wide range of audio files which are not all actually finally used. This may take up an unnecessarily large amount of disk space. The Infoline allows you to immediately see how many of the files are actually in use and helps you decide if you need to remove some of the unused media, or remove all of the unused media using the 'Remove Unused Media' command (Pool menu).

The Pool Search function

Clicking on the Search button in the toolbar opens a search window in the lower half of the Pool (Figure 10.5).

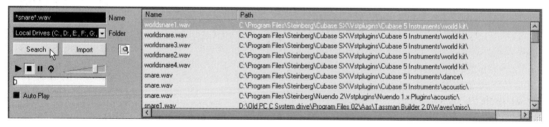

Figure 10.5
Using the Pool's Search function to find a snare drum

The search function behaves in much the same way as the search functions available in any standard operating system. Enter the file name or extension into the search field. The asterisk ('*') symbol may be used as a wild card. For example, to find all those wave files in your system which contain 'snare' somewhere in their name, enter *snare*.wav (see Figure 10.5).

Getting to know the Pool

This section targets the key functions of the Pool.

Auditioning clips

You can audition any clip or region by selecting it and pressing the Play button on the toolbar. Loop playback is achieved by activating the Loop button. However, probably the easiest way to audition a clip is to click on the waveform image in the Image column. (Figure 10.6). Playback commences from the position at which you click.

Figure 10.6
Audition a clip by clicking on the waveform image

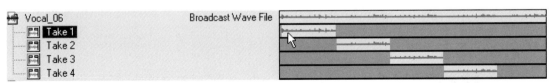

Importing clips

Import Medium

To import an audio or video clip (or a number of clips) directly into the Pool, click on the Import button. This opens an Import Medium dialogue where you can select a file (or a number of files) of one of the supported types from your hard disk or other storage media. Click on Open to import the chosen file(s). At this point, an Import Options dialogue appears (Figure 10.7). Here, you can make a copy of the selected files in the Project's working directory and, if applicable, convert the file(s) to the sample rate and/or resolution of the current Project. Making a copy of the files in the working directory is highly recommended since you can then work with them independently without fear of interfering with work in other projects or applications. The Import Medium dialogue is also opened by selecting 'Import Medium' in the Pool menu.

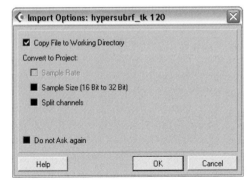

Figure 10.7
Import Options dialogue

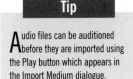

Tip

Audio files can be auditioned before they are imported using the Play button which appears in the Import Medium dialogue.

Tip

Cubase SX allows the importing of audio media in the following file formats: Wave (.wav), AIFC and AIFF (.aif), REX (.rex), REX 2 (rx2), Sound Designer II (.sd2), Wave 64 (.w64), MPEG Layer 3 (.mp3), MPEG Layer 2 (.mp2), MPEG (.mpeg), Ogg Vorbis (.ogg), and Windows Media Audio (.wma). For video media, Cubase SX supports the following file formats: Quick Time Video (.mov and .qt), AVI Video (.avi), and MPEG video (.mpg).

Import Audio CD

Cubase SX features an Import Audio CD function for importing audio CD tracks directly into the program without using additional CD audio grabbing applications. This scores high for many Cubase SX users since the use of sample and drum loop audio CD's is now very popular. To help still further, the 'Import From Audio CD' dialogue allows you to audition each audio track before importing and select a name and folder for the file(s). To import from an audio CD proceed as follows:

- Insert an audio CD into the CD drive of your computer. Open the 'Import From Audio CD' dialogue by selecting Import Audio CD in the Pool menu (the 'Import From Audio CD' dialogue may also be opened by selecting Import/Audio CD in the File menu). (Figure 10.8).

Figure 10.8
Open the 'Import From Audio CD'
dialogue

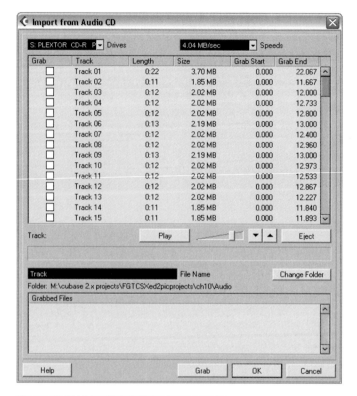

Figure 10.9
Audition the CD tracks using the
dialogue's arrow buttons or the play
button

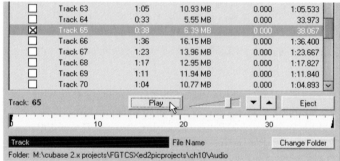

- If you have more than one CD drive in your system, select the correct CD drive in the Drives menu at the top of the dialogue. Audition the CD tracks by selecting a track in the track list and clicking on the up or down arrow buttons below the lower right corner of the list (Figure 10.9). These play a small section of the first and last parts of the audio track. You can use the up/down arrow keys of the computer keyboard to step through the tracks and you can play the whole track by selecting the Play button.
- If required, choose an alternative folder for the imported audio file(s) using the Change Folder button. This would normally be left at its default setting which is the working Audio folder for the current project. Enter a name for the file(s) in the File Name field (Figure 10.10). This is used as the generic name for importing one or more tracks from the audio CD. To select more than one track hold Ctrl/Command while clicking on the CD track check boxes.

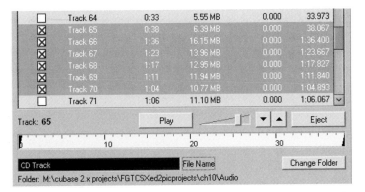

Figure 10.10
Enter a generic name for the chosen
audio CD track(s) in the file name field

- Click on the Grab button to import the audio CD track(s). A blue percentage
  meter registers the progress of the import operation (Figure 10.11).

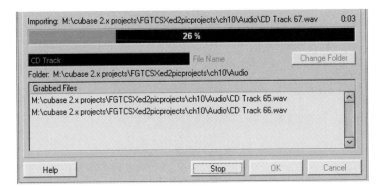

Figure 10.11
Click on the Grab button to import the
audio CD tracks

When the import operation is complete click on the OK button to close the
Import From Audio CD dialogue. At this point one of two things happens as follows:

1   If the Pool was the active window when you selected the 'Import Audio CD'
    function, the audio tracks are imported into the Pool only (Figure 10.12).
2   If the Project window was the active window when you selected the
    'Import Audio CD' function, the audio tracks are imported into the Pool
    AND events are also created for them in the Project window.

Figure 10.12
The imported audio CD tracks in the Pool

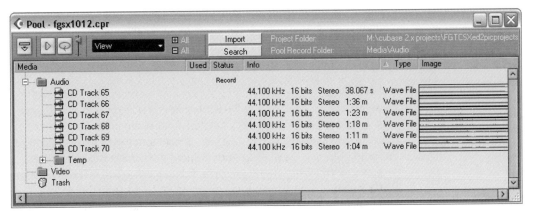

Renaming clips

Clips are renamed by clicking once on the currently selected clip name. Enter a new name into the name field in the standard fashion (Figure 10.13). The renaming of clips should be approached with caution since re-naming a clip also re-names the referenced audio file on hard disk. This is especially hazardous if you are renaming clips which reference audio files which are located outside of the Project's working directory (those marked with the cross symbol in the Status column).

Figure 10.13
Approach renaming of clips with caution since this also renames the associated file on hard disk

Copying clips

Clips are copied by selecting New Version in the Pool menu (Figure 10.14). This makes a copy of the currently selected clip but does not create a new audio file for the clip (i.e. the clip references the same audio file as the original clip). An incremental number is added to the copy to differentiate it from the original.

Figure 10.14
Select New Version in the Pool menu to copy a clip

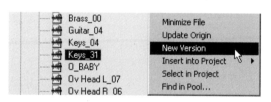

Dragging and dropping clips

Clips may be freely dragged from the Pool and dropped directly into the Project window. When using drag and drop, an event is created for the clip on the track and at the position at which you release the mouse button. A blue marker line and position box show the current drop position before you release. To use drag and drop techniques, proceed as follows:

• Place the Pool in a position where it does not obscure the Project window event display. There must be at least one audio track visible.
• Click on the chosen clip icon (to the left of the clip name) and drag. A dotted rectangle representing the clip appears.
• Drag the clip into the Project window event display.
• Release the mouse button at the appropriate position. A new event is created which is referenced to the dragged clip. The event is created at the position at which the mouse button was released and is moved to the nearest beat according to the current Snap value (if the Snap button is activated).

As well as dragging clips out of the Pool, audio and video files can be dragged directly into the Pool (or Project window) from your computer's desktop or from the file handling software of the operating system (such as Windows Explorer). This is a useful alternative to using the regular import functions.

Deleting clips

There are three ways of deleting clips as follows:

1 Deletion from the Pool only. This removes the clip from the Pool but does not remove the referenced file from the hard disk.
2 Deletion from the Pool and from the hard disk. This removes the clip from the Pool and also permanently deletes the referenced file from the hard disk.
3 Deletion from the Pool only or from the Pool and the hard disk by removing unused media. This operation is achieved using the 'Remove Unused Media' function in the Pool menu.

Deleting from the Pool only

To delete a clip from the Pool only proceed as follows:

- Select the clip in the Pool and press Backspace or Delete on the computer keyboard (or select Delete from the Edit menu).
- If the clip is used, a warning dialogue appears (Figure 10.15). Click on Remove to remove all occurrences of the clip from the event display.
- After clicking on Remove, a further dialogue appears giving a choice of removing the clip from the Pool or moving the clip into the Trash folder. Select 'Remove from Pool' to remove the clip from the Pool only (Figure 10.16). The clip is deleted from the Pool but the associated file on hard disk remains.

Tip

Newly recorded audio events which are deleted from the Project window without saving in the current session are automatically placed in the Trash folder.

Figure 10.15 (left)
Clip is used warning dialogue

Figure 10.16 (right)
Select 'Remove from Pool' to remove the clip from the Pool only

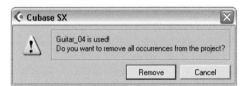

Deleting from the Pool and from the hard disk

To delete a clip from the Pool and from the hard disk proceed as follows:

- Select the clip in the Pool and press Backspace or Delete on the computer keyboard (or select Delete from the Edit menu).
- If the clip is used, a warning dialogue appears (Figure 10.15, above). Click on Remove to remove all occurrences of the clip from the event display.
- After clicking on Remove, a further dialogue appears giving a choice of removing the clip from the Pool or moving the clip into the Trash folder. Select Trash (Figure 10.17). This moves the clip into the Trash folder. The Trash folder is an intermediary storage area before the final deletion of the clip and its referenced file on hard disk. Clips may be stored there indefinitely and you can restore a clip at any time by dragging it from the Trash folder into the other media folders.
- To finally delete clips and their associated files on hard disk, select Empty Trash (Pool menu). This opens a final Warning dialogue giving you the choice to Erase or Remove from the Pool (Figure 10.18). Choosing

Figure 10.17 (left)
Select 'Trash' to move the clip into the Trash folder

Figure 10.18 (right)
Select 'Empty Trash' in the Pool menu and then Erase in the final Warning dialogue to permanently delete clips and their associated files on hard disk (Caution: this operation cannot be undone!)

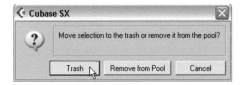

Remove from the Pool removes the clips in the Trash folder from the Pool but does not erase the associated files on hard disk. Choosing Erase permanently deletes all clips currently stored in the Trash folder and also permanently deletes their associated files on hard disk! CAUTION: THIS OPERATION CANNOT BE UNDONE!

Removing Unused Media

To remove all unused clips from the project proceed as follows:

- Select 'Remove Unused Media' from the Pool menu.
- In the dialogue which appears, select 'Remove from Pool' if you wish to remove the clips from the Pool only but retain the referenced files on hard disk. Select 'Trash' if it is your intention to remove the clips from the Pool and permanently delete the referenced files on the hard disk.
- All unused media is removed from the Pool according to the choice you have made in the previous step.

Removing all the unused clips from a project is an operation you might undertake when the Pool has become cluttered with a large number of unused clips after lengthy experimentation or the auditioning of miscellaneous material. If you are in the habit of auditioning audio material from a number of different locations outside of the current Project's working directory then you should, above all, NOT use the Trash folder when using 'Remove Unused Media'. In this case, select 'Remove from Pool' to remove the clips from the Pool only.

Finding events, clips and missing files

Find the events referring to the currently selected clip in the Pool

To find all events which refer to a clip, select the clip in question in the Pool. Select 'Select in Project' from the Pool menu. This immediately selects all those events in the Project window which refer to the clip. This operation also functions with multiple selections.

Find the clip referenced by the currently selected event in the Project window

Conversely to the above example, it is also useful to find the clip referenced by any one event in the Project window. To achieve this, select the event in question in the Project window. Select 'Find Selected in Pool' from the Audio menu. If it is not already open, the Pool window is automatically opened with the corresponding clip selected.

Finding missing files

Whenever you open a Project which contains files which have been moved, renamed or otherwise changed either outside of Cubase SX or as a result of manipulations in another Project, a 'Resolve Missing Files' dialogue appears. This allows you to locate or search for the missing files at the time of the opening of the project or, if you close the dialogue, you can search for the files at a later time using 'Find Missing Files' in the Pool menu. This opens the same 'Resolve Missing Files' dialogue (Figure 10.19).

The Resolve Missing Files dialogue features the following options:

Info

Deleting clips in Cubase SX is deliberately NOT simplistically easy. There is one major reason for this: to avoid the accidental permanent deletion of clips and their associated files on hard disk. The Trash folder gives you the option of keeping absolutely all the files associated with a project right up until the last moment – it is a kind of 'safety buffer' between keeping and finally deleting the files on disk. Use Empty Trash only when you are 100% sure that you no longer need the files contained therein.

Tip

Clips may be dragged directly from the Audio and Video folders into the Trash folder if they are not currently in use. Conversely, any clip may be dragged from the Trash folder into the Audio and Video folders.

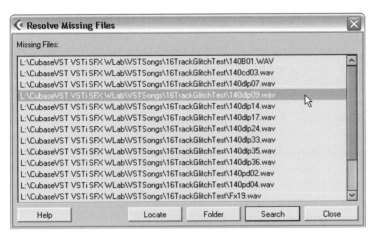

Figure 10.19
Use the 'Resolve Missing Files' dialogue
upon opening the Project, or at a later
stage, to find missing files

- Locate – allows you to manually search and locate the file on your
  system. This is suitable for circumstances where you may know where the
  file is located and already have some idea of how it was renamed or
  otherwise changed.
- Folder – allows the selection of a specific folder in which to locate the
  missing file using the Locate button. This suits circumstances where you
  already know the folder location of the missing file.
- Search – opens a search window (Figure 10.20) where you can specify a
  file name in the Name field, and where to search for the missing file, using
  the 'Search Folder' button. An asterisk (*) may be used as a wild card for
  generic search operations. For example, the search operation shown in
  Figure 10.20, searches for all wave audio files which contain "Vocal" in the
  first five letters of the file name. Once a file has been accepted, by clicking
  on the Accept button, Cubase SX attempts to automatically map all other
  missing files by searching in the same folder as the accepted file.

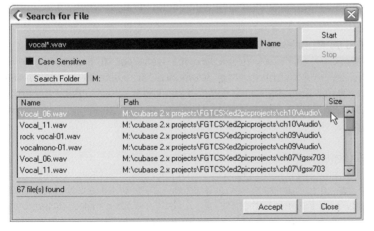

Figure 10.20
'Search for File' window for searching for
missing files

Avoiding missing file problems

There may be occasions when you simply cannot find the missing files. Of
course, the consequences of this depend very much upon the importance of
the files which are missing. Unfortunately, if an important file has gone miss-

ing and remains missing despite your best efforts to find it, then there is no real way to re-create it other than to re-record from scratch.

The good news is that if you follow strict procedures for recording, saving, backing up and clip and file management then you should never suffer from any missing files at all. There are three essential ways of avoiding missing files as follows:

1 *Always* copy any media to the working directory of the project when importing.
2 *Never* permanently delete clips and their associated files for media which is located outside of the working directory of the project.
3 *Never* move, rename or delete the project's audio files in another application or using the file management tools of your operating system.

Other precautionary measures include making an archive backup of the entire project either to a second hard drive or to removable media, such as CD or zip disk, using external applications or saving to a new folder while remaining in Cubase SX using 'Save Project to New Folder' (File menu). See 'Archiving your Cubase SX Projects' and 'Switching to a new Project folder and making backups', below.

If you suffer from missing files as a result of a mistake or when you have intentionally permanently deleted a number of files but the clips are still located within the project, you may wish to delete them. To achieve this, select 'Remove Missing Files' from the Pool menu.

The only types of missing audio files which are recoverable are edit files. If an edit file is missing and marked as 'Reconstructible' in the Status column of the Pool, then it is possible to recreate the file by selecting 'Reconstruct' in the Pool menu.

Editing and processing clips

Clips may be processed directly using the Process or Plug-in options in the Audio menu. Audio processing in the Pool is best achieved using the Quick menu (Right click/Ctrl click) with the clip selected. The Quick menu gives direct access to all the available offline audio processing options in your system in the lower part of the menu display (Figure 10.21). When using audio processing at the clip level, processing is applied to the whole clip unless otherwise specified in the dialogue of the processing option itself (see Chapter 9 for more details about the offline processing options).

Audio clips may be edited in detail by opening them in the Sample editor. To achieve this, double click on the clip icon to the left of the clip name in the Pool or select the clip and press Ctrl + E/Command + E. When the Sample editor is opened using a clip, there is no Show Event button available on the toolbar.

Figure 10.21
Use the Quick menu for rapid access to the audio processing options in your system

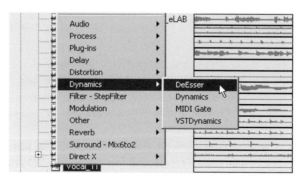

Minimising and freezing clips

Selecting 'Minimize File' in the Pool menu permanently deletes all unused sections of the currently selected clip(s). This is useful when you want to minimise the amount of disk space which is taken up by a project (for example, prior to archiving). The operation involves permanent deletion of audio data on hard disk and the clearing of the entire edit history for the clip. For these reasons, the Minimize File function should be used with great caution.

'Freeze Edits' (Audio menu) allows you to make all audio processing and applied effects a permanent part of the data. If there are several clips which refer to the same audio file you must choose the new version option in the dialogue box which appears, in order to proceed with the Freeze Edits function. If the target clip is a single edit version and no other clips refer to the same audio file, the dialogue box gives you the option of replacing the original clip or creating a new one. If you are 100% sure that you will never need to revert to a previous edited version of the clip, select Replace. Using the Freeze Edits function 'Replace' option is useful when you want to reduce the amount of disk space which is taken up by a project. Like 'Minimize File' above, the operation involves permanent deletion of audio data on hard disk and the clearing of the edit history for the clip. It should therefore be approached with great caution. If in doubt, always create a new version and leave the original intact.

Archiving your Cubase SX projects

Archiving is usually understood to mean making a final backup version of a fully completed project and copying this onto removable media for long term storage. When archiving has been successfully completed the original projects can be deleted from the hard disk. This frees up hard disk space and provides a method by which you can build up a library of all your Cubase SX projects.

Archiving is often a two stage process involving, firstly, optimising the size of the completed project using the 'Prepare Archive' function (Pool menu) and, secondly, transferring this reduced version to removable storage media such as CD or DVD. You can also use 'Save Project to New Folder' (File menu) for the first stage which is a good way of creating a copy of the whole project (if you decide to use this method then follow the procedure outlined in 'Switching to a new Project folder and making backups', below). This has the advantage of leaving the original project intact. Exactly how you reduce the size of the project depends on what kind of archiving is taking place. If the archive is for a project which is totally finished then you may want to reduce the size as much as possible. Projects which may need re-working are probably best archived in their original state, unless they contain particularly large amounts of unused media.

To prepare a project for archiving proceed as follows:

- Select 'Prepare Archive' in the Pool menu (Figure 10.22). 'Prepare Archive' checks for missing files, verifies that all files referenced by the clips in the Pool are contained within the working folder of the project, and gives you the option to use Freeze edits to make all audio processing a permanent part of the data.
- If there are any missing files in the project a dialogue appears giving you the option to find them (Figure 10.23). Selecting Find opens the 'Resolve

Caution

Minimize files and freeze edits operations cannot be undone!

Caution

Archiving which involves deletion of data from the hard disk should be approached with extreme caution.

Figure 10.22
Select 'Prepare Archive' in the Pool menu

Figure 10.23
Missing Files warning dialogue

Figure 10.24
Prepare Archive 'Freeze edits' dialogue

Figure 10.25
The Pool is ready for archiving

Missing Files' dialogue. Selecting Cancel abandons the Prepare Archive operation. A project which contains missing files is not considered suitable for archiving purposes. If the missing files cannot be found anywhere on your system then, in order to proceed further with the Prepare Archive procedure, you must remove the missing files using the 'Remove Missing Files' function (Pool menu).

- When there are no missing files, the Prepare Archive process moves on to the next stage. Another dialogue appears giving you the option to Freeze edits (Figure 10.24). This allows you to make all audio processing and applied effects a permanent part of the data and operates in the same manner as the main Freeze Edits function (Audio menu). Selecting 'Freeze' freezes ALL processed clips in the project and involves permanent changes to the audio data on hard disk (see 'Minimising and Freezing', above, for more details). The Freeze button should therefore be used with caution. Selecting 'No' conducts no freeze operations on the clips in the Pool.
- After having completed the previous step, Prepare Archive ensures that all audio files referenced by the clips in the Pool are contained within the working folder of the project. Any files which are located outside of the project folder are automatically copied into the working directory. Upon completion, Cubase SX considers that the project is ready for archiving and a dialogue to confirm this appears (Figure 10.25).
- Copy the overall Project folder to your chosen storage medium using an external application or the file handling software of your operating system. For example, to archive to CD, drag the archive Project folder into the appropriate location in your chosen CD burning application and burn the CD in the normal manner.

What really needs to be archived?

When archiving, you do not necessarily need to copy absolutely all the files which are contained within the Project folder. For example, if you used the Freeze edits option you do not need to save the Edits folder since all the audio files are now contained within the default Audio folder. Neither do you need to save the Fade and Image folders since fade and image data can be recreated when the project is opened again in Cubase SX. Any files with the extension .csh may also be omitted from the archive since, these too, are recreated when the project is re-opened. If you wish to reduce the size of your archive still further, you may like to start the archiving process by removing all the unused media in the Pool using the 'Remove Unused Media' function in the Pool menu (see 'Remove Unused Media', above).

Who is responsible?

The above outlines just one archiving method. Bear in mind that this is not the only way of archiving your work. The above procedure should not be understood as a completely foolproof way of archiving your projects since archiving requirements can vary enormously. The above procedure should therefore be viewed as a rough guide. This text assumes no responsibility for decisions made about whether or how you reduce the size of your audio files, whether you delete any audio files, or any other decision made with regard to the safety of your data. These decisions remain the sole responsibility of the reader.

Tip

Successful archiving of your Cubase SX projects relies upon a thorough and complete understanding of the Pool and all the functions in the Pool menu. Before embarking on serious archiving tasks, re-read this chapter thoroughly and consult the Cubase SX user documentation.

Switching to a new Project folder and making backups

There are occasions when you need to save the entire project to a new location at some stage after the project has begun. This might occur if you start your session with a generic default project or if you decide that you wish to continue development of an existing project under a new name in a completely separate and independent project folder. For these purposes, use 'Save Project to New Folder' in the File menu. This saves a complete copy of the whole project including all audio and edit files to a different existing folder or to a newly created folder. 'Save Project to New Folder' also serves as a way of making a backup copy of your entire project prior to archiving to removable storage media such as CD or DVD. To use 'Save Project to New Folder', proceed as follows:

Tip

When working on important projects it is a good idea to make regular backups onto CD-R or CD-RW. This is easily achieved by copying the Project folder in your CD writing application. Alternatively, copy/drag the Project folder to a backup location on your hard disk. When doing so, make sure you don't move the Project folder instead of copying it.

- Select 'Save Project to New Folder' in the File menu. This opens a Select Directory dialogue. Select a location on your hard disk and click on the Create button (Figure 10.26). Enter the name of your new Project folder in the Create New Directory dialogue.
- Click on the OK button to open the Save to Folder Options dialogue (Figure 10.27). Here, you can specify a new name for the project and choose to 'Minimize' all audio files, 'Freeze' all edited files and 'Remove' all unused files. These options act upon ALL the files in the project when it is saved. See 'Minimising and freezing' and 'Remove Unused Media', above, for details of what these options do. The implications of these functions when used with 'Save Project to New Folder' are less dangerous than in certain other circumstances, since you are saving copies of all data to a new location. The original project and all its associated media remain untouched in the original Project folder.

Figure 10.26
Select a location on the hard disk and create a new directory

Figure 10.27
Specify the name and choose the save options in the Save to Folder Options dialogue

When saving is complete, the path to the original Project folder is automatically closed and the newly saved Project is automatically opened in a single active Project window.

Practical Pool techniques

The following sections describe a number of typical project scenarios where it is both practical and desirable to use the Pool.

The Pool as a reservoir

The Pool need not always be open to import media and you need not always use the Import Medium option in the Pool menu. Importing can be achieved just as easily using the Import option in the File menu. This imports the media directly into the event display. However, if you are auditioning a large number of files, as might occur when working with drum loops or searching for sound effects, the event display may quickly become cluttered with miscellaneous material. In this case, it is more practical to import into the Pool alone using the Pool's Import button. In this context, the Pool might be viewed as a reservoir of raw material and this raw material might be further organised into sub-folders within the main Audio folder (Figure 10.28). Remember that before importing you can audition the files using the play button in the Import Medium dialogue and you can also import a number of files at the same time.

Figure 10.28
The Pool as a reservoir for audio material organised into sub-folders

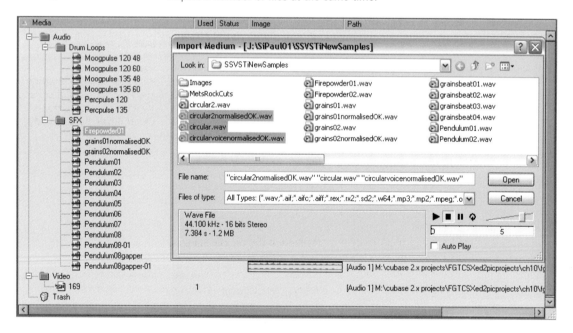

The Pool as a simple list

While proceeding with your work you may wish to occasionally view the clips which have been created in the project and how much disk space the project is currently using. You may also need to drag clips from the Pool into the Project window. For these and other routine operations, it is sufficient to open the Pool, in reduced form, as a simple list to the right of the Project window (Figure 10.29). To achieve this, resize the Pool window and place it in the desired position. Set the width of the window so that you can see the Media and Use columns only. It may also be appropriate to make sure you have access to the import button in the top right of the resized window. This

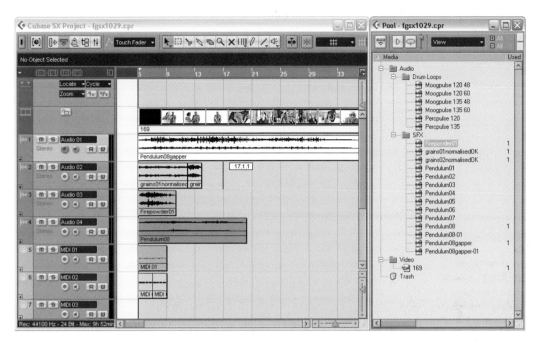

means that you can still quickly import media into the Pool. Activate the Infoline so that you can see how many audio files are in the Pool, how many are currently used, and their total size in megabytes. You can view more entries in the media list and different columns using the vertical and horizontal scroll bars. It is also a practical position from which to drag and drop clips into the Project window. When using drag and drop, an event is created for the clip on the track and at the position at which you release the mouse button. A blue marker line and position box show the current drop position before you release.

The Pool as an insert database

Thanks to the origin time information which is retained in the header data of Broadcast Wave audio files, the Pool can be used as an insert database. Broadcast Wave audio files retain information about the time position at which they were originally recorded and in Cubase SX this origin time can be viewed and edited in the Origin Time column in the Pool. This is particularly useful if you have imported a group of Broadcast Wave audio files from another project or another application since, using the origin time information, you can insert the material into the event display and retain the relative time positions of the different sections of the audio. Equally, Broadcast Wave audio files exported from Cubase SX can be easily arranged according to their origin times in a second Cubase SX project or in an external application (such as Nuendo).

Let's imagine that you have imported a group of Broadcast Wave audio files from an external application which include various instruments of a multitrack recording of drums, bass and guitar. To insert them into the event display at their original positions, select all the clips concerned in the Pool and then select 'Insert into Project – At Origin' in the Pool menu (Figure 10.30).

Figure 10.29
Resizing the Pool window to display a simple media list is practical for a range of operations including dragging and dropping clips into the Project window

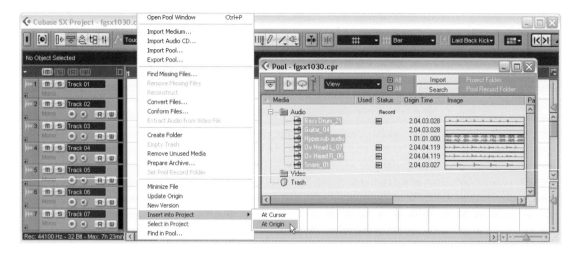

Figure 10.30
Use 'Insert into Project – At Origin' to retain the relative time positions of imported Broadcast Wave audio files

Events are created, beginning on the currently selected track, according to the origin times of each clip, thereby retaining the relative positions of the audio material as originally recorded.

The Pool as a file conversion utility

Selecting the 'Convert Files' and 'Conform Files' functions in the Pool menu provide two ways of using the Pool as a file conversion utility.

For creative, corrective and other reasons you may wish at various moments to convert the sample rate, bit depth, number of channels or file format of one or a number of audio files. To achieve this in the Pool, select the clip(s) you wish to process and select 'Convert Files' from the Pool menu. In the Convert Options dialogue (Figure 10.31), select the combination of changes you wish to make in the four conversion menus. Selecting Keep in any of the fields means that this attribute of the audio file will not be changed in the conversion process.

Figure 10.31
Convert Options dialogue

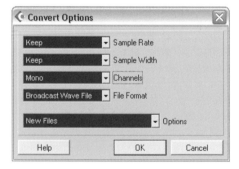

The Options field gives you the choice of three conversion methods:

1 New Files – creates a converted copy of the original file in the Project Audio folder and adds a new clip to the Pool which points to the converted copy. The original clip and audio file remain on the hard disk and in the Pool and the original clip points to the original unconverted file.

2 Replace Files – converts and replaces the original file in the Project Audio folder. The clip which used to point to the original now points to the converted file. CAUTION: THIS OPERATION CANNOT BE UNDONE!

3 New + Replace in Pool – creates a converted copy of the original file in the Project Audio folder but does not replace the original, which remains on the hard disk. The clip which used to point to the original now points to the converted copy.

Using files from multiple sources often results in a range of different file types listed in the Pool but you may prefer that all the files in a project conform to the specifications chosen in the Project Setup window. To achieve this, select 'Conform Files'. Conform Files forces all files to conform to the same sample rate, bit depth and file type as specified in the Project Setup window (Project menu). Upon selection, a dialogue gives you the option of keeping the original files in the Project Audio folder and creating new files (Keep), or replacing all the files in the Pool and the Project Audio folder (Replace) (see Figure 10.32). CAUTION: THIS OPERATION CANNOT BE UNDONE!

Figure 10.32
Conform Files Keep/Replace dialogue

Importing and exporting the Pool

The Pool is usually saved as an integral part of the project but it can also be imported and exported independently. This might be useful if you need to include a number of audio files from another project in the current project or if you need to import/export the Pool from/to Steinberg's Nuendo, which recognises the same Pool file format. When a Pool file is imported, the clips contained therein are added to those currently in the Pool. For the clips contained in an imported Pool to be correctly referenced to the files on hard disk, the files themselves must be located in their original folders as indicated by the path names.

To import or export the Pool, select Import Pool or Export Pool from the Pool menu. Pool files are given the extension '.npl'.

Tip

Before exporting the Pool, create a special folder using Create Folder (Pool menu) and drag all the clips into it. When you later import the Pool into another Cubase SX or Nuendo project all the clips are neatly packaged in their own folder and are easier to find among any clips already in the current Pool.

Mixing and EQ

Mixing in Cubase SX involves similar tools to those found in a traditional recording studio. You are provided with a virtual mixing console, (known simply as the Mixer), which includes EQ controls, auxiliary sends, insert points and automation. You also have a virtual effects rack with various reverb, delay, modulation, distortion and other effects supplied as standard. In Cubase SX, you can mix both audio and MIDI tracks in the same virtual console.

Mixing is a curious combination of art and science and to achieve successful results can take years of experience and training. If you are completely new to the field and have just started mixing, then you should perhaps not be surprised to find that music production is not as easy as it sounds.

The quality of the recordings we hear on commercial CD releases and every day on the radio or television is taken for granted but when you begin to attempt to achieve similar results, even with a tool like Cubase SX, it soon becomes obvious that there are an enormous number of parameters involved.

This is not to say that it is impossible to achieve a good result without any prior experience of music production and mixing, but simply that it will certainly require a lot of patience, perseverance and the extensive use of, sometimes, the most under-valued tool in your arsenal, your ears! If you do not know how to listen then you do not know how to mix.

We have already touched upon various aspects of recording, routing and processing in Chapters 2, 3, 5, 7 and 9 which helped you become familiar with the recording and virtual studio aspects of the program. This chapter proceeds to the deeper level of how you mix all your tracks together into a composite whole. It explores the Mixer and the main functions relevant to mixing and EQ. It provides specific mixing guidelines and mixing techniques to help you get a better mix and its EQ 'Hot Zone' charts help you dial in to the relevant frequencies of popular musical instruments to help you get the most out of Cubase SX's EQ section. Real-time audio effects, MIDI effects and automation are outlined separately in Chapters 12, 14 and 15.

Preliminaries

In the recording studio, the mixing stage tends to become packaged as an entirely separate entity. However, mixing cannot be completely separated from the rest of the recording process.

In popular music, the producer/engineer is often building the mix from the very first recording. As each musician adds their part, the sound image of the final mix gradually takes shape. Alternatively, in classical music, the sound image often relies on the use of high quality, strategically placed microphones in, hopefully, an ideal acoustic recording environment. The mix is already largely decided at the moment of recording and any mixing which occurs is rather different from that which takes place with multi-track recordings in popular music.

In any kind of recording, mistakes made during the track laying stage are also apparent when you come to do the mix, probably more so. Each stage in the sound recording chain contributes to the final result and great care must be taken when the signal is actually recorded.

Similar considerations exist when recording MIDI tracks except that, at the time of recording, you are probably more concerned with the quality of the performance than the quality of the sound. The sound can always be changed at a later stage by changing the sound program on the MIDI device. However, even though the prime consideration might be to capture a magical performance, the chosen sound might radically affect the rest of your mix if you change it at the mixing stage. Any such changes should therefore be approached with great care.

What is mixing?

Having stated that mixing cannot be completely separated from the rest of the recording process, it remains the point at which the various elements of your recording endeavours come to fruition. The sounds you have carefully recorded are fine tuned, and reverb, EQ and other effects and processing are applied, all of which give the music that polished, finished sound. Unfortunately, it is also the point at which a collection of well recorded tracks can be destroyed by a poor mix!

But how could we define what mixing actually is? Essentially, it is the setting of all the levels of a multi-track recording in order to achieve a well-balanced stereo (or surround) result. Balance is the key word for mixing. The stereo image must be carefully balanced so that it is not weighted too heavily to the left or right and different instruments might be mixed more 'forward' or 'back' in the mix, producing a sense of depth and focus. The mix should not be too 'boomy' at the bass end or too 'harsh' in the upper frequencies. Despite careful attention at the track laying stage, some sounds may still need corrective EQ, and EQ may be used to carefully blend or highlight sounds, or for other creative purposes. The mix often incorporates reverb and other effects, which must be carefully mixed with the source sounds. Certain tracks also benefit from additional processing, like compression or noise gating, and the whole mix might be processed through a loudness maximiser or multi-band compressor to boost the final level.

Ten golden rules for recording and mixing

To help create a better mix with a Cubase SX system, remember the following guidelines:

1   Do not make recordings which sound bad and expect to 'fix it in the mix'. It is better to have recordings which already sound good and then you can improve them in the mix.

2   When recording with a microphone, take the time to ensure that it is placed in the best possible position to get the optimum sound quality. Even a very small change can make a difference. Be aware of the acoustic environment in which you are making the recording.

3   Use a good quality microphone and the right model for the application.

4   Make sure that you record at an optimum level whilst also avoiding distortion.

5   Monitor all recordings and the mix through good quality studio monitors.

6   When creating the mix, pan the sounds to appropriate positions across the stereo image and also attempt to achieve some depth in the sound field. The bass drum, snare drum, bass instrument and lead vocal in popular music are usually panned to the centre of the stereo image.

7   Do not over-use reverb or any other effect when creating the mix.

8   Do not over-use EQ. When using microphones, attempt to get the right sound at the time of the recording by experimenting with microphone choice and position, rather than immediately resorting to EQ. Boosting frequencies is not the only way of using EQ, cutting frequencies is often preferable. EQ is best viewed as a way to improve (or creatively change) already well-recorded sounds and to provide a subtle means of balancing and blending the sounds in the mix.

9   Use your ears and do not abuse them by monitoring at abnormally loud sound levels. Take plenty of breaks during the mixing session. After two to three hours of listening to the same sounds the ear becomes fatigued and is less sensitive to the upper frequencies.

10 As far as possible, know every aspect of Cubase SX and the peripheral equipment you are using.

These 'rules' only exist as a guide and, where appropriate, the rules can be broken. There are not always pre-set methods of achieving the desired results and some of the most important developments in music production have occurred as a result of creative experimentation.

The Mixer

In Cubase SX the Mixer takes centre stage in the mixing process and, just like a real-world mixing console, it is important to know all of its functions to get the best results.

The Mixer is laid out like a conventional console with a series of vertical modules, (or strips), each of which controls an Audio, MIDI, Group, VST instrument, FX or Rewire channel (Figure 11.1). To the left and right of the central channel area there are the input and output buss strips, responsible for routing signals into and out of the program. Audio and MIDI channel strips are linked to their corresponding tracks in the Project window and the order of the channels follows the order of the tracks displayed in the Track list. Channels are shown when the corresponding tracks are present in the Project window or when a VST instrument, FX or Rewire device is activated within the system. Group, VSTi, FX and Rewire channels are always shown to the right of the Audio and MIDI channels. To open the Mixer, select 'Mixer' in the Device menu or press F3 on the computer keyboard.

Figure 11.1
The Mixer

The Mixer is displayed in normal or extended mode according to the setting of the normal/extended icon in the Common panel (see below for details). In normal mode, you have access to all the basic channel settings including the volume, pan, mute, solo, read, write, edit channel settings, EQ and effects bypass, monitor enable and record enable controls. In extended mode, you have access to the inserts, EQ or send parameters for each channel or you can display an overview, meters or surround panner (where applicable). The extended view is helpful when you are working on the EQ for a number of channels at the same time (for example), rather than opening the channel settings window separately for each channel.

Manipulating the Mixer controls is largely mouse-based unless you have the luxury of an external control surface. The main points of contact include the following:

- The faders and pan controls are moved by clicking and dragging on the controls. Holding Ctrl (PC) / Command (Mac) and clicking once on a fader resets the fader to 0dB. Holding Ctrl (PC) / Command (Mac) and clicking once on a pan control resets the pan to the centre position. Hold Shift to make fine level and pan adjustments.
- When a channel EQ is active, the EQ bypass button is illuminated in green. Clicking once on an active EQ bypass button disables the EQ, at which time the EQ bypass button is illuminated in yellow.

- When a channel effect Insert or Send is active, the Bypass Insert and Disable Send buttons are illuminated in blue. Clicking once on an active Insert or Send button disables all insert or send effects for the channel, at which time the bypass button is illuminated in yellow.
- Clicking on the edit button (labelled with a lower case 'e') opens the Channel Settings window where you can assign effects and adjust the EQ for the channel.
- Clicking on the mute button ('M') mutes the channel at which time the mute button is illuminated in yellow.
- Clicking on the solo button ('S') solos the channel at which time the solo button is illuminated in red and all other channels are muted.

Common panel

The left-most panel of the mixer is known as the Common panel (Figure 11.2). This is used to manage the settings of the Mixer on a global level. Changes made here affect all, or specific types, of mixer channels.

The upper-most buttons of the Common panel (those on the extended part of the Mixer) allow you to quickly change the extended view between insert, EQ, send, surround panner, large scale meters or channel overview. The Common panel is particularly useful when you wish to, for example, instantly de-activate all the mute or solo buttons after complex muting and soloing operations and

Figure 11.2
The Common panel

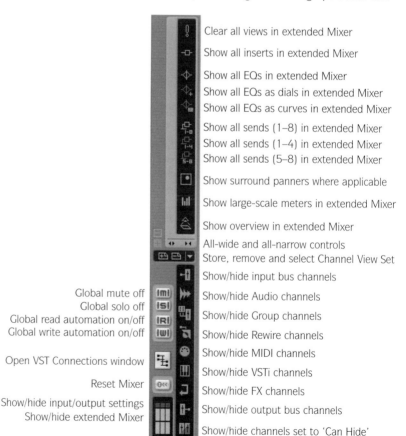

Clear all views in extended Mixer

Show all inserts in extended Mixer

Show all EQs in extended Mixer
Show all EQs as dials in extended Mixer
Show all EQs as curves in extended Mixer

Show all sends (1–8) in extended Mixer
Show all sends (1–4) in extended Mixer
Show all sends (5–8) in extended Mixer

Show surround panners where applicable

Show large-scale meters in extended Mixer

Show overview in extended Mixer

All-wide and all-narrow controls
Store, remove and select Channel View Set

Show/hide input bus channels

Global mute off
Global solo off   Show/hide Audio channels
Global read automation on/off   Show/hide Group channels
Global write automation on/off   Show/hide Rewire channels

Show/hide MIDI channels
Open VST Connections window
Show/hide VSTi channels

Reset Mixer   Show/hide FX channels

Show/hide input/output settings
Show/hide extended Mixer   Show/hide output bus channels

Show/hide channels set to 'Can Hide'

helps ensure that you are reading all the available channel automation in the mix when you activate the global Read button. The channel selection menu (lower downward pointing arrow) is good for selecting channels by name when you have a large number of tracks in the mix and, also with complex mixes in mind, the channel type show/hide buttons help you view only those channel types you really need to see, (including showing or hiding the input and/or output busses). Clicking on the 'All narrow' icon allows you to see around thirty channel faders on an average 17 inch monitor. This is great for getting an overview of your mix. Also check out the 'Hide channels set to Can Hide' option which hides all those channels which have 'Can Hide' activated in their own dedicated menus. The current Mixer view may be saved as a presets in the Channel View Set menu.

Audio channels

The number of Audio channels featured in Cubase SX is virtually unlimited and depends upon the processing power of the host computer. The Mixer expands automatically according to how many tracks you add. Each Audio channel strip can be mono, stereo or surround/multiple channel, depending on the configuration you choose when the track is first created. All channel formats feature a single channel fader and a single set of function buttons. The only difference with stereo and multiple channel strips is that they include dual or multiple meters (and a surround panner where applicable). Apart from these minor differences, each Audio channel strip contains the same set of parameters and these are outlined in Figure 11.3.

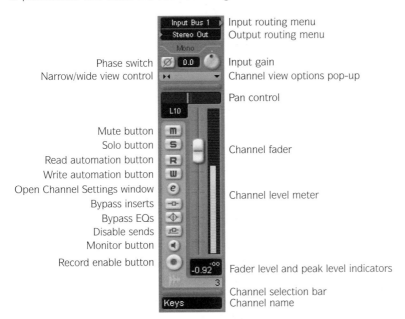

Figure 11.3
Audio channel control functions

MIDI channels

Like regular Audio channels, the number of MIDI channels in Cubase SX is also virtually unlimited and depends upon the processing power of the host computer and the polyphony limitations of your peripheral MIDI devices. Once again, the Mixer expands according to how many MIDI tracks you add.

> **Tip**
>
> De-activate all mute or all solo buttons in the Mixer by clicking on the Unmute All or De-activate All Solo buttons in the Common panel.

> **Tip**
>
> When using the Mixer to create a mix, it is not always convenient if channels are automatically record enabled when selected. To disable automatic record enabling, open Preferences/Editing and disable 'Enable Record on Selected Track'.

Tip

Hold Shift while moving a channel fader or pan control to make fine adjustments.

MIDI channels behave in much the same way as their audio counterparts except that when you move the channel fader you are sending MIDI Volume messages and when you move the pan control you are sending MIDI Pan messages to the receiving MIDI device. The MIDI channel strips feature mute, solo, read, write, edit channel settings, bypass, record and monitor enable buttons which behave similarly. It is important to bear in mind that when you move the controls on a MIDI channel strip you affect MIDI data only, you are NOT directly controlling the audio itself. As mentioned elsewhere in this book, MIDI is NOT audio, it is a set of digital instructions (see Chapter 5 for full details about MIDI theory). MIDI channels control external MIDI devices, onboard VST Instruments or Rewire devices. Each MIDI channel strip contains the same set of parameters and these are outlined in Figure 11.4.

Figure 11.4
MIDI channel control functions

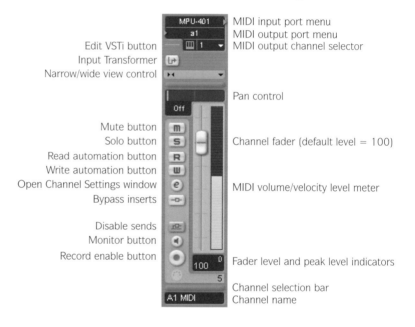

FX channels

FX channels are specialised channels which function as 'containers' for the send effects within a project. Each FX channel might be viewed as an effects device, as found in the effects rack of a traditional recording studio. An FX channel is similar to a regular audio channel but is designed to process signals routed from the auxiliary sends of regular Audio, Group, VSTi and Rewire channels. An FX channel normally contains an effect assigned as an insert in its insert panel which is chosen at the time the FX channel is added to the project. Signals routed from the auxiliary sends of other channels are processed with this effect or, for more elaborate send processing, several effects may be assigned in series in the insert slots of the FX channel. The fader of the FX channel acts as the return level for the effect. You can also pan and EQ the FX channel as desired and the channel parameters may be automated.

Traditionally, effects used as send effects have their 'wet/dry' mix set to fully 'wet' (100% 'wet'). In this configuration, the FX channel produces only the wet signal, while the channel from which the send signal is being routed produces only the dry signal. Most of the time, FX channels are designated as stereo since most of the effects supplied with Cubase SX have stereo outputs. It is equally possible to create a mono FX channel if you are using a mono effect. Auxiliary send signals are routed in mono for mono audio channels and in stereo for stereo audio channels. Pan controls in the routing section of the send panel in the Audio Channel Settings window allow the panning of the send signal between the left and right sides of the stereo input of the effect assigned to the FX channel. The output routing of an FX channel is normally to the master stereo output buss.

Group, VST Instrument and Rewire channels

In addition to the audio, MIDI and FX channels, the Mixer displays Group channels and, (if any are activated), VST Instrument and Rewire channels. Group channels are added using the usual Add track function but VST Instrument and Rewire channels are present when the relevant device is active within the system. All these channel types handle audio signals.

Group channels are buss channels (mono, stereo or multiple) to which any number of regular Audio channels (and also VST Instrument and Rewire channels) may be routed. Channels are routed to a Group by selecting a Group output in the output routing menu above each channel strip. Group channels themselves may be routed to another Group channel if the target Group channel has a higher number than the source Group channel. Group channels are created by adding a Group channel using the Add track function (Project menu). These appear in the Group tracks folder in the Project window. The function buttons and general operation of Group channels are similar to regular audio channels, with the exception of the record enable and monitor buttons which are not present.

Groups are extremely useful for dividing your mix into separate sub-mixes. For example, if you were mixing four channels of backing vocals and wanted to apply the same compression, EQ and reverberation to all of them, it might be easier to mix them to a Group first and apply the treatment from there (this also minimises the load on the CPU). Likewise, once you have established a drum mix, it might be easier to balance its level with the rest of the mix by sending it to a Group. In both these cases, it is also easier to arrange the stereo pan position of each voice/instrument by soloing the Group to listen to it in isolation from the rest of the mix. Where appropriate, any mix might be broken down into its constituent parts and each sent to a different Group. This might include stereo kit, vocals, rhythm instruments, pads, strings and so on. Each Group could then be processed in some way and carefully mixed to the master stereo output buss or routed to separate hardware outputs via additional busses.

VST Instrument channels are also shown in the Mixer. In order to be displayed they must first be activated in the VST Instruments panel. The VST Instruments panel is opened by selecting VST Instruments in the Devices menu or pressing F11 on the computer keyboard. An instrument is activated when you make a selection from the pop-up menu which appears when you click in the window of one of the slots. The function buttons and general operation of VST Instrument channels are similar to regular Audio channels, with the exception of the record enable and monitor buttons which are not present. VST Instrument channels feature an additional edit button below the regular buttons which directly opens the graphical user interface for the instrument. (See Chapter 17 for more details about VST Instruments).

Rewire channels are displayed in the Mixer when the audio channels from a Rewire equipped application (such as Propellerhead Reason) are directed to Cubase SX via Rewire. Rewire allows the real-time streaming of digital audio into SX from such things as software synthesizers and drum modules. The function buttons and general operation of Rewire channels are similar to regular Audio channels, with the exception of the record enable and monitor buttons which are not present.

Channel Settings

The insert, EQ and send settings for the mixer channels are adjusted in a number of locations, including in the extended section of the Mixer and in the Channel Settings window (opened by clicking on the channel's edit button). The channel settings may also be adjusted in the Inspector in the Project window (see Chapter 4 for details).

Adjusting the controls in the extended section of the Mixer

The insert/send assignments and EQ configuration can be immediately viewed and edited on any channel by activating the extended Mixer. The channel must be in 'wide' mode in order to view the extended channel strip. You can choose what to view in each channel's pop-up options menu (Figure 11.5) or globally for all channels by clicking on the appropriate symbol in the Common panel.

Audio insert effects are activated individually in the Inserts section for each channel in the extended Mixer. Insert effects are assigned by clicking in one of the Insert effects slots and choosing an effect from the pop-up menu (Figure 11.6). There are a total of eight insert effects slots. Insert effects are arranged in series i.e. the signal passes through each effect in turn. The output of each effect provides the input for the next effect in the following slot. However, inserts 1-6 are pre-fader and inserts 7-8 are post-fader insert points. The post-fader insert points are intended for processing which is best applied after the channel's fader, (such as limiting for peak level control).

Figure 11.5
Choose what to view in the extended part of the Mixer using the channel's pop-up options menu

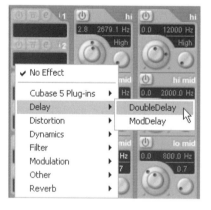

Figure 11.6
Assigning an insert effect in Insert slot 2 of an Audio channel

An audio Send effect must first be present on an FX channel before it is available in the Send effects slots in the Mixer. To create an FX channel you simply add it to the project using the usual Add function, (Project menu), at which time you choose the effect required from the pop-up plug-in menu (for more details see 'FX channels', above). Send effects are assigned in the Send effects section of an extended Mixer channel by clicking in one of the Send effects slots and choosing an effect from the pop-up menu. To actually send the channel signal to the effect, increase the corresponding Send effects level using the Send mini-fader (Figure 11.7). There are a total of eight send effects slots. Send effects are arranged in parallel i.e. they are added to the original signal. The relative levels of the original (dry) version and the effected (wet) version of the signal are carefully mixed together for the desired result.

The EQ for Audio channels may be set up in the extended part of the Mixer using 4-band EQ sections arranged in a classic mixing console layout with a choice of control knobs or mini-faders. (EQ is outlined in more detail below).

The MIDI insert and send effects sections of the Mixer are implemented in a similar manner to the Audio effects sections and can be accessed in the extended section of the Mixer. Clicking once in any of the insert or send effects fields in the MIDI insert or send sections opens a pop-up menu from which you can choose one of the available MIDI effects (Figure 11.8). Here, you need to bear in mind that you are affecting MIDI data and not audio signals, but the logical structure of applying the effects remains very similar to the audio equivalent. There are four insert effect and four send effect slots.

Figure 11.7
Setting the send level in send slot 1 of an audio channel

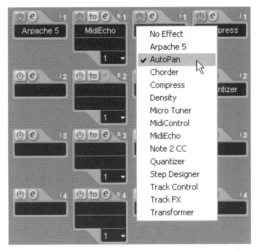

Figure 11.8
Assigning insert and send effects on MIDI channels is handled in a similar manner to Audio channel effects

Info

Audio and MIDI effects are explained in more detail in Chapters 12 and 14.

Channel Settings windows

The other main method of assigning insert and send effects and adjusting EQ is to use the Channel Settings window. The Channel Settings window is opened for each channel by pressing the edit button ('e'). The Channel Settings window varies between channels which handle audio and those designated as MIDI channels. The advantage of the Channel Settings windows is that you can see all of the insert, send and EQ settings simultaneously and the EQ section features an EQ curve display where you can make adjustments graphically (see the EQ section, below, for a detailed explanation).

Audio channel Settings

The Channel settings window is opened by clicking on the edit button ('e') on the channel strip. For Audio, Group, FX, VSTi and Rewire channels, the Channel Settings window (Figure 11.9) features a duplicate of the channel

Figure 11.9
Audio channel settings window

fader, an insert effects section, an EQ section with four modules and EQ curve display, and a send effects section. There are also a number of reset and control buttons.

The channel fader, insert and send section parameters function in the same manner as in the main Mixer window (as outlined above). The EQ section features an EQ curve display in which you can quickly create custom EQ curves and a useful presets menu (see the 'EQ' section, below, for more details). Also worthy of mention are the 'Initialise channel' and 'Reset EQs' buttons which initialise the entire channel or just the EQ section to Cubase SX's default values (Caution: use with care since you cannot go back to the channel's previous settings once it is initialised). The Select Channel menu in the lower left corner allows you to switch between channels of any type in the same open window. Each new channel chosen in the menu replaces the current channel shown and opens the appropriate type of Channel settings window.

MIDI Channel Settings

The MIDI Channel settings window is opened by clicking on the edit button ('e') on the channel strip of a MIDI channel (Figure 11.10).

The MIDI Channel Settings window features a duplicate of the channel fader, an insert effects section, and a send effects section. All channel fader, insert and send section parameters function in the same manner as in the main Mixer window (as outlined above). The Select Channel menu in the lower left corner allows you to switch between channels of any type in the same open window. Each new channel chosen in the menu replaces the current channel shown and opens the appropriate type of Channel settings window.

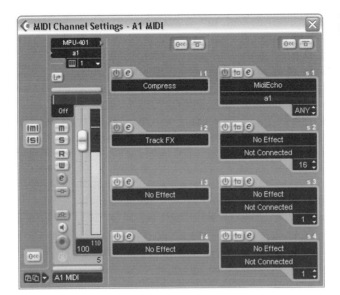

Figure 11.10
MIDI Channel Settings window

Info

The output buss section of the Mixer includes an Audition buss. This is a dedicated buss which cannot be removed and is found under the Studio tab in the VST Connections dialogue. It is designed for the direct auditioning of audio material and bypasses all EQ and effects. Audio is directed to the Audition bus when you use the audition tools in the Project window, Audio Part editor or Sample editor and when you use the editors' local playback and loop controls. This helps with auditioning when working in fine detail and allows you to set up a separate audition level to the main stereo out level.

Input and Output busses

The main input and output busses appear on either side of the regular channels in the Mixer (input busses on the left and output busses on the right, as shown in Figure 11.11). Input busses provide control of any incoming signals from the audio hardware's inputs while output busses provide control of signals which are being routed back out to the 'real' world via the audio hardware's outputs. The manner in which the input and output busses are connected to the audio hardware is managed in the VST Connections window (see Chapter 2 for coverage of VST Connections). The input and output busses may be mono, stereo or multiple channel format. Input busses are used primarily for the recording of input signals (see Chapter 3 for details of setting up an input buss for recording). Here, we are concerned with the use of output busses, which normally provide master level control and sound processing for the entire mix.

Figure 11.11
The input and output busses to the left and right of the regular Mixer channels

Figure 11.12
Stereo output bus
with inserts section
set up for a stereo
mix

By default, the regular Mixer channels are routed to the first stereo output buss which, in turn, is usually assigned to the first pair of stereo outputs in the audio hardware. The output routing for regular Mixer channels is chosen in the input/output routing menus above each channel. If the input/output routing menus are hidden, click on the 'Show input/output settings' symbol in the Common panel to display the menus above the channels. (For more details about output routing, see the section entitled 'The Output path' in Chapter 7). When mixing to stereo most of the output menus of the regular channels are set to the same stereo master output buss. The channel fader on this buss provides the master fader for the whole mix.

By activating the extended Mixer you can see the inserts section for the stereo master output buss. Using the inserts section, you can implement effects and processing which affect the whole mix. The output buss insert effects routing is similar to that for regular channels i.e. the signal passes through each effect in the rack in descending order. However, for stereo mixing, only effects with a stereo input and stereo output can be used. The insert effects slots on an output buss are primarily intended for processing which is suitable for a final stereo mix or mastering. This includes such things as limiters, compressors, loudness maximisers, noise reduction processors and denoisers. Inserts 1-6 are pre-fader and inserts 7-8 are special post-fader insert points. The post-fader insert points are intended for processing which is best applied at the very end of the signal chain after the fader, such as limiting and dithering. (For mastering techniques see Chapter 13).

Multiple buss and surround configurations

Users with multiple I/O hardware may configure their system for surround sound or other multiple input/output configurations. Multiple channel surround busses or a number of extra busses may be added to the system in the VST Connections window, depending upon the number of available hardware inputs/outputs (see Chapter 2 for more about the VST Connections window and see Chapter 16 for more details about surround sound). Busses added in the VST Connections window appear in the Mixer to the left (for input busses) and to the right (for output busses) of the regular audio, MIDI and other channel types.

Input busses are mainly used for recording purposes and are outlined in chapters 2 and 3. Output buss assignments might involve surround configurations, where a single buss is all that is needed to control a 5.1 surround output, or multiple output configurations where additional mono or stereo busses are used to route signals to other parts of your audio system (see Figure 11.13).

Once activated, additional output busses are available in other parts of the system. For example, any Audio channel can be assigned to any of the available output busses in the output selection menu of the channel strip. The extra busses find many uses in a Cubase SX system such as routing signals to separate hardware outputs for external processing or mixing, routing effects sends to the processing and effects in an external effects rack, or for setting up an auxiliary headphone mix.

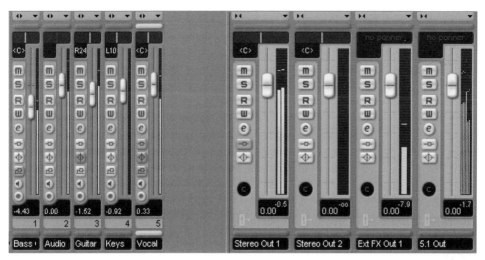

Figure 11.13
After having been activated in the VST Connections window, additional output buses appear in the Mixer to the right of the regular channels

EQ

EQ is an abbreviation for 'equalisation', the process of increasing or decreasing the levels of different frequency bands within a sound signal for corrective or creative purposes. Essentially, EQ involves combining the actions of various different types of filter but, whereas filters are normally concerned with removing frequencies, EQ allows both the reducing and the boosting of chosen bands of frequencies within the signal. One of the most popular implementations of EQ is known as parametric EQ. This allows you to select a frequency band almost anywhere within the signal, adjust the width of this frequency band and increase or decrease its level.

Cubase SX provides four bands of parametric EQ per channel. These are arranged as modules which can be viewed and adjusted in the extended part of the Mixer (Cubase SX only) in the Channel Settings window or in the Inspector.

EQ in the Mixer window

In the Mixer, the layout of the EQ controls resembles the style of a classic real-world console and you have the choice of viewing the parameters as control knobs or mini-faders (Figure 11.14). The advantage of viewing the EQ sections in the extended part of the Mixer is that you can adjust the EQ for a number of related tracks simultaneously and you maintain a good overview of your EQ settings. This is similar to the way you might work with a real-world console.

EQ in the Channel Settings window

To open the Channel Settings window for a channel click on the channel edit button. The Channel Settings window shows the EQ section as four modules and an EQ curve display in the central area of the window (Figure 11.15).

The EQ curve display provides visual feedback of the EQ settings and an alternative method of manipulating the frequency and gain parameters. Frequency is shown on the horizontal axis and gain on the vertical axis. Clicking in the display activates a numbered handle and its corresponding module. The handle can be dragged to any position and allows the adjustment of frequency and gain simultaneously. Double-clicking on a handle

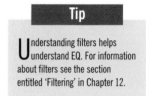

> **Tip**
>
> Understanding filters helps understand EQ. For information about filters see the section entitled 'Filtering' in Chapter 12.

Figure 11.14
EQ sections for two Audio channels in the Mixer displayed with classic control knobs and with mini-faders

Figure 11.15
The EQ section in the Channel Settings window

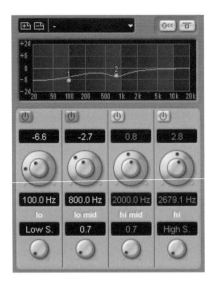

deletes it and de-activates its corresponding module. Moving the handles in the EQ curve display is a great way of intuitively adjusting the EQ while listening to the sound. This is one of the main advantages of adjusting the EQ in the Channel Settings window.

Tip

In the EQ curve display, press Ctrl/Command while dragging a handle to change the gain only, press Alt while dragging a handle to change the frequency only, or press Shift while dragging a handle to change the Q only.

EQ details

Controls

To help you understand the EQ section in more detail, Figure 11.16 shows the functions of one EQ module in isolation.

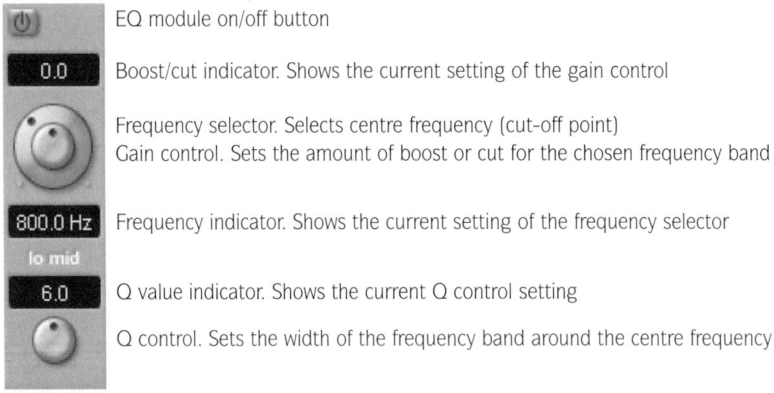

Figure 11.16
EQ control functions (as displayed in the Channel Settings window)

EQ module on/off button

0.0   Boost/cut indicator. Shows the current setting of the gain control

Frequency selector. Selects centre frequency (cut-off point)
Gain control. Sets the amount of boost or cut for the chosen frequency band

800.0 Hz   Frequency indicator. Shows the current setting of the frequency selector
lo mid

6.0   Q value indicator. Shows the current Q control setting

Q control. Sets the width of the frequency band around the centre frequency

The default operation of all modules is in parametric EQ mode. EQ modules 2 and 3 are available in parametric EQ mode only. Modules 1 and 4 can be used in parametric EQ mode or switched to low shelving/high-pass or high shelving/low-pass modes. These modes are activated by setting the Q control knobs for modules 1 and 4 to their lowest or highest setting. The modes function as follows:

- Low shelving – changes the module's characteristics to those of a low shelving filter providing overall low frequency boost or cut below the selected frequency cut-off point.
- High-pass – changes the module's characteristics to those of a high pass cut-off filter where all frequencies below the selected frequency cut-off point are significantly reduced and all those above pass through unchanged.

- High shelving – changes the module's characteristics to those of a high shelving filter, providing overall high frequency boost or cut above the selected frequency cut-off point. The opposite of the low shelving filter.
- Low-pass – changes the module's characteristics to those of a low pass cut-off filter where all frequencies above the selected frequency cut-off point are significantly reduced and all those below pass through unchanged. The opposite of high-pass mode.

Additional parameters

The EQ section (as displayed in the Channel Settings window) features a number of other parameters located above the modules. These operate as follows:

- Store button (+) – stores the current EQ settings to a preset. A default preset name is added to the preset menu. The default name can be changed later by double-clicking on the preset name field.
- Remove button (-) – removes the currently displayed preset from the preset menu.
- Preset menu – contains all EQ presets. Click on the downward pointing arrow to open the menu. Presets are selected from the list by clicking on the preset name. To enter a new name double-click on the preset name field.
- Reset button – resets all four EQ modules to Cubase SX's default EQ settings.

Figure 11.17
Parametric EQ controls

Theory

This section quickly outlines the theory behind parametric EQ once again. This is of value to those who are new to EQ'ing. The essential pre-requisites for a parametric EQ are a gain control, a centre frequency selector and a Q control. The frequency selector allows you to tune the EQ to the frequency band you wish to process and the Q control governs the 'width' of this band, (otherwise known as the bandwidth). The gain control provides the means to boost or cut the chosen frequencies. Figure 11.17 provides a graphical view of these main controls.

Practice

Now, bearing the theory in mind, let's conduct an experiment with a single Cubase SX EQ module. Try the following:

- Activate a single EQ module while playing a complex signal, (such as a rhythm guitar or a drum performance), through the chosen Audio channel.
- Set the gain control to -24dB to radically cut the chosen frequencies.

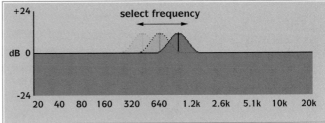

Frequency control

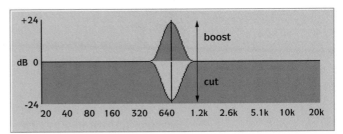

Gain control

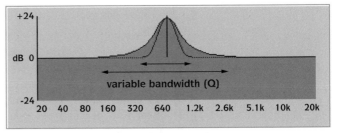

Q control

- Set the Q control to 6.0 (centre position).
- Slowly sweep the frequency selector from the maximum to the minimum position.

As you sweep the frequency selector you notice the change in the sound as the cut frequency band sweeps down through the spectrum. The effect is particularly apparent between 100Hz and 5kHz and as you reach the lower part of the frequency range the sound becomes more treble biased as the bass and lower-mid frequencies are reduced in level. Using this kind of technique you can, for example, tune into unwanted frequencies to correct a sound which was recorded with too much middle, or too much bass. Try the same experiment with the Q control set to different values.

EQ Summary

Cubase SX's EQ section provides a convenient means of shaping your sounds for both corrective and creative purposes. The inclusion of parametric EQ, high and low pass cut-off filters and high and low shelving filters means that Cubase SX's EQ section matches the performance of that found on many real-world mixing consoles. The preset storage facilities are particularly welcome since any EQ configuration can be saved for later recall and instant comparisons can be made between different settings. For further tips on using EQ see the following 'Mixing decisions' section and 'EQ Hot Zone' charts, below.

Mixing decisions

At this point in the chapter you should have a good grasp of the parameters involved in the mixing process and how you might use the basic mixing features of Cubase SX. For more details about the real-time effects and processors supplied with the program, see Chapters 12 and 14. The facilities provided in Cubase SX are very high quality and very comprehensive but, no matter how many channels or how many effects and processors you have, you still have to actually DO the mix. Above all, this involves listening very carefully and making a large number of decisions based on what you hear. The following section focuses on the key elements of your mix and helps you make the right decisions.

Mixing tips

The 'Ten golden rules for recording and mixing', above, help with the basic decisions involved in the recording and mixing process but here are some additional tips to help you create a better mix:

- If you are mixing pop or rock material, the bass drum, snare drum and bass instrument are invariably panned to the centre of the stereo image along with the lead vocal. The bass sounds tend to be mixed fairly dry (i.e. with little or no reverb). Carefully mixing the drum kit and bass first is a good way of laying the foundations for the rest of the mix.
- The different sounds in a drum kit should not be panned excessively wide as this can give the rather odd impression that the drummer has very long arms!
- If you have a lead vocal in your mix it should normally be in the centre of the stereo image and more 'up-front' than the other sounds. It would

also normally be treated with reverberation. The correct balance of the 'dry' (original) and 'wet' (reverberant) signals of the vocal sound and their balance with the rest of the mix is crucial, as is the choice of reverb type. Beware of adding too much reverb.

- The vocal or other lead instrument may be difficult to hear because it is being masked by the frequencies from other instruments. Rather than trying to excessively boost the sound you wish to hear, try instead cutting some of the frequencies of the sounds in the same register. For vocals, try cutting some of the accompanying instruments between around 2kHz to 4kHz and slightly boosting the vocal itself in the same frequency range. To add still more presence to the vocal try slightly boosting at around 3kHz.

- The perceived distance, location and depth of a sound in the mix is determined by its relative level, its high frequency content and the delay/reverberant characteristics which surround it (especially the early reflections). Cutting the high frequency content and adding subtle early reflections (or delay) can move a sound 'back' in the mix. Reducing the level of the direct sound and adding a slight amount of reverberation can increase the perceived distance of the sound still further. Careful use of short delays (less than 40ms) on monophonic sources helps give them depth and directional focus. For depth enhancement, avoid surrounding all your sources with excessive reverb. Inevitably, this results in a cloudy, unfocused mix.

- Some instrumental and vocal performances produce wildly fluctuating signal levels. These are difficult to mix since sometimes they are too loud and sometimes too soft. Applying mild compression can help control this type of unmanageable signal. The problem can also be resolved by riding the faders as part of a manual or automated mix.

- If the mix is sounding 'muddy' attempt to clarify the definition of the main instruments in the mix by slightly boosting their most prominent frequencies. However, beware of boosting multiple instruments at the same frequency range; attempt to differentiate the sounds by giving each instrument its own EQ space. Your mix may also be sounding 'muddy' due to a confused and 'boomy' bass end. In this case, try using some low frequency broad band cut on the bass instruments centred between around 200 and 250Hz.

- If the mix is sounding 'harsh', identify which instruments are producing this harshness and cut the offending frequencies. Upper frequency 'hard edge' usually occurs somewhere between 1kHz and 3kHz so try cutting in this range. Many instruments can be softened by applying a broad band cut centred between 3kHz and 4kHz. To add more 'warmth', try a moderate broad band boost centred around 200Hz on selected instruments.

- Sounds to which you have applied corrective or creative EQ may sound good within the mix but odd or unnatural when listened to in isolation. This is normal. If it sounds right in the mix then it IS right. It is standard practice to subtly adjust the EQ for various chosen sounds to help blend them together and provide each instrument with its own EQ space.

- Do not try to achieve a mix by continually raising levels and boosting EQ frequencies since, not only will it sound like an aural battlefield, you will also quickly run out of headroom on the master faders.

- As you add more sounds to the mix try to keep some kind of focus on the overall sound image you are trying to create. Many engineers listen to one or more mixes of established artists, before and during the mix session, as a point of comparison with their own mix.

- Judging the mix clearly, especially after having worked on it for some time, is not always easy. Some engineers recommend listening to the mix from outside the mixing room with the door open. This technique often shows up faults with the mix which were not obvious when you were in front of the speakers. Strange but true!

- As well as performing the mix in one take, do not be afraid to also try recording the mix in separate sections. These can be edited together at a later stage.

- If your mix is to undergo further editing and processing at a later mastering stage, do not apply noise-shaped dither and truncate to 16-bit at the mixdown stage. Instead, mix to a high-resolution format, such as 32-bit float or 24-bit. Noise-shaped dither is applied later, as the last step in the mastering session, prior to truncation. Global fades in and out are also best left to the mastering session.

- When you have completed the mix, try listening to it on different audio systems such as a regular hi-fi system, a walkman or a car hi-fi system. Try also listening to the mix on high quality headphones. If it sounds like you intended on all systems then you have probably created a good mix.

The above tips help with a number of issues which may be encountered during the course of a mixing session but only knowledge, experience and practice will produce the 'perfect' mix. To help you on your way to getting things sounding better, the following section is dedicated to highlighting the important frequency ranges for a number of popular musical instruments.

EQ Hot Zones

This section highlights the important frequency ranges or 'hot zones' for a number of popular musical instruments in the form of 'EQ Hot Zone' charts. This helps you to tune in to the relevant frequencies for corrective or creative purposes using Cubase SX's onboard EQ section or a third party developer EQ plug-in effect. EQ is an important tool in any mix but, as explained in Chapter 7, if your sounds are already well recorded, you shouldn't need to use much EQ to get the desired result. Using EQ in the mix should be more about blending sounds together rather than correcting poor recordings.

How to use the EQ Hot Zone charts

The first thing to bear in mind before using the following EQ Hot Zone charts is that you cannot adjust a chosen frequency band in a sound if that frequency band is not already present in the signal. For example, you cannot enhance the so-called 'air' or 'sheen' of a vocal track between 14kHz and 20kHz if this frequency range is not present in the recording. All you will add is hiss. Similarly, you cannot easily boost the 80Hz sub-bass region of a bass drum if it was originally recorded with a sharp high-pass filter set at 100Hz. Also bear in mind that you cannot make accurate EQ adjustments if your monitoring equipment or headphones are not capable of accurately reproducing the whole of the audible frequency range.

Each EQ Hot Zone chart displays two EQ curves. The upper curve shows the key areas within the frequency spectrum where the chosen instrument may be boosted for specific creative or corrective purposes. The effect of boosting is indicated for each zone. Similarly, the lower curve (the dotted line) shows the key areas within the frequency spectrum where the chosen instrument may be cut for specific creative or corrective purposes. Likewise, the effect of cutting is indicated for each zone. The amount of boost or cut shown for the curves is only a rough (and conservative) estimate and may vary considerably for each treated sound. There are, therefore, no hard and fast rules for the amounts of boost or cut. Going beyond the amounts indicated usually gives more extreme results, which might be suitable for radical creative effects or radical correction. Where appropriate, suitable high-pass or low-pass filter settings are indicated by the lower curve (dotted line).

Above all, the curves shown in the charts are NOT intended as overall EQ settings which you would want to re-create in their entirety in Cubase SX's EQ curve display. They merely show those frequency bands which are useful for the specific effects indicated. The EQ Hot Zone curves were created using 'typical' source sounds in each category. However, the accuracy of the curves cannot be guaranteed for all sounds in the same category since the tone colour and spectral components of sounds vary enormously. Mixing cannot be reduced to the sonic equivalent of painting by numbers. The charts are therefore usable as rough guides to help you quickly tune in to the key frequency ranges of your sounds. You may well need to fine tune the EQ settings for the final result and you must, at all times, use your ears and your own judgement.

Depending on the nature of your creative or corrective task, you might need to use only one part of the curve, as in the case of a 'boomy' bass drum, or several parts of the curve, as in the case of a vocal with too much 'hard edge' and not enough 'warmth'. For a boomy bass drum, try a moderate broad band cut centred around 300Hz, as indicated in the EQ Hot Zone Bass Drum chart (see Figure 11.20, below). This corrective EQ setting is easily created in Cubase SX's EQ section by dragging a handle to the appropriate position in the Channel Settings EQ curve display and setting an appropriate Q value using the Q control knob (Figure 11.18). Alternatively, click on the frequency field and type in the centre frequency. Then adjust the gain and Q by ear using the control knobs.

For a cold, piercing vocal, try a little boost centred around 300Hz and a subtle broad-band cut centred around 1.5kHz or perhaps a sharper cut at around 3kHz, as indicated in the EQ Hot Zone Vocals chart (see Figure 11.31, below). The corrective EQ setting for this vocal problem is easily created in Cubase SX's EQ section by dragging handles to the appropriate positions in the Channel Settings EQ curve display and setting the appropriate Q values using the Q control knobs (Figure 11.19). Alternatively, click on the frequency field and type in the centre frequencies. Then adjust the gains and Q controls by ear using the control knobs.

EQ Hot Zone charts

Figures 11.20 to 11.31 show the EQ Hot Zone charts for a selection of popular musical instruments and vocals.

Figure 11.18
Curing a 'boomy' bass drum in Cubase SX's EQ curve display using the EQ Hot Zone Bass Drum chart shown in Figure 11.20

Figure 11.19
Correcting a cold, piercing vocal in Cubase SX's EQ curve display using the EQ Hot Zone Vocals chart shown in Figure 11.31

Figure 11.20

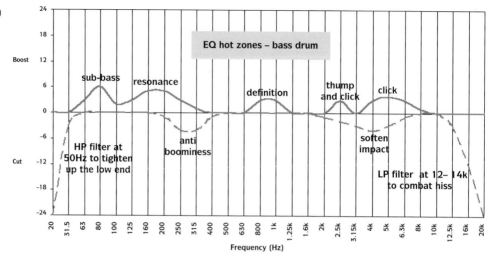

Figure 11.21

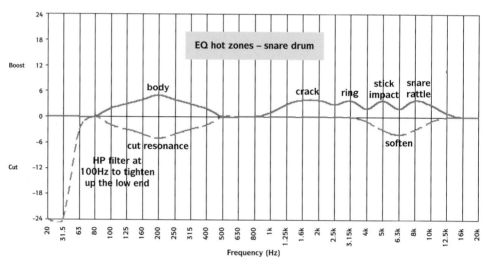

Figure 11.22

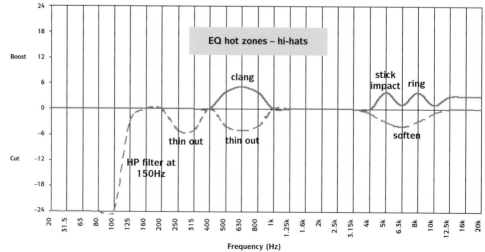

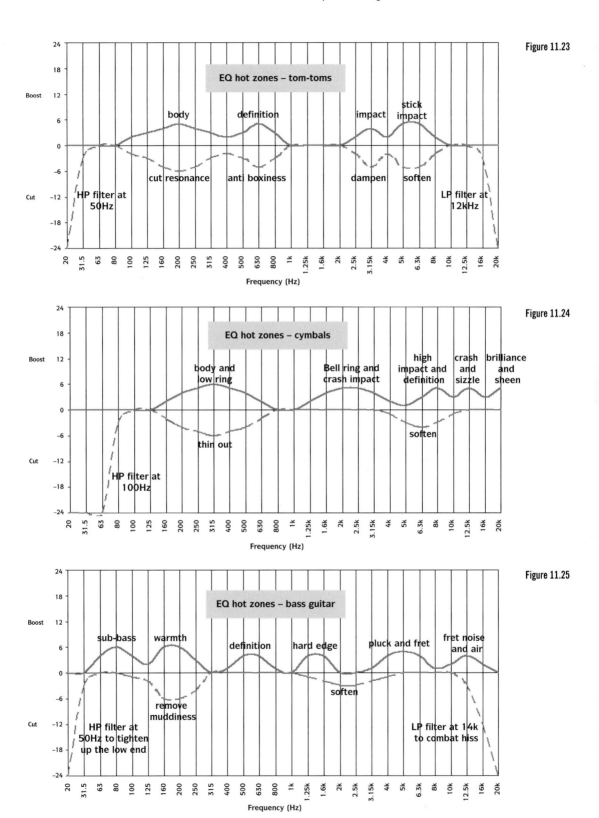

Figure 11.23

Figure 11.24

Figure 11.25

Figure 11.26

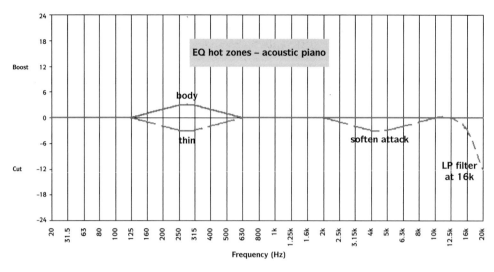

Figure 11.27

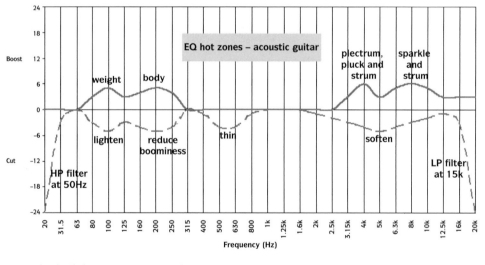

Figure 11.28

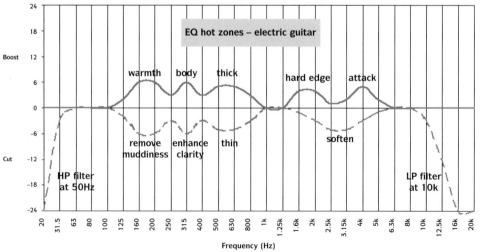

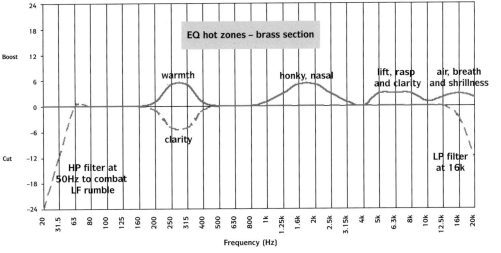

Figure 11.29

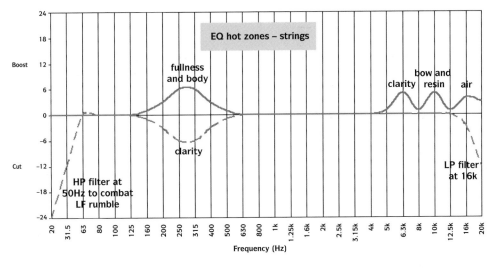

Figure 11.30

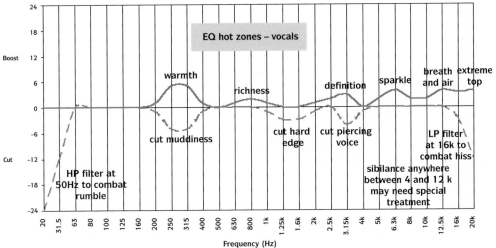

Figure 11.31

Mixing strategies

Designing your own mixing layout in Cubase SX

The first thing you might like to do before proceeding with a mix is to set up Cubase SX's working environment so that it is optimised for the kinds of mixing tasks you may need to perform. This is rather like the traditional recording studio when the engineer resets all the faders, dials and buttons on the console before proceeding with mixing. You could open all the relevant windows that you might need for the mixing session, place them in convenient positions on the screen and pre-load your favourite effects and processors. The window layout you design may be saved as a workspace in the Window menu.

Figure 11.32 shows a screen layout optimised for mixing. The VST Performance window is open so that you can keep an eye on the current CPU load. This is important if you tend to use a large number of real-time effects in your mixes. Ideally, the CPU load should not average much higher than 50 -60%. A reduced Project window forms part of the layout, where the Marker track has been made larger than the other tracks. The Marker track helps you find your way around the musical arrangement and is especially useful if you have set up Cycle Markers. A reduced Transport panel is displayed for basic transport needs. Mixer 2, (opened from the Devices menu), is displayed next to the Project window, configured to show the FX channels only. This provides quick access to the send effects return levels and channel settings edit buttons. The Mixer itself is shown in reduced mode below the other windows.

Figure 11.32

Cubase SX mixing layout

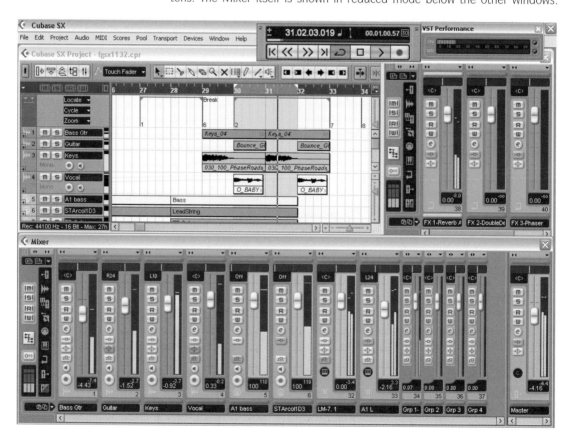

The Mixer can, at any time, be extended so that you can make detailed insert, send and EQ adjustments in the extended channel strips.

If your mixing layout goes beyond the limits of your screen this is not a big disadvantage since you can always use the main scroll bars to quickly move around. Equally, you can scroll through the channels in the Mixer using the Mixer window's scroll bar when there are too many channels to fit in your Mixer window width. Alternatively, use the left/right arrow keys on the computer keyboard to scroll/select the channels.

Once you have set up a satisfactory layout you can save it as a Workspace (Window/Workspaces/New workspace). Your mix environment may now be recalled at any time from the Organise workspaces dialogue (Alt + Pad 0) or using a key command (by default, Alt + Pad 1 to Pad 9). See Chapter 20 for more details about Workspaces.

Using Group channels as effects returns

Rather than the usual FX channels, Group channels provide an alternative method of managing send effects returns within the Mixer. Instead of activating an effect in an insert slot of an FX channel, you activate it in an insert slot of a Group channel. You may then route a send signal from the auxiliary send of an Audio channel to the Group channel, in the same manner that you would route it to an FX channel.

Since a Group channel can be set up to behave in much the same way as an FX channel, some users may wonder what is the real difference between the two channel types. The answer is that there is not much difference in their basic functionality. However, the signal of a Group channel set up as a send effect can be routed to other Group channels, which may also be set up as send effect channels. This means that you could route a signal to a Group set up for a delay effect, and then route the delay signal to a Group set up for reverb. This kind of arrangement is good for setting up multiple effects for creative sound processing. Although you can route one Group channel to another, the destination Group must be higher than the source. Group channels also feature auxiliary sends whereas FX channels do not have send slots and FX channels cannot be routed to other FX or Group channels. However, assigning send effects to FX channels helps clarify the logical flow of your routing and allows you to show/hide all your send effects more easily in the Mixer.

For both Group and FX channels, the outputs of the effects used in the inserts would normally be set to 100% wet so that the channel faders control the level of the wet signal only, while the level of the dry signal is governed using the fader on the original source Audio, VSTi or Rewire channel.

Useful solo functions

When you solo an Audio, VSTi or Rewire channel with an active auxiliary send routed to an FX channel, the FX channel is also automatically soloed. This is helpful when you wish to listen to a soloed track complete with any effects which have been applied to it. Group channels behave in a similar fashion. If, however, you wish to hear the channel dry, then click on the mute button of the FX channel before activating solo. Any other channels you want to listen to when activating a solo button can be 'protected' from the soloing action using the solo defeat function. To activate solo defeat, hold Alt and click on the solo button of

<table>
<tr><td>

Tip

For creative multiple effects processing use a chain of effects in the insert slots of a single FX or Group channel. Try placing a simple level-control plug-in between each effect in the chain (such as the ToolsOne plug-in supplied with Wavelab). This allows boost or attenuation of the effects level passed on to each effect in the chain.

</td></tr>
</table>

the chosen channel. Now when you activate the solo button of another channel, the 'solo defeated' channel is not muted. To de-activate the solo defeat function, hold Alt and click on the solo button of the 'solo defeated' channel a second time.

Integrating external effects

While the supplied plug-in effects are adequate, processing such as reverb is still often best handled using an external unit. A common requirement is the need to integrate the external unit into the mixer of Cubase SX so that you can use it in much the same way as an internal plug-in. Luckily, Cubase SX features a special External FX plug-in module designed specifically to make the integration of external effects a painless process. This is possible only if you have audio hardware with multiple inputs and outputs, since you need to route the effects signal out of and back into Cubase SX via additional busses, (separate from the main input/output busses). To integrate an external send effect, proceed as follows:

- Open the VST Connections window (Devices menu or press F4) and select the External FX tab. Add a new External FX buss and activate the desired input and output ports corresponding to the physical inputs and outputs to which you are connecting the external unit. Name the new buss as appropriate. Leave the delay, send gain and return gain columns at their default zero settings (Figure 11.33)

Figure 11.33
Set up the External FX buss in the VST Connections window

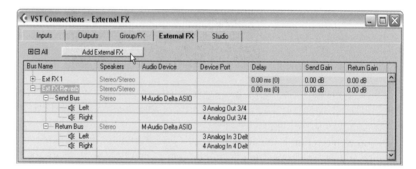

- Connect your external effects device to the physical inputs and outputs associated with the new External FX buss you created in the previous step.
- In the Mixer, add a new FX channel (Project/Add track/FX channel). In the pop-up dialogue which appears adjust the configuration to match the number of channels on the external unit (usually mono or stereo). Select the External Plugins sub-menu and choose the appropriate external effect from the list (Figure 11.34). You have now created a send effect which routes the send and return signals to/from the external device.
- When the external FX channel is first created, the External FX interface appears automatically on the screen (Figure 11.35). Here you can adjust the send and return levels and, if necessary, configure the delay time so that Cubase SX can compensate during playback. A delay time may be required if your external unit introduces latency into the signal path. (Note that the latency of your audio hardware has already been taken into account in this process and should not be entered here). Typically, the latency time is 0ms or values between 0.5 and 2ms, depending upon

Figure 11.34
Create a new External FX channel

the external device. Compressor/limiters are likely to introduce slight latencies and should be set up carefully. To help find out the exact time required, the interface features a 'ping' button. This sends a short pulse to your external unit and measures the time it takes to come back via the return line. When measuring the latency in this way, temporarily reduce all delay parameters in your external unit to zero or use a bypass button (if available) to avoid measuring the delay in the effect rather than the latency in the signal path.

Figure 11.35
Set up the External FX settings in the External FX interface

- If the external unit is a reverb device you would normally set it up to produce a 100% wet signal at its output since, here, we have created a send effect.
- You can now send a signal to the external effect in exactly the same way as you would for an internal send effect. Choose an audio-based track to which you wish to apply the effect and open its send panel. Activate the External effect in one of the send slots. Adjust the send level using the minifader in the send slot, as usual. Insert effects may be set up in a similar manner.

Using the Mixer context menu

Right clicking (PC)/Command clicking (Mac) anywhere on the Mixer display opens the Mixer context menu (Figure 11.36)

The Mixer context menu is a multi-purpose menu for linking channels, adding channels, saving/loading selected channel settings or all the current Mixer settings, and for meter management. The options function as follows:

- Link/Unlink channels – links two or more channels together so that moving the fader, mute, solo, monitor or record enable controls on one of the linked channels simultaneously moves the same controls on all the other linked channels. To link channels, select two or more channels in the Mixer by clicking on the selection strip (just

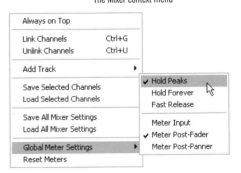

Figure 11.36
The Mixer context menu

Tip

To change a single parameter in a group of linked channels hold Alt on the computer keyboard.

above the name field) while holding the Shift key on the computer keyboard (alternatively for consecutive channel selections use the left/right arrow keys while holding Shift on the computer keyboard). Select Link Channels in the Mixer context menu to implement the link. Link Channels is immediately useful for grouping channels together for common tasks, such as muting the backing vocals in a mix, lowering the volume of linked string channels while maintaining their relative levels, or soloing all the drum tracks.

- Save/Load Selected channels – saves or loads the current settings of the selected channel(s). All parameters are saved or loaded. When loading a multiple channel file, only the currently selected channels are affected. For example, if you selected six channels when you saved the file then, to load all six channels, you must manually select six channels when you load the file. Good for copying settings between multiple tracks in the same mix or in an alternative version of the same project.
- Save/Load all Mixer settings – saves or loads all the current parameter settings for all channels in the Mixer, including the input and output busses. This is like taking a global snapshot of the whole Mixer. Good for re-initialising the Mixer to your preferred settings prior to commencing a mix and for copying mixes between different versions of the same project. This function does not add channels when there are less channels in the destination Mixer than in the saved file.
- Global Meter Settings – features a number of options for changing the behaviour of the meters. When 'Hold Peaks' is activated a horizontal line at the peak level of the signal remains in the display for a short time. The hold time is chosen in File/Preferences/VST (the default time is 3 seconds). When 'Hold Forever' is activated the highest peak in the signal is held permanently in the meter display, which is helpful for keeping an eye on the maximum peaks in the signal. When 'Fast release' is de-activated, the meters react slightly more slowly to changes in the signal allowing you to see more clearly the average peak level. When 'Fast Release' is activated, the meters behave in a manner similar to peak program meters (PPM) and react extremely quickly to show all the peaks in the signal. This is good for recording highly dynamic signals where you may wish to monitor the transient peaks more clearly in order to avoid digital distortion. The 'Meter Input', 'Meter Post-Fader' and 'Meter Post-Panner' settings allow you to see the levels on the channel meters either before the channel fader, after the channel fader (but before the pan control) or, finally, after both the channel fader and the pan control. In Meter Input mode, you are viewing the meter level of the source audio as recorded on hard disk (or of the incoming audio signal if you are looking at an input buss). Meter Input mode is normally used when recording (see Chapter 3 for more details). In Meter Post-Fader mode, you are viewing the level of the signal after it has passed via the channel fader. In Meter Post-Panner mode you are viewing the level of the signal after it has passed via the channel fader and the pan control. Post-Panner mode is relevant to stereo signals only where the pan position you choose is now reflected in the channel meter. Many sound engineers claim that Post-Panner mode is more intuitive and visually logical to use.
- Reset Meters – resets all meters simultaneously. Helpful if you are measuring levels over a specific passage or checking for clipping.

Other useful Mixer techniques

Other useful Mixer techniques include the following:

- Various simple key commands make life easier when using the Mixer. For example, use the left/right arrow keys on the computer keyboard to select the channels. Hold Shift while pressing the left/right arrow keys to make multiple channel selections. Use the up/down arrow keys to change the fader level of a single selected channel or a number of selected channels. Use 'M' to mute and 'S' to solo a single selected channel or a number of selected channels.

- Automatic record enabling of channels upon selection is not convenient for most mixing purposes. To disable automatic record enabling upon channel selection, open File/Preferences/Editing and disable 'Enable Record on Selected Track'.

- The settings of one channel can be copied to another using standard copy and paste techniques. Select the channel which you wish to copy from and select Ctrl (PC) / Command (Mac) + C on the computer keyboard to copy the settings. To paste the setting to another channel, select the target channel and select Ctrl (PC) / Command (Mac) + V on the computer keyboard to paste the settings. Settings may be copied from one Project window to another.

- During mixing you are likely to concentrate on specific passages using Cubase SX in cycle playback mode. To make this quicker and easier, it is well worth setting up a number of cycle markers in the Marker track. Hold Ctrl (PC) / Command (Mac) and drag with the pointer or pencil in the Marker track to insert a cycle marker over the selected range. Open the cycle marker pop-up menu and make a selection from the list to move the left and right locators to the start and end of the chosen cycle marker range. Alternatively, press Shift + G to start immediate loop playback around the currently selected cycle marker.

- When using Send effects, there are times when you do not want the channel fader to affect the level of the signal going to the effect. In these circumstances, use the Pre-fader button (next to the on/off and edit buttons in the Send effect slots). When the Pre-fader button is in the default de-activated state (the post fader setting), the channel fader affects the signal level going to the effect, i.e. lowering the channel fader reduces the level of the channel and simultaneously reduces the signal level which is routed to the effect. When the Pre-fader button is activated (the pre-fader setting), the channel fader no longer affects the signal level which is routed to the effect, i.e. lowering the channel fader reduces the level of the channel only and the signal is still sent to the effect at the level set in the effects slot. A pre-fader setting might suit an autopan effect when you want to hear the effects signal only. Here you would reduce the fader level of the dry signal to its minimum, leaving only the effects signal audible. A pre-fader setting is also good for special effects. For example, try setting up a pre-fader send to a reverb effect and then slowly fade out the dry signal to leave the reverberant signal only. This creates the illusion of the sound disappearing into the distance.

Figure 11.37
Audio channel and stereo output bus
signal flowchart (for stereo mixing)

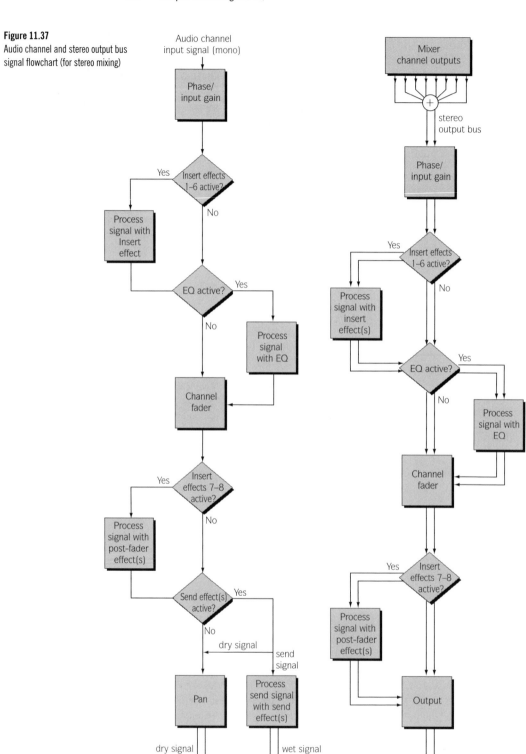

Mixer routing

To help further clarify your mixing tasks, Figure 11.37 shows a flowchart of the signal as it passes through an Audio channel and a master stereo output buss and the order in which the effects and EQ are applied. It is helpful to remember the overall order in which effects and EQ can be applied in an audio-based channel; i.e. Insert effects 1-6, followed by EQ, followed by Insert effects 7-8, followed by Send effects.

Mixing down

The final mix

The final mix involves mixing down the multi-track audio into a stereo or multi-channel/surround format. Depending on your preferences and overall system resources, this can occur using a variety of techniques. The main choices are as follows:

1 *Mixing down using an external console.* Here, the signals from the tracks in Cubase SX are routed to an external console via the digital or analogue outputs of your audio hardware. The final mix takes place using the faders and controls of the external console. The mix is transferred to the final medium, such as analogue tape, DAT or CD recorder, via the outputs of the external mixer.

2 *Mixing down to external media using the virtual Mixer in Cubase SX.* In this case, the final mix takes place entirely within Cubase SX. The mix is transferred to the final medium via the analogue or digital outputs of your audio hardware. This technique suits mixing down to analogue tape, DAT or external CD recorder and offers the possibility of an automated mix within Cubase SX, when your external console does not feature automation.

3 *Mixing down to an audio file using the virtual Mixer in Cubase SX and the Export/Audio Mixdown function* (the audio file is stored on the hard disk of the host computer). In this case, the final mix takes place entirely within Cubase SX. The mix is transferred directly to the hard disk as an audio file in the format specified in the Export/Audio Mixdown dialogue. This allows you to produce high-resolution audio files suitable for later compilation into the tracks for an audio CD or other final media (see below for details of the Export/Audio Mixdown function).

The third option tends to be the most popular choice among Cubase SX users since it is convenient and helps maintain the quality of the audio. If you are using this option and your mix is to undergo further editing and processing at a later mastering stage, do not apply dithering and do not truncate to 16-bits. Instead, choose a high-resolution audio format in the Export/Audio Mixdown dialogue, such as 32 or 24-bit/44.1, and mix down without dithering. Global fades in and out are also best left to the mastering session. However, if no mastering stage is envisaged, use dithering and choose 16-bit/44.1kHz in the Export/Audio Mixdown dialogue when you wish to produce an audio file which is suitable for burning onto an audio CD. See Chapter 13 for full details about mastering and dithering.

Info

The precise routing order for a signal passing through an Audio channel runs as follows:

1 phase switch
2 input gain
3 inserts 1-6
4 EQ
5 pre-fader aux send
6 channel fader
7 inserts 7-8
8 post-fader aux send
9 pan.

Integrating the MIDI tracks in your final mix

If you are using option 1, as outlined above, the audio signals from your external MIDI devices are easily integrated into the final mix by routing them into the channels of the external console. However, if you are using Export/Audio Mixdown to export your final mix as an audio file, all MIDI tracks which are triggering the external MIDI devices in your system are NOT included in the mix. Cubase SX has no way of knowing what audio signals your external units are producing. The solution is to bounce the audio outputs of your external MIDI devices onto regular audio tracks within Cubase SX, before proceeding with the final mix. This technique is explained fully in the section entitled 'How do I include my MIDI recordings when I use Export / Audio Mixdown?' in Chapter 5.

Export/Audio Mixdown

Export/Audio Mixdown provides a way of creating a stereo (or surround format) audio file of the whole mix. It also allows you to create an audio file from any passage and any track combination within your project. The latter is useful for bouncing several tracks and their effects into a single mono or stereo audio file to free up space in the project and on the hard disk. This also helps conserve processing power. A wide range of file formats are available. The Export/Audio Mixdown dialogue is opened by selecting Export/Audio Mixdown in the File menu (see Figure 11.38).

Figure 11.38
The Export/Audio Mixdown dialogue

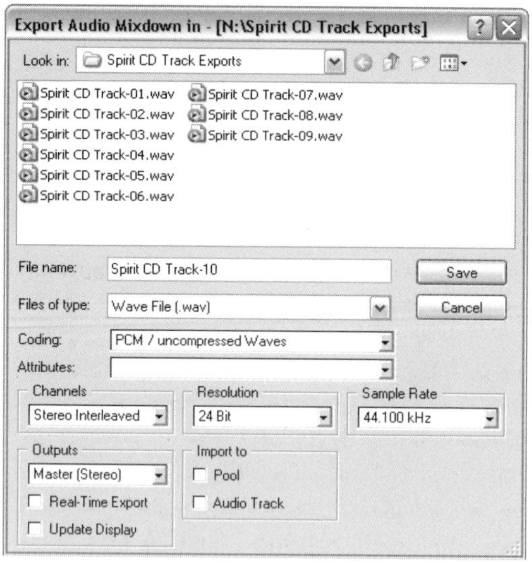

Export/Audio Mixdown allows you to transfer your entire mix as heard on the chosen stereo (or multichannel) output buss into a single audio file. You can also export individual channels. The function operates on all non-muted audio-based channels (Audio, Group, VSTi, FX and Rewire) between the left and right locators. The basic procedure for mixing down using Export/Audio Mixdown is as follows:

- Move the left and right locators to the start and end points of the passage in the project you wish to mix down. This could be a few bars or the whole length of the project. Mute all tracks which you do not wish to include in the mix.
- Audition the selected passage to make sure that the mix is exactly what you need and, if necessary, make any final adjustments.
- Open the Export/Audio Mixdown dialogue and select the file type, number of channels, resolution and sample rate for the destination file. Wave is the standard file type in PC systems and AIFF is the standard file type in Mac systems. For internet and website applications, MPEG and Real Audio file types are available.
- If you intend to mix down to a final stereo file to be used for the creation of an audio CD, Stereo Interleaved, 16-bit, 44.1kHz are the correct settings. If it is a final audio file to which no further processing is to be applied, you would also need to apply dithering when truncating the bit-depth (e.g. reducing the bit-depth from 24-bit to 16-bit). Dithering is applied in slots 7 or 8 of the chosen output buss (see Chapter 13 for more details about dithering).
- If your mix is to undergo further editing and processing at a later mastering stage, do not apply noise-shaped dither and truncate to 16-bit at the mixdown stage. Instead, mix to a high-resolution format, such as 32-bit float or 24-bit. Noise-shaped dither is applied later, as the last step in the mastering session, prior to truncation.
- Choose the output buss you wish to mix down in the outputs menu. For mixing down a stereo mix, select the stereo output buss to which all the channels in the Mixer are routed.
- Decide whether you would like the resulting file to be automatically imported back into Cubase SX. Activate 'Import to Pool' / 'Import to Audio Track' as required.
- Select a folder and a name for the new file and, after verifying that you have made the correct settings in the dialogue, click on the Save button.

| **Info** |

If an External FX plug-in is active within the project, Export/Audio Mixdown is always conducted in real-time mode. This is necessary in order to capture the real-time output of the external effects device.

In the above procedure, make sure you set the left and right locators to appropriate positions. When placing the right locator, it is preferable to leave a gap of one or two bars after the audio tracks have finished to take into account any reverberation tail or other effects which may spill over beyond the end point of the music.

Using Export/Audio Mixdown to create a stereo file of a whole mix results in an audio file which has not suffered any degradation due to being transferred from one medium to another and, if it is a final 16-bit/44.1 audio file, it can be assembled with other similar files to create the tracks for a CD. If you have a CD-R drive, you can burn a sequence of 16-bit/44.1kHz audio files to an audio CD using an audio CD burning application.

If your mix is to undergo further editing and processing at a later mastering stage, you would normally choose a high-resolution audio format, such as 32-bit float or 24-bit, in the Export / Audio Mixdown dialogue. Mastering often takes place in a specialised mastering and CD burning application like Steinberg Wavelab or Bias Peak, but excellent results may also be obtained using Cubase SX for the mastering session and a separate CD writing application for burning the CD. See Chapter 13 for full details about mastering and dithering.

Other possibilities for exporting audio include the creation of:

- MP3 and Real Audio files for multimedia applications
- Multiple-channel interleaved files
- Split stereo or split multi-channel files
- Mono files

If you encounter difficulties when using Export/Audio Mixdown, try activating 'Real Time Export' in the Export/Audio Mixdown dialogue. This takes longer but may provide a solution. Also make sure that none of your tracks have their monitor buttons activated, as this blocks transfer of the channel's data during the export process.

Mixer moves

To help you in your various mixing tasks, the following table provides a summary of some of the default key commands and practical mixer moves:

Table 11.1 Mixer moves

Key selected		Mouse action	Result
PC	Mac		
F2	F2	–	opens the Transport panel
F3	F3	–	opens the Mixer
F4	F4	–	opens VST Connections window
F11	F11	–	opens VST Instruments panel
F12	F12	–	opens VST Performance meter
M	M	–	mutes selected channel(s)
S	S	–	solos selected channel(s)
ctrl	cmnd	click once on fader	resets fader to 0dB
ctrl	cmnd	click once on pan control	resets pan position to centre
Shift	Shift	move fader or pan control	changes setting in fine amounts
–	–	click on channel headroom indicator	resets headroom indicator
–	–	double-click on channel strip name	opens channel name entry pop-up
L/R arrow	L/R arrow		selects next consecutive channel
U/D arrow	U/D arrow		changes volume fader level of selected channel

Audio effects

Cubase SX is supplied with a wide range of audio effects and processors. These are found in the Plug-ins sub-menu of the Audio menu or in the pop-up menus of the audio-based channel insert slots and are designed principally for real-time processing. Real-time processing is that which takes place at the same time as the music is playing, as opposed to the offline processing available in the Process menu, which takes place when you are not in playback mode. However, to maximise the flexibility of the program, all plug-in effects may also be applied as offline processes.

Plug-ins are audio processing and effects modules which can be added to the effects panels of Cubase SX as and when you need them. They do not usually function as stand-alone programs and, therefore, always require a host (like Cubase SX) in which to run. As well as the plug-ins supplied with the program, you can add additional Steinberg and third party developer plug-ins and, as you are probably already aware, there are literally hundreds to choose from. Because of its open-endedness, the plug-in concept offers possibilities beyond the normal confines of the core program. Plug-ins open up whole new worlds of audio processing to the Cubase SX user and endow the program with a large degree of expandability and flexibility within a single software environment. This allows users to build their own virtual studio according to their budget, their system resources, and the kind of project they are working on.

Plug-in formats and standards

Plug-ins are supplied in a number of different formats, each of which suits the host program in which they are intended to run. The popular formats relevant to Cubase SX include VST (Windows and Mac OS X) and Direct X (Windows only). These are the dominant plug-in standards.

VST plug-ins run in all VST compatible applications including, of course, Cubase SX. Although the plug-ins supplied with the program are essentially VST plug-ins, they are designed to run in Cubase SX alone and cannot be used in other programs.

The Windows version of Cubase SX also recognises Direct X plug-ins. Direct X is an application-independent standard developed by Microsoft for the handling of audio, video and multimedia tasks in Windows operating systems. Cubase SX recognises the Direct X protocol and, when any Direct X plug-ins are installed within the system, a new sub-menu appears in the Plug-ins menu.

Direct X is also sometimes referred to as Direct Show and a large number of Windows-based applications support it. Due to its popularity, many third party developers produce Direct X effects and processors, since their product is assured compatibility with a larger number of host programs.

VST and Direct X plug-ins normally incorporate a graphical user interface which runs in a separate window within the host application. This is where you manipulate the control parameters for the device and save and load presets.

Audio effects in theory

In the quest for instant results, the theoretical aspects of audio signal pro-cessing are often forgotten. However, taking some time to understand the theory can help you achieve better results. Before proceeding to descriptions of the supplied effects and how to handle them, this section, therefore, cov-ers the theoretical aspects of the main effects and processing techniques you are likely to encounter in your use of Cubase SX.

Audio effects and audio processing refer to a number of methods by which you can modify an audio signal for creative or corrective purposes. To be exact, effects are generally those techniques which modify the sound for creative pur-poses and often involve adding elements to the signal (such as reverb, delay and chorus). Processing tends to mean the modification of signals for correc-tive purposes and often involves subtracting elements from the signal (such as compression, gating and filtering). However, these latter kinds of processing can also be used for creative effects. For the sake of convenience, 'audio effects' as used in this text is taken to mean all types of audio effects and audio processing. The essential thing to remember is that all effects and processing involve the modification of the original sound in some way.

Audio effects can be divided into a number of categories and, conve-niently, these match the default sub-menu categories of the Plug-in menu of Cubase SX. The categories include delay, distortion, dynamics, filter, modu-lation, reverb and 'other' types of processing.

Info

The phenomenon that delays of less than 30–40 ms are fused with the direct sound is known as the Haas effect (discovered by Helmut Haas in 1951). Haas also found that short delays help the ear locate the direction of the original source, like the early reflections in a reverberant space. The careful use of short delays across the stereo sound field therefore helps place mono sources at specific positions within the stereo image and adds depth and focus to the mix.

Delay

Delay is the replication of a signal which occurs at a set time after the origi-nal. When the delayed signal is clearly distinguishable from the original, (usu-ally when the delay time is increased to around 30ms or more), this is classed as a particular type of delay known as echo. Delay effects often involve repeating echos, produced by adding an amount of feedback to the delay cir-cuit. Delay is also an essential element when producing effects like chorus and flanging (see Modulation, below) and plays a part in reverb devices where a pre-delay controls the length of time between the original sound and the onset of the reverberation effect.

The concept of delay is easily understood by the majority of users but, nowa-days, surrounded by ever more exotic effects, it tends to be under-valued. In sound processing, delay and echo are terms which essentially refer to the same thing but, strictly speaking, an echo is a sound reflection separated from the original sound by more than 30ms (as outlined above). Before 30ms the ear perceives the reflections as part of the same sound i.e. they are fused into one. After 30ms the ear begins to differentiate the original and the delayed signal.

This is important to remember since it can help you achieve the desired effect when programming delay devices like Cubase SX's Double Delay or Mod Delay.

Delay devices feature a relatively simple set of controls which usually include the following parameters:

- Delay time – sets the time delay for the replication of the signal, usually measured in milliseconds.
- Feedback – determines the proportion of the delay which is fed back to the input, thereby controlling the number of repeats for the delay line.
- Pan – pans the delayed signal to different positions in the stereo image (in a stereo delay device).
- Mix – controls the mix of the original (dry) signal and the effects (wet) signal.

Bearing in mind the 30ms threshold, ADT effects (Automatic Double Tracking) are created using delay times of around 30 to 60ms with no, or very little, feedback. ADT simulates the effect of doubling the sound, since the ear perceives the delayed signal as a separate event but the delay time is not great enough for it to become detached from the original sound. As you increase the delay time beyond 50-60ms and increase the feedback, other kinds of effects, such as 'slap-back' echo, are possible. Here we begin to clearly differentiate the delayed and the original signal. If you also manipulate the stereo imagery by delaying one channel by a different amount to the other you can create pseudo-stereo effects. As you increase the delay time still further special effects such as 'ping pong' echoes and multiple echo effects become possible. 'Ping pong' is the term applied to an echo which 'bounces' a number of times between each channel of the stereo image. With longer delay times, all kinds of special effects can be created and, in Cubase SX, the timing of the echoes can be tuned to the tempo of the music using the tempo sync features.

If needed, you can also work out the delay times for any given tempo with a calculator, using the following equation:

delay (in seconds) = (240/ current tempo)/note value

where note value equals four for a quarter note, eight for an eighth note, sixteen for a sixteenth note and so on.

Distortion

Distortion is the adding of extra frequencies to a sound signal using a non-linear audio process. This results in a change in the waveform. Distortion can be of the unwanted type, such as that encountered when you record at too high a level on a digital recording medium, or it can be of the wanted type, such as the warm characteristics of tube amplifiers or mildly overdriven analogue tape. Distortion of the wanted type usually involves the adding of extra harmonics based upon the most prominent frequency components in the original signal. Distortion is referred to by a number of different names including saturation, overdrive and 'fuzz'.

The effect of applying distortion ranges from the subtle addition of analogue warmth (simulated tape saturation) to cold digital recordings, to the explosive and powerful production of 'fuzz' electric guitar sounds. Subtle analogue tape saturation effects often use only small amounts of third-harmonic distortion and apply this distortion to the loudest peaks in the signal. 'Fuzz' or overdrive type effects are produced by adding more harmonics to the signal, where lower-order harmonics (second, third, fourth and fifth) produce a 'musical' thickening of the sound and the addition of higher-order harmonics produces more metallic results. Subtle overdrive and extreme fuzz effects can be heard and viewed in Cubase SX's Overdrive plug-in, where the display represents the number and amplitude of the harmonics added to the signal (regulated using the Drive parameter).

Since distortion often involves an obvious change in the waveform of the signal, it is useful to see exactly how in a graphical representation. Generally, a more complex waveform equates to more harmonics in the signal. Cubase SX's supplied QuadraFuzz effect adds harmonic distortion to the signal according to a number of transfer functions (Shape buttons). A transfer function is essentially a 'go-between' shaping function which determines the relationship between an input and an output signal. Changing the shape of the function produces distortion in the output. Figure 12.1 shows what QuadraFuzz adds to a clean guitar signal when the top, middle and lower Shape buttons are selected (using the 'Light Fuzz' preset). Each button produces progressively more distortion in the signal. (See also 'QuadraFuzz' in the section entitled 'The supplied audio effects', below).

Figure 12.1

The effect of QuadraFuzz's Shape buttons. A clean guitar signal (left) is treated with three instances of distortion using the top, middle and lower Shape buttons respectively, resulting in progressively more distortion.

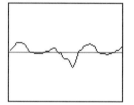
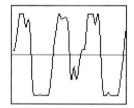
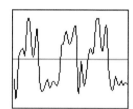
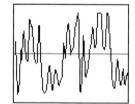

Dynamics

Dynamics processing involves the automatic control of the level of the signal in various ways and includes the techniques of compression, limiting, expansion and gating. These are important concepts in audio processing and it is therefore worth persevering with the theory if you are not already familiar.

In simple terms, when you compress a signal, loud parts become quieter and quiet parts become louder; compression converts a large dynamic range into a smaller dynamic range. When you expand a signal, loud parts become louder and quiet parts become quieter; expansion converts a small dynamic range into a larger dynamic range. Compressors and expanders are automatic gain control devices. Compressors start to reduce the gain of an audio signal when the level rises above a set threshold and expanders reduce the gain as the level falls below a set threshold.

The amount of compression or expansion is usually described in terms of a ratio, (e.g. 2:1, 10:1 20:1, infinity:1). When an infinitely high ratio of compression is applied to an input signal, the output does not increase above the threshold no matter how much level is applied at the input. This is a particular type of compression known as limiting. When an infinitely high ratio of expansion is applied to an input signal, the output reduces to zero as soon as the input drops below the threshold. This is a particular type of expansion known as gating, (also known as noise gating). Therefore, compression and limiting can be grouped into the same category, and expansion and gating can be grouped into another.

Compression and limiting

There are normally a number of standard controls which govern the compressor/limiter process and these are as follows:

• Threshold – sets the level at which compression begins to occur. When the input signal goes above the threshold, the output signal from the device is attenuated, (reduced in level), according to the ratio set with the ratio control.
• Ratio – varies the amount of gain reduction. A ratio of 2:1 indicates that for every 2dB the input level rises above the threshold level there will be a 1dB increase in the output level. A ratio of 10:1 indicates that for every 10dB the input level rises above the threshold level there will be a 1dB increase in the output level and so on. Note that a ratio of 1:1 indicates that there is no change in gain between the input and output levels.
• Attack time – determines the rate at which the compressor attenuates the output level after the threshold has been exceeded.
• Release time – determines the rate at which the compressor returns to its normal output gain after the input signal has fallen below the threshold level.
• Gain makeup – since compression often involves an overall reduction in output level many compressors incorporate a 'makeup' control to increase the level after compression.

Compressor/limiters also generally feature soft-knee or hard-knee characteristics. Soft-knee is when compression begins gradually a number of dB's below the threshold, whereas hard-knee is when the compression begins more suddenly at the threshold level. Soft-knee compression tends to sound more natural and transparent to the listener whereas hard-knee compression produces a more obvious effect.

The relationship between the input level, output level and ratio is best viewed in diagrammatic form as in Figure 12.2. The compressor section display in Cubase SX's VST Dynamics and Dynamics plug-ins resembles this same graphical format, as we shall see later.

Figure 12.2 shows the threshold set at –20dB. When the ratio is set at 2:1, an input level exceeding the threshold by 10dB results in a 5dB attenuation in the output level. When the ratio is at infinity:1 the output level remains at

Figure 12.2
Compressor/limiter input and output levels for different ratios

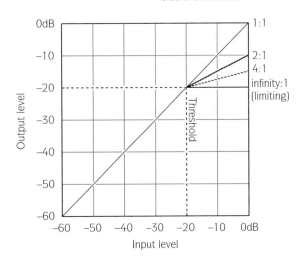

–20dB no matter how high the input level rises above the threshold.

Settings for the threshold and ratio vary enormously depending on the input signal but, as an initial starting point, a resulting gain reduction of between 5 – 10dB might be expected. To achieve this the threshold might be set around 10 – 15dB below the maximum peaks in the signal and the ratio might be set between 2:1 and 10:1. The gain makeup might then be set to bring the output back up to the required level. The attack and release times are very important for the resulting characteristics of the compressed signal and can be used for a variety of creative effects.

For example, setting a slow attack time (20-50ms) on a bass guitar or lead guitar allows the initial impact of each note to pass through unhindered before the compression takes effect. This maintains the original attack characteristics of the sound while still compressing the rest of the signal, allowing it to cut through in the mix and adding punch. (Try release times around 20-50ms and ratios between 5:1 and 15:1).

Conversely, a slow attack time on a rock vocal sound, which you are attempting to level out, might not be appropriate. The slow attack may allow too many of the initial transients to pass through unhindered, thereby negating the levelling effect you are trying to achieve. For many vocal applications, a faster attack (5-15ms) may be more suitable. (Try release times around 100ms and ratios between 3:1 and 6:1).

The choice of release time is also paramount in creating the desired effect. Too short or too long a release time can result in undesirable audible 'pumping' or 'breathing' side-effects, so the release time must be set carefully. A fast release time (less than around 20ms) can increase the perceived level of the natural decay of an instrument. This can be used to increase the 'body' of, for example, a drum sound. Conversely, you may wish to emphasise the actual 'hit' of the drum, in which case you might set a slow release time combined with a moderately slow attack time.

Compressors are often used to increase the average signal level to make sounds and mixes seem louder and to even out the level of wildly fluctuating signals so that they can be managed more easily in the mix. However, the parameters must be set very carefully in order to avoid unwanted side-effects, especially when compressing a whole mix. This can sometimes result in one dominant instrument producing undesirable reduction in the level of the rest of the mix whenever it is playing. In addition, note that when you are using the gain makeup control to increase the level after compression, you are also increasing the noise floor by the same amount. This is an unavoidable side-effect of compression which can sometimes become obtrusive, particularly if the original signal already contains high levels of background noise. In the case of compressing a whole mix, a multi-band compressor is often more appropriate.

Compressors and limiters are often found in the same device but the applications of pure limiting are different from those of compression. Limiters are generally used to stop a signal passing above a set threshold, no matter how loud the input becomes, (sometimes referred to as 'brickwall' limiting). Limiting devices are characterised by very fast attack and release times, so that fast transients can be detected and corrected very quickly. The threshold for limiting is normally set quite high, so that only the transient peaks are attenuated while the rest of the signal passes through unaffected.

Tip

Setting both the attack and release time of a compressor very fast (less than 1-2ms), together with a threshold set for the peaks in the signal, can produce desirable distortion in the individual cycles of the waveform. Try ratios between 2:1 and 6:1. Used in a very subtle manner, this can simulate the effect of tape saturation, adding warmth to the signal.

Tip

As well as controlling the wanted parts of the signal, compression may also result in an increase in the level of some of the unwanted parts of the signal, such as interference or headphone spill between sung vocal lines. To avoid this effect, try firstly using expansion / gating to reduce the level of the interference and then apply the compression.

Expansion and gating

Expansion and gating are the opposites of compression and limiting and, once again, the precise characteristics are best viewed in diagrammatic form (see Figure 12.3).

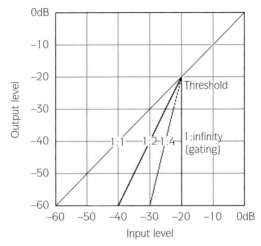

Figure 12.3
Expander/gate input and output levels for different ratios

Although expanders have their uses, most of this section concentrates on the use of one particular kind of expander, commonly known as the noise gate. A noise gate is a very high ratio expander. If the input signal falls below a pre-set threshold the output is radically attenuated. This is extremely useful for eliminating the unwanted noise and interference which may be present in between the wanted sections of a musical performance. Figure 12.3 shows the behaviour of an expander/noise gate whose threshold has been set at –20dB.

Typically, expander/noise gates feature the following control features:

- Threshold – sets the level at which expansion begins to occur or the gate begins to close. When the input signal goes below the threshold, the output signal from the device is attenuated according to the ratio set with the ratio control.
- Ratio – varies the amount of gain change. A ratio of 1:2 indicates that for every 1dB the input falls below the threshold there is a 2dB decrease in the output. A ratio of 1:infinity indicates that as soon as the input falls below the threshold the output is radically attenuated (i.e. the signal is gated). Classic gating devices feature fixed infinite ratios with no ratio controls. Instead, the gating action is regulated with a threshold (as above) and a floor or gain control which determines by how many dB the signal is attenuated when it falls below the threshold.
- Attack time – determines the rate at which the expander/noise gate opens (to allow the signal through) when the signal rises above the threshold.
- Release time – determines the rate of attenuation when the signal has fallen below the threshold.
- Hold time – controls the length of time for which the level of the signal is guaranteed to be held before attenuation occurs.

The attack control of noise gates are normally endowed with very fast attack times in order to be able to cope with sounds which have rapid attack tran-

Info

Frequency-conscious gating, as implemented in Cubase's VST Dynamics and Dynamics plug-ins, is particularly useful for gating live drum recordings which are suffering from leakage between microphones. This involves filtering the side-chain signal which triggers the gate so that it emphasises only the frequency range of the wanted instrument. For example, tuning the filter to the frequency bandwidth of the bass drum makes the gate sensitive to the bass drum alone. This means that the gate only opens when the bass drum is playing and any leakage into the bass drum mic from the snare and hi-hats is minimised.

sients such as drum and percussion sounds. This ensures that the first part of the sound opens the gate quickly enough so that it passes through unhindered. However, sounds with slower attack characteristics benefit from slower noise gate attack times in order to avoid the audible click which can sometimes occur when the gate is opened abruptly.

The hold time is used to determine how long the gate remains open and, once it starts to close, the release time determines the rate at which the signal fades away.

As well as their usual noise elimination function, noise gates can also be used creatively to modify the envelope of the signal. For example, special effects can be created by intentionally slowing down the attack portion of a sound using a slow attack setting, or the 'body' of the sound can be attenuated with a fast release time to produce staccato effects.

Filtering

A filter is a device which attenuates one or more chosen frequency bands within a sound while allowing the others to pass through unchanged. In the same way as a coffee filter 'filters' the larger particles of coffee from the source coffee mixture, or an air filter 'filters' the larger particles of air-born dust from the air, a sound filter 'filters' various sound particles (harmonics) from the raw source sound which passes through it. Various types of sound filter are available but the essential idea of all sound filters is that of a device which modifies the harmonic structure of the sound which passes through it.

The filter type determines what kind of filtering action takes place on the source signal. Each filter type has specific characteristics which are fundamental to the manner in which the filtering action takes place. The main filter types include low-pass, high-pass, band-pass and band-reject. Each filter features a cut-off frequency. This determines the frequency at which the filter begins to have an effect. In the case of a low-pass filter those frequencies below the cut-off point are allowed to pass through unchanged while those above are significantly reduced. The cut-off point of a low-pass filter therefore regulates the overall 'brightness' of the tone. Resonance is another attribute of most filters and this is also referred to as Q or emphasis. This emphasises the frequencies around the cut-off point thereby regulating the 'sharpness' or resonant character of the tone. Other aspects of filter design include filter slope characteristics, phase response and the implementation of envelope generators to control the action of the cut-off frequency.

Filter types

The four basic types of filter are low-pass, high-pass, band-pass and band-reject. Variations and combinations of these are known by different names such as notch filtering and parametric EQ. The use of filters in the pure sense implies the cutting of frequencies, whereas EQ implies the cutting and the boosting of the chosen frequencies (see Chapter 11 for more details about EQ). Understanding the action of the four basic filter types can lead to a better understanding of EQ and is the first step in becoming familiar with filtering in general.

Filter types are generally recognised by their amplitude response. This is shown on a graph of amplitude against frequency (see Figures 12.4 to 12.7, below). Each filter type is characterised by one part of the frequency spectrum which is allowed to pass through, known as the pass band, and another part of the spectrum which is significantly reduced, known as the stop band. The point at which the filtering action begins, (when the amplitude response passes from the pass band to the stop band), is known as the cut-off frequency (or cut-off point). There is always a transitional area between the pass band and the stop band. The rule for defining the exact point for the cut-off frequency is generally accepted as that point where the signal has fallen 3dB below the level of the pass band. It is, therefore, true to say that a significant number of frequencies below (or above) the cut-off point will have already been attenuated (cut) before the cut-off point itself is reached.

Low-pass
A low-pass filter allows those frequencies below the cut-off point to pass through with little change while those above are significantly reduced.

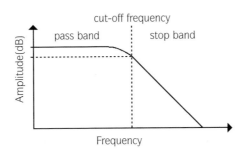

Figure 12.4
Amplitude response of a low-pass filter

High-pass
A high-pass filter significantly reduces those frequencies below the cut-off point while those above are allowed to pass through with little change (the opposite of the low-pass filter).

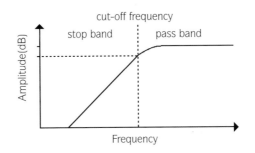

Figure 12.5
Amplitude response of a high-pass filter

Band-pass
A band-pass filter allows a band of frequencies to pass through between two cut-off points while significantly reducing frequencies both above and below the pass band. The mid-point of the amplitude response curve is referred to as the centre frequency and the frequency range between the lower and upper cut-off points is known as the bandwidth.

Figure 12.6
Amplitude response of a band-pass
filter

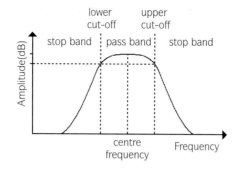

Band-reject

A band-reject filter attenuates (rejects) a band of frequencies between two cut-off points while allowing the rest of the signal to pass through with little change (the opposite of the band-pass filter). The mid-point of the amplitude response curve is referred to as the centre frequency and the frequency range between the lower and upper cut-off points is known as the bandwidth.

Figure 12.7
Amplitude response of a band-reject
filter

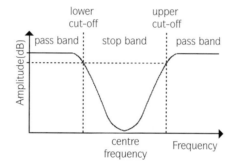

Filter slopes

In its most basic form, a low-pass filter (for example) is regulated using a single parameter, the cut-off frequency. This governs the point at which the upper frequencies in the sound begin to be reduced, (attenuated), thereby controlling how the spectrum is modified. However, this attenuation takes place according to a slope as the filter passes between the pass band and the stop band. This slope describes the rate at which the upper frequencies are attenuated and is generally measured in terms of dBs per octave. The slope varies according to the manner in which the filter has been designed. In voltage-controlled circuitry, for example, the rate is governed, among other things, by the number of resistors and capacitors used in the circuit. A simple passive filter with one resistor and one capacitor in the circuit is known as an RC filter and this has an attenuation slope of 6dB per octave. Other common rates include 12dB per octave, 18dB per octave and 24dB per octave. These slopes can be plotted graphically in terms of relative attenuation against frequency.

Filter resonance (emphasis)

Resonance can be defined as the frequency or frequencies at which an object vibrates in sympathy with itself or with external vibrational phenomena.

Filters, too, can be endowed with this kind of behaviour. Passive RC filters have no resonant frequencies and simply filter the source according to their amplitude and phase response. However, active filters are often designed to produce a boost in the response around the cut-off frequency.

Most filtering plug-ins include a parameter which is used to regulate the amount of resonance (see Cubase SX's StepFilter). The parameter is commonly referred to as resonance, emphasis or Q. Figure 12.8 shows what happens to a low-pass filter's amplitude response for low, high and maximum resonance values.

When the resonance control parameter is set to low or medium positions the bandwidth of the emphasised frequencies is quite wide and they are only boosted by a small amount (Figure 12.8a). For higher resonance values the bandwidth of the emphasised frequencies is quite narrow and they are boosted by a large amount (Figure 12.8b). As the resonance is increased the lower frequencies are progressively attenuated. At maximum resonance the lower and upper frequencies virtually disappear from the filtered signal leaving a single harmonic which oscillates at the cut-off frequency (Figure 12.8c). In the latter case, an amount of the source signal normally still passes through.

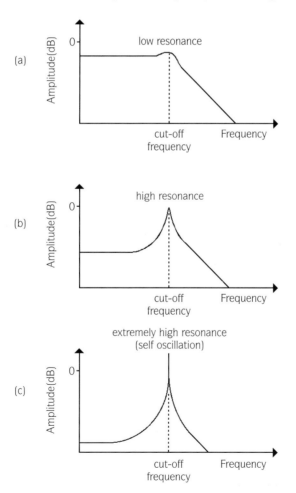

Figure 12.8
The effect of resonance on a low-pass filter's amplitude response

The effect of resonance can be summarised as follows: resonance results in the emphasising of a narrow band of frequencies (harmonics) located around the cut-off point. This narrow band can be moved around within the frequency spectrum by changing the frequency of the cut-off point. This results in effects which are particularly pleasing to the ear. At extreme resonance values, when the filter enters a state of self-oscillation (as in Figure 12.8c), special effects and pitched tones can be produced.

The resonant low-pass filter has, more than any other filter type, been responsible for some classic subtractive synthesis effects and is excellent for producing the filter sweeps commonly used in dance music. Cubase SX's Step Filter plug-in allows the simultaneous changing of both the cut-off frequency and the resonance in synchronisation with the current tempo of the project. Setting up a medium to high resonance level and then sweeping the cut-off frequency up and down has been used in innumerable synth patches and dance tracks. As well as its implementation in low-pass filters, resonance is also commonly implemented in high-pass filters.

Using filters

In addition to the sweeping effects described above, filters can also be used to produce pseudo-stereo effects, comb-filter effects, wah-wah effects and such things as AM radio and telephone simulations. In a corrective sense, filters are particularly useful for hum and hiss removal and band-limiting (check out the Q10 Renaissance Equalizer and Linear Phase EQ plug-ins supplied by Waves for the more advanced uses of filters and EQ).

Modulation

Modulation encompasses a wide range of effects including chorus, flanging, and phasing and the, perhaps slightly lesser known, techniques of amplitude modulation, frequency modulation and ring modulation. Modulation is the modification of the characteristics of one signal using a second signal. The modulating signal could be an LFO (a low frequency oscillator) or some other kind of signal somewhere in the audible range. For example, simple modulation effects include vibrato and tremolo. Vibrato is a form of frequency modulation where the frequency (or pitch) of the target signal is modulated by an LFO. Tremolo is a form of amplitude modulation where the amplitude level of the target signal is modulated by an LFO.

Chorus, flanging and phasing

Although the classic modulation effects like chorus, flanging and phasing are easily recognisable, the ways in which they are produced in modern effects devices may not be so obvious.

Chorus is an effect produced by passing a signal through one or more delay lines and modulating the delay time(s) with an LFO. The result is mixed with the original signal. The modulation of the delay times produces changes in the perceived pitch and timing, and phase cancellation effects, creating the illusion of an ensemble of sound sources. It was first conceived as a means of attempting to make a single musical performance sound like more than one performer.

Flanging is a similar effect created by mixing a delayed version of a signal with the original and modulating the delay time with an LFO whilst also applying an amount of feedback. This produces phase cancellation effects which are heard as a comb filter effect sweeping up and down within the frequency spectrum.

Phasing is created by mixing a phase-shifted version of a signal with the original and modulating the phase shifting with an LFO whilst also applying an amount of feedback. Similar to flanging, phasing is also perceived as a comb filter effect sweeping up and down within the frequency spectrum, but the swept frequency bands are not always harmonically related to the target signal.

Amplitude modulation, frequency modulation and ring modulation

Amplitude modulation, frequency modulation and ring modulation tend towards more esoteric effects and are implemented in sound synthesis, as well as sound effects devices.

Amplitude Modulation is achieved by modulating the amplitude of one audio signal by another signal where both signals are in the audible range. Using simple sine waves for the modulator produces a signal containing the target signal and two sidebands which are the sum and difference frequencies of the target signal and the modulating signal. Applying amplitude modulation where the modulating signal is an LFO produces tremolo effects. When the modulator is not an LFO (i.e. when it is in the audible range), the result tends towards densely packed inharmonic frequencies added to the signal.

Frequency modulation is probably better known for its uses in sound synthesis. In FM, the frequency of one signal is modulated by another. Applying frequency modulation where the modulating signal is an LFO produces vibrato effects. When the modulator is not an LFO (i.e. when it is in the audible range), multiple frequencies known as sidebands are added to the signal.

Ring modulation is a special kind of amplitude modulation where the target signal and the modulating signal are multiplied to produce the sum and difference of their frequencies in the output. Unlike amplitude and frequency modulation, the original frequency of the source signal is not present in the output. Typically, this produces science fiction alien effects for speech and metallic tones for pitched sounds.

Reverb

Reverb is an abbreviation for reverberation. Reverberation is an effect produced by a multiple series of echos occurring after the original sound in an acoustic space. It is characterised by three distinct phases, as shown in Figure 12.9. Reverberation is found in virtually every acoustic space and its characteristics vary enormously depending on the size of the space and the kinds of materials and objects found therein.

Figure 12.9 approximates what takes place in a real reverberant space. Firstly, the original sound arrives directly from the source to the listener's ear. After a short pause the first reflections from the surfaces of the room (or other acoustic space) are heard; these are known as early reflections. This is then followed by a complex mass of multiple reflections as the reflected sounds continue to bounce off the various surfaces. The amplitude of these multiple reflections decays exponentially to form what is commonly known as the reverb tail. In real reverberant spaces (especially in large ones), the upper frequencies decay at a faster rate than the rest of the signal.

The aim with virtual reverb plug-ins is to re-create the same kind of behaviour. However, the first thing you may notice when comparing different

Info

The early reflections within reverberation are crucial in giving the treated sound a sense of depth and focus, and clarify the location of the direct sound. Careful manipulation of early reflections can enhance the clarity, shape and depth of sounds within the mix.

Figure 12.9
The three phases of reverb

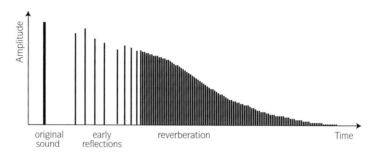

devices is that reverb units are not all created equal. Convincing reverberation remains difficult to replicate artificially and requires a large amount of processing power to achieve the best results. Cubase SX's Reverb A and Reverb B achieve very good results considering the small amount of processing power they use.

Other

There are of course a multitude of other effects which do not necessarily fit neatly into any particular category. These include devices such as Cubase SX's Grungelizer, which adds crackle, noise and distortion to your signals, and Bitcrusher, which adds noise and distortion to signals by truncating the bit resolution. Other miscellaneous effects and processing techniques include vocoding, loudness maximisation, bass maximisation, stereo enhancement, spatial image processing, harmonic excitement, sonic optimisation, 'psychoacoustic' enhancement, and noise, click and hum removal.

Setting up audio effects in Cubase SX

In Cubase SX, real-time audio effects may be assigned as insert effects or send effects. There are no strict rules about which effects are assigned to which kind of effects slots but, for example, not all of the supplied effects are suitable for use as insert effects, and reverb effects are almost always assigned as send effects (see below for precise recommendations). The effects routing structure of the Mixer is similar to that found in a classic real-world console (see Info box, left).

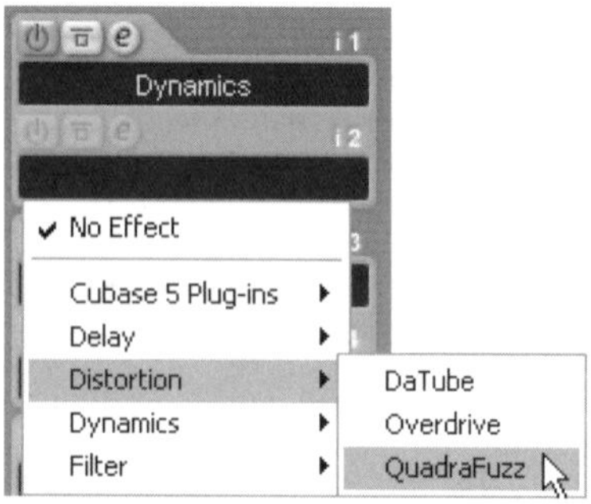

Insert effects

Insert effects are assigned by clicking in any of the Insert effects slots of an Audio, Group, VSTi, FX, Rewire channel or an input/output buss, at which time a pop-up menu appears containing the plug-ins available in your system (Figure 12.10).

Insert effects slots do not feature any level controls since the signal simply passes through each insert effect in turn. Insert effects assignments are unique for each channel and each time you activate an insert effect you also activate an additional instance of the chosen plug-in effect. This, of course, uses processing power so, while insert effects are invaluable, they tend to use more system resources than send effects. Each channel in the Mixer has a total of eight Insert slots. Effects are assigned to the Insert slots in the extended part of the

---

Info

The precise routing order for a signal passing through an Audio channel runs as follows:

1 phase switch
2 input gain
3 inserts 1-6
4 EQ
5 pre-fader aux send
6 channel fader
7 inserts 7-8
8 post-fader aux send
9 pan.

Figure 12.10
Assigning an effect in an Insert effects slot

channel strips in the extended Mixer, in the Channel Settings window or in the Inspector.

Insert effects differ from send effects in the manner in which the signal is routed. There is no separation of the dry and effect signals. Instead, the signal passes directly THROUGH the effects 'in series' (see Figure 12.11). When more than one insert effect is activated, the signal passes through each in turn, in descending order. Note that the channel audio signal is routed directly to the first insert effect's input, (i.e. it has not yet passed via the channel fader and is commonly known as the 'pre-fader' signal). However, the level of this signal may still be changed using the input gain control for the channel. After having passed through one or more of Insert effects slots 1-6, the output from the effect(s) is routed via the EQ section (if active), channel fader, and pan control to the chosen output buss. The signal level going into insert effects 1-6 is NOT affected by the channel fader level since they are pre-fader. Inserts 7 and 8 are special case post-fader slots which are suitable for processing which benefits from coming after the channel fader, such as limiting. Slots 7 and 8 are particularly useful when used in an output buss for final limiting, loudness maximisation or dithering during a mix or mastering session. In general, insert effects are best suited to processing like compression, expansion, limiting, noise gating, EQ, filtering and distortion. Chorus, phasing and similar effects also work well as insert effects.

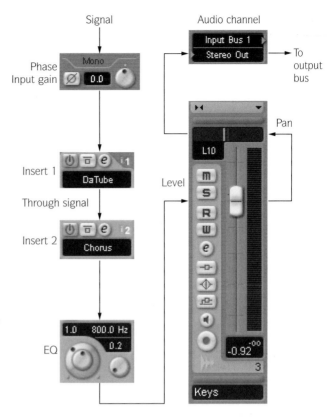

Figure 12.11
The routing configuration for Insert effects (slots 1-6)

Send effects

Send effects are managed using FX channels. The effect is actually assigned as an insert effect on the FX channel, which may at first seem confusing. The first thing to do when setting up a send effect is to add an FX channel to the project. This is achieved in the same way as for other channel types by using the Add function (Project menu). The Add FX channel dialogue allows you to choose an effect for the new FX channel (Figure 12.12). The effect for the channel may be changed at a later time, or other effects may be added, in the Insert slots for the FX channel.

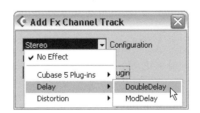

Figure 12.12
Choosing an effect for an FX channel in the Add FX channel dialogue

Figure 12.13
Assigning a send effect in a send effects slot

Once an FX channel is activated in the project, you can send signals to it for processing from the auxiliary send slots of any of the audio-based channels. Send effects are assigned by clicking in any of the send slots for the channel, at which time a pop-up menu appears containing the FX channels and other routing destinations (Figure 12.13). The send level is regulated using the mini-fader of the effects slot. Send effects can be chosen on as many audio-based channels as required, in any order, and with unique send levels for each slot. This saves on processing power since, for example, any number of audio channel sends can use the same reverb effect which you have activated only once in a single FX channel.

Each channel in the Mixer has a total of eight send slots. The send slots are assigned in the extended part of the channel strip in the extended Mixer, in the Channel Settings window or in the Inspector. The routing configuration for send effects is similar to a traditional mixing console. Figure 12.14 traces the signal as it is split between the 'dry' and the 'wet' signal paths, in a typical post-fader send configuraton. The 'dry' signal passes through the pan

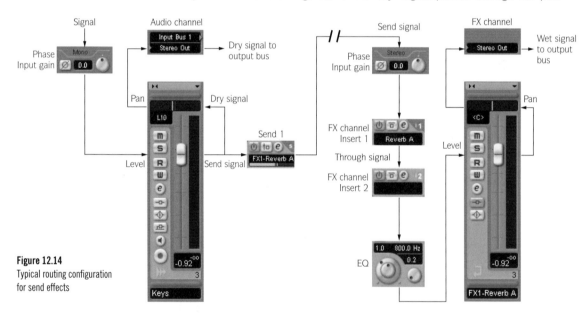

Figure 12.14
Typical routing configuration for send effects

control of the channel strip, as usual, and is routed to the chosen output buss. The send ('wet') signal is routed (post-fader) via the send level and the effect in the FX channel to the chosen output buss, where it joins the dry signal in the mix. The FX channel fader controls the level of the effects return.

With FX channels, the effect (wet) signal is added 'in parallel' to the dry signal in the mix via the FX channel fader, which is usually routed to the same output buss as the dry signal. A suitable mix between the dry and wet signals is achieved by balancing the fader level of the source channel (dry) and the fader level of the FX channel (wet). Under normal circumstances, the 'mix' control in the user interface of the effect in the FX channel is set to 100% wet. This ensures that the FX channel governs only the wet signal and the source Audio channel governs only the dry signal.

Each send is routed either pre or post-fader. If it is pre-fader (i.e. with the pre-fader switch activated), then the signal is routed to the FX channel before it arrives at the channel fader (in this case, the channel fader level does NOT influence the send level). If it is post-fader (i.e. with the pre-fader switch de-activated), then the signal passes via the channel fader before it is routed to the FX channel (the channel fader level influences the send level). Post-fader is the default setting.

You may wonder how the pre-fader switch might be useful. Practical uses include occasions when the channel fader has been set rather low and does not provide enough signal for the effect send; in this case the pre-fader signal provides more level. The pre-fader switch also allows you to fade a signal in the mix without also fading any effect applied to it. This can be used for special mixing techniques. For example, if you fade a sound which has pre-fader reverb added to it, the result gives the impression that the sound is disappearing into the distance as the dry signal diminishes whilst the reverberation signal remains.

Send effects are best suited to effects like reverb, delay and chorus. Virtually any of the supplied effects included in the Delay, Modulation and Reverb categories in the Audio/Plug-in menu might be assigned as send effects.

Info

S end signals to stereo effects can be panned in the routing section of the send panel of the Channel Settings window.

Common GUI functions for audio effects

The graphical user interface (GUI) for any of the currently active effects can be opened by clicking on the edit button of the slot corresponding to the effect. The edit buttons are labelled with a lower case 'e' and are found in all channel effects slots in the Mixer, in the Channel Settings window and in the Inspector. All GUIs for the effects open in a separate window similar to that shown in Figure 12.15.

Figure 12.15
The graphical user interface for the supplied Symphonic effect

Basic GUI functions

The GUI parameters common to most effects include an 'On' button, a file menu, a presets menu and, where appropriate, an output and/or mix fader. An effect is activated (or de-activated) in the GUI by clicking the On button, at which time it is illuminated in blue. The file menu allows you to save and load banks of presets or individual presets to/from hard disk (Figure 12.16).

The presets menu allows you to choose a preset from the currently loaded presets (Figure 12.17). The number of available preset slots varies between effects. To find out how many preset program slots are available for each plug-in, take a look in the 'Number of programs' column in the Plug-in Information window (Devices menu).

Figure 12.16
Use the file menu to save and load banks
and single effects to/from hard disk

Figure 12.17 (right)
Use the preset menu to load preset
effects

The output fader is for setting an appropriate level for the output of the effects device. This varies according to the application. The mix fader determines the mix between the wet and dry signal which passes to the output (Figure 12.18). When used as a Send effect, the mix fader is normally best set to 100% wet and, when used as an Insert effect the wet and dry signals might be provisionally set to equal proportions. Here the final setting invariably needs to be fine tuned.

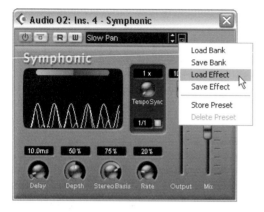

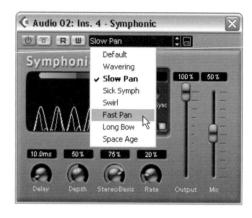

There are, of course, a number of effects which do not feature any of the common control parameters. The general rule is that all visible parameters can be manipulated in some way by clicking and dragging with the mouse. All effects parameter changes made as part of a mix can be automated by activating the Read and Write buttons found next to the On button. In the case of those Cubase SX effects which feature a graphical display of the control settings, clicking and dragging directly in the display changes two relevant parameters simultaneously. This is excellent for automation purposes and can help create inspiring sound effects.

Figure 12.18
Use the mix fader to set the proportion of wet and dry signal

Tempo sync controls

Where applicable, the supplied effects feature tempo sync controls. These allow the synchronisation of various parameters (such as LFOs and delay times) to the current tempo of Cubase SX. Activating the tempo sync button for an effect enables the tempo sync menu. This is opened by clicking on the field next to the tempo sync button (Figure 12.19).

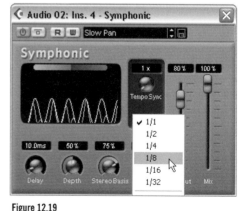

Figure 12.19
Activate tempo sync and open the note value menu next to the button

The tempo sync menu contains a list of note values which determine the division of the bar which Cubase SX uses for synchronisation purposes. For example, setting this to 1/8 where a delay time is concerned produces repeated delays at 1/8 note intervals, or setting this to 1/1 where an LFO controlling auto pan is concerned produces a panning effect which occurs once in each bar.

The supplied audio effects

There now follows descriptions of a selection of the audio effects supplied with the program. These are listed in the same order in which they are found in the Plug-ins menu and are therefore arranged according to the categories outlined at the beginning of this chapter.

ModDelay

ModDelay is a time or tempo based delay device featuring pitch modulation of the delayed signal (Figure 12.20).

Figure 12.20
ModDelay

The interface includes the following parameters:

* Feedback – regulates the number of times the delay signal is repeated. Range: 0 – 100%.
* Delay Time – sets the delay time when tempo sync is not activated. Range: 0 – 9999ms.
* Tempo sync – multiplies the delay time of the tempo sync setting by a factor of x1 to x10.
* Tempo sync pop-up menu – sets the division of the bar which is used to create the tempo synced delay signal. Range: whole note to 1/32 note, whole note triplets to 1/32 note triplets, dotted whole note to dotted 1/32 note.
* Delay mod – regulates the amount of pitch modulation applied to the delay signal. Range: 0-100%.
* Mix slider – determines the proportion of wet and dry signal output from the effect where 0% is no effect and 100% is fully wet. Range: 0-100%

User guide

ModDelay is a simple delay device with standard feedback and delay time controls and the additional tempo synchronisation facility. The delay modulation parameter adds chorus-like richness to the effect which sets it apart from standard delay devices. For an exaggerated example of the use of modulation check out the 'Swirl' preset. This might suit fuzz guitar. For spot delay effects try the 'Bounce' preset. ModDelay is suitable for use as an Insert effect or a Send effect.

It is *not* a good idea to actually record delay effects with the sound unless you are sure that the effect is an integral part of the sound's character. Delay is best applied at the mixing stage. It can be used on almost any sound in the mix but is particularly suitable for lead guitar, saxophone and vocals and on featured elements in the mix, such as solos or special effects. Bass sounds do not generally benefit from delay treatment. Too much delay can result in a confused and messy mix so, as with all effects, it should not be over-used.

Double delay

DoubleDelay is a tempo-based dual delay device (Figure 12.21).

The interface includes the following parameters:

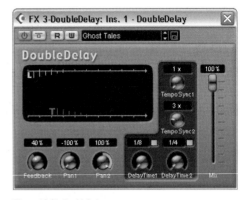

Figure 12.21 DoubleDelay

- Feedback – sets the number of repeats for both delays simultaneously. Range 0 – 100%.
- TMP sync 1 – multiplies the delay time of delay line 1 by a factor of x1 to x10 when in tempo sync mode.
- TMP sync 2 – multiplies the delay time of delay line 2 by a factor of x1 to x10 when in tempo sync mode.
- Pan 1 – sets the panoramic position for delay line 1. Range –100% to +100%.
- Pan 2 – sets the panoramic position for delay line 2. Range –100% to +100%.
- Delay time 1 – determines the delay time of delay line 1 when not in tempo sync mode. Range: 0 – 0.9999ms.
- Delay time 2 – determines the delay time of delay line 1 when not in tempo sync mode. Range: 0 – 0.9999ms.
- Tempo sync menu 1 – sets the division of the bar which is used to create the tempo synced delay line 1 signal. Range: whole note to 1/32 note, whole note triplets to 1/32 note triplets, dotted whole note to dotted 1/32 note.
- Tempo sync menu 2 – sets the division of the bar which is used to create the tempo synced delay line 2 signal. Range: as above.
- Mix slider – determines the proportion of wet and dry signal output from the effect where 0% is no effect and 100% is fully wet. Range: 0-100%

User guide

The graphic display shows delay line 1 in the upper part of the display (shown in light blue) and delay line 2 in the lower part of the display (shown in dark blue). The horizontal axis represents delay time and the vertical axis represents pan position (with the left channel in the upper half of the display and the right channel in the lower half of the display). The delay position for each delay line is shown by a thick vertical line. Feedback is displayed as repeat events after the input event. The delay time and the pan position for each delay line can be changed by dragging the thick vertical lines directly in the display.

DoubleDelay is supplied with a number of useful presets which make good starting points for the creation of your own effects. It can be used on almost any sound in the mix and produces excellent stereo, tempo synced delay and special effects. It is particularly suitable for lead guitar, saxophone, vocals, and tempo sync delays for synthesizer sequences. Try 'Follow Me' or 'Ghost Tales' on sequenced synth lines.

DaTube

DaTube is a classic saturation device emulating the sound of a tube amplifier (Figure 12.22). The interface features three simple parameters as follows:

Figure 12.22
DaTube

- Drive – determines the amount of pre-gain before the signal enters the amplifier. More drive gives more saturation. Range: 0 – 100%.
- Balance – regulates the proportion of dry and effects signal where 100% gives maximum drive effect. Range 0 – 100%.
- Output – determines the final output level of the amplifier. Range: – infinity to 0dB.

User guide

Of course, the best feature of DaTube is its virtual vacuum tube which lights up when it receives a signal! A neat device which works well for giving edge and definition to guitars and warmth and character to cold synth parts. It performs best with sounds with plenty of top and helps give lightweight rhythm guitars more definition in the mix. The relationship between the drive and output settings is important where a high drive setting often benefits from a low output setting. Take a listen to the presets to hear how this relationship works. 'Warm Distortion' makes a good starting point for fine tuning the settings. DaTube is better suited as an Insert effect but may also be used as a Send effect.

Overdrive

Overdrive is a distortion device for the simulation of electric guitar amplifiers and the creation of classic fuzz guitar effects (Figure 12.23).

The interface includes the following parameters:

- Speaker simulation on/off – when activated, simulates the sound of a speaker cabinet.
- Factory styles menu – sets the choice of algorithm for the simulated guitar amplifier.

Figure 12.23
Overdrive

- Bass – bass frequency tone control. Range: +/– 15dB.
- Mid – mid frequency tone control. Range: +/– 15dB.
- Hi – high frequency tone control. Range: +/– 15dB.
- Drive – sets the amount of distortion (overdrive) for the unit. Range: 0 – 100%.
- Input slider – regulates the level of the input signal. Range: +/–15dB.
- Output slider – regulates the level of the output signal. Range: +/–15dB.

User guide

Overdrive is useful if you are a guitarist using Cubase SX who does not already have an external amplification system or pre-amplifier. It is more adaptable than a pure distortion device and can add a very wide range of tonal characteristics to a guitar signal. The unit can be treated much like a regular guitar amplifier in the way that you set it up. Once you have chosen the basic algorithm in the Factory styles menu it is then a matter of balancing the various tone and level controls to achieve the desired character for the sound. Activating the speaker simulation produces a more rounded and warmer sound. Overdrive can, of course, also be used to process any other (non-guitar) type of signal.

The supplied presets make good starting points for creating your own effects but most seem to be set with the output too high. The 'Lead Drive' preset is good for lead guitar but try taking down the output slider by 3 – 6dB. It is better suited as an Insert effect but may also be used as a Send effect.

QuadraFuzz

QuadraFuzz is a sophisticated multi-band distortion device providing level control in four frequency bands both before and after distortion. In addition, the width of each frequency band is user-configurable (Figure 12.24).

Figure 12.24
QuadraFuzz

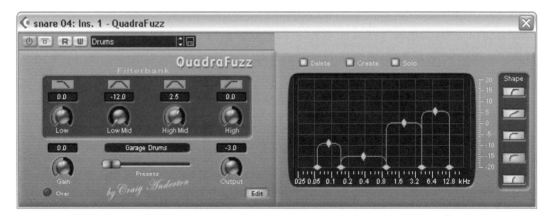

The interface features the following parameters:

In the main section:

- Gain dial – determines the overall input gain for the device. The 'Over' clipping LED is illuminated if you apply too much input gain. Range: −20dB to +20dB.
- Low, Low mid, High mid, High dials – regulate the outputs from the four frequency bands *after* distortion. Range: −12dB to +12dB.
- Output dial – regulates the overall output level. −20dB to +20dB.
- Preset slider – allows the selection of the available presets in the current bank.
- Edit button – opens the extended editing section (see below).

In the extended section:

- Dual function input level / frequency band selector display – the frequency spectrum is divided into four zones according to the positions of four user-configurable selector bands. These bands act upon the input signal *before* distortion. The level of each band is changed by dragging the top handle vertically. Note that this level affects the overall gain set with the main panel's Gain control and can therefore cause clipping, (indicated by the the 'Over' clipping LED). The frequency crossover points for each band is adjusted by dragging the lower handles horizontally. Scale: −20dB to +20dB (vertical), 25Hz to 22kHz (horizontal).

- Transfer shape selector buttons – determine the transfer function which produces the distortion effect (five buttons).
- Delete button – deletes the currently selected preset.
- Create button – stores the current settings as a preset. All presets are saved with the project. However, for presets to be globally available you must use Cubase SX's save and load functions at the top of the edit window.
- Solo button – solos the currently selected frequency band allowing you to hear the distortion effect in one band alone.

User guide

QuadraFuzz was originally a hardware circuit designed by Craig Anderton, hence the Craig Anderton signature on the front panel. Spectral Design have expanded on the original concept by providing control over the width of the frequency bands before distortion. This, coupled with the fact that you have control over the level of the frequency bands both before and after distortion, produces a distortion device of extremely wide ranging capabilities.

You can use QuadraFuzz as mainly a preset device by operating in the main window only, and testing the unit with the supplied presets shows how you can create effects of extreme subtlety through to manic overdrive. The heart of the device is in the edit window and this is where you need to go if you want to radically change the existing presets or create your own. Like many distortion devices, you need to maintain a balance between the input and output stages since applying radical distortion can create radical level changes. Try using the solo button while making changes in the frequency band selector display. This helps you judge more precisely the result of each change you make.

The distortion itself is applied to the signal according to your choice of transfer function (Shape button). A transfer function is a function which governs the relationship between the amplitude of an input and output signal which pass through it. Changing the shape of this function affects the waveform of the output signal in various ways, producing different types of distortion. The shapes you see on the buttons give a rough indication of the kind of transfer function which has been used in each case and the lower the button you select the more harmonics are added to the signal. The point to remember here is that the harmonic distortion is only added to those parts of the signal you choose using the frequency selectors, and how much distortion applied to each band depends on the levels you set.

QuadraFuzz is, of course, well suited to the production of all types of fuzz guitar effects but it is also excellent for synth sounds and for subtly highlighting or completely mangling drum and percussion sounds. It might also be used for adding subtle warmth and character to certain frequencies within a mix. QuadraFuzz is suitable for use as an Insert effect or a Send effect and, for subtle treatments within a mix, might occasionally be used as a Master effect.

DeEsser (Cubase SX only)

DeEsser is a semi-automatic de-essing device designed by SPL and Steinberg. De-essing refers to the process of removing over-emphasised 's' sounds (otherwise known as 'sibilance') from vocal recordings. (Figure 12.25)

Figure 12.25 DeEsser

The interface features the following parameters:

- S-reduction – controls the amount of 's' sound which is removed from the signal. For most applications, settings between 3 and 7 are recommended. Range: 0-10.
- Level display – shows the amount of 's' reduction which is taking place. Range: –20db to 0dB (in 2dB steps).
- Auto threshold button – when activated, DeEsser continually tracks the amplitude of the input signal and provides a constant amount of de-essing regardless of level variations. When de-activated, DeEsser uses a fixed threshold for its de-essing determined by the level of the S-reduction dial.
- Male/Female buttons – changes the operation of DeEsser to suit the male voice (sibilance reduction around 6kHz) or the female voice (sibilance reduction around 7kHz).

User guide

Traditionally, de-essing involves using an equaliser and a compressor. The vocal signal is passed through the compressor in the usual way but the action of the compressor is governed by an equalised version of the signal inserted into the 'side chain'. The side chain of a compressor is a second feed from the input which determines how gain reduction should take place (based upon threshold, ratio, attack and release controls). In the case of de-essing, the signal inserted into the side chain is equalised to a narrow bandwidth at the frequency of the sibilance. By carefully adjusting the compressor's threshold, ratio, attack and release, gain reduction occurs according to the sibilance level only.

The advantage of DeEsser is that it saves you the potential headache of configuring this setup manually. Due to its simplicity DeEsser is very quick to configure. The disadvantage is that it does not allow you to fine tune the frequency to that of the particular sibilance you are trying to correct. The reality is that a sibilance problem might occur anywhere between 4 to 12kHz, although it is true to say that most problems do occur in the approximate frequency ranges used by DeEsser.

When setting up the controls in general and when using the presets 'Male Heavy' and 'Female Heavy', be careful with the setting of the S-reduction dial. At higher levels, the de-essing action can cut into the vocal a little too much. DeEsser would normally be used as an Insert effect on the vocal track. However, if you wish to apply DeEsser after a channel's built-in EQ stage, this can only be achieved if you insert DeEsser in slots 7 or 8. Alternatively, use a high quality EQ plug-in in a slot BEFORE DeEsser, when using insert slots 1 to 6.

MIDI Gate

MIDI Gate (Figure 12.26) provides a manner in which you can 'play' your audio tracks using MIDI input as a gate trigger signal. When MIDI Gate is applied to an audio track the immediate effect is silence but when you trigger MIDI gate from a live MIDI keyboard, or from an existing MIDI track, the audio signal is allowed to pass through according to the timing of the notes and the settings on the control panel.

The interface features the following parameters:

Figure 12.26
MIDI Gate

- Attack – determines the speed with which the gate opens after the unit has received a MIDI trigger note. Range: 0 – 500ms.
- Hold – determines the length of time for which the gate is sure to remain open once it has been triggered. Range: 0 – 3000ms.
- Release – determines how long it takes for the gate to close after having been opened. Range: 0 – 3000ms.
- Note to Attack – determines whether and by how much the pitch of the incoming MIDI notes affects the attack setting. A setting of 0 switches this function off. Range: 0 – 127.
- Note to release – determines whether and by how much the pitch of the incoming MIDI notes affects the release setting. A setting of 0 switches this function off. Range: 0 – 127.
- Velocity to VCA – determines how much MIDI velocity effects the amplitude of the audio output. At a setting of 0, MIDI velocity has no effect on the output level. At a setting of 127, MIDI velocity has maximum effect on the output level. Range: 0 – 127.
- Hold mode – in Note Off mode, the gate is held open until the MIDI Note off point and ignores the Hold time setting. In Note On mode, the Hold time is taken into consideration and the hold action starts at the moment a Note on message is received.

User guide

To configure MIDI Gate for use on an audio track proceed as follows:

- Choose the audio track you wish to process and activate MIDI Gate as an Insert effect in one of the Insert effects slots. (The immediate effect is to silence the audio track since the track is now gated by the MIDI Gate).
- Create a new MIDI track using Add/MIDI Track (Project menu) or choose an existing MIDI track.
- Choose MIDI Gate as the output in the 'out' field of the MIDI track.
- If you intend to trigger your audio track live from a MIDI keyboard select the MIDI track and ensure that the monitor button (or the record enable button) is activated so that incoming MIDI data is passed through to the

MIDI gate. Commence playback. When you play the keyboard the audio track is triggered.

- If you intend to trigger your audio track from a recorded MIDI track select the MIDI track and ensure that neither the monitor button nor the record enable button are enabled. Commence playback. The audio track is triggered according to the notes on the MIDI track and the settings on the MIDI Gate.
- Adjust the parameters of MIDI Gate according to the effect you require.

MIDI Gate is excellent for creating rhythmic effects and works particularly well when triggered by a tightly sequenced monophonic synth part. In this respect, check out the possibilities of using the Step Designer MIDI effects module for controlling MIDI gate (see Chapter 13). The settings shown in Figure 12.26 make a good starting point when triggering from a recorded MIDI track. When using a MIDI keyboard for live triggering, try working in cycle record mode (Overwrite mode) just in case you stumble upon a great musical idea.

VST Dynamics

VST Dynamics (Figure 12.27) is a multiple process dynamics plug-in.

VST Dynamics features auto gate, auto level, compressor, softclip and limiter processors, each of which is activated by clicking on the processor label buttons. It is designed to be used as an Insert effect on regular Audio channels. The signal flow through VST Dynamics is shown in the lower right corner of the window.

There now follows a description of each processor module in the VST Dynamics window:

Figure 12.27
VST Dynamics

Auto Gate

Auto Gate is a noise gate conforming to the standard features of similar real-world devices but with the addition of threshold auto-calibration, a look-ahead predict function and frequency conscious triggering. Gating is a form of dynamic processing most often used for the cutting of unwanted signals below a set threshold, such as the unwanted noise and interference which may be present in between the wanted sections of a vocal performance. (See the section entitled 'Audio effects in theory' at the beginning of this chapter for more details about gating).

Auto Gate features the following controls:

- Trigger Frequency Range – allows the triggering of the gate using a selectable range of frequencies in the input signal. When the trigger frequency range slider is set to the Off position the opening of the gate is triggered by the whole of the input signal. When it is set to On the gate is triggered by the frequency range set in the frequency range display. The frequency range can be adjusted by moving the green handles and you can monitor which part of the signal is being selected by switching the trigger frequency range slider to Listen.
- Threshold – sets the threshold level for the gate. When the input signal rises above this threshold the gate is opened to let the signal through. When it falls below this threshold the signal is attenuated (cut). When the Calibrate button is activated the threshold level is set automatically according to the current signal. This is useful for automatically finding the correct threshold level for the background noise in a recording. To set the correct level when using Calibrate, play a segment of the unwanted noise only. The noise will then be cut when no other signal is present. Range: –60dB to 0dB.
- Attack – determines the rate at which the gate opens when the input signal rises above the threshold. When the Predict button is activated the gate looks ahead in the audio material and registers which parts of the signal exceed the threshold. This information is then used to trigger the gate at precisely the right moment. Range: 0.1 to 100ms.
- Hold – controls the time for which the gate is guaranteed to be held open once it has been triggered. Range: 0 to 1000ms.
- Release – determines the rate of attenuation when the signal has fallen below the threshold and after it has been held for the set Hold time. When the Auto button is activated the release time is automatically adjusted according to the audio material itself. Range: 10 to 1000ms.

The Auto Gate display also features LEDs indicating when the gate is being triggered. This provides useful visual feedback about the gate's behaviour.

Auto Level

Auto Level is an automatic level control device designed to even out the signal level differences in audio material. It boosts low level and attenuates high level signals. This is good for automatically increasing the level of signals which are too low in relation to the rest of the mix.

Auto Level features the following controls:

- Threshold – sets the level above which processing starts to take place. Signals below the threshold are not affected. Range: –90dB to –10dB.

- Reaction time – sets the speed with which the level is adjusted. This should be set according to the characteristics of the audio material. Use the Fast setting for material with very sudden changes in level and the Mid and Slow setting for material with more gradual changes in level.

Compressor

Compressor is a standard audio compressor. Compressors convert a large dynamic range into a smaller dynamic range. In other words, when you compress a signal, loud parts become quieter and quiet parts become louder.

Compressor features the following controls:

- Threshold – sets the level above which compression starts to act. Signals below the threshold are not affected. Range: –60dB to 0dB.
- Ratio – sets the compression ratio for those parts of the signal which rise above the threshold. A ratio of 4:1 means that for every 4dB the input signal rises above the threshold, the output signal will increase by only 1dB. Range: 1:1 to 8:1.
- Attack – determines the rate at which the compressor begins to act upon the signal after the threshold has been exceeded. Short attack times compress the impact of the first part of the signal while slow attack times allow the first part of the signal to pass through unprocessed. Range: 0.1 to 100ms.
- Release – determines the rate at which the compressor returns to its normal output gain after the input signal has fallen below the threshold level. When the Auto button is activated the release time is adjusted automatically according to the audio material. Range: 10 to 1000ms.
- Makeup Gain – provides output level adjustment to compensate for changes in level due to compression. Range: 0dB to +24dB

Compressor also features a gain reduction meter, indicating how much gain reduction is taking place, and a compression characteristic graphic display, indicating the characteristics of the compression curve as governed by the threshold, ratio and makeup controls. (See the section entitled 'Audio effects in theory' at the beginning of this chapter for more details about compression).

Soft Clip

Soft Clip is an automatic gain control device which has no user-adjustable parameters. It is designed to make sure that the output level never exceeds 0dB and to generate 'tube-like' warmth in the treated signal. Soft Clip begins processing when the input signal rises above –6dB and this is indicated in the meter display when the level indicator rises into the yellow, orange and red zones. No processing is taking place when the level indicator is in the green zone.

Soft Clip is a useful alternative to the Limiter section and is particularly suitable for digital audio signals which are sounding cold and brittle.

Limiter

Limiter is a simple two parameter limiting device. Limiters are generally used to stop the output signal passing above a set threshold, no matter how loud the input becomes. The threshold for limiting is normally set quite high, so that only the transient peaks are reduced in level while the rest of the signal passes through unaffected.

Tip

As well as controlling the wanted parts of the signal, compression may also result in an increase in the level of some of the unwanted parts of the signal, such as interference or headphone spill between sung vocal lines. To avoid this effect, try firstly using expansion / gating to reduce the level of the interference and then apply the compression.

Limiter features the following controls:

- Threshold – sets the threshold at which peak limiting starts to take effect. The output level never rises above this setting, no matter how loud the input becomes. Input signals below the threshold setting are not affected. Range: –12 to 0dB.
- Release control – controls the time it takes to return to normal gain after a peak above the threshold has been reduced in level. When the Auto button is activated the release time is adjusted automatically according to the audio material. Range: 10 to 1000ms.

A red LED indicates when limiting is taking place.

Using all VST Dynamics processor modules at the same time is rarely appropriate since their functions are often duplicated. For example, Soft Clip and Limiter are both limiting devices so, for almost all applications, using both simultaneously would be unnecessary. Similarly, if you have achieved the desired dynamic control using Auto Level it may be unnecessary to also use Compressor. But, of course, there are no strict rules and each case must be judged on its own merits. Often, the best approach with dynamics processing is to have a clear idea of what you want to achieve before you begin. This helps identify which processors you really need to use.

Dynamics
The Dynamics plug-in is the same as VST Dynamics except that it does not include the Auto Level and Soft Clip modules and the order in which the signal passes through the modules is user-configurable.

StepFilter
StepFilter is versatile step-based and static filter device suitable for rhythmic, tempo-linked and traditional filtering effects (Figure 12.28).

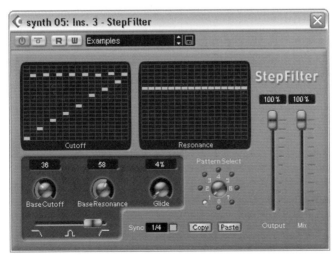

Figure 12.28
StepFilter

The interface features the following parameters:

- Cut-off point step display – a 16 step entry grid which functions when the tempo synchronisation button (Sync button) is activated. The horizontal axis represents 16 note divisions at the resolution chosen in the tempo sync field (see below). The vertical axis represents the cut-off frequency setting which is chosen using a draggable blue marker.
- Resonance step display – a 16 step entry grid which functions when the tempo synchronisation button (Sync button) is activated. The horizontal axis represents 16 note divisions at the resolution chosen in the tempo sync field (see below). The vertical axis represents the resonance setting which is chosen using a draggable blue marker.
- Base cut-off dial – determines the base frequency for the cut-off frequency i.e. the values shown in the cut-off point step display are relative to the value chosen here. Range: 0-100.
- Base Resonance dial – determines the base value for the resonance amount i.e. the values shown in the resonance step display are relative to the value chosen here. Range: 0-100.
- Glide dial – implements smooth transitions between each filter step. Range: 0 – 100%.
- Filter mode slider – selects low-pass, band-pass and high-pass filter types, (see the section entitled 'Audio effects in theory' at the beginning of this chapter for more details about filter types).
- Pattern selector – provides eight internal storage slots for the saving of cut-off and resonance patterns. These are saved with the current project but for global availability you must save them with the file save options at the top of the window.
- Copy and Paste buttons – provide copy and paste functions for copying cut-off and resonance patterns. This helps build up variations on the same theme.
- Sync button – activates/de-activates tempo synchronisation.
- Tempo sync field – offers a choice of tempo synchronised note value settings which determine the resolution of the cut-off point step display and resonance step display. Click on the tempo sync field to open the pop-up menu. Range: whole note to 1/32 note, whole note triplets to 1/32 note triplets, dotted whole note to dotted 1/32 note.
- Output slider – regulates the level of the output signal. Range: 0 – 100%.
- Mix slider – determines the proportion of wet and dry signal output from the effect where 0% is no effect and 100% is fully wet. Range: 0-100%

User guide

The first thing to try with StepFilter is to play a drum loop in cycle playback mode and check out the various patterns in the 'Examples' preset. Try changing the tempo sync value to 1/8, 1/16 and 1/32 notes with pattern 1 selected. Next, listen to the effect of changing the base cut-off and base resonance dials. Be careful with your speakers (and your ears!) at high resonance levels since this can produce piercing ringing effects. Now move on to the cut-off and resonance displays themselves. Simply drag the mouse in the displays to set up your own patterns. The cut-off and resonance values of the two displays are stepped through simultaneously.

If you want just straight filtering, de-activate the sync button. At this point in time, all step sequencing functions are de-activated. However, the first markers in each of the cut-off and resonance displays remain active as do the base dials and the filter type slider. StepFilter is an extremely expressive and responsive device, even in this static mode and, if you wish, the movements you make can be automated by activating the Read and Write buttons (see Chapter 15 for more information about automation).

StepFilter is superb for setting up filtering effects on dance tracks and works wonders with drum loops. Virtually any other kind of material can also be processed. StepFilter is normally used as an Insert effect but might have its uses as a Send or Master effect.

Chorus

Chorus (Figure 12.29) is a classic chorus effect device featuring up to four delay taps for producing rich, multi-layered chorus effects.

The interface includes the following parameters:

Figure 12.29
Chorus

- Frequency – sets the modulation rate. Range: 0 – 5Hz
- Delay – governs the intensity of the chorus effect. Range: 0 – 5ms.
- Stages – adds up to three more delay taps for producing a richer, multi-layered chorus effect. Range: 1 – 4.
- Mix slider – determines the proportion of wet and dry signal output from the effect where 0% is no effect and 100% is fully wet. Range: 0 – 100%

User guide

The display window of Chorus features a graphic representation of the parameter settings. Increasing the frequency modulation of the signal using the frequency dial results in more waveform cycles appearing in the display (more waveforms = more rapid modulation). Increasing the delay time using the delay dial results in less delay signal forms appearing inside each waveform cycle (less delay density = longer delay times). Increasing the stages dial results in up to three more 'shadow' waveforms appearing behind the first one. This produces a richer chorus effect. Increasing the frequency and delay dials to higher values results in more obvious chorus effects while lower values are more subtle. Any detuning of the signal is more obvious at higher frequencies.

The supplied presets are designed more for sound effects than standard chorus treatments so you may need to do some initial work creating your own presets. The 'default' setting is a good all-round chorus effect which sweetens just about any target signal. Try the settings in Figure 12.29 for bass guitar.

Chorus is a versatile effect which is good for treating bass, guitar, strings and organ sounds and anything that needs thickening or sweetening. It is suitable for use as an Insert or Send effect.

Flanger

Flanger is a classic flanging device with additional stereo and tempo-based features (Figure 12.30).

Figure 12.30
Flanger

The interface includes the following parameters:

- Feedback – changes the intensity of the flanging effect by feeding back the delayed signal to the input. Higher settings produce more resonant and pronounced sweeping effects. Range 0 – 100%.
- Delay – sets the initial delay time for the delayed signal. This controls the frequency range of the flanging effect with lower delay times producing high frequency sweeping effects and higher delay times producing mid and low frequency sweeping effects. Range: 0-100ms.
- Depth – sets the depth of the modulation effect. Range: 0 – 100%.
- Rate – sets the frequency rate of the modulation effect. Range 0 – 5Hz.
- Stereo basis – sets the characteristics of the stereo image of the effect where 0% is mono, 50% matches the original stereo signal and 100% is maximum stereo enhancement.
- Shape sync – changes the shape of the waveform of the modulating signal.
- Tempo sync dial – multiplies the delay time of the tempo sync setting (see below) by a factor of x1 to x10.
- Sync button – activates/de-activates tempo sync mode.
- Tempo sync pop-up – offers a choice of tempo synchronised note value settings in tempo sync mode, providing a way of matching the sweeping of the flange effect to the tempo of the music. Range: whole note to 1/32 note, whole note triplets to 1/32 note triplets, dotted whole note to dotted 1/32 note.
- Output slider – regulates the level of the output signal. Range: 0 – 100%.
- Mix slider – determines the proportion of wet and dry signal output from the effect where 0% is no effect and 100% is fully wet. Range: 0 – 100%

User guide

The display window of Flanger features a graphic representation of the parameter settings. Increasing the frequency rate of the delay modulation using the rate dial results in more waveform cycles appearing in the display (more waveforms = more rapid modulation). Increasing the delay time using the delay dial results in less delay signal density inside each waveform cycle (less delay density = longer delay times).

As the intensity of the effect is increased (using the feedback dial), the delay signal is represented more brightly in the display (it changes from green to bright blue). The amplitude of the modulating waveform is increased/ decreased according to the position of the depth dial and its shape can be modified with the shape sync dial.

Flanger benefits from the inclusion of tempo synchronisation and stereo enhancement. The supplied presets make good starting points for creating your own effects. Try the 'Slow Helix' preset on electric or acoustic guitar. Certain sounds may need level adjustment after flanging since low frequency sweeps often push the output signal higher than the original. Like chorus, flanging is a versatile effect which can be used on a wide variety of sounds. It is popular for special effects with vocals, strings and guitar and helps thicken and sweeten any sound in need of enlivenment. Flanger is suitable for use as an Insert or Send effect.

Metalizer

Metalizer is a variable band-pass filtering device with tempo or time based frequency band modulation (Figure 12.31).

The interface includes the following parameters:

Figure 12.31
Metalizer

- Feedback – regulates the resonance of the effect. Higher settings produce more resonance. Range 0 – 100%.
- Sharpness – governs the narrowness of the band-pass filter. Higher settings produce a narrower pass band and thus a sharper tone. Range 0 – 100%.
- Tone – regulates the frequency content of the effect. Lower settings emphasise the mid-range frequencies while higher settings emphasise the upper frequencies. Range 0 – 100%.
- Modulation on/off button – when activated, moves the band-pass filter up and down the frequency axis to produce 'wah-wah' effects.
- Modulation speed dial – regulates the speed of the modulation effect according to a frequency in Hertz, if the sync button is de-activated (Range: 0 – 10Hz), or according to a note division of the bar, if the sync button is activated.
- Tempo sync pop-up – offers a choice of tempo synchronised note value settings in tempo sync mode, providing a way of matching the modulation effect to the tempo of the music. Range: whole note to 1/32 note, whole note triplets to 1/32 note triplets, dotted whole note to dotted 1/32 note.
- Sync button – activates/de-activates tempo synchronisation.
- Mono/stereo button – toggles between mono or stereo output.
- Output slider – regulates the level of the output signal. Range: 0 – 100%.

- Mix slider – determines the proportion of wet and dry signal output from the effect where 0% is no effect and 100% is fully wet. Range: 0 – 100%

User guide

Metalizer produces a range of effects from flange-like sounds and wah-wah to extreme notch filtering effects. The heart of Metalizer is the sharpness dial. This governs the essential quality of the effect and the higher its setting the narrower the band-pass filter, as shown in the graphic display. The tone and feedback dials affect the high frequency and resonant content of the effect and this is reflected in the display by the density and brightness of the waveform inside the filter curve. Switching in the filter band modulation allows time or tempo based modulation of the filtered frequency band up and down the frequency axis for the production of classic wah-wah and other swept filter effects. The mono/stereo button is a welcome feature since it helps create simple centred monophonic effects as well as those which are swept across the stereo image. Clicking and dragging directly in the graphic display allows the simultaneous adjustment of the sharpness and tone controls.

Metalizer is excellent for wah-wah and other filtering effects and is particularly suitable for the production of special effects. It works best on harmonically rich sound sources like strings, distortion guitars and complex synth sounds. Metalizer is suitable for use as an Insert or Send effect.

Phaser

Phaser is a classic phasing device featuring tempo synchronisation and stereo enhancement (Figure 12.32).

The interface for Phaser includes the following parameters:

- Feedback – changes the intensity of the phasing effect by feeding back more of the phase shifted signal to the input. Higher settings produce more pronounced 'swooshing' effects. Range: 0 – 100%.
- Stereo basis – sets the characteristics of the stereo image of the effect where 0% is mono, 50% matches the original stereo signal and 100% is maximum stereo enhancement.

Figure 12.32 Phaser

- Rate – sets the frequency rate of the phaser effect, (when tempo sync is de-activated). Range: 0 – 5Hz.
- Tempo sync dial – multiplies the note value for the tempo sync phasing (see below) by a factor of x1 to x10.
- Sync button – activates/de-activates tempo synchronisation.
- Tempo sync pop-up menu – offers a choice of tempo synchronised note

value settings, providing a way of matching the 'swooshing' of the phase effect to the tempo of the music. Range: whole note to 1/32 note, whole note triplets to 1/32 note triplets, dotted whole note to dotted 1/32 note.

- Output slider – regulates the level of the output signal. Range: 0 – 100%.
- Mix slider – determines the proportion of wet and dry signal output from the effect where 0% is no effect and 100% is fully wet. Range: 0 – 100%

User guide

The display window of Phaser features a graphic representation of the parameter settings. Increasing the feedback dial results in a larger waveform in the display and increases the intensity of the characteristic phase 'swooshing' effect (larger waveform = more intense effect). Increasing the frequency rate of the phaser effect using the rate dial or tempo sync menu results in more waveform cycles appearing in the display and a more rapid phasing effect (more waveforms = more rapid phasing).

Phaser benefits from the inclusion of tempo synchronisation and stereo enhancement. The supplied presets make good starting points for creating your own effects. Like chorus and flanging, phasing is a versatile effect which can be used on a wide variety of sounds. It is popular for special effects with vocals, strings and guitar and helps thicken and sweeten any sound in need of enlivenment. Phaser is suitable for use as an Insert or Send effect.

Symphonic

Symphonic is a hybrid autopan, chorus/flange and stereo enhancement device (Figure 12.33).

The interface includes the following parameters:

- Delay – sets the delay time for the symphonic effect. Higher delay times produce a more pronounced effect. Range: 0 – 100ms.
- Depth – sets the depth of the symphonic effect. Range: 0 – 100%.
- Stereo basis – sets the characteristics of the stereo image of the effect where 0% is mono, 50% matches the original stereo signal and 100% is maximum stereo enhancement.

Figure 12.33
Symphonic

- Rate – sets the frequency rate of the modulation of the symphonic effect. Range 0 – 5Hz.
- Tempo sync dial – multiplies the note value for the tempo sync phasing (see below) by a factor of x1 to x10.
- Sync button – activates/de-activates tempo synchronisation.
- Tempo sync pop-up – offers a choice of tempo-synchronised note value settings, providing a way of matching the modulation rate of the symphonic

effect to the tempo of the music. Range: whole note to 1/32 note, whole note triplets to 1/32 note triplets, dotted whole note to dotted 1/32 note.
- Output slider – regulates the level of the output signal. Range: 0 – 100%.
- Mix slider – determines the proportion of wet and dry signal output from the effect where 0% is no effect and 100% is fully wet. Range: 0 – 100%

User guide

The display window of Symphonic features a graphic representation of the parameter settings. When tempo sync is active, increasing the tempo sync dial results in more and smaller waveforms in the display and increases the speed of the modulation of the symphonic effect (more waveforms = a more rapid modulation effect). Increasing the delay dial moves the beginning of the waveform to the right of the display and increases the phasing-like element in the symphonic effect. Increasing the depth dial results in more amplitude in the waveform in the display and a more intense effect (larger waveform = more depth). Like tempo sync, increasing the rate dial results in more and smaller waveforms appearing in the display and a corresponding increase in the rate of the modulation of the symphonic effect. The stereo basis dial increases the stereo enhancement of the effect and can be used in conjunction with the rate and tempo sync features to create autopan effects.

Symphonic is a versatile effect which is particularly suitable for string, pad and guitar sounds. It works best with harmonically rich sounds and is designed primarily to process stereo signals. It produces good autopan effects. The supplied presets make good starting points for creating your own effects. Symphonic is suitable for use as an Insert or Send effect.

Tranceformer

Tranceformer is a ring modulation device (Figure 12.34).

Tranceformer accepts an input signal and frequency modulates it with a variable frequency oscillator (Tone dial) to produce a ring modulation effect. A second oscillator (Speed dial) is used to apply LFO pitch modulation to the Tone oscillator. The interface includes the following parameters:

- Tone – governs the frequency of the main frequency modulating signal. Range: 1 – 5000Hz.
- Speed – regulates the speed of the second oscillator when the pitch modulation on/off button (below) has been activated. Range: 0 – 10Hz (if the sync button is de-activated). Whole note to 1/32 note, whole note triplets to 1/32 note triplets, dotted whole note to dotted 1/32 note (if the sync button is activated).
- Depth – determines the

Figure 12.34 Tranceformer

depth of the pitch modulation. Range: 0 – 100%.
- Waveform buttons – determine the type of waveform which produces the pitch modulation effect. Sine, square, sawtooth, reverse sawtooth and triangle waveforms are available.
- On/off button – activates/de-activates pitch modulation.
- Mono/stereo button – determines whether the effect output is in mono or stereo.
- Sync button – activates/de-activates tempo synchronisation.
- Output slider – regulates the level of the output signal. Range: 0 – 100%.
- Mix slider – determines the proportion of wet and dry signal output from the effect where 0% is no effect and 100% is fully wet. Range: 0 – 100%.

User guide

The display window of Tranceformer features a graphic representation of the parameter settings. When pitch modulation is switched off (on/off button) the frequency modulating waveform appears above the middle line in the display. When it is switched on it appears inside the modulating waveform. In both cases, the number of waveforms becomes more dense as the Tone dial is increased, producing a corresponding increase in the frequency modulation effect. The Depth dial controls the amount of pitch modulation. Clicking and dragging directly in the graphic display allows the simultaneous adjustment of the Tone and Depth controls.

Tranceformer is excellent for the creation of special effects and strange, other-worldly sounds. It can be used to great effect on vocals and speech. It also has its uses in the creation of unusual drum and percussion parts and may also be applicable to special guitar and synthesizer effects. Some of the more interesting effects are achieved by using very low Tone, Depth and Speed settings. Check out the 'Saw Falling' and 'Low Pad Vibe' presets and try settings of around 70Hz for Tone with 1% Depth and 0.1Hz Speed (pitch modulation On) for alien speech effects. Tranceformer is suitable for use as an Insert or Send effect.

Reverb A

Reverb A is a reverberation device for the simulation of rooms and acoustic spaces (Figure 12.35). It is available in Cubase SX only.

The interface includes the following parameters:

- PreDelay – sets the delay between the initial sound and the onset of the reverb. Range: 0 – 100ms.
- Room size – governs the size of the simulated room. Range: 20 – 100%
- High Cut – filters out the high frequencies in the reverb signal producing a more 'mellow' and natural sounding effect. Range: –15dB to 0dB.
- Low Cut – filters out any unwanted low frequencies, reducing any 'boominess' which may be present with larger room sizes and longer reverb times. Range: –15dB to 0dB.
- Reverb time – sets the duration of the reverb. Range: 0.20secs – 'forever!'.

Figure 12.35
Reverb A

- Mix slider – determines the proportion of wet and dry signal output from the effect where 0% is no effect and 100% is fully wet. Range: 0 – 100%

User guide

The interface for Reverb A features a graphic representation of the parameter settings. Room size is displayed as a re-sizeable cube, reverb time as a three dimensional reverberation waveform which stretches further into the distance as the time is increased and pre-delay as a reverberation waveform which begins at a greater or smaller distance from a loudspeaker, depending on the delay time. The interface also features an input level meter, which is helpful.

Reverb A is a good all-rounder and thanks to the high cut and low cut parameters produces convincing reverberation even at longer reverb times. (Note: at the time of writing the high cut and low cut dials were labelled in reverse order). It does not quite match the performance of some high-end reverb plug-ins but it can still be recommended for drums, vocals, and any other sound. Try the 'Ice' preset on vocals. The supplied presets make good starting points for creating your own effects.

Reverb A would normally be used as a Send effect and in this capacity the Mix slider would usually be set to 100% wet. (See the section entitled 'Audio effects in theory' at the beginning of this chapter for details about the theory of reverb).

Roomworks

Roomworks is a reverberation device for the simulation of rooms and acoustic spaces (Figure 12.36). It is a more advanced unit than the supplied Reverb A and B plug-ins and benefits from a more elaborate set of controls (with a corresponding increase in the amount of CPU power required to run the plug-in). The interface includes the following parameters:

- High shelf input filter – provides high frequency cut or boost (-18dB to +6dB) above the selected frequency cut-off point (250Hz – 22kHz). This filtering is pre-reverb.
- Low shelf input filter – provides low frequency cut or boost (-18dB to +6dB) below the selected frequency cut-off point (25Hz – 6kHz). This filtering is pre-reverb.

Figure 12.36
Roomworks

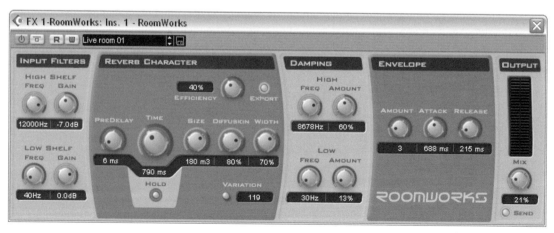

- Efficiency – determines the liveliness (amount of absorption) in the simulated room (0-100%).
- Export button – when enabled, optimises the reverb signal for maximum quality during Export/Audio Mixdown operations.
- pre-delay – sets the delay between the initial sound and the onset of the reverb (0-500ms).
- Time – sets the duration of the reverb (100ms – 20s).
- Size – governs the size of the simulated room (20 – 250 cubic metres).
- Diffusion – determines the amount of diffusion in the simulated room (0 – 100%).
- Width – governs the width of the stereo effect of the reverb (0 – 100%).
- Hold button – when enabled, holds the reverb effect infinitely.
- Variation button – each time this button is pressed a new variable is introduced into the reverb algorithm to create a slightly different sound.
- High frequency damping filter – dampens or emphasises the high frequency content (10% – 400%) around the chosen cut-off point (500Hz – 22kHz). This filtering is post-reverb.
- Low frequency damping filter – dampens or emphasises the low frequency content (10% – 400%) around the chosen cut-off point (25Hz – 1kHz). This filtering is post-reverb.
- Envelope amount, attack and release controls – trims the overall contour of the reverberation result.
- Mix – determines the proportion of wet and dry signals at the output (0% = dry, 100% = wet). If you are using the unit as a send effect, activate the Send button which locks the mix output at 100% wet.

User guide

Roomworks stands up well against mid-range hardware units. It's main strengths are the pre and post reverb filtering which allow excellent fine tuning of the character of the reverb. After setting up the pre-delay, time, size and diffusion parameters to achieve a basic sound, the real soul of Roomworks is found in the high and low damping controls. Juggling the four parameters of the damping section allows the creation of a wide range of effects. The overall shape of the results can be still further modified using the controls in the envelope section.

The unit is supplied with a good range of presets. It works particularly well with drums and can place snares and overall kits in a variety of reverberant spaces with convincing ease. It also provides adequate results for vocals if you do not have access to a high end hardware unit. It excels at producing small and medium sized room simulations.

Roomworks would normally be used as a Send effect and in this capacity the Send button would usually be activated to provide a 100% wet signal from the unit. (See the section entitled 'Audio effects in theory' for more details about the theory of reverb).

Chopper

Chopper is an amplitude modulation device featuring five modulation waveforms (Figure 12.37). Amplitude modulation involves a periodic change in the amplitude level of a signal. This can be used to produce such things as tremolo effects and, when set to stereo, can also produce autopan effects. The interface includes the following parameters:

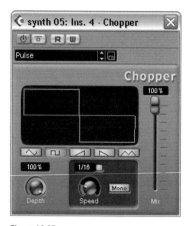

- Waveform buttons – for selecting the type of oscillator waveform used to produce the amplitude modulation effect. The choice is between sine, square, sawtooth, reverse sawtooth and triangle waveforms.

Figure 12.37
Chopper

- Depth – regulates the depth of the amplitude modulation effect. Range: 0 – 100%.
- Sync on/off button – determines whether the output of Chopper is synchronised to the tempo of Cubase SX or not. When de-activated, the speed button (described below) is regulated in terms of frequency (hertz). When activated (illuminated) the speed button is regulated in terms of note values.
- Speed – regulates the rate of the amplitude modulation in terms of frequency (0 – 50Hz), when the Sync button is de-activated, and in terms of note values when the Sync button is activated.
- Tempo sync pop-up – offers a choice of tempo-synchronised note value settings, providing a way of matching the amplitude modulation rate to the tempo of the music. Range: whole note to 1/32 note, whole note triplets to 1/32 note triplets, dotted whole note to dotted 1/32 note.
- Mono/stereo button – determines whether the output is mono or stereo. When set to stereo, Chopper can be used for autopan effects.
- Mix slider – determines the proportion of wet and dry signal output from the effect where 0% is no effect and 100% is fully wet. Range: 0 – 100%

User guide

Chopper produces excellent tremolo effects for guitar and other instruments and allows the speed of the tremolo to be tuned to the tempo of the song using the sync and speed parameters. When used as an insert for a stereo channel or as a Send effect the unit serves as a convenient autopanner, the speed of which can be easily tuned to the tempo of the song.

Chopper can be used to add interest to otherwise lifeless sounds. It is particularly useful for enlivening synthesizer parts and can introduce tempo related beats into any kind of sustained note. For example, processing a sustained note using the unit as an Insert effect with the waveform set to square or reverse sawtooth, the mode set to stereo, the sync button activated and the speed set to a 1/16 note value, produces a pleasing synth pulse effect. For further enhancement follow this effect with flange (see Flanger above). Chopper is also good for 'chopping up' vocals and speech for special effects. Chopper is suitable for use as an Insert or Send effect.

Grungelizer

Grungelizer (Figure 12.38) is a device for producing noise, interference and ageeing effects for your digital recordings. The parameters include:

Figure 12.38 Grungelizer

- Crackle – adds crackles and pops to the signal, as found on scratched vinyl recordings. The speed of the imaginary vinyl record can be changed between 33, 45 or 78rpm.
- Noise – adds high frequency hiss to the signal.
- Distort – mildly distorts the signal.
- EQ – filters the signal, progressively taking out the body of the sound as the value is increased.
- AC – adds 50Hz or 60Hz mains hum to the signal.
- timeline – accentuates all the other settings by a progressively greater amount as the dial is turned back in time to the year 1900.

User guide

The first question you might ask with regard to the Grungelizer is why would you want to add all this interference to your perfect digital recordings!? The answer is that the digital world is sometimes just too clean! Adding 'dirt' can sometimes give a sound more character. You may also need to artificially 'age' some element in a music production, such as a vocal, or a special effect or you might just want your guitar to sound as dirty as possible. You may also need to replicate the sound of a vintage 78 record made in 1920.

For experimental purposes, try using just one of the dials alone in conjunction with the timeline dial. For example, used alone, the EQ dial is a filter which effectively takes out more of the body of the sound the higher it is set and this can be handy as a hybrid tone control. The distort dial provides a mild distortion effect which can be used to add subtle character to lifeless synth sounds. Used carefully, the Grungelizer can be a surprisingly welcome addition to your effects rack.

Additional effects

Of course, any number of other plug-in effects may be added to your Cubase SX system. At the time of installation, you also had the option of installing the plug-ins which were supplied with previous versions of the program.

Many of these are well worth exploring and the Karlette delay unit and the Mysterizer are particularly recommended. These are outlined below:

Karlette

Karlette is a multi-tap delay device emulating the characteristics of a tape loop echo unit (Figure 12.39). The interface for the unit features four identical delay lines and includes the following parameters:

For each delay line:

Figure 12.39
Karlette

- Delay time – sets the delay time in milliseconds or in note values depending on the status of the sync button (see below).
- Volume – sets the volume for the delay line.
- Damp – filters the upper frequencies of the delay signal so that repeat echoes are progressively dampened.
- Pan – pans the delay signal in the stereo image.
- Feedback – determines the proportion of the delay which is 'fed back' to the input, thereby controlling the number of repeats for the delay line.
- Sync – determines the tempo-related behaviour of the unit. When the sync button is activated the display of each delay line is shown in note values and the actual delay time becomes directly related to the tempo of Cubase SX. Changing the tempo of the program will now automatically adjust the delay times so that the repeats are always synchronised. When the sync button is de-activated the unit is no longer tempo driven and delay times are entered in milliseconds.
- Wet/dry slider – controls the mix of the dry input signal and the treated (wet) signal. When used as a send effect this would normally be set to fully 'wet' and when used as an insert it would normally be set somewhere in between the two according to the mix required.

User guide

Karlette can be used as an ordinary delay line, as a multi tap delay device or as a virtual emulation of a tape echo unit. The general theory of delay is outlined in the 'Audio effects in theory' section (above). Multi tap and tape loop echo deserve further explanation before we go on to explore the details of using Karlette.

Multi tap delay refers to a special kind of delay system where a number of separate delay lines are available simultaneously, each with their own volume, pan and feedback controls. This allows the creation of effects with multiple delay times and multiple pan positions. It is often used for creating effects where the delay repetitions sweep across the stereo image or travel in circular or cyclic patterns.

Many years ago, before technology supplied the digital alternative, echo effects were produced by tape loop echo units. These devices were very popular among guitarists of the 1960's and were responsible for some classic sound effects. The essential design involved a short loop of recording tape which was directed past erase, record and three or more playback heads. The erase head cleaned off the previous pass, the record head recorded the input signal and the playback heads replayed this signal slightly later. The delay effect was a function of the actual distance of the playback heads from the record head and multiple repeats could be achieved by feeding the delay signal back to the input (feedback). Karlette has been designed with this kind of system in mind.

For a normal stereo delay effect try the following procedure. De-activate the sync button and turn down the volume of the third and fourth delay lines. Set the first and second delay lines to 400ms (or some other equal value), pan them hard left and hard right and turn up the volume of both to maximum. Set a 30% (300) feedback value in the left channel and a 50% (500) feedback value in the right channel. This produces a delay effect which sweeps left and then fades to the right. Simple but effective. If you would like to use the same effect in sync mode, activate the sync button and set the first and second delay lines to 1/4 note values.

For a multi tap delay effect try the following procedure. Activate the sync button and set the delay lines to 1/8 note, 1/4 note, dotted 1/4 note and 1/2 note values respectively. Adjust the first pair of pan controls to 'L40' and 'R40' positions and the second pair of pan controls to 'L50' and 'R50' positions. Adjust all delay lines for 50% (500) feedback and set the levels to read 0, −6, −12 and −18dB respectively. Set the damp controls to values of 100, 200, 400 and 600 respectively. This produces a multiple 'ping pong' echo effect which is good for special effects and which, although it is rather complex, will sit in time with much of your rhythmic material.

For an authentic tape loop echo effect try the following. De-activate the sync button, set the delay lines to 1848, 1877, 1906 and 1935ms and adjust the volume dials to read −2, −3, −4 and −5dB. Adjust the damp controls to values of 750, 820, 900 and 990, the feedback controls to 550, 650, 750 and 850 and set all pan controls to the centre position. Any input will now be repeated according to four slightly different independent loop times. This is an attempt to simulate the behaviour of the playback heads of a real-world unit where the repeats tended to become smeared. The first delay time is derived from four times the duration of a quarter note at 130bpm (4 x 462ms) and it is this which gives the loop its basic tempo. The high damp settings quickly reduce the upper frequencies in the signal, also emulating the behaviour of the real thing. For special effects, try changing the delay times and the pan positions.

Karlette is a useful alternative to Cubase SX's other delay units and can achieve special effects not available on most other delay devices. The sync feature is ideal for automatically adjusting delay times to the tempo of the song, if this is what the song needs. Karlette works well with lead guitar, lead synth, saxophone and most other solo instruments. It is excellent for the creation of sound effects and tape loop echo simulations. It is suitable for use as an Insert or Send effect.

Mysterizer

Mysterizer (Figure 12.40) is a unique multi-effects processor based upon the manipulation of effects parameters relative to the x-y position of a marker in the display.

The interface includes the following parameters:

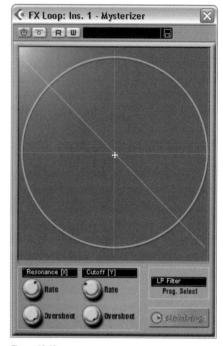

Figure 12.40
Mysterizer

- x-y display screen – allows the placing of a position marker which controls two parameters of the chosen effect type (Program Select menu). The x axis (horizontal) is arranged with the lowest value on the left and the highest on the right. The y axis (vertical) is arranged with the lowest value at the top and the highest at the bottom.
- Rate dial (x axis) – determines how fast the white marker moves towards the target position you specify on the x axis.
- Rate dial (y axis) – determines how fast the white marker moves towards the target position you specify on the y axis.
- Overshoot dial (x axis) – determines the distance with which the white marker 'misses' the target position and bounces back and forth on either side on the x axis.
- Overshoot dial (y axis) – determines the distance with which the white marker 'misses' the target position and bounces back and forth on either side on the y axis.
- Program selection menu – steps through a selection of popular effects. For each selection, the two parameters which are available for manipulation on the x and y axes are shown in the (X) and (Y) info fields below the display area. The following effects are available: low-pass filter, high-pass filter, band-pass filter, distortion, ring modulation, comb-delay, mono delay, and stereo delay.

User guide

Mysterizer features a simple but powerful user-interface. The position marker plots a position on the x and y axes of the display which affects two parameters of the chosen program type. When you click once anywhere in the blue display window the position marker is moved to that position but, here's the twist, the marker does not have to move directly to the point at which you clicked, it can also be made to bounce back and forth on both the x and y axes gradually moving closer to the target. This action occurs at the rate set with the rate control and at the distance set with the overshoot control. In practice, this gives the impression of the position marker bouncing wildly around the target point like in some kind of abstract computer game. Of course, this has a corresponding effect on the sound being processed. For example, if you choose the low-pass filter in the program select field the x axis is set to resonance and the y axis is set to cut-off. As the marker changes position, the resonance and cut-off are tweaked accordingly, resulting in some remarkable real-time sound effects. Experiment with the other program selection options. Comb Delay and Ring Modulation produce good results.

By activating the Read and Write buttons you can automate the movements of the position marker and the marker can also be controlled according to MIDI note input if you assign the MIDI out of a MIDI track to Mysterizer. In the latter case, MIDI velocity controls the x axis position and MIDI note value controls the y axis position. Mysterizer is suitable for use as an Insert or Send effect.

Combination processing

If you have enough processing power you can achieve some creative effects by using more than one unit as an Insert effect. Try the following combinations:

- Compression followed by overdrive distortion (typically used by guitarists to achieve more sustain).
- Compression followed by filtering.
- Delay followed by chorus/flange.
- Distortion followed by chorus/flange.
- Chorus/flange followed by chorus/flange.
- Tremolo followed by autopan.
- Reverb followed by phasing.
- Filtering followed by delay.

Experimentation can yield some surprisingly good effects and if you are feeling really adventurous try using combinations of three or four effects/processors. In addition to using Insert effects, you could also simultaneously incorporate one or more Send effects. (Also see 'Combination processing' in Chapter 9.)

Info

Using multiple Insert effects can quickly use up your computer's processing power. Check out the current CPU load in the VST Performance window (Devices menu). Ideally, the CPU load should average no more than 50 – 60%.

Plug-ins from other developers

There are a wide range of plug-ins available from other developers (for more details see the websites listed in the Plug-ins section of Chapter 22). Of particular note, are the UAD powered plug-ins, which run on a dedicated PCI card installed in the computer, resulting in less strain on the CPU, and the similarly functioning TC electronics powercore system. Also high on the list come the excellent plug-ins supplied by Voxengo and PSP Audioware. Among the wide range of plug-ins from PSP Audioware comes their renowned PSP Vintage Warmer (Figure 12.41). Vintage Warmer provides analogue tape simulation effects and limiting. It helps remedy the problems of Cubase SX users suffering from cold, brittle or characterless digital recordings and works equally well on individual tracks, whole mixes or as a mastering effect.

Figure 12.41
PSP Vintage Warmer

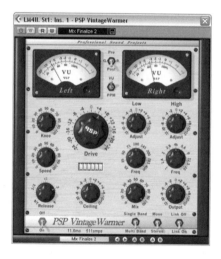

Plug-in information

To see an overview of all the plug-ins installed in your system, select 'Plug-in Information' from the Devices menu. This opens the Plug-in Information window (Figure 12.42) where the plug-ins are arranged in a list with columns showing the important characteristics of each device. Here, you can check out the number of inputs and outputs, the latency, the number of parameters, and how many program slots are available for storing presets, for each plug-in. The leftmost column allows you to de-activate those plug-ins you never use by unchecking the tick box. This de-activates the plug-in in Cubase SX but it remains installed on your computer. You can, at any time in the future, re-activate it. Using the tabs at the top of the window you can view the installed Direct X and MIDI plug-ins.

Figure 12.42
Plug-in Information window

		Name	Nb I/C	Category	Vendor	VST V	Delay	Use Delay Comp	Nb Para	Nb Prog	Old	Modified	Path
✔	1	Reverb A	2 / 2	RoomFx	Spectral Design	2.2	0	✔	6	8	R	4/23/2002	C:\Program Files\Steinberg\Cubase
✔	1	Reverb B	2 / 2	RoomFx	Spectral Design	2.2	0	✔	5	8	R	4/23/2002	C:\Program Files\Steinberg\Cubase
✔	-	Reaktor4 FX 2x8	2 / 8	Spacializer	Native Instrumer	2.3	0	✔	1000	128	R	7/29/2003	C:\Program Files\Steinberg\VstPlug
✔	-	SurroundPan	2 / 6	Spacializer	Steinberg Media	2.3	0	✔	23	1		8/6/2003	C:\Program Files\Steinberg\Cubase
✔	-	SurroundPanSX1.x	2 / 6	Spacializer	Steinberg Media	2.3	0	✔	20	1		8/6/2003	C:\Program Files\Steinberg\Cubase
✔	2	DeEsser	2 / 2	Mastering	Spectral Design	2.2	683	✔	3	4	R	4/12/2002	C:\Program Files\Steinberg\Cubase
✔	-	Magneto	2 / 2	Mastering	Spectral Design	2.2	296	✔	6	4	R	8/19/2003	C:\Program Files\Steinberg\Cubase
✔	-	MultibandCompressor	2 / 2	Mastering	Spectral Design	2.2	950	✔	7	10	R	8/19/2003	C:\Program Files\Steinberg\Cubase
✔	-	uv22	2 / 2	Mastering	Spectral Design	2.2	0	✔	3	4	R	4/26/2002	C:\Program Files\Steinberg\Cubase
✔	-	uv22 hr	2 / 2	Mastering	Spectral Design	2.2	0	✔	3	4	R	8/26/2002	C:\Program Files\Steinberg\Cubase
✔	-	a1	0 / 2	Synth	Waldorf	2.2	0	✔	99	128	R	4/30/2003	C:\Program Files\Steinberg\Cubase
✔	-	cs40	0 / 2	Synth	Steinberg	2.2	0	✔	25	16	R	10/16/200'	C:\Program Files\Steinberg\Cubase
✔	-	HALion	0 / 18	Synth	Steinberg Media	2.3	0	✔	3920	1	R	10/6/2003	C:\Program Files\Steinberg\VstPlug
✔	-	JX16	0 / 2	Synth	maxim digital auc	2.0	0	✔	40	64	R	10/22/200'	C:\Program Files\Steinberg\Cubase
✔	-	Kontakt	0 / 12	Synth	Native Instrumer	2.2	0	✔	0	1	R	9/10/2002	C:\Program Files\Steinberg\VstPlug
✔	-	lm-7	0 / 2	Synth	Steinberg	2.2	0	✔	38	3	R	4/23/2002	C:\Program Files\Steinberg\Cubase
✔	-	LM-9	0 / 2	Synth	Steinberg	2.2	0	✔	19	2	R	8/15/2001	C:\Program Files\Steinberg\Cubase
✔	-	Neon	0 / 2	Synth	Steinberg	2.2	0	✔	14	16	R	8/15/2001	C:\Program Files\Steinberg\Cubase
✔	-	Reaktor4	2 / 8	Synth	Native Instrumer	2.3	0	✔	1000	128	R	7/28/2003	C:\Program Files\Steinberg\VstPlug
✔	-	vb-1	0 / 2	Synth	Steinberg	2.2	0	✔	6	16	R	4/16/2002	C:\Program Files\Steinberg\Cubase
✔	-	BitCrusher	2 / 2	Effect	Steinberg Media	2.2	0	✔	5	5	R	4/18/2002	C:\Program Files\Steinberg\Cubase
✔	2	Chopper	2 / 2	Effect	Steinberg Media	2.2	0	✔	8	9	R	4/24/2002	C:\Program Files\Steinberg\Cubase
✔	2	Chorus	2 / 2	Effect	Spectral Design	2.2	0	✔	5	8	R	4/18/2002	C:\Program Files\Steinberg\Cubase
✔	1	DoubleDelay	2 / 2	Effect	Spectral Design	2.2	0	✔	12	8	R	4/12/2002	C:\Program Files\Steinberg\Cubase
✔	2	Dynamics	2 / 2	Effect	Spectral Design	2.2	0	✔	25	8	R	4/24/2002	C:\Program Files\Steinberg\Cubase
✔	3	Flanger	2 / 2	Effect	Spectral Design	2.2	0	✔	11	8	R	7/18/2002	C:\Program Files\Steinberg\Cubase
✔	2	Metalizer	2 / 2	Effect	Steinberg Media	2.2	0	✔	9	9	R	4/24/2002	C:\Program Files\Steinberg\Cubase
✔	1	ModDelay	2 / 2	Effect	Spectral Design	2.2	0	✔	7	8	R	4/12/2002	C:\Program Files\Steinberg\Cubase
✔	1	Overdrive	2 / 2	Effect	Spectral Design	2.2	0	✔	8	8	R	4/12/2002	C:\Program Files\Steinberg\Cubase
✔	2	Phaser	2 / 2	Effect	Spectral Design	2.2	0	✔	8	8	R	4/12/2002	C:\Program Files\Steinberg\Cubase
✔	-	Q	2 / 2	Effect	Spectral Design	2.2	0	✔	35	10	R	8/19/2003	C:\Program Files\Steinberg\Cubase

Plug-in Information

VST Plug-ins   DirectX Plug-ins   MIDI Plug-ins

Shared VST Plug-ins Folders

C:\Program Files\Steinberg\VstPlugins   Add...   Change...   Remove

Update

Mastering

What is mastering and what is a master?

Traditionally, 'mastering' is a final editing and processing stage which comes after mixing. Officially, this stage is referred to as 'pre-mastering', since it takes place before the 'real' master (the 'glass master') is produced at the CD duplication factory. For most of us, 'mastering' is understood to mean the same as 'pre-mastering'. Here, you might adjust the final sound quality using any combination of EQ, compression, expansion, loudness maximisation, stereo processing, harmonic excitation, dithering or other processes, and you might also adjust the order, spacing, lengths and levels for a group of mixes intended as the tracks for a CD.

In broad terms, a 'master' is a final high quality recording from which copies can be made. This could be a master produced within Cubase SX or the master (or pre-master) produced after a final mastering stage in other software or in a professional mastering house. For commercial releases, the mastering stage often takes place under the direction of a highly experienced professional mastering engineer. While professional mastering of your mixes is likely to give better quality results, doing it yourself and producing your own 'factory-ready' CD master is certainly possible (CD duplication plants readily accept masters in red-book CD audio format).

Many Cubase SX users wish to perform their own final mastering step to maximise the quality of their recordings prior to duplicating for demo purposes or for commercial release. If you intend to produce a production master CD yourself, bear in mind that the CD writing process is prone to error, especially if you use a poor quality CD recorder and poor quality media. To avoid errors, always use a high quality CD recorder and the best media. Also, work in a clean, dust-free atmosphere and never touch the surface of the master compact disc. If you are duplicating your own audio CDs for demo purposes, it is still worth working within strict guidelines to avoid problems.

Mastering decisions

The way you approach mastering is highly dependent upon the nature of your project and your personal preferences, but assembling the tracks for a CD master would normally involve the following steps:

- General editing decisions such as removing clicks, topping and tailing and adjusting track lengths

Info

Mastering is the final stage in a chain of processes which contribute to the production of a finished musical work or recording project. These processes include: composition, arrangement, performance, recording, mixing and mastering.

Info

For serious CD pre-mastering purposes, CD writers manufactured by Plextor are highly recommended.

Info

Many professional mastering houses master to DDP (Disc Description Protocol) on Exabyte tape. This helps optimise results since DDP is not subject to the same error rate and handling difficulties as CDR.

- Deciding the track order and the spacing between tracks
- Expansion/compression, equalisation and other sound processing decisions
- Fading, leveling and limiting decisions
- Dithering and truncating the bit-depth to 16-bit
- CD track indexing and burning of the final Red Book audio CD

The mastering stage may be the first time that you hear your group of finished mixes one after the other and at this point you may hear some surprising differences between the overall sound quality and perceived loudness of each track. These are the kinds of elements which need correction during the mastering session, so that you finish up with a homegenous set of tracks. However, it is important to bear in mind that the way in which you use sound processing on a stereo mix at the mastering stage is very different to the way in which you use it on individual instruments at the mixing stage. For example, emphasising the snare using EQ also affects the vocal and bringing out the bass drum may also affect the bass guitar. The sound processing settings for mastering, therefore, are likely to be far less radical. In this context, it is vitally important that you use an accurate monitoring system, otherwise the subtleties of the mastering process cannot be judged correctly.

If your mixes are already sounding exactly the way you wish then further modification with mastering processing may no longer be necessary. In this case, it may then be just a matter of deciding the track order and the spacings, dithering and truncating to 16-bit and indexing and burning the CD.

> ### Tip
>
> To get a better idea of the average loudness of each CD track, select the CD track event and use the Statistics function in the Audio menu. Compare the 'Average' RMS power levels for each CD track, (the lower-most values in the Statistics window).

Mastering in Cubase SX

Although it may be preferable to use a specialised program for mastering (such as Steinberg Wavelab or Bias Peak), almost all of the mastering steps suggested above can be applied within Cubase SX. The one exception is the final step of creating track indexes and burning the CD. Cubase SX is NOT designed for the detailed preparation of the track list for a CD and integrated CD burning is NOT included. For some suggestions about how to approach CD burning, see 'Burning the CD', below.

The remainder of this section details how to set up Cubase SX for a mastering session and suggests some mastering plug-in chains for the insert slots of the stereo master output bus.

Creating a mastering template

Cubase SX is supplied with a mastering template called 'Stereo Mastering for Audio CD' but it is a good idea to create your own personalised version which you can use to start each mastering session. This streamlines the project for the usual mastering operations. Try the following :

- Select 'New Project' in the File menu.
- In the dialogue which appears, click on 'Empty'. Select the directory where you wish to create the folder for the project and click on the 'Create' button. Enter a name for the new project folder in the 'Create new directory' pop-up box which appears. Click on OK to open the empty project.

- In the Project Setup dialogue (Project menu), enter a suitable length for the project in the Length field. If you are assembling a number of tracks for a CD demo you might like to enter the normal audio CD duration (74 minutes). Select 'seconds' in the Display format field. Enter your preferred sample rate and record fomat in the respective fields (32-bit float is recommended for mastering projects).
- Open the Mixer in extended mode and reduce its horizontal size to a minimum. Hide the input buss and make sure the stereo master output buss is visible at the extreme right position. Select 'Meter' in the output buss pop-up menu to show the large scale meters in the upper part of the display. Arrange the Mixer window behind the Project window so that only the stereo master output bus is visible on the right of the screen (see Figure 13.1). This provides you with easy access to the master stereo fader and displays a helpful stereo level meter which is always visible while you work on your mastering project.
- Activate and then de-activate the Write button in the stereo master output bus. This adds the output buss automation sub-track in the Project window (in the Input/Output Channels folder). This might be used for creating automated fades in and out.
- With the output buss sub-track selected, open the Inspector and select the Inserts panel (this is the Inserts panel for the stereo master output buss). Here, you can set up your chain of mastering plug-ins in the Insert slots. You might like to activate the UV22HR (or other) dithering plug-in in slot 8. For CD mastering set the UV22HR to Normal / 16-bit. If desired, add other processors in the remaining slots.
- Add the marker track. This is invaluable for marking the starts (and ends) of your CD tracks and edit points.
- Add two stereo audio tracks in the Project window. Name the first track 'CD tracks' and the second 'Edits' (for example). The first track is for your CD tracks and the second is for rough editing purposes. (This is assuming that you intend to pass all the CD tracks through the same mastering processing of the stereo master output buss. However, if it is your intention to apply separate real-time processing on each CD track then you may need to put each song on a different audio track in the Project window. Alternatively, you could automate the processing). Resize all tracks as appropriate.
- If required, activate the large scale Time Display and VST Performance windows from the Device menu. A large time display is easier to see and helps if the Transport panel time displays are hidden. The VST performance window helps you keep an eye on the current CPU overhead.
- Activate the Transport panel. Try using it in 'Jog Scrub and Markers' mode, selected from the pop-up menu. This may be all you need for mastering. Configure the Project window toolbar. For example, try setting the Snap mode to 'Shuffle'. In Shuffle mode all events on a track are tightly snapped one against the other and the order may be changed by dragging one event in between two others. This is excellent for quickly re-ordering the CD tracks.
- For spacing, try preparing empty audio events of various lengths (1, 2 and 3secs, for example) and store these on the 'Edits' track. In shuffle

mode these can be inserted between two CD tracks at any time by holding Alt and dragging a copy of the event to the desired join between two tracks. A green insert marker is displayed.

- Your setup should now resemble Figure 13.1. Save the project as a template using 'Save as template' (File menu). Enter a name such as 'stereo mastering' into the pop-up dialogue to save the project in the Templates folder. Now, whenever it is your intention to do a mastering session, you can load your mastering template from the list of templates which appears when you select 'New Project' (File menu).

Figure 13.1
Stereo mastering template in Cubase SX

Typical mastering plug-in processing chains

The processing chains shown below might typically be found in the insert slots of the stereo master output bus during a mastering session. While it is possible to use various of the supplied plug-ins for mastering purposes, mastering quality EQ, compression and limiting normally requires high precision plug-ins designed specifically for the purpose. Therefore, some of the plug-ins shown in these examples are from the Waves range. To get started with mastering try the following processing chains:

1 High quality mastering

A high-quality mastering chain featuring the Waves Masters plug-ins, for linear phase equalisation, linear phase multi-band compression, loudness maximisation/limiting, and dithering. Alternatives from the plug-ins supplied with Cubase SX are shown in brackets.

Figure 13.2
High quality mastering plug-in chain featuring the Waves Masters plug-ins

- Slot 1: Waves Linear Phase EQ (or the supplied 'Q' EQ)
- Slot 2: Waves Linear Multiband Compressor (or the supplied Multiband Compressor)
- Slot 7: (post master bus fader): Waves L1 or L2 Ultramiximiser (or VST Dynamics limiter section in slot 7 and UV22 HR in slot 8)

2 Classic mastering chain for adding warmth and character

A digital mix suffering from a cold, brittle quality might benefit from the higher quality Q plug-in or the warmth of the Waves Renaissance EQ. Using Magneto or PSP Vintage Warmer can help add warmth to the signal. Overall, this chain includes equalisation, compression, analogue style tape saturation and limiting. If you are using the VST Dynamics limiter section make sure that the red LED only lights up occasionally (i.e. you need to be limiting the peaks only).

- Slot 1: 'Q' EQ plug-in or Waves Renaissance EQ
- Slot 2: Multiband Compressor or Waves Renaissance Compressor
- Slot 3: Magneto (or try PSP Vintage Warmer)
- Slot 7: VST Dynamics (using soft clip or limiter section only) or Waves L1 Ultramaximizer (without IDR)
- Slot 8: (post master bus fader): Apogee UV22 HR dithering

Figure 13.3
Mastering plug-in chain for warmth and character

All stages in these mastering chains are optional and individual plug-ins can be bypassed using their respective bypass buttons. Depending upon the application and desired result, the order of the EQ and compressor plug-ins may be reversed. Unless you wish to impose radical changes upon your mixes for creative effect, the settings for most mastering processors must be set with great subtlety and precision. If the mix is already sounding exactly as you want to hear it, then it may not need any mastering processing at all (except for dithering).

Mastering processing settings

This section briefly covers the kinds of settings you might need when using plug-ins for mastering purposes (bear in mind that appropriate settings depend entirely upon the signal you are processing). Due to the often specialist require-ments of mastering, reference is also made to the Waves range of plug-ins. These are NOT supplied as part of Cubase SX. The settings for plug-ins when used in mastering applications are likely to be far less radical than those used for processing during the tracking and mixing stages. This is especially true of EQ, compressor and limiter settings. Let's examine how you might adjust the controls in a mastering chain featuring EQ, compressor and limiter plug-ins.

EQ settings for mastering

Flattering the mix

A dull mix may need to be flattered at the mastering stage, either to re-inforce a weak bass end or to bring out the detail and 'air' in the upper frequencies, or both. A common problem is that the mix has too much activity in the mid frequencies. This tends to mask the other frequencies in the signal and may also result in a harsh sounding mix. Correcting these issues might involve slightly boosting the lower and upper frequencies whilst also attenuating the mid frequency band (or it may require just one of these measures). The target low frequency band is usually that below around 150Hz. Boosting here should always be approached with great subtlety since too much bass just adds boominess. The 'air' frequencies are in the region between 15kHz to 20 kHz but beware of boosting too much as this may give the impression that your mix is now sounding thin. Attenuating the mid frequencies might involve a wide and extremely subtle curve somewhere between 1 and 6kHz. Beware of cutting the frequencies too much as this can seriously upset the balance (any adjustments to the all-important mid-frequences should always be kept to an absolute minimum). These measures sometimes produce an EQ curve which resembles a smile, hence this kind of EQ is commonly referred to as a 'smile curve'. Try the settings shown in Figure 13.4.

Figure 13.4
Subtle curve for flattering the mix in the supplied Q plug-in

Adding warmth

The Waves Linear Phase EQ is designed to be as transparent as possible. This means that, even if you impose a fairly radical EQ curve, any undesirable side-effects are likely to be minimal. The common undesirable side-effect inherent in many other EQ devices is phase shifting between the different frequency bands resulting in loss of clarity and harshness. Digital mixes sometimes suffer from a cold, brittle quality to the sound and the last thing you want to do is process the signal with an EQ which adds still more harshness. Waves Linear Phase EQ provides a solution. To warm up your mix, try setting the Linear Phase EQ to similar values to those shown in Figure 13.5. This resembles the smile curve shown above but is a slightly more radical curve designed to add warmth and air to a harsh, congested mix. Flatten the curve slightly if the settings are too radical for your own mix.

Figure 13.5
Waves Linear Phase EQ for adding warmth

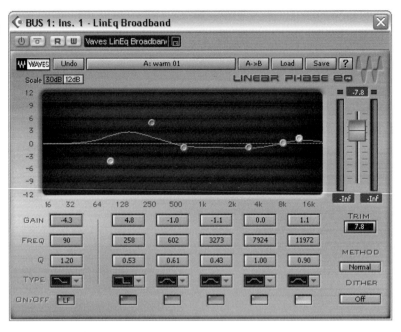

Compression settings for mastering

Wideband compression

Classic wideband compression devices may be used to add punch and dynamic movement to a mix whilst also controlling the average level of the signal. When using Waves Renaissance Compressor, C1 or the supplied Dynamics plug-ins for mastering, try very gentle ratios between 1.01 and 1.5 : 1 with thresholds between -30 and -50dBFS to add coherence and density. Gentle control can also be achieved with slightly higher ratios between 1.1 and 3 : 1 and a high threshold between -3 and -5dBFS. Try starting with an attack of around 100ms and a release of 250ms and then adjust to taste.

In the case of the Waves Renaissance Compressor plug-in try the 'Mastering Opto 1' preset as a starting point. Try setting a threshold of around -15dB, lower the release to around 250ms and add around 3dB of gain. Leave all other controls in their default positions. This is good for density and punch. Alternatively, try the Dynamics processor supplied with Cubase SX with the following compressor settings. Threshold: between -20 and -30dB, ratio: 1.3 : 1, attack: 100ms, release: auto, and makeup gain: +2dB. Also activate the limiter in the Dynamics plug-in with the threshold at -0.5dB and auto release active. This ensures that the transient peaks in the signal are kept under control.

Subtle compression can often be applied in a fairly transparent manner but may produce a 'smearing' or 'blurring' of the transients and a dulling of the overall sound. It is also true to say that the lower frequencies in a composite signal tend to dominate the attack and release of the compression. This can produce an undesirable effect where, for example, the bass line dictates the dynamic changes in the upper frequencies. A still worse effect of this is 'hole punching' where sudden low frequency energy may severely reduce the level of the rest of the signal, producing a virtual dropout in the perceived loudness of the signal.

Multi-band compression

Multi-band compressors (like the supplied Multiband Compressor, and the Waves C4 and Linear Multiband Compressors) can help overcome some of the undesirable effects of wide band compression. Multi-band compressors split the input signal into a number of frequency bands so that you can apply a different amount of compression/expansion to each band. However, these devices are more difficult to use and can easily ruin a good mix if set up incorrectly.

Using multiband compression for frequency selective dynamics processing
This example uses the supplied Multiband Compressor to increase the level of a bass drum which was mixed too low and reduce the high frequency level of a vocal which becomes harsh during loudly sung passages. Ordinary EQ or wideband compression are not ideal for these kinds of tasks. However, using multiband compression, you can dial in to the frequency range of the problem instrument or voice and expand or compress to emphasise or de-emphasise the sound as required. Assuming that the above two problems are occurring in the same mix, proceed as follows:

Tip

Any processing which affects the crucial mid-band frequencies in the mix (between around 250Hz and 6kHz) should be approached with subtlety and caution, since it is easy to disturb the natural internal balance of the main instruments if you use radical or inappropriate settings.

- Open the Multiband Compressor in an appropriate insert slot in the master bus inserts panel.
- In the user interface, load the default preset. This featues three frequency ranges. Using the diamond shaped handles, adjust the mid-band so that its lower frequency threshold is set to around 100 to 120Hz and its upper frequency threshold to around 6kHz.
- While listening to the mix, select the lower frequency band so that its curve is highlighted in the breakpoint curve display. Insert a series of breakpoints near the lower left corner above the line to form a curve similar to that shown in Figure 13.6. Here you are applying low level upward compression (low level expansion). When the curve is above the diagonal, the level is increased. This means that gain is applied to the mid level bass frequencies in the signal. You could try narrowing the frequency range of the lower band to tune in to the bass drum more precisely. The net effect is more bass drum without processing the other frequency ranges in the mix.
- Now select the upper frequency band so that its curve is highlighted in the curve display. This time insert a series of breakpoints near the upper right corner below the line to form a curve similar to that shown in Figure 13.6. Here you are applying downward compression near the threshold where the vocal becomes harsh during the loud passages. Whenever the vocal becomes loud and harsh the upper frequencies are compressed downwards, hopefully without an obvious effect on the other instruments in the mix. You may need to narrow the frequency range of the upper band to avoid taking out too much 'air' from the mix.
- Notice how we have achieved the above effects without processing the mid band. This is helpful since the mid band is responsible for the main body of a mix, including the natural internal balance of the vocals, snare and dominant instruments. If the mid-band is already sounding right it is best not to touch it.

Figure 13.6
Multiband Compressor curves to
simultaneously emphasise a bass drum
and tame a harsh vocal

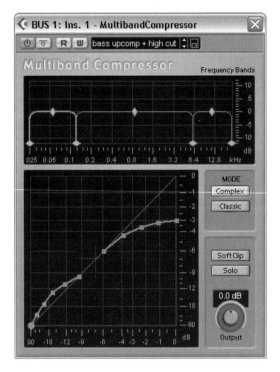

Using multiband compression to add punch and density

This example uses the Waves Linear Multiband Compressor to add overall punch to a mix using upward compression. It is assumed here that you are processing rock or pop music (which perhaps features a drum kit mixed slightly too low). The idea is to attempt to bring out the kit and add punch to the overall mix. Proceed as follows:

- Activate the LinMB plug-in in a slot in the stereo output bus. Load the 'Upward Compressor +3dB' preset from the factory presets.
- Switch off ARC.
- Using the Gain master control, increase the gain of all frequency bands to +5.
- Using the Range master control, reduce the range of all frequency bands to -5.
- Using the Attack master control while observing the mid frequency band, adjust the mid frequency band attack to approximately 43ms. All other bands are adjusted relative to this value.
- Using the Release master control while observing the mid frequency band, adjust the mid frequency band release to approximately 150ms. All other bands are adjusted relative to this value.
- While listening to the mix, lower the threshold of all bands simultaneously using the Threshold master control. Try settings between around -25 and -15dB.
- If the red LEDs above the LinMB's master faders become illuminated, click on the Trim button to reduce the output level. Alternatively, adjust the output level manually. The LinMB should now resemble Figure 13.7.

For a successful result you need to tweak the above settings to match the characteristics of your own mix. Try setting the attack and release times so

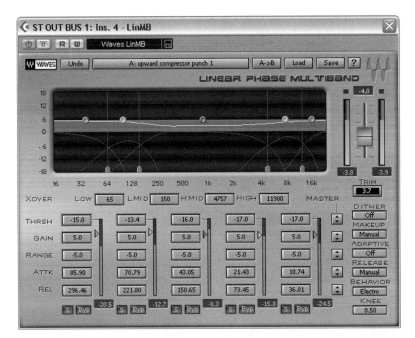

Figure 13.7
Waves Linear MultiBand upward
compression for adding punch and
density to a mix

that the compression line in the display moves up and down in rhythm with the music. A moderate attack time allows the transients of the drums and percussion to cut through thereby emphasising the rhythm. To increase the emphasis on the rhythm you may need to increase the attack time still further. You can achieve similar results using the above values in the Waves C4 Multiband Parametric processor.

Limiting and loudness maximisation settings for mastering

Limiting is generally used in mastering when you want to control the highest peaks in the signal without affecting the body of the sound. The threshold for limiting is therefore usually set very high, and attack times are typically set extremely fast to ensure that sudden transients are kept under control. For maximum transparency and preservation of the natural dynamics of the signal, aim for gain reduction of no more than 6dB. After this the effect starts to draw attention to itself. Once the peaks have been reduced, gain can be applied to the overall signal to provide what is commonly known as loudness maximisation. This results in a significant increase in the perceived loudness since the average level is increased. Greater peak reduction and more extreme loudness maximisation might suit club and hard rock mixes.

Peak limiting and loudness maximisation are the two primary functions of the Waves L1 and L2 Ultramaximizers. The L1 limits and maximises the signal automatically using a lookahead system which anticipates the signal peaks and reshapes them. A threshold control determines the amount of peak gain reduction. The more you lower the threshold into the body of the incoming signal the higher the output level is pushed up towards the output ceiling. The output ceiling ensures zero-overshoot brickwall limiting for the final output signal. The L2 is similar but has been designed specifically with mastering functions in mind and differs from the L1 in providing 9th order noise shaping and ARC (automatic release control). Like the L1 it is intended to be placed in the last plug-in slot in the chain, AFTER the stereo master bus faders.

Cubase SX does not feature plug-ins of this level of sophistication but adequate limiting may be achieved using the soft limit or limiting modules of the Dynamics and VST Dynamics plug-ins, placed in the 7th slot and followed by UV22 HR dithering in the 8th slot (i.e. both AFTER the stereo master bus faders). When using these plug-ins make sure that the limiter's red clipping indicator lights up only occasionally.

With all these limiters, DO NOT set the final output threshold to the maximum 0dBFS. An out ceiling of between -3dB and -0.3dB is more appropriate. This avoids possible clipping errors which may occur if the recording is later played back on poorly designed equipment. The Waves recommended maximum output ceiling for mastering applications is -0.3dB.

Figure 13.8
Typical Waves L1 Ultramaximizer CD mastering setup featuring limiting, loudness maximisation and IDR dithering

Dithering

What is dithering?

A reduction in the bit depth of a digital audio signal means that you are now expressing the audio with shorter wordlength samples. This results in a slight loss in the definition of low level signals, since reducing the wordlength means that you have had to throw away some of the least significant bits. Without processing, this manifests itself as a particular kind of low level non-linear distortion known as quantisation noise. Dithering involves adding a low level controlled noise to the signal and takes into account the least significant bits before they are discarded. This converts the low-level distortion into a more friendly linear noise or 'hiss' and preserves some of the integrity of the original signal. Using a process known as noise shaping, the more friendly noise is re-distributed to parts of the audio spectrum where it is less obvious to the ear. The net result is enhanced clarity and spaciousness.

Dithering is most often applied at the point just before you convert a high resolution file (such as 24-bit) to a lower resolution file (such as 16-bit). For CD mastering purposes in Cubase SX, this is normally when you are producing the final 16-bit master audio file using Export/Audio Mixdown (see Chapter 11 for details about the Export/Audio Mixdown function).

When to use dithering in Cubase SX

All internal audio processing in Cubase SX is performed at 32-bit float resolution, so if you are using the Export/Audio Mixdown function to create an audio file of lesser resolution then you may need to use the dithering options supplied with Cubase SX (or those included with other plug-ins such as the Waves L1 or L2). To be exact, dithering should be applied in the following cases:

- When using the Export/Audio Mixdown function (File menu) to create a final master audio file of any bit depth less than 32-bit float (i.e. 24-bit, 16-bit or 8-bit).
- When mixing down to an external medium, such as DAT, (where the standard bit depth is 16-bit).

When truncating the bit depth from 32-bit float to 24-bit as an interim process, some experts recommend using dither without noise shaping and preferably TPDF dither, although Steinberg consider this to be rather a matter of taste than necessity. At the mixing stage, if it is your intention to perform a final mastering stage at a later date, try mixing down without dither to a high resolution file. Apply noise-shaped dither only as the last step before truncation during the mastering session.

Loading a dithering plug-in

Cubase SX is supplied with the Apogee UV22 HR dithering plug-in which supports dithering to all the popular bit resolutions (see Figure 13.10). Cubase SL is supplied with the very similar Apogee UV22 dithering plug-in which is identical to the UV22 HR except that dithering is to 16-bit resolution only. Dithering is always applied after the master faders and, in the case of Cubase SX, this means loading the dither plug-in in slots 7 or 8 of the stereo master output bus inserts panel. In Cubase SL, it means loading the dithering plug-in in slot 4 of the master bus inserts panel. The following description outlines the use of the Apogee UV22 HR plug-in. The use of the UV22 is very similar. To load the Apogee UV22 HR plug-in proceed as follows:

- Open the extended Mixer and show the stereo master output bus channel strip (if it is not already visible).
- Click in the name field of slot 8 and select 'uv22 hr' from the Other sub-menu of the effects pop-up menu (Figure 13.9).
- Upon selecting the UV22 HR plug-in, the graphical user interface is opened automatically (Figure 13.10).

IMPORTANT

Noise-shaped dithering is normally a once-only operation performed as the very last step in the mastering process. It is best not to re-apply noise-shaped dither to audio that has already been subject to this process. If you intend to conduct a final mastering stage in a specialised mastering application (or in Cubase SX) do not apply noise-shaped dither at the mixing stage. Instead, mix down to a high-resolution file without dither (24-bit or 32-bit float). At the mastering stage, import this file into the mastering application and apply noise-shaped dither as the very last process just before truncation to produce the final 16-bit master audio file.

Info

See chapter 11 for details about the Export/Audio Mixdown function.

Figure 13.9
Select uv22 hr from the Other sub-menu

Figure 13.10
The Apogee UV22 HR plug-in

Apogee UV22 HR dithering functions

The UV22 HR dithering plug-in incorporates an advanced dithering algorithm developed by Apogee. It features the following parameters:

- Normal – this provides the best all-round type of dithering.
- Low – applies a lower level of dither noise to the signal.
- Autoblack – when activated, the dither noise is muted when there are silent passages in the signal.
- Bit Resolution – specifies the intended bit resolution of the final audio result. The choice is between 8, 16, 20 and 24-bit.

Using dithering

As with any processing, you must use your ears to decide if the dithering settings you have chosen give the desired result. However, given that dithering is intentionally an extremely subtle kind of processing, it may be difficult to perceive the results. To get a feel for what dithering can do for you, try a test procedure of producing an audio mixdown file (File/Export/Audio Mixdown) at a resolution of 8-bits both with and without dithering. Preferably, use an audio file which includes some low level material. Listen to the difference between the two files. Now try the same experiment with 16-bit files.

The most important thing to remember when you use dithering is that the bit depth should be matched to the intended bit-resolution of the final file. For CD mastering, set the UV22 HR plug-in to normal / 16-bit.

If you are using the Waves L1 or L2 Ultramaximizers, Waves recommend a number of combinations of IDR dither and noise shaping. The most important of these are as follows:

- type 1, normal (24, 20, or 16-bit) - general purpose high-quality use (CD mastering, may be edited or EQ'ed at a later stage)
- type 1, ultra (16-bit) - high resolution CD master (no further editing)
- type 2, ultra (24, 20 or 16-bit) - low noise/high resolution

The bit depth you set relates to the intended bit resolution of the final audio file or other destination. Option 1 (type 1 / normal), above, is a good choice for standard CD mastering.

Recommended order of use of plug-ins for mastering

Placing plug-ins in a chain may result in undesirable interaction between the different processes. The following is a suggested order for some of the common pre-mastering processing steps to avoid problems and to arrive at a final version of the recording (suitable for duplication or manufacture):

- De-essing
- Equalisation
- Expansion/compression
- Harmonic excitement
- Reverberation
- Stereo imaging / MS processing
- Sample rate conversion (e.g. downsampling from 88.2kHz to 44.1kHz)
- Limiting/level maximisation

- Dithering
- Truncation (e.g. reduction of the bit depth from 24-bit to 16-bit)

This list is certainly not the only way of ordering the processes. For example, depending on the application, the order of equalisation and expansion/compression might be reversed. Compressing after EQ produces a smoother result but may undo some of the settings of the EQ if the threshold is set inappropriately. EQing after compression allows you to adjust the EQ parameters with more clarity, knowing that EQ changes are not changing the action of the compressor. Limiting is often placed after sample rate conversion since the conversion process can result in slight level increases, (although the ideal position for sample rate conversion is probably just before dithering). Of course, for many projects you do not need to downsample and so you can ignore the latter issues.

As for dithering and bit reduction, take care that you do not confuse these processes with downsampling! The most important rule for dithering is that it is normally a once-only final step just before bit reduction.

Downsampling issues

Using Cubase SX for downsampling (using the 'Sample Rate' field in the Export Audio Mixdown dialogue) is not advisable if limiting and dithering are at the end of your mastering chain, since this places sample rate conversion AFTER limiting and dithering. It may be better to do the downsampling in one pass WITHOUT limiting, dithering and truncation, and then re-import the downsampled audio file for these final stages in a second pass. If your project is destined to be duplicated on CD, try starting off with the standard CD sample rate of 44.1kHz and maintain this sample rate throughout the project. In this way you do not subject your file to the possible damage caused by poor quality sample rate conversion.

The quality of Cubase SX's sample rate conversion when using Export Audio Mixdown is not adequate for all professional applications. For the best quality you are advised to use a dedicated sample rate conversion plug-in at the appropriate position within the chain, or to do the final stages of your mastering processing in an external editor. Wavelab features a high quality sample rate conversion plug-in known as the Crystal Resampler. Alternatively, try a stand-alone application like Voxengo's r8brain Pro.

Quality control

Overusing plug-in effects can damage the pristine quality of your digital recordings, especially if you are working with 16-bit files. Almost all audio processing (even simple gain changes) increases the wordlength of the audio, (e.g. after processing, a 16-bit signal might be expressed in 32-bit float resolution). If you were to print this processed signal back to 16-bit, bit reduction and loss of low level detail results. Do this once and the effect is, admittedly, minimal. Do it a number of times to a number of signals and the cumulative effect results in a slight loss of transparency and detail.

To help maintain quality, start with high resolution sources (e.g. 24-bit/44.1kHz) and try to maintain this high resolution for as long as possible

Info

Not all of the mastering processes shown here are covered by the Steinberg and Waves range. In addition, although Cubase may be used for mastering, Steinberg Wavelab, Bias Peak (or similar) are preferable for dedicated mastering and CD burning tasks.

Tip

Using the 'Sample Rate' field in the Export Audio Mixdown dialogue to downsample may not give the best results. To minimise damage to your audio files, use a separate high quality sample rate conversion plug-in. Alternatively, if your project is destined to be duplicated on CD then start off with the standard CD sample rate of 44.1kHz and maintain this sample rate throughout the project.

Info

The full details of truncation, dithering and downsampling are beyond the scope of this text. Those readers needing more in-depth coverage are advised to consult specialist texts or to search the internet.

throughout the processing chain. Avoid printing effects one at a time to the same audio file. Multiple effects processing is best applied in a single pass. Where possible, keep effects in real-time until the final mix (if your computer's processing power permits). Of course, the latter is not possible when you are using the off-line processing in the Processing menu. Use only high quality plug-ins which have at least a 32-bit float internal resolution. If it is your intention to carry out a final mastering stage in Cubase SX or other software, do not truncate the bit-depth or use noise-shaped dither at the mixing stage. Instead, mix to a high resolution file without noise-shaped dither (try 32-bit float). Avoid applying noise-shaped dither more than once in the same project.

These steps help you get a better result when you finally arrive at the mastering stage. With mastering you are aiming to squeeze the final 10% of quality out of your completed stereo mixes but remember; if a mix is already sounding excellent then it may need no further processing other than dithering and truncation to 16-bit. One of the greatest skills of mastering engineers is knowing just how much processing is required and when to leave a mix alone.

Burning the CD

As outlined above, Cubase SX does not include integrated track indexing and CD burning functions. You must therefore conduct the final burning and organisation of the CD in other software (e.g. Steinberg Wavelab, Bias Peak, Ahead Software Nero, Roxio Easy CD Creator, Roxio Jam and others). The first dilemma is deciding exactly how you are going to mix down the final 16-bit audio; as one long audio file containing all the tracks, or as separate files, one for each track on the CD. This decision is largely dictated by the capabilities of your chosen CD editing and burning software. Some applications allow you to split a single audio file into a number of tracks, others require each track as a separate file. In both cases, if you have carefully spaced your tracks in Cubase SX you will need to duplicate this in the burning software. One approach is to make a careful note of the pauses between each track and enter these manually. Most CD burning software allows you to adjust the pauses. However, bear in mind that the data on audio CDs is divided up into frames, where there are 75 frames per second and each frame contains 588 stereo samples. On an audio CD you can only ever start a CD track at the beginning of a frame. This can lead to subtle problems when adjusting start times and pauses between tracks. Normally, small amounts of silence are inserted to ensure that track starts and ends do not get cut off when the CD is played. Luckily, most CD burning software takes care of these finer points automatically, as long as the timing requirements of your CD remain relatively simple (if in doubt stick to spacings of whole seconds).

Once the track list and suitable pauses have been entered you should carefully audition the CD once more to make sure that it sounds as intended. When you proceed to the actual burning of the CD, ALWAYS use disc-at-once mode since this ensures that the CD is recorded in one pass without interruption (as opposed to track-at-once which results in the writing laser being turned off between each track). Also, experts recommend the use of 2 x to 4 x burning speed to minimise writing errors.

MIDI effects

As well as audio effects, Cubase SX is supplied with a range of real-time MIDI effects. These are found in the Send and Insert panels of each MIDI channel. MIDI editing has traditionally been an offline ('permanent') process but, with MIDI effects, the emphasis has changed. Manipulating MIDI data in real-time encourages new horizons of creativity and experimentation.

Like their audio counterparts, MIDI effects are plug-in modules which can be added to the effects panels of MIDI channels as and when you need them. In addition to the plug-ins supplied with the program, you can add additional MIDI effects using, for example, third party developer plug-ins created in the Cakewalk MFX format (Windows users only). For this purpose, Steinberg supply an MFX wrapper (available from the Freeware section of the Steinberg website) which, when installed, enables compatibility with the MFX standard.

Tip

If you are looking for MFX MIDI effects try Ntonyx (www.ntonyx.com) who are independent suppliers of Cakewalk MFX-compatible MIDI plug-ins. For these to function, you must install the MFX wrapper.dll file supplied by Steinberg in the Freeware section of their website. Place the .dll file in the Components folder in the Cubase SX directory.

The difference between MIDI effects and audio effects

The MIDI effects structure and routing is similar to that found with audio effects but with the following very important differences:

1 MIDI effects are for the real-time processing of MIDI data. They do NOT act upon audio data in any way.
2 Unlike audio Send effects, MIDI Send effects are unique to each MIDI track and are *not* assigned for global use by all MIDI channels. There is no send level involved with MIDI Send effects.
3 Since you are processing a sequence of digital instructions rather than an audio signal, the results of certain effects may not be directly comparable to their audio counterpart.

Setting up MIDI effects in Cubase SX

In Cubase SX, real-time MIDI effects may be assigned as Insert effects or Send effects. There are no strict rules about which effects are assigned to which kind of effects slots but, for example, if real-time compression or quantizing of a MIDI track were required, the 'Compress' or 'Quantizer' plug-ins would normally be assigned as MIDI Insert effects. Send effects might suit those occasions when you wish to route the Send data to a different MIDI device to the source (you can assign the target MIDI device separately in the Send effects slots).

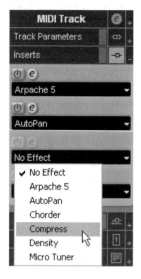

MIDI Insert effects

MIDI Insert effects are assigned in the Insert panel of a MIDI channel strip in the expanded Mixer (Cubase SX only), in the MIDI Channel Settings window or in the Inspector (Figure 14.1). Each MIDI track has a total of four Insert slots. Click on an Insert effect field to open the MIDI effects pop-up menu.

MIDI Insert effects differ from MIDI Send effects in the manner in which the data is routed. There is no separation of the track and effect data. Instead, the MIDI data passes *through* the effects 'in series' (see Figure 14.2). When more than one insert effect is activated, the signal passes through each in turn, in descending order. The destination MIDI device is that which is assigned for the MIDI track. Note that, with multiple Insert effects, the data received by each effect is that which is output by the preceding effect in the panel. Therefore, depending on the effects used, the final output may not resemble the original input data at all.

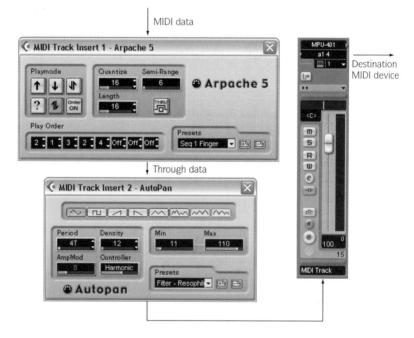

Figure 14 .2
The routing configuration for MIDI Insert effects

MIDI Insert effects are suited to almost all MIDI effects but, of course, the suitability depends upon the intended result. There are no hard and fast rules.

MIDI Send effects

MIDI Send effects are assigned in the Send panel of a MIDI channel in the expanded Mixer, in the MIDI Channel Settings window or in the Inspector (Figure 14.3). Each MIDI track has a total of four Send slots. Click on a Send effect field to open the MIDI effects pop-up menu.

With MIDI Send effects, the MIDI track's data is routed to the destination MIDI device as usual (via the output port chosen in the 'out' field) and a copy of the data is also sent 'in parallel' to the MIDI effect (assigned in the Send effects slot). The data produced by the Send effect is routed to a destination device according to the MIDI port and MIDI channel chosen in the Send effects slot (Figure 14.4). The destination device for the Send effect data may be the same device as the MIDI track or any other MIDI device in your system. Unlike audio Send effects, each assigned MIDI Send effect is unique to the MIDI track and there is no assignment of MIDI Send effects in a globally available MIDI Send effects panel.

Figure 14.3
MIDI Send effects are assigned using the Send slots in the Send panel of a MIDI channel

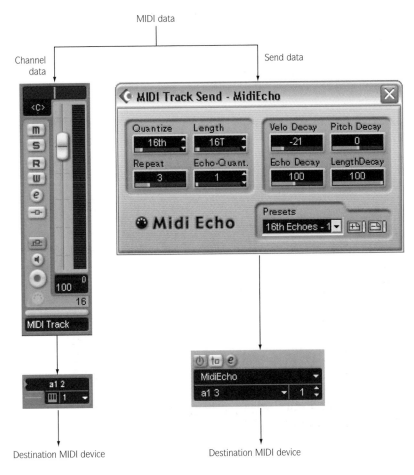

Figure 14.4
The routing configuration for MIDI Send effects

It is not always appropriate that the data from the Send effect is sent to the same MIDI device as the MIDI track since the effects data may cancel out or interfere with the source MIDI data. Such a case may occur with the MidiEcho effect, where the MIDI echo data may coincide unfavourably with the source data, producing double notes, velocity problems and cancellation effects. If you are using an external multi-timbral MIDI device, try routing the Send effect data on a separate MIDI channel set to the same sound. If you are using a VST Instrument, try activating a second instance of the instrument or sending the echo data on another channel, if it has multi-timbral capability. Using the Send effects to route the MIDI data to a completely different device and sound patch is, of course, valuable for creative purposes.

MIDI Send effects are best suited to MIDI plug-ins like MidiEcho, Micro Tuner, Track FX and Transformer but there are no hard and fast rules.

Common graphical user interface functions for MIDI effects

The graphical user interface (GUI) for any of the currently active MIDI effects can be opened by clicking on the edit button of the slot corresponding to the effect. The edit buttons are labelled with a lower case 'e' and are found in all effects slots in the Mixer, in the MIDI Channel Settings window and in the Inspector. Most GUIs for the MIDI effects open in a separate window similar to that shown in Figure 14.5. When opened from the Inspector, some of the effects open within the Inspector itself. If required, you can force these kind of effects to open in a separate window by pressing Alt while making an effects selection.

Info

Like audio effects, MIDI effects use the processing power of your computer, albeit a smaller amount than their audio counterparts. However, generating large amounts of additional MIDI data can result in MIDI bottlenecks so, depending upon your MIDI interface and the polyphony of your MIDI devices, there are limits to the number of MIDI effects which can be run simultaneously.

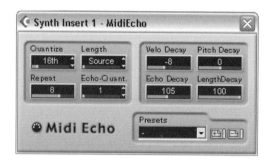

Figure 14.5
The graphical user interface for the MidiEcho effect

Basic GUI functions

Many MIDI effects include a Presets menu which is opened by clicking on the downward pointing arrow next to the Presets field (Figure 14.6). You can add your own presets by clicking on the plus (+) folder symbol next to the Presets menu and you can delete the currently chosen preset by clicking on the minus (–) symbol folder. Any stored presets are globally available to all projects.

Figure 14.6
Use the Presets menu to store and recall MIDI effects presets

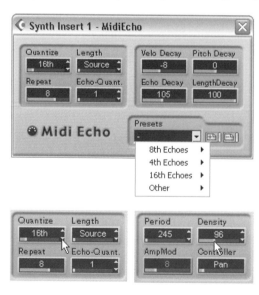

MIDI Effects are active as soon as they are selected in the Inserts or Sends sections and therefore do not feature an On button. Another common attribute are dual action value fields which feature a slider control or up/down arrows for changing the settings. The slider control often changes the value in ticks and the up/down arrows often change the value in note values.

Figure 14.7
Make adjustments in the MIDI effect value fields using the up/down arrows (left) or the slider control (right).

The supplied MIDI effects

There now follows descriptions of the supplied MIDI effects. These are listed in the same order in which they are found in the MIDI effects menu.

Arpache 5

Arpache 5 is an arpeggiator MIDI plug-in. Typically, an arpeggiator is a device which automatically steps through the notes in a held chord. The speed and order of the playback of the notes are regulated by various settings on the device. Arpache 5 generates arpeggios by transforming MIDI input data. The parameters allow the creation of standard arpeggios, random arpeggios and arpeggios which follow a user-specified note order.

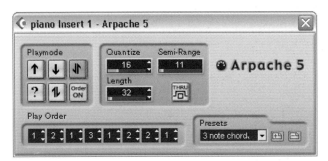

Figure 14.8
Arpache 5

Arpache 5 features the following parameters:

- Playmode buttons – determine the playback order for the arpeggio. The options include up, down, down + up, up + down, random ('?') and Order. The Order button allows you to set the playback order according to the settings in the Play Order fields (see below).
- Quantize – determines the playback speed according to a note value related to the project tempo. The value can be changed using the mini slider or the up/down arrows. Range: 1/32 note triplets to whole note values.
- Length – regulates the length of each playback note according to a note value related to the project tempo (changed using the mini slider or the up/down arrows). Range : 1/32 note triplets to whole note values.
- Semi-Range – determines the pitch range of the playback in semitones starting from the lowest input note. For example, a setting of 12 ensures that all arpeggiated notes are within the same octave (12 semitones) and any higher notes are transposed down. A setting of 24 allows the arpeggio to be automatically transposed in as many octaves as are available within the range.
- Thru – when activated, all notes arriving at the input of the arpeggiator are passed through to the output. When de-activated, the input notes are not passed through to the output. For standard arpeggio behaviour, Thru would be de-activated.
- Play Order – when the Order button is activated (illuminated) the playback order is determined according to the settings in the play order fields which represent each step in the arpeggio in incremental time

position order. The numbers you choose for each field specify which note from the input chord is allocated to each time position step, counting from the lowest note in the chord.

User guide

Info

For more elaborate arpeggiator effects, try the 'Arpache SX' MIDI plug-in supplied with the program. Arpache SX features advanced velocity and sorting modes as well as a special sequencer mode which allows you to use the interaction between a MIDI part and the MIDI input as the basis for the arpeggio.

To set up Arpache 5 for standard arpeggiator purposes proceed as follows:

1 Select a MIDI track and activate the Record Enable or Monitor buttons so that you can play live through the track.
2 Set the output port of the MIDI track to an appropriate MIDI device, (try the supplied A1 VST Instrument). Select a suitable sound. If you are using the A1 synth, try the ' Nice'n'Fine' preset in the Lead section.
3 Activate the Arpache 5 MIDI plug-in as an Insert effect on the chosen MIDI track. In its traditional role as a regular arpeggiator, Arpache is normally assigned as an Insert.
4 In the Arpache 5 interface, activate the down + up button, set Quantize to 8, Length to 32 and Semi-Range to 11.
5 Hold down a three note chord comprising of C3, E3 and G3 on your MIDI keyboard (or any other three note chord). The settings in 4) above produce an arpeggio which steps through the notes in the held chord in ascending and descending order, at a speed corresponding to $1/8^{th}$ note intervals at the current project tempo. Each playback note has a $1/32^{nd}$ note duration.
6 Try changing the Semi-Range to 12. This causes the lowest note to step up an octave on each cycle of the arpeggio. Try changing the speed by setting the Quantize value to 16.
7 Try activating the random ('?') button to produce a randomised playback order. Check out the effect of the other Playmode buttons and try setting up your own custom playback order by activating the Order button and entering values into the Play Order fields (values of 1, 2, 1, 3, 1, 2, 2, 1 give good results with three note chords).

AutoPan

AutoPan is an LFO-like oscillation device for MIDI Controller data. It allows the continuous modulation of any chosen Controller between a specified value range. Autopan is suitable for producing automatic MIDI panning effects (the continuous modulation of MIDI Controller 10). It might also be applied to the modulation of Controllers 71 and 74 which control cut-off and resonance in many MIDI devices. In this way, you can set up automated tempo related modulations of the cut-off and resonance parameters of a synthesizer.

` ` ` ` **Figure 14.9**
AutoPan

AutoPan features the following parameters:

- Waveform selector buttons – determine the modulation waveforms applied to the chosen MIDI Controller. The range of these waveforms is scaled according to the minimum and maximum parameters. The first five buttons apply the wave shapes as indicated on the button. The sixth button applies a random shape. The seventh and eighth buttons apply ascending and descending periodical envelopes respectively, where the duration of each section of the curve follows the value chosen in the period parameter.
- Period – determines the speed of one modulation cycle. For example, if you set this to '4th', a modulation cycle is repeated once every quarter note. The period can be set according to note values (with the up/down arrows) or ticks (with the mini-fader).
- Density – controls the density of the MIDI controller events which are used to describe the modulation effect produced by Autopan. Here, higher values mean a smoother curve. However, it is recommended that you do not set the density too high since producing a large number of Controller events can cause MIDI transmission problems.
- AmpMod – controls the overall length of the periodical envelopes (selected using the seventh and eighth waveform selector buttons as described above). Here, a setting of 4 results in a periodical envelope which is repeated every 4 beats.
- Controller – allocates the target MIDI Controller to which the modulation effect is to be applied. Pan (Controller 10), Sound Variation (Controller 70), timbre/harmonic (Controller 71) and brightness (Controller 74) are possible targets but the suitability of each controller depends upon the MIDI implementation in the target device. (See Appendix 3 for a list of all MIDI Controllers).
- Min and Max – determine the lower and upper limits of the waveform thereby regulating the scale and range of the modulation effect.

User guide

AutoPan is an ingenious MIDI plug-in which can be used for all kinds of automated modulation effects. Unfortunately, MIDI devices often suffer from 'zipper' noise when the Pan Controller is modified in real-time so using Autopan for one of its prime purposes may not always be successful. However, with other MIDI controller targets AutoPan performs extremely well. For example, to set up an automated modulation of the cut-off parameter of the supplied A1 VSTi, proceed as follows :

1 Select a MIDI track and allocate the output port to the supplied A1 VST Instrument. Select the 'Thrash Lead' preset.
2 Record a simple test sequence of notes over a length of 4 bars or use an existing 4 bar MIDI recording. Here, the 4 bars is important since it is the length of time over which the cut-off parameter is to be modulated.
3 Activate the AutoPan MIDI plug-in as an Insert effect on the chosen MIDI track.
4 In the Autopan interface, click on the sine waveform button, select a Period of '7680' (double click in the Period field to enter the value), select a Density of 12 and set the Controller field to Brightness (Controller 74). Set a minimum value of 10 and a maximum of 110. With a Period of '7680' the modulation cycle has a duration of 4 bars

(since by default there are 7680 ticks in 4 bars).

5 Commence playback and listen to the effect of the modulation in the A1 VSTi. To see the action of the modulation open the A1 interface by clicking on the VSTi edit ('e') button and observe the cut-off dial. If everything is functioning correctly you should see the dial move slowly back and forth throughout the 4 bar sequence.

6 Try changing the speed by setting the AutoPan Period value to 1280 or 1920.

7 Check out the effect of setting the Period to 8th, AmpMod to 8 and selecting the last Waveform Selector button on the right.

Chorder

Chorder is a MIDI chord creation device for the triggering of chords from single MIDI input notes. Chorder functions in three modes, each of which changes the manner in which the chords are triggered. The three modes are as follows:

Figure 14.10
Chorder

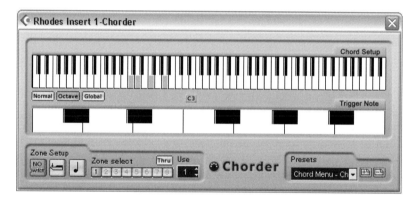

- Normal mode – allows the assignment of a different chord to each note on the MIDI keyboard. In this mode, there are two keyboards in the display. The lower keyboard is where you select the trigger note and the upper keyboard is where you assign the chord which corresponds to this trigger note.
- Octave mode – allows the assignment of a different chord to each note name in one octave such that playing the same note at any octave (e.g. C2, C3, C4) triggers the same chord. In this mode, the display features a one octave lower keyboard where you specify the trigger note and a full range upper keyboard where you assign the chord which corresponds to this trigger note at all octaves.
- Global mode – in this mode you assign a single chord which is triggered by all MIDI input notes. This chord is transposed according to the pitch of the incoming MIDI note. In this mode, the display features a single keyboard where you assign the chord which is to be triggered.

The basic behaviour of Chorder, therefore, revolves around the choice of mode. You can also implement up to eight chord variations per trigger note. These are triggered according to velocity or note range. To set up the variations, proceed as follows :

1 Select the trigger note onto which you wish to apply the variations.

2 Select the Velocity symbol button or the Note symbol button according to whether you want to trigger the variations by velocity zone or note range.

3 Specify how many variations you wish to apply in the Use field (next to the zone select buttons).

4 Select the first Zone select button and set up the chord variation in the keyboard in the display.

5 Select the other Zone select buttons in turn and set up the other chord variations up to the number specified in the Use field.

6 When Velocity has been chosen as the switch for the variations, the normal velocity range (1–127) is divided into equal zones according to the number of zones chosen in the Use field. The variations are triggered according to the velocity with which you strike the keys.

7 When Note Range has been chosen as the switch for the variations, you play one note on the keyboard to choose the base note and a second higher note to select the variation. The difference in semitones between the two notes selects the corresponding variation.

User guide

To become familiar with Chorder proceed as follows :

1 Select a MIDI track and activate the Record Enable or Monitor buttons so that you can play live through the track.

2 Set the output port of the MIDI track to an appropriate MIDI device and select the program of your choice. Try using an electric or acoustic piano sound.

3 Activate the Chorder plug-in as an Insert effect on the chosen MIDI track.

4 Click on the downward pointing arrow of the Presets menu and select 'Song Builder' from the Chord menu. This is a multiple chord preset created in Normal mode.

5 Play single notes on your keyboard. The Song Builder preset has chords assigned to all notes between C2 and B6. The octaves contain the major, minor, 7th, minor 7th and major 7th chord shapes. As indicated by the preset name, this might be useful for building up a chord pattern for a song.

6 Try also selecting the 'Chord Selection' preset. This operates in Octave mode and contains more esoteric chords which are useful for jazz styles.

Compress

Compress is a MIDI velocity processor which compresses or expands the velocity values of the notes which pass through it. This has the effect of reducing the peak velocity values and, thereby, reducing the overall range of the velocity data (compression), or increasing the peak velocity values and, thereby, increasing the overall range of the velocity data (expansion).

Compress features the following parameters:

• Threshold – determines the velocity value above which compression or expansion begins.

• Ratio – determines the amount by which velocities above the threshold are changed. When the ratio is greater than 1 (e.g. 2:1, 3:1) compression occurs. When the ratio is less than 1 (e.g. 1:2, 1:4) expansion occurs. A ratio of 1:1 results in no change in the data.

• Gain – heavy compression or expansion may push the velocities outside of the usual range (1–127) so that all processed notes have a velocity at

Tip

When you fist load Chorder the interface contains no chord assignments. It is a good idea to save this as an initialisation preset (named as 'Reset', for example). This is then globally available to all projects and may be used to initialise Chorder whenever you need to start with a blank sheet.

Figure 14.11
Compress

the minimum or maximum values. Where this is not the desired result, the gain setting brings the velocities back into a meaningful range by adding or subtracting a fixed velocity to/from the data. You would normally use negative gain settings for expansion and positive gain settings for compression.

User guide

The precise effect of the ratio parameter is not immediately apparent, but the use of some simple arithmetic and a calculator helps clarify the issue. Let's take two MIDI notes, one with a velocity of 60 and another with a velocity of 45. Applying compression to the notes with a threshold of 50 and a compression ratio of 2:1 results in the following:

- The note with a velocity value of 45 is ignored in any compression process since it falls below the threshold. The MIDI note with a velocity of 60 rises above the threshold by a value of 10. This note must therefore be included in the compression process.
- The value by which the note rises above the threshold is divided by the first figure in the compression ratio. This gives 10/2 which equals 5.
- To calculate the final value of the note the result of 5 is added to the threshold value. 50 + 5 = 55. The new velocity value of the note is now 55 instead of 60.
- The final velocities for the two notes are 45 and 55. The velocity difference between the two notes has been compressed.

Applying expansion to the same source notes with a threshold of 50 and a compression ratio of 1:2 results in the following:

- The note with a velocity value of 45 is ignored in the expansion process since it falls below the threshold. The MIDI note with a velocity of 60 rises above the threshold by a value of 10. This note must therefore be included in the expansion process.
- The value by which the note rises above the threshold is multiplied by the second figure in the expansion ratio (1:2). This gives 10 * 2 which equals 20.
- To calculate the final value of the note the result of 20 is added to the threshold value. 50 + 20 = 70. The new velocity value of the note is now 70 instead of 60.
- The final velocities for the two notes are 45 and 70. The velocity difference between the two notes has been expanded.

Try substituting other threshold and ratio values in the above calculations. Although making music does not require an in-depth knowledge of mathematics, understanding these processes can help you get better results from the Compress plug-in.

Control

Control is a simple control panel for MIDI Controller data. You can select up to eight different controllers in the fields on the right side of the window. The value for each is set in the corresponding fields on the left. Typical uses include:

Figure 14.12
Control

- tweaking the settings of a synth patch in a MIDI device which responds to MIDI Controller data.
- remote control of devices which respond to RPN and NRPN MIDI data.
- setting basic controllers like modulation, pan, volume and portamento.
- sending Local Ctrl On/Off and other MIDI mode messages.

Density

Density is a random MIDI note filter which adds new notes or deletes existing notes to/from the data which passes through it. It features a single parameter. When this is set to 100%, no change occurs in the processed data. When set lower than 100% various notes are randomly filtered from the processed data. When set higher than 100% various notes are randomly added to the processed data.

Figure 14.13
Density

Density is worth trying on MIDI drum and percussion parts and on synth sequences. Used on its own or in combination with other MIDI plug-ins it can help invent new patterns and new musical ideas. It is also helpful when musical arrangements have become repetitive. It works best on monophonic MIDI parts since it produces unpredictable results with chords.

Micro Tuner

Micro Tuner is a microtuning plug-in for VST Instruments and those external MIDI devices which support micro-tuning. This allows you to set up the tuning of the target device to an alternative tuning system to the standard equal temperament tuning (also known as equal tempered tuning). Equal temperament tuning divides the octave into twelve equal intervals and this is the standard tuning system used in the West. However, other classical and experimental tunings are possible and these can add variety and interest to musical arrangements. Micro Tuner is supplied with a number of tuning system presets including Harmonic, Pure Major, Pure minor, Mean Semitones, Pythagorean and so on.

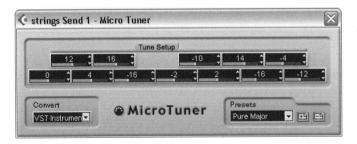

Figure 13.14
Micro Tuner

The interface features 12 value fields arranged as the keys of one octave on a musical keyboard. Tunings are adjusted in cents (one hundredth of a semitone) by clicking and dragging in the value fields. A Convert parameter adjusts the plug-in for use with VST Instruments (default) or with external MIDI devices (in real-time or non real-time modes).

User guide

In its standard role, Micro Tuner would be used as an Insert effect to change the tuning of the target MIDI device. However, it might also be used as a MIDI Send device routed to a second instance of the same instrument/sound.

Tip

For thickening and chorus effects, Micro Tuner can be used as a Send effect routed to a second instance of a VSTi or another MIDI channel in a multi-timbral device. Set the effect sound to the same sound patch as the main MIDI track. Try using the 'Pure Major' preset.

This allows you to use the microtunings for thickening and chorus effects. This is particularly good for, strings, choirs and pads and for really big sounds you can assign several instances of Micro Tuner, each tuned slightly differently.

In addition to the supplied presets try the following:

0, –10, 23, –25, –14, –2, 10, 2, –8, 6, –4, –12 (Raga Bhairava)
0, 12, 4, –6, 8, –2, 10, 2, 14, 6, 18, 10 (Raga Kafi)
0, –6, –4, –2, –8, 2, –8, –2, –4, –6, 0, –10 (Valotti and Young)

MidiEcho

MidiEcho produces delay, chorus and pitch-shift effects. It acts upon the MIDI data only and does not directly affect the audio signal of the target MIDI device in any way. For the initial testing of MidiEcho it is suggested that a simple piano MIDI part is targeted. Assign MidiEcho as an Insert effect, set the parameters to the same values as those shown in Figure 13.15 and play the chosen part in cycle playback mode. Experiment with the Quantize, Repeat and Velo Decay parameters to produce different echo effects.

Figure 14.15
MidiEcho

The parameters of MidiEcho function as follows:

- Quantize – determines the speed of the echoes relative to the current tempo. This value can be regulated in terms of ticks using the mini slider (480 ticks = a quarter note) or in terms of note values using the up/down arrow keys (Range: between 1/32T and 1/2 notes).
- Length – sets the length of the echoed note events. Regulated in terms of ticks using the mini slider (480 ticks = a quarter note) or in terms of note values using the up/down arrow keys. Using the slider you can set the length to 'Source' which means that the echoes have the same length as the MIDI input notes.
- Repeat – determines the number of echo repeats for each incoming MIDI note. Range: 1–12.
- Echo-Quant – sets up a quantizing grid which regulates where the echoes fall allowing you to set up rhythmically correct echoes regardless of the other settings. A setting of '1' disables the effect of this parameter.
- Velo Decay – determines a velocity amount which is added or subtracted to/from each echo repeat, thereby simulating a crescendo or decay effect. Range –36 to +36.
- Pitch Decay – determines a pitch amount in semitones which is added or subtracted to/from each echo repeat, thereby changing the pitch of each consecutive echo, producing ascending and descending pitch sequences. Range –36 to +36.

- Echo Decay – adds or subtracts a number of ticks to each successive echo repeat to produce accelerated or decelerated echo effects. A setting of 100 produces no change. A setting or less than 100 produces echoes which speed up. A setting or more than 100 produces echoes which slow down.
- Length Decay – determines an amount by which the length of each echo repeat note is reduced to produce echo note lengths which are progressively shortened. A setting of 100 produces no reduction of the length and values under 100 produce progressively more reduction.

User guide

To start using MidiEcho it is a good idea to set the Length to 'Source'. This ensures that you will at least hear the source MIDI notes. In its first implementation in Cubase SX, MidiEcho does not respond well to live MIDI input and works best with pre-recorded MIDI parts. Bear in mind that the processing relies upon adding to existing MIDI note data and could, in certain circumstances, produce undesirable delays in the data flow of the rest of the music. This depends upon the density of the events in the arrangement.

Try the following settings as starting points for your own experiments (Table 14.1):

Table 14.1 MidiEcho plug-in starting points							
Quantize	Length	Repeat	Echo-Quant	Velo-Decay	Pitch Decay	Echo Decay	Length Decay
16th	32th	10	1	−12	0	100	100
16T	32th	4	1	−20	0	108	100
4th	Source	7	9	−20	0	118	100
16T	47	10	1	−12	0	98	100
4th	63	5	3	−12	0	99	100
32T	47	3	1	−12	12	99	100

Note 2 CC

Note 2 CC generates MIDI controller events whose value is determined by the pitch of the incoming MIDI notes. The higher the pitch, the higher the value of the controller. One MIDI Controller is assigned at any one time. Assigning MIDI Controller 7 (Main Volume) results in keyboard tracking of the volume, where the sound becomes louder the higher you play. Assigning MIDI Controller 10 (Pan) results in keyboard tracking of the stereo position which is suitable for piano, organ, drum and percussion sounds. Note 2 CC produces a new Controller event for every pitch and with busy polyphonic parts might create confusing results. Note 2 CC is therefore best for monophonic MIDI tracks.

Figure 14.16
Note 2 CC

Quantizer

Quantizer is a basic MIDI note timing correction plug-in. Whereas the main Quantize functions of Cubase SX operate primarily as an offline process,

Figure 14.17
Quantizer

Quantizer is valuable for experimenting with the feel of a track in real-time. The strength parameter is valuable since it allows real-time 'iterative-style' quantizing where notes are pulled towards the quantize value (when it is set to less than 100%) as well as hard quantizing (when it is set to 100%). However, the plug-in does not possess the same range of parameters as the main Quantize features (see Chapters 5 and 6 for more details about Quantize).

Quantizer features the following parameters:

- Quantize – determines the resolution of a position-based 'quantize grid' which is imposed upon incoming MIDI notes. The resolution is defined in terms of a note value. Notes which pass through Quantizer are moved onto the nearest divisions of the bar as defined by this note value (in conjunction with the other parameters). Range: dotted 1/4 note to 1/32 note.
- Swing – adds a swing (shuffle) factor to the quantize function, where every second note position on the grid is pushed to the right (so that it falls slightly later).
- Strength – regulates the strength of the quantize function in terms of a percentage. For example, a strength setting of 50% means that notes are moved towards the grid by reducing the note's current distance from the nearest grid line by 50% (similar to iterative quantize). A strength setting of 100% forces all notes directly onto the nearest grid line (hard quantize).
- Delay ms – delays (positive values) or advances (negative values) the notes which pass through Quantizer.

Step Designer

Step Designer is a monophonic MIDI step sequencer. MIDI note data is generated by drawing events in the upper half of the grid which displays time on the horizontal axis and pitch on the vertical axis (1 octave at a time). Velocity values, gate times and two MIDI controllers may be controlled for each note by dragging the corresponding value sliders in the lower half of the display. The time display is divided into 32 steps, each of which represents a note division of the bar between 1/128th and 1/2 notes. The overall length of the pattern is variable between 1 and 32 steps.

Step Designer features a control panel above and to the left of the main display which includes the following parameters:

- Pattern – determines the current pattern number. Each instance of Step Designer holds up to 100 different patterns.
- Copy and Paste buttons – these are used to copy and paste the data from one pattern to another. This is excellent for creating variations of the same pattern.
- Reset and Random buttons – the Reset button resets Step Designer to its default startup settings (an empty pattern). The Random button generates a random sequence of notes in the currently displayed pattern (replaces any existing notes in the current pattern).
- Length – determines the overall length of the pattern between 1 and 32 steps.

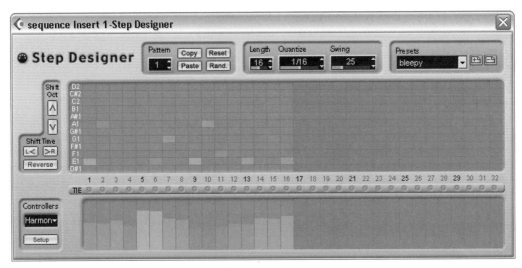

Figure 14.18
Step Designer

- Quantize – determines the length of each of the 32 steps in the sequence in terms of a note value between 1/128th and 1/2 notes.
- Swing – imposes a swing feel upon the pattern, where every second note position on the grid is pushed to the right (so that it falls slightly later). A higher percentage produces more swing.
- Presets menu – allows the storage and recall of preset patterns.
- Shift octave buttons – move the pitch display up or down by one octave at a time.
- Shift time buttons – moves the order of the notes to the left or right where notes which are pushed off the end of the pattern are re-inserted at the opposite end of the sequence. This is excellent for creating pattern variations and changing the feel.
- Reverse – reverses the note order of the pattern.
- Controllers section – provides a selection menu which determines what data is visible in the lower half of the display. The Setup button opens a dialogue where you can select which two MIDI controllers are to be targeted by Step Designer (this is globally set for the current instance of Step Designer and cannot be individually set for each pattern).

User guide

To generate your own pattern in Step Designer proceed as follows:

1 Assign Step Designer as an Insert effect on a MIDI track. Note that Step Designer blocks all MIDI thru activity on the track so is best suited to an empty MIDI track.
2 Allocate the MIDI output port of the track to a suitable MIDI device and sound patch. For this exercise, try using the supplied A1 VST Instrument set to the 'Plain Bass Lead' preset. (The A1 is a good target device for experimenting with Step Designer since, in the A1 interface, the Controller numbers are displayed in the central information field for each parameter when you move the mouse over the parameter control. This can help you find which Controllers are to be assigned in the Controller section of Step Designer).

3 Select a length for the pattern in the length field. The default 16 step setting is suitable for experimentation.

4 Select the quantize value for each step in the Quantize field. Once again, the default 1/16 note setting is suitable for experimentation.

5 Drag the mouse left to right across the note event display. A series of note events are inserted as small graphical rectangular blocks. This is a very quick manner of entering note data. You may prefer to enter a pre-defined series of notes, in which case you should click in the appropriate pitch position for each step.

6 Drag the mouse across the velocity display in the lower half of the window. All velocity values are adjusted according to the position of the mouse. This is a very quick manner of entering velocity data. You may prefer to enter more precise velocity values, in which case you should drag the velocity levels for each step individually.

7 Commence playback of Cubase SX. The pattern entered in Step Designer plays back synchronised to the current project tempo, in a continuous loop.

8 During playback, try editing the notes and velocity data.

9 Click on the Controllers menu and select the Gate option. Edit the gate times of the notes in the lower part of the display. The gate times affect the lengths of the notes in the pattern.

10 Select the Harmonic or Brightness controllers in the Controllers menu. Edit the Harmonic and Brightness values in the lower part of the display. This produces real-time changes of the resonance and cut-off parameters in the A1 VSTi. Open the A1 interface to observe the movement of the parameters.

11 Click on the Setup button to assign other controllers to Step Designer. Experiment with the value settings of the chosen controllers

Other techniques

There are a number of techniques which can help you get more out of Step Designer. Try the following:

Tip

Step Designer works well with analogue-style synth sounds. It is excellent for producing filter sweep effects in dance tracks. Try using Step Designer with the supplied A1 VSTi (the '1/16 sequenzer' patch and many of the bass sounds work well). Step Designer also gives great results when used with Native Instruments' Pro52/53 VSTi.

• click and drag vertically on the note list on the left of the note display to slide the octave up or down. Note that moving notes in the current pattern 'off-screen' results in a note name appearing in the display indicating the presence of notes in other octaves. This is helpful for keeping track of the notes in multi-octave patterns.

• click on any of the Tie indicators (the strip between the upper and lower sections of the interface) to tie any note to the preceding note, for longer note durations. Ties can be implemented on any number of successive steps in the pattern and the tied note always takes on the pitch of the note to which it is attached. Changing the pitch of tied notes moves all tied steps simultaneously.

Automating pattern changes

It is possible to automate pattern changes in Step Designer by drawing data onto the appropriate automation track. To achieve this proceed as follows:

1 Right click/Command click on the MIDI track where Step Designer is assigned and select 'Show Automation' from the pop-up menu. By default, the Volume automation track appears.

2 Click on the small downward pointing arrow to open the automation selection menu. Select 'More'.

3 In the Add Parameter dialogue which appears, select 'Pattern Select' (usually last in the list). The automation track for Pattern Select is now displayed in the Project window.

4 Activate Read on the Pattern Select automation track. Draw a single automation handle on the automation curve and move it vertically while observing the Pattern field in the Step Designer interface. As you move the automation curve the pattern number changes.

5 Draw automation points on the Pattern Select automation track at the points corresponding to where you want your pattern changes (click on the blue line with the pointer tool to create new automation handles). For this kind of change you need two automation points vertically placed at the pattern change position.

6 To determine which pattern you are selecting, place the project cursor after the pattern change point and move the last automation point vertically. Observe the resulting pattern change in the Step Designer interface. For more information about editing automation curves, see Chapter 15.

Track Control

Track Control provides three control panels for standard GS and XG General MIDI devices. This allows remote control of standard GM parameters in GS/XG compatible MIDI devices. Panels are selected in the menu at the top of the interface. The options include GS Basic Controls, XG Effects and Sends and XG Global. The Off button sets all parameters to their lowest value without sending out any MIDI data. The reset button resets all controls to their default values and sends out the corresponding MIDI messages. (See Appendix 4 for more details about General MIDI).

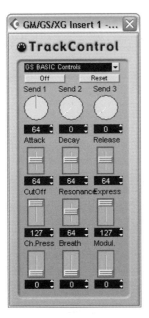

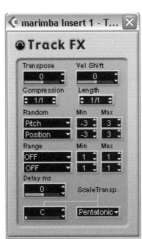

Figure 14.19 (left)
Track Control

Figure 14.20 (right)
Track FX

Track FX

Track FX is a duplicate of the Track Parameters section of the MIDI Inspector but includes additional Scale Transpose and Delay parameters. Scale Transpose forces all incoming MIDI notes to conform to the chosen musical scale. A wide range of scales are available including standard major, harmonic minor and melodic minor and also the more esoteric Arabian, Balinese, Hungarian, Chinese and so on.

Scale Transpose works well for the discovery of new melodies and ideas when used in conjunction with Track FX's Random parameter which can be set to pitch. Try setting the minimum and maximum Random setting to around –3 and +3 and select pitch as the target. Select your choice of scale and then use any MIDI melody as input.

The delay parameter adds or subtracts a time in milliseconds to push the incoming MIDI data backwards or forwards in time.

For details of the other parameters in Track FX see the section entitled 'The Inspector' in Chapter 4.

Transformer

Transformer is almost identical to Logical Editor except that it processes the data in real-time. This allows the application of elaborate MIDI processing functions without permanently affecting the data.

Transformer's functions include deleting, transforming and inserting data based upon user-configurable filters. The filter is set up in the upper part of the window and the action which should take place upon the filtered data is defined in the lower half of the window.

Figure 14.21
Transformer

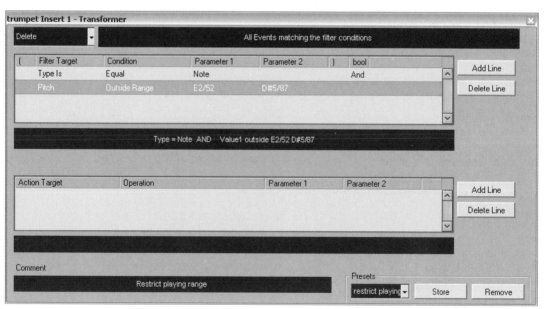

A statement in plain English describing a simple Transformer function might run as follows :

If the incoming MIDI message type is an Aftertouch message delete it.

This translates into the window as follows:

- In the upper Filter section, set the Filter target to 'Type', set the condition to 'Equal' and Parameter 1 to 'Aftertouch'.
- Ignore the Action section.
- Choose Delete as the function mode in the upper left menu.

This results in the deletion of all aftertouch messages from the incoming data.

Taking a look in the pop-up menus of the various columns reveals that some very sophisticated filtering and transformation actions are possible. Try loading some of the presets to see how more complex functions are set up. You may also like to consider the following two examples.

Setting a filter to restrict the input range for a chosen instrument

For restricting the MIDI input to the playing range of a trumpet, for example, proceed as follows:

- In the upper Filter section, set the Filter target column to 'Type', the Condition column to 'Equal' and the Parameter 1 column to 'Note'.
- Click on the Add Line button. Set the Filter target column to 'Value 1' (Pitch), the Condition column to 'Outside Range' and the Parameter 1 and 2 columns to 'E2 (52)' and 'D#5 (87)'.
- Choose Delete as the function mode in the upper left menu.

The result is the real-time deletion (or filtering) of any notes outside the chosen range. This kind of filter is excellent for keeping within the natural note range of an instrument, if a sense of realism is what your music needs.

Changing pitch bend into pan data

To set a transformation which changes pitch bend into pan data proceed as follows:

- In the upper Filter section, set the Filter target column to 'Type', the Condition column to 'Equal' and the Parameter 1 column to 'Pitchbend'.
- In the lower Action section, add two lines using the Add Line button. For the first line, set the Action target column to 'Type', the Operation column to 'Set to fixed value' and the Parameter 1 column to 'Controller'. For the second line, set the Action target column to 'Value 1', the Operation column to 'Set to fixed value' and the Parameter 1 column to '10' (Pan Controller number).
- Choose Transform as the function mode in the upper left menu.

The result is the real-time transformation of pitch bend messages into pan data. This is good for the real-time application of pan data using your master synth's pitch wheel. Of course, many more configurations are possible and, by using more data lines in each section, extremely complex filters and data transformations can be designed. Any efforts made with Transformer will serve you well when you use the main Logical editor.

How do I make the MIDI effects a permanent part of the data?

The data produced by the MIDI effects can be made a permanent part of the data using 'Merge MIDI in Loop' in the MIDI menu (Figure 14.22).

Figure 14.22
Merge MIDI in Loop dialogue

Merge MIDI in Loop merges all non-muted MIDI events between the left and right locators in a new MIDI part which is created on the currently selected MIDI track. If there is already MIDI data on the destination track you can choose to overwrite it or merge all the data.

To use Merge MIDI in Loop proceed as follows:

- Adjust the left and right locators to encompass the MIDI passage you wish to merge.
- Mute all those MIDI tracks you do *not* wish to include in the merge operation or, if you are working on a single track, you could use its solo button.
- Select a destination MIDI track.
- Select 'Merge MIDI in Loop' from the MIDI menu.
- Activate the 'Include Inserts' and/or 'Include Sends' options to include the MIDI effects you wish to be merged.
- Activate the 'Erase Destination' option if you wish to erase the current MIDI part on the destination track and replace it with the merged data. For example, this would be the case, if you were working on a single MIDI part and wished to make its MIDI effects a permanent part of the data. Erasing the destination avoids double notes.
- De-activate the 'Erase Destination' option if you do NOT wish to erase the current MIDI part on the destination track and wish to merge all the chosen data with it. Remember that merging the data from a single part onto the same track means that you are merging the data with itself, which results in double notes.

Tip

'Merge MIDI in Loop' does not function on tracks which have not been assigned to a MIDI output port (i.e. those whose output ports are displayed as 'Not Connected').

MIDI effects combinations

Multiple MIDI effects combinations arranged in the Inserts slots works particularly well for producing creative manipulations of MIDI data. Try the following:

Arpache followed by Autopan

To produce an arpeggiated synth sequence featuring automatic modulation of the cut-off of the supplied A1 VSTi, assign Arpache followed by Autopan as Insert effects on a MIDI track whose output port is assigned to the supplied A1 VSTi set to the '1/16 sequenzer' patch. Set up the parameters as shown in Figure 14.23 and try holding down C1 and D1 on your MIDI keyboard. To hear the effect of Autopan you must activate playback. Autopan does not function if Cubase SX is in stop mode.

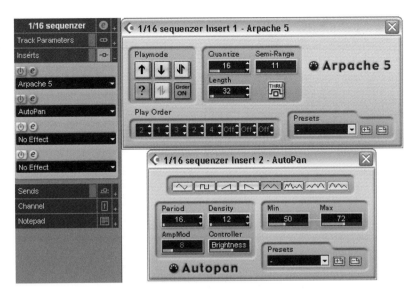

Figure 14.23
Arpache followed by Autopan

Arpache followed by Density

To produce automated hi-hats, assign Arpache followed by Density as Insert effects on a MIDI track whose output port is assigned to the supplied LM7 VSTi. Set up the parameters as shown in Figure 14.24 and hold down F#1, G#1 and A#1 (closed, pedal and open hi-hats). Arpache generates the notes. Density randomly deletes certain events. This produces hi-hat variations. Try different Play Order settings in Arpache and different Density settings to generate other variations.

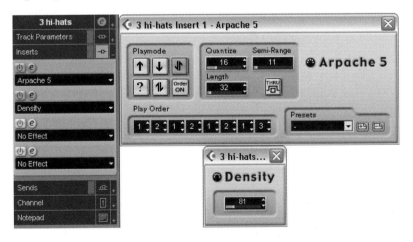

Figure 14.24
Arpache followed by Density for automated hi-hat variations

Arpache followed by Midi Echo

To produce a classic arpeggiated synth with synchronised MIDI echoes assign Arpache followed by Midi Echo as Insert effects on a MIDI track whose output port is assigned to the supplied A1 VSTi set to the 'Nice'n'Fine' patch. Set up the parameters as shown in Figure 14.25. This setup is suitable for playing live through the MIDI track or for being triggered from a pre-recorded MIDI part. Try holding down C2 and G2 (or C2 and F2).

Figure 14.25
Arpache followed by Midi Echo

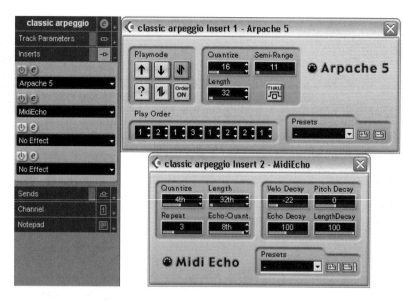

Step Designer followed by Density followed by Track FX

This combination shows how Cubase SX can generate approximations of a musical performance. Assign Step Designer followed by Density followed by Track FX as Insert effects on a MIDI track whose output port is assigned to a Rhodes electric piano patch (or some other piano sound). Set up the parameters as shown in Figure 14.26. The Step Designer pattern is random, generated by clicking on the Random button. A Swing setting of 50 gives the pattern some character. This pattern of notes passes through the Density plugin which adds notes to the pattern, producing chord-like structures. The pitch of these is further randomised in the Track FX plug-in which also adds/subtracts a random length to/from the notes. A Pentatonic Scale Transpose setting makes it all sound more musical. Try playing back at a tempo of around 105 bpm. This combination just happens to produce a result which sounds something like a drunken jazz pianist! Experiment with the settings.

Figure 14.26
Step Designer followed by Density followed by Track FX

Automation

Mix automation is considered a standard requirement in professional recording studios. It allows the producer, sound engineer or musician more scope to produce the best possible mix and gives instant recall of a mix which was performed on a previous occasion. Automation normally includes various dynamic mixer fader and control movements which took place throughout the course of the mix. The movements are recorded on the fly and any changes can be overdubbed as many times as necessary in order to achieve the desired result. Cubase SX includes similar automation features and, as well as automation of the faders, pan controls, and switches on the Mixer channel strips, it includes automation of all EQ controls, all plug-in effect controls, and all VST instrument controls.

Basic automation

Basic automation can be recorded in Cubase SX using two methods:

1 Activating the Write buttons and recording the movements of the controls in real-time.
2 Opening an automation 'subtrack' in the event display and drawing an automation curve.

Basic automation using the Read and Write buttons

The Read (R) and Write (W) buttons are found on every channel strip in the Mixer. The buttons are duplicated in the Track list and in the Inspector. Read and Write buttons are also found on each plug-in effect interface and each VST Instrument interface.

To start using automation, create a new project or open an existing test project. Make sure you have two or three audio tracks recorded in the project. Set up Cubase to cycle on a suitable passage and open the Mixer (press F3 on the computer keyboard). Arrange a layout in a similar manner to Figure 15.1, so that you can see both the Mixer and the Project window. For most Cubase SX projects, it is standard practice to leave one or two empty bars at the start of the project. This can be useful for any automated Mixer settings you may wish to implement before the music actually starts. In Cubase SX, make sure that 'Touch Fader' automation mode is activated in the Project window toolbar.

To record automation in the Mixer proceed as follows:

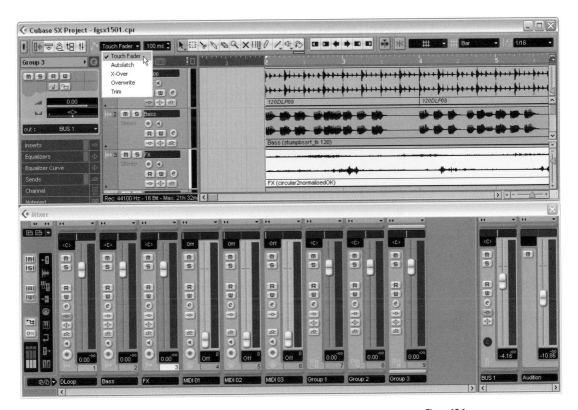

Figure 15.1
Arrange the layout of your project like this before recording any automation

- Activate the Write button on one of the Audio channels in the Mixer (Figure 15.2). An active Write button is illuminated in red.
- Start playback in Cycle mode and simply move the fader of the Audio track you Write enabled (Figure 15.3).

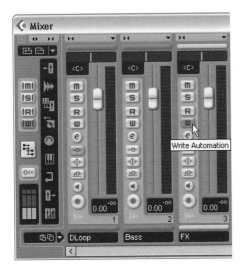

Figure 15.2
Activate the Write button for an Audio channel

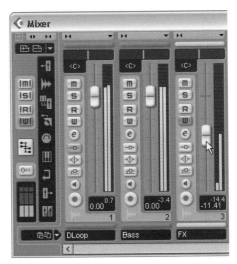

Figure 15.3
Move the fader while in normal playback mode

- Stop moving the fader after the first cycle and activate the Read button for the track. An active Read button is illuminated in green. On subsequent laps of the cycle, the fader moves according to the manipulations you made on the first lap of the cycle (Figure 15.4).

Figure 15.4
Activate the Read button for the Audio channel

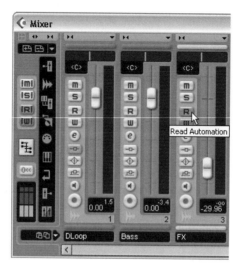

- Stop playback. Right click/Command click on the corresponding track in the Track list in the Project window. Select 'Show Used Automation' from the pop-up menu (Figure 15.5).

Figure 15.5
Select 'Show Used Automation' from the Track list pop-up menu

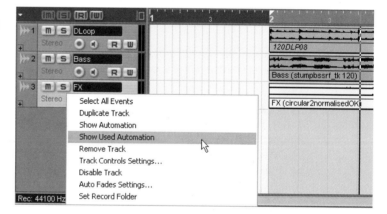

- Show Used Automation opens the automation subtrack(s) for the Audio track. Alternatively, you can click on the small plus (+) symbol in the lower left corner of the track in the Track list. If you have manipulated the channel fader, then an automation curve representing the fader movements is now shown in the event display (Figure 15.6). Automation events are shown as small black markers (handles) and these govern the actual shape of the curve.
- Grab one of the handles in the automation curve using the Pointer tool (Object Selection tool) near to the current position of the Project cursor

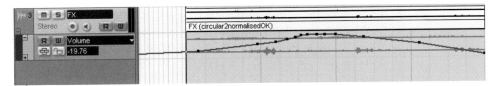

and drag it vertically up and down (Figure 15.7). This changes the shape of the curve and simultaneously changes the level shown on the channel fader. Manipulating the automation handles in the subtracks is the main automation editing technique (covered in more detail in the section entitled 'Edit the Automation', below).

Figure 15.6
The automation curve in the Volume automation subtrack in the event display

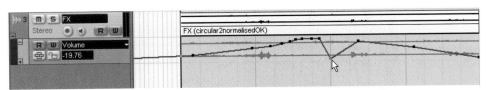

Basic automation by drawing automation curves in the subtracks

It is sometimes more appropriate to draw an automation curve in the event display rather than moving controls manually. Such a case might occur if you wanted to produce a simple fade in or some kind of panning manipulation. Manipulating the curves in the event display is also the main editing technique for existing automation data (covered in more detail in the section entitled 'Edit the Automation', below).

Figure 15.7
Drag an automation handle in the event display to change the shape of the curve

Let's imagine that you want to pan one of your sounds from the left to the centre position at the start of the mix. To achieve this in the event display, proceed as follows:

• Right click/Command click on the track to which you wish to apply a pan effect in the Track list. Select 'Show Automation' from the pop-up menu (Figure 15.8).

Figure 15.8
Select 'Show Automation' from the Track list pop-up menu on the chosen track

• By default, the Volume automation subtrack appears. Click on the small downward pointing arrow in the subtrack name field and select 'Pan Left-Right' from the pop-up menu (Figure 15.9).
• Activate the Read button for the Pan Left-Right subtrack in the Track list. Select 'Beat' in the Grid Quantize menu and select the Line tool from the

Figure 15.9
Select 'Pan Left-Right' from the
subtrack pop-up menu

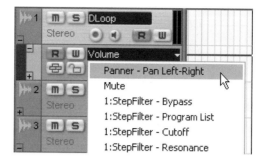

Project window toolbar. Draw a line at the appropriate position in the
event display to produce the pan effect of your choice (Figure 15.10).

Figure 15.10
Use the Line tool to draw a pan
automation curve in the 'Pan Left-Right'
subtrack

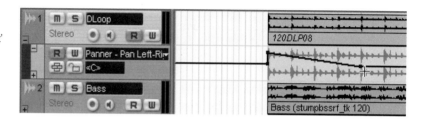

- Activate playback to hear the result. Adjust and experiment with the
curve as required.

Figure 15.11
Try the other Draw tools to create
different shaped automation curves

- Try using the other Draw tools in the toolbar and different Grid Quantize
menu settings to create different shaped automation curves (Figure 15.11).

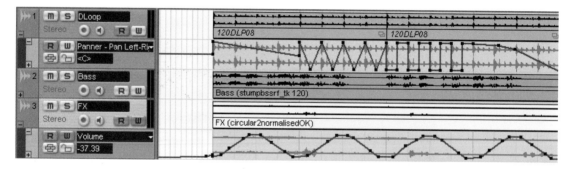

More automation

The subtrack pop-up menu as shown in Figure 15.9, above, does not show
all the available subtracks. To select other subtrack types, select the 'More'
option (Figure 15.12). The "More' option opens the Add Parameter dialogue
from where you can select the automation subtrack of your choice (Figure
15.13).

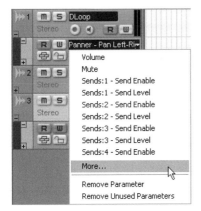

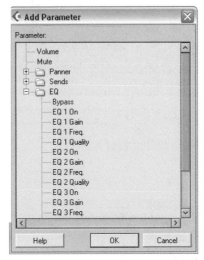

Figure 15.12 (left)
Select other subtrack types using the 'More' option

Figure 15.13 (right)
The Add Parameter dialogue for selecting other subtrack types

Info

The 'automation return time' field (next to the automation mode menu) determines how long it takes for the automation to revert back to the existing automation curve after new data has been written in Touch fader mode.

Automation modes

Cubase SX provides five automation modes in the toolbar of the Project window. The modes operate as follows:

- Touch Fader – automation starts to be written when you click on a control during playback and continues until you release the mouse button. This is the standard automation mode for recording movements 'on the fly'.
- Autolatch – automation starts to be written when you click on a control during playback. The last set value for the control continues to be written until you stop playback or de-activate the Write button. In this mode, the release of the mouse button does not switch off the automation. Good for writing static mixes over a looped section.
- X-Over – automation starts to be written as soon as you click on a control during playback. The last set value for the control continues to be written until the new automation curve crosses a point on the existing curve (or until you stop playback or de-activate the Write button). For successful operation, both the Read and Write buttons should be activated. In this mode, the release of the mouse button does not switch off the automation. Good for writing fades up to a set level on the existing curve.
- Overwrite mode – automation starts to be written for volume faders only, at their currently set values, AS SOON AS YOU COMMENCE PLAYBACK. The last set value for the control continues to be written until you stop playback or de-activate the Write button (like Autolatch). This function should be used with caution since you can easily overwrite wanted automation, but it is good for writing static volume fader mixes over a specific section or for re-setting all faders to 0dB.
- Trim mode – automation starts to be written when you click on a control during playback and continues until you release the mouse button. When trim mode is selected, the faders of channels with their Write buttons activated are temporarily reset to the mid position. When you write the

Tip

An excellent way of viewing the behaviour of the different automation modes is to write the automation while viewing the corresponding subtrack in the Project window event display. With the Write button active, each time you click on a control the track header in the Track list turns red to indicate that automation is being recorded.

automation, the changes affect the existing curve relative to the movements of the fader above or below the mid-point. More importantly, Trim mode can be used to change the automation between the left and right locators when Cubase SX is in stop mode. Proceed as follows: find the automation you wish to trim in the automation subtracks in the event display, set the left and right locators around the events, select Trim mode, activate Write on the appropriate channel(s) and then move the fader(s) up or down.

Automating your mix

It is assumed here that you are already familiar with basic mixing in Cubase SX and have read Chapter 11 of this book. You cannot really tackle automation until you have a clear idea of what mixing itself actually involves. For a global overview, your attention is drawn to the sections entitled 'Preliminaries', 'What is mixing?', 'Ten Golden rules for recording and mixing' and 'Mixing decisions' in Chapter 11. This helps you focus on some of the issues you are likely to encounter when using automation. Bear in mind that automated mixing is not a separate magical process, it is merely one of a number of tools (albeit a rather special tool) that you can use to get a better mix. The decision to use it or not is a function of the artistic and technical imperatives of your mix.

Experimenting with automation (as in Basic Automation, above) helps you become familiar with the possibilities. However, using automation in an actual mix reveals that there are many other considerations which govern exactly how and why you might use it. One of the things to avoid is using automation just because it happens to be available. This might produce a mix with lots of intricate automation but you may lose the focus of what kind of mix the music really needs. A better approach is to think about your mix in terms of its overall musical and artistic structure and then define what this implies technically. For example, consider the following basic questions:

- Do you need to separately fade in any of the instruments?
- Do you have any panning effects in mind for any parts of the arrangement?
- Do you need to 'ride' the fader of a problem track to help it 'sit' correctly in the mix?
- Do any of the channels need to be muted/unmuted throughout the course of the mix?
- Do you need to produce filter sweep effects on a VSTi or MIDI synth?
- Do you intend to perform an overall fade out at the end of the music?

Any of these options could be candidates for automation. Why? Because they all involve dynamic mixer control changes. Automation might also involve jumping from one static mix configuration to another and not necessarily smooth, continuous changes. In addition, if you do not have an external control surface, simultaneous manipulations of multiple controls in a complex mix are actually impossible with a single mouse. In this sense, automation is a necessity in Cubase SX.

Of course, your mix may not need automation at all. It may simply require the same settings throughout the entire length of the project. This is perfectly acceptable since it is not a crime to not use automation!

Step-by-step automation project

1 Prepare for the mix

This project uses a forty eight bar musical arrangement as test material (Figure 15.14). This is no more than a skeleton structure which is intended for demonstration purposes only. Your own material may imply a more sophisticated approach but the key steps remain the same.

Figure 15.14
Target material for mix automation

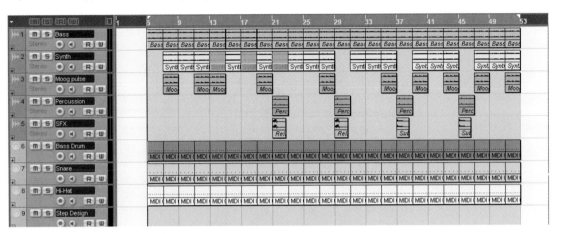

The target material in Figure 15.14 includes five Audio tracks: bass, synth, Moog synth pulse effect, percussion and SFX; and four MIDI tracks: bass drum, snare drum, hi-hat and a monophonic sequence track produced by the supplied Step Designer MIDI plug-in. The MIDI drum tracks trigger the sounds in a HALion VSTi sampler and the Step Design MIDI sequence triggers the supplied A1 VSTi synth.

Preparing for the mix in the global sense would normally involve adjusting the Mixer, and perhaps some of the other windows in Cubase SX, to suitable settings. Various suggestions about how to do this are outlined in the section entitled 'Mixing strategies' in Chapter 11. You may already have a suitable layout saved as a Window Layout in the Window menu (Figure 15.15).

Before commencing with the final mix you would normally set up a basic mix (outlined below). However, before starting any kind of mix, try thinking about the structural shape you intend to impose. This invariably has consequences for any automation you might need to apply. For example, the intentions in the target material outlined here are the following:

- to fade in the bass drum, snare and hi-hat separately.
- to set up a simultaneous panning effect on the synth and Moog pulse sounds in the introduction.
- to set up a left-right panning effect on the percussion track.
- to mute the A1 Step Designer sequence on all but ten separate bars within the arrangement.
- to implement a global fade out at the end of the track.

All these elements imply the use of automation.

During mixing you are likely to concentrate on specific passages using

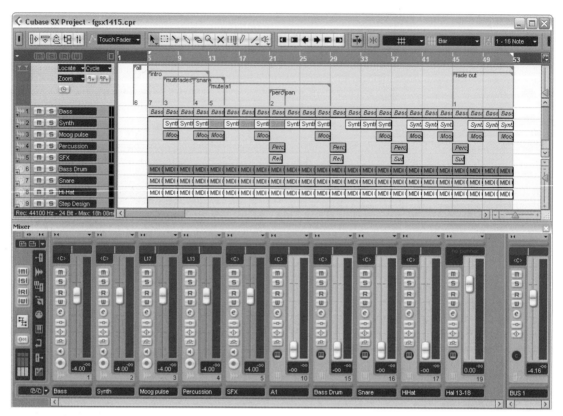

Figure 15.15
Use a layout suitable for mixing

Cubase SX in cycle playback mode. This is particularly true when writing automation. Here, the cycle markers could encompass the specific passages where the automation is required. For this purpose, it is well worth setting up a number of cycle markers in the Marker track before the mix begins (Figure 15.16).

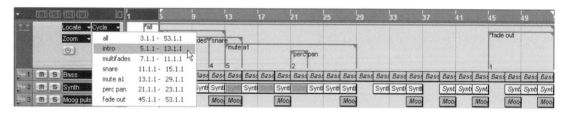

Figure 15.16
Help manage your mix by marking the structure of the musical arrangement using Cycle Markers in the Marker track

Hold Ctrl (PC) / Command (Mac) and drag with the pointer or pencil in the Marker track to insert a cycle marker over the selected range. Open the cycle marker pop-up menu and make a selection from the list to move the left and right locators to the start and end of any chosen cycle marker range. Alternatively, double click on the cycle marker in the Marker track. To start loop playback around the currently selected cycle marker, press Shift + G.

Other preparative measures include labeling the Mixer channels and tracks (if needed), re-arranging the track order in the Project window and hiding channels that you do not wish to see in the Mixer using the Common panel show/hide buttons (and using the 'Hideable' option in the pop-up channel menus).

2 Set up a basic mix

Before starting with any specific automation you may wish to set up a basic startup mix in the Mixer which sets all your faders and relevant controls to various default settings (Figure 15.17). Set this up *without any write buttons activated*. At this stage you are not writing automation, you are setting up a basic mix. The settings you make are used by Cubase SX as the basic default values for each control before any automation is applied. Try using a passage where all tracks in the mix are playing. The controls you set might include basic fader, pan, EQ and effects settings. Remember, it is important *not* to use the Write buttons on the channels at this stage.

Figure 15.17
Set up a basic mix in the Mixer with *no* automation buttons activated

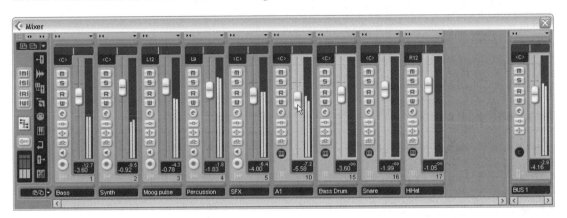

3 Write the automation

This is where you start to fill in the details of your mix. The automation can take place in between other mixing tasks or you could concentrate on it as a separate process. In any case, it forms part of the overall process of gradually building the sonic image you want to hear. Let's apply the automation, as outlined in the 'Prepare for the mix' section, above. (Your own mix may, of course, feature different automation.) Proceed as follows:

> **Tip**
>
> To adjust the resolution of the automation data, use the Automation Reduction slider in Preferences/Editing.

Fading in the bass drum, snare and hi-hat separately

- Set up the left and right locators around the section of the intended fade ins. In this case, the section is marked with a cycle marker called 'intro' (Figure 15.18). Here, it is decided to implement the automation on the VST Instrument channels and not on the MIDI channels which trigger this VST Instrument.

Figure 15.18
Set up the left and right locators around the section of the intended fade ins

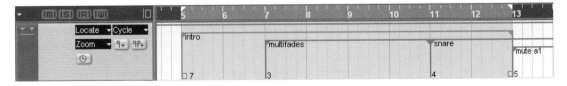

- Ensure that both the Read and Write buttons are de-activated on the relevant channels in the Mixer. Since this section involves fade ins from silence, move the faders for the bass drum, snare drum and hi-hat to their lowest positions (Figure 15.19).

- Make sure you have activated the 'Touch Fader' automation mode on the Project window toolbar. Activate the Write buttons of the three drum tracks and activate cycle mode.Start playback and move the bass drum fader at the appropriate moment to create a bass drum fade in over the required bars. Activate its Read button and verify your fade on the next lap of the cycle. Adjust as necessary. Proceed with the snare and hi-hat channels in the same manner (Figure 15.20).

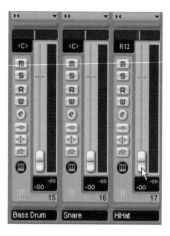

Figure 15.19
Move the faders for the bass drum, snare and hi-hat to their minimum values in the Mixer

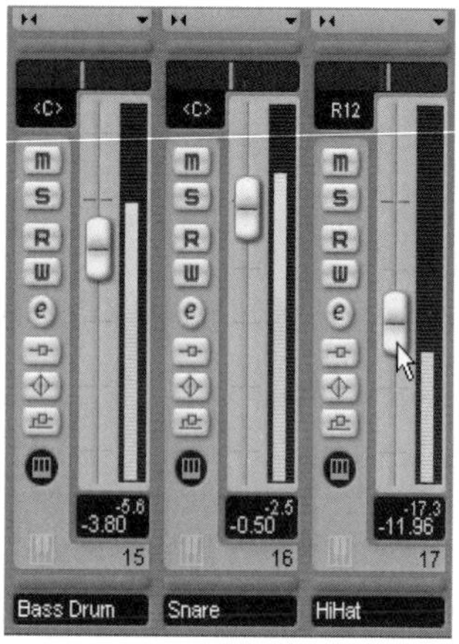

Figure 15.20
Write the automation in the Mixer using the channel faders

- Automation for VST Instrument channels appears in a track in the Project window named 'VST Instrument Automation'. This track becomes available at the moment you activate the Write button on the VSTi channel. Open the automation subtracks of the VST Instrument Automation track to view the automation curves for the bass drum, snare and hi-hat (Figure 15.21). Notice here how the bass drum is faded in first followed by the hi-hat and then the snare. This adds interest to the musical introduction.

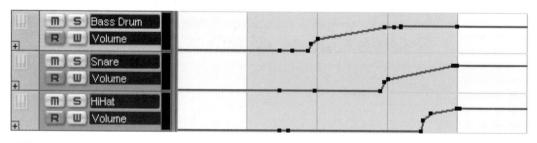

Figure 15.21
The resulting volume automation curves for the bass drum, snare and hi-hat in the Project window event display

- If you are not satisfied with the results, you could re-write the offending parts of the automation using the channel faders or edit the automation events in the Project window (editing automation in the Project window is explained in more detail below).

Setting up a simultaneous panning effect on the synth and Moog pulse tracks

- Set up the left and right locators around the section of the intended pannings. In this case, the pannings are to take place over bars 7 and 8 (2 bars). The effect involves the simultaneous panning of both sounds from opposite sides of the stereo image to meet in the centre.
- Ensure that both the Read and Write buttons are de-activated for the relevant channels in the Mixer. This automation features the synth sound panned from left to centre and the Moog pulse panned from right to centre. Before commencing to write the automation, move the pan control for the synth channel to the left and the pan control for the Moog pulse channel to the right (Figure 15.22).
- Make sure you have activated the 'Touch Fader' automation mode on the Project window toolbar. Activate the Write buttons of the two tracks and activate cycle mode. Start playback and move the synth pan control at the appropriate moment. Slowly drag it to the centre position over the required two bars (Figure 15.23). Activate its Read button and verify your pan on the next lap of the cycle. Adjust as necessary. Proceed with Moog pulse channel in the same manner but pan it from the opposite side.

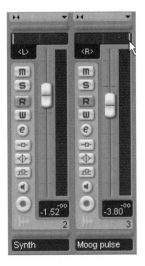
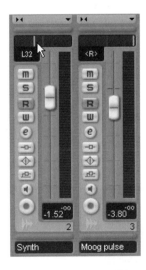

Figure 15.22 (left)
Move the pan control for the synth channel to the left and that for the Moog pulse channel to the right

Figure 15.23 (right)
Write the automation in the Mixer using the pan controls

- Open the automation subtracks of the synth and Moog pulse tracks in the Project window to view the pan automation curves (Figure 15.24).
- If you are not satisfied with the results, you could re-write the offending parts of the automation using the channel pan controls or edit the automation events in the Project window (editing automation in the Project window is explained in more detail below).

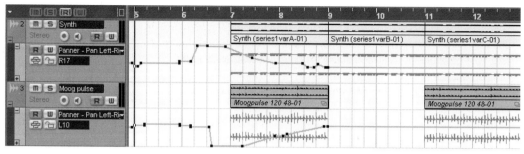

Figure 15.24
The resulting pan automation curves for synth and Moog pulse tracks in the Project window event display

Figure 15.25
The pan automation curve for the percussion sound in the Project window event display

Setting up a left-right panning effect on the percussion track

- This is similar to the previous step ('Setting up a simultaneous panning effect …') but takes place on the percussion channel in bars 21 and 22. Rather than panning from one side to the centre, this effect pans the sound left to right. Proceed in a similar manner to the above except pan the sound from the left all the way to the right. Open the pan automation subtrack of the percussion track in the Project window to view the pan automation curve which should resemble Figure 15.25.

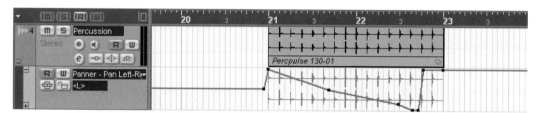

Muting the A1 Step Designer sequence on all but ten separate bars within the arrangement

Step Designer is a MIDI step sequencer available as a MIDI effect (see Chapter 13 for details). This outputs a monophonic pattern of MIDI notes which can be directed to any available MIDI device. In the demonstration piece, the MIDI output of Step Designer is routed to the A1 VST Instrument.

Step Designer plays continuously whenever you are in playback mode so including it in a piece of music means that you usually need to find a way of changing the pattern or muting the output so that it fits in with the rest of your musical arrangement. For changing the pattern, see 'Automating pattern changes' in the Step Designer section in Chapter 13. For muting the output, you can either mute the MIDI output from Step Designer by changing to an empty pattern or mute the audio from the triggered MIDI instrument (in this case the A1). For the latter solution, proceed as follows:

Figure 15.26
Set up the left and right locators to encompass the section where you intend to mute/unmute the track

- Set up the left and right locators to encompass the bars where you intend to mute/unmute the A1 synth track. In this case, the section is marked with a cycle marker called 'mute A1' (Figure 15.26).

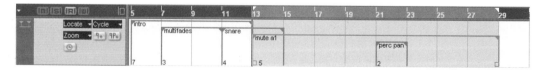

- In the demonstration piece, the sequence is in a muted state more often than it is in an unmuted state. For this reason it is a good idea to set the channel's default status to mute button 'on'. Ensure that both the Read and Write buttons are de-activated on the relevant channels in the Mixer. Since the default status of the track is 'mute on', activate the mute button on the A1 VST Instrument channel (Figure 15.27).
- Make sure you have activated the 'Touch Fader' automation mode on the Project window toolbar. Activate the Read and Write buttons of the A1 VST Instrument channel and activate cycle mode. Start playback and de-activate and re-activate the mute button at the appropriate points in time. Verify the mute manipulations on the next lap of the cycle. Adjust as necessary.
- Automation for VST Instrument channels appears in a track in the Project window named 'VST Instrument Automation'. This track is available only after you have written some automation. Open the automation subtracks of the VST Instrument Automation track and find the automation curve for the A1 VSTi (Figure 15.28). Notice here how the mute curve has only

Figure 15.27
Activate the mute button on the A1 VST Instrument channel

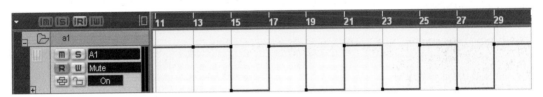

two settings. When the line is in the upper part of the subtrack the mute button is activated. When the line is in the lower part of the subtrack the mute button is de-activated.

Figure 15.28
The resulting mute button automation for the A1 VSTi track

Implement a global fade out at the end of the track

If your mix is to undergo a mastering stage at a later date, global fades in

Figure 15.29 (left)
Set up the left and right locators to encompass the fade out

and out are best left to that time. This exercise assumes no further processing after the mix. Here, a global fade out is created using the output bus fader. Proceed as follows:

Figure 15.30
Write the overall fade out in the Mixer using the stereo output bus fader

- Set up the left and right locators to encompass the bars where you intend to create the fade out. In this case, the fade occurs over the final eight bars of the music (Figure 15.29).
- Activate the Write button of the output bus in the Mixer and activate cycle mode. Make sure you have activated the 'Touch Fader' automation mode on the Project window toolbar. Start playback and move the Master fader at the appropriate moment to create a fade out over the required bars. Activate the Read button and verify your fade on the next lap of the cycle. Adjust as necessary (Figure 15.30).
- Automation for the output bus channel appears in a folder in the Project

Figure 15.31
The resulting Master fader automation curve in the Project window event

window named 'Input/Output Channels'. This is available only after you have written some automation in the output bus channel. Open the folder to view the automation curve for the fade out (Figure 15.31).

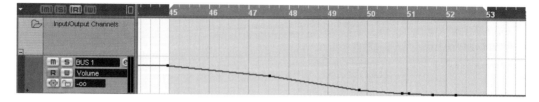

4 Edit the automation

Figure 15.32
Overview of the resulting automation in the Project window event display

Before proceeding to any detailed editing take a look at all the resulting automation curves of your mix in the Project window event display (Figure 15.32). Select 'Show Used Automation for all tracks' in the Track list Quick menu.

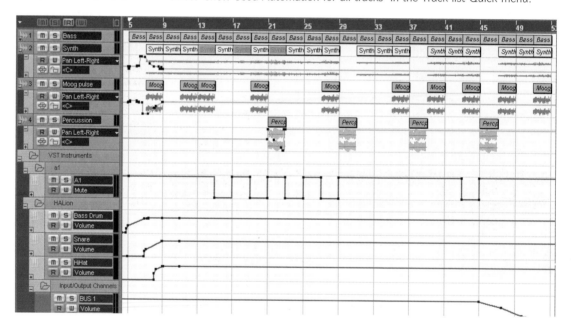

Editing techniques

The automation data is shown as small black markers or handles along the length of the automation curves and it is these which govern the actual shape of the curve. These are known as automation events. Automation events may be edited using the standard mouse and tool techniques of the Project window, as outlined in Chapter 4. The following are some of the most useful techniques:

- Select one or more automation events by dragging a box around the relevant area in the subtrack using the Pointer tool (Object selection tool). Alternatively, step through the events using the left/right arrows on the computer keyboard. Selected automation events are displayed in red.

- Delete one or more automation events by selecting them and pressing the Backspace or Delete keys on the computer keyboard. Alternatively, use the Eraser tool.
- Copy a group of automation events using Ctrl + C. Paste the copied events by moving the Project cursor to another position in the subtrack and pressing Ctrl + V. The copied events overwrite the chosen section from the Project cursor position. Alternatively, use the Range Selection tool to move (or copy by pressing Alt) the events to a new position.
- Click on any automation event and drag it to a new position to change the shape of the curve. Movements snap to the current snap resolution.
- Write a single new automation event by clicking once anywhere along the automation line.
- Write multiple new automation events by dragging any of the draw tools (pencil, line, parabola and so on) in the automation subtrack.

Cleaning up

Manually writing automation in the Mixer often results in small errors and these might show up as irregularities in the automation curves. For example, the pan curve for the synth track in Figure 15.32 is not as accurate as it could be. To smooth the curve proceed as follows:

- Zoom in to the pan subtrack so that you can see the individual automation events clearly (Figure 15.33). Set up the left and right locators and activate playback in cycle mode. In this way, you can make all edits 'on the fly' and hear the results on the next lap of the cycle.

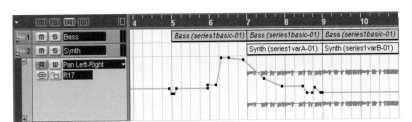

Figure 15.33
The pan automation events before editing

- Delete the first group of pan events before bar 7 and move one of the handles to the left pan position at the very beginning of bar 7 (Figure 15.34). Activating the Snap button helps with getting the correct bar position. The left pan position corresponds with the uppermost position in the automation curve.

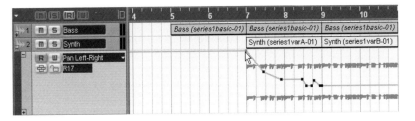

Figure 15.34
Delete the first group of pan events and move one of the handles to the left bar position at the beginning of bar 7

Figure 15.35
The resulting smooth pan over two bars

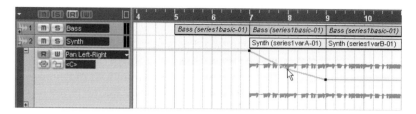

- Thin out the events between bars 7 and 8 and move the event located at the beginning of bar 9 to the centre pan position. Create a suitable curve between the event at bar 7 and the event at bar 9 (Figure 15.35). This gives you a smooth pan from the left to the centre pan positions over two bars.
- Tidy up the other events in the same manner. Bear in mind that it may not be appropriate to make all automation scientifically correct. Leaving some of the rough edges may be what gives your mix its character. Above all, avoid the habit of working visually. The aim is not to produce a visually perfect event display but to produce a good sounding mix. Always listen very carefully as you make each change and preferably work in cycle playback mode. If the automation sounds best 'rough and ready' then leave it that way.

Moving and copying automation

Moving or copying automation events in the Project window event display are common requirements. Moving is useful for those occasions when the timing of individual events or a group of events is not quite right. Copying saves time when you have a number of repetitive sections of automation. When copying and moving regular Audio and MIDI events in the Project window, the automation events are automatically attached and copied/moved with them, if 'Automation Follows Events' is enabled (Edit menu). See 'Automation Follows Events' below. Here, we look at how automation events are copied and moved independently.

Three methods of independently moving groups of automation events are as follows:

1   Select the Object selection tool and drag a selection box around the group of automation events. Press Ctrl/Command + X to cut the events. Place the cursor at the position at which you wish to paste the automation events. Press Ctrl/Command + V to paste the events.
2   Select the Range selection tool and drag in the appropriate subtrack(s) (or normal tracks) to select the area of interest. Once selected, click in the shaded area (at which time a hand appears) and drag the selection to a new location.
3   Select the Object selection tool and drag a selection box around the group of automation events. Click on any one of the selected events and drag the whole group horizontally backwards or forwards along the track. The horizontal movement is magnetic to the current snap resolution and you can only drag the group as far as the next event in the subtrack.

Tip

When moving automation handles, activate the Project window infoline. The infoline displays the start time and value of the event as you drag it. This helps place the events with greater precision. Alternatively, click directly on the value field in the infoline to activate a slider which may be used to change the value of the event.

Two methods of independently copying groups of automation events are as follows:

1 Select the Object selection tool and drag a selection box around the group of automation events. Press Ctrl/Command + C to copy the events. Place the cursor at the position at which you wish to paste the copied automation events. Press Ctrl/Command + V to paste the events.

2 Select the Range selection tool and drag in the appropriate subtrack(s) (or normal tracks) to select the area of interest. Once selected, press Alt on the computer keyboard, click in the shaded area (at which time a hand appears) and drag a copy of the selection to a new location.

Automation follows events

If you enable 'Automation follows events' in the Edit menu, any automation data found in the same range is automatically attached to regular Audio and MIDI events when they are moved or copied. This provides one of the easiest methods of moving and repeating automation data. For example, in the step-by-step automated mix outlined above, we set up a panning effect on the percussion track which panned the sound left to right over two bars (see 'Setting up a left-right panning effect on the percussion track' above). The two bar percussion passage actually occurs four times in total. To make the panning effect happen each time the percussion event occurs, all we do is enable 'Automation follows events' (Edit menu), delete the three instances of the percussion event which do not feature automation and replace them with copies of the percussion event with automation. The result is shown in Figure 15.36.

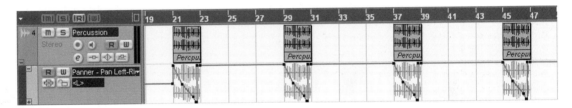

5 The completed automation

Figure 15.37 shows the completed automation subtracks in the Project window event display (including a number of additional automated passages). There is almost certainly a lot more work involved to complete your mix but the above steps provide you with most of the tools you need to go on to produce more sophisticated results.

Figure 15.36
Enable 'Automation follows events' and copy the percussion Audio event, to produce four instances of the same automated pan effect

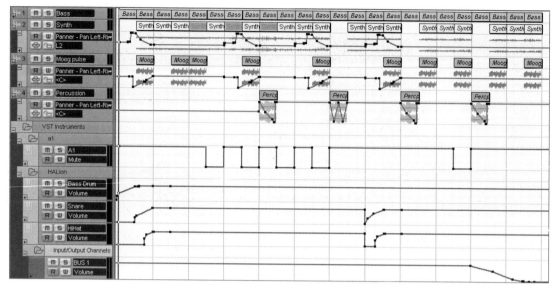

Figure 15.37
The completed automation in the Project window event display

Creating snapshots of the mixer settings

It is not always appropriate to use automation for dynamic movements of the controls. There are many occasions when you simply need to change from one group of settings to another, instantaneously. Each group of settings might be referred to as a snapshot; a non-dynamic mix which remains static for a given number of bars. For example, a common technique involves setting up separate static mixes for the intro, verse, chorus, middle eight and solo sections. The technique outlined below is best suited to Cubase SX in Autolatch mode (although it is possible to achieve similar results with Touch Fader mode).

To set up a static mix for your chosen sections proceed as follows:

• Select Autolatch mode in the Project window toolbar (Cubase SX only).

Figure 15.38
Click on the Write button in the Common panel to globally activate all channel Write buttons

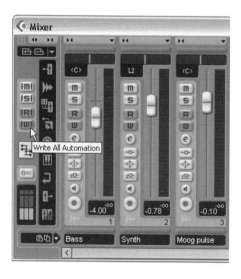

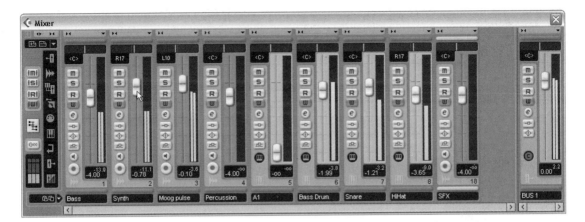

- Set up the left and right locators to encompass the first passage of music where you wish to implement a static mix. Select the Cycle button on the Transport panel. Click on the Write button in the Mixer Common panel. This activates the Write buttons globally for all channels (Figure 15.38).
- Commence cycle playback and set up the Mixer controls for the first section (Figure 15.39). The last set value for each control continues to be written until you stop playback or de-activate the Write button. After moving any controls make sure you continue to write the data for at least one whole cycle in order to write the values over the full length of the passage.
- Set up the left and right locators to encompass the second passage of music where you wish to implement a static mix. Select the Cycle button on the Transport panel. Make sure the Write button is still activated on all channels. Commence cycle playback and set up the Mixer controls for the second section (Figure 15.40). After moving any controls make sure you continue to write the data for at least one whole cycle in order to write the values over the full length of the passage.
- Continue in a similar manner to write as many static mix sections as required. When you have finished, de-activate the Write buttons. Click on the Read button in the Mixer Common panel to activate the Read buttons globally for all channels. Commence playback from the start of the music. During playback, you should see the controls change as you pass from one static mix to the next.

Figure 15.39
Commence cycle playback and set up the Mixer controls for the first section

Figure 15.40
Commence cycle playback and set up the Mixer controls for the second section

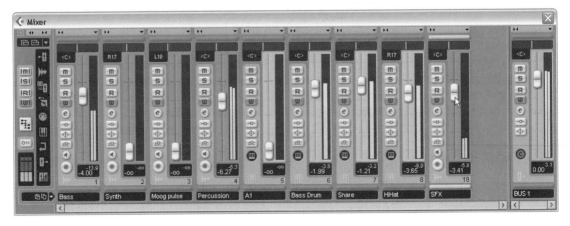

Info

The Insert effects bypass switch for Audio, Group and VSTi channels is not automatable.

What exactly can be automated?

Cubase SX allows automation of almost all of the mixing parameters. These include the following:

Audio, Group, VSTi and 1/0 bus channels

Channel faders
Pan controls
Mute buttons
Channel strip EQ bypass switches
Channel strip FX Send bypass switches
Enable, frequency, gain and Q controls for all EQ modules
Send effects on/off switches
Send effects levels
Send effects pre/post switches
Insert effects parameters and program selection

MIDI channels

Channel faders
Pan controls
Mute buttons
Track Parameters on/off switch
Transpose, velocity shift, random and range in the Track Parameters section
Insert effect on/off switches
Send effect on/off switches
Insert effect parameters
Send effect parameters

Plug-in automation

Send effects parameters and program selection
Master effects parameters and program selection
VST Instrument parameters and program selection

Surround sound

Surround sound implies the use of a multiple channel sound diffusion system where there are speakers behind and to the side of the listener as well as in front. Most surround sound configurations have their historical foundations in the film industry, which began using multichannel formats as long ago as the early 1950s. Early implementations involved a number of channels to the front of the listener and one to the rear, known as the effects channel. Early 70mm widescreen cinemas featured five channels across the cinema screen and a surround channel which fed multiple speakers to the rear and sides of the auditorium. As widescreen cinema fell out of fashion the need for a large number of channels across the front became obsolete. In the 1970s Dolby Laboratories encouraged the use of a surround sound system based upon three main screen channels (left, centre and right), with two low frequency bass extension channels and one surround channel to the rear. The centre channel was traditionally used for dialogue. The company also developed a 70mm format featuring a stereo surround channel. This was the forerunner of the 5.1 channel Dolby Digital Surround format.

At this point, you may well ask why Cubase SX should need to be equipped with surround sound when this is largely the domain of the film industry. The answer lies in the fact that, in recent times, there has been a convergence of the film sound, television sound and record industries such that they no longer work in isolation, and surround sound has become an accepted common standard among all three. In addition, surround systems are finding their way into more and more homes and the DVD-Audio disc aims to bring multichannel surround sound to the general consumer market (possibly eventually replacing standard audio CDs). Surround mixes are already a common occurrence in the audio industry. Cubase SX is ready to help you create your surround mix if you should need to.

Demystifying surround sound

In recent times, surround sound has been championed by two organisations: the aforementioned Dolby Laboratories and DTS (Digital Theatre Systems). One of the main differences between the two systems is that the audio data stream for Dolby Surround is stored on the filmstrip itself (between the sprocket holes) whereas the audio data for DTS is stored on a separate laser disc. The audio encoding algorithms for both methods involve data compression techniques and both systems are already available on many DVDs and music CDs. Both use the same kind of multiple channel sound formats in order to be compatible with the current hardware installed in cinema auditoriums.

The popular 5.1 channel surround configuration is a special implementation of the standard surround setup known as 3/2. The standard 3/2 configuration forms the essential reference system for surround sound. It features a left, centre and right channel in front of the listener and left surround and right surround channels to the rear (Figure 16.1).

Figure 16.1 shows the five speakers of a basic surround setup. '3/2' simply means three channels to the front and two to the rear. As mentioned above, the front centre channel has its origins in the film industry where it is used for dialogue. 5.1 channel surround adds an additional specialised channel to the basic 3/2 system known as the LFE channel ('Low Frequency Effects' or 'Low Frequency Extension' channel). This is the '.1' in the '5.1' name (Figure 16.2). There are many derivations of this in other surround configurations like 3/2/1, 5/2/1, 6.1 and 7.1. In all these cases, the '1' refers to an LFE channel. The other numbers refer to the number of full-bandwidth speakers featured in the surround system and, in the first two cases, how they are distributed between the front and rear parts of the listening space.

In the film industry, the LFE channel traditionally handles sub-bass frequencies between 20Hz to around 80Hz. This is used for

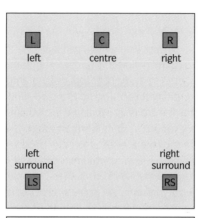

Figure 16.1
3/2 system for surround sound

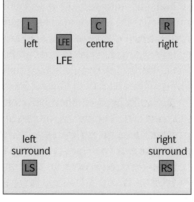

Figure 16.2
'5.1 channel' surround sound

material which will not compromise the end result if the program is reproduced on a system which cannot handle the low frequencies or does not feature an LFE channel. In may ways, the LFE channel is intended as an optional effects channel and is not considered as an essential element which must be used in order to conform to the 5.1 (or similar) standard.

Once a surround mix has been created it has to be encoded to conform to the chosen surround format. This is achieved using special software and hardware (not included in Cubase SX). For example, to create media suitable for playback in 5.1 channel Dolby Digital format, the multiple audio files created by a surround mix must be converted into a data stream known as AC-3. At the time of playback, the AC-3 data is decoded into the intended playback format using multichannel audio playback hardware featuring Dolby Digital decoding. In fact, the AC-3 data stream may be decoded for mono, stereo or 5.1 channel surround playback and so represents an adaptable format.

Common surround sound formats

The common surround formats include the following:

- *Dolby Stereo (Dolby Surround)* – Dolby Stereo is a four channel surround format developed in the 1970s for the film industry featuring left, centre, right and monophonic surround channel (of limited bandwidth). This is sometimes referred to as LCRS. In the early days of home theatre, it was possible to decode the left, right and surround channel information using early Dolby Surround decoders.
- *Dolby Pro Logic* – early 'home-theatre' Dolby Surround decoders could not derive a centre channel. The introduction of the Dolby Pro Logic format allowed the decoding of the centre channel and helped create a sound quality equivalent to cinema auditoriums in the home theatre environment. Dolby Pro Logic II improved matters further since it was capable of producing five channel surround (left, centre, right, left surround, right surround) from Dolby Surround encoded material, and also enhanced surround reproduction from any other unencoded stereo signal. The surround channels for Pro Logic II featured full bandwidth reproduction.
- *5.1 channel digital surround* – a digital surround format featuring five discrete full bandwidth channels and one limited bandwidth low frequency effects (LFE) channel. These are arranged as left, centre, right, in front of the listener and left surround, right surround to the rear. Traditionally the low frequency effects channel is located between the left and centre channels in front of the listener (see Figure 15.2). At the time of writing, 5.1 channel digital surround sound is implemented by two organisations, Dolby Laboratories and DTS (Digital Theatre Systems).
- *Dolby Digital 5.1* – the Dolby implementation of 5.1 channel surround sound. This involves conversion of the six discrete audio channels into a digital data stream known as AC-3. The AC-3 data stream is later decoded using proprietary Dolby decoding equipment. Dolby Digital is the most popular surround format for DVD (Digital Versatile Disc).
- *DTS* – a similar 5.1 surround system to Dolby Digital. In the film industry, the DTS audio data stream is stored on a separate laser disc whereas the Dolby audio data stream is stored on the filmstrip itself. When used on DVD the DTS digital data stream is recorded on the medium itself. The DTS system uses slightly less compression and some experts claim that it has a superior sound quality.
- *6.1 channel digital surround* – a surround format similar to Dolby Digital 5.1 but with an additional centre surround channel to the rear. 6.1 formats include Dolby Digital EX and DTS ES.
- *7.1 channel digital surround* – a surround format similar to Dolby Digital 5.1 but with additional left and right side speakers or, in the case of the proprietary SDDS 7.1 format (Sony Digital Dynamic Sound), left centre and right centre front channels to handle wide screen cinema.

Setting up the surround features in Cubase SX

General Setup

For full surround reproduction the Cubase SX user needs audio hardware connected to the host computer which is capable of producing the number of audio outputs required for the chosen surround format. For example, standard 3/2 would require five audio outputs and 5.1 channel surround would require six. Of course, the sound reproduction system would also need to feature multiple speakers and amplifiers to match the number of channels of the chosen format.

Creating a surround output buss

You configure the output of Cubase SX for surround sound by creating a surround output buss in the outputs section of the VST Connections window, selected from the Devices menu. Proceed as follows:

- Open the VST Connections window and click on the outputs tab.
- Click on the Add button to open the Add bus dialogue. The choice of formats provided in the Configuration menu includes mono, stereo, LRCS, standard 3/2 (5.0), 5.1 surround and various other left/right/centre/surround/LFE permutations and quadraphonic (Quadro) formats (Figure 16.3). Most of these are described above. Quadro allows the setting up of mixes based upon the four channel quadraphonic format devised for vinyl records in the early 1970s.
- Select a surround format from the Configuration menu. Since it is such a popular format many readers may choose the 5.1 surround format. Once chosen, the details of the new surround buss are displayed in the VST Connections window (Figure 16.4). Make sure that the channels are routed to the appropriate output ports of your audio hardware.

Figure 16.3
The Add output bus dialogue allows you to add an output buss in your chosen surround format

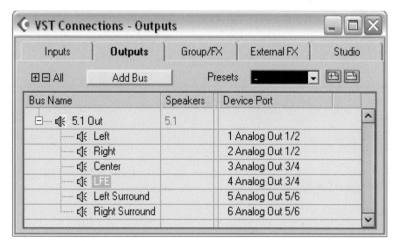

Figure 16.4
5.1 surround buss in the VST Connections window

- When you create a new surround buss, a surround output channel strip is added in the Mixer (Figure 16.5). The meters follow the order of the channels as listed in the VST Connections window (from left to right).

Figure 16.5
5.1 surround output bus channel in the Mixer

At this point, any audio-based channels routed to the surround buss may be mixed in surround, using the surround panner. The surround panner is available only when a surround buss is chosen in the output routing menu.

Using surround channels

Regular Audio tracks are normally in mono or stereo format but when they are added to the Project they can also be assigned as surround channels in the Add track dialogue. A surround channel is appropriate for playback of multichannel interleaved files. Libraries of 5.1 surround files of this type are already available.

Surround format channels are also applicable to software samplers which include 5.1 surround support, such as Steinberg's Halion sampler. In this case, the last six outputs of Halion (outputs 13-18) are configured as a 5.1 surround output and these appear in Cubase SX's Mixer on a dedicated 5.1 VSTi surround channel. Multichannel interleaved samples recorded in 5.1 surround and loaded into Halion can now be triggered, and heard via Cubase SX (Figure 16.6). Try the supplied '5.1 Movie SFX' program. Notice how the 5.1 VSTi channel (Hal 13-18) does NOT feature a surround panner since the surround panning of a 5.1 source is not adjustable within Cubase SX. All other functions of a 5.1 channel operate just like regular mono and stereo channels.

Figure 16.6
Halion's 5.1 surround output appears as a 5.1 VSTi channel (Hal 13-18) in the Mixer

Mixing surround sound

To commence mixing for surround sound you would normally route all channels in the Mixer to the surround output bus. This is selected in the output routing pop-up menu in the upper section of the channel strip (Figure 16.7).

Alternatively, you can route a channel signal directly to any of the surround outputs using the other routing options in the menu. When a surround output is chosen for regular audio-based channels, a miniature surround panner replaces the normal pan control in the Mixer channel strip (Figure 16.8). This allows you to graphically place the sound within the surround soundfield. The current position is indicated by a blue marker. You can move the position of the marker by clicking and dragging within the display. A slightly larger version of the surround panner is available in the extended part of the Mixer.

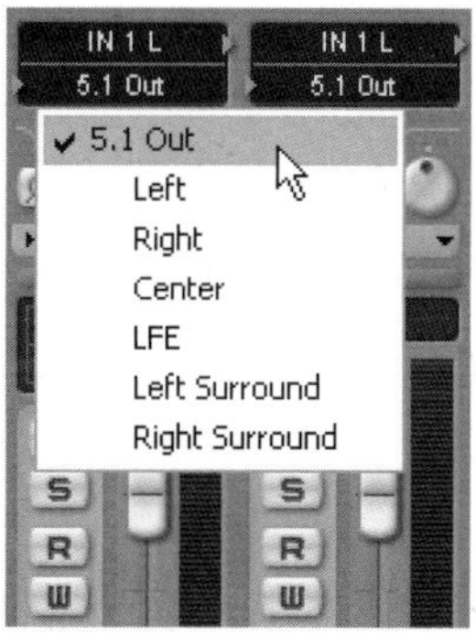

Using the surround panner plug-in

For more elaborate control of the surround pan position, double click on the surround panner control in the channel strip. This opens the more detailed surround panner interface (Figure 16.9).

The surround panner interface displays a representation of the speaker configuration for the chosen surround format. The level of each channel is indicated next to each virtual speaker where 0dB represents the full power of the source audio signal. The level is also indicated graphically by thick blue lines which appear at each virtual speaker. The relative levels of the channels are controlled by dragging a ball within the display, at which time the blue lines change length and the levels indicated are updated. Any of the channels can be switched off by Alt-clicking on the speaker icon. Modifier keys facilitate the moving of the ball as follows:

- Holding Ctrl/Command + Shift while dragging in the display restricts movement to the x axis (horizontal) only.
- Holding Ctrl/Command while dragging in the display restricts movement to the y axis (vertical) only.
- Holding Alt while dragging in the display restricts movement to the diagonal between the top left and lower right corners.
- Holding Ctrl/Command + Alt while dragging in the display restricts movement to the diagonal between the lower left and top right corners.

If you have a wheel mouse you can move the ball using the wheel where no modifier key provides horizontal movement, holding Ctrl provides vertical movement and holding Shift in either case allows movement in fine increments. To ensure the correct functioning of wheel movements, make sure the mouse pointer is inside the SurroundPan display.

The lower part of the interface features the following:

- Mode menu – this governs the manner in which the speakers are distributed around the listening position. Standard and Position modes

Figure 16.7 (left)
Select the surround output bus in the Mixer channel output routing pop-up menu

Figure 16.8 (right)
The miniature SurroundPan control in the Mixer channel strip

Figure 16.9
The surround panner plug-in interface

Tip

Hold Alt while moving a Divergence dial in the SurroundPan interface to move all three Divergence dials simultaneously.

produce aligned front speakers as found in a cinema auditorium and Angle mode implements speakers which are equi-distant from the listening position. The default setting is Standard mode.

- Mono/stereo pop-up – determines the manner in which the single mono marker or dual stereo markers move around the display. This is particularly relevant for stereo signals where the movement of the right channel marker is mirrored on the x axis or the y axis, or both simultaneously. ëMono Mixí is the default setting for mono channels and 'Y-Mirror' is the default for stereo channels. The left and right channels of a stereo signal routed through a surround panner set to Mono Mix are added together before entering the plug-in. A mono signal routed through a surround panner set to a stereo mode is split into two channels before entering the plug-in.
- Centre level dial – determines the percentage by which the centre channel provides the centre image where 100% results in full use of the centre channel, (in which case the left and right front channels are reduced in level when the marker is in the central vertical area), and 0% results in zero use of the centre channel, (in which case the left and right front channels are raised in level when the marker is in the central vertical area). When the centre channel has been reduced to 0% the left/right front channels behave like a regular stereo setup where the centre sound is produced by the in-phase signals of the left and right source signals.
- LFE dial – determines the amount of the source signal which should be routed to the LFE channel. This is relevant only when the surround configuration includes an LFE channel(as in 5.1 surround).
- Divergence dials – control the differentiation of the distribution of the source signal between the different channels where levels higher than 0% result in a less exclusive distribution. i.e. the higher the percentage on the dial the less differentiation between the corresponding channels.

Exporting a surround sound mix

Once you have completed a surround mix you may wish to export it for later encoding in the chosen surround format. For this purpose, Cubase SX's Audio Mixdown function (File menu) features two additional options in the Channels section pop-up menu (Figure 16.10).

For a 5.1 channel surround mix, the surround options function as follows:

- N. Chan. Split – for a 5.1 surround mix (for example) results in the export of six mono audio files corresponding to each of the channels. The length of the files corresponds to the positions of the left and right locators. The files can later be imported into another application for encoding in the chosen surround format.
- N. Chan. Interleaved – for a 5.1 surround mix (for example) results in the export of a single multiple channel interleaved file where each channel corresponds to one of the surround channels. The length of the file corresponds to the positions of the left and right locators. This is not a common format and so may not be recognised by all other applications.

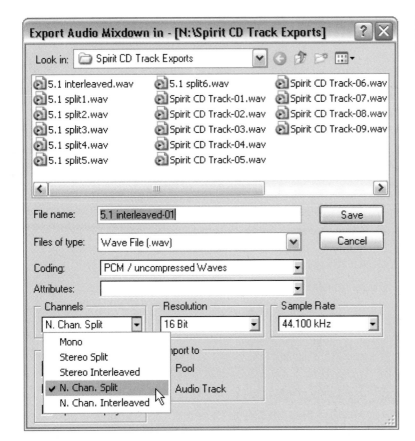

Figure 16.10
The surround export options in the Audio Mixdown dialogue

For other surround formats, the number of mono audio files or channels included in the multiple channel interleaved file produced is dependent upon the number of channels used in the surround output bus, as chosen in the Audio Mixdown output menu.

Windows users may export an encoded 5.1 surround file by selecting 'Windows Media Audio Pro' in the 'Files of type' menu. The resulting WMA surround file is recognised by Windows Media 9 capable programs under Windows XP only. Other operating systems are unable to decode the surround information.

VST instruments

This chapter outlines the installation and basic use of VST Instruments within Cubase SX and describes some of the VST Instruments supplied with the program.

What are VST Instruments?

VST is an abbreviation for 'Virtual Studio Technology' or 'Virtual Studio' and was introduced by Steinberg in 1996 for their Cubase VST MIDI+Audio sequencing software. VST Instrument is an abbreviation for 'Virtual Studio Instrument' and the term is often shortened still further to read 'VSTi'.

VST-compatible audio effects and processing units come in the form of 'plug-ins' which can be added to the host software when required (as described in Chapter 12). VST 2.0 technology took this concept one stage further by introducing a special kind of plug-in which allows the transmitting and receiving of MIDI data as well as audio. This encouraged the development of more sophisticated regular plug-ins but, more importantly, it inspired the development of software synthesis and sampling instruments which can operate within the convenient environment of the host software. These became known as VST Instruments.

A VST Instrument could be a software synthesizer or sampler, a software drum module or some other virtual sound-making device and, once activated inside the host software (e.g. Cubase SX/SL), it can be played via MIDI using an external MIDI keyboard or triggered from an existing MIDI track. In many respects, VST Instruments behave in the same way as their real-world counterparts, the only major difference being that they reside inside your computer.

System requirements and performance issues

VST Instruments require a VST 2.0 (or later) host application like Steinberg Cubase SX/SL and most run on both the PC and Mac computer platforms. Cubase SX should already be running successfully on the computer before you install a VST Instrument. Once installed, the VST Instrument may be loaded from a menu and activated inside Cubase SX similar to a regular plug-in effect. The sounds are triggered via MIDI, either in real-time using an external MIDI keyboard (or other controller) or from a recorded MIDI track. There are a number of computer hardware factors which affect the performance and playability of a VST Instrument. Paramount among these are CPU speed, the amount of RAM memory and audio hardware latency.

CPU speed and RAM

Software synthesis, software sampling and software effects processing are CPU-intensive activities. The number of voices available for any software instrument is, therefore, directly related to the amount of CPU power available. The drain on CPU power varies according to the number of notes being played simultaneously and according to the complexity of the tone being produced by the instrument. Many software samplers and sample-based drum modules require substantial amounts of RAM in order to run smoothly. This is particularly true for those which use disk-streaming techniques where greater use of RAM memory results in less strain on the hard disk.

Latency

Latency is the delay between the input and output of a digital audio system (expressed in samples or milliseconds). All digital audio systems take a small amount of time to respond to a user input and process the data through their hardware and software. This affects real-time performance with VST instruments since it imposes a slight delay between the moment you press a note on your MIDI keyboard and the moment you hear the sound from the instrument. If the delay is too long then it becomes impossible to play in real-time. (Real-world electronic musical instruments also suffer from a similar delay). For real-time performance, the audio hardware should preferably be capable of latency times of less than 10ms. Achieving this requires a professional-quality audio card/hardware with a special ASIO driver. (See relevant internet sites and software/hardware developer documentation for precise details of ASIO drivers and hardware system recommendations).

The supplied VST Instruments

Cubase SX is supplied with a number of VST instruments, including the A1, Monologue and Embracer synthesizers, the LM7 drum module and the VB1 bass synthesizer. These are pre-installed on the computer in the 'Vstplugins' folder alongside the regular plug-ins. VST instruments from previous versions of the program are also available on the installation DVD.

Installing third party developer VST Instruments

There are a wide range of VST Instruments supplied by third party developers (see Table 17.4 at the end of this chapter). These are installed on your computer in a similar fashion to regular plug-ins. Follow the installation instructions supplied with the chosen VST Instrument and, when complete, you normally find the relevant file(s) located in the Cubase 'vstplugins' folder alongside the regular plug-in files. In some cases, you may need to manually drag the installed plug-in file into the vstplugins folder. When you next launch Cubase SX, the newly installed VST Instrument is added to the list of available instruments within the software.

Activating and using VST Instruments

Before you can play or open the graphical user interface for a VST Instrument it must first be activated in one of the slots of the VST Instruments panel. This is opened by selecting 'VST Instruments' in the Devices menu or by pressing

Figure 17.1
VST Instruments panel

Figure 17.2
Click on a VST Instrument slot to open
the pop-up selection menu

Figure 17.3 (right)
Click on the Edit button to open the
interface for the VSTi

F11 on the computer keyboard (Figure 17.1).

To load a VST Instrument into one of the panel's slots, click on a blank name field. This opens a pop-up menu containing the VST Instruments which are available on your system (Figure 17.2).

Selecting a VST Instrument from the menu loads it into the slot and its name appears in the name field. The instrument is activated/de-activated by clicking on the slot's power button. Once activated, the appropriate number of VST Instrument channels is automatically created in the Mixer (VST Instruments like HALion, Kontakt, Model E, Battery and DR-008 feature multiple output channels). Just like regular audio channels, VSTi channels are used to regulate the volume, pan position, EQ and routing of the audio output signal from the instrument.

To open the GUI (graphical user interface) for the VST Instrument click on the edit button (lower case 'e') in the VST Instrument slot (Figure 17.3).

In order to trigger the VST Instrument via MIDI you must first allocate the output port of a MIDI track to the instrument. If you intend to trigger the instrument live from a MIDI keyboard, you must also allocate an appropriate MIDI input port for the MIDI track.

Select a MIDI track and click in the 'out' field in the basic settings section of the Inspector. This opens the pop-up output menu where the name of any currently active VST Instruments are found alongside the other output ports (Figure 17.4). Select the desired VST Instrument and choose an appropriate MIDI channel (not necessary with all VST Instruments since many are permanently set to Omni mode). With the Record enable button or the Monitor button activated you can now play the VST Instrument from an external MIDI keyboard. If desired, you can make a recording onto the chosen track. You can also trigger the VST Instrument using an existing pre-recorded MIDI track if you set the track's output port to the VST Instrument.

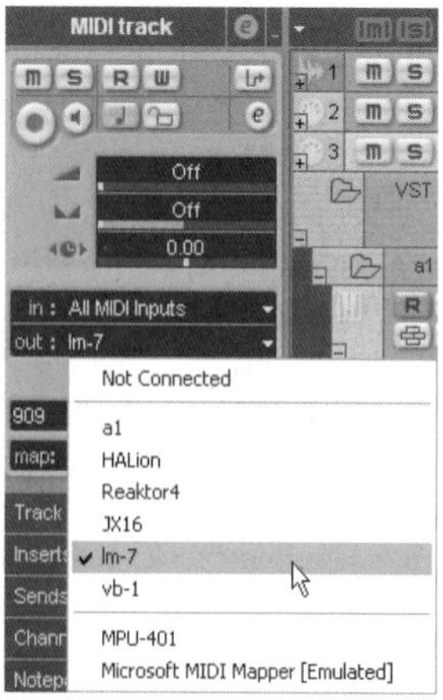

Figure 17.4
Allocate a MIDI track to a VST Instrument in
the 'out' field

VST Instrument automation in Cubase SX

Automation of VST Instrument parameters is achieved by activating the Write button in the GUI window of the instrument and recording the movements of the controls in real-time (Figure 17.5). The automation is written in normal playback mode; activating the record button on the Transport panel is NOT necessary. To play back the automation, activate the Read button in the GUI window of the VST Instrument.

Figure 17.5
To record the movements of the controls, activate the Write button in the GUI window of the VST Instrument

Alternatively, automation may be created in the VST Instrument Automation subtracks in the Project window. When you first activate a VST instrument, a VSTi device track and a number of VSTi audio tracks appear in the Project window. The VSTi device track and associated sub-tracks are used to edit any automation already recorded and may also be used to create automation data from scratch using the Draw tools (Figure 17.6).

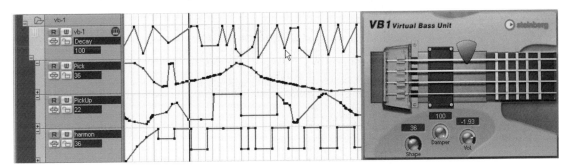

VSTi automation is excellent for producing filter sweeps and special effects and can add an extra dimension to synthesizer parts. For example, try using the Draw tools in the VST Instrument Automation subtracks in the Project window to create shapes which modulate the values of the filter cutoff, resonance and drive controls of the supplied A1 synthesizer (Figure 17.7). Make sure the Read button is activated in the VSTi interface window.

Figure 17.6 (above)
Create or edit VST Instrument automation in the VST Instrument Automation subtracks in the Project window

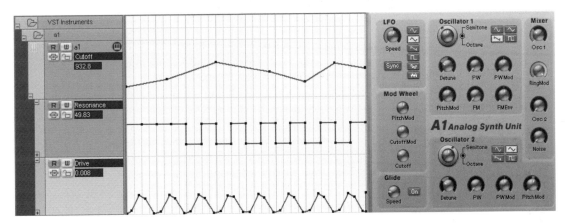

Figure 17.7
Modulating the cutoff, resonance and drive controls of the supplied A1 synth using automation curves in the VST Instrument Automation subtracks

Converting VSTi tracks into regular audio tracks

MIDI tracks which trigger VST Instruments can be directly converted into audio files for use on regular audio tracks using Cubase SX's Export/Audio Mixdown function in the File menu. Export/Audio Mixdown exports non-muted VSTi tracks (and audio tracks) between the left and right locators to an audio file. This is helpful when your computer is running out of system resources since regular audio tracks use less CPU and less RAM than VSTi tracks. (See Chapter 11 for details of Export/Audio Mixdown.)

Instrument Freeze

An alternative to the above technique for freeing up system resources is to use the Instrument Freeze function. This allows you to freeze the performance of a VST instrument so that it is played back from a 'ghost' audio track rather than being calculated in real-time. Instrument Freeze takes into account all non-muted MIDI parts which are triggering the chosen VST instrument and operates over the entire length of the Project. To freeze an instrument, proceed as follows:

- Make sure that the VST instrument performance plays back exactly as required, including activating the appropriate Read buttons if you have recorded any automation.

- Set Length in the Project Setup window (Project menu) to no longer than the length of the Project.

Figure 17.8
Freezing the A1 VSTi

- Open the VST Instruments panel from the Devices menu (or press F11 on the computer keyboard).

- Locate the VSTi slot for the instrument you wish to freeze and click on its 'Instrument Freeze' button to the left of the slot (Figure 17.8).

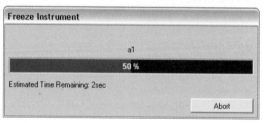

- In the 'Freeze instrument options' dialogue which appears, you can choose to freeze the instrument only, in which case any insert effects on the VSTi channel(s) are not frozen with the instrument, or you can choose to freeze both the instrument and any insert effects on the VSTi channel(s). A further option 'Unload instrument when frozen' helps free up still more computer resources by unloading the VSTi after the freeze operation. This is particularly welcome for RAM hungry sampler plug-ins like Halion and Kontakt.

The resulting 'ghost' audio file is stored in a new Freeze folder, located in the Project folder. All MIDI tracks/parts and VSTi device tracks relevant to the frozen instrument are now greyed out and cannot be edited. However, the

VSTi audio channels remain active and operate as if you are still triggering the VST instrument in the normal way. Frozen VST instruments can at any time be un-frozen by clicking on the Instrument Freeze button a second time.

The supplied VST Instruments

There now follow descriptions of the VST Instruments supplied with the program.

A1 Synthesizer

The A1 (Figure 17.9) is a classic virtual analogue synthesizer featuring two oscillators, a resonant filter, an LFO and a built-in chorus/flanger. It has a maximum polyphony of 16 voices and 128 program slots.

Figure 17.9
The A1 analogue synthesizer

Control Interface

The GUI for the A1 features the following:

Oscillator section The A1 has two similar oscillators. These feature tuning controls which can be adjusted in semitone or octave steps and waveform selector buttons providing sine, triangle, sawtooth and pulse shapes. The oscillators may be detuned in semitone steps and when a pulse waveform is chosen pulse width and pulse width modulation controls allow the changing of the width of the waveform between square and narrow pulse widths and the modulation of the width according to the LFO. The pitch of both oscillators may also be modulated by the LFO. Oscillator 1 features FM and FM Envelope parameters. When using FM, it is recommended that you reduce the output level of oscillator 2 to zero in the mixer section. The FM control regulates how much the frequency of oscillator 1 is modulated by oscillator 2. The FM envelope control determines how much the filter envelope affects the frequency modulation.

LFO section The LFO section provides a low frequency oscillator signal which is used to modulate the pulse width or pitch of the oscillators, or the cut-off frequency of the filter. A sync button enables synchronisation of the LFO to the current tempo of Cubase SX. Sine, triangle, sawtooth, square, sample and hold and random waveshapes are available.

Mixer section The mixer section features Osc 1 and Osc 2 parameters which regulate the levels of oscillators 1 and 2. A ring modulation parameter determines the level of the ring modulation (multiplication) of oscillators 1 and 2. A noise parameter determines the amount of white noise to be added to the overall signal. To use the noise generator alone, reduce the levels of oscillators 1 and 2 to zero.

Filter section After being mixed the composite signal is routed to the filter section. This consists of a resonant filter with 12dB-per-octave or 24dB-per-octave filter slope characteristics. Four filter types are available including low pass, high pass, band pass and notch. The cut-off control determines the cut-off or centre frequency for the different filter types. The resonance control emphasises the frequencies around the cut-off point for all filter types. A drive parameter adds distortion to the signal. The Envelope control regulates the amount of modulation of the cut-off frequency by the filter envelope and the Velocity control determines the amount of modulation of the cut-off frequency according to the velocity of incoming MIDI notes. The Cutoff mod parameter determines how much LFO modulation is applied to the filter cut-off and the Keytrack control allows the modulation of the cutoff frequency according to pitch (keyboard tracking). A standard ADSR envelope (attack, decay, sustain, release) controls how the value of the cut-off frequency evolves over time. The ADSR parameters are adjusted using the rotary controls or by clicking and dragging directly in the envelope display.

Amplifier section The amplifier section features a standard ADSR envelope which determines how the amplitude level of the sound evolves over time. The ADSR parameters may be adjusted using the rotary controls or by clicking and dragging directly in the envelope display. A volume slider controls the overall level of the output and a velocity slider determines how much the velocity of incoming MIDI notes affects the level.

Chorus/Flanger section The A1 features a Chorus/Flanger section. This includes a speed control for regulating the modulation rate of the effect's LFO, a feedback control for regulating the sweeping characteristics of the sound and a depth control for regulating the LFO modulation depth. A Quad button produces a richer multi-tap chorus effect. Overall the Chorus/Flanger section adds stereo width, sweetens and enriches sounds.

Mod Wheel section and Glide control The Mod Wheel section determines how the modulation wheel affects pitch modulation, cut-off modulation and the cut-off frequency. This is important for real-time performance control with the modulation wheel of the controller keyboard. The pitch modulation control regulates how much the LFO affects the pitch of the sound relative to the modulation wheel position; this is useful for setting up vibrato and pitch

Info

For more details about filters, see the section entitled 'Audio effects in theory / Filtering' in Chapter 12.

sweep effects. Cut-off modulation regulates how much the LFO affects the cut-off frequency relative to the modulation wheel position; this is good for automatic wah-wah and similar filtering effects. Cut-off regulates how much the modulation wheel affects the cut-off frequency; this is applicable to sweeping the cut-off frequency of the filter in real-time performance. The Glide control applies a portamento effect to melodic input where the pitch glides from one note to the next rather than changing instantaneously. The speed control governs how quickly the pitch glides between notes.

User guide

Preliminary experiments with the A1 revolve around the choice of waveform and the relative tunings of oscillators 1 and 2. The FM, FMEnv and RingMod controls are rich sources for new timbres and the Drive parameter in the Filter section helps give sounds definition and character. The inclusion of chorus and flange effects adds to the final identity of sounds and the graphical envelope windows help you set up envelopes quickly and easily. The A1 is a highly adaptable synthesizer which is particularly suited to the creation of bass, pad and synth lead sounds and sound effects. It is a good instrument for testing MIDI effects and in this context benefits from the information field in the centre of the GUI which shows the name, value and associated MIDI controller number as you pass the mouse pointer over each control.

Steinberg VB1

The VB1 is a virtual model of a bass guitar. It features 4 note polyphony and has 16 program slots.

The VB1 GUI features an image of the working parts of a bass guitar. These can be moved around within the interface to produce different tones. The five elements which can be manipulated are as follows:

- Pick position – regulates the attack and tone, assuming a 'mellow' character when positioned far from the bridge and a 'bright' character when positioned close to the bridge. When positioned above the pickup, the sound becomes more 'plucked'.
- Pickup position – regulates the tone of the sound, where a position close to the bridge picks up more upper harmonics from the virtual strings and a position far from the bridge produces a 'hollow' sound.
- Shape control – determines the shape of the impulse waveform which provides the initial virtual 'pluck' of the string.
- Damper control – applies a dampening action to the vibration of the virtual strings.
- Volume control – regulates the output volume.

Updating sounds on the VB1 involves manipulating the moveable objects of the interface with the mouse. To create bass sounds with very 'sharp' attack characteristics set the dampening control to its most

Figure 17.10
The VB1 virtual bass synth

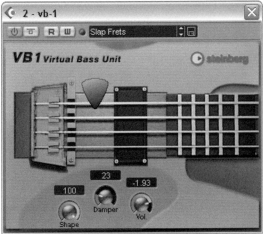

dampened setting and the shape control to its maximum setting. Adjust the pickup and pick positions to achieve the required final result. To create more synth-like tones try moderate dampening, with the shape control set between 0 and 50, and the pick at its furthest position from the bridge.

Although only equipped with five parameters, the VB1 is capable of producing a wide variety of bass sounds. It works best in the lower octaves. It is particularly good at producing plucked tones and works well when combined with other VST Instruments to produce composite bass sounds.

LM7 drum module

The LM7 is a virtual drum module which uses samples loaded into RAM memory to produce its sounds (Figure 17.11). It has 24-bit resolution and 12 voice polyphony. It features 12 drum pads each of which has volume, tuning and pan control.

Figure 17.11
LM7 drum module

Control interface

The LM7 GUI features twelve drum pads in the lower half of the window arranged in two rows of six pads with their corresponding volume and tuning sliders in the upper half of the display. A global velocity control determines how much the velocity of incoming notes affects the amplitude of the LM7 output, where 0% is no effect and 100% is maximum effect. The panorama control can be set individually for the currently selected pad (indicated by a yellow LED) and controls the pan position of each sound in the stereo image. A volume slider provides overall level control.

User guide

The LM7 drum sounds are triggered by clicking on the pads with the mouse or according to incoming MIDI notes from a MIDI track or live MIDI keyboard. When a pad is triggered its LED is illuminated.

The LM7 is a highly accurate drum module. Once the MIDI part has been recorded, the samples are triggered with pin-point accuracy which is difficult to match in a real-world unit. The load on the CPU is minimal since the LM7 triggers samples which are loaded into RAM memory. The LM7 is good for demos and basic arrangements and the 909 drum set's closed hi-hat is an ideal target for the Metronome's MIDI click.

Drum sets are loaded and saved in banks of three sets using the File menu above the GUI. The drum sets are selected using the program menu.

Combining Cubase with applications from other developers

You can significantly augment the creative potential of Cubase SX/SL by combining it with some of the more elaborate applications and VST Instruments supplied by other developers, especially those featuring modular synthesis environments and sampling. This is particularly relevant for those using Cubase SX for electronic music composition, orchestral composition/arranging, and sound effects creation. Favourites include Propellerhead Reason software synthesis studio (not actually a VSTi), Native Instruments Reaktor sound studio, Native Instruments Kontakt software sampler, Applied Acoustics Systems Tassman physical modelling synthesizer, and Steinberg Halion sampler. Reason is not available as a VSTi but is easily integrated into Cubase using the Rewire protocol, while the others may be integrated as standard VST Instruments. These applications provide much more than ordinary VSTi software synthesizers and musical instruments; they are often complete studio, synthesis, sampling, sequencing and sound processing environments in their own right. Reason provides analogue synthesizers, samplers, drum machines and effects together with sequencing, mixing and patching features, all within an intuitive virtual rack environment. Kontakt is a powerful software sampler in an elegant and easy-to-use virtual rack, supplied complete with its own on-board convolution effect (for convincing reverberation) and an outstanding library, the cornerstone of which is a special version of the Vienna Symphonic Orchestra sample collection. Tassman provides a modular environment where you can build your own musical instruments based upon physical modelling, for truly authentic re-creations of acoustic instruments as well as hybrid instruments never heard before. Reaktor is probably the ultimate modular sound studio, allowing you to build your own instruments and effects and providing a vast library of synthesizers, samplers, effects, drum machines and sequencers (Figure 17.12). All these applications integrate well into the Cubase software environment.

Figure 17.12
Reaktor's Space Drone synthesizer in action in Cubase SX

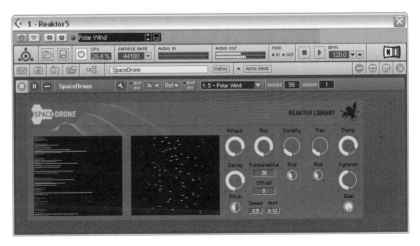

Summary

VST Instruments provide a convenient means of accessing high quality sound sources within the convenient environment of Cubase SX. All that is required to trigger the sounds is one external keyboard connected to your computer via MIDI and a low latency audio card. This arrangement cuts down on your need to have a large scale MIDI network and therefore saves physical space in your recording studio/working environment. In addition, VST Instruments do not develop electronic faults and are not subject to the usual wear-and-tear suffered by real-world instruments.

The only drawback is that running VST Instruments alongside audio tracks and plug-ins requires a rather powerful processor. If the CPU load becomes a problem try using Instrument Freeze or convert your VST Instrument tracks into audio tracks (these options put less strain on the CPU). Unlike MIDI tracks which trigger external MIDI devices, MIDI tracks which trigger VST Instruments can be converted directly into audio data.

There are now an extremely wide range of VST Instruments available, representing a vast array of different instrument types and synthesis techniques. Table 17.1 lists some of the main developers and their products.

Table 17.1 VST Instruments list

Developer	VST Instrument	Description
Antares	Kantos	Audio controlled software synthesizer
Applied Acoustics	Tassman	Modular synthesizer based on physical modelling
Applied Acoustics	Lounge Lizard	Electric piano
Arturia	Storm	Virtual multi-module studio
Big Tick	Angelina	Vocal pad synthesizer (using formant synthesis)
Big Tick	Cheeze Machine	String ensemble synthesizer (Free)
Bitheadz	Unity AS-1	Virtual analogue synthesizer
Bitheadz	Unity DS-1	Sampler
Bioroid	Turntablist Pro	Turntable emulation and scratch mixer
Bitshift Audio	pHATmatic	REX file player
Bitshift Audio	pHATmatic Pro	Loop player and sample slicer
Bojo	Impulse	Virtual analogue synthesizer
Bojo	Organ One	Organ
Desaster Development	Ruction	Sample sequencer
Edirol	HyperCanvas	GM sound module
Edirol	SuperQuartet	Sample-based sound module
Emagic	EVP73	Electric piano
FXpansion	DR-002	Freeware basic virtual drum machine
FXpansion	DR-008	Modular drum synthesis/sample player
FXpansion	Mysteron	Theremin emulation (Free)
GForce	MTron	Mellotron emulation
Girl	Girl	Sample/loop manipulator and sequencer

Table 17.1 VST Instruments list (cont)

Developer	VST Instrument	Description
Green Oak	Crystal	Modular synthesizer
IK	Sample Tank	Sample player/sound module
Image Line	DX10	FM synthesizer
Image Line	Wasp	Virtual analogue synthesizer
Jorgen Aase	Energy Pro	Step sequencer/synthesizer
Koblo	Gamma 9000	Drum synthesizer
Koblo	Stella 9000	Polyphonic sampler
Koblo	Vibra 1000	Mono virtual analogue synthesizer (Free Mac only)
Koblo	Vibra 6000	Mono virtual analogue synthesizer
Koblo	Vibra 9000	Advanced virtual analogue synthesizer
Lin Plug	Gakstoar Alpha	Virtual analogue synthesizer (2 oscillator version)
Lin Plug	Gakstoar Delta	Virtual analogue synthesizer (4 oscillator version)
Lin Plug	Rupsta Gamma	Virtual drum machine
LoftSoft	FM Heaven	FM synthesizer
mda	DX10	FM synthesizer (Free)
mda	ePiano	Electric piano (Free)
mda	JX10	Virtual analogue synth (Free)
mda	Piano	Piano (Free)
MHC	Space Synthesizer	Ambient texture synthesizer
Muon Software	Atom Pro	Simple but powerful virtual analogue synthesizer
Muon Software	Tau Pro	TB303-style acid bass synth emulation
Muon Software	Electron	Virtual analogue synthesizer
Muon Software	Positron	Virtual analogue synthesizer
Native Instruments	Absynth	Modular synthesizer
Native Instruments	Battery	Sample-based drum and percussion module
Native Instruments	B4	Hammond B3 tonewheel organ emulation
Native Instruments	FM7	FM synthesizer
Native Instruments	Kontakt	Sophisticated sampler
Native Instruments	Reaktor Session	Reaktor ensemble player
Native Instruments	Pro-53	Prophet 5 analogue synthesizer emulation
Native Instruments	Reaktor	Powerful modular synthesizer/rhythm processor/software sampler
PlugSound	Vol. 1: Keyboards	Sample-based sound module
PlugSound	Vol. 2: Fretted	Sample-based sound module
PlugSound	Vol. 3: Drums	Sample-based sound module
PlugSound	Vol. 4: Hip Hop Toolkit	Sample-based sound module
PlugSound	Vol. 5: Synth	Sample-based sound module
reFX	Quadra SID 6581	C-64 SID chip emulation synthesizer
rgcAudio	Pentagon I	Virtual analogue synthesizer (4 oscillators)
rgcAudio	Square I	Virtual analogue synthesizer (3 oscillators)
rgcAudio	Triangle I	Virtual analogue synthesizer (Free)

Table 17.1 VST Instruments list (cont)

Developer	VST Instrument	Description
rgcAudio	Triangle II	Virtual analogue synthesizer (Free)
Spectrasonics	Atmosphere	Dream pad sound module based on sampling
Spectrasonics	Stylus	Vinyl remix groove and sample manipulation module
Spectrasonics	Trilogy	Electric, acoustic and synth bass module
SpeedSoft	Virtual Sampler	Software sampler
SpeedSoft	VX 7	FM synthesizer
Steinberg	D'cota	Advanced analogue, spectrum and wave impulse synthesis
Steinberg	Groove Agent	Virtual drummer
Steinberg	HALion	Sophisticated software sampler based on hard disk streaming
Steinberg	Hypersonic	Virtual music workstation
Steinberg/MDA	JX16	Virtual analogue synthesizer
Steinberg	LM4 MK II	Virtual drum machine (18 drum pad version)
Steinberg	Model E	Minimoog Model D analogue synthesizer emulation
Steinberg	Neon	Basic virtual analogue synthesizer
Steinberg	Plex	Restructuring synthesizer by Wolfgang Palm
Steinberg	The Grand	Grand piano
Steinberg	VB-1	Virtual bass guitar
Steinberg	Virtual Guitarist	Rhythm Guitar module
Synapse	Junglist	Virtual analogue synthesizer
Synapse	Plucked String	Plucked string synthesizer based on physical modelling
Synapse	Scorpion	Virtual analogue synthesizer
TC Works	Mercury-I	Virtual analogue synthesizer
TC Works	Spark Modular	Modular synthesizer
Tobybear	Deconstructor	Sample manipulator
Tobybear	Electric Cowboy	Guitar synthesizer based on physical modelling
Virsyn	Cube	Additive synthesizer
Virsyn	Tera	Modular synthesizer
Waldorf	Attack	Drum and percussion synthesizer
Waldorf	PPG Wave 2.V	PPG Wave 2.2 wavetable synthesizer emulation

The Tempo track

In Cubase SX, tempo is managed in two modes: Fixed tempo mode and Tempo track mode. These operate as follows:

- Fixed tempo mode – is when the tempo button in the Transport panel is de-activated. In this mode, the tempo of Cubase SX follows the single Fixed tempo shown in the Transport panel.
- Tempo track mode – is when the tempo button in the Transport panel is activated. In this mode, tempo-based audio and MIDI tracks (those set to musical time base) follow the tempo changes of the Tempo Track.

The Tempo Track editor is for creating and editing tempo and time signature changes (Figure 18.1). It is opened by selecting Tempo Track from the Project menu, or by pressing Ctrl/Command + T on the computer keyboard. (All time signature settings are active both in fixed and tempo track modes.)

The Tempo Track editor is dominated by the tempo display area which shows tempo in beats-per-minute (bpm) on the vertical axis and time in the chosen time format on the horizontal axis. Tempo events are shown as small square handles along the length of the tempo curve. The shape of the curve is changed by dragging the existing handles to new locations or drawing a new curve. The shape of the curve is modified according to the curve type selection where 'jump' mode produces instantaneous tempo changes at each tempo event position, whereas 'ramp' mode produces smooth, gradual

Figure 18.1
The Tempo Track editor

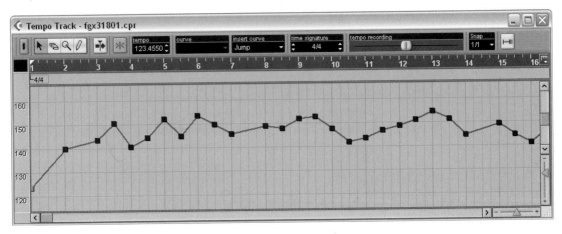

changes between one event and the next. Time signature events are shown in the time signature strip below the ruler.

The Tempo Track editor toolbar

Figure 18.2
The Tempo Track editor toolbar

The Tempo Track editor toolbar features the following:

- Object Selection, Eraser, Zoom and Draw tools – the Object Selection (Pointer) tool is for selecting events by clicking on individual events or dragging a selection box around a group of events. Selected events are shown in red. Once selected the event(s) can be dragged to a new position or edited in the tempo or time signature fields. The Eraser is used to delete unwanted events. The Zoom tool governs the zoom factor of the display and allows you to zoom in to the tempo curve for detailed editing. The Draw tool is used to draw a new tempo curve or add a new time signature.
- Autoscroll – when activated the display follows the position of the project cursor. When de-activated the display remains static and ignores the position of project cursor.
- Snap – governs the snap resolution for the placing of inserted or moved tempo events in the display. When activated, events are placed at the beginning of each bar (when the ruler shows 'bars and beats'), or according to the visible vertical grid lines (when the ruler shows other time formats). The number of visible vertical grid lines depends upon the horizontal zoom setting. When Snap is de-activated events are inserted/moved with no regard for the bar positions or vertical grid lines.
- Tempo field – shows the tempo of the currently selected tempo event. The tempo value can be changed by clicking on the small up/down arrows or by double clicking on the value field and entering a tempo directly using the computer keyboard.
- Curve field – shows, and allows the editing of, the curve type of the currently selected tempo events.
- Insert Curve field – governs the curve type when inserting tempo events using the Draw tool.
- Signature – shows the values of the currently selected time signature event. The time signature can be changed by clicking on the small up/down arrows or by double clicking on the value field and entering a time signature directly using the computer keyboard.
- Tempo recording slider – allows the recording of tempo events in playback mode. This is useful for creating natural-sounding tempo manipulations while listening to the music (works best with MIDI and sliced audio arrangements).

> **Tip**
>
> Use the Zoom tool to quickly zoom in or out of the display. Click once in the display to zoom in and double click to step back through the previous zoom settings.

Exploring the Tempo Track editor

Creating a tempo curve

To create a test tempo curve proceed as follows:

- Activate tempo track mode in the Transport panel and open the Tempo Track editor.
- Activate the Snap button and select 'Ramp' in the Insert Curve field.
- Select the Draw tool and click and drag in the tempo display to create your own test curve. With bars and beats in the ruler and the Snap button active, events are inserted on the first beat of each bar (Figure 18.3).

Figure 18.3
Create a test tempo curve in the Tempo Track editor

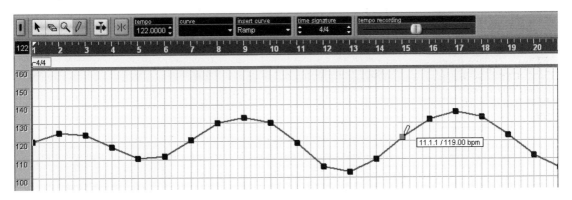

When inserting or moving tempo events, the precision of each tempo value depends upon the vertical zoom setting, where high zoom factors allow the insertion of tempo events whose values include fractional changes in tempo (such as 120.42, 121.62, 122.78bpm or similar). With lower vertical zoom factors the tempo values are always whole integer numbers (such as 120, 121, 122bpm).

Editing the tempo curve

To change the curve type proceed as follows:

- Press Ctrl/Command + A to select all tempo events.
- Select 'Jump' in the Curve field. The shape of the curve is modified as shown in Figure 18.4. You can also modify the shape of specific sections; 'jump' and 'ramp' characteristics can exist within the same curve.

Figure 18.4
Changing the curve type to 'Jump' mode

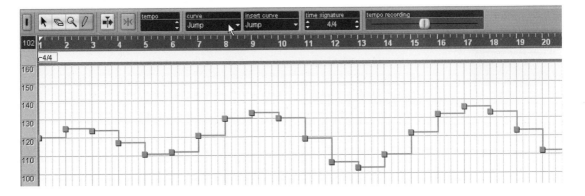

To move one or more tempo events proceed as follows:

- Select one or more tempo events using the Object Selection tool.
- Drag the event(s) to the desired location and release the mouse. The shape of the tempo curve is changed accordingly (Figure 18.5).

Figure 18.5
Moving a group of tempo events

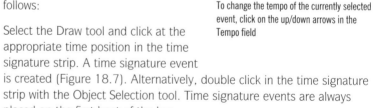

Tip

y selecting 'Increment/Decrement on Left click and drag' in Preferences/User Interface/Controls/ Value Box, you can change the value in the Tempo field by clicking and dragging directly in the field.

To edit the value of a single event in the Tempo field proceed as follows:

- Select the event whose tempo you wish to change.
- Click on the up/down arrows in the Tempo field to change the tempo in whole integer values (Figure 18.6). For precise values click directly in the Tempo field and enter the required tempo using the computer keyboard.

Inserting and editing time signature events

To insert time signature events proceed as follows:

- Select the Draw tool and click at the appropriate time position in the time signature strip. A time signature event is created (Figure 18.7). Alternatively, double click in the time signature strip with the Object Selection tool. Time signature events are always placed on the first beat of the bar.

To edit a time signature event proceed as follows:

- Select the time signature event. A selected time signature event is shown with a red marker box.
- Click on the left or right up/down arrows to modify the appropriate element of the time signature (Figure 18.8).

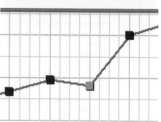

Figure 18.6
To change the tempo of the currently selected event, click on the up/down arrows in the Tempo field

Figure 18.7
Click in the time signature strip with the Draw tool to insert a time signature

Figure 18.8
To change the currently selected time signature click on the up/down arrows in the Time Signature field

Time display format in the ruler

The display characteristics of the ruler can be changed between linear 'bars and beats' and linear time using the options in the lower section of the pop-up ruler options menu. This is opened by clicking on the arrow button to the right of the ruler (Figure 18.9).

Selecting 'Bars+Beats Linear' results in a display where each bar in the ruler is represented by the same horizontal distance, regardless of any tempo changes (Figure 18.10).

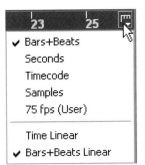

Figure 17.9
Click on the arrow button to the right of the ruler to open the pop-up time display options menu

Tip

There is always at least one tempo event and one time signature at the start of the project. These first events cannot be deleted. Bear in mind, however, that the first tempo event in tempo track mode and the fixed mode tempo may be set to different values.

Figure 18.10
The Tempo Track display in 'Bars+Beats Linear' mode

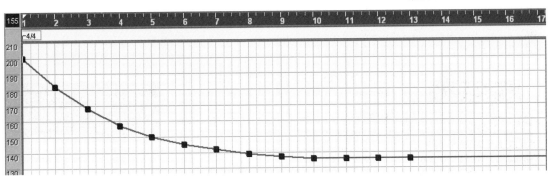

Selecting 'Time Linear' results in a display where the distance between each bar in the ruler becomes greater as the tempo is decreased (Figure 18.11).

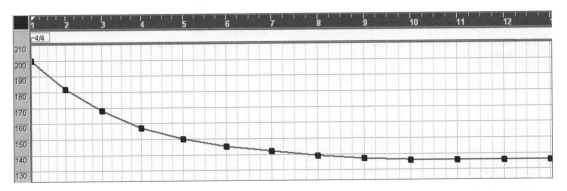

Figure 18.11
The same curve in 'Time Linear' mode

Why use tempo changes?

Tempo changes are not essential for music created with Cubase SX. However, the fact remains that the tempo of most music created using live musicians varies either subtly or dramatically. The changes in tempo add to the liveliness and 'feel' of the performance. Almost all great musical performances involve tempo changes but there are no hard and fast rules about exactly how the changes should be applied. Musical scores often involve tempo-related directions in addition to the notes themselves but, in the context of tempo, no two musical performances are ever exactly identical.

General guidelines for song forms include increasing the tempo on all the choruses and going back to the original tempo for the verses. More subtle manipulations might include wider tempo variations in the early stages of the music and lesser tempo variations as the piece progresses, giving the impression of a group of musicians 'settling' into the 'groove'. Hook lines might benefit from slight tempo increases to generate excitement.

Matching the tempo of Cubase SX to the tempo of a musical performance

There are several methods of matching the tempo of Cubase SX to that of an audio recording of a musical performance. The most immediate and practical technique is to use the 'Merge tempo from tapping' function. This adjusts the tempo according to a sequence of MIDI notes you have recorded in time with the music. Alternatively, you can adjust the tempo using the Time warp tool. The following is a two-stage procedure which uses a combination of these techniques to help you match the tempo with great ease and accuracy. Proceed as follows:

Stage 1

- Activate Tempo track mode on the Transport panel.
- If it is not already present, import the recording of the musical performance onto an Audio track. Activate Linear time base (shown by a clock symbol) on the chosen audio track (Figure 18.12).

Figure 18.12
Activate Linear time base on the chosen Audio track

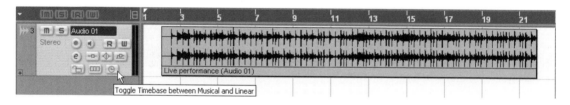

- Select or add a MIDI track. Activate Linear time base and record enable the track.

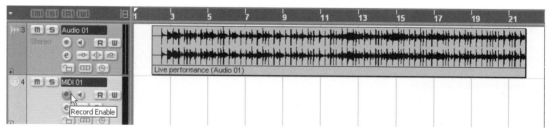

Figure 18.13
Record enable a MIDI track and set it to Linear time base

- Activate record and tap on the MIDI keyboard in time with the audio material. Try using an open hi-hat or rimshot sound recorded at quarter note intervals and start on the first downbeat of the first bar (Figure 18.14).

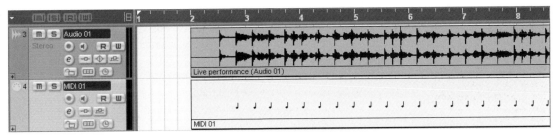

Figure 18.14
MIDI events recorded in time with the music at quarter note intervals

- Play back the recorded MIDI events and make sure their positions correspond to the timing of the audio material. If necessary, edit the positions of the MIDI events in the Key editor (with the Snap button de-activated).
- Select the recorded MIDI part and select 'Merge tempo from tapping' in MIDI/Functions. Select the desired resolution (in this case, quarter notes) and tick 'Begin at Bar Start' (Figure 18.15).
- Clicking on OK in the 'MIDI Merge Options' dialogue inserts tempo events into the tempo track according to the positions of the MIDI notes. Mute the MIDI track and play back the performance with the metronome click activated. The tempo of the click now matches the musical performance. Open the Tempo Track editor if you need to view/edit the tempo events (Figure 18.16).

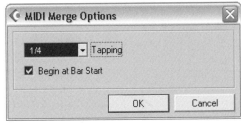

Figure 18.15
Choose the resolution for the tempo events in the 'MIDI Merge Options' dialogue

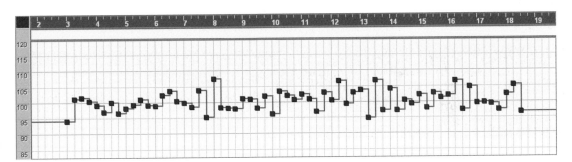

If your MIDI notes were recorded with sufficient accuracy, the first stage of this process may be all you need to establish an accurate tempo map of the musical performance. However, if you need still greater accuracy try completing the second stage outlined below.

Figure 18.16
The resulting tempo events in the Tempo track editor. In this case, the tempo fluctuates around 100bpm

Stage 2
- Add the Marker track in the Project window and set it to linear time base.
- Select the audio event and open the Sample editor.
- Click on the Hitpoint edit button or select 'Calculate hitpoints' in Audio/Hitpoints to calculate hitpoints for the audio material (Figure 18.17).

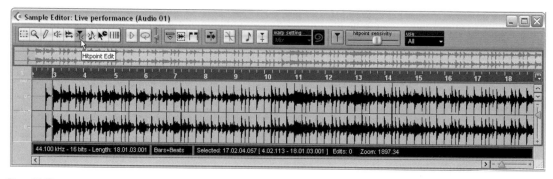

Figure 18.17
Select the audio event, open the Sample editor and select 'Calculate hitpoints' in the Audio/Hitpoints sub-menu

- After having created the hitpoints, adjust the sensitivity slider on the toolbar so that the hitpoints appear at quarter note intervals (i.e. use the same timing resolution as you used in stage 1). Try selecting All in the Use menu or, if you have defined the audio tempo, try 1/4 note. Verify the audio segments by clicking between each pair of hitpoints with the play tool. The objective is to avoid the creation of too many hitpoints, especially those placed closely together, whilst also attempting to end up with at least one hitpoint at each quarter note position. The result when aiming for hitpoints at quarter note intervals resembles Figure 18.18. Do not be too concerned if there are not hitponts at absolutely all the quarter note positions as here we are aiming for a good guide, rather than absolute perfection.

Figure 18.18
Hitpoints created in the Sample editor for the main 'hits' of the musical performance

Figure 18.19
Markers in the Marker track (created from the Hitpoints)

- Select 'Create markers from hitpoints' in the Audio/Hitpoints sub-menu. This creates markers in the Marker track at the positions of the hitpoints. Go back to the Project window to view the markers in the Marker track (Figure 18.19).

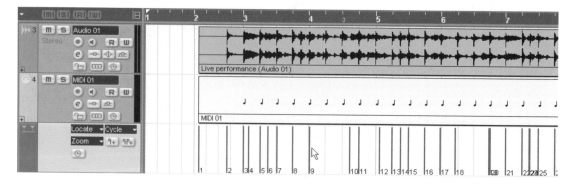

- Select the Time warp tool (in the default Warp grid mode). At this time the tempo events produced in stage 1, (above), appear in the ruler (Figure 18.20).

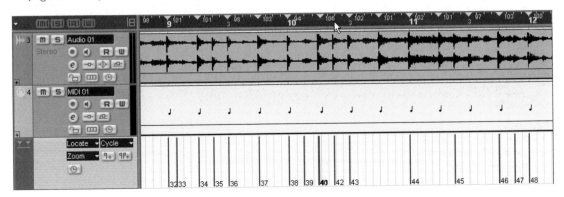

- In the Project window toolbar, activate the Snap button, set the Snap mode menu to events and the Grid type menu to Beat. With Snap mode set to events, the marker events become 'magnetic'.
- A short vertical line appears whenever you place the Time warp tool in the event display at the same position as an existing tempo event (those visible in the ruler). By clicking at this position you can drag the corresponding tempo event to the nearest 'magnetic' marker (the tempo event 'snaps' to the marker), (Figure 18.21). If there is no marker at the position, you may need to drag the tempo event manually with the Snap button de-activated. In this case, line up the tempo event visually to just before the peak in the waveform which corresponds to the 'hit' of the beat.

Figure 18.20
With the Time warp tool selected, the existing tempo events appear in the ruler

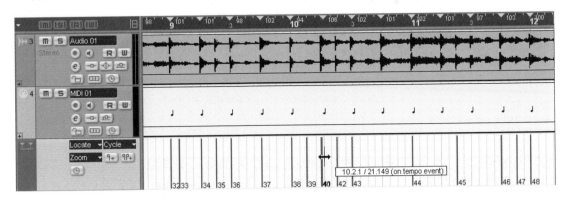

- Work through the tempo events in a similar fashion, lining them up with the nearest marker events. If the tempo events appear to be dragged too far off the tempo, the marker concerned may be inaccurate. Use your judgement while listening to the material in playback mode and seek out the best position for each event. Many tempo events are likely to be already in the correct position.

Figure 18.21
Drag the tempo events to the nearest markers in the event display

The techniques outlined in this second stage help you refine the data created in stage 1 to produce an extremely accurate tempo map. Creating hit-points and converting them to markers in the event display effectively provides you with rhythmic 'anchor points' upon which you can 'hang' your tempo events.

Synchronisation

Synchronisation refers to the technique of running two or more devices in perfect time with each other. This is required in Cubase SX systems which include external devices such as video tape recorders, tape machines, hard disk recorders, sequencers and drum machines. The devices must be connected together in some way so that they are all 'aware' of their time positions relative to the other units in the system. This is achieved using a time encoded signal (timecode). Digital systems may also require the use of word clock or some other clock reference signal. One of the units in the system is chosen as the 'master' device and the others are chosen as 'slaves'. The master device generates the reference code for the system and the other units synchronise themselves to this. Precisely how this is achieved depends upon the application. Positional synchronisation techniques may be divided into two main categories: bar-based synchronisation and time-based synchronisation.

Info

The synchronisation of digital audio/video devices usually requires two signals: 1) timecode and 2) clock. Timecode is a positional reference which tells the system 'where' it should be. Clock is a frequency rate reference which tells the system at 'what speed' it should be going.

Bar-based synchronisation

This involves sending MIDI Clock between units which keeps them synchronised in terms of bar position and tempo. This is an older, entirely MIDI based technique which is recommended only when there is no other solution. A typical use includes the synchronisation of external sequencers and drum machines which do not feature MTC (MIDI Time Code).

MIDI Clock includes a static MIDI message transmitted 24 times per quarter note and Start, Stop and Continue messages. Song Position Pointer (SPP) messages are invariably also included in the transmitted data. The receiving device responds according to the Start, Stop and Continue messages and calculates the tempo at which it should be running by measuring the time between each MIDI Clock message. The additional Song Position Pointer messages are used for calculating the current position within the song. This allows fast forward and rewind operations and the possibility of starting at any point within the music. (Before Song Position Pointers, synchronisation could only be achieved by commencing playback from the start of the song).

Time-based synchronisation

This involves the use of 'time-stamped' code which provides an absolute time-based reference for synchronisation purposes. This comes in the form of SMPTE / EBU time code or MIDI time code (MTC). Time-based synchronisation using SMPTE / EBU time code or MIDI Time Code is preferable to bar-referenced synchronisation since it is more accurate and is tempo-independent.

Time code has its origins in the film industry where the time stamped information was measured in terms of a number representing hours, minutes, seconds and frames. The resolution of the code was determined by its frame rate (e.g. 24 frames-per-second) and this was originally how many film frames passed through the camera per second. This kind of time code has been adopted for audio purposes and is now widely used in various forms throughout the audio industry.

SMPTE is an abbreviation for the Society of Motion Picture and Television Engineers and time code is often referred to by this name, (pronounced 'simptee'), since this organisation was the first to establish a time code standard. However, strictly speaking SMPTE time code is only one standard, as used in the USA. The other is EBU Time Code as used in Europe (established by the European Broadcasting Union).

The different types of time code can be told apart by the manner in which they are stored and transmitted and by their frame rates. Time code is transmitted as Longitudinal Time Code (LTC), Vertical Interval Time Code (VITC) or MIDI Time Code (MTC) and these are defined as follows:

- Longitudinal Time Code (LTC) – the code is recorded as a stream of audio pulses on an audio track. LTC is commonly used for audio work and video productions.
- Vertical Interval Time Code (VITC) – this code is embedded within the video picture (in a gap when the cathode ray is briefly switched off) and is popular for video editing.
- MIDI Time Code (MTC) – this is a special kind of time code with a slightly lower resolution than LTC which is transmitted via MIDI.

Time code varies in the number of frames per second for the encoded signal. This is known as the frame rate and could be one of the following:

> 24 fps – traditional 35mm film rate.
> 25 fps – European standard for audio and video (EBU).
> 30 fps – USA standard for audio work (30 Non-Drop).
> 30 dfps – rarely used format.
> 29.97 fps – USA television and video non-drop frame format (29.97 Non-Drop).
> 29.97 dfps – USA television and video drop frame format (29.97 Drop).

The basic format for all time code is hours : minutes : seconds : frames. When greater accuracy is required, the frame is divided into 80 subframes. For audio work, it is normal practice to use 25 fps in Europe and 30 fps in the USA. LTC and MTC time code at the latter frame rates are the most likely types of time code with which you will come into contact during your use of Cubase SX.

Synchronisation in digital systems

The problems

The synchronisation of digital audio devices presents new problems which were not apparent in analogue systems. When operating in internal mode (i.e. when not synchronised to another unit) each device plays back its audio according to the timing of its own internal digital clock (audio clock). Slaving one digital audio device to another unit using timecode alone results in time-based synchronisation, but audio playback in the slaved unit is still referenced to its own internal digital clock. In effect, various parts of the same system are synchronised to different clocks. This results in a system where fractional timing drift may occur, sometimes causing digital pops and clicks.

Slaving Cubase SX to external units such as tape machines suffers from this problem, especially when the SX project contains audio material. Under normal circumstances, when Cubase SX is not slaved to an external device, both the MIDI and audio data are locked to the same clock (the digital audio hardware's internal clock). However, when Cubase SX is slaved to an external device using timecode (MTC), the positional reference of the program is governed by the incoming timecode, while the clock reference for the audio data is still locked to the internal audio clock. Due to variations in tape speed and/or audio clock speeds, this can result in timing drift between the audio recorded in Cubase SX and the audio recorded in the external unit and/or the MIDI data. The problem may manifest itself as a loss of clarity or as phasiness in the sound quality.

The solutions
Word Clock
A popular solution to the problem outlined above is the use of word clock. One unit is chosen as the single master timecode and word clock source (usually the unit where A/D conversion takes place), and all other units are slaved to this device. Word clock keeps the sample rates of digital audio hardware in synchronisation by using a clock which is referenced to the transferred data bits, normally at the same rate as the sample rate chosen for the digital audio system. Using word clock requires audio hardware equipped with word clock connectors. Many digital audio signals, such as S/PDIF, AES/EBU and ADAT, are self-clocking since the clock reference is embedded within the signal. With these interfaces, lock can therefore be achieved without the use of word clock, (however, locking to word clock is likely to provide better jitter-free performance).

ASIO Positioning Protocol (APP)
APP is a relatively new technology designed to ensure sample accurate positioning between suitably equipped devices. It requires audio hardware with an ASIO 2.0 driver which includes APP functionality, and the ability to read positional information in the external device (see the electronic documentation and the Steinberg website for more details about APP).

Synchronising without Word Clock
It is worth bearing in mind that some of the synchronisation problems outlined above are relevant to those systems where Cubase SX is slaved to an external device. You may encounter less problems if you are running a system where Cubase SX is always the master device. Equally, if you are synchronising Cubase SX to devices whose timing clocks are very stable, such as another computer or a hard disk recorder, then you may encounter minimal problems if you synchronise using time code without a reference clock. However,

the fact remains that a system synchronising digital devices without a reference clock (such as word clock) cannot guarantee accurate long-term timing (the longer the audio recording, the more apparent becomes the timing drift).

If you intend to set up your system without Word Clock, it helps if you use time code which was generated from your audio hardware. For this and other purposes, Cubase SX is supplied with a 'SMPTE Generator' plug-in (explained in the next section).

The SMPTE Generator plug-in

Cubase SX is supplied with a SMPTE Generator plug-in (Figure 19.1). This can be used as an Insert effect on any audio track. The audio track is routed to the appropriate output of your audio hardware and recorded onto the intended time code track of the external device. The generation of the time code may be linked to the project ruler by activating the link button. In this case, time code generation begins from the current location of the project cursor when you press Cubase SX's play button. The frame rate matches the frame rate set in the Project Setup window (Project menu). Otherwise, deactivate the Link button and press the Generate button. This generates time code at the chosen frame rate beginning from the specified start time.

Figure 19.1
The SMPTE Generator plug-in

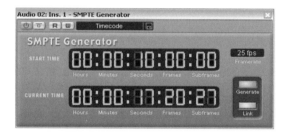

As well as providing a convenient time code source, the SMPTE Generator is also useful for becoming familiar with the various different types of SMPTE, particularly if you do not have any prior experience with time code. However, be careful when routing the time code through your audio system. Reduce the volume level before pressing the generate button to avoid damage to your speakers or to your ears!!

Setting up synchronisation in Cubase SX

It is important to have a basic understanding of the different types of time code, as outlined in the above sections, since you may come into contact with them in the peripheral equipment which you connect to your audio system. However, internally, Cubase SX recognises only MIDI Time Code (MTC), ASIO Positioning Protocol (APP) or VST System Link as timecode sources. The practical synchronisation of Cubase SX to external audio hardware, like tape recorders or hard disk recorders, often implies the use of a hardware synchronisation device (synchroniser) which converts SMPTE / EBU time code into MTC. For professional applications, the synchroniser would also provide Word Clock for the system. A typical synchronisation setup of this type might resemble Figure 19.2. (For APP alternatives and VST System Link information see the Steinberg website).

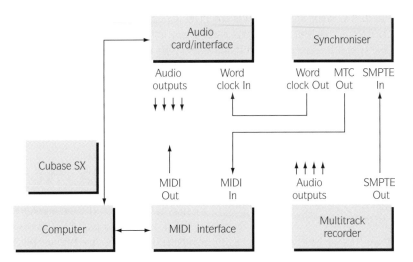

Figure 19.2
Cubase SX slaved to a multitrack tape or hard disk recorder featuring synchronisation via time code and Word Clock

Synchronisation in Cubase SX is managed in the Synchronisation Setup dialogue opened from the Transport menu (Figure 19.3). This is used to select the timecode source, the MIDI Machine Control status, the drop out and lock behaviour, and the MIDI input and output ports for MIDI Machine Control in/out, MTC in/out and MIDI Clock out.

Tip

VST System Link allows the sending of audio, MIDI, transport and synchronisation data between two or more computers with sample-accurate resolution. This involves connecting machines together via digital cables between ASIO audio cards and means that you can build a network of awesome processing power.

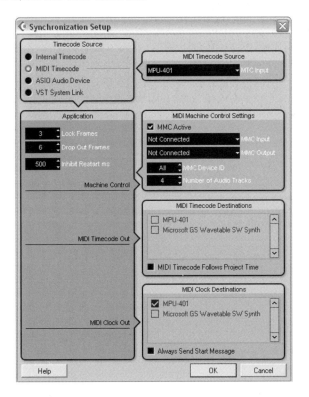

Figure 19.3
The Synchronisation Setup dialogue

When Cubase SX behaves as the slave to an external device using MTC, you need to set the appropriate MIDI Input for the time code, a start time which Cubase SX uses as the beginning of the project (in the Project Setup dialogue Start field), and activate the Sync button on the Transport panel (press 'T' on the computer keyboard). In this configuration, Cubase SX commences playback in synchronisation with the external device when it receives time code with the same or a greater value than the set start time.

Practical synchronisation in Cubase SX

Cubase SX as the master device using MIDI clock

Cubase SX cannot be slaved to an external device using MIDI Clock since it does not recognise incoming MIDI Clock messages. Due to the technical limitations of MIDI Clock, it is not considered a suitable format for providing master timing control of Cubase SX. However, Cubase SX can generate MIDI Clock and therefore behave as the master device for external devices which recognise the data. MIDI Clock is suitable for the synchronisation of external sequencers and drum machines. To set up synchronisation using MIDI Clock, proceed as follows:

• Connect a MIDI cable between the appropriate physical MIDI output port of your MIDI interface and the MIDI input of the drum machine or external sequencer.
• Enable the reception of MIDI Clock data in the external MIDI device.
• Open the Synchronisation Setup dialogue in Cubase SX by selecting 'Sync Setup' in the Transport menu (Figure 19.4).

Figure 19.4
Select Sync Setup in the Transport menu

Metronome Setup...	
Metronome On	C
Precount On	
Sync Setup...	
Sync Online	T
Retrospective Record	Shift+Pad *

• In the Synchronisation setup dialogue, activate the appropriate MIDI port in the 'MIDI clock destinations' section (Figure 19.5).

Figure 19.5
Activate the appropriate MIDI port in the Sync Setup 'Send MIDI Clock' section

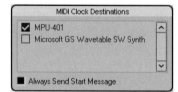

MIDI Clock Destinations
☑ MPU-401
☐ Microsoft GS Wavetable SW Synth
■ Always Send Start Message

• Click on OK to leave the dialogue. Press play in Cubase SX to send the MIDI Clock messages. The receiving device plays back synchronised to Cubase SX.

MIDI Clock may also be the solution if you are recording the MIDI data from a non-MTC equipped drum machine or sequencer into Cubase SX. In this case, configure Cubase SX in the same manner as above, but also connect a second MIDI cable from the MIDI out of the external device to a MIDI input port of your MIDI interface. In this setup, MIDI Clocks are transmitted via the MIDI output of Cubase SX to the slaved device and the MIDI note data from the external unit is sent back to Cubase SX via the second MIDI cable. Activating record in Cubase SX records the incoming data onto a record enabled MIDI track.

Cubase SX as the master device using MIDI time code

Using Cubase SX as the master device is a popular solution when synchronising external multitrack machines and video recorders and, in many circumstances, is a better solution than using it as the slave. Proceed as follows:

- Connect a MIDI cable between the appropriate MIDI output port of your MIDI interface and the MIDI input of the external device.
- Enable the reception of MTC in the external device.
- Set Cubase SX and the external device to the same frame rate. In Cubase SX, set the frame rate in the Project setup window (Project menu). For most situations you would choose 25 or 30fps.
- Set the start time for Cubase SX in the Project setup window (Project menu). Also set an appropriate start time in the external unit.
- In the Sync Setup dialogue, activate the appropriate MIDI port in the 'MIDI timecode destinations' section (Figure 19.5a).
- Click on OK to leave the Sync Setup dialogue. Press play in Cubase SX to send MTC. The receiving device plays back synchronised to Cubase SX.

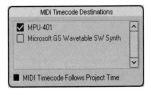

Figure 19.5a
Select the appropriate MIDI output port for the MTC in the 'MIDI timecode destinations' section

Cubase SX as the slave device using MIDI time code

As outlined above, MTC is a particular kind of time code which can be transmitted through an ordinary MIDI cable. MTC supports 24, 25, 30 and 30 drop frame formats. The device which sends the MTC to Cubase SX could be a synchroniser which converts SMPTE time code into MTC or, perhaps, another sequencer. A synchroniser is often used to provide an interface between a multitrack tape or hard disk recorder and a computer based sequencer, like Cubase SX, and this forms the main subject matter of this section.

Before synchronisation can occur with the multitrack recorder, one of the tracks must be striped with time code (although some devices produce their own time code signal without using a track). After striping, this code is routed to the time code input of the synchroniser which drives the rest of the system. In this example, the synchroniser converts the SMPTE time code into MTC, which is routed to the computer and Cubase SX via a MIDI cable connected to the MIDI interface.

To set up Cubase SX with a multitrack recorder and a synchroniser which converts SMPTE time code to MIDI time code, proceed as follows:

- If required, stripe a track of the multitrack recorder with SMPTE/EBU time code. For this task you could use Cubase SX's SMPTE Generator plug-in (as described above).

- Ensure that your synchroniser is correctly connected to the multitrack recorder (normally time code output of the multitrack recorder connected to the time code input of the synchroniser) and that the MTC out from the synchroniser is connected to the MIDI In of your MIDI interface.
- If you are using Word Clock, ensure that the Word Clock output from the synchroniser is connected to the Word Clock input of the audio card/audio hardware device.
- In the Synchronisation Setup dialogue, set Timecode Source to MIDI Timecode. Select the MIDI port for the incoming MTC in the 'MIDI Timecode source' input pop-up menu (Figure 19.6).

Figure 19.6

Set the Timecode Source to MIDI Timecode and select the MIDI port for the incoming MTC in the Synchronisation Setup dialogue

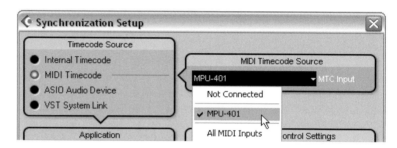

- Select the appropriate start time, frame rate and display offset (if required) in the Project Setup dialogue (Project menu) (Figure 19.7).

Figure 19.7

Select the start time, frame rate and display offset in the Project Setup dialogue

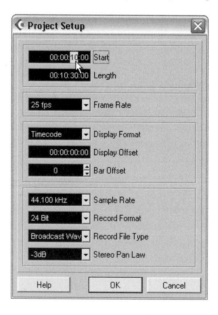

- Click on the Sync button on the Transport panel to activate synchronisation (or press T on the computer keyboard).
- Cubase SX is now ready to slave to any incoming MTC. Rewind the multitrack recorder to before the start time of the project and commence playback. When Cubase SX receives time code on or after the project start time, Cubase SX begins playback, in synchronisation with the multitrack recorder.

Cubase SX automatically chases and locks to each new position selected on the external device. In the Synchronisation Setup dialogue, the Drop Out and Lock Time options dictate the speed with which Cubase SX reacts to the incoming code, as follows:

- Lock Time specifies the number of correct frames of time code required before Cubase SX locks to it.
- Drop Out Time specifies the number of incorrect frames (or drop outs) which are tolerated before Cubase SX abandons synchronisation.

Synchronising Cubase SX with a tape recorder using MIDI Machine Control (MMC)

Cubase SX provides support for external devices which recognise MIDI Machine Code (MMC). MMC is a special part of the MIDI protocol which specifies MIDI messages for the control of such things as tape transports.

The use of MMC is a two-way process involving both MMC messages and MTC. It requires both the MIDI input and MIDI output of the tape recorder to be connected to Cubase SX. MMC messages are transmitted from the MIDI output of Cubase SX to the MIDI input of the tape recorder, which controls the transport and other functions. The tape recorder transmits MTC to the MIDI input of Cubase SX and this locks the two machines in synchronisation. The process usually requires the recording of time code onto one track of the tape recorder and this is converted into MTC during playback.

To set up your system and the Synchronisation Setup dialogue for use with a tape machine which supports MMC, proceed as follows:

- Ensure that the MIDI in and out cables are correctly connected between the tape recorder and Cubase SX and that time code has been recorded onto one track of the tape. Adjust the tape recorder set-up for MMC operation.
- In the Synchronisation Setup dialogue, set Timecode Source to MIDI Timecode. Select the MIDI port for the incoming MTC in the MIDI Timecode Settings 'MIDI Input' pop-up. Activate 'MIDI Machine Control' in the Machine Control section. Select the MIDI input and output ports for the MMC in the MIDI Machine Control Settings section (Figure 19.8)
- Select the appropriate start time, frame rate and display offset (if required) in the Project Setup dialogue (Project menu).
- Make sure that System Exclusive data is filtered (ticked) in the Preferences/MIDI Filter/Thru section (File menu).
- Activate the Sync button on the Transport panel.

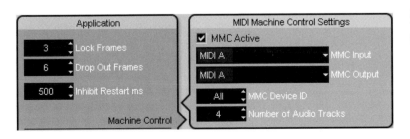

Figure 19.8
Typical Synchronisation Setup settings for MMC operation

- Press the play button on the tape recorder and play the tape for a short section to allow Cubase SX to lock to the current time code position.
- Stop the tape and press play in Cubase SX. If all is well, the tape rolls back to just before the current time position in Cubase SX and commences playback. After a second or two Cubase SX commences playback in sync with the tape recorder and, thereafter, all Cubase SX transport buttons, including play, stop, fast forward and rewind, control the transport of the tape recorder.

Production tips and power tools

This chapter outlines a number of tips, techniques, high-power macro commands and workspaces which help you on your way to becoming a Cubase power user. The emphasis here is on speed and efficiency, so if improving your productivity and workflow is a priority then this chapter is essential reading. The topics covered explore some of the lesser known aspects of Cubase SX as well as finding new ways of using common functions.

100 speed tips

The following is a comprehensive list of tips for enhancing speed and getting the best out of Cubase SX. The text is divided into a number of logical categories to help you find the tip you need.

Saving and file handling

1   Select Ctrl/Command + Alt + S to save the project with an incremental number automatically appended to the file name. The latter function is valuable for making regular saves of the latest version of your work as the project progresses. If things go wrong in the current version you can always revert to an earlier version.

2   Name your audio files in a meaningful way – Re-name your audio tracks before starting to record. Cubase SX uses the track name for the name of the audio file which is written to the hard disk and, by using meaningful names rather than the default 'Audio 1', 'Audio 2' etc., the files are easier to recognise if you need to find them individually at a later stage. A take number is chronologically appended to the file name for each new recording on the same track.

3   To avoid missing file problems and confusion store each Cubase SX project in its own separate folder. The program is designed with the idea of storing each project file and all its associated audio, edit and image files within a single overall folder. You can have several versions of the same project within the same folder but storing completely different projects within the same folder is to be avoided.

Navigation and zooming

4   To navigate quickly between different sections of your music without dropping out of playback, activate play and hold the numeric keypad '+' key to fast forward the project cursor. Release the key to instantly go back into normal playback mode. Try the same thing with the '-' key. Hold Shift to increase the wind speed.

5   Configure the wind speed when holding down Shift and the keypad '+' and '-' keys in Preferences/Transport/Wind Speed Options. Try activating 'Adjust to Zoom' with a Fast wind factor of 3.

6   An alternative method of setting the positions of the locators is to click in the ruler while pressing Ctrl (PC) / Command (Mac) to set the position of the left locator and click in the ruler while pressing Alt to set the position of the right locator.

7   If you are fine tuning the start of a range selection at high magnification in the Sample editor and lose visual contact with the start point, proceed as follows: stop playback, de-activate and re-activate the autoscroll button (press F twice), press L on the computer keyboard. Finally, de-activate the autoscroll button before re-commencing playback in order to not lose the start point.

8   Use the Zoom tool to quickly zoom in or out of the display. Click once in the display to zoom in and double click to zoom out.

9   To achieve a full horizontal and vertical view of all events in the project, hold Shift and click once with the zoom tool in the event display.

10   To zoom in to a specific range, make a range selection using the Range selection tool followed by 'Zoom to selection'. Use 'Undo zoom' to go back to the previous zoom setting. Assign key commands to 'Zoom to selection' and 'Undo zoom' (try 'Z' and 'Alt + Z').

Event editing

11   In the Project window, click with the right mouse button (PC)/ Ctrl + click (Mac) in empty space to open the context sensitive Quick menu. Hold down a modifier key (Ctrl/Command, Shift or Alt) to open a pop-up toolbox instead. To reverse the Quick menu / pop-up toolbox functionality select 'Pop-up toolbox on right click' in Preferences / Editing.

12   To repeat a number of consecutive events in the Project window select Repeat in the Edit menu (Ctrl/Command + K) and enter the number of repeats required in the pop-up dialogue. Alternatively, select the object selection tool and point at the lower right corner of the event while pressing Alt (until the pencil symbol appears). Drag to the right to repeat the events (the number of repeats is shown in a pop-up box).

13   To create a crossfade between two audio events, drag one audio event so that it overlaps slightly with another. Press the 'X' key on the computer keyboard. A default crossfade is created. Double click on the crossfade area to modify the crossfade curve characteristics.

14   To cut and paste range selections within events with automatic splits and re-alignment of following events, use the range selection tool with delete time, cut time and paste time (Edit menu/Range). Delete time deletes the range selection and moves all following events leftwards to close the gap. Cut time is similar but also copies the deleted range to the clipboard. Paste

time copies the clipboard at the start point of the range selection and moves all following events rightwards to make room for the pasted data.

15   Use 'select all events' from the track list Quick menu to select all events on the currently selected track.

16   Hold down any modifier key when renaming a track to rename all events/parts on that track to the same name. Alternatively, select several events and change the name on the infoline.

17   When using the main editors, press 'P' and the divide key (numeric keypad) on the computer keyboard to set the left and right locators and cycle playback to the selection. The cursor now cycles within the selected part (between the left and right locators) and does not scroll off the edge of the window while you are in the editor.

18   To split all selected events at the same point, select a number of events in the Project window and click on any one with the split tool. Alternatively, use the 'split at cursor' and 'split loop' commands in the edit menu.

19   As an alternative to the split tool for splitting events, press Alt and click with the object selection tool.

20   To delete all events on a track which come after the horizontal position at which you click, select the erase tool and click in the display while pressing Alt.

21   To create empty audio or MIDI parts in the Project window, press Alt and drag with the object selection tool. This is often more convenient than the standard 'draw tool and drag' technique.

22   To nudge a selected event back or forward in time in the event display, use Ctrl + left arrow and Ctrl + right arrow (default key commands for nudge left and nudge right). The nudge resolution is determined by the current ruler setting and the grid settings in the Project window toolbar.

23   To copy events from one project to another, drag and drop between two open Project windows. This works for both audio and MIDI events.

24   To find the length of any range, or group of events, activate the snap button and choose Events in the snap menu. Select the range tool and drag across the required range (the range snaps to the starts/ends of events). The length of the selection is shown in the length field of the infoline in the same time format as that chosen in the ruler.

Markers

25   To add standard markers, click on the add marker button found in the track list section of the Marker track or press the insert key on the computer keyboard. Standard markers are placed at the current location of the project cursor. Alternatively, add markers freely anywhere in the Marker track using the draw tool or 'on the fly' using the insert key while listening to the music or watching a video.

26   To add cycle markers, click on the add cycle marker button found in the track list section of the Marker track. Cycle markers are placed between the current positions of the left and right locators. Alternatively, press Ctrl/Command and drag the object selection or draw tool over the desired range for the cycle.

27   Instant cycle playback – Select a cycle marker and press Shift + G. This places the left and right locators at the start and end of the cycle

marker and automatically commences playback in cycle mode.

28 To ensure key command functionality for recalling cycle markers (by default, Shift+Pad 1 to Shift+Pad 9), de-select the 'number lock' key on the numerical key pad.

29 When you have created hitpoints in the Sample editor you can generate markers at the hitpoint positions by selecting Create Markers in the Audio/Advanced sub-menu. This is helpful when lining up tempo events to audio hits using the time warp tool in the Project window, since the tool is magnetic to the markers.

30 In order to clarify the Marker track display in the Inspector, you may find it more practical to see the description column next to the marker ID number. To achieve this, change the position of the description column by dragging the column header to the left in the Inspector.

Key commands

31 Key commands do not exist for workspaces numbered above 9. If you prefer to avoid the mouse for activating higher numbered workspaces, use Alt/Option + Pad 0 to open the 'Organise workspace' dialogue. Once open, use the up/down arrows to navigate the list of workspaces. Press return to activate the currently selected workspace. Press Alt/Option + F4 to close the dialogue.

32 Assign a key command to 'Transport – Restart' so that you can instantly restart playback from the last registered start point. If you are a PC user try assigning the Home key.

33 Try reversing the default key commands for 'Zoom – Zoom to Selection' (Alt + S) and 'Project – Setup' (Shift + S). This helps navigate within the Sample editor, where you can now use Shift + F to zoom to the whole clip, Shift + E to zoom to the event, Shift + S to zoom to the current selection, and Shift + G to loop around the current selection. In other words, all the common zoom and loop key commands now use the Shift modifier key which is easier to remember and easier to use.

34 Assign a key command to 'Transport – StartStop Preview' (try Alt + spacebar) and use this to start and stop local playback within the Sample editor or Pool. This is useful for playback of the whole clip or for playback of a range selection.

35 If you frequently need to manually activate/de-activate the monitor button for channels/tracks, assign a key command to the 'monitor' command in the Key Commands dialogue. Try 'Ctrl + Shift + M'.

MIDI

36 When activating MIDI effects in the Inspector, the parameters of certain devices open within the Inspector itself. If this is not convenient, you can force the effect to open in a separate window by pressing Alt while making the selection.

37 To quickly select all notes of the same pitch in the Key editor, hold down Ctrl/Command and click on the relevant key in the virtual keyboard to the left of the main display.

38 The pop-up programs menu for VSTi and external MIDI devices (Inspector) is good for auditioning sounds on the fly. Step through the

sounds in the list using the up/down arrow keys on the computer keyboard. Also try entering the name of the type of sound you are looking for in the filter at the top. All sounds containing the text you enter are then shown in the list.

39   Use the 'Edit VST instrument' button on the toolbar of the MIDI editors to quickly open the user interface for a VST instrument while working in the editor. If the 'Edit VST instrument' button is not visible on the toolbar, select it from the toolbar pop-up menu, (to open the menu click with the right mouse button (PC)/Ctrl + click (Mac) on the toolbar).

40   If you want to export a MIDI sequence as a Standard MIDI File and the track concerned uses a drum map, use 'O-Note Conversion' (MIDI menu) to transpose the notes before exporting. This ensures that the correct sounds are triggered.

41   To 'humanise' the effect of Over quantize, try adding a few ticks in the Random Quantize setting of the Quantize Setup dialogue.

42   Get logical – When you find yourself involved in MIDI editing tasks which seem laboriously repetitive and time-consuming, remember the Logical editor. This editor often provides effective solutions to labour intensive editing and may even help avoid repetitive strain injury!!

43   Increase the Key editor vertical zoom resolution to reveal the note names inside each event on the grid.

44   To insert a series of notes at the same pitch in the Key editor, select the paint tool and drag it across the grid while pressing Ctrl/Command. To control the insert resolution, activate the snap button and select the desired quantize value in the Quantize type menu. Set the Length Q menu to 'Quantize Link'.   Alternatively, press Alt and move the object selection tool (pointer) near to the end of an existing note and then drag across the grid. The chosen note is repeated over the range you drag.

45   Use the Controller lane presets menu in the lower left corner of the MIDI editors to organise instant recall of multiple controller lanes.

46   Click on the Edit In-Place button in the Inspector for MIDI tracks to show/hide the Edit In-Place editor. Alternatively, use the default key command: Ctrl/Command + Shift + I.

Audio editing

47   To remove fades and crossfades, select the events containing the fades using the Object selection tool, or select the range containing the fades using the range selection tool, and then select 'Remove Fades' in the Audio menu.

48   The Snap point of an audio event in the Project window is visible as a vertical blue line (when it is not in its default position at the start of the event). In the Project window, the Snap point may be modified using 'Snap point to cursor' (Audio menu). The Snap point is also adjustable in the Sample editor.

49   Multiple Sample editors may be opened simultaneously when you are working on several clips at the same time. This is useful for copying, pasting and merging audio between different clips.

50   To merge the current contents of the clipboard with the existing audio in the Sample editor use the Merge Clipboard function in the Process menu.

51   To avoid clicks when splitting events, try activating 'Snap to Zero

crossing' in Preferences/Editing/Audio (File menu). Don't forget to de-activate this tick box after editing is complete since this may cause unwanted side-effects in other Cubase SX editing operations.

52 When using the Process functions for editing in fine detail in the Sample editor, always work with the Snap to zero button activated. This avoids clicks and glitches between the processed and unprocessed parts of the audio clip.

53 To make the tempo of Cubase SX fit the length of an audio event containing a drum loop you need to know its length in beats. Select the loop event, enter the beat length into the Beat Calculator (Project menu) and click on 'At Tempo Track Start' to change the tempo of Cubase SX to that of the loop. This assumes that the length of the event containing the loop has already been edited to last for a precise number of bars and beats.

54 In the Audio Part editor, use the Play tool (loudspeaker icon) with the 'Edit active part only' button de-activated, to quickly switch between and audition the contents of each event/track/lane.

55 To avoid clicks between audio slices after increasing the tempo, set up auto fades in the Auto fades dialogue for the track. Tick 'auto crossfades' and deselect 'use project settings'. Try between 15ms and 30ms for the crossfade. Alternatively, try activating the fade in and fade out options with a 5ms to 10ms fade time.

56 To merge the attack of one drum sound with the decay of another, open the Sample editor, select a sound using the range selection tool and copy it to the clipboard. Select a second sound with which you wish to merge the copied sound. Open the Merge Clipboard dialogue (Audio/Process menu). Try setting the percentage slider to its '100% copy' position and adjust the pre-crossfade to between 50 and 100ms. Activate the pre-crossfade tick box. Fine tune the settings while in Preview mode. When satisfied click on the Process button.

57 To mix and match sound slices between different drum loops, open a number of synchronised sliced loops (or Rex files) simultaneously in the Audio Part editor. Use the mute and other tools on the different events to create new rhythms and arrangements.

58 To drag and drop a range selection directly from the Sample editor into the Project window, hold Ctrl on the computer keyboard, click in the highlighted selection and drag into the event display.

59 To time stretch multiple audio events in the Project window by the same stretch factor, proceed as follows: 1) Select the desired events and select 'Bounce selection' in the Audio menu. Select 'replace' in the dialogue which appears. 2) With the bounced events still selected, select 'Find selected in Pool' (Audio menu). The Pool is opened automatically with the bounced clips selected. 3) Select Timestretch in the Process menu and stretch the selected clips in the Pool as appropriate (after processing, the ends of some events in the event display may need dragging to the right).

60 To tile two or more Sample editors on the screen, select the audio events to be edited and select Window/Minimize All, followed by Return, followed by Window/Tile horizontally. When you are finished editing, close the editor windows and select Window/Restore All.

Mixer

61   When using the Mixer to create a mix it is not convenient if channels are always automatically record enabled when selected. To disable automatic record enabling, open Preferences/Editing and disable 'Enable Record on Selected Track'.

62   Open the user interface for a VST Instrument directly from the Mixer by clicking on the lower 'Edit VST instrument' button in the VST Instrument channel strip.

63   To change a fader level for a single channel in a group of linked channels in the Mixer, hold Alt on the computer keyboard while making the change.

64   When dragging a handle in the EQ curve display, press Ctrl/Command to change the gain only, press Alt to change the frequency only, and press Shift to change the Q only.

65   To make A/B comparisons between the equalised and unequalised signal, click on the channel's Bypass EQs button (green = EQ enabled, yellow = EQ disabled).

66   Try activating File/Preferences/Editing/Mixer selection follows project. In this mode, the contents of an open Channel Settings window automatically follows your track or mixer channel selection. This is useful for keeping track of all the channel settings when switching between tracks/channels.

67   Any combination of channels in the Mixer can be temporarily hidden by activating the 'Can Hide' option found in each channel's pop-up menu. Show/hide the chosen channels by activating/de-activating the 'Hide channels set to Can Hide' icon in the left panel.

68   Prepare for the mix – For mixing purposes you might wish to open suitably sized Project and Mixer windows with perhaps the Transport panel closed. You could also include the Time display and VST Performance windows suitably placed within the screen space. Save your layout as a Workspace using Window/Workspaces/New Workspace.

69   To copy the settings of one channel to another in the Mixer proceed as follows: 1) select the source channel and press Ctrl/Command + C to copy the channel settings to the clipboard. 2) select the target channel and press Ctrl/Command + V to paste the contents of the clipboard to the chosen channel. (Alternatively, use the copy/paste icons in the lower left corner of the Mixer).

70   Combine plug-in effects for creative purposes – Creative effects can be achieved by using more than one effect in the insert slots. Try the following: compressor followed by fuzz (typically used by guitarists to achieve more sustain), fuzz followed by chorus/flange, echo followed by chorus/flange, chorus/flange followed by chorus/flange, tremolo followed by autopan, reverb followed by phasing, filtering followed by delay.

71   In the Mixer, hold Shift while moving a channel fader or pan control to make fine adjustments.

72   Use 'Save selected channels' and 'Load selected channels' in the Mixer quick menu to save/load channel templates for channel input busses (for recording specific sources) or for preset playback settings for audio channels.

73   To regulate the overall level of an audio based channel after automation has been applied, use the Wavelab-supplied 'Tools One' plug-in (or similar)

inserted into slot 7 or 8 of the channel (i.e. post fader). Alternatively, for one or more automated channels, change the output routings to a Group and apply overall level changes using the Group channel fader.

74   To apply master buss reverb or delay which continues after the master fader has been fully attenuated (for example, on fade outs when mixing or mastering), insert the reverb or delay effect in insert slots 7 or 8 of the master buss (i.e. post fader).

75   To set a number of tracks in the Project window or channels in the Mixer to the same input or output buss, select the chosen tracks/channels and change the input/output menu selection of any one while holding Alt. With MIDI tracks, the menu change operates upon all tracks when holding Alt or, alternatively, only upon selected tracks if you hold down the Shift key.

Automation

76   To change the recording resolution for automation data, adjust the Automation Reduction slider in Preferences/Editing.

77   When moving automation handles, activate the Project window infoline. The infoline displays the start time and value of the event as you drag it. This helps place the events with greater precision. Alternatively, click directly on the value field in the infoline to change the value of the event.

78   An excellent way of viewing the behaviour of the different automation modes is to write the automation while viewing the corresponding subtrack in the Project window event display. With the Write button active, each time you click on a control the track header in the Track list turns red to indicate that automation is being recorded.

79   To clarify the display of automation data in the Project window, activate 'Show Track colours' at the top of the track list and use the pop-up Track colour selector for each automation sub-track to choose an appropriate colour.

Import/Export

80   Easy import – you can import multiple audio files in the file selection dialogue which appears after using the Import medium function (Pool menu). It is also possible to drag and drop audio (and standard MIDI files) directly from the desktop into the event display.

81   Easy export – if you are suffering from missing audio tracks or silence after using Export/Audio Mixdown, make sure that no tracks have been left in monitor mode. This can easily occur when using 'Tapemachine Style' or 'While Record Enabled' monitor modes since selected tracks automatically activate their monitor buttons when in stop mode or when record enabled. Tracks set to this status are NOT included in the audio mixdown (when mixing down from a bus, such as Bus 1). So, before the mixdown check that all monitor buttons are de-activated.

82   Keep the reverb – When using Export/Audio Mixdown take care that any reverberation tail which may occur after the audio tracks themselves does not get cut off due to the right locator being placed too close to the end point of the audio events. Add two or more bars safety margin to the right locator position.

83 To copy tracks between projects, use Export/Selected Tracks and Import/Track archive (File menu).

Pool

84 To find the current maximum peak amplitude and the average loudness of an audio clip, select the clip in the Pool and then select Statistics from the Audio menu. The resulting Statistics window shows the maximum peak amplitude (Peak Amplitude), which means the single highest peak found in the selection, and the average RMS power (Average), which means the average loudness of the signal.

85 Before exporting the Pool, create a special folder using Create Folder (Pool menu) and drag all the clips into it. When you later import the Pool into another Cubase SX or Nuendo project all the clips are neatly packaged in their own folder and are easier to find among any clips already in the current Pool.

86 To view more details about Broadcast Wave files in the Pool, click in the Info column for the file to reveal a pop-up info box.

87 To find out the total size taken up by the audio files in a project, activate the Show info button in the Pool (see the Total Size field).

88 To sort the audio files used in a project alphabetically or by type, date or path, click on the relevant column header in the Pool.

Miscellaneous

89 Try setting Preferences/Editing/Controls/Value Box to 'Increment/Decrement on Left Click and Drag'. This means that by clicking on a value field and dragging the mouse position vertically you can instantly change values in a fast, fuss-free way. The technique works well when adjusting the start, end, volume, fade in, fade out or transpose values for a selected event in the Project window Infoline. It is also good for adjusting length, pitch, velocity and channel data in the Key and Drum editor Infolines, and for changing the tempo (in fixed mode).

90 Undo/redo editing using the undo/redo functions in the Edit menu or by pressing Ctrl + Z (undo) or Ctrl + Shift + Z (redo). Step back through your edits using the Edit history window (select 'History' in the Edit menu).

91 While in the Project window, you can select tracks using the up/down arrow keys. While in the Mixer, you can select tracks using the left/right arrow keys. Several tracks/channels can be selected simultaneously by holding the Shift key while pressing the arrow keys. By default, selecting also record enables the tracks and the Shift + arrow combinations therefore provide a quick method of record enabling multiple tracks.

92 Ctrl/Command click on the click, tempo and sync buttons to open the Metronome, Tempo and Sync Setup windows respectively.

93 To name all parts dragged onto a track according to the track's name, activate 'Parts get track name' in Preferences/Editing. This is useful for copying parts between instruments in a MIDI orchestral project (for

example), where you might use a template with the tracks already named according to the instruments in the orchestra.

94 To implement tempo changes over a specific range without affecting the rest of the tempo in the project, proceed as follows: 1) Select a range in the event display using the Range selection tool. 2) Select the Time warp tool in normal mode. 3) Click within the selected range to enter a tempo event. Additional tempo events are automatically added at the start and end of the selected range. Tempo changes may now be freely added within the selected range without affecting the rest of the tempo structure of the project.

95 For instant loop playback of the currently selected event in the event display press Shift + G (Transport menu/loop selection).

96 To activate/de-activate Play Order mode without opening the Play Order editor or Play Order controls in the Transport panel, click on the Play Order button in the track list (drag the vertical split point to the right if you cannot see it).

97 In Windows systems, if you see wingdings in the Score editor instead of notes, open the Fonts folder in the Control panel and refresh the contents by selecting 'Refresh' in the View menu (or press F5 on the computer keyboard). If this does not solve the problem try downloading Steinberg's scorefonts file at
ftp://ftp.steinberg.net/download/pc/Cubase_SX/misc/scorefonts.zip

98 Save different Project startup settings as templates. Select 'Save as template' in the File menu and choose a suitable name in the 'Save as template' dialogue. The template is now available in the templates list when you select 'New project' (File menu). Templates are useful for creating startup projects for working with 24 track audio, 16 track MIDI, 2 track mastering and so on, or for pre-configuring the system for use with advanced VSTi sampler/synthesizers like Halion and Reaktor.

99 Know how to use your hard disks – experts recommend using two hard disk drives with Cubase SX; one for the system and program files and one for the project and audio files. This has been found to increase performance and it is easier to maintain the audio disk. For large capacity hard disks it is preferable to create several smaller sized partitions since this allows easier defragmentation and management of data.

100 Back up your data. Although hard disk failure is not a common occurrence, backing up your data is essential if you wish to avoid the potentially disastrous situation of losing all your files. Popular back-up media include: hard drives in removable caddies, external firewire drives, zip or jaz discs, recordable CD and DVD.

Info

If any of the tips outlined here are particularly useful to you, copy them into Cubase's notepad (Project menu) along with your own tips/notes and save this as part of your default project. That way, your favourite tips and info are always available when you start up a new project.

Macro magic

The macro section of many Cubase SX setups often remains empty because, while users are aware that macros can be enormously powerful, few have the time or the patience to create their own. This section shows you how and also provides you with a time-saving startup library of powerful ready-made macros.

What are macros?

Macros are user-configurable 'super functions' made up of a number of basic functions strung together in a logical sequence. They are very powerful since a large number of moves can be reduced to a single key command. Functions that you use one after the other repetitively can now be selected at lightning-fast speed via a macro command, resulting in dramatically increased efficiency and productivity. Macros are managed in the Key commands window.

Key commands window

The macro commands are found in the lower section of the Key commands window, opened by selecting 'Key commands' in the File menu (Figure 20.1). To see the current list of macros click on the 'Show/Hide macros' button. If you are new to macros there may be no macros in the list when you first go there. New empty macros are created by clicking on the 'New macro' button. A command is added to the new macro by selecting a function from the upper half of the window and clicking on the 'Add command' button. You can keep on adding functions to the macro to create an elaborate sequence of commands. Once created, a key command may be assigned to the macro in the macro section in the upper half of the window. This means that the macro can now be activated with a single keystroke.

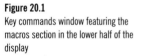

Figure 20.1
Key commands window featuring the macros section in the lower half of the display

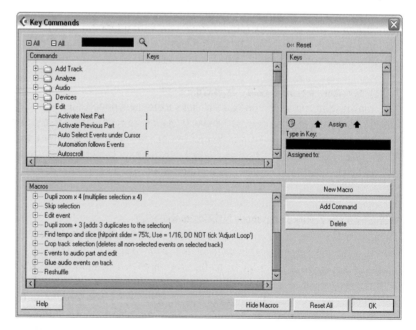

Macro library

The following is a list of both simple and advanced macros designed to enhance your use of Cubase SX and to teach you how to create your own macros by example. Each entry features the macro name, the suggested key command, the list of functions which make up the macro, and a brief description of what the macro does and how it can be used.

1 Bounce audio track [Key command – F7]

Designed to select all events on the currently selected audio track and bounce them all into one single audio event which overwrites all the original events in the event display. This creates a new file on the hard disk and a new clip in the Pool (regardless of what you choose in the Replace dialogue which appears).

2 Bounce all audio tracks [Key command – Shift+F7]

This macro bounces all audio tracks into events of the same length, based upon the range of the overall project. This is particularly useful when you need to export multitrack audio material into another audio application which does not recognise regular global file exchange formats; you can maintain the relative positions of the audio events simply by starting all files at the same time position.

3 Merge MIDI track [Key command – F8]

Similar to the audio version above, this merges all MIDI parts on the currently selected MIDI track and bounces them all into one single MIDI part which overwrites all the original parts in the event display (depending upon your choice in the 'Erase destination' option in the MIDI Merge options dialogue which appears).

4 Merge all MIDI tracks [Key command – Shift+F8]

This macro merges all non-muted MIDI parts in the event display into a single MIDI part on a new MIDI track. Useful for creating type 0 standard MIDI files or for mixing down a number of MIDI drum parts into a single composite part. (Assumes that the pointer tool is selected).

5 Crop selection [Key command – typewriter '=']

This macro uses the lock command to shield the current selection from the delete command and its action is similar to an image crop function as found in image editing software. All you do is select one or more events on the currently selected track and when you select this macro all other non-selected events on the track are deleted. It is intended for operation on the currently selected track only.

6 Dupli zoom x 2 [Key command – Ctrl/Command+F2]

Doubles the number of instances of the current range selection, automatically zooms in to the currently used area of the event display and reselects the duplicated section. It is designed to be used after having made a selection with the range selection tool (double-click on an event, for example) and may be repeated as required (by pressing the assigned Key command a number of times). Repeating the macro results in useful musical numbers. For example, selecting an event with the range selection tool and pressing

Macro 1
Edit – Select All on Tracks
Audio – Bounce

Macro 2
Tool – Range tool
Edit – Select all
Audio – Bounce
Tool – Select tool
Navigate – Up
Navigate – Down

Macro 3
Edit – Solo
Edit – Select All on Tracks
Transport – Locators to Selection
MIDI – Merge Midi in Loop
Edit – Solo

Macro 4
Edit – Select All
Transport – Locators to Selection
Add Track – MIDI
MIDI – Merge MIDI in Loop

Macro 5
Edit – Lock
Edit – Select All on Tracks
Edit – Delete
Edit – Select All on Tracks
Edit – Unlock

Macro 6
Transport – Locate Selection
Edit – Duplicate
Transport – Locators to Selection
Transport – Set Left Locator
Edit – Left selection side to cursor
Zoom – Zoom Full

Ctrl/Command+F2 (the suggested key command) gives two duplicates, pressing it twice in succession gives four duplicates, pressing it three times gives eight duplicates, pressing it four times gives sixteen duplicates... and so on. The number of duplicates for each selection of the macro is always doubled. This is particularly useful when working with drum loops. If required, the zoom command may be left out of the macro. Note that all the events between the left and right locators are reselected. This allows you to use the macro for 'multiplication' rather than 'addition'. For a meaningful result, always use the range selecton tool with this macro.

7 Dupli zoom x 4 [Key command – Ctrl/Command+F4]

Quadruples the number of instances of the current range selection, automatically zooms in to the currently used area of the event display and re-selects the duplicated section. It is designed to be used after having made a selection with the range selection tool (double-click on an event, for example) and may be repeated as required (by pressing the assigned Key command a number of times). Repeating the macro results in useful musical numbers. For example, selecting an event with the range selection tool and pressing Ctrl/Command + F4 (the suggested key command) gives four duplicates, pressing it twice in succession gives sixteen duplicates, pressing it three times in succession gives sixty four duplicates... and so on. The number of duplicates for each selection of the macro is always quadrupled. This is useful when working with drum loops and you can build up a large number of duplicates very quickly. If required, the zoom command may be left out of the macro. Note that all the events between the left and right locators are reselected. This allows you to use the macro for 'multiplication' rather than 'addition'. For a meaningful result, always use the range selecton tool with this macro.

8 Dupli zoom + 3 [Key command – Ctrl/Command+F3]

A simpler macro than the 'dupli zoom' multiplication macros outlined above. This simply 'adds' three duplicates to the current selection and zooms in to the used area of the display. It may be used repetitively but it always adds three duplicates and so does not always produce a musically meaningful number of events. It provides an alternative to the standard repeat command selected by pressing Ctrl/Command + K. Other similar macros could be designed for other musically useful numbers of repeats. If required, the zoom command may be left out of the macro.

9 Edit event [Key command – Alt+E]

Sets the left and right locators to the currently selected event, opens the relevant editor, zooms in, selects the range of the event and commences loop playback. This macro automatically organises your event selection ready for editing purposes and functions well with all event types. For a more stable view switch off autoscroll in the relevant editor.

10 Events to audio part and edit [Key command – Ctrl/Command+Alt+E]

Puts the currently selected audio events into an audio part and opens the Audio Part editor. Simple but very useful. Ideal for editing multiple audio takes which have been recorded in cycle recording mode.

Macro 7

Transport – Locate Selection
Edit – Duplicate
Edit – Duplicate
Edit – Duplicate
Transport – Locators to Selection
Transport – Set Left Locator
Edit – Left selection side to cursor
Zoom – Zoom Full

Macro 8

Transport – Locate Selection
Edit – Duplicate
Edit – Duplicate
Edit – Duplicate
Transport – Locators to Selection
Transport – Set Left Locator
Zoom – Zoom Full

Macro 9

Transport – Locators to Selection
Edit – Open
Zoom – Zoom to Locators
Edit – Select Event
Transport – Loop Selection

Macro 10

Audio – Events to Part
Transport – Locators to Selection
Edit – Open
Zoom – Zoom Full

11 Make loop from range selection [Key command – Alt+A]

Before using this macro you are strongly advised to make a backup of the audio clip in question. The macro is designed to make an audio event from a range selection in the Sample editor. Before activating the macro, double-click on the chosen audio event to open the Sample editor and select the required range using the range selection tool. Here, it is assumed that you wish to 'extract' a rhythmic loop from the rest of the audio in the event. Upon activation, the macro sets the tempo definition loop to your chosen range selection and then adjusts the length of the audio event in the event display. Next, the Sample editor is closed and then re-opened with the focus on the newly sized audio event. (From here, you might like to adjust the audio tempo definition manually before creating hitpoints and slicing the audio, or before activating musical mode, for example).

Macro 11
Tool – Audio Tempo Definition Transport – Locators to Selection Audio – Set Audio Event from Loop Edit – Open Close Editor

12 Punch range setup [Key command – Ctrl+#]

This macro prepares Cubase SX for the 'Punch range record' macro outlined below (Macro 13). It assumes that no punch buttons have already been acti-vated on the Transport panel and requires the preparation of suitable workspace and zoom presets. The zoom presets menu is found to the left of the horizontal zoom slider in the lower right corner of the Project window. The workspace presets menu is found as a sub-menu in the Window menu. The action of the macro runs as follows: 1) The Transport panel punch out button is activated. 2) A workspace, containing settings for a suitably sized Project window with a visible Transport panel, is selected. 3) A zoom preset set for a 10-15 second horizontal view (or some other suitable zoom setting) is select-ed. 4) A second zoom preset set to a four row vertical track size is selected. 5) The range tool is selected ready to make a selection for the punch in.

Macro 12
Transport – AutoPunch Out Workspaces – Workspace 2 Zoom – Zoom Preset 2 Zoom – Zoom Tracks 4 Rows Tool – Range Tool

13 Punch range record [Key command – #]

Designed to make punch-in recording easier, this macro gives a two bar pre-roll before your chosen range selection and automatically punches in and out of record mode at the start and end points. Although it is not essential, the procedure works better if you have already prepared the way using the 'Punch range setup' macro, outlined above. In any case, before starting to punch record using this macro, ensure that the cycle, punch in and pre-roll buttons are de-activated on the Transport panel and that the punch out but-ton is activated. Select any section of your music using the range selection tool. You are now ready to start punch recording. This macro works even when a range over several tracks is selected, at which time simultaneous recording on all tracks takes place. You are also free to record on both audio and MIDI tracks at the same time. You would most often use the range selec-tion tool to govern where recording takes place but the macro also works !when you select events with the object selection tool. Overall, this macro is excellent for all kinds of detailed punch in work and, if necessary, makes it easy to punch in over the same section a large number of times. (If you need a post-roll after the recorded section, activate the post-roll button and enter a post roll value in the Transport panel). This macro works best with 'Enable record on selected track' active (Preferences/Editing) and with 'Tapemachine style' selected (Preferences/VST).

Macro 13
Transport – AutoPunch In Transport – Locators to Selection Transport – To Left Locator Transport – Step Back Bar Transport – Step Back Bar Transport – Start

Macro 14

Transport – Set Marker 9
Transport – To Left Locator
Transport – Step Back Bar
Transport – Step Back Bar
Transport – Play until Next Marker

Macro 15

Transport – Locators to Selection
Navigate – Right
Transport – To Right Locator
Edit – Cut
Edit – Paste

Macro 16

Transport – Locators to Selection
Transport – To Right Locator
Transport – Set Marker 9
Transport – To Left Locator
Transport – Set Right Locator
Transport – To Marker 9
Transport – Set Left Locator
Transport – To Right Locator
Transport – Step Back Bar
Transport – Start

14 Punch range playback [Key command – ']

This macro makes it easy to audition what you have just recorded with the above punch range record macro (Macro 13). It sets marker 9 at the current position of the cursor (which would normally be found placed just after the recording), rewinds to the start of the recorded section, steps back two bars and then plays back the passage up to marker 9. The macro may be used repetitively but for successful operation you should allow playback to reach marker 9 before recommencing.

15 Reshuffle [Key command – Alt+R]

Shuffles the next event back to the end point of the current event selection. This macro always works on the next event to the right of the current selection and may be used repetitively. For a successful result, you must also select the track concerned. The outcome is the closing of all the gaps between events so that they appear consecutively on the track. Good for pulling events back together after fine tuning the start and/or end points or after edits in the Sample editor which change the length of the event (excellent when editing speech, for example).

16 Skip selection [Key command – Shift+\]

Based on the automatic skip macro supplied with the program, use this macro to skip the current range or event selection by reversing the left and right locator positions. After the skip range is created, this macro steps back one bar and automatically starts playback so that you can immediately audition the effect of the skip. (For a successful skip effect, the cycle button must be activated on the Transport panel).

Workspaces

What are workspaces?

Workspaces are complete window layouts which may be stored or recalled at any time, allowing you to quickly adapt your working environment to the task at hand. They come in two varieties:

1 'Workspaces'

'Workspaces' contain the layout and contents of the windows stored at various moments within the active project. They may be recalled within the active project only and are not available globally to other projects. A workspace includes window sizes, window positions, Project window track sizes, horizontal zoom resolutions, horizontal and vertical scroll positions, ruler time settings, tool selection, mixer configuration, Transport panel configuration and so on. Essentially, most of what you can see on the screen at any given moment while working on your project may be saved as a workspace. It's a bit like taking a snapshot. This is excellent for workflow.

2 'Workspace presets'

Once created, regular workspaces may also be stored as presets known as 'Workspace presets'. These are globally available to all projects. 'Workspace presets' store the main windows only and do not include all the details within each window. However, they have the advantage of being globally available to all projects and are useful for setting up generic window layouts for primary tasks such as recording, editing and mixing.

Organize workspaces dialogue

Workspaces are managed using the 'Organize Workspaces' dialogue which is opened by selecting Window/Workspaces/Organize, or pressing Alt + Pad 0 (Figure 20.2). This displays the list of available workspaces in the current project to the left, and the list of globally available workspace presets to the right.

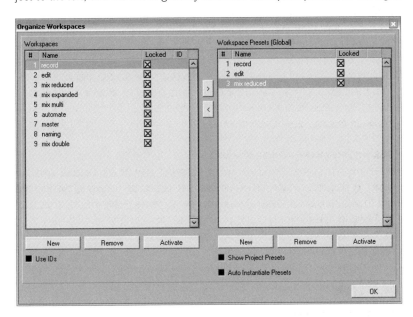

Figure 20.2
Organize workspaces dialogue

There is always at least one 'active' workspace which is indicated by a grey selection bar in the list, even if you have not yet created any workspaces in the current project. In the latter case, the default active workspace appears named as 'Main' in the list. New workspaces may be created at any time by clicking on the 'new' button. The stored data is based upon the positions and contents of the currently open windows in the project. When you create a new workspace you are obliged to name it in the list.

You can activate any existing workspace by double-clicking in its number (#) column or by selecting it and clicking on the activate button. A workspace may be locked by clicking in its box in the locked column, which keeps the selected workspace in its original form regardless of how you change the windows in the project. This means that you always go back to the original stored workspace each time you select it. To store a workspace as a preset which is available globally to all projects, move it from the left column into the right column using the arrow buttons between the two lists. If required, workspace presets on the right may be moved back to the left workspace list in a similar manner. Activating 'Auto instantiate presets' automatically copies global workspace presets into the list on the left if there are not already workspaces

Unlock Active Workspace	Alt+Pad .
New Workspace	Alt+Pad /
Organize...	Alt+Pad0
✔ (1.) - record	Alt+Pad1
(2.) - edit / punch	Alt+Pad2
(3.) - edit / pool	Alt+Pad3
(4.) - mix reduced	Alt+Pad4
(5.) - mix expanded	Alt+Pad5
(6.) - mix multi	Alt+Pad6
(7.) - automate	Alt+Pad7
(8.) - master	Alt+Pad8
(9.) - naming	Alt+Pad9
More...	

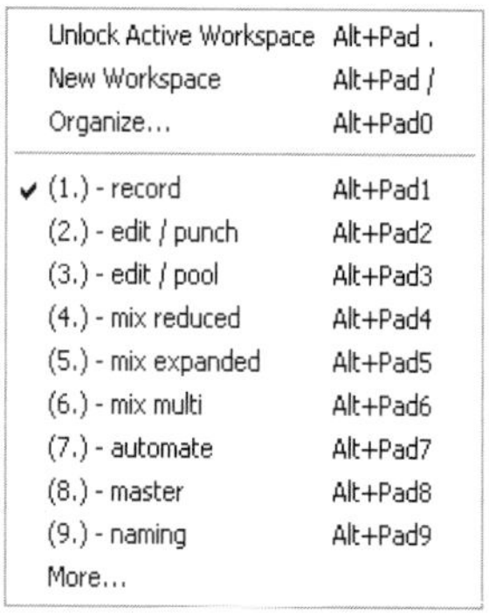

Figure 20.3
Workspaces sub-menu showing the default key commands

created for the current project. This is useful when creating new projects. Activating 'Use IDs' allows you to re-number the workspaces in !the ID column regardless of their position in the list. This is helpful when recalling specific workspaces using key commands (Alt + Pad 1-9) since the keypad numbers now refer to the ID numbers and not the list numbers.

Handling workspaces and workspace key commands

Handling workspaces requires a little practice. The first rule to keep in mind is that you are always working within the active workspace. Secondly, this active workspace can either be locked or unlocked. If it is locked, you are not actually changing what is stored in the workspace if you adjust the current window layout. However, if it is unlocked, the contents are immediately changed if you make any adjustments. A very good and easy tip for keeping an eye on your workspace status is to observe the number in brackets next to the Window menu. The number within the brackets specifies the currently active workspace, and the presence or non-presence of a full-stop next to the number denotes its locked/unlocked status. For example, '(1)' means that the active workspace is number 1 and it is unlocked, whereas (1.) means that the active workspace is number 1 and it is locked.

The Organize workspaces dialogue is helpful for the overall management of workspaces but the default key commands are often better when creating and using workspaces during the heat of a recording session. The relevant key commands can be found next to the menu items in the workspaces sub-menu (Figure 20.3).

The basic sequence of events to create a workspace using the key commands runs as follows:

1   Set up the windows in the project as required (or use the current layout).
2   Press Alt + Pad / to create a new workspace. Enter a name into the pop-up dialogue.
3   Press Alt + Pad . to lock the workspace.
4   Press Alt + Pad 1-9 to recall the workspaces you create.
5   Press Alt + Pad . a second time to unlock the workspace if you need to update it.

Workspaces for workflow

Like macros, workspaces help improve your workflow. This section explains exactly how this comes about by describing the creation of three commonly required workspaces. As you no doubt already know, the primary functions of Cubase include recording, editing and mixing; so why not set up personalised workspaces with these functions in mind, each with the specific tools and window layouts needed to make each task easier? The following sections describe how to do this. Each workspace is suitable for saving as a workspace preset, thus becoming available to all projects. However, since some of the details within the windows are not stored in workspace presets, you may also wish to save the setups as regular workspaces within your default startup project.

Info

The workspaces shown here are designed for a single 17 inch monitor. Dual monitor systems offer considerably more elaborate possibilities since you have more screen estate to play around with.

A workspace for recording

Of course, configuring the screen environment for recording varies greatly depending on the specific recording task at hand; audio recording might need different on-screen elements to MIDI recording and each project would undoubtedly feature variations in the number of tracks being used. However, there are a number of common factors involved. For most projects you would at least need to see the Project window and the Transport panel. The recording workspace outlined here also features the Mixer and the Pool (see Figure 20.4). It is assumed that the project already contains a number of audio and MIDI tracks added to the track list and that the overall system and VST connections are fully tested and operational.

Figure 20.4
A workspace for recording. Here, the first take of the recording session is underway.

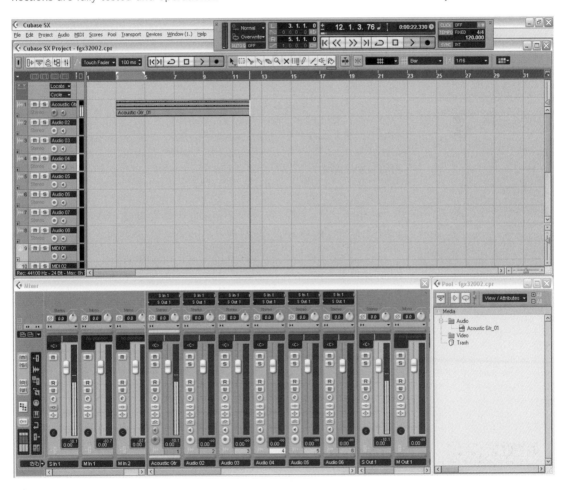

At first sight, the screen layout shown in Figure 20.4 looks a simple affair but the secrets of this workspace are in the details inside each window. Overall, the workspace includes a reduced Project window with the Mixer open below and the Transport panel open above. Space has been allocated next to the Mixer for a small-sized Pool window. To grasp the logic of this workspace we need to consider the audio recording process itself (MIDI recording considerations are similar). Here, it is assumed that you need to record an external source, such as a live musical performance via a microphone. Like all recordings of this type, the first thing you need to verify in Cubase is the level of the input signal. Hence, this workspace features the Mixer with the input busses visible. You are therefore ready to monitor/adjust the input level immediately and can keep an eye on input levels throughout the recording session. Next, you would probably decide which channel you are going to record on and set its input buss. You may also need to adjust the output buss assignation. To accommodate this, the workspace features the input/output menus visible on all channels. The main output busses are also already visible so you can adjust/monitor the overall output level. The Transport panel includes the performance meter, record mode, locators, main transport, and master and sync sections. You therefore have instant access to the punch-in, punch-out, pre-roll, post-roll, click and tempo parameters, as well as the obvious record modes and main transport buttons. In the Project window itself, the tracks are set to a vertical size of 2 rows allowing you a view of the record and monitor buttons and of the events in the event display as they get recorded (1 row may also be appropriate if you need to see more tracks simultaneously). The Inspector, Infoline and Overview switches are de-activated, (although you may prefer to open the Inspector for certain detailed audio and M!IDI recording operations). The open Pool window in the corner helps you keep an eye on the actual audio clips/files as they get recorded which, with this window size, are displayed as a simple list.

A workspace for event editing

Designing a workspace for event editing is potentially much simpler than the recording example above, since all you probably need is the Project window maximised to show the greatest amount of event display possible (see Figure 20.5). A suitable track row size is chosen to get a good view of the events (in this case 4 rows), the Infoline is activated to display information about each event as it is selected, and the active Overview helps you navigate and zoom within the whole project. An open Inspector might be helpful if you are editing MIDI program selection or MIDI channel parameters, or when you need to quickly open the interface for a VST Instrument. The Transport panel is also shown and features the Marker section to help with navigation, the jog wheel for detailed lining up of the cursor position/edit point and the master level control to adjust the overall level while editing (without having to open the Mixer).

A workspace for mixing

Any workspace designed for mixing would, of course, include the Mixer. The workspace shown in Figure 20.6 is dominated by the extended Mixer with a rather 'squashed' Project window reduced to its minimum vertical height. The screen width shown here allows around 15 mixer channels to be displayed in wide mode. The input and output busses have been hidden to allow a greater number of regular channels to be displayed simultaneously. (Conveniently, these Mixer details are included within each stored workspace). The Project window features a slightly larger Marker track to help navigate within the project and regular tracks with their row size reduced to the minimum. When the Marker track is selected, the markers are also shown in list form in the open Inspector to the left. The left/right locators in the ruler are available for selecting specific ranges along the time line. To help still further with navigation the

Figure 20.5
A workspace for editing where the event display is made as large as possible

Figure 20.6
A workspace for mixing featuring the extended Mixer dominating the screen space

Transport panel is reduced to just the locator and marker sect!ions, providing buttons for moving the cursor left/right locator positions or to the first fifteen markers. (Note that the main Transport buttons can be displayed on the Project window toolbar if you do not wish to use the standard keypad short-cuts). The time display helps when Cubase is linked to other machines via time code and the performance meters help you keep an eye on the CPU load.

What's so good about workspaces?

Using any one of the above workspaces in isolation might be useful but the real advantage of workspaces is being able to instantly switch between them at any stage during the evolution of a project. This is very liberating. Think about it; rather than approaching your workflow in standard 'do all the recording, do all the editing and then mix it' fashion, you can now instantly and effortlessly jump between different streamlined environments. Of course, the advantages do not end there; you can store a workspace at any moment throughout the development of your project and go back to that particular view at any time in the future. Furthermore, you can create workspaces suit-able for all kinds of other everyday Cubase tasks, such as tiling multiple editors; opening multiple insert effects interfaces; organising reduced, extended and multiple Mixer layouts; tiling a large-scale Pool window alongside the Project Browser… the possibilities are endless.

Recommended reading

Some readers may wish to enrich their knowledge of the subjects related to the use of Cubase SX. There are a wide range of books available on MIDI, sequencing, sound recording and digital audio and the following list should help you find what you need:

Anderton, Craig 'MIDI for Musicians', (Amsco Publications, 1995), 120pp.

Borwick, John 'Microphones – Technology and Technique', (Oxford: Focal Press, 1990), 241pp.

Borwick, John ed. 'Sound Recording Practice', (Oxford: Oxford University Press, 1996), 616pp.

Buick, Peter and Lennard, Vic 'Music Technology Reference Book', (PC Publishing, 1995), 160pp.

Clackett, Dave 'Handbook of MIDI Sequencing', (PC Publishing, 1996), 244pp.

De Furia, Steve and Scacciaferro, Joe 'The Sampling Book', (Omnibus Press, 2002), 152pp.

Everest, F. Alton 'The Master Handbook of Acoustics', (New York: TAB Books, 1994), 452pp.

Gibson, David 'The Art of Mixing', (Music Sales Limited, 1997), 127pp.

Harris, John 'Recording the Guitar', (PC Publishing, 1997), 156pp.

Howard, David M. and Angus, James 'Acoustics and Psychoacoustics', (Oxford: Focal Press, 2nd edition, 2001), 416pp.

Huber, David Miles 'The MIDI Manual', (SAMS, 1991), 268pp.

Huber and Runstein 'Modern Recording Techniques', (Oxford: Focal Press,1997), 496pp.

Katz, Bob 'Mastering Audio: The Art and the Science', (Focal Press, 2002), 319pp.

Kirk, Ross and Hunt, Andy 'Digital Sound Processing for Music and Multimedia', (Oxford: Focal Press, 1999), 352pp.

Lehrman, Paul 'Midi for the Professional', (Music Sales Corp., 1993), 239pp.

Massey, Howard 'Behind the Glass', (Backbeat UK, 2000), 224pp

Mellor, David 'Recording Techniques for Small Studios' (PC Publishing, 1993), 208pp.

Millward, Simon 'Sound Synthesis with VST Instruments', (PC Publishing, 2002), 277pp.

Ortiz, Joe and Pauly 'Beat It! (MIDI drum programming)', (PC Publishing, 1997), 114pp.

Owsinski, Bobby 'The Mixing Engineer's Handbook', (Music Sales Limited, 1999), 234pp.

Poyser, Debbie and Johnson, Derek 'Fast Guide to Propellerhead Reason', (PC Publishing, 2005), 410pp

Rona, Jeffrey and Wilkinson, Scott (Editor) 'The Midi Companion', (Hal Leonard Publishing Corp, 1994), 96pp.

Rothstein, Joseph 'MIDI – A Comprehensive Introduction', (Oxford: Oxford University Press, 1992), 226pp.

Rumsey, Francis 'The Audio Workstation Handbook', (Oxford: Focal Press, 1996), 286pp.

Russ, Martin and Rumsey, Francis (Editor) 'Sound Synthesis and Sampling', (Oxford: Focal Press, 1996), 400pp.

Stavrou, Michael 'Mixing with your Mind', (Flux Research, 2004), 300pp. (available from: www.mixingwithyourmind.com)

Waugh, Ian 'Making Music with Digital Audio (Direct to disk recording on the PC)', (PC Publishing, 1997), 250pp

White, Paul 'Creative Recording 2 – Microphones and Recording Techniques', (Music Maker Books, 1995), 99pp.

White, Paul 'Home Recording Made Easy', (Sanctuary Publishing,1997), 205pp.

White, Paul 'MIDI for the Technophobe', (Sanctuary Publishing, 1997), 184pp.

Useful websites

The internet is a very good resource for the latest information about Cubase SX and related products. The following lists some websites which may be of interest :

Steinberg Cubase

Steinberg main website	www.steinberg.net
Cubase.net forum	forum.cubase.net

Plug-ins

Antares	www.antarestech.com
Arboretum	www.arboretum.com
Audio Ease	www.audioease.com
BBE Sound	www.bbesound.com
dB-audioware	www.dB-audioware.com
DSP FX	www.dspfx.com
FXpansion	www.fxpansion.com
IK Multimedia	www.ikmultimedia.com
Izotope	www.izotope.com
Intelligent sounds and music	www.ismism.de
Native Instruments	www.native-instruments.com
Princeton Digital	www.princetondigital.com
Prosoniq	www.prosoniq.com
PSP	www.pspaudioware.com
SIR (Impulse Response Processor)	www.knufinke.de/sir
Sonic Foundry	www.sfoundry.com
Tascam	www.tascam.co.uk
T.C. Electronics powercore	www.tcelectronic.com
UAD powered plug-ins	www.mackie.com/uad-1
Virtos Audio	www.virtos-audio.com
Voxengo	www.voxengo.com
Wave Arts	www.wavearts.com
Waves	www.waves.com

MIDI plug-ins

Franck's MIDI plug-ins	www.midi-plugins.de
Nicolas Fournel	www.nicolasfournel.com
Ntonyx MIDI effects	www.ntonyx.com
Tencrazy	www.tencrazy.com

VST Instrument developers

Applied Acoustics Systems	www.applied-acoustics.com
Arturia	www.arturia.com
Bioroid	www.bioroid.com
Bitshift Audio	www.bitshiftaudio.com
Bojo	www.bojo.dk
Delaydots	www.delaydots.com
Edirol	www.edirol.com
Fxpansion	www.fxpansion.com
GMedia Music	www.gmediamusic.com
Green Oak	www.greenoak.com
Image Line	www.fruityloops.com
Lin Plug	www.linplug.com
LoftSoft	www.loftsoft.co.uk
Maz sound tools	www.maz-sound.de
mda	www.mda-vst.com
Muon Software	www.muon-software.com
Native Instruments	www.native-instruments.com
reFX	www.refx.net
rgcAudio	www.rgcaudio.com
Spectrasonics	www.spectrasonics.net
Steinberg	www.steinberg.net
Synapse Audio	www.synapse-audio.com
TC Works	www.tcworks.de
Tobybear	www.tobybear.de
Ultimate Sound Bank	www.plugsound.com
VirSyn	www.virsyn.de
Yellow tools	www.yellowtools.de

Audio cards/hardware

Apogee	www.apogeedigital.com
Creamware	www.creamware.com
Creative	www.creative.com
Echo	www.echoaudio.com
Edirol	www.edirol.com
E-MU	www.emu.com
ESI (Ego Systems Inc.)	www.esi-pro.com
Focusrite	www.focusrite.com
Korg	www.korg.com
Lexicon	www.lexiconpro.com
Mackie	www.mackie.com
Mark of the Unicorn (MOTU)	www.motu.com
M Audio	www.midiman.com
Metric Halo	www.mhlabs.com
RME	www.rme-audio.com
T.C. Electronics	www.tcelectronic.com
Turtle Beach	www.tbeach.com
Yamaha	www.yamaha.com

Soundbanks and samples

Convolution impulse responses	www.noisevault.com
FM sounds	www.thedx7.co.uk
Groundloops sampled loops	www.groundloops.com
KVR VSTi sound libraries	www.kvraudio.com
PrimeSounds sample library	www.primesounds.com
Reaktor (Len Sasso)	www.swiftkick.com/reaktor.html
Reaktor (Paul Swennenhuis)	www.midiworld.org/AuReality
Reaktor (Wave In Head)	www.waveinhead.de
Sonomic	www.sonomic.com
Sound ideas	www.sound-ideas.com
Tassman library	ww.hvsynthdesign.com
Time and space	www.timespace.com
WizooSounds sample library	www.wizoosounds.com

Sound synthesis, synthesizers and music technology

Hammond organ	theatreorgans.com/hammond/faq
Mellotron	members.aol.com/tronpage
Mellotron	www.mellotron.com
Moog	www.moogmusic.com
Moog synthesizers	moogarchives.com
Synthesizers and synthesis	www.vintagesynth.org
Synthesizer history	www.obsolete.com/120_years
Synthesizer information and links	www.synthesizers.com
Synth zone	www.synthzone.com

General interest

Acousti Products	www.acoustiproducts.com
Acoustics	www.mhsoft.nl
Acoustics	www.ethanwiner.com/acoustics.html
Acoustic analysis	www.etfacoustic.com
Analogx utilities	www.analogx.com
audio CD A/B tests	www.theabcd.com
audio comparison CDs	www.3daudioinc.com
Audio forums	www.audioforums.com
Audio production database	www.note2.com
Auralex acoustics	www.auralex.com
Apple website	www.apple.com
Arbiter Group PLC	www.arbitergroup.com
Carillon	www.carillondirect.com
CD-Recordable FAQ website	www.cdrfaq.org
Computer Music Magazine	www.computermusic.co.uk
Computer isolation boxes	www.iso-box.com
Digital domain	www.digido.com
Electronic music publishing	www.raw42.com
Electronic music website	www.em411.com
Future Music magazine	www.futuremusic.co.uk
Hard drive performance (DskBench)	www.sesa.es
Kustom PCs	www.kustompcs.co.uk

KVR Audio plug-in resources	www.kvraudio.com
Mac audio and music site	www.macmusic.org
Metal grille pop-shields	www.stedmancorp.com
MIDI Farm	www.midifarm.com
MIDI utilities	www.midiox.com
Millennium Music	www.millennium-music.biz
Musician's Tech Central	www.musicianstechcentral.com
Music XP website	www.musicxp.net
PC hardware analysis	www.cpuid.com
Plug-in Spot VSTi resources	www.pluginspot.com
Pro audio network	www.digitalprosound.com
Pro audio reference	www.rane.com/digi-dic.html
Professional recording resources	www.prorec.com
Project studio handbook	theprojectstudiohandbook.com/directory. htm
Quiet PC	www.quietpc.com
Recording Industry network	www.artistpro.com
Red Submarine	www.sub.co.uk
Rightmark audio analyser	audio.rightmark.org
Shareware Music Machine	www.hitsquad.com
Silent PC components/cases	www.antec.co.uk
Silent PC components/cases	www.paq.ltd.uk
Silent PC review	www.silentpcreview.com
Softpedia general utilities	www.softpedia.com
Sonic Spot resources	www.sonicspot.com
Sound on Sound magazine	www.soundonsound.com
Studio design	www.johnlsayers.com
Studio design (SAE)	www.saecollege.de/reference_material
Studiospares	www.studiospares.com
Studio tips	www.studiotips.com
Tom's PC hardware guide	www.tomshardware.com
University of York	www.york.ac.uk/inst/mustech
Utilitygeek general utilities	www.utilitygeek.com
Virtual Guitarist website	www.bornemark.se
VST central VSTi listings	www.vstcentral.com
Windows optimisation	www.ccleaner.com

23

Glossary

ADC Analogue-to-digital converter. A device which converts analogue data, such as an audio signal from the real world, into digital data (a sequence of numbers) which can be retained in computer memory or stored on digital media such as hard disks, DAT, CD and DVD.

ADSR Attack, Decay, Sustain, Release. A four-breakpoint envelope type used to control how the amplitude of a sound evolves over time. ADSR envelopes are also used to control the spectral evolution of a sound by modulating the cut-off frequency of a filter.

AES Audio Engineering Society. International organisation responsible for setting standards in the audio industry.

AES/EBU A digital signal interface standard agreed by the Audio Engineering Society and the European Broadcasting Union. The AES/EBU digital interface is a professional alternative to the S/PDIF standard.

Aftertouch The action of applying pressure to one or more keys of a musical keyboard after the onset of a note or chord. Also referred to as 'Channel Aftertouch' or 'Channel Pressure', it is transmitted via MIDI as Aftertouch messages and affects all notes present on the same MIDI channel by the same amount. It can be used to produce various real-time performance effects such as volume or brightness modulation and vibrato.

AGP Accelerated Graphics Port. Slot found on a computer's motherboard designed to accept graphics cards. Advantageous for audio since using an AGP graphics card optimises the use of the computer's resources and is unlikely to interfere with audio performance.

Algorithm A clearly defined, step-by-step set of instructions designed to achieve the completion of a specific task. Algorithms are invariably translated into computer programming languages and used as the building blocks for computer programs.

Aliasing A particular type of digital audio distortion which manifests itself as additional frequency components which do not form part of the original audio signal. This

occurs when a signal has been sampled at too low a sampling rate to accurately capture the details of the high frequency components.

All-pass filter A filtering device which involves delaying frequency components by varying amounts and mixing the result with the original signal. Unlike conventional filtering, no attenuation in the amplitudes of the frequencies takes place.

AM Amplitude Modulation. A sound effect achieved by modulating the amplitude of one audio signal (the carrier) by another signal (the modulator). When the modulator is an LFO, tremolo effects are produced. When both signals are in the audible range, a more complex signal containing the carrier and the sum and difference frequencies of the carrier and modulator is produced (sometimes used for sound synthesis).

Amplifier A device which increases or decreases the amplitude of a signal which passes through it.

Amplitude A measure of the depth of the compression and rarefaction cycles of a sound signal where the peak amplitude is the point of maximum displacement from the mid-point of the signal's waveform. The amplitude contributes to the perceived loudness of the signal.

Analogue In audio, refers to a sound signal whose waveform has a value at every point in time. There are no discrete steps between each point and an analogue recording is usually that which has been made onto audio tape. Also used to describe analogue synthesis (as opposed to digital synthesis).

Arpeggiator A device for automatically repeating a group of notes in a cyclic pattern, usually by stepping through the notes of a chord which is held down on the musical keyboard.

ASIO Audio Stream Input Output. Computer protocol developed by Steinberg for handling audio recording and playback in digital audio systems.

Attack The shape and duration of the first part of a sound event where the amplitude rises from zero to its peak level (as implemented in an ADSR envelope).

Attenuation The reduction of the amplitude of a sound signal (or of a component within the signal).

Balance i) describes the relative levels of two or more sound elements (for example, when setting up a mix on a mixing console). ii) MIDI Controller 8. Used to adjust the relative levels of two components of a sound.

Band-pass filter A filter which allows a band of frequencies between two cut-off points to pass through with little change while significantly attenuating frequencies both above and below the pass band.

Band-reject filter A filter which significantly attenuates a band of frequencies between two cut-off points while allowing the rest of the signal to pass through with little change.

Bandwidth i) The range between two frequency points within the spectrum of an audio signal. ii) The overall frequency range of the spectrum of an audio signal.

Bank Select A combination of MIDI Controllers 0 and 32. A Bank Select message is usually immediately followed by a Program Change and allows switching to as many as 16384 different Banks.

BIOS Basic Input Output System. A program at the root level of a computer system for controlling its elementary operations.

Bit Acronym for 'binary digit'. The smallest unit of information in a binary number, represented as a 1 or a 0.

Bit depth The number of levels of measurement available in a digital audio system during A/D and D/A conversion. For example, a 16-bit system features 65536 possible discrete values which can be used to measure the amplitude of an audio signal. Greater bit depth results in greater dynamic range.

Boot A term used to describe starting a computer. This can take the form of a 'cold start', when the computer is booted from its switched off state, and a 'warm start', when the computer is restarted in its switched on state.

BPM Abbreviation for Beats Per Minute. Musical tempo expressed as the number of beats which occur in one minute. For example, at a tempo of 60BPM each beat of the bar has a duration of one second.

Breath Controller A breath operated device connected to a synthesizer used to change the volume or timbre of a sound. It is transmitted via MIDI as Controller 2.

Byte An 8-bit binary number (e.g. 0011 1010), creating the fundamental unit of measurement for computer

media. A kilobyte (Kb) is 1,024 bytes, a megabyte (Mb) is 1,024 kilobytes and a gigabyte (Gb) is 1,024 megabytes.

Buffer Temporary storage area used to store data as it flows in, out and through a computer system.

Carrier In frequency modulation, amplitude modulation and ring modulation, the carrier is the audio signal to which modulation is applied. The carrier normally governs the perceived pitch of the resulting tone.

CD ROM Compact Disc Read Only Memory. A read-only CD containing data which can only be read by a computer CD drive and not an audio CD player.

Cent One hundredth of a semitone. A unit in musical instrument tuning systems used for fine adjustments of pitch.

Centre frequency The centre point of the passband or stopband in a band-pass or band-reject filter.

Chorus An effect produced by passing a signal through one or more delay lines and modulating the delay time(s) with an LFO. The result is mixed with the original signal. The modulation of the delay times produces changes in the perceived pitch and timing, creating the illusion of an ensemble of sound sources.

Comb filter A filter comprised of multiple amplitude response curves (or resonances) located at harmonic intervals relative to a chosen fundamental frequency. Passing a signal through such a filter emphasises the chosen harmonics in the source sound and can often change its perceived pitch.

Compressor An automatic level adjustment device which normally results in loud parts of the signal becoming quieter and quiet parts becoming louder. Compression converts a large dynamic range into a smaller dynamic range.

Control Change A type of MIDI message used to control various parameters other than the musical notes. Control Change messages contain information about the Controller number (0 - 127) and its value (0 - 127). Each Controller number has a specific function and the more commonly used Controllers include modulation (01), breath control (02), main volume (07), pan (10), expression (11) and sustain pedal (64).

CPU Central Processing Unit. The main processor or chip controlling the operations of a computer, usually found on the main circuit board (motherboard).

Cross modulation The interconnection of the outputs of two oscillators to eachother's frequency inputs resulting in a complex frequency-modulated signal.

Cut-off The frequency at which the response of a filter passes from the pass band to the stop band (or vice versa), i.e. the frequency at which the filter starts to have an effect.

DAC Digital-to-analogue converter. A device which converts digital data into analogue data. For example, before we can hear the music on an audio CD, the digital information picked up by the read head of the CD player must first be converted into analogue form which can be processed by an amplifier and speaker system and, finally, sensed by the ear as sound vibrations in air.

DAT Digital Audio Tape. Digital audio recording format using 3.81mm wide tape in small cassettes. Began as a consumer format but later became widely accepted in the professional audio industry. Features include 16-bit and 24-bit recording and playback at 44.1kHz or 48kHz and various tape lengths up to 120mins.

Decay i) As part of an envelope (e.g. ADSR), describes the shape and duration of a second part of a sound event where the amplitude falls from its peak level to its sustain level. ii) In general terms, describes how a sound fades away to silence.

Decibel (dB) A unit of relative measurement of sound level between audio signals on a logarithmic scale. For example, increasing the level of an input signal by 6dB results in an output which is double the amplitude of the original. Attenuating the level by 6dB results in an output which is half the amplitude.

Delay A replication of a signal which occurs at a set time after the original. Used in audio for delay, echo, chorus, flanging and other effects.

Digital Digital systems handle information as numerical data. For example, a digital waveform is measured as a succession of discrete points in time (samples), each of which is represented by a value (the maximum range of which forms the bit depth [or wordlength]). The quantity of these samples within a given time frame forms the sample rate. The audio on a CD is recorded at 16-bit/44.1kHz, i.e. 44,100 16-bit wordlength samples per second.

Distortion A non-linear audio process which adds extra frequencies to the signal, thereby changing its waveform.

Dither Audio processing technique which counteracts quantisation noise in digital audio recordings. Quantisation distortion occurs at very low levels when there are not enough bits in the system to accurately measure the signal. Noise shaped dithering involves converting the quantisation distortion into another kind of signal and re-distributing it to parts of the audio spectrum where it is less obvious to the human ear.

DMA Direct Memory Access. Describes access to RAM without passing through the main processor.

Download The process of loading a file from another system, such as from the internet or other network, into one's own computer.

Driver Software which provides the communication protocol between a hardware device and the operating system of the host computer. The hardware is usually set up and initialised via the driver software.

DSP i) Digital Signal Processing. The processing of signals using digital microprocessors. ii) Digital Signal Processor. A special computer chip which has been optimised for the high-speed numerical computations required for the processing of audio signals.

DVD Digital Versatile Disc. 5 inch diameter disc with around seven times the capacity of a regular compact disc, able to store data in computer, audio and video formats. DVD-A (DVD-Audio) is a high-quality format for stereo and multichannel audio.

EBU European Broadcasting Union, an organisation responsible for setting audio and broadcasting standards in Europe.

Echo A particular kind of delay where the delayed signal is clearly distinguishable from the original, often involving repeating echos. Delay effects may be classed as echo when the delay time is increased to around 30ms or more, (i.e. when the ear begins to clearly differentiate the delayed and original signals).

EIDE Enhanced Integrated Drive Electronics. A standard for fast data transfer between the host computer and mass storage devices, such as hard drives and CD ROM drives.

Emphasis See Resonance

Envelope The shape of a sound's amplitude variations over time (usually plotted on a graph of amplitude against time with break-points for each stage in the sound's evolution). One of the most common envelope shapes is the ADSR envelope.

Envelope Generator (EG) A device which generates a time-varying control signal (envelope) used to modulate the amplitude of a sound (usually based upon a set of values entered by the user). Envelope generators are also commonly used to modulate the frequency of the cut-off point of a filter.

Equalisation (EQ) Increase/attenuation of the levels of different frequency bands (e.g. bass, mid and treble) within a signal for corrective or creative purposes.

Expression MIDI Controller 11. Used to change the volume of a note while it is sustaining.

FAT File Allocation Table. A small area of a computer's hard drive containing an index which is used to keep track of all data stored on the disk.

Feedback Circuit which allows the connection of the output signal back to the input, producing additional frequency components within the signal, (when used for overdrive and saturation effects), or for creating echo repeats, (when used for delay effects).

FFT Abbreviation for Fast Fourier Transform. An optimised version of the Fourier Transform (Joseph Fourier), a mathematical procedure for calculating the frequency components of a sound from the waveform.

Filter A device which attenuates one or more chosen frequency bands within a sound while allowing the others to pass through unchanged.

Firewire Data communication standard also referred to as IEEE-1394 (Institute of Electrical and Electronic Engineers). Supports the serial transfer of data at 400Mbit/sec or 800Mbit/sec and allows hot-plugging of peripheral devices.

Flanging An audio effect created by mixing a delayed version of a signal with the original and modulating the delay time with an LFO while also applying an amount of feedback.

FM Frequency Modulation. A sound synthesis technique (or effect) where the frequency of one signal (the carrier) is modulated by another (the modulator). In the sound synthesis sense, FM implies that both frequencies are within the audible range and when this is the case multiple frequencies known as sidebands are added to the signal.

Frequency The number of times a periodic sound wave oscillates per second, measured in hertz (Hz).

Frequency domain The representation of a sound signal on a graph of amplitude versus frequency. This shows the spectrum of the signal.

Fundamental The lowest frequency component within a periodic soundwave and normally that which gives the tone its perceived pitch.

Gain A measure of the increase in relative amplitude level between the input and output of an amplifier.

Gate i) An audio device which radically attenuates the level of an input signal when it falls below a certain threshold. Used especially to filter out unwanted background noise and interference in the inactive parts of speech or musical performance. ii) The time between the moment a note is

triggered by pressing a key on a musical keyboard (key on) and when the note is ended by releasing the key (key off).

General MIDI (GM) An addition to the MIDI protocol, (not formally a part of the MIDI Specification), providing a standard set of rules for patch mapping, drum and percussion note mapping, multi-timbrality, polyphony and various other elements. Roland introduced an enhanced version of the GM standard known as GS (General Standard) and Yamaha introduced similar enhancements known as XG (Extended General MIDI).

Harmonic Component within a sound whose frequency is a whole integer multiple of the fundamental.

Headroom The difference between the current level of a recorded signal and the maximum output level of the recording medium.

Hertz (Hz) A unit for measuring frequency. It expresses the number of oscillations per second of a periodic soundwave. The greater the number of hertz, the higher the perceived pitch of the sound.

Hexadecimal A base sixteen numbering system often used by computer programmers as an alternative to decimal or binary systems. The decimal numbers 0-9 are expressed as 0-9 in hexadecimal and decimal 10-15 are expressed as the letters A-F. Hexadecimal numbers have much more in common with the way that computers actually work than decimal numbers and they are less cumbersome than binary numbers. Thus they have proved extremely efficient for the analysis and understanding of computer data.

Hold pedal Middle foot pedal featured on acoustic pianos which, when pressed down, sustains the concurrently played note(s) but allows any subsequent notes to be played normally for as long as the pedal is held down. A similar foot pedal is featured on some electronic musical keyboards to create a similar effect. In MIDI-based applications the pedal action is transmitted using MIDI controller 66, (also referred to as sostenuto).

High-pass filter (HPF) A filter which significantly attenuates the frequencies below a chosen cut-off point while allowing those above to pass through with little change.

HTML Hypertext mark-up language. A language used in the creation of web pages.

Internet Global network of computers interconnected via telephone lines. The internet is now the largest information resource in the world and provides a wide range of services and entertainment.

ISP Internet Service Provider. Internet users must subscribe to one of the ISPs which provide access to the internet.

Jumper A small clip for connecting pins on a circuit board to enable hardware re-configuration. Jumpers are found on such things as computer motherboards, extension cards and hard drives.

Latency The delay between the user input and the time it takes for a real-time digital audio system to respond and process the data through its hardware and software.

Level A measure of the amplitude of an audio signal.

LFO Abbreviation for low frequency oscillator. A type of oscillator which operates below the normal hearing range, often used for modulating a second oscillator to produce vibrato, tremolo and other modulation effects.

Limiter A peak level control device used to reduce the gain of the input signal when the input level exceeds the chosen threshold. A limiter is usually characterised by a very fast attack time and gain reduction which acts upon only the loudest peaks in the signal.

Logarithmic A manner in which to manage scales involving very large numbers and helpful in music and acoustics for understanding the human perception of sound intensity and frequency. The ear's response to these phenomena is logarithmic and not linear. For example, plotting frequency on a graph logarithmically shows equal pitch intervals (an equal distance between successive octaves) rather than a linear plot which shows equal frequency intervals (a doubling of the distance between successive octaves).

Loudness The subjective response of the ear to the amplitude of a sound signal.

Loudness contour The shape of the amplitude of a sound as it evolves over time. The same meaning as envelope shape (see envelope, above).

Low-pass filter (LPF) A filter which significantly attenuates the frequencies above a chosen cut-off point while allowing those below to pass through with little change.

Master keyboard A MIDI equipped keyboard (often with no sound generating circuitry) used to control a network of MIDI modules and devices. Sometimes referred to as a 'mother keyboard'.

MIDI Musical Instrument Digital Interface. A data communication standard, first established in 1983, for the exchange of musical information between electronic musical instruments and, subsequently, computers. This involves the serial transfer of digital information, (MIDI Messages), via 5 pin DIN connectors. MIDI Messages are governed by a pre-defined set of rules and syntax known as the MIDI Specification.

MIDI Channel A channel for the sending and receiving of MIDI messages between devices. MIDI specifies 16 separate channels and each MIDI device can be set to be receptive to messages on one of these channels or, in the case of a multi-timbral instrument, on several specified channels at the same time.

MIDI Clock A timing related MIDI Message embedded in the MIDI data stream. MIDI Timing Clocks are sent 24 times per quarter note and along with Song Position Pointer, Start, Stop and Continue messages are used to synchronize MIDI-based sequencers, drum machines and other MIDI devices. Unlike SMPTE/EBU Time Code, MIDI Timing Clock is tempo-dependent.

MIDI Controller A type of MIDI Message used to control various musical parameters other than the notes themselves, such as Modulation, Volume and Pan. Controllers are also referred to as 'Continuous Controllers' and 'Control Change messages'.

MIDI Event MIDI data once it has been recorded into a MIDI-based sequencer. This is in contrast to 'MIDI Message' which refers to the same data as it is being sent down the MIDI cable.

MIDI File A standardised file format providing a way of transferring MIDI data between different software sequencers, hardware sequencers and computer platforms. There are three types of MIDI File: Type 0 stores the data as a single stream of events, Type 1 contains multiple parallel tracks and Type 2 allows sets of independent sequences to be stored in a single file. Type 1 is the most popular format.

MIDI In 5 pin DIN socket found on all MIDI-equipped devices used to receive MIDI data.

MIDI interface A hardware interface which provides a link between a computer and external MIDI devices, normally providing at least one MIDI input and one MIDI output with more advanced units providing multiple MIDI sockets and synchronization facilities.

MIDI Machine Control (MMC) An addition to the MIDI Specification to facilitate the control of tape transports and other devices.

MIDI Message A short sequence of MIDI data which passes a discrete instruction or command to the receiving device. MIDI Messages include such things as Note On, Note Off, Polyphonic Pressure, Control Change, Program Change, Aftertouch, and System Exclusive messages.

MIDI Mode An operational mode governing how a MIDI device manages data on different MIDI Channels and whether it performs polyphonically or monophonically. There are 4 modes including Mode 1 (Omni On/Poly);

response to messages on all MIDI channels and polyphonic, Mode 2 (Omni On/Mono); response to messages on all MIDI channels and monophonic, Mode 3 (Omni Off/Poly); response to messages on chosen MIDI channel(s) and polyphonic, Mode 4 (Omni Off/Mono); response to messages on chosen MIDI channel(s) and monophonic. Most units power up in Mode 3.

MIDI Out 5 pin DIN socket found on all MIDI equipped instruments used to send MIDI data.

MIDI Thru 5 pin DIN socket found on most MIDI equipped instruments providing a copy of the MIDI data received at the MIDI In. In other words, the data passes through the unit on to a further destination.

MIDI Time Code (MTC) A type of time code which is sent via MIDI, used to synchronize MIDI-based sequencers and other MIDI devices. Similar to SMPTE/EBU time code, MTC is an absolute timing reference measured in hours, minutes, seconds and fractions of a second and so does not vary with tempo.

Modulation i) The modification of one signal by another to produce effects (e.g. vibrato and tremolo). For real-time performance, the intensity of the modulation effect is controlled by the modulation wheel found on the control panel of electronic musical keyboards. Modulation is transmitted via MIDI as MIDI Controller 1. ii) The basis for FM and AM sound synthesis techniques.

Modulator i) The control signal which applies a modulating effect to a second signal. ii) The modulating part of a carrier:modulator pair of oscillators in FM synthesis.

Multi-timbral The ability of a synthesizer or module to produce several different sounds at the same time controlled on different MIDI Channels.

Native processing Digital audio processing involving the computer's own processor and other resources rather than external digital signal processing hardware.

Noise A sound comprised of randomly distributed and inharmonic frequency components.

Notch filter A specialised type of band-reject filter which significantly attenuates a very narrow band of frequencies between two cut-off points while allowing the rest of the signal to pass through with little change.

Note On A MIDI message produced by pressing a key on a musical keyboard (or by the onset of a pre-recorded MIDI event). A Note On message starts the sounding of a musical event. It contains information about the Pitch and the Velocity of the note.

Note Off A MIDI message produced by releasing a key on a musical keyboard (or by the termination of a pre-recorded MIDI event). A Note Off message starts the release phase of a musical event. It contains information about the Pitch of the note to be switched off and the Velocity with which the key was released.

Octave An interval in pitch between two tones corresponding with a doubling (or halving) of the frequency. In Western music there are 12 notes in each octave.

Operating system An organised collection of software at the next level up from BIOS which enables the user to communicate with the computer. The operating system provides the interface between BIOS and the applications running on the computer.

Oscillator A device which produces a periodic, alternating signal. Oscillators are used for generating periodic waveforms of a given amplitude and frequency.

Overtone Spectral component in a composite sound signal located at a higher frequency than the fundamental.

Pan The panoramic position of a sound within the stereo image. Most devices with two or more audio outputs feature a pan control. Pan data is transmitted via MIDI as Controller 10.

Parametric EQ Flexible signal filtering arrangement based upon a centre frequency selector, a Q control and a gain control. The centre frequency selector allows you to tune in to the frequency band you wish to process, the Q control regulates the width (filter slope characteristics) of this band and the gain control provides the means to boost or cut the chosen frequencies.

Patch A configuration of the controls of an electronic or software synthesizer which creates a specific sound. Also referred to as program, voice, sound or preset. Each patch can usually be stored in the instrument's memory for later recall.

PCI Peripheral Component Interconnect. A PCI bus is a standard computer slot for cards and extension boards and is widely used for connecting audio cards.

PCM Pulse Code Modulation. Coding scheme involving the conversion of binary numbers into electronic pulses and fundamental to the conversion of analogue signals into digital form during the sampling process.

Phase The relationship between two or more components of a waveform (or of separate signals) in terms of the relative position of the compression and rarefaction parts of their waveforms. Phase is expressed in degrees.

Phasing An audio effect created by mixing a phase-shifted version of a signal with the original and modulating the phase shifting with an LFO while also applying an amount of feedback.

Pink noise A sound signal whose acoustical energy decreases (as the frequency increases) at a rate of 3dB-per-octave. This results in a signal with equal acoustical energy in each octave. Pink noise is useful in acoustic measurements since it approximates the frequency spectrum of typical audio signals and produces a flat response on a constant Q spectrum analyser.

Pitch The subjective response of the ear to the frequency of a sound signal.

Pitch Bend Variation of the pitch of a sounding note (e.g. the bending of a note on a guitar). It is transmitted via MIDI as Pitch Bend data and on electronic keyboards is usually applied in real-time using a pitch wheel on the control surface of the instrument.

Plug and Play A standard developed by Microsoft and Intel to enable extension cards and peripheral hardware to be automatically recognised and installed in PC computer systems.

PMCD Pre-Master CD. A special format, originally developed by Sonic Solutions, to allow glass masters to be cut directly from CD-R. Sometimes used (probably wrongly) to describe any Red-Book-standard CD-R master from which a glass master can be made for mass CD duplication.

Pole An element in filter design responsible for the characteristics of the filter slope between the pass band and the stop band where a 1-pole filter results in a filter slope of 6dB per octave, a 2-pole filter gives a slope of 12dB per octave, a 4-pole filter gives a slope of 24dB per octave and so on.

Polyphonic Having the capacity to play more than one note simultaneously.

Portamento A sliding of pitch between consecutively played notes (similar to glissando).

Program Change A type of MIDI message used to remotely change the Program number or patch in a MIDI device. There are 128 available program numbers but when used in conjunction with Bank Select messages the number of possible program slots is significantly expanded.

Pulse wave A periodic sound wave containing odd-numbered harmonics similar to a square wave but with certain harmonics in the series missing. Pulse waves are characterised by their pulse width which is the proportion of one complete cycle for which the waveform remains in the compression (or positive) part of its waveform. A pulse wave with a pulse width of 1/n lacks each nth harmonic.

PWM Pulse Width Modulation. The cyclic modulation of the pulse width of a pulse wave using an LFO as the modulator.

Q A measure of the selectivity and filter slope characteristics of a filter, where low Q values select a wide bandwidth and high Q values select a narrow bandwidth. Also referred to as resonance and emphasis.

Quantisation The process of transforming a continuous analogue signal into a series of discrete values during analogue-to-digital conversion.

Quantisation noise A noise produced when converting very low level audio signals, due to insufficient bit depth (lack of resolution). The noise results from the rounding up or down of some of the least significant bits used to express the signal and is heard as a 'graininess' in the sound reproduction.

Quantize A term used in hardware and software sequencers to describe the action of automatically moving recorded notes onto the nearest fraction of a bar according to a quantize value. For example, using a quantize value of 16 (meaning 1/16 notes) shifts all inaccurately played notes onto the nearest 1/16 division of the bar. More elaborate methods of quantizing material include moving notes 'towards' a quantize value according to a percentage (iterative quantize) and moving notes according to a pre-recorded 'feel' template (groove quantize).

RAM Random Access Memory. Volatile memory for the temporary storage of data.

Real-time Instantaneous output (or result) from an input. Real-time digital audio processing refers to processing where there is virtually no delay between the input signal and the processed output signal. Recording music into a sequencer in real-time means that the performance is recorded instantaneously as it is played, much like recording onto a tape recorder.

Release The shape and duration of the final part of a sound event where the amplitude falls from its sustain level to zero.

Resonance The frequency or frequencies at which a device or object vibrates in sympathy with itself. Many filters are endowed with resonant behaviour normally characterised by a boost in the frequencies around the cut-off point. The shape and intensity of this boost in frequencies is regulated by a resonance control (often also referred to as Q or emphasis).

Resynthesis Analysis-synthesis technique where an existing sample is analysed and arranged into a set of parameters and values (e.g. pitch, amplitude and phase for each harmonic) which are used as the basis for synthesizing a new sound.

Reverberation Multiple series of reflections occurring after the original sound in an acoustic space. Also known as reverb, reverberation is characterised by three phases: the original sound which arrives directly from the source to the listener's ear, after a short pause the early reflections from nearby surfaces and finally a complex mass of multiple reflections which fade to silence (known as the reverb tail).

Ring modulation Amplitude modulation technique where two oscillator signals are multiplied to produce the sum and difference of their frequencies in the output. The original frequency of the source signal is not present in the output.

ROM Read Only Memory. Memory with fixed contents which cannot be overwritten.

SACD Super Audio Compact Disc. A high fidelity CD format utilising DSD (Direct Stream Digital) technology, developed by Sony and Philips. Rivals the DVD-A format.

Sample i) A snapshot of a digital audio signal at one moment in time. ii) A recorded segment of digital audio.

Sampler Musical instrument which allows the recording, editing, modifying and playback of segments of digitally recorded sound.

Sampling rate In digital audio recording the sampling rate is the number of times an analogue signal is measured per second during the process of analogue-to-digital conversion. For example, the audio on a CD is recorded at a sampling rate of 44.1kHz, i.e.: 44,100 samples per second.

Sample resolution See 'Bit depth'.

Sawtooth wave A periodic sound wave containing all the harmonics in the natural harmonic series with the level of each harmonic at 1/n that of the fundamental (where n = the harmonic number). A sawtooth wave has a saw-shaped waveform, hence its name.

SCSI Small Computer System Interface. A communication buss system available in several standards, supporting fast data transfer speeds (up to around 240Mbit/second) and the connection of several devices on the same buss (usually hard drives).

Semitone A shift in pitch of half a tone. In mathematical terms, a change in pitch of one semitone is achieved by multiplying or dividing the frequency by 1.0595. The keys on a piano keyboard are arranged in one semitone steps.

Signal-to-noise (S/N) ratio The ratio of the signal level to the noise level in a system, usually expressed in decibels (dB's). The larger the value of the S/N ratio the lower the level of the background noise.

Sine wave A pure, periodic sound wave based upon the mathematical sine function containing a single component at the fundamental. A sine wave has a sinusoidal waveform.

SMPTE Society of Motion Picture and Television Engineers. An American organisation responsible for setting film and audio standards and recommended practices. For convenience, time code is often referred to as 'SMPTE' (pronounced 'simptee') but, in fact, this is only one type of time code.

Song Position Pointer A MIDI message often included when synchronizing MIDI devices using MIDI Timing Clocks. It allows the slaved instrument to be synchronized to the same position in the music as the master instrument after fast forward and rewind operations.

S/PDIF Sony Philips Digital InterFace. A digital signal interface standard often found on audio cards, DAT machines and other devices. S/PDIF sockets take the form of RCA phonos.

Spectrum A representation of a sound in terms of its constituent components at one point in time or averaged over a chosen time frame. Expressed graphically in the frequency domain as vertical lines (or peaks) where each line represents a component at a different frequency and amplitude. A spectrum gives a good idea of a sound's timbral quality.

Square wave A periodic sound wave containing all the odd-numbered harmonics in the natural harmonic series with the level of each harmonic at 1/n that of the fundamental (where n = the harmonic number). A square wave has a square-shaped waveform, hence its name.

Steady-state The segment within the envelope of a sound event where the timbre and amplitude is relatively constant. It is within this part of the sound where a loop can be applied using sampling techniques for the artificial sustaining of a note.

Step-time A method of entering notes into a sequencer one step at a time (also referred to as Step input). The pitch, position and duration for each entry is pre-determined and after input is complete the music can be played back at any tempo. Step-time provides a useful method of entering notes into a sequencer when real-time performance is either too fast or too complicated.

Sustain The part in the evolution of a sound event which determines the amplitude level which sustains for as long as the note is held.

Sustain Pedal A foot pedal on acoustic and electronic pianos used to produce a sustaining of all played notes for as long as the pedal is held down. MIDI Controller 64 (also known as the Damper pedal).

Synthesizer An electronic or software-based musical instrument specialised in the creation of a wide range of tones and sound textures beyond those encountered in conventional musical instruments. A synthesizer is normally endowed with a performance interface (a musical keyboard), a control interface (GUI or front panel controls) and a synthesis engine (sound processing circuitry).

System Exclusive A type of MIDI Message allowing non-standardised communication between MIDI devices. Used for the transfer of Manufacturer Specific System Exclusive and also Universal System Exclusive data. Manufacturer Specific System Exclusive includes a unique ID for each manufacturing company and might be used to change or control almost any parameter in the receiving device as deemed appropriate by the manufacturer. Universal System Exclusive data includes MIDI Machine Control, MIDI Show Control, Sample Dump Standard, MIDI File Dump, General MIDI On and General MIDI Off.

Timbre Tone colour, or harmonic structure which gives a sound its sonic identity.

Time Code A time encoded signal recorded onto audio or video tape for time and point location and synchronisation purposes. It is sometimes referred to as 'SMPTE' (pronounced 'simptee') but, in fact, SMPTE is only one standard, as used in the USA. The other is EBU Time Code as used in Europe. Time code is measured in hours, minutes, seconds, frames and subframes.

Time domain The representation of a sound signal on a graph of amplitude versus time. This shows the waveform of the signal.

Tremolo A periodic variation in the loudness of a tone produced by modulating its amplitude with a low frequency oscillator (LFO), usually set in the range between 1 and 10Hz.

Triangle wave A periodic sound wave containing all the odd-numbered harmonics in the natural harmonic series with the level of each harmonic at $1/n^2$ that of the fundamental (where n = the harmonic number). A triangle wave has a triangle-shaped waveform, hence its name.

Trigger A short pulse which instructs a synthesizer to start a process like the sounding of a note or the generating of an envelope.

USB Universal Serial Bus. High speed data communication standard allowing the serial transfer of data at up to 12Mbit/second for USB 1 and 480Mbit/second for USB 2. Due to its superior data transfer speed USB 2 is the preferred option for audio and MIDI applications. Allows hot-plugging of peripheral devices.

VCA Voltage Controlled Amplifier. Type of amplifier used in analogue synthesis where the gain is regulated by a control voltage.

VCF Voltage Controlled Filter. Type of filter used in analogue synthesis where the cut-off frequency is regulated by a control voltage.

VCO Voltage Controlled Oscillator. Type of oscillator used in analogue synthesis where the frequency is regulated by a control voltage.

Velocity The speed (or force) with which a key is pressed or released on an electronic keyboard instrument. Normally, the harder a key is struck the louder the resulting note and the higher the velocity value. Velocity might also be used to affect the brightness, vibrato, sustain or some other expressive element within the sound. It forms part of the actual MIDI note data, (the third byte of Note On and Note Off messages), and does not assume a separate MIDI data category.

Vibrato A periodic variation in the pitch of a tone produced by modulating its frequency with a low frequency oscillator (LFO), usually set in the range between 1 and 10Hz. Vibrato produces a characteristic 'warbling' effect and is usually applied during the sustain part of the sound.

Virtual analogue Simulated analogue synthesis using digital signal processing techniques in software synthesis instruments.

Volume i) Generic term for loudness, amplitude or level. ii) MIDI Controller 7. Used to regulate the volume of notes in a MIDI recording. Also referred to as Main Volume.

VSTi Abbreviation for VST Instrument (Virtual Studio Instrument).

Waveform The shape of a sound wave when represented on a graph of time versus amplitude. Typical synthesized periodic waveforms include sawtooth, square, triangle and pulse.

White noise a sound signal whose acoustical energy remains the same for any given linear bandwidth within the frequency spectrum. White noise produces a 'hissing' sound.

Appendix 1
Computer hardware

Those with at least a superficial understanding of what goes on inside their computer are likely to get more out of Cubase SX. However, the first thing that Cubase SX users should bear in mind is that computer hardware and software changes extremely quickly and it is therefore difficult to keep up with the latest developments. While it is acknowledged that the specifications of your computer are important for system performance, this book is dedicated to Cubase SX itself and not to in-depth computer coverage. Any information contained in this appendix should therefore be regarded as additional to the main focus of the text. For more detailed coverage of computers readers are advised to consult the relevant books, magazines and websites. For precise computer recommendations for Cubase SX consult the Steinberg user documentation or the Steinberg website.

There now follows coverage of the basic hardware components of a computer and how these elements are likely to affect the Cubase SX user.

Motherboard concerns

The motherboard is a large circuit board inside the computer to which almost all other components are connected in some way. It is the central hub of activity and includes a wide range of slots and sockets. These generally include connectors for the CPU, RAM, hard drives, CD ROM / DVD drives, and serial and parallel ports. Also included are expansion ports for peripheral devices such as PCI (Peripheral Component Interconnect), AGP (Advanced Graphics Port), USB (Universal Serial Buss) and Firewire which may be used to connect audio hardware devices, MIDI interfaces, graphic cards, SCSI cards, printers and so on. The motherboard also contains the BIOS (Basic Input Output System).

Each motherboard features what is known as a chipset. Each chipset is endowed with the characteristics required to communicate with the latest processors, RAM and hardware devices. Motherboards and their chipsets are continually updated in order to maintain compatibility with the latest developments in computer hardware. For example, different kinds of motherboards are required for AMD processors and Intel Pentium processors.

Processor choice

The processor or CPU (Central Processing Unit) is effectively the brain of the computer where the calculations and processing of data takes place. Processor speeds are measured in GHz (gigahertz) and, in general, the faster the speed the shorter the performance time for any given operation. Processor types and speeds are continually changing but, for Cubase SX, the fastest currently available Intel or AMD processors are recommended for the PC and the fastest currently available

G4/G5/Core processors are recommended for the Mac. Due to the rapid rate of change in the computer industry, you are advised to check the latest magazines and catalogues to find out the current state of affairs in the computer processor market.

RAM matters

With ever more memory-hungry operating systems and computer applications, lots of RAM is essential to run your system smoothly. RAM is an abbreviation for Random Access Memory. This is a temporary storage area and, when computations need to be performed, the data required is first stored there and then accessed at high speed by the computer's processor. If there is insufficient RAM the hard disk is used as a virtual memory expansion area. This slows things down since access to data on the hard drive is slower than access to RAM. Any such slowing down of the computer's performance may not be so important for non-musical programs but for real-time applications which use native audio processing, like Cubase SX, optimal access to high speed RAM is essential for smooth operation. The amount of available RAM (among other things) directly affects how many audio tracks, plug-ins and virtual instruments your system can handle. It also affects the smooth operation of software sampling instruments which use RAM as a storage area for sample data. It therefore pays to have as much RAM as possible and 512MB or more is recommended for the best results.

The hard disk

The hard disk is where the operating system, program applications (including Cubase SX) and all other important data is stored permanently. When it is needed, this data is retrieved from the hard disk and processed in other parts of the system. Large and fast hard drives are essential for optimum Cubase SX performance. Size is important for giving you enough space to record all your data and speed affects the rapidity with which data can be retrieved from the disk (which, in turn, affects the number of simultaneous audio tracks you can run in Cubase SX).

Digital audio eats up hard disk space extremely quickly. Recording 16-bit audio at the usual 44.1kHz sampling rate (CD quality) takes up 5MB of disk space per mono minute. This means that a CD in its final stereo format would need around 600-700MB of disk space. When you record multiple tracks in Cubase SX your space requirements are likely to be much greater. If you intend to use high resolution 24-bit and 32-bit float audio then your disk space requirements are increased still further. However, size is not the only consideration when choosing a hard drive.

Multi-track digital audio puts heavy demands on the speed and efficiency of the drive. Large amounts of data must be transferred from the disk to the audio hardware in the fastest possible time. The data stream for each track is accessed in rotation and the data blocks on the disk may not always be found in convenient locations. For 16-track audio the read head of the drive is effectively attempting to be in sixteen different places at the same time so that you can hear your audio with no delay and in perfect synchronisation. In reality, the data is stored in advance in a buffer which helps speed up the rate of data transfer. Add to this the fact that the hard disk may also be expected to simultaneously record during playback, then you can begin to appreciate why the hard drive needs to be particularly efficient. The main indicator of hard drive performance is the sustained data transfer rate (DTR). The DTR is the amount of data which can be read from the disk within a given time frame, measured in MB per second. Other indicators include the average access time, the average time it takes for the read head to find and retrieve a piece of data on the disk, and the rotation speed. Common rotations speeds include 5400, 7200 and 10,000rpm. 7200rpm or better is recommended for audio applications.

Although a single hard disk can produce adequate results, the use of two (or more) hard disk drives is highly recommended for audio-based computer systems. One drive is used for the system and program files, and the other is used for the project and audio files. This arrangement can significantly increase your track count and makes it easier to maintain and defragment the audio drive.

The choice of hard drive revolves around two interface types: ATA / IDE (Advanced Technology Attachment / Integrated Drive Electronics) and SCSI (Small Computer Systems Interface). Furthermore, there are two types of ATA / IDE drives, Parallel ATA (PATA) and Serial ATA (SATA).

ATA / IDE hard drives include controller hardware on the drive itself which manages the input and output of the data. ATA refers to the interface specification and IDE refers to the device type. Most drives are of an improved IDE type known as Enhanced IDE (EIDE) and their mode of data transfer is Ultra DMA (Ultra Direct Memory Access). Direct memory access allows data to be transferred to and from the hard drive without using the CPU. This results in a more efficient use of the system's resources since the CPU can engage in other calculations while the hard drive transfers data to and from RAM. Drives of this type are sometimes referred to as ultra ATA or ultra DMA. Traditional parallel ATA drives (PATA) are slowly being replaced by serial ATA drives (SATA). These use a serial interface which provides faster sustain transfer rates.

SCSI drives require a host adapter which provides the interface between the drive and the computer. There are various SCSI interface types known as SCSI 1, SCSI 2 and wide SCSI. Many audio professionals use SCSI drives since they generally have better RPM speeds and superior sustained data transfer rates. SCSI hard drives either fit inside the computer case or are found as separate stand-alone units. External SCSI devices are portable between different host computers, (as long as they are equipped with a SCSI interface). This means that the same drive could be attached to any one of a number of computers and several SCSI devices may be attached in sequence to a single host computer. In this sense, SCSI drives are more flexible than Ultra DMA EIDE drives.

Whatever kind of hard drive you use for your Cubase SX setup, remember to organise a method of backing up your data. Hard drives can develop faults, and system crashes can result in damage to data on the disk. Popular back-up media include: hard drives in removable caddies, external firewire drives, zip or jaz discs, recordable CD and DVD. Although hard disk failure is thankfully not a common occurrence, backing up your data is essential if you wish to avoid the potentially disastrous situation of losing all your files.

Audio hardware

Installing suitable audio hardware in your computer system is very important for the successful operation of Cubase SX. By audio hardware we mean a single audio card, a combined audio card with hardware interface or a separate audio device linked to the computer in some way (via USB or Firewire connectors, for example). Audio hardware could also mean the internal audio hardware of the host computer as in the case of Mac computers.

The audio hardware should be capable of recording and playing back digital audio using the hard drive to store the data. Audio hardware for computers commonly falls into the following categories:

- Budget stereo in/out devices - these normally feature digital audio recording capability, a MIDI interface, (usually on a dual joystick/MIDI port D-type socket) and MIDI synthesizer and/or sampling facilities. A card of this description is often a consumer card designed primarily for the games market.
- High-end audio cards and hardware featuring multiple inputs and outputs. These devices usually include an external rackmount unit or break-out box and have been designed with the professional recording industry in mind. Such devices are normally suitable for connection to both Mac and PC computers and they are the preferred choice for Cubase SX users.

For use with Cubase SX the audio hardware should:

- be able to record and play back stereo digital audio using the hard drive as the storage medium
- be a stereo or multiple input/output device with at least 16-bit resolution and 44.1kHz sampling rate
- be compatible with the operating system or have a separate ASIO driver (Audio Stream Input Output)

The main factors to bear in mind before choosing your audio hardware can be summarised as follows: the signal-to-noise ratio (or dynamic range), the bit resolution of the A-to-D and D-to-A converters, the THD and frequency response figures, the number of line/mic inputs and outputs, the MIDI and digital I/O, the on-board synthesizer features (if you need them), the ADAT facilities (if you need them), ASIO driver availability, expected latency figures and so on. The presence of digital in and out sockets is also important, especially if you intend to record from or mix down to DAT (Digital Audio Tape) or other digital media. Digital I/O improves the quality of both the record and playback path.

Latency is an increasingly important issue when choosing audio hardware for use with Cubase SX. Low latency is essential if you are hoping to monitor your recordings via Cubase SX or if you are intending to trigger VST Instruments live via MIDI, and it also improves the general responsiveness of the software. All professional audio hardware is supplied with dedicated ASIO drivers which help reduce the latency figures to acceptable levels. A well written ASIO driver can reduce latency to around 3-10ms and those products quoting similar figures are preferable.

If you are considering hardware with analogue ins and outs the bit resolution of the analogue-to-digital and digital-to-analogue converters should be taken into account. Although it is not always the case, a higher bit resolution usually means a better signal-to-noise ratio and better overall sound quality. Of similar importance is the bit resolution of the internal signal path which should be as high as possible.

No matter how fast your processor and no matter how much RAM you have, the actual sound quality is finally governed by the audio hardware. However, this is not to say that if you have first class audio hardware you are guaranteed a high quality audio result - you also need to have a high quality microphone, (if you are recording vocals or live instruments), and, if the signal is passing through a mixing console, then this too must be of the highest quality possible. In addition, you must be monitoring the results through a good amplification and speaker system. In other words, all stages in the recording and playback path should be of optimum quality. Your audio hardware might be viewed as a kind of cross-roads along this audio path - it is at the critical point in the recording and playback processes.

Graphics card

Computers require a graphics card in order to produce the image we see on the monitor screen. This is normally installed in the AGP port (Accelerated Graphics Port) of the motherboard. Graphics cards contain an amount of on-board RAM. The more RAM available, the greater the number of possible colours and the greater the potential resolution of the images produced. More importantly, more RAM means that graphics operations are less likely to interfere with audio operations. For Cubase SX, it is sufficient to use a 16-bit display quality but higher bit depths are unlikely to detract from the audio performance. Popular screen resolutions for Cubase SX might be anywhere between 1024 x 768 pixels to 1600 x 1200 pixels, depending upon the screen size and monitor specifications. Dual or triple monitor setups are popular among Cubase SX users and for this purpose a graphics card with dual or triple output ports is required. Output ports can be of the standard VGA variety or DVI. DVI is a digital interface which helps improve image quality. It is also recommended that you use a graphics card featuring passive cooling (i.e. no fan) since this helps cut down the overall noise of the computer.

The DVD/CD drive

A DVD-ROM drive is essential to install the latest versions of Cubase SX since the program is supplied on a DVD-ROM disc. Luckily, DVD-ROM drives are a standard feature of most currently available computers, and most DVD-ROM drives can read both DVD-ROM and CD-ROM discs. DVD-ROM stands for Digital Versatile Disc Read Only Memory and describes a type of read-only disc similar to standard CD-ROMs (Compact Disc Read Only Memory). DVDs can store more data than CDs. Most computer programs are now supplied on DVD-ROM or CD-ROM.

A variation on the DVD/CD-ROM drive is the DVD/CD-RW drive (DVD/CD Recorder). This allows you to write and read data to/from DVDs or CDs using DVD and CD recordable media. DVD/CD-R discs allow you to write data only once on the DVD/CD whereas DVD/CD-RW discs allow you to write data on the same disc many times. Recordable DVDs and CDs are extremely popular among Cubase SX users for backup purposes and for recording audio CDs. Cubase SX can directly import the data from standard audio CDs using the Import Audio CD option. To burn your own Red Book audio CD requires additional software (such as Wavelab, Sound Forge or Bias Peak).

A DVD/CD drive does not have to be enormously fast for Cubase SX. Drives are supplied in a variety of speeds such as 32 speed, 48 speed and so on, and most are adequate for general purpose use. The speed refers to the number of times faster the data is transferred to/from the disc when compared to an ordinary audio CD drive. However, for serious CD burning it is more the overall accuracy which is important. High precision drives supplied by Plextor (or similar) are recommended for this purpose.

The monitor

Standard CRT (cathode ray tube) type colour monitors come in 15 inch, 17 inch, 19 inch, 21 inch and greater sizes. Due to price considerations some are tempted to buy the smallest monitor but, for use with Cubase SX, this is a false economy. The absolute smallest monitor this book recommends is 17 inch. Cubase SX needs space to spread out and the use of multiple windows and their organisation on the screen demands a lot from the monitor.

TFT-LCD flat-screen monitors are an excellent alternative to standard CRT type computer monitors since their use results in less eye strain and general fatigue and they take up less space in cramped studios. In addition, CRT type monitors may cause significant hum when used near instruments such as electric guitar and electric bass, whereas TFT-LCD monitors do not produce this effect. The availability of more cost-effective flat-screen monitors means that the reign of the archaic technology that is the CRT type monitor may soon be over (thankfully!). TFT-LCD monitors are the preferred choice for Cubase SX users.

Remember that the monitor is one of the most important points of contact you have with the program and you may spend an awful long time gazing into it. As well as size, it is important to have a monitor capable of giving a crisp, clear image. Some monitors have superior focus, brightness and colour. A flat image screen can cut down on image distortion and those monitors with an anti-glare coating are easier to look at. For added protection when using a CRT type monitor, an optical glass anti-glare filter is recommended.

The keyboard and mouse

Of all the peripheral devices surrounding the computer, the keyboard and mouse are the most familiar. They provide points of tactile contact with the machine and methods by which we can give it instructions.

For Cubase SX, it pays to know how to use these basic tools and what to look for in the hardware sense. Some Cubase SX users may not think that learning to type has anything to do with creating music; they are probably right, but if you are the kind of user who must search for each letter and symbol before you type it, then you are going to be handicapped in your use of Cubase SX and, for that matter, most other computer software. Naming tracks, saving songs and using keyboard shortcuts all require some level of keyboard skill. So, if you are going to use the keyboard, you may as well choose one which is comfortable and then become very familiar with it. The basic advice here is try before you buy. Some of the cheaper keyboards are not very pleasant to use and for the faster typist may not be sensitive enough. The final choice is a personal matter.

As for the mouse, the most comfortable shape and size depends on the characteristics of your hand. The final choice is, once again, a personal matter but it pays to make some comparisons between different models. Some users may prefer a trackball, where the cursor position is regulated by a rolling ball in the top part of the device. A wheel mouse is useful in Cubase SX for scrolling within the Project and other windows. Other possibilities include the use of wireless and optical keyboards and mice. These offer considerable flexibility if you need to move from one desktop/instrument location to another, and an optical mouse can be used on a wider range of surfaces than a standard mouse.

Noise issues

Unfortunately for computer users in general and particularly for musicians and recording studios, most computers make a certain amount of noise. This can prove extremely obtrusive when you are trying to listen to your latest musical masterpiece. Most of the noise comes from the various fans inside the computer case and the CD and hard drives.

A number of specialist PC computer suppliers provide computers which have been built specifically with noise minimisation and audio work in mind. These normally feature ultra quiet power supplies and hard drives housed in special acoustic enclosures. Computers of this type (or other low-noise alternatives) are the preferred option for Cubase SX users.

Appendix 2
MIDI messages

MIDI messages

The following table shows some of the most common MIDI messages. All data is shown in hexadecimal notation with the decimal equivalent below.

Table A2.1 MIDI messages

Message type	Function	Status byte	Data byte	Data byte	Data byte	Comments
Channel Voice messages						
Note off	Terminates a note event	8nH 128	kkH kk	vvH vv	–	kk = key number (0-127), vv = velocity (0-127)
Note on	Starts a note event	9nH 144	kkH kk	vvH vv	–	kk = key number (0-127), vv = velocity (0-127)
Polyphonic key pressure	Polyphonic key pressure	AnH 160	kkH kk	vvH vv	–	pressure for each individual key, kk = key number, vv = pressure
Control change	Generic control function	BnH 176	ccH cc	vvH vv	–	for wheels, switches, pedals etc. cc=controller no., vv =control value
Program change	Changes receiver's program number	CnH 192	ppH pp		–	pp = program number (0-127)
Channel key pressure	Channel key pressure (Aftertouch)	DnH 208	vvH vv		–	vv = amount of pressure applied (0-127)
Pitch bend	Changes pitch of notes on same channel	EnH 224	ffH ff	ccH cc	–	ff = fine changes (0-127), cc = coarse changes in pitch (0-127)

Table A2.1 MIDI messages (cont)

Message type	Function	Status byte	Data byte	Data byte	Data byte	Comments
Channel Mode messages						
Control change	Reset all controllers	BnH 176	79H 123	00H 0	–	resets all controllers to their default values
Control change	Local on/off	BnH 176	7AH 122	vvH vv	–	disconnects keyboard from sound-making circuitry (0=Off, 127=On)
Control change	All notes off	BnH 176	7BH 123	00H 0	–	terminates all currently playing notes
Control change	Omni mode off (all notes off)	BnH 176	7CH 124	00H 0	–	the receiver responds only to messages sent on its MIDI channel
Control change	Omni mode on (all notes off)	BnH 176	7DH 125	00H 0	–	the receiver responds to messages on all MIDI channels
Control change	Mono mode on/poly mode off (all notes off)	BnH 176	7EH 126	vvH vv	–	the receiver responds monophonically, vv = no of channels
Control change	Poly mode on/mono mode off (all notes off)	BnH 176	7FH 127	00H 0	–	the receiver responds polyphonically
System messages (a number of examples)						
System Exclusive	Manufacturer-specific	F0H 240	iiH ii	nnH-nnH nn - nn	F7H 247	ii = Manufacturer ID (0-127), nn - nn = almost any sequence of data dependent on function of message, F7H = end of the SysEx message
Active sensing	Transmitting instrument saying 'I am still here'	FEH 254	–	–	–	message transmitted every 300ms
MIDI clock	MIDI timing clock for sychronisation	F8H 248	–	–	–	message transmitted 24 times per quarter note
System reset	Resets receiver to power-up state	FFH 255	–	–	–	initialises all parameters to their default state

Table A2.1 MIDI messages (cont)

Message type	Function	Status byte	Data byte	Data byte	Data byte	Comments
Commonly used Control Change messages						
Control change	Modulation	BnH 176	01H 1	vvH vv	–	01H (1) = modulation, vv = modulation amount (0-127)
Control change	Breath controller	BnH 176	02H 2	vvH vv	–	02H (2) = breath control, vv = breath control amount (0-127)
Control change	Foot controller	BnH 176	04H 4	vvH vv	–	04H (4) = foot pedal control, vv = control amount (0-127)
Control change	Channel volume (Main volume)	BnH 176	07H 7	vvH vv	–	07H (7) = main volume, vv = volume level (0-127)
Control change	Pan	BnH 176	0AH 10	vvH vv	–	0AH (10) = pan, vv = pan value (0-127)
Control change	Expression	BnH 176	0BH 11	vvH vv	–	0BH (11) = expression, vv = control value (0-127)
Control change	Sustain pedal	BnH 176	40H 66	vvH vv	–	40H (66) = sustain pedal, vv = control value (0-63 = Off, 64-127 = On)

Notes

All message data is shown in hexadecimal notation with the decimal equivalent below.

n in the Status byte is a value between 0 and 15 designating one of the sixteen MIDI channels.

cc, ff, ii, kk, pp, vv are values between 0 and 127.

Appendix 3
MIDI controllers

No	Controller	No	Controller	No	Controller	No	Controller
0	Bank Select MSB	32	Bank Select LSB	64	Damper pedal on/off	96	Data increment
1	Modulation wheel	33	Mod wheel LSB	65	Portamento on/off	97	Data decrement
2	Breath control	34	Breath control LSB	66	Sustain pedal on/off	98	NRPN LSB
3	Undefined	35	Undefined	67	Soft pedal on/off	99	NRPN MSB
4	Foot controller	36	Foot controller LSB	68	Legato Footswitch	100	RPN LSB
5	Portamento time	37	Portamento time LSB	69	Hold 2	101	RPN MSB
6	Data Entry	38	Data entry LSB	70	Sound Variation	102	Undefined
7	Channel Volume	39	Channel Volume LSB	71	Timbre	103	Undefined
8	Balance	40	Balance LSB	72	Release Time	104	Undefined
9	Undefined	41	Undefined	73	Attack Time	105	Undefined
10	Pan	42	Pan LSB	74	Brightness	106	Undefined
11	Expression	43	Expression LSB	75	Sound Control #6	107	Undefined
12	Effect control 1	44	Effect control 1 LSB	76	Sound Control #7	108	Undefined
13	Effect control 2	45	Effect control 2 LSB	77	Sound Control #8	109	Undefined
14	Undefined	46	Undefined	78	Sound Control #9	110	Undefined
15	Undefined	47	Undefined	79	Sound Control #10	111	Undefined
16	Gen Purpose #1	48	Gen Purpose #1 LSB	80	Gen Purpose #5	112	Undefined
17	Gen Purpose #2	49	Gen Purpose #2 LSB	81	Gen Purpose #6	113	Undefined
18	Gen Purpose #3	50	Gen Purpose #3 LSB	82	Gen Purpose #7	114	Undefined
19	Gen Purpose #4	51	Gen Purpose #4 LSB	83	Gen Purpose #8	115	Undefined
20	Undefined	52	Undefined	84	Portamento Control	116	Undefined
21	Undefined	53	Undefined	85	Undefined	117	Undefined
22	Undefined	54	Undefined	86	Undefined	118	Undefined
23	Undefined	55	Undefined	87	Undefined	119	Undefined
24	Undefined	56	Undefined	88	Undefined	120	All Sound Off
25	Undefined	57	Undefined	89	Undefined	121	Reset All Controllers
26	Undefined	58	Undefined	90	Undefined	122	Local control on/off
27	Undefined	59	Undefined	91	FX 1 Reverb Depth	123	All notes off
28	Undefined	60	Undefined	92	FX 2 Trem Depth	124	Omni mode off
29	Undefined	61	Undefined	93	FX 3 Chorus Depth	125	Omni mode on
30	Undefined	62	Undefined	94	FX 4 Celeste Depth	126	Mono on/Poly off
31	Undefined	63	Undefined	95	FX 5 Phaser Depth	127	Poly on/Mono off

Appendix 4
General MIDI

For the convenience of those using General MIDI (GM) synths and modules and in order to avoid some of the confusion which can arise on the subject, this appendix outlines the essentials of the General MIDI protocol. There are three main types of General MIDI devices:

- GM – General MIDI. The first GM standard devised by Roland.
- GS – General Standard. The same as General MIDI but with additional features devised by Roland.
- XG – Extended General MIDI. The same as General MIDI but with additional features devised by Yamaha.

The essential idea of GM/GS/XG MIDI synths and sound modules is that they all share a common language. A MIDI sequence played back using one GM module will sound much the same on any other GM module. Cubase SX provides the "track Control' MIDI effect plug-in which allows the editing of various GS/XG parameters. In addition, to select programs using GM names, activate the GM device in the MIDI Device manager window (Device menu) and select the GM device in the 'out' field of the MIDI track. You can now select GM programs by name rather than number.

The following outlines the basic practical protocol for all GM/GS/XG devices, (note that the full GM protocol encompasses many more parameters than those described here):

- A minimum of 24-voice polyphony.
- Multi-timbrality on 16 MIDI channels where each channel can play a variable number of voices from the available polyphony.
- Drum sounds are always on MIDI channel 10, and each drum is allocated to a specific MIDI note number (as shown below in the 'Standard GM drum map' table).
- The sounds available comply with the program numbers and 128 presets of the standard bank of GM sounds, as in the following table:

Table A4.1 Standard bank of General MIDI sounds

No	Name	No	Name	No	Name	No	Name
1	Piano 1	9	Celesta	17	Organ 1	25	Nylon-str. Gt.
2	Piano 2	10	Glockenspiel	18	Organ 2	26	Steel-str. Gt.
3	Piano 3	11	Music box	19	Organ 3	27	Jazz Gt.
4	Honky-tonk P.	12	Vibraphone	20	Church organ	28	Clean Gt.
5	E. Piano 1	13	Marimba	21	Reed Organ	29	Muted Gt.
6	E. Piano 2	14	Xylophone	22	Accordion Fr	30	Overdrive Gt.
7	Harpsichord	15	Tubular bell	23	Harmonica	31	Distortion Gt.
8	Clav	16	Santur	24	Bandneon	32	Gt. harmonics
33	Acoustic Bass	41	Violin	49	Strings	57	Trumpet
34	Fingered Bass	42	Viola	50	Slow Strings	58	Trombone
35	Picked Bass	43	Cello	51	Syn. Strings 1	59	Tuba
36	Fretless Bass	44	Contrabass	52	Syn. Strings 2	60	Muted Trumpet
37	Slap Bass 1	45	Tremelo Str.	53	Choir Aahs	61	French Horn
38	Slap Bass 2	46	Pizzicato Str.	54	Voice Oohs	62	Brass 1
39	Synth Bass 1	47	Harp	55	SynVox	63	Synth Brass 1
40	Synth Bass 2	48	Timpani	56	Orchestral Hit	64	Synth Brass 2
65	Soprano Sax	73	Piccolo	81	Square Wave	89	Fantasia
66	Alto Sax	74	Flute	82	Saw Wave	90	Warm Pad
67	Tenor Sax	75	Recorder	83	Syn. Calliope	91	Polysynth
68	Baritone Sax	76	Pan Flute	84	Chiffer lead	92	Space Voice
69	Oboe	77	Bottle Blow	85	Charang	93	Bowed Glass
70	English Horn	78	Shakuhachi	86	Solo Vox	94	Metal Pad
71	Bassoon	79	Whistle	87	5th Saw Wave	95	Halo Pad
72	Clarinet	80	Ocarina	88	Bass & Lead	96	Sweep Pad
97	Ice Rain	105	Sitar	113	Tinkle Bell	121	Gt. Fret Noise
98	Soundtrack	106	Banjo	114	Agogo	122	Breath Noise
99	Crystal	107	Shamisen	115	Steel Drums	123	Seashore
100	Atmosphere	108	Koto	116	Wood Block	124	Bird
101	Brightness	109	Kalimba	117	Taiko	125	Telephone 1
102	Goblin	110	Bagpipe	118	Melo Tom 1	126	Helicopter
103	Echo Drops	111	Fiddle	119	Synth Drum	127	Applause
104	Star Theme	112	Shannai	120	Reverse Cymb.	128	Gun Shot

Table A4.2 Standard GM drum map

Note	No	Drum name	Note	No	Drum name
C1	36	Bass Drum	D3	62	Mute High Bongo
C#1	37	Side Stick	D#3	63	Open High Conga
D1	38	Acoustic Snare	E3	64	Low Conga
D#1	39	Hand Clap	F3	65	High Timbale
E1	40	Electric Snare	F#3	66	Low Timbale
F1	41	Low Floor Tom	G3	67	High Agogo
F#1	42	Closed Hi-Hat	G#3	68	Low Agogo
G1	43	High Floor Tom	A3	69	Cabasa
G#1	44	Pedal Hi-Hat	A#3	70	Maracas
A1	45	Low Tom	B3	71	Short Whistle
A#1	46	Open Hi-Hat	C4	72	Long Whistle
B1	47	Low Middle Tom	C#4	73	Short Guiro
C2	48	High Middle Tom	D4	74	Long Guiro
C#2	49	Crash Cymbal 1	D#4	75	Claves
D2	50	High Tom	E4	76	High Wood Block
D#2	51	Ride Cymbal 1	F4	77	Low Wood Block
E2	52	Chinese Cymbal	F#4	78	Mute Cuica
F2	53	Ride Bell	G4	79	Open Cuica
F#2	54	Tambourine	G#4	80	Mute Triangle
G2	55	Splash Cymbal	A4	81	Open Triangle
G#2	56	Cowbell	A#4	82	Shaker
A2	57	Crash Cymbal 2	B4	83	Castanets
A#2	58	Vibraslap	F0	29	Scratch Push
B2	59	Ride Cymbal 2	F#0	30	Scratch Pull
C3	60	High Bongo	A0	33	Metronome
C#3	61	Low Bongo	B0	35	Acoustic Bass Drum

Appendix 5
Additional software

While Cubase SX is undoubtedly a powerful music creation and audio editing tool, many users may wish to expand the possibilities with additional software. For music production and sounds effects creation popular choices include Native Instruments Kontakt and Reaktor, Propellerhead Reason, Applied Acoustics Systems Tassman, Tascam Gigastudio and Steinberg Halion (for more details see page 387). For audio editing, CD and DVD creation check out Steinberg Wavelab, Bias Peak or Sony Sound Forge. Wavelab (Figure A5.1) has established a very good reputation among mastering engineers. It includes leading edge audio editing, restoration and analysis tools, and for the creation of audio CDs and DVDs provides the intuitive and easy-to-use audio montage window. Other features include high quality DIRAC time stretching and pitch shifting, Crystal Resampler professional sample rate conversion, K system metering, effect morphing, batch processing and a Spectrum editor for surgical editing in both the time and frequency domains.

Figure A5.1

Steinberg Wavelab for audio editing, restoration, analysis and CD/DVD creation

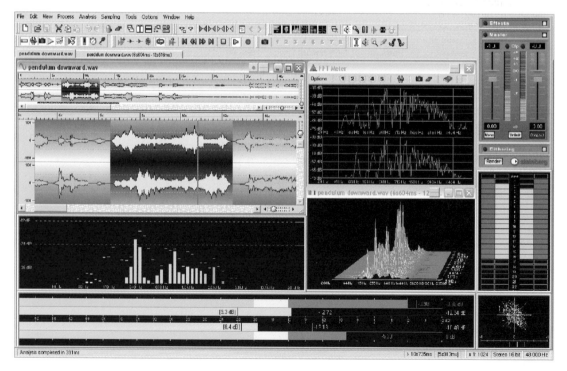

Index